ROMAN SYRIA

AND THE NEAR EAST

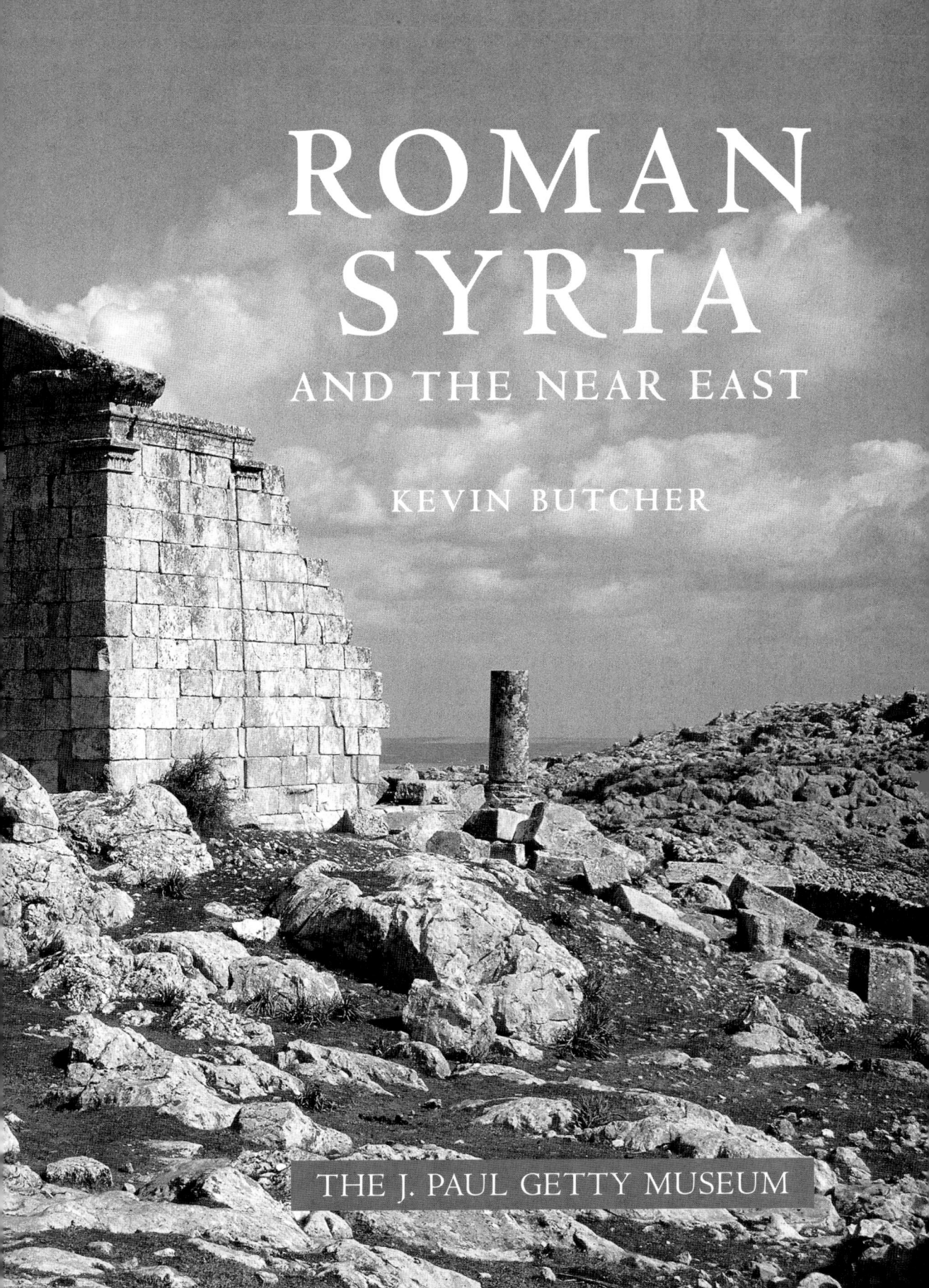

ROMAN
SYRIA
AND THE NEAR EAST

KEVIN BUTCHER

THE J. PAUL GETTY MUSEUM

To my grandparents, Jack and Dora Jones

First published in the United Kingdom in 2003
by The British Museum Press
A division of The British Museum Company Ltd
46 Bloomsbury Street, London WC1B 3QQ

First published in North America in 2003
by Getty Publications
1200 Getty Center Drive, Suite 500
Los Angeles, California 90049-1682
www.getty.edu

Christopher Hudson, Publisher
Mark Greenberg, Editor in Chief

Designed and typeset in Photina by Martin Richards
Printed in Spain by Grafos

Library of Congress Cataloging-in-Publication Data

Butcher, Kevin.
  Roman Syria and the Near East / Kevin Butcher.
    p. cm.
  ISBN 0-89236-715-6
  1. Syria--History--333 B.C.--634 A.D. 2. Middle East--History--To 622.
  3. Rome--History--Empire, 30 B.C.--284 A.D. 4. Romans--Syria. I.
    Title.
  DS96.2.B87 2003
  939'.43--DC21
                      2003006252

CONTENTS

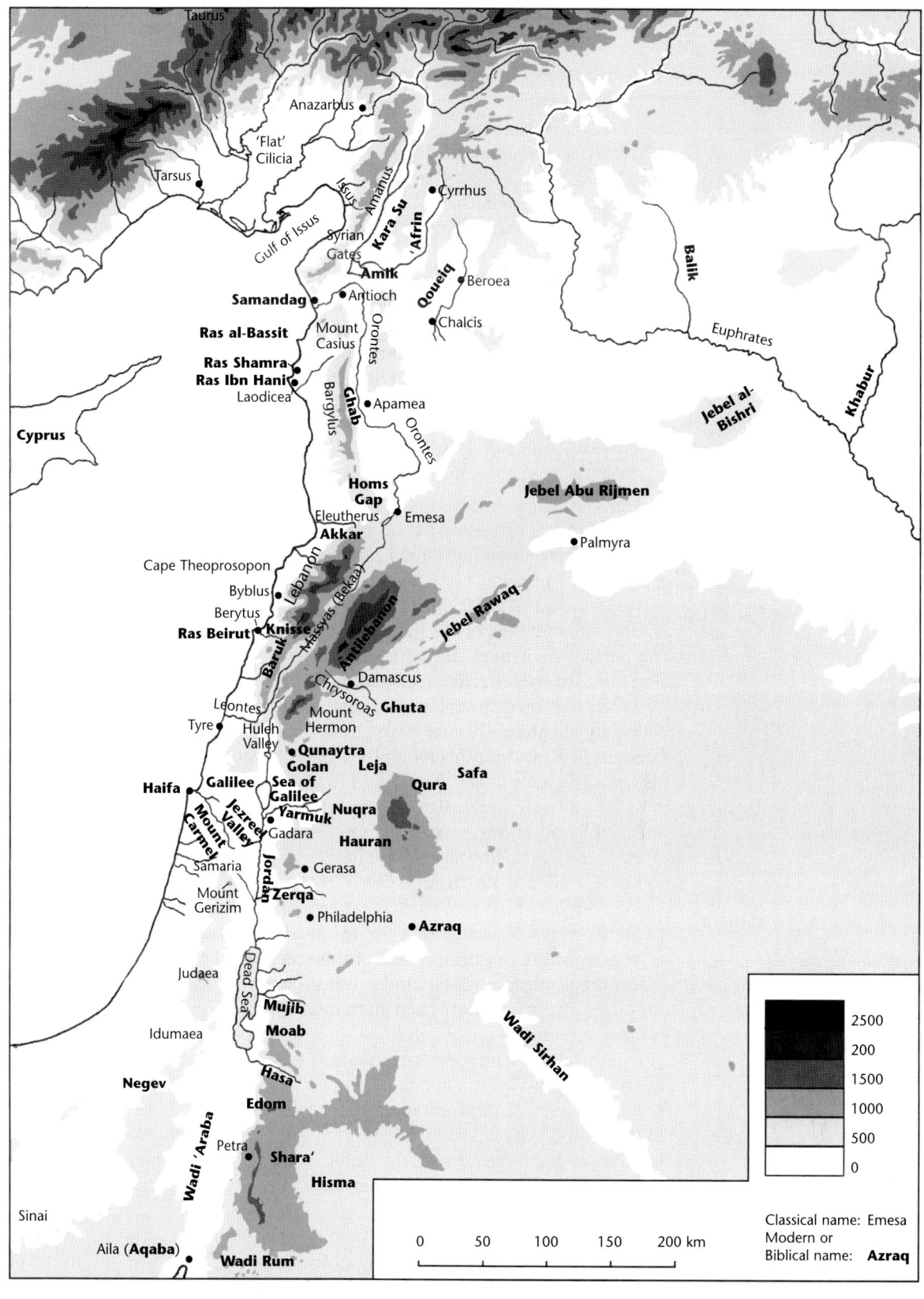

Taurus

Anazarbus •

'Flat' Cilicia

Tarsus •

Cyrrhus •

Kara Su

Afrin

Amik

Syrian Gates

Gulf of Issus

Issus

Amanus

Beroea •

Qoueiq

Samandag •

• Antioch

Mount Casius

Chalcis •

Balik

Euphrates

Ras al-Bassit

Ras Shamra
Ras Ibn Hani •

Laodicea •

Ghab

Bargylus

Apamea •

Orontes

Orontes

Jebel al-Bishri

Khabur

Cyprus

Jebel Abu Rijmen

Homs Gap

Eleutherus

Emesa •

Palmyra •

Cape Theoprosopon

Akkar

Byblus •

Lebanon

Jebel Rawaq

Berytus •

Ras Beirut •
Knisse

Baruk

Massyas (Bekaa)

Antilebanon

Damascus •

Ghuta

Leontes

Chrysoroas

Tyre •

Huleh Valley

Mount Hermon

Qunaytra •

Leja

Safa

Haifa •

Galilee

Golan

Sea of Galilee

Qura

Mount Carmel

Jezreel Valley

Yarmuk

Nuqra

Gadara •

Hauran

Samaria

Jordan

Gerasa •

Mount Gerizim

Zerqa •

Philadelphia •

Azraq •

Judaea

Dead Sea

Wadi Sirhan

Mujib

Idumaea

Moab

Negev

Hasa

Edom

Wadi 'Araba

Petra •

Shara'

Hisma

Sinai

Aila (**Aqaba**) •

Wadi Rum

	2500
	200
	1500
	1000
	500
	0

0   50   100   150   200 km

Classical name: Emesa
Modern or
Biblical name: **Azraq**

PREFACE AND ACKNOWLEDGEMENTS

This is a book about Syria and the Near East under Roman rule. The subject is enormous, and the present volume, which is intended for the interested non-specialist, makes no claim to be authoritative or comprehensive. I have chosen themes and problems which I think are interesting, and because many of these fields of study are not my speciality I have relied extensively on the expertise of others. Even so, trying to marshal the vast array of magisterial writings on the subject into a coherent shape is a humbling experience, and no doubt I have ridden roughshod over a number of research topics which deserved more thorough and careful analysis in my attempt to condense the material into an essay of 200,000 words. The difficulties are compounded by the fact that although the literature on Roman Syria and the Near East – in the form of articles and specialist books on specific subjects - is extensive, it is only recently that detailed scholarly syntheses have emerged and some of the major problems and areas for study have been defined. I can appreciate why this is so; the effort and knowledge required to draw all the information together and to provide new insights leave me in awe of the scholars who have compiled such studies. Where there is debate, I have endeavoured to present different views, but it would be impossible to examine every area of dissent even among the topics explored. The select bibliography is not intended to be comprehensive, but provides references for the text and pointers for those interested in pursuing particular themes. For the sake of brevity the footnotes are not extensive and are used only to reference quotations.

I have also tried to explore and emphasize material culture in many of the following chapters. This has been given weight over texts and inscriptions not because I believe that this kind of evidence is somehow superior but because this is where recent work has begun to contribute considerably to the discussion. By material culture I mean not only architecture and building phases on sites, which form the essence of traditional archaeological approaches in the Roman east, but also pottery and other ceramics, coins, stone, glass and other kinds of evidence which have yet to make their full impact on the Roman archaeology of the region, such as environmental remains and the findings of surface surveys. To look at everything in detail over such a wide region would, of course, be unrealistic in a book of this scope, and I can only touch on many fascinating subjects which under other circumstances or at the hands of another writer might have been given more space. We are at a very elementary stage in our understanding of things great and small, like pottery distributions, coin circulation, settlement patterns, land use and ownership, the relationship of cities to their hinterland and that all-important social unit, the village. Most major sites remain largely unexcavated, and promise to reveal many surprises in the future. Where possible I have tried to refer to objects, sites and standing buildings which can be seen by visitors to the region today. In a number of cases I might have chosen other examples, but I have preferred those with which I am personally familiar.

In transliterating modern place names I have not tried to maintain any particular consistency. A glance at any of the literature about sites in this region

Fig. 1. Map of the region.

will make it clear that there is no generally agreed convention for rendering non-Latin alphabets. I have tried to employ commonly encountered forms, but readers should be aware that there are often several variants. I have generally used Latinized versions of Greek place names; with personal names I have tended to use whatever is most familiar.

It remains for me to thank friends and colleagues who took time to read drafts of this book. A special debt of gratitude is owed to Pierre-Louis Gatier, David Graf, Jean-Baptiste Yon and the otherwise anonymous referees for doing battle with the penultimate version of the text in its entirety and at very short notice. Their constructive comments, criticisms and encouragement have helped persuade me that my attempt to condense such a huge topic into a single volume was not a totally reckless enterprise. Needless to say that they bear no responsibility for what follows. Thanks are also due to others who looked at earlier drafts, suggested changes, or provided additional bibliography: Andrew Burnett, Nadia El-Cheikh, Richard Duncan-Jones, Philip Grierson, Phil Freeman, Erica Hunter, Simon James, Sarah Jennings, David Kennedy, Henry Mallorie, Phil Mills, Peter Parr, Tim Potter, Paul Reynolds, and Gary Young. I have also benefited much from discussions of things Roman with Dominic Perring, Helga Seeden, Reuben Thorpe and Tim Williams. In addition I must thank Dr Khaled al-As'ad for his kindness and hospitality during visits to Palmyra, and students of archaeology at the American University of Beirut, with whom I have explored some of the more obscure sites in the region, and who over the years have contributed to the debates on some of the themes covered here.

The photographs and illustrations are sometimes intended to be supplementary to the text, rather than merely illustrative. Most of the photographs, maps and drawings are mine, but I should also like to thank Peter Guest, Erica Hunter, Michael Robinson, Wolfgang Leschhorn and the Trustees and photographers of the British Museum for making their photographs available to me, and to Paul Reynolds for providing a drawing of a Hellenistic fish plate.

I also owe a profound debt of gratitude to Nina Shandloff and to Charlie Mounter at The British Museum Press and to the book's designer, Martin Richards, for taking this seemingly interminable project through to its conclusion. Thanks also to the copy editor, David Rose, for heroically calculating imperial equivalents for my metric measurements. Finally, it is customary to thank one's spouse or partner for his or her patience and forbearance during the period of writing; but I think my wife, Marguerite, has shown tolerance beyond measure. The same would apply to our son Tristan, though he is presently too young to express any opinion (or, indeed, much forbearance). To them I promise that life will be different in the aftermath.

FOREWORD

Roman Syria. The writer is responsible for the choice of words, the reader for their interpretation. Nevertheless in what follows I shall attempt to explain what I intend by these words, to constrain the readings and prevent misunderstandings. I use the word *Roman* here not so much as a cultural shorthand, but as a chronological bracket. The limits set are therefore political: from the Roman annexation in 64 BC to the Battle of the Yarmuk in AD 636, when the region was lost to the Roman empire and became a prize for the Muslim Arab armies. One can certainly find major political, social and cultural discontinuities within this enormous span of time, and thus object to my calling the empire of Justinian or Heraclius 'Roman', but equally one can find continuities, which if anything is a consequence of the Roman empire's skill at reinventing itself while retaining enough symbols to appear as a continuum. I find it no more problematic to combine the empire of Augustus and Heraclius into a single narrative than the commonplace welding of fifth-century-BC Athens and second-century-AD Rome together under the rubric 'antiquity'.

Some subdivision of this seven-hundred-year period is necessary, however. The term 'republic' traditionally covers the Roman empire before Augustus (down to 27 BC), and I have retained this. I have used the terms 'early empire' or 'early Roman' to mean what is often termed the Principate, from Augustus to Diocletian (27 BC to AD 284), and 'late empire' or 'late Roman' for the period that follows, down to the Muslim conquest. The term 'Byzantine' has been employed to signify the empire after the conquest, with one exception which is a concession to common usage: 'Byzantine' is normally used to describe imperial coinage after the monetary reform of Anastasius in AD 498 (see chapter 6).

That much about the term 'Roman' can be taken as assumed in this work. The term is also a cultural one, although this usage is more problematic. In any case Greek or 'Graeco-Roman' culture (some equally difficult terminology) is more appropriate in this context, and for this reason I have extended the chronological bracketing a little to include a brief discussion of the Hellenistic period at the beginning. It is argued that the establishment and promotion of cities by Hellenistic rulers produced abrupt discontinuities that for many communities constituted the beginnings of a new civic identity and communal history. If these discontinuities cannot be demonstrated clearly for the Hellenistic period, they were certainly in place in the Roman. The history of Roman imperialism in the region is closely allied with fortunes of the Greek-style city state and Hellenism, and the Hellenistic period was formative in shaping this political and cultural geography. The position taken here is that the main traits of 'Graeco-Roman' culture were inseparable from power relations, between the imperial authorities and local ones, and between local elites and their social inferiors. Lack of space has meant that the question of the survival of 'Graeco-Roman' culture after the Muslim conquest cannot be examined here, but there is certainly a good case for seeing various forms of continuity from Roman to Muslim rule, with a stronger discontinuity occurring in the eighth century after the Abbasid revolution that overthrew the Syrian-based Umayyad dynasty.

Syria is an ill-defined, impure geographical notion which accords well with the complex and ill-defined social and religious identities explored in the final part of this book. The terms 'Syria and the Near East' could be understood as alternative titles for the same thing, but I have not chosen them for this reason and that is not what is intended here. The book has two levels of focus: a more detailed one, concentrating mainly on the region occupied by the modern Syrian Arab Republic and Lebanon (but also including parts of Turkey) which can be considered, however vaguely, to constitute 'Roman Syria'; and a more general one, drawing on evidence from a wider region, including Jordan, Israel/Palestine and what in antiquity was known as Mesopotamia (but which is now divided between Turkey, the Syrian Arab Republic and Iraq), which could be considered the 'Near East'.

There are several reasons for these two layers of 'resolution'. One is practical. In a book of this length it is not possible to explore the entirety of the 'Near East' in detail. The amount of material is simply too great, and too varied. Prior publications have also shaped the choice of emphasis. There are many excellent general works on Judaea/Palestine and Arabia, and I have not sought to compete with these. The wealth of evidence for these regions would produce a bias that would overshadow the rest. For studies of sites such as Jerusalem, Caesarea Maritima, Scythopolis, Medaba, and many other important places in these areas, the reader is advised to consult other sources. Nevertheless these regions have produced important evidence that has a direct bearing on 'Roman Syria', and it would be otiose to discard this information entirely. For this reason archaeological sites and finds that might be better described as being located in the 'Near East' or 'Syrian region' rather than Syria proper are discussed in the chapters that follow.

Furthermore, the two layers do not have clearly defined boundaries. To separate something called 'Roman Syria' from a broader 'Near East' engenders problems of its own, for it would mean attempting to devise a more rigorous definition than that offered above and imposing geographical limits to the evidence. I am not sure that the former rigour can be achieved, or that the latter imposition is desirable. Such an exercise would entail the concoction of questionable political or ethnic circumscriptions for a material culture that refuses to be bound by such contingent frontiers, ancient or modern. Scholars might be able to agree on those places that ought to be included in a survey of 'Roman Syria', but they would not necessarily concur about what ought to be excluded. The ancient sources themselves fail to provide any clear guidelines to follow, and trying to define 'Syria' in terms that the Romans might have understood is especially difficult for the long period covered by this book. It meant different things at different times. While most of this 'Near Eastern' region at some time or other made up the province, and later the provinces, of Syria, some parts subsequently acquired different names: Arabia, Palaestina, Phoenice (the evolution of the provinces is examined in chapter 3). Other parts were never part of a province called Syria but were nonetheless sometimes referred to, however vaguely, as Syrian. Suffice to say that it is difficult to pinpoint where Roman Syria stops and other parts of the Near East begin, and I have not sought to make a precise distinction here.

The geography of Syria and the Near East does not lend it any special unity, other than as the area between the eastern shore of the Mediterranean and the Euphrates river. It forms only a part of what is sometimes referred to as the

Fertile Crescent (a curved band of good agricultural land stretching from Mesopotamia across northern Syria and down to Egypt), and only a portion of the area inhabited by speakers of Semitic languages. Part of the problem of defining the region lies in the inability to characterize it geographically and culturally as a single entity. When I use the terms 'Syrian' or 'Syrians' these are not to be understood as specific political or cultural designations, or as implying any cultural or ethnic unity. They are used simply as shorthand for things and people inhabiting the Syrian region. To some this might seem to be doing an injustice to the cultural and historical diversities of a region which they may feel ought to be given another name; any name, in fact, as long as it is not Syria. It is difficult to avoid the identity politics of modern nation states in the region, where the past is often used in highly creative ways to define who the inhabitants are, or, as is commonly the case with the definition of identities, who they and their forebears are *not*: not-Arab, not-Syrian, not-Phoenician, not-Jewish and so on. Until the Sykes-Picot agreement of 1915 and the ensuing French and British mandates following the collapse of Ottoman rule, 'Syria' was frequently used by geographers and historians (and by Syrian nationalists) to denote what would now be called the 'Near East'. The latter term is currently in vogue, but like 'Middle East', 'Levant' or 'Orient', it has its detractors, who object to the fact that it defines the region in terms of a position relative to the West, or Europe, as if it had no autonomy from them. A century and a half ago the Balkans was the 'Near East'; now it has discarded its mere relative position and become part of autonomous Europe. Preferring 'Near East' over 'Syria' in the title of this book might seem more appropriate to some, but it would imply that an equal focus has been brought to bear on the south, which it has not. It appears that no single term for the region suits everyone, and in calling, for example, the cities of the region 'Syrian', I am not endorsing the claim of any modern ideologies.

Roman Syria and the Near East were of course part of a much larger frontier zone bordering on the great state to the east ruled first by the Parthians and then by the Sasanians, and events within other parts of this zone often had a bearing on the region covered here. As a result it will occasionally be necessary to turn to these neighbouring areas: particularly Parthian- and Sasanian-ruled Mesopotamia (with its common cultural ties with Syria); Armenia (which Rome disputed with the Parthians and Sasanians); and the vast peninsula of Arabia (from which the Muslim conquerors of the seventh century came).

Geography

The basic geography may be divided into three regions: a coastal strip with hills or high mountains behind it; a north - south rift valley to the east of that; and finally the eastern steppe and desert zones. This approach emphasizes differences in the availability of the most valuable commodity in the region: water. Vegetation, settlement and ease of communications were all affected by its availability, and, perhaps more than anything else, water shaped the human geography of Roman Syria and the Near East.

The coast possesses small plains, fertile and watered by rivers and seasonal streams, usually dominated by a backdrop of high mountains or hills and sometimes divided by mountainous spurs which reach to the sea. These great mountain chains form a barrier, running north - south: the Amanus (fig. 2); the Jebel Akra (ancient Mount Casius); the Jebel Ansariyeh (ancient Bargylus),

Fig. 2. Clouds on the Amanus, the mountain range dividing Syria from Cilicia, seen from the Amik Plain north-east of Antioch.

and the high Lebanon range. Both the Jebel Ansariyeh and the Lebanon are anticlines which have fractured, so that their coastal flanks form relatively gentle slopes but their eastern sides fall away steeply to the plains of the Ghab and Bekaa respectively. South of the Lebanon range the coastal plain widens a little, although it is broken by the spur of Mount Carmel which lies above the modern port of Haifa. The coastal zone south of Haifa is low-lying, with few anchorages suitable for harbours. Behind the plains lies the hill country of Samaria and Judaea, and south of Judaea the plateau of the Negev desert.

There are few lowland passes through the coastal mountain chains. The principal route through the Amanus was known in antiquity as the 'Syrian Gates', a high pass between the inland plain of Antioch (the modern Amik plain) and the plain of Issus on the coast. It was used extensively in ancient times. The River Orontes breaks through to the sea between the Amanus and Mount Casius, providing the city of Antioch up river with a vital link to the Mediterranean. The Homs Gap is a corridor lying between the Ansariyeh and Lebanon ranges, through which the Nahr al-Kabir (the ancient River Eleutherus) flows, and this pass links the upper reaches of the Orontes valley and Emesa with the coastal plain of Akkar and the sea. The littoral known as Phoenicia was effectively separated from the hinterland by the huge ridges of the Lebanon mountains, snow-capped in winter and a long climb at any time of year (colour plate 1). The lowest pass through this range is between the Jebel al-Knisse and the Jebel Baruk, east of Beirut (the ancient port of Berytus), but another higher pass also provided access to the Bekaa from the mountains above Byblus. The lower hills to the south proved less of an obstacle, with many routes providing access to the fertile valley of the Jordan or the arid lands of the Dead Sea and the Wadi 'Araba. One of the most prominent in this region is the Jezreel valley, dividing Galilee from Samaria.

Immediately behind the mountains is a series of river valleys formed by geological faults. The north-western part of Syria is dominated by the Orontes (the modern Asi river), which follows a fault line northwards from the Bekaa valley in Lebanon to reach the sea near Antioch. Until recently parts of the valley were marshy and prone to flooding in winter, especially in the plains of the Ghab, near Apamea, and the Amik, near Antioch. Another river valley, that of the Kara Su, a tributary of the Orontes, flows south along the eastern edge of the Amanus mountains and fed what was until recently a marshy region of the Amik plain. A second river flowing south into the same marshes is the 'Afrin, which has its source in the Kartal Dag range, to the north of the ancient city of Cyrrhus.

The sources of the Orontes and another river, the Litani (ancient Leontes), lie in the broad and well-watered rift of the Bekaa valley (ancient Massyas). This is the area between the Lebanon on the west and, on the east, the Antilebanon range (the Jebel ash-Sharqi) and the high dome of Mount Hermon (Jebel ash-Sheikh). Although it is a valley, the floor of the Bekaa is about 1000 metres (3280 feet) above sea level. The central and southern part of the Bekaa is extremely fertile, but the northern part, which slopes down towards Homs, is much more arid, and the Orontes cuts a deep channel through it, making irrigation difficult. The Litani begins only a few kilometres below the source of the Orontes, flowing southwards on the eastern side of the Lebanon range before it turns to meet the Mediterranean north of the port of Tyre. A third river, the Jordan, which begins in the south-western reaches of Mount Hermon, does not reach the Mediterranean at all. Instead it flows south along a deep channel which descends below sea level, first through the Huleh valley and into the basin which forms the Sea of Galilee, and finally through the Jordan valley into the Dead Sea. From the Dead Sea, the Wadi Araba forms a continuation of the rift valley, extending south to the Gulf of Aqaba on the Red Sea and dividing the Negev from the Shara' range which extends along its eastern side (colour plate 2).

Much of inland Syria beyond the mountains and river valleys is characterized by dry steppe and semi-desert. This constitutes the third zone, often labelled as Rome's desert frontier. There are, however, stretches of cultivable land, and much of it is not strictly a desert. Indeed, the northernmost parts of Syria, the limestone and basalt hills between the great Euphrates bend and the Mediterranean, are well-watered and have long sustained a large population (fig. 3). In the centre of this region, more or less halfway between the Orontes and the Euphrates, is the city of Aleppo (classical Beroea). Aleppo is surrounded by fertile plains, and can not only rely on adequate rainfall but can also draw water from the Qoueiq river which flows through the city. The Qoueiq goes on to supply the region around the ancient city of Chalcis, before it expires, landbound, in a marsh. There are other rivers that drain from the highlands into the steppe in this way, providing water for settlement and agriculture. In the Antilebanon mountains is the source of the Barada river, the ancient Chrysoroas, which flows east to water the Ghuta oasis, on the edge of which lies Damascus.

The interior of Syria and the Near East is further broken up by mountains

and plateaux, a number of which are remnants of volcanic activity. Mountain chains run north-east of Damascus towards the Euphrates: the Jebel Rawaq, the Jebel Abu Rijmen north of Palmyra, and the Jebel al-Bishri. A direct route across Syria between Damascus and the Euphrates ran along the line of these mountains via the oasis of Palmyra. The Jebel Rawaq and Jebel Abu Rijmen more or less mark the line where the mean annual rainfall drops below 200 millimetres (8 inches; the lower limit for annual crop raising without special irrigation techniques - see fig. 56), and to their south lies the real desert of Syria and Arabia. Much of it is characterized by gravel plains, but there are variations - the black basalt lava-flows and rocks of Safa in the desert south-east of Damascus, or river silts, sandstone and windblown sand towards the Euphrates. This southern desert is generally quite high, over 500 metres (1640 feet) above sea level, sloping gradually down towards the Euphrates in the east. West of this steppe and desert zone, and south of Damascus, lie the 'lava-lands' of the Hauran, including the high volcanic massif of the Jebel Druze (now also called the Jebel al-'Arab), a mountainous region covered in small volcanic craters and cones. From this region extend two major lava-flows, the Qura and the Leja. The Leja separates the Damascus region from the Nuqra, a broad, fertile plain in the heart of the lava-lands. Other extinct volcanoes to the west in the Golan and Mount Hermon created lava-fields north of Qunaytra, and this volcanic basalt stretches south to the valley of the Wadi Yarmuk. The lava-lands receive sufficient rains to make them fertile, and a finger of this climate extends further south to water the western side of the Transjordan plateau (the high area of limestone hills east of the Jordan, the Dead Sea, and as far south

Fig. 3. The Euphrates at Zeugma. View from the acropolis, with the site of the Hellenistic city of Apamea on level ground on the opposite side, to the right.

as the Shara' range). Four seasonal rivers, the Yarmuk, Zerqa, Mujib and Hasa, flow west from the plateau down to the rift valley of the Jordan and the Dead Sea. This fertile western side of the Transjordan plateau supported its principal ancient cities, such as Gadara, Gerasa and Philadelphia. Further east the plateau receives little rain, and the true desert begins. From near the oasis of Azraq, located near the south-eastern corner of the lava-lands, extends the Wadi Sirhan, which once formed a major route into the greater Arabian peninsula. In the south the plateau culminates in the massif of the Shara', which then drops down to the Hisma depression, beyond which lie the Hijaz and central Arabia.

The easternmost landmark in this region is the Euphrates, which has its origins in Anatolia. Initially this river flows towards the Mediterranean, but in northern Syria it turns south-east towards the Persian Gulf. For much of its course it passes through desert, but the fact that it is navigable along most of its length meant that in antiquity this river provided a vital link between the north and Babylonia and the Gulf. Two important tributaries in Mesopotamia, the Balikh and the Khabur, meet the Euphrates along its middle reaches.

The Structure of this Book

I hope that the above explains what I intend by 'Roman Syria and the Near East', chronologically and geographically. It remains to explain how this book is arranged. It is divided into four sections. The first, 'Grand Narratives', provides a general historical framework to orient the reader in the chapters that follow. It is not intended as a comprehensive history of the region. The second section, 'Organizing Space and Time', deals with the impact of Rome on the political makeup of the region and on the basic structures that gave rhythm and order to everyday life. The Greek-style city state was a key element in Roman manipulation of these structures, more so, it would seem, than any other institution, including the Roman army. However, the army was important in the development of a communications infrastructure, and these changes had an effect on civilian life. The third section, 'Production and Consumption', covers more strictly economic matters, such as the relation between city and countryside, the exploitation of the landscape and the influences of economic processes on 'Hellenization' or 'Romanization'. The chapter 'Portable Antiquities' considers the integration of Syria and the Near East into the state tax system and the wider world of Mediterranean trade. Again the city state emerges as an important player in the provincial economy. The fourth and final section, 'The Construction of Communities', examines the institutions that provided a sense of social identity for the peoples of the region: the city state; language and culture; religion; and the Roman army. The chapters try to cover a lot of ground, but they cannot encompass everything. Some popular subjects which receive detailed treatment in other general works - for example, Roman roads, forts and army units, provincial governors, Rome and the Jews, and the 'caravan trade' – are given less space here than might be anticipated. There are many more things that could have been said about these important themes, but they have been better said elsewhere and the reader is encouraged to consult the bibliography for further reading.

Hellenism and Greek culture are of course a central feature of this period, even if they are difficult concepts to define. Under Alexander the Great the 'Greek World' had come to encompass the 'Near' and 'Middle East', and because the West claims Greece as part of itself, the period and region covered by this book have long been a battleground, between the champions of the Western tradition who seek to determine its essential Greekness, and those who are looking to emphasize the 'authentic' and indigenous lurking beneath a Western veneer. Hellenism has been seen as 'a first "europeanization" of the Near East',[1] and for romantic Hellenists, Syria and the rest of the 'East' became an irredeemably foreign entity with the Muslim conquests, detached from Western destiny: 'So utterly gone and extinct is that old world, so alien is the sordid present ... that [a European traveller in the Levant] becomes aware of a closer kinship between himself and some of these fragments of antiquity than exists between himself and the living people of the land'. So wrote E. R. Bevan on the opening page of his great work, *The House of Seleucus*, published in 1902, but similar sympathies continue to be expressed. For those interested in indigenous origins, the Western tradition either corrupted or had no real impact. Recently a study has emphasized the 'hollowness of Roman rule in the Near East'[2] by reference to eastern origins. Both camps in this clash of East and West have been able to appeal to either 'Graeco-Roman' or 'indigenous' origins or archetypes to support their case because both elements are present, or appear to us to be present. Perhaps this search for origins is rooted in the idea that by uncovering a thing's origin we discover something genuine and legitimate about it. Hence, possibly, the interest in the origin of what is called 'frontality' in Palmyrene art (chapter 8), the origin of the so-called 'Hippodamian' plan of cities (chapter 7), or the question of whether 'Phoenician' identity in the Roman period was a direct continuation of some earlier one (chapter 8). By choosing the Hellenistic period as the beginning of my narrative I would seem to be siding firmly with the Hellenist camp, and indeed I do view the impositions of the Hellenizing imperial powers as an important break with the past. But there is a significant difference between the origin of a thing and its meanings to contemporaries. Origins and archetypes are not explanations in themselves, and the persistence of a form over time does not necessarily mean that it was somehow less passive or less susceptible to corruption, or, to use a term redolent of social Darwinism, that it possessed a greater capacity for survival. The symbols and codes cultures employ to provide a sense of social identity for their members may change without the members sensing any severe discontinuities. A form may persist but its meaning change, or meaning may persist but the form change (see chapter 8).

Inevitably this debate between Hellenizers and Indigenizers has turned to the question of identities. Many of the broader identities that we can see expressed in Roman Syria were political creations of the Hellenistic and Roman periods: city state; commune of the imperial cult; province. This would seem to vindicate the Hellenist standpoint, because these institutions were 'Graeco-Roman', but we might question how natural it is for individuals to identify with a single 'ethnic' or 'cultural' group (something which is often implicit in modern identity politics), rather than employing various different identities according to context. Ethnicity, culture and identity are difficult concepts to pin down, and even if they appear to overlap (so that one can speak of ethnic or cultural identity), they cannot be treated as the same thing. Thus the question 'Was there a distinct Syrian culture?' is not quite the same as 'Was there a distinct Syrian identity?' Hoping for a clear resolution to either question is probably futile. The social identities that we can detect now at such a remove are unlikely to have been the only ones to exist. Individuals can identify themselves with several different (and sometimes contradictory) social institutions: tribe; religion; guild; city; and so on. It is difficult enough to analyse these traits in modern societies, let alone in the distant past. There is always the fear that we might project identities on to peoples of the past that they never had, but to some extent such projections are unavoidable. In using general concepts like 'Graeco-Roman', 'Greek city', 'baetyl-worship' or 'late antiquity' we are probably projecting identities and meanings which contemporaries would not have recognized, but the analysis of the institutions and categories that appear to generate identities requires some level of generality. Nevertheless, caution is advisable. The local and the particular seem to have been important to the inhabitants of the region, especially in the case of religions (chapter 9), and it is in the local and particular that the Indigenizers have their best case, rather than in recourse to any general 'oriental' identity or culture.

East or West? Perhaps we should choose neither, for both are identities projected on to the past, and instead we should try to grant the peoples of the region some autonomy from these discourses. They were not an eternal, immutable part of the 'orient' hiding behind a classical veneer, from which the West would do better to learn, nor were they the passive victims of superior cultural entities. They were active participants in a network of social relations, imperial and otherwise, with a capacity for appropriating and using cultural symbols of different origin for their own ends. Cultures and identities are constructed, performative and historically situated rather than innate and unchanging. Even the identities of East and West are fluid, contingent and ascribed. Indeed, it is perhaps ironic that the seventh century AD witnessed not only the creation of a great 'Eastern' politico-cultural world empire centred on what was once 'Hellenized' Syria, but that for many modern scholars in the West, the near-eclipse of the Roman empire at this time should be seen as marking the beginning of the 'Byzantine' empire and the transformation of this formerly 'Western' power into an integral part of the 'East'.

18

LIST OF RULERS

Seleucid kings

Seleucus I Nicator
(312-280 BC)
Antiochus I Soter
(280-261 BC)
Antiochus II Theos
(261-246 BC)
Seleucus II Callinicus
(246-226 BC)
Seleucus III Ceraunus
(226-223 BC)
Antiochus III the Great
(223-187 BC)
Seleucus IV Philopator
(187-175 BC)
Antiochus IV Epiphanes
(175-164 BC)
Antiochus V Eupator
(164-162 BC)
Demetrius I Soter
(162-150 BC)
Alexander I Balas
(150-145 BC)
Demetrius II Nicator,
(145-140, 129-125 BC)
Antiochus VI Dionysus
(145-142 BC)
Diodotus Tryphon
(142-138 BC)
Antiochus VII Euergetes
(138-129 BC)

Alexander II Zebinas
(128-123 BC)
Seleucus V (125 BC)
Cleopatra Thea (125 BC)
Cleopatra and Antiochus
VIII Grypus
(125-121 BC)
Antiochus VIII (121-96 BC)
Antiochus IX Cyzicenus
(113-95 BC)
Seleucus VI Epiphanes
Nicator (95-94 BC)
Demetrius III Philopator
(95-88 BC)
Antiochus X Eusebes
Philopator (94-83 BC)
Antiochus XI Epiphanes
Philadelphus and Philip
I Philadelphus (93 BC)
Philip I (93-83 BC)
Antiochus XII Dionysus
(88-84 BC)
(Tigranes of Armenia,
83-69 BC)
Antiochus XIII Asiaticus
(69-64 BC)
Philip II Barypous
(c. 68-64 BC)

Parthian (Arsacid) kings

Arsaces I (c. 238-211 BC)
Arsaces II (c. 211-191 BC)
Phriapatius
(c. 191-176 BC)
Phraates I (c. 176-171 BC)
Mithradates I
(c. 171-138 BC)
Phraates II (c. 138-127 BC)
Artabanus I
(c. 127-123 BC)
Mithradates II
(c. 123-88 BC)
Gotarzes I (c. 90-80 BC)
Orodes I (c. 80-77 BC)
Sinatruces (c. 77-70 BC)
Phraates III (c. 70-57 BC)
Mithradates III
(c. 57-54 BC)
Orodes II (c. 57-38 BC)
Pacorus I (c. 39 BC)
Phraates IV (c. 38-2 BC)
(Tiridates, usurper in the
west, 26 BC)
Phraataces (c. 2 BC - AD 4)
Orodes III (4-6)
Vonones I (8-12)

Artabanus II (10-38)
Vardanes I (40-45)
Gotarzes II (40-51)
(Vonones II, usurper,
c. 51)
Vologaeses I (51-78)
(Vardanes II, usurper,
55-58)
Vologaeses II (77-80)
Pacorus II (77-105)
(Artabanus III, usurper,
80-81)
Vologaeses III (105-147)
(Osroes I, usurper,
109-129)
(Parthamaspates, Roman
nominee, 116)
(Mithradates, usurper,
c. AD 140)
Vologaeses IV (147-191)
(Osroes II, usurper,
c. AD 190)
Vologaeses V (191-208)
Vologaeses VI (208-222)
Artabanus IV (213-224)

Sasanian shahs of Persia

Ardashir I (224-241)
Shapur I (241-272)
Hormizd I (272-273)
Bahram I (273-276)
Bahram II (276-293)
Bahram III (293)
Narseh (293-303)
Hormizd II (303-309)
Shapur II (309-379)
Ardashir II (379-383)
Shapur III (383-388)
Bahram IV (388-399)
Yazdgard I (399-420)

Bahram V Gor (420-438)
Yazdgard II (438-457)
Hormizd III (457-459)
Peroz (457-484)
Balash (484-488)
Kavad I (484, 488-497,
499-531)
Zamasp (497-499)
Khusrau I Anushirvan
(531-579)
Hormizd IV (579-590)
Bahram VI Chobin
(590-591)

Roman emperors

Usurpers are only mentioned
when relevant to the text.

Julio-Claudian dynasty
Augustus (27 BC - AD 14)
Tiberius (14-37)
Caligula (37-41)
Claudius (41-54)
Nero (54-68)

Galba (68-69)
Otho (69)
Vitellius (69)

Flavian dynasty
Vespasian (69-79)
Titus (79-81)
Domitian (81-96)

'Adoptive' emperors
Nerva (96-98)
Trajan (98-117)
Hadrian (117-138)

Antonines
Antoninus Pius (138-161)
Marcus Aurelius and Lucius
Verus (161-169)
Marcus Aurelius (169-177)
Marcus Aurelius and
Commodus (177-180)
Commodus (180-192)
Pertinax (193)
Didius Julianus (193)
(Pescennius Niger, usurper
in the east, 193-194)
(Clodius Albinus, usurper
in the west, 193-196)

Severan dynasty
Septimius Severus
(193-198)
Septimius Severus and
Caracalla (198-209)
Septimius Severus,
Caracalla and Geta
(209-211)
Caracalla and Geta
(211-212)
Caracalla (212-217)
Macrinus (217-218)
Elagabalus (218-222)
Severus Alexander
(222-235)

The 'soldier emperors'
Maximinus I Thrax
(235-238)
Gordian I and Gordian II
Africanus (238)
Balbinus and Pupienus (238)
Balbinus, Pupienus and
Gordian III (238)
Gordian III (238-244)
Philip I the 'Arab' (244-246)
Philip I and Philip II
(246-249)
Trajan Decius (249-251)
Trajan Decius and
Herennius Etruscus (251)

Hostilian and Trebonianus
Gallus (251)
Trebonianus Gallus and
Volusian (251-253)
Aemilian (253)
(Uranius Antoninus,
usurper in Syria c. 253)
Valerian and Gallienus
(253-260)
(Macrianus and Quietus,
usurpers in the east,
260-261)
(Postumus, usurper in the
west, 259-268)
Gallienus (260-268)
Claudius II (268-270)
Quintillus (270)
Aurelian (270-275)
(Vaballathus, usurper in
the east, 271-272)
Tacitus (275-276)
Florianus (276)
Probus (276-282)
(Saturninus, usurper in the
east, c. 278)
Carus (282-283)
Carus and Carinus (283)
Carus, Carinus and
Numerian (283)
Carinus and Numerian
(283-284)
Carinus (284-285)
Diocletian (284-286)

The Tetrarchy
Diocletian and Maximianus
(286-305)
Galerius and Constantius I
Chlorus (305-306)
(Constantine I, usurper in
the west, 306)
Galerius and Severus II
(306-307)
(Maxentius, usurper in the
central provinces,
306-312)
(Maximianus, 2nd reign as
usurper in the west,
306-307)
(Maximianus and
Constantine I, usurpers
in the west, 307-308)
Galerius and Licinius
(308-309)
Galerius, Licinius,
Maximinus II Daia and
Constantine I (309-311)
Licinius, Maximinus II and
Constantine I (311-313)
Licinius and Constantine I
(313-324)

Dynasty of Constantine
Constantine I (324-337)
Constantine II, Constans
and Constantius II
(337-340)
Constans and Constantius
II (340-350)
Constantius II (350-361)

(Magnentius, usurper in
the west, 350-353)
Julian (361-363)
Jovian (363-364)
Valentinian I and Valens
(364-367)
Valentinian I, Valens and
Gratian (367-375)
Valens, Gratian and
Valentinian II (375-378)
Gratian and Valentinian II
(378-379)
Gratian, Valentinian II and
Theodosius I (379-383)
Valentinian II, Theodosius I
and Arcadius (383-392)
Theodosius I and Arcadius
(392-393)
Theodosius I, Arcadius and
Honorius (393-395)

*Eastern Roman ('Byzantine')
Empire*
Arcadius (395-402)
Arcadius and Theodosius II
(402-408)
Theodosius II (408-450)
Marcian (450-457)
Leo I (457-473)
Leo I and Leo II (473-474)
Leo II (474)
Leo II and Zeno (474)
Zeno (474-491)
(Leontius, usurper in the
east, 484-488)
Anastasius I (491-518)
Justin I (518-527)
Justin I and Justinian I
(527)
Justinian I (527-565)
Justin II (565-578)
Tiberius II (578-582)
Maurice Tiberius (582-602)
Phocas (602-610)

Heraclian dynasty
Heraclius (610-613)
Heraclius and Heraclius
Constantine (613-638)
Heraclius, Heraclius
Constantine and
Heraclonas (638-641)
Heraclius Constantine and
Heraclonas (641)
Heraclonas (641)
Constans II (also called
Constantine III)
(641-654)
Constans II and
Constantine IV (654-668)
Constantine IV, Heraclius
and Tiberius (668-681)
Constantine IV (681-685)
Justinian II (685-695)
Leontius (695-698)
Tiberius III (698-705)
Justinian II, 2nd reign, and
Tiberius (705-711)

Bistahm (591-597)
Khusrau II Parvez (591-628)
(Hormizd, usurper? c. 593)
Kavad II (628)
Ardashir III (628-630)

Shahrbaraz (630)
Buran (630-631)
Azarmidukht (631)
Khusrau III? (c. 629-631)
Khusrau IV? (c. 631-637)

Hormizd V (631-632)
Yazdgard III (632-651)

All dates AD unless otherwise noted

PART I
GRAND NARRATIVES

I AN INCIDENTAL ANNEXATION

In 64 BC a Roman general met with a local king at the city of Antioch in northern Syria and told the king that he was out of a job. Of this fact ancient writers were certain; but they differed as to the motives. Some thought it a question of legitimacy, and that the king had proved himself unworthy in some way. Others considered it a matter of security, that the king was incapable of defending Syria against 'the despoiling raids of Jews and Arabs.'[3] Whatever the case, it was this meeting which marks the beginning of the Roman province of Syria, and it was for reasons of legitimacy or security that Rome justified the annexation of an area far more extensive than the kingdom in question.

The protagonists in this curious historical event were Antiochus XIII Asiaticus, a Seleucid dynast whose ancestors had once ruled an empire from the Hellespont to India, and the general Gnaeus Pompeius Magnus, better known in English as Pompey the Great. As far as we know Antiochus did not dispute Pompey's judgement. In his earlier relations with Rome the king had accepted his position as a sort of client, dependent on the favours of Roman patrons far more powerful than himself. Now Pompey would claim the kingdom by right of conquest, even though Antiochus had been an ally rather than an adversary of Rome.

Antiochus was a rather minor casualty in a much grander struggle between the Romans and two more dangerous and powerful eastern kings, Mithridates VI Eupator of Pontus and Tigranes of Armenia. It is this struggle that led to the Roman annexation of Syria, and a brief outline of that struggle is necessary to place the dismissal of Antiochus XIII in context. During the later second and

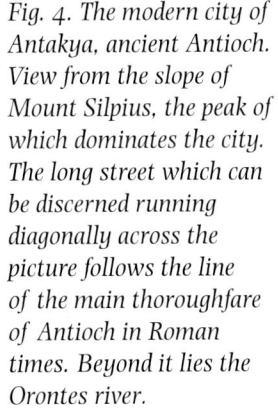

Fig. 4. The modern city of Antakya, ancient Antioch. View from the slope of Mount Silpius, the peak of which dominates the city. The long street which can be discerned running diagonally across the picture follows the line of the main thoroughfare of Antioch in Roman times. Beyond it lies the Orontes river.

early first centuries BC Rome had been aggressively extending her influence in the eastern Mediterranean, and even in those regions relatively remote from direct interference, rulers had become wary of acting too openly against Roman interests. By the beginning of the first century BC many of the weaker states in the eastern Mediterranean, which generally sought safety in alliances with whatever superpower offered them the greatest security, were beginning to judge that their best chances lay in compacts with Rome. Kings, however, were used to making diplomatic alliances with other kings, and they often found it difficult to steer their way safely through the constantly shifting policies and political intrigues of the ruling aristocracy at Rome. Roman intentions were hard to discern, because the Roman state had no consistent, long-term policy in its dealings with the eastern Mediterranean states, and each of the succession of generals appointed to deal with the kingdoms adopted a different strategy. As Roman aristocrats, these generals were in competition with others of their kind to acquire wealth and honours, and such things could best be attained by securing a high-profile military command. As the Roman empire expanded, the glittering prizes grew ever greater, until the commanders were fighting for supreme control of the empire itself.

Nevertheless there were still some alternatives to Rome in the first half of the first century BC. Some kings commanded sufficient wealth and resources to act independently and even to stand against the Romans, and these powerful rulers were always casting around for allies. Yet joining an alliance against Rome was not a choice to be made lightly, even for a powerful state. While the expansion of the Roman empire cannot have seemed inevitable to contemporaries, the history of the period provided plenty of cautionary examples to illustrate what happened to those who tried to block her expansion. Mithridates VI of Pontus, however, challenged Rome in a bloody dispute which raged for more than two decades. The focus of the conflict was in Asia Minor, but the complexity of dynastic intermarriages among eastern rulers could easily lead to other kings and regions becoming involved. When the Roman general Lucius Lucullus won a major victory over Mithridates in 71 BC, the defeated king escaped and sought sanctuary with his son-in-law Tigranes, the king of Armenia. Lucullus knew that even in defeat Mithridates was very resourceful, and demanded that the Armenian king hand over the fugitive, to prevent the enemy rallying anti-Roman support and raising another army.

It was this chain of events that led indirectly to Rome's annexation of Syria, and it is perhaps appropriate that Armenia should have played such a central role from the very beginning, because in the centuries that followed the kingdom was a territory bitterly disputed between the Romans and their eastern neighbours the Parthians and Persians, with its political disposition influencing imperial strategies along their respective frontiers. Tigranes had begun his reign (c. 96 BC) as a vassal ruler of the vast and powerful Parthian empire, but in the years following his accession a dynastic civil war in the Parthian realm had allowed him to embark on an ambitious scheme of conquest, southwards into the western parts of the Parthian empire, and westwards to absorb what remained of the enfeebled Seleucid kingdom in Syria. At its greatest extent the empire of Tigranes stretched from the Mediterranean to the Caspian sea.

The arrival of Mithridates in Armenia must have proved an embarrassment to Tigranes, who was then at the zenith of his power. Nevertheless the Roman demand was refused. Lucullus retaliated by invading Armenia (69 BC) and

Fig. 5.1. Silver tetradrachm with a portrait of Antiochus XIII Asiaticus, the last Seleucid king. BM 1927-4-3-87.

Fig. 5.2. Silver tetradrachm with a portrait of Tigranes of Armenia. BMC 2.

destroying its capital, Tigranocerta. The Armenian royal governor of Syria withdrew his army to help defend the homeland. Tigranes' empire disintegrated, leaving local rulers, formerly subject to the Armenian king, negotiating for recognition with the new Roman power-broker. For the Romans the invasion had been a great success, although by invading a kingdom which had been carved out of lands claimed by both the Parthians and the Seleucids, Lucullus was leading Rome into an entirely new sphere of affairs. It is hardly surprising, then, that as Tigranes' power collapsed the general found himself courted by embassies from the Parthian ruler and the Seleucid claimant, Antiochus XIII, both kings wanting to recover the lands of which they had been deprived by Tigranes.

It is somewhat ironic that Antiochus XIII owed his throne to the conflict that eventually ended with his dismissal. During Tigranes' occupation of Syria the Roman Senate had recognized Antiochus as rightful heir to the Seleucid realm, and now, as the Armenian forces withdrew, Lucullus did the same. He posed no direct threat to Roman interests (even if some of his more powerful ancestors had been formidable opponents), and his kingdom consisted of a small and unstable domain centred on the city of Antioch and the fertile plain of eastern Cilicia. Strategically the kingdom was not particularly vital to Rome, although it did control a major land route from Cilicia into Syria via the Belen Pass (the 'Syrian Gates') in the Amanus mountains.

To some extent, then, Antiochus appeared to have the backing of Rome, and he could perhaps hope to occupy his throne as a Roman 'client king'. But events changed quickly, with unfavourable consequences for Antiochus. His kingdom was disputed by a relative, and other petty rulers in northern Syria threatened his control of the hinterland. He may even have lost his kingdom to his rivals by the time Pompey arrived. More importantly, Mithridates of Pontus had eluded the Romans, and this proved to be Lucullus' undoing. The fugitive king made his way home to Pontus, raised a new army and inflicted a resounding defeat on the Roman legions there. The Senate and the People of Rome replaced Lucullus with Pompey, who in a brilliant campaign drove Mithridates overseas (where he later died) and received the formal submission of Tigranes. The Armenian king forfeited his empire but was allowed to retain his ancestral kingdom.

Pompey then took it upon himself to settle affairs in the power vacuum left by the withdrawal of Tigranes from Syria. The empire of Tigranes was Roman by right of conquest, although there were Parthian claims to consider. Syria, however, had never been part of the Parthian kingdom. Pompey could have chosen not to interfere, leaving the region as a patchwork of small independent political entities, as it had been immediately prior to Tigranes' invasion. It is unlikely, however, that such an option was entertained when the alternative was so much more promising: the extension of Roman influence and control over the east. It was a question of finding out what the states of Syria were like and whether any of them would offer resistance. The political makeup of the region was complex and potentially unstable, which offered Pompey an excuse to intervene to ensure order and security. In the north-west Antioch was the capital of what remained of the Seleucid kingdom. Further east a dynast called Dionysius controlled the cities of Hierapolis and Beroea, and to the north of these lay the large kingdom of Antiochus I of Commagene. The regions south of Antioch and the principality of Dionysius included a number of city states such as Apamea as well as small principalities and areas inhabited by nomadic tribes, some of which may have been the 'Jews and Arabs' that Pompey invoked as an excuse for dismissing Antiochus. The Phoenician cities of the coast were independent states, although some were controlled by overlords characterized as 'tyrants'. The south was dominated by three large kingdoms: the Hasmonaean, Nabataean and Ituraean. Between these three was an inland enclave of city states which later became known collectively as the Decapolis (Ten Cities).

Whether Pompey regarded the Parthians as a major threat or not is unclear. Even if he did not, there was always the chance that, if left alone, the relatively small states in Syria might gravitate towards the eastern superpower. The Parthians had shown an interest in Syria in the past, and may have aimed at reducing the Seleucids to vassal status during the troubled years prior to the rise of Tigranes. This would have given them access to the Mediterranean, making their kingdom as formidable as any that Rome had yet faced in the east. The Parthians were certainly in a position to build a world-empire centred on Mesopotamia, and even if (as some have argued) they had no pretensions to further western conquests, they were clearly a challenge to Roman interests. Syria was easy prey for the Parthians and Rome; it was merely a question of which power was best able to take it and then control it. To the Romans the region could have strategic value as a launching point for further aggression against the Parthians or the Ptolemaic kingdom of Egypt. Furthermore, the cities and kingdoms of Syria were wealthy, although revenues would have to be offset against the expenses of maintaining armies in the region. We cannot be certain that all of these considerations were weighed up (and Pompey, being a very ambitious individual, was probably acting out of a desire for personal glory as well), but the decision to annex Syria found its first expression in the dismissal of Antiochus XIII. This event marked the beginning of Roman interference and influence, which was to have a profound effect on the communities of Syria and the Near East. As it turned out, Pompey's political and military gamble of annexation paid off in Rome's favour, although there was nothing assured about the permanence of Roman rule in Syria at this early stage.

In the spring of 63 BC Pompey left Antioch and marched south with an army, extorting money, executing 'tyrants', and reducing the power of some of the native principalities. He seems to have posed as the champion of the Greek-style city states, 'liberating' them from the rule of tyrants and dynasts. A civil war in the Hasmonaean kingdom of Judaea drew him further south, where his interventions changed the power structure and extent of the Jewish state, and brought the war to an inconclusive pause. He had planned an attack on the Nabataeans but did not press this after intervening in Judaea. Instead he appointed his deputy, Marcus Aemilius Scaurus, as governor pending a proper senatorial appointee, and departed Syria, leaving Scaurus with two legions.

Pompey had not greatly altered the political makeup of Syria, although the fact of Roman rule now meant that the status of a community was decided by Rome rather than through the community's independent interactions with its neighbours. The more powerful could negotiate better deals, but Roman control of status, favours and obligations could not be challenged except through open rebellion. For the city states, 'freedom' presumably came at a cost, in the form of tribute to Rome. The major dynasts, as 'friends' of Rome, may not have had to provide tribute at all, although at least one found it prudent to bribe Pompey to retain his throne. At this early stage Rome had not yet established for certain who were friends and who were enemies. The Seleucids had been deposed, and hostile or potentially rebellious elements had been removed where these were recognizable. The boundaries of Roman power in the region had not been established, although a symbolic border with the Parthian realm along the Euphrates river was to become political reality in later years. The new province of Syria was geographically and politically vague and amorphous, but Pompey may have had a model in mind when he decided to annex the region. He had justified the dismissal of Antiochus XIII by implying that his restoration would only lead to instability. As the conqueror of Tigranes, Pompey had the right to appoint or dismiss local rulers as he judged fit, but his subsequent actions may have stretched the terms of his senatorial appointment, which was to make war on Mithridates and Tigranes, and not to campaign in Syria. The Syrian acquisitions of Tigranes were less extensive than the region which Pompey now claimed, and, if anything, the Roman province of Syria resembled the Syrian provinces which Antiochus' ancestors had ruled. Through the deposition of Antiochus XIII the Roman state could pose as the legitimate successor of the Seleucids in Syria, providing a fiction of continuity which at the same time justified imperial expansion. The kingdom of Antiochus XIII was very small, but his removal looks like a critical gesture signifying Roman intentions: the Romans would bring order to Antiochus' ancestral domains.

Syria before Rome

The Seleucid kingdom had been carved out of Alexander the Great's empire, itself created through conquest of the Persian empire. Many characteristics of these later empires can be detected in the Persian empire, which straddled Mesopotamia, stretching westwards into Syria, Asia Minor and Egypt, and eastwards into Iran, Afghanistan and Pakistan. The rule of Persia's Achaemenid kings was sanctioned by divine right, and the empire associated with the person of the king. Submission to the king, who was the source of justice and order, was the only major imperial demand expected of all the empire's subjects. In spite of the centralized, despotic nature of their rule at the centre of the empire, the Achaemenids accepted and carefully managed the diverse cultures of the provinces through a policy of decentralized authority, permitting, or perhaps accepting, a high degree of local autonomy. Although most high administrative posts were reserved for Persians, some governors were of local origin, and Persian rule is characterized in the sources as lenient and fostering cosmopolitanism by allowing local elites to remain in charge of their native lands and peoples and to maintain their own traditions. As their empire expanded, the Achaemenids adopted and adapted the local forms of social control. Persian imperialism did not, it seems, involve imposing Persian culture on everyone. However, an education system provided a cohesive ideology for the elites of the empire, although its form of transmission appears to have been predominantly oral rather than literary. Thus, in spite of the looseness of Persian political control and the diversity of the empire's cultures, the diffusion of elite culture gave the empire an impressive degree of integrity. The king's powers were extensive *across* communities through his relations with the elites, but could not always be applied intensively *within* communities.

Evidence for the Persian period in Syria is poor, and the quality of the information varies from place to place. It has been assumed that the region was not heavily urbanized, except for the Phoenician coast, where the Persians actively supported cities, but the paucity of evidence from outside Phoenicia hardly allows us to be certain. Many Hellenistic cities were founded on old sites whose population and status in the Persian period is unknown, and which can be determined only through confident archaeological identification of their Persian phases. Our best evidence comes from the Phoenician cities, which provided ships and sailors for the Persian fleet. In their long-distance economic contacts all over the Mediterranean the Phoenician states were encouraged by the Persian rulers. Thus Phoenicia benefited from its position on the periphery of the Persian empire. The cosmopolitan nature of Achaemenid rule is evident in the art of Phoenician cities like Aradus, Byblus and Sidon. Local rulers are depicted in Persian dress, but their badges of office and coin types often combine local, Persian, Egyptian and Greek elements. In certain ways the Phoenician cities resembled the independent city states of Greece, and in spite of their conflicts with Athens and its allies as agents of Persian imperialism, they were open to Greek influences. Greek marbles were imported, and the highly Hellenized styles of some of the sculpture suggest Greek, or Greek-trained sculptors at work. Elite burials indicate the adoption or adaptation of a variety of traditions: the Phoenician upper classes were buried in sarcophagi of Egyptian style, Lycian style and, perhaps in imitation of philhellene Persian elites in Asia Minor, in imported Greek marble sarcophagi with elaborate figured reliefs of thoroughly Greek style. Architectural elements make it clear that the cities also boasted buildings of Achaemenid imperial style. The coastal regions at least demonstrate a network of overseas exchanges and a lively hybridization of cultures, but one cannot speak of a deliberate policy of 'Persianization'.

With Alexander the Great's invasion of the Persian empire, and the death of its king Darius in 330, the entire Persian dominion became a Macedonian prize. This event marked the beginning of what since the nineteenth century has been called the Hellenistic period. Although it signalled a new phase of elite power, many regions of the Hellenistic east witnessed the continuity of traditions, and the Persian ideas of the king as the embodiment of empire, decentralized control through local rulers, and a widely diffused imperial elite culture were maintained by Alexander and his successors, although now the imperial elite culture was Greek and had a strong literary bias. Greek became the language of the court and high-level administration from the Mediterranean to India, and colonies and settlements of Greek-speakers were established all across the former Persian domains. This does not necessarily mean that local cultures in the heavily colonized regions declined, although in many parts of Syria their persistence through the Hellenistic period is hard to trace. The impact of Macedonian rule during the few years between Alexander and the establishment of the great Hellenistic kingdoms of

Fig. 6. Part of the sanctuary of Eshmun near Sidon: the Persian phase of the complex included this series of terraces which have been likened by some to a Mesopotamian ziggurat.

the Seleucids and Ptolemies is difficult to assess. Along the Mediterranean coast of Syria and Palestine, which was the area most receptive to foreign imports and ideas, excavations have revealed that the cities were importing significant quantities of black-gloss pottery from Athens at the end of the fourth century, probably in conjunction with other more perishable goods which have left little or no trace. There was a notable influx of Greek and Macedonian settlers in the late fourth and early third centuries BC. Alexander established a standardized coinage in gold, silver and bronze which circulated widely throughout his empire, although this operated in conjunction with local coinages in some areas. A universal currency was convenient for long-distance trade, yet, as we will see in chapter 6, it was not a prerequisite for widespread economic links between different parts of the Mediterranean or elsewhere. But like Greek literacy a universal currency, stamped with the symbols of a central authority, contributed to the diffusion of an imperial ideology and power over wide areas.

The Seleucid kingdom took its name from the founder of the dynasty which ruled it for two and a half centuries. Although it tends to be called a 'Syrian' empire, Syria formed only a part of the kingdom, and its origins in Babylonia (rather than Syria proper) mark the Seleucid kingdom as a Middle Eastern empire, which, like its Achaemenid and Alexandrian predecessors, was centred on the Fertile Crescent. Seleucid history began inauspiciously. In 320 BC a young Macedonian officer named Seleucus was appointed governor of Babylon, but he was forced out in the complex power struggle between generals that followed Alexander's death. For the next two decades a large part of Alexander's empire was dominated by the governor of Phrygia, Antigonus the One-Eyed. Other governors, particularly Ptolemy of Egypt and Lysimachus of Thrace, feared for their own positions and formed an alliance against Antigonus. Seleucus, now Ptolemy's protégé, retook Babylon in 312 BC and, allied with both Ptolemy and Lysimachus, drove Antigonus into Asia Minor, finally defeating him in Phrygia in 301. In the division of territory that followed, Seleucus was given northern Syria, which remained Seleucid territory for the next two and a half centuries, and Ptolemy occupied the south. Seleucus went on to defeat Lysimachus, and found himself presiding over an empire stretching from the western coast of Asia Minor to India. Babylonia remained the keystone to his possessions, a bridge between the eastern and western halves of his empire which any rival would have to cross in order to conquer the whole.

The impact of Seleucid rule on the culture and political geography of Syria is examined below, and we will return to it at various points in the chapters which follow. The impact of Ptolemaic rule in the south, which lasted for about a century, is rather more difficult to evaluate, because there is not a great deal of evidence available. Some scholars explain the relative lack of evidence by arguing that there was comparatively little development in the south under the Ptolemies, who preferred to rule through traditional forms of government rather than encouraging the development of Greek cities as the Seleucids appear to have done (fig. 7). Like the Seleucids the Ptolemies founded settlements, although the extent of the programme of urbanization (if it could be called such) appears to have been much less ambitious than the Seleucid one, and it is often impossible to distinguish city from fortress given the evidence available to us. Among the more important Ptolemaic foundations were

Ptolemais, founded at the coastal site of Akko, Philadelphia (Amman), Berenike (Aqaba), and Scythopolis in Galilee.

The Seleucid period was a crucial phase in the diffusion of Greek culture in Syria. For a start, it witnessed the development of a programme of urbanization based on the model of the Greek *polis*, which was also the form of local government most favoured by Rome in the eastern Mediterranean. The programme had been initiated by Alexander, but it was Seleucus and his son Antiochus I who carried it forward by founding numerous cities in their empire. Northern Syria was one of the regions that received particular attention. Some of the work there was probably done by Antigonus the One-Eyed, but Seleucus and his descendants deserve credit for fashioning northern Syria into an urbanized region with great centres like Antioch, Seleucia, Laodicea, Apamea, Beroea, Chalcis, Hierapolis and Zeugma. The Seleucid foundations not only provided Greek and Macedonian colonists with land and a familiar lifestyle organized around the institution of the *polis*; they were also intended

Fig. 7. The unfinished palace of the Tobiad Hyrcanus at Tyros (Iraq al-Amir), Jordan. First half of the second century BC. The Tobiads were a Jewish dynasty installed in the region of Ammanitis under the Ptolemies and then the Seleucids.

to operate on behalf of the rulers as instruments of economic and political control over their respective hinterlands. The four great 'sister cities' known collectively as the Tetrapolis, which consisted of the ports of Seleucia and Laodicea and the two cities of Antioch and Apamea in the Orontes valley, dominated the rich agricultural lands of the north-west. New foundations were given dynastic names, or formerly existing settlements were refounded with dynastic names, a deliberate act which associated the landscape and political geography of the empire with the family of the king, and not merely with the person of the king himself. Although the major foundations ceased after Antiochus I, there are hints that many Seleucid cities witnessed substantial growth during the second century BC. Seleucus' urban network persisted through the Roman period, being supported and augmented under Roman rule.

To what extent the Seleucids found it prudent to legitimate their rule through association with the Achaemenids as well as Alexander the Great and the Macedonians cannot be known for certain, but it is worth noting that Seleucus was the only full-blooded Macedonian of the dynasty. Like many other Macedonian officers he had been married to a Persian on Alexander's instructions; unlike those other officers he made a point of staying married to her after Alexander's death. Their son and successor Antiochus I was therefore half-Persian, and all subsequent members of the dynasty had Persian blood. The capable Antiochus continued the work of consolidation initiated by his father, elaborating on the system of symbolic identity for the Seleucid empire. He initiated a universal dating system, the Seleucid era, which began in 312 BC, the year Seleucus recovered Babylonia. This association of time itself with the dynasty stood in marked contrast to the traditions employed by rival dynasties, which dated by regnal years of kings or other traditional systems. It is perhaps ironic that the era was so successful that it outlasted memory of the dynasty itself, and later became known as the 'era of Alexander' or 'of the Greeks' (see chapter 2). Antiochus may also have been responsible for organizing civic cults of Seleucus. In these Seleucus was worshipped as the founder of the city, so that the dynasty became intimately linked to notions of civic identity. Seleucus became an ancestral figure for citizens within the empire as well as for the dynasty itself, and as with the Seleucid era these civic cults continued to be observed in Roman times. And whereas Seleucus had legitimized his rule by continuing to issue coinage using the designs employed by Alexander the Great, Antiochus began issuing coins with portraits of himself and his father. Thenceforth it was commonplace to find portraits of the reigning king on Seleucid coins, in contrast to coins of other Hellenistic dynasties who legitimized their rule through portraits of Alexander or a founding ancestor, or patron deities. The Seleucids were liberated from the need to refer constantly to founder figures on their coinage, perhaps because other media, such as time itself, helped to provide this form of legitimation.

Seleucus' successors spent much of their time fighting rivals in Asia Minor, southern Syria and Palestine and the eastern provinces. Seleucid ambitions in the Mediterranean arena led to fierce competition with other Hellenistic kingdoms there: the Ptolemies of Egypt, the Attalids of Pergamum and the Antigonids of Macedonia. The need to be close to this arena is thought to have been a major reason for the westward shift of the Seleucid empire's core and its eventual concentration in Syria. Even Seleucus I had found it prudent to appoint his son Antiochus as joint king, to administer the eastern half of the empire, while Seleucus himself supervised diplomacy and conflict with his western rivals. But this westward shift may be partly the bias of our sources: Greek writers, who were mainly concerned with events in the Mediterranean basin. Generally speaking, the bias of our sources ensures that whenever the Seleucid kings moved east, they move out of history, and only rarely do we have any details of their activities there. Wars and problems in the western part of the empire during the second half of the third century BC suggest that the Seleucid empire was starting to decline, but it is almost impossible to determine what was happening in Mesopotamia and the vast eastern provinces for much of this period.

Decline or no, it was Antiochus III 'the Great' (222-188 BC) who is credited with consolidating Seleucid rule in the eastern parts of his empire and in Asia Minor, and, more significantly for us, with wresting southern Syria and Palestine from the Ptolemies. The conquest of the south effectively made the whole region part of the Seleucid kingdom (and may explain why Pompey could regard the south as much the victor's prize as the north). Antiochus' involvement in politics further west brought him into conflict with a new Mediterranean power: Rome. During the first decade of the second century BC the Romans started interfering in Greece, and by doing so encroached upon the ambitions of Antiochus. The king's attempts to extend his influence there led to an all-out war in which the Romans defeated him on the Greek mainland, and then struck at him in Asia Minor. It is all too easy to see the Roman victory as ordained, but at the time it cannot have seemed so. The Seleucid kingdom was among the richest and most formidable powers in the ancient world, and this struggle would determine who was to dominate the eastern Mediterranean for the foreseeable future. Thus when Antiochus was completely defeated at the Battle of Magnesia in 190/189 BC and the Romans imposed a heavy fine on the Seleucid kingdom, forcing Antiochus to relinquish Asia Minor, the focus of Mediterranean power shifted decisively westwards, and the discourse of power among the Hellenistic kingdoms was increasingly framed by reference to the city on the Tiber. The Taurus mountains were to be recognized as the western boundary of the Seleucid empire, and the rest of Asia Minor was to be surrendered to other states and kingdoms, most of which were Rome's allies. The Seleucid kingdom remained powerful, but the damage done to royal prestige encouraged Seleucid client rulers on the peripheries of the empire to make bids for independence. The loss of Asia Minor perhaps inhibited the empire's ability to compete with many other important Mediterranean states effectively, and the heavy indemnity imposed by Rome may have engendered a financial crisis in the kingdom for several years until the fine was paid (though this is far from certain). Another factor contributing to Seleucid decline was the frequent warfare between rival claimants to the Seleucid throne in the second half of the second century BC. These disturbances were often sponsored by Rome and other Hellenistic kingdoms, so Syria, as the most accessible part of the empire for these rival powers, tended to be the battleground for these disputes rather than other more easterly areas of the empire. The increasing concentration of royal activity in Syria, and need for the kings to reside and protect their interests there, led to neglect of other regions.

In the second century BC Rome was still too far away to achieve control of the Seleucid empire. But while the Battle of Magnesia was the last major clash between Rome and the Seleucids, the Romans continued to meddle in eastern affairs in a somewhat erratic manner, which proved detrimental to Seleucid power. Rome had demanded hostages from Antiochus III after the Battle of Magnesia, and used these to manipulate the succession, which subsequently divided the royal house into warring factions. Secessionist regimes, such as the Maccabees of Judaea, could count on Roman support, if not physical aid. Antiochus IV Epiphanes (175-164 BC) complied with a Roman ultimatum that he abandon newly won conquests in Ptolemaic Egypt, which seriously threatened the balance of power in the eastern Mediterranean. Rome lent nominal support to a usurper, Alexander Balas, who in 150 BC overthrew the legitimate Seleucid monarch Demetrius I. For the Romans, a weak Seleucid kingdom was better than a strong one, although indirectly, and probably unwittingly, the Roman contributions to Seleucid decline assisted the rise of the Parthians. The Babylonian keystone of the Seleucid empire was to fall to this new eastern rival rather than to Rome. As a result, the power that eventually eclipsed that of the Seleucids in most of their former territories was not Rome, but this dynasty which had its origins in Central Asia.

The early history of the Parthian kingdom is obscure; they used an era going back to 247 BC, but what event this Parthian year zero commemorated is uncertain. The rulers were known as the Arsacid dynasty (after its founder,

Fig. 8. Silver tetradrachm of Antiochus III. BMC 28.

Arsaces) and they ruled over an Iranian tribe who were originally nomadic and known as the Parni. The tribe and its kings became known collectively as Parthians after the old Achaemenid province in northern Iran where they first established themselves as an important power. The Parthian kingdom remained under Seleucid influence until about the time of its formidable king Mithridates I (*c.* 171-138 BC), who captured Iran and southern Mesopotamia (Babylonia) from the Seleucids and even took the Seleucid king Demetrius II prisoner (140 BC). His successor and namesake Mithridates II (*c.* 123-87 BC) consolidated Parthian rule in the new territories and, as a result of a diplomatic accord with the Chinese emperor Wu-Ti, established a trade link which later became the so-called 'Silk Road', a channel of trade between China and the west which the Parthians jealously (and very profitably) controlled. For the Seleucids, Parthian control of Iran and Babylonia severely reduced the resources of their kingdom and lessened their chances of recovering what was lost.

No longer in possession of Asia Minor, and with the steady incursions of the Parthians to the east, the Seleucid empire declined rapidly during the second half of the second century BC. The reign of Alexander Balas (150-145 BC) was particularly disastrous. The Parthians under Mithridates I established themselves in the east, the Ptolemies gained a temporary influence over Syria, and following Alexander's death the Seleucid kingdom entered into a prolonged feud between the sons of Demetrius I and Alexander Balas' successors. The Parthians took Babylonia and defeated two Seleucid armies sent to recover the keystone. Rulers were forced to make concessions of independence to many of the wealthier and more powerful cities: Tyre in 126/125 BC, Tripolis in 112/111, Sidon in 111 and Seleucia in 109/108. The Jews established an independent state, as did other groups in the region, and by the end of the second century BC the Seleucid kingdom was effectively reduced to northern Syria, north-western Mesopotamia and the plain of eastern Cilicia. Disputes over the succession continued, contributing to further decline. Yet it was from an unexpected quarter – from Tigranes of Armenia – that the final blow to the Seleucid kingdom came. There is a claim that Tigranes invaded at the invitation of the Antiochenes, who were weary of the constant, internecine strife of the Seleucids. More probably Tigranes took advantage of an already weakened kingdom and a population which no longer identified strongly with the dynasty to achieve his own, opportunistic ends. Civil wars had no doubt divided and destroyed loyalty to an empire embodied in the person and blood line of the king. After a long period of relative invisibility, local cultures of Syria and the Near East begin to emerge into our view at the end of the Seleucid empire, as regional powers asserted themselves. Yet it was not only the non-Greek element of the subject population that broke with the Seleucids; the Greek city states did so as well. The Seleucid experiment of linking their hegemony with the Greek-style *polis* ultimately failed.

That ultimate failure should not overshadow the Seleucids' tremendous success down to the middle of the second century BC. But when studying Seleucid imperialism we are faced with the difficulty of differentiating between uniquely Greek institutions and standard imperial ones, and with distinguishing what was unique about the Seleucid empire. There are various similitudes and differences. In their struggles with their western rivals one might detect a continuation of Achaemenid and Alexandrian claims to a universal world-empire. If so, this distinguishes the Seleucids from other Hellenistic kingdoms, which do not seem to have aspired to world conquest, and seen in this light the confrontation between Antiochus III and Rome was a clash of similar imperial aspirations. Antiochus III established an imperial ruler cult (not to be confused with civic founder cults), but in doing so he may have had similar cults established by the Ptolemies in mind. An understanding and respect for established cultures in the empire which they ruled was a characteristic the Seleucids shared with the Achaemenids, but this did not prevent them from encouraging the development of Greek cities, a form of cultural imperialism which distinguishes them from the Persians. In the third century the Seleucids were great supporters of urbanization, perhaps believing that a network of cities would help to reinforce their rule. This support is thought to have declined after the death of Antiochus I, but a revival of the tradition (albeit on a less grand scale) occurred under Antiochus III and Antiochus IV. Following the conquest of the south by Antiochus III the city of Berytus (formally renamed Laodicea in Canaan) expanded significantly in size. The city's orthogonal layout suggests planned expansion, although this seems to have adhered to an earlier, probably Persian, plan. The conquest of the south was accompanied by the adoption of the universal Seleucid era there. Ptolemaic coinage was demonetized and quickly replaced with Seleucid issues. Passing references in the textual sources refer to the adoption of Greek institutions by native cities of the Phoenician and Palestinian coast. Such actions indicate that Seleucid imperialism, however we define it, remained vigorous into the second century.

The archaeological evidence is patchy, but it points to cultural patterns that we might expect of an empire, Greek or otherwise. Cities and towns which were settled by Greek colonists, or those on the coast with easy access to the Mediterranean world, exhibit greater Hellenization of their material culture than villages and the countryside. In other words there was greater diffusion of Greek culture and symbols horizontally, between the cities and elites, than vertically from the cities and elites to the mainly rural lower classes. The majority of the population remained speakers of Semitic languages, and the further down the social scale, the less likely these people were to be Hellenized. Even among the elites local styles of art and architecture were sometimes blended with Greek and Achaemenid imperial styles, producing what is sometimes called a 'hybrid' material culture. Old, pre-Hellenistic pottery forms were often retained under the Seleucids, alongside new, Hellenistic types, suggesting that this hybridization extended to the preparation and display of food. Even so, pottery made in Greece and Asia Minor spread extensively through the Seleucid empire, and was imitated locally. The Hellenistic pottery forms of Syria do not show the same degree of Hellenization as those of Asia Minor, in that a smaller range of shapes is imitated. It has been tentatively suggested that Greek colonists had a major part to play in disseminating these Greek-style imitations and their originals. In places where Greek colonies were few, we find few imitations and local forms are predominant. Furthermore, the forms imitated at places inland, far from the Mediterranean, are those of the main period of colonization, in the late fourth and early third centuries BC. These forms were retained, suggesting little further influence (which coincides with the fact that there were no large influxes of Greek colonists after the middle of the third century). The difficulties of transmitting Greek culture vertically through the local rural populations are suggested by the fact that the proportions of Greek and Greek-style fine ware pottery are much higher in towns and cities than on

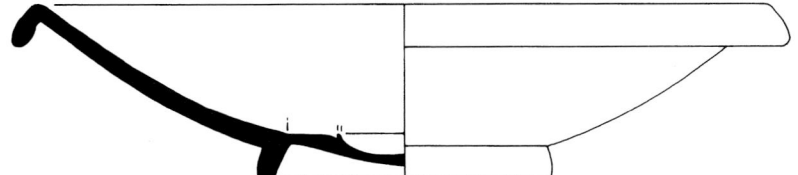

Fig. 9. Hellenistic fish plate from the excavations in Beirut. This particular form was made at Antioch.

rural sites. A common Greek type, widespread on Hellenistic sites of the region, is the so-called fish plate, which is a dish with an overhanging rim and a floor sloping down to a central depression (fig. 9). The form seems to have emerged at Athens *c.* 400 BC. Its distinctive shape was likely to have been related to a very specific (and very Greek?) function, although it is unlikely that this was confined to serving fish as the modern name for the shape suggests. Various other bowl and plate forms are typically Greek, and imported or imitated in both fine and coarse ware. Local or regional imitation could have led to a decline in imports of the originals. This seems to have happened in the case of Attic black-gloss forms, popular in Syria in the late fourth century, which were supplanted by Syrian copies. Antioch appears to have been a major centre of fine ware production, and from the mid-third century BC the city began exporting a new, mould-made form, the so-called Megarian bowl (also produced at other centres in the eastern Mediterranean), all over the coastal regions of Syria. This in turn was imitated locally. From the middle of the second century a new gloss ware, known nowadays as Eastern Sigillata A, was produced on a massive scale somewhere in the region, probably at or near Antioch or in eastern Cilicia. Although it was originally made with black or brown glosses in addition to red, as the industry continued to grow during the first century BC red (the favoured colour of most Roman sigillata wares) became predominant. It may be no coincidence that these changes to Eastern Sigillata A parallel the decline of the Seleucids and the advent of Rome in Syria, and production of this ware was unhindered by the Roman annexation (see p. 200). Finds of Rhodian amphoras in southern Mesopotamia and the Persian Gulf provide tantalizing hints of long-distance trade between the Mediterranean and these regions under Seleucid rule. The absence of later amphoras may mean that this trade was cut short by Parthian invasion, but at present the evidence is very limited. Greek pottery forms are thus a potential index of the level of Seleucid imperialism and links with the Mediterranean world, even if there are many regional and local variations in pottery assemblages.

The Seleucids tend to receive less notice in general accounts of the ancient world than their rivals the Ptolemies or the Antigonids (no doubt because the written sources for them are so much poorer), and Seleucid history is usually framed in terms of a slow decline following early years of promise. In narratives of Middle Eastern history they feature as an interlude in the accounts of Achaemenid, Parthian and Sasanian imperialism. The oral traditions of the Parthians and Sasanians eventually succeeded in expunging the Seleucids from collective memory in Iran. Yet although the Seleucid kingdom was supplanted by Rome and the Parthian realm, and was eventually all but forgotten, some of the institutions which the Seleucids created and supported had a profound influence, as will be shown in later chapters. Furthermore, Roman claims to a universal empire and its highly Hellenized culture made it a suitable successor to the Seleucids in Syria and the Near East.

2 ROME, SYRIA, PARTHIANS AND PERSIANS

Pompey's 'settlement' of 64-63 BC did not result in the recognition of an agreed boundary between what was Roman and non-Roman. Yet a boundary of sorts was clearly present, dividing Roman possessions from Parthian. Syria and Mesopotamia were now politically separated between one empire ruled by Latin-speaking Italian elites and another controlled by a Parthian-speaking aristocracy. The Euphrates became both a symbolic and a very real political boundary, even if in cultural terms the river served as a highway, bringing greater homogeneity to the local cultures that existed along its banks. From the very beginning this boundary was problematic. Some would see it as unnatural, an artificial frontier circumscribing the potential offered to the power which, like the Achaemenids and Seleucids, managed to straddle Iran, Mesopotamia and Syria. The Euphrates was a temporary compromise between two contenders, Rome and the Parthians, both perhaps aiming at a world-empire. It would take a number of defeats east of the river for the Romans to realize that further expansion across this symbolic divide would be extremely difficult. But renewed attempts at conquest in the second century AD suggest that the Roman ideology of a universal empire continued to conflict with what was practically possible.

The political and military history of Rome's eastern frontier can be portrayed as a struggle between Rome and two successive states to the east, the empires of the Parthians and Sasanian Persians, to create a world-empire which incorporated the whole of the Fertile Crescent. According to this view, a geographical precondition for a superpower was to acquire control of the Fertile Crescent together with Iran and the eastern Mediterranean. These regions were axial to Achaemenid, Seleucid and Muslim power, and the marginalization and rapid decline of Seleucid power can in part be attributed to the loss of Iran and southern Mesopotamia after the mid-second century BC. However, such a narrative may obscure what the different contenders thought they were doing, and what they hoped to achieve. Nevertheless any historical account of Roman Syria can scarcely ignore Rome's conflicts with its neighbours and the strategies that were adopted by both sides. The Parthian and Sasanian states were the most serious rivals to Roman imperialism until the Muslims in the seventh century. An ideology of eternal victory may have made it difficult for Rome to accept these rivals on equal terms, even if repeated military campaigns demonstrated that a Roman conquest was likely to be impossible. With the Parthians Rome tried to adopt the superior position of patron, attempting to treat the Parthians like vassals through the taking of hostages, or by imagery of submissive Parthians bending to Roman will. For a brief period the Sasanians were able to turn the tables, taking the emperor Valerian captive, portraying the Sasanian king victorious over a succession of Roman emperors, and even compelling Rome to pay tribute – although this latter humiliation could perhaps have been viewed by Rome as one of her regular subsidies to barbarians beyond the frontiers.

In spite of their power it is very easy to exaggerate the threat posed by these eastern states. The bulk of Rome's armies were concentrated on the Rhine and

Danube frontiers; if some estimates are accurate, nearly half of the forces available to Rome in the second century were deployed there. Less than a quarter were stationed in the east. The centralized, 'civilized' Parthian and Sasanian states were perhaps less of a continual threat than the decentralized forces on the northern frontiers, and therefore did not require a perpetual show of force; and although serious, wars with the two eastern empires were more intermittent and could often be resolved by the opposing heads of state reaching an understanding. During times of peace both sides could regard each other as a partner in shielding civilization from barbarism, whereas this can hardly have been the case in Rome's relations with her northern neighbours. Moreover, many of the eastern troops were not positioned to participate frequently in attacks across the Euphrates, being posted to Judaea or Arabia, where they were used to police the local population and to control nomads. Consequently major wars in the east required concentrating troops at a mustering-point and bringing in reinforcements from abroad. If the empire was divided between more than one emperor, as it frequently was from the mid-third century onwards, it was sometimes difficult to request troops from one's colleagues, whose priorities lay elsewhere. A divided empire restricted the abilities of emperors to conduct large-scale offensives aimed at conquest of the Fertile Crescent (assuming that that was their aim). Roman forces in the east could serve as a deterrent, but they were not necessarily well suited to offensives.

Conflicts also arose for control of states positioned in the interstices between the empires. Whoever had influence in Armenia could also dominate Mesopotamia and the regions to the north, such as Colchis and Iberia. For both Rome and her eastern rivals domination of Armenia was strategically crucial, and long-term peace could be achieved only through a resolution which allowed both powers a way of controlling it simultaneously.

ROME AND THE PARTHIAN KINGDOM

The Parthians

Our knowledge of the Parthian state comes as much from Roman and Sasanian writings as from the Parthian kingdom itself, and it is perhaps unwise to place too great a weight on such sources. This means it is rather difficult for us to discern what Parthian imperialism meant. Mithridates I adopted the custom of styling himself king of kings, and it is perhaps he who emphasized a link between the royal Parthian house of the Arsacids and the Achaemenids. There are reports from Roman sources that the Parthians took this connection seriously with regard to their dealings with Rome, regarding themselves as the rightful inheritors of the Achaemenid empire, which included Syria, Asia Minor and Egypt. They may also have posed as the legitimate successors of Alexander the Great. The Roman historian Tacitus mentions the 'menacing terms' with which the Parthian king Artabanus in AD 35 referred to 'the old boundaries of the Persian and Macedonian empires, and to his intention of seizing the territories held first by Cyrus and afterwards by Alexander.'[4] Some modern commentators have questioned the veracity of these Parthian objectives, and they may, of course, be the product of Roman rhetoric and scare-mongering, but they could also indicate that Rome considered the Arsacid rulers a serious threat, and that the Parthians were indeed regarded as the successors to the dangerous Persian kings who had menaced the Greek world from the sixth to the fourth century BC.

The king and court exercised government over a variety of states, which were administered by nobles and vassal-kings. Some self-governing Greek cities founded by Alexander and the Seleucids were included in the political makeup of the empire. In very general terms the political geography of the Parthian realm was not too far removed from the initial arrangements of the Romans in Syria, where a complex array of semi-independent political entities was administered by a few imperial officials (see chapter 3). Arsacid right to rule was legitimized by a claim to be connected by blood to the Achaemenids, and by a claim to have been appointed by heaven as God's viceroy on earth. Like the Achaemenids the Arsacids were Zoroastrians, although they appear to have been very tolerant of other religions in their empire. The status of Parthian kings was far above that of their subjects. As with the Seleucids and Ptolemies, royal blood was of paramount importance for kingship and a defining feature of their state; hence it was difficult for outsiders to challenge the legitimate line, and most, if not all, usurpers were related to the ruling Arsacid dynasty until the successful challenge of the Sasanian Ardashir in the AD 220s.

Nobles and vassal kings contributed soldiers and military assistance to their king, to whom they were presumably bound by an oath of loyalty. Little is known about the hierarchies of the Parthian kingdom, although there is some evidence to suggest that Seleucid court titles were adopted. The Parthian elite was far more stable than the Roman elite with regard to the continuity of power within families: some of the noble clans, such as the Suren, remained influential under the Sasanians, long after the dynasty's fall. Although they might not covet supreme power for themselves, the great families exercised a high degree of influence over internal politics, even to the extent of overthrowing and assassinating unsatisfactory rulers. This might explain why Parthian kings were generally cautious in their dealings with the Romans: a king's reputation among the aristocracy rested on his success, and aggression was always a gamble. A council of nobles appointed the king, and the Suren family reserved the right to crown him. Some interpret the relationship between the royal and subordinate families as antagonistic, one that pitted the powers of the core against those of the periphery, with the king trying to assert central authority over the nobles, who preferred control to be less centralized. If so, it was a struggle in which the nobles eventually gained the upper hand and weakened the Parthian kingdom. But it also confirms the impression that the Parthian nobility colluded in Arsacid right to rule, rather than challenging this ideal. Overall, the relatively loose structure of Parthian power proved satisfactory in both the defence and government of the empire; vassal-states maintained their identities and privileges and this may be one of the reasons why they were more likely to resist the imposition of government by another power such as Rome.

The Parthian language was used at court and for administration, but many other languages were spoken in the empire. Not all of them were literary: Armenian was not written at all until the fifth century AD. The use of Greek on coins and royal inscriptions is notable; a conscious continuation, perhaps, of Seleucid traditions. It is worth noting that late Seleucid silver coins, and Roman imitations of them (see chapter 6), appear to have circulated in Parthian

Mesopotamia alongside Parthian coins down to the very end of Parthian rule, while their counterparts with portraits of Roman emperors did not. The Seleucids may therefore have served as an additional source of legitimation for Arsacid rule, at least in the first centuries of their empire. The symbols of Parthian royalty mixed Greek and Persian elements: the white cloth diadem of Hellenistic kings mingled with long hair, beards, torcs, long-sleeved jackets and trousers. Parthian coins gave the kings Greek titles, and the ruling class is credited with taking some active interest in Greek culture. We are told that when news reached the Parthian court of the defeat of a Roman invasion force in 53 BC, they were watching a performance of Euripides' *Bacchae*. One of the greatest Greek geographers, Isodore of Charax, came from a Parthian vassal-kingdom at the head of the Persian Gulf. A school of philosophy was established in Babylon. Cities like Seleucia on the Tigris were granted autonomy in their own affairs. However, this may not mean that any special respect was reserved for the Greeks: the Parthians, as heirs of the Seleucids, respected whatever local cultures existed and employed Greek symbols of power to stress their own legitimacy and continuity. But Greek was only one of many cultures persisting under Parthian rule. Texts from Babylonia show traditional Babylonian religions continuing as they had under the Seleucids, and in other parts of their empire local cultures passed from one dominion to the other uninterrupted. A turning-point in the Hellenization of the Parthian west came in the first century AD, when the Greek city of Seleucia on the Tigris revolted against Parthian rule and held out for seven years before surrendering. The excavators suggest that following the re-establishment of Parthian control, buildings began to incorporate Parthian elements, whereas before the styles were mainly Greek. The two-columned porticoes placed at the entrances to large halls found in the phase between the second century BC and first century AD dropped out of use, and instead the vaulted hall or *iwan*, typical of Parthian architecture, became the characteristic architectural element. From the first century AD onwards, the Greek element in Parthian royal iconography begins to decline. On coins the Greek inscriptions become degraded to the point of unintelligibility, and are accompanied by Parthian inscriptions. By the time that the Sasanian kingdom was established, the Parthians seem to have forgotten the 'real' history of the Achaemenids and Macedonians, having replaced those traditions with epics from eastern Iran, which in turn were used by the Sasanians to help legitimize their dynasty. The break with the past may have been assisted by the fact that the Parthians had no tradition of written history of the sort practised in the Roman empire, and relied more heavily on oral recitals from memory. Without the backup of writing it was relatively easy to manipulate collective memory in order to replace one tradition with another over a few generations.

The Parthian realm was under a lot of pressure by the second century AD, with the rise of the Kushan kingdom to the east and Roman attacks in the west. But it was still able to put up shows of strength, such as the invasion of Syria under Marcus Aurelius in the 160s, and defeat of the emperor Macrinus in AD 217. Internal rebellion, rather than external attack, brought Arsacid rule to an end; yet Roman aggression contributed significantly to its decline.

From Pompey to Augustus

The first formal encounter between the Parthian kingdom and Rome had been in Anatolia in 92 BC, to discuss mutual interests there, but Rome was not drawn into Parthian affairs until Lucullus' invasion of Armenia. The defeat of Tigranes and his submission to Pompey placed Rome in the position of power-broker in the region. Roman armies marched through northern Mesopotamia and south into Adiabene, and the Parthian inability to challenge them, coupled with the fact that Tigranes had been able to take their land, no doubt convinced many members of the Roman elite that the Arsacids could be subdued. The history of subsequent Roman-Parthian conflicts was to prove that judgement unsound. Nevertheless, prior to the Roman annexation of Syria it looked as if Rome might rapidly achieve domination over Armenia and Mesopotamia as well.

The decades following Pompey's annexation were marred by civil wars in the Roman world, in which cities and allies had to supply money and military assistance to the different factions. The period also witnessed intermittent attempts to conquer Mesopotamia by ambitious commanders. Appointment as governor of Syria provided Roman aristocrats with opportunities for personal enrichment and military glory: Aulus Gabinius accepted too many bribes and had enemies in Rome who could bring him down; his successor in office, Marcus Licinius Crassus, was perhaps more impervious to slander but not to Parthian weapons. Gabinius had been planning a campaign across the Euphrates; and Crassus had the forces – seven legions – to realize such a campaign. In 53 BC he invaded Mesopotamia, intent on conquest and plunder, but instead led a Roman army to disaster at Carrhae. Crassus and three quarters of his soldiers were killed by the Parthians, and in the aftermath of the defeat local rulers sought to curry favour with the Arsacids. The nomadic Rhambei, who dwelt in the steppe on the west bank of the Euphrates in the vast region north of Palmyra, transferred their allegiance to the Parthian king, and between 51 and 50 Parthian forces were active in northern Syria. The Roman province was under threat little more than a decade after its annexation.

Some sort of political instability in the Arsacid realm may explain why the invaders did not manage to secure northern Syria, particularly after a violent civil war broke out between Pompey and Julius Caesar. Most of the Roman troops in the province were withdrawn to assist Pompey's cause, and the cities were forced to provide finance, recruits and ships. All to no avail; in 48 Pompey lost the war and fled to Egypt, where he was killed. The Antiochenes, wary of being seen to help the loser, had refused to grant him asylum in Syria.

Caesar toured the east shortly after Pompey's death. The civil war was over, but the Roman world was still polarized into pro- and anti-Caesarian factions. The great general honoured cities such as Laodicea and Antioch, and his compacts with local dynasts requested that they should consider it their duty to safeguard Roman interests in Syria. But which Roman interests, given that there were two camps? In the summer of 46 BC a rumour circulated that Caesar was dead, and this was sufficient to provoke a renegade Pompeian called Caecilius Bassus to demonstrate where his sympathies lay. In the aftermath of Pompey's defeat Bassus had fled to Tyre, a city which he now seized. From there he managed to win over the Syrian legions and engineered the murder of Caesar's nephew Sextus, who had been appointed governor. Bassus gained the support of local dynasts and the Parthians. He established his headquarters in the fortress of Apamea and resisted Caesarian attempts to overthrow him. In 44 the governors of two provinces in Asia Minor arrived with huge armies and besieged Bassus at Apamea, without success. But in the same year Julius

Caesar was assassinated in Rome, and his 'republican' murderers began organizing their armies for a struggle against Caesar's supporters. One of these republicans, Gaius Cassius Longinus, arrived in Syria in 43. He had governed the province after the death of Crassus, and may have been able to make use of old connections there to secure his power base. Cassius won over both rebel and Caesarian legions and Bassus was able to step down without losing face. The republicans also initiated negotiations with the Parthian king, sending an envoy, Quintus Aetius Labienus, to the Parthian court to ask for military assistance.

Cassius withdrew most of the Roman troops to join the republican forces in Macedonia for the final confrontation with Caesar's supporters. The defeat of the republican forces at Philippi in 42 led to a temporary peace in the Roman empire, but the two principal beneficiaries of the victory at Philippi, Mark Antony and Caesar's heir Octavian, soon began to quarrel. Antony placed two of the defeated republican legions in Syria, which, as it turned out, was an error of judgement. At the Parthian court, Cassius' envoy Labienus and King Orodes decided to launch an invasion of Syria, to be led by the Roman commander and the king's son Pacorus. They overwhelmed the republican legions (some of whom deserted), and while Labienus led an expedition west into Asia Minor, Pacorus took his armies south, accepting the submission of Syrian states as he went. The Roman province was lost to the Parthians (40 BC), who now acquired their outlet on the Mediterranean.

Tangible evidence of the invasion is sparse. Coins issued at Antioch and Apamea during the Parthian occupation show that the cities abandoned new dating systems which had been adopted under the Romans and reverted to dating by the Seleucid era (which they had used prior to the Roman annexation). Labienus himself struck gold and silver coins with his own portrait, probably in Asia Minor rather than Syria. Overall the rapid disintegration of Roman control illustrates the precarious nature of their rule in Syria at this time; but the subsequent collapse of Parthian domination does not suggest that the invaders were any more secure. Antony had problems dealing with the increasingly hostile machinations of Octavian, but in 39 he sent a deputy, Publius Ventidius Bassus, with an army to recover the east. Ventidius' campaign was remarkably successful; in the engagements Labienus and Pacorus were killed, and the Parthian army was forced to withdraw. The Roman commander then set about restoring Roman control of the Syrian province. This proved to be a complex task; many states and dynasts now had reason to oppose Rome, being either Parthian appointees, such as the Hasmonaean Antigonus in Judaea, or had conspicuously aided the Parthians, such as the Phoenician island state of Aradus, and Antiochus I, king of Commagene. Ventidius besieged Antiochus in his capital, Samosata, forcing him to capitulate, and the Roman Senate, exasperated with a prolonged dynastic feud between the Hasmonaeans of Judaea, appointed the Idumaean Herod as king in their place (p. 95). The siege of Aradus ended in 37, and Herod finally overthrew his Hasmonaean rival with Roman assistance.

With Syria secured, Antony began preparations for an invasion of the Parthian kingdom. Revenge for Carrhae had been high on the agenda of empire: Caesar had planned a campaign which was cut short by his assassination, and the intervening years had been occupied with internal conflicts. Initially Antony attempted to cross into Mesopotamia at Zeugma. However, he found the opposite bank of the Euphrates too strongly defended by the Parthians, so he marched north and east via Armenia. His army was more than twice the size of Crassus' force, but his invasion of the Parthian realm proved inconclusive. In 34 he made Armenia a Roman province after deposing its king, yet this was hardly compensation for his failure to secure a worthy victory over the Parthians. During these years Antony's position worsened as his financial and political situation deteriorated. War with Octavian looked increasingly likely, and he worked to gain the support of local dynasts and the Ptolemaic queen Cleopatra, which in Cleopatra's case meant making concessions of territory to her. In 37 - 36 the Ptolemaic queen had acquired coastal cities between Orthosia and Berytus, Damascus, the Ituraean kingdom of Chalcis, and lands which belonged to Herod and the Nabataeans. A son of Antony and Cleopatra, Ptolemy Philadelphus, was declared king of Syria, Phoenicia and part of Asia Minor, and another son made king of Armenia. If these arrangements had any political reality, Antony was unable to enforce them, for he was soon obliged to withdraw his forces for a final battle with Octavian.

Fig. 10. Auspicious moment: relief from the sanctuary on Mount Nemrut showing the horoscope of Antiochus I of Commagene, thought to depict the configuration of the stars when Pompey confirmed him as king, on 7 July 62 BC: Jupiter, Mercury, Mars and the Moon are in conjunction with Leo.

The Parthians did not attempt to invade Syria in retaliation, but they took advantage of the Roman withdrawal from Armenia to set up a descendant of Tigranes as king there. When Antony was defeated at Actium in 31 BC, Syria fell into the hands of Octavian. Late in 30 BC, with Antony and Cleopatra dead and Egypt annexed to the empire, Octavian arrived in the province, and local communities had to negotiate their status with yet another Roman warlord. Among them were the dynasts who had supported Antony. Of these some, like Herod, were successful in convincing Octavian of their value to his regime; others were not so successful, and were deposed. However, once the situation in the east had stabilized, the deposed dynasties were restored. This was a clear indication that eastern dynasts were reliant on imperial favour, and that the emperor could depose or instate kings at will. But it was also a sign that Rome would respect some of the existing configurations of power – for the moment.

Favours were also extended to or retracted from cities. During his later visit to Syria in 20 BC Octavian, now styled Augustus, deprived Sidon and Tyre of their liberty 'for dishonouring the treaties which they had struck with Rome'.[3] Rewards and punishments had been meted out to cities under the republican generals, and the demands of loyalty would see the same happen under the emperors. The first few decades of Roman rule had hardly been easy for the communities of the region.

Julio-Claudian Diplomacy

Under Augustus Syria became an imperial province, its governors being appointed by the emperor rather than the Senate. The province was still relatively isolated from the rest of the Roman empire, being almost completely separated from the Roman provinces of Asia Minor by the client kingdom of Cappadocia. The legionary garrisons were all stationed in the north, and there was no major military presence in the south. Should military intervention in the south prove necessary, as it did on occasions such as rioting following the death of Herod in Judaea, the Syrian governor would normally have to bring forces from the north. Quite apart from the time this would take and the logistical problems encountered in organizing supplies, any removal of troops from the north would also expose the province to potential attack from the Parthians. Fortunately for Rome, the Parthian kingdom's political and military fortunes appear to have been waning, and it is difficult to gauge the extent of the Parthian threat in this period. But the lessons learned from the failures of Crassus and Antony were well taken. Instead of all-out attack on Parthian territory, Roman efforts shifted to greater reliance on diplomatic intrigues. In this Augustus and his successors directed much of their efforts towards securing Roman influence over Armenia (see below).

Troubles in the Parthian kingdom could prove advantageous to Rome. Renegade Parthian usurpers realized that the Roman empire could be used as a refuge, and such pretenders could be kept by Augustus as bargaining-counters in any negotiations with Parthian kings, or be persuaded to launch attacks on the kingdom from Roman territory. Octavian was faced with a situation of this sort right at the beginning of his reign. In *c.* 30 BC the legitimate Parthian king, Phraates IV, defeated a usurper, Tiridates, who fled to Syria with his supporters, taking Phraates' son with him as a hostage. Tiridates was allowed to remain in Syria, and from here the usurper made an attack on Mesopotamia. Although he issued coins in 26/25 BC styling himself 'Friend of the Romans'[6] it is not clear whether Rome offered him any military or financial support. Phraates rapidly gained the upper hand, and both sides appealed to Augustus. In 20, after prolonged negotiations and threats of war, a settlement was reached: Tiridates was to remain in Roman territory, to be maintained at Roman public expense as king-in-exile. Phraates' son was sent back to his father, and in return Phraates surrendered the Roman military standards captured from Crassus and Antony.

Augustus exploited the return of the standards for its immense symbolic value; the failed campaigns against the Parthian kingdom had done serious damage to Rome's self-image as a perpetually victorious empire, and the settlement could be hailed as a kind of Parthian submission. Augustus and his stepson Tiberius were in Syria at the time that the negotiations were completed, but it is not known whether Tiberius, who received the standards, travelled to the Euphrates to take charge of them from the Parthians. The concept of the Euphrates as a boundary received political reinforcement a few years later when an island in the river was used as the site for negotiations by Augustus' grandson Gaius Caesar and the Parthians (AD 1/2), and in Strabo's great geographical work composed during the reign of Augustus, the Euphrates is described in specific terms as the boundary of the Parthian empire. Such recognition presumably meant formal acceptance of an autonomous Parthian sphere of affairs.

In order to secure the succession and prevent civil war Phraates retained his chosen heir and sent his other children to Augustus. The acceptance of Parthian hostages at Rome illustrates how complex were relations between the two great powers. The securing of royal hostages had long been standard

Roman practice from potentially dangerous vassals, or kingdoms beyond the boundaries of the empire, but it is hard to view the Parthian realm in a client's role with regard to Rome. Augustus no doubt wanted the Arsacids to be seen that way. Parricide was not unusual in the Parthian royal house, and rulers had good reason to fear their offspring (Phraates himself was said to have killed his father Orodes and his brothers). But if the arrangement was intended to be of mutual advantage to both sides, it did not have that result. The death of Phraates still led to a civil war, in which the Parthian nobles supported various contenders. Augustus acceded to the demands of at least one faction to send Vonones, one of the hostages, but if this was an attempt to gain influence over the Parthian throne it failed. Vonones was driven out of Parthian territory, and was eventually forced to retire to Syria.

The complex history of relations between Rome and the Parthians cannot be covered here in any detail. One of the reasons why that history is so complex is that the reigning Parthian kings were frequently challenged by other members of their family, leading to periods of instability and civil conflicts, with both sides attempting to accommodate themselves with Rome. The troubled reign of Artabanus (c. AD 10-38) resulted in various accords and hostilities between him and the emperors, none of which led to all-out war. Artabanus threatened to invade Syria, and was especially anxious that the Romans remove Vonones to a safe distance from the border of his empire. Even after the death of Vonones, Tiberius still held some of the Parthian hostages, and used at least two of these against Artabanus, releasing them in the hope that they would attract sufficient following to undermine the authority of the king. The usurpers' bids for power were unsuccessful, but they helped weaken the Parthian regime. A peace was concluded in 37 under Caligula. At a meeting on the Euphrates, the Romans formally recognized Artabanus as king of the Parthian realm and in exchange received a son as hostage. But the death of Artabanus not long after, and a subsequent civil war in the kingdom, made the treaty increasingly irrelevant, so that by 49 the emperor Claudius was prepared to support another pretender, Meherdates, in his unsuccessful bid to secure the Parthian throne.

The Disposition of Armenia

During the reign of Tiberius (AD 14-37) most of the eastern frontier came under direct Roman control. In Asia Minor the kingdom of Cappadocia was annexed, as was the kingdom of Commagene in Syria. Direct Roman control now extended all along the upper reaches of the Euphrates. These changes were supervised by Tiberius' nephew Germanicus, who was sent to the east with *imperium* (the power to act as the emperor's proxy) in AD 17. Among Germanicus' achievements while in the region was a diplomatic settlement in Armenia. This kingdom, which lay to the east of the newly consolidated Roman frontier, had been a bone of contention between Rome and the Parthians before, and emerged once again as a problem in the early first century AD. When his bid to control his ancestral kingdom failed, the renegade Vonones had attempted to install himself as king of Armenia, without success. Following that incident the Armenian throne had remained vacant until Germanicus appointed a neutral nominee, Zeno of Pontus (who was given the throne name Artaxias III). The choice proved satisfactory to Artabanus, Rome and the Armenians, even though it meant that the Armenian rulers were no longer descended from the royal house that had produced kings like Tigranes. But after Zeno's death, the Romans and Parthians disputed the succession and another solution was needed. At the end of Claudius' reign (54) the new Parthian king, Vologaeses I, tried to resolve the issue in his favour by invading Armenia and installing his brother Tiridates on the Armenian throne.

This pre-emption by the Arsacids prompted Claudius' successor Nero to break with the Augustan preference for diplomacy and to organize a retaliatory strike. The emperor appointed a highly competent general, Corbulo, to command the neighbouring Roman province of Galatia-Cappadocia. Corbulo invaded Armenia in 58 and drove Tiridates out, installing a Roman nominee called Tigranes in his place. Roman hegemony had been affirmed by military power, but the situation remained unstable. Corbulo was then given the governorship of Syria, from whence presumably he could monitor events. Tigranes proved to be a menace; he was openly hostile to his Parthian neighbours, and before long provoked a Parthian invasion of his kingdom. With this the two empires appeared to be on the brink of a major conflict. War was averted by a combination of diplomatic compromise and military threat. Nero's government proposed that Tiridates be reinstated, on condition that he travelled to Rome to be crowned by the emperor. The Parthians, however, were able to gain control of Armenia and even defeated a Roman army there. The Roman response was to elevate Corbulo to an extraordinary command over the eastern legions of Galatia-Cappadocia and Syria, making it clear that unless Roman demands were met, there would be a war over Armenia. Eventually, under pressure, Vologaeses agreed, and Tiridates travelled to Rome. Although this settlement under Nero was acceptable to both sides, the political realities of an Arsacid on the Armenian throne compromised the Roman position more than the Parthian. For the remainder of the first century, however, it proved a satisfactory compromise. The Arsacid rulers of Armenia were nominal vassals of Rome, receiving their crowns from the emperors.

An Unsustainable Lightness?

An equally serious crisis under Nero was internal: the Jewish revolt, which began in AD 66. There had been frequent religious and political crises in Judaea since the death of Herod in 4 BC, but under Claudius and Nero the situation worsened. It seems likely that Rome, used to ruling through elites, misjudged the degree to which the elites it had backed in Judaea commanded popular support. The incident provides a fascinating insight into the strengths and weaknesses of the Roman system of 'government without bureaucracy' (see chapter 3), and what happened on those rare occasions where the pro-Roman elites were unable to control the masses. A riot in Jerusalem led to the death of the pro-Roman high priest and the city being seized by the rebels. The revolt spread throughout Judaea, prompting the governor of Syria to march south with a legion, a large number of auxiliaries and supporting troops from client rulers. The rebels successfully defeated the Roman army, and to all intents and purposes much of Judaea was lost to Rome. Nero responded by appointing another capable general, the future emperor Vespasian, and giving him a command separate from that of Syria. A new province was created specially for him: Judaea. The only drawback was that he would have to pacify it. Vespasian set about his task with characteristic vigour. In 67 he arrived with three legions and began reducing Galilee. By 68 the Romans had regained control of much of Judaea, so that in the summer of 69 when Vespasian began his bid for empire in the civil conflict with his rival Vitellius, he could leave his son Titus to prosecute the siege of Jerusalem and the rebel strongholds of Herodium, Masada and Machaerus. In the following year Jerusalem was taken and the Temple sacked. The three fortresses still held out, but these were taken one by one over the years between 70 and 74.

The crisis of military power in the south illustrates the frailty of Roman rule in Syria and the lack of political integration at this point. Archaeology also presents us with a picture of local indifference to the discourse of Roman power. Regional architectural styles, incorporating non-classical elements of decoration and design, are still apparent in many parts of the province, in contrast to the high degree of homogeneity observed from the later first century AD (see chapter 8). Many local Syrian city coinages lack the imperial portrait under Augustus and his Julio-Claudian successors, in contrast with neighbouring Asia Minor or Egypt where the use of the imperial portrait as a communal symbol of the Roman empire was commonplace. However, we should beware of extending the apparent lightness of political and military integration to the economy as well. Pottery and glass show clear economic links with Italy and the rest of the Mediterranean in the Julio-Claudian period (see chapter 6). Indeed, trade with Italy seems to have declined in the later first century, at precisely the time when political and military integration was increased. This fact may reflect the development and growth of regional markets. A link between the improvement of transport and communications, the development of regional supplies for goods, and the spread of Roman military power through the province of Syria is a plausible one; armies could be stationed only in those regions where adequate infrastructures for supplies existed (though

some would argue that the army was responsible for developing those infrastructures). The slow advance of the army into more remote regions, observed from the later first century onwards, must reflect advances in that infrastructure. Furthermore, there are clear signs that Roman intrusion into the social structures and cultural life of the peoples of the province had already begun with the annexation under Pompey, although this process seems to have accelerated under Augustus. These are themes explored in the chapters which follow.

Flavian Consolidation

The reign of Vespasian proved to be a crucial one in the development of the Syrian province. In 72 the kingdom of Commagene, which had been annexed and restored twice under the Julio-Claudians, was permanently added to the province of Syria. With this a substantial stretch of the upper Euphrates, facing Parthian Mesopotamia, became a military frontier under direct Roman control. Other dynasties disappeared in later years. It is thought that Emesa was annexed between 72 and 78/79 (the dynasty is last heard of in 72: see chapter 3). When the Herodian king Agrippa II died *c.* 92/93, under Vespasian's son Domitian, his large kingdom in the south was also annexed, so that by the reign of the emperor Nerva (AD 96-8) of the Near Eastern 'client' kingdoms only the Nabataean realm remained. There is also good evidence for improvements to military infrastructure for communications and supplies. A project of canalization around Antioch, much of which involved the army, is thought to have been for military purposes. A milestone of AD 75 shows that a Roman road was being constructed across the Syrian steppe, probably between Palmyra and Sura on the Euphrates, giving Rome direct access to the middle Euphrates valley from central Syria. But how far Roman control extended down the Euphrates at this point is uncertain.

All of these changes point to greater military integration and the expansion of direct Roman control under Vespasian. However, some scholars have drawn attention to the fact that changes were already taking place at the end of Nero's reign, in connection with the compromise of Corbulo's settlement. These included the acceptance of Parthian domination over Armenia as a military fact, regardless of the symbolic relationship between Armenia and Rome. This acceptance probably explains why the kingdom of Pontus in northern Asia Minor was annexed in 64/65, further extending direct Roman control over the eastern frontier. Flavian military activities even further to the north-east, aimed at securing the Caucasus against the Sarmatians, may also have a Neronian origin. To the south Damascus, which had possibly been under Nabataean control for much of the first century, was certainly brought under direct Roman control by *c.* 63. The huge central Anatolian region of Galatia-Cappadocia was elevated to a military province under Corbulo, but whether it retained its status in Nero's later years is unknown. If not, it had recovered this status under Vespasian, who had two legions there. The upper Euphrates became a military frontier with an Armenian 'buffer' beyond, flanking Parthian Mesopotamia.

Vespasian's actions can be interpreted in the light of Corbulo's Armenian settlement, but it may also have aimed at securing Syria for offensives against the Parthians. We know very little of relations between the Parthian kings and the Flavian emperors. Vespasian rejected a proposal by the Parthian king

Fig. 11. Roman bridge on the road between Samosata and Zeugma, probably built by legionaries of the legio IV Scythica, *which spans the Cendere river (the ancient Chabinas), a tributary of the Kahta river, which is itself a tributary of the Euphrates. Both ends were originally flanked by a pair of columns with Latin dedications by the four cities of Commagene to Septimius Severus, his wife Julia Domna, and their sons Caracalla and Geta; the column naming Geta was removed after his murder by Caracalla in 212. Traces of an earlier inscription remain on one of the columns, perhaps dating to Flavian times; the bridge and road may have been part of a more general programme of consolidation and development under the Flavians.*

Vologaeses for a joint Parthian-Roman defence of the Caucasus against the troublesome Sarmatian tribes beyond, and turned down offers of Parthian assistance in the civil war against Vitellius (though this may be because the offer came too late). The king of Commagene was deposed on a charge of colluding with the Parthians, but there may be nothing to this accusation which provided a pretext for the Roman invasion. There are vague hints of some sort of hostilities slightly later in Vespasian's reign. Parthian support during the reigns of Titus and Domitian for two impostors pretending to be Nero look very much like a response to Roman support for pretenders in the Parthian realm. In the past the Romans had intended to undermine the authority of aggressive Parthian kings or to exploit periods of political instability by this means. The Flavians had usurped the empire, so now the Parthians sponsored false Julio-Claudian claimants. It is difficult to assess the seriousness of these incidents, and like the Roman-sponsored usurpers in the Parthian territory, the false Neros attracted an impressive following, but neither proved a serious challenge to Flavian authority. Nevertheless impostors had occasionally succeeded in the past: the career of the Seleucid usurper Alexander Balas was proof that under the right circumstances such a strategy (in that case pretending to be a son of Antiochus IV) could work.

The evidence thus hints at a 'grand strategy' of consolidation under the Flavians, without which the period of aggression against the Parthian kingdom in the second century would have been less feasible. It enabled Rome to embark on a scheme of annexation beyond the Euphrates. It may also have been prompted by the realization that, during the Jewish war, internal rebellion could threaten the security of the east.

Aggression and Expansion

The second century witnessed the full integration of Syria and the Near East into the eastern Roman empire on all fronts: cultural, political and military. Syrian elites began to enter the Senate, and the ruling classes of the province embraced the cultural movement sweeping the eastern Mediterranean known as the Second Sophistic (see chapter 8). Regional architectural styles declined and were replaced by more homogeneous imperial forms. Cities constructed the sorts of buildings we associate with the 'Graeco-Roman' city: public fountains, theatres, hippodromes, colonnaded streets. The emperor's portrait became a common device on local civic coins. The century saw the advance of the military into the Syrian and Arabian steppe and desert, and by the early third century Roman power had advanced down the middle Euphrates as far as Bijan island (see below). There was a Roman military presence at the Azraq oasis in Arabia, and possibly one at Jauf, some 400 kilometres (250 miles) east at the far end of the Wadi Sirhan. In Armenia and northern Mesopotamia, Rome began to gain the upper hand. Invasions of southern Mesopotamia (Babylonia) failed to secure any permanent control, but by the end of the century most of northern Mesopotamia was under Roman rule or influenced by Rome.

In 106 the Nabataean kingdom was annexed, becoming a province called Arabia, separate from the province of Syria. The motives for the annexation are obscure. The transition does not appear to have involved any major military activity. It is assumed that Rabbel II, the last Nabataean king, had died before his kingdom was incorporated. In any case, the legate of Syria seems to have occupied the kingdom without opposition. If this was part of a strategy leading to the emperor Trajan's invasion of the Parthian kingdom, it is hard to see how the two events were linked. It can be regarded as a strengthening of direct Roman rule by annexing the last major 'client' kingdom of the east, but Trajan's campaigns in Mesopotamia brought a new one into the empire by encompassing Osrhoene, the kingdom centred on the city of Edessa. Economic motives, such as the seizure of the lucrative trade routes through the Nabataean kingdom, are possible, but it is debatable to what extent Roman conquests were motivated by economics. Rabbel may have followed the example of certain earlier 'client' kings by bequeathing his kingdom to the Roman people on his death, leaving Rome with a legitimate claim and little option but to intervene. But all this is speculation; nothing is known of the circumstances.

The annexation of Arabia had not brought Trajan to the region, but shortly after this he turned his attention to the east. The Parthian kingdom was divided between Vologaeses III and the usurper Osroes. Osroes had attempted to impose a king of his own choosing in Armenia, violating the settlement reached under Nero. The instability of both the Armenian and Parthian kingdoms allowed Trajan to achieve something which had eluded Crassus and Mark Antony, and which the emperors of the first century had not sought: a decisive Parthian victory.

Trajan's Parthian war was the first in a succession of major Roman offensives against its eastern neighbour. In the autumn of 113 the emperor set out for the east, rejecting Parthian requests to show support for the Armenian succession and not to prosecute the war. The following year he annexed the Armenian kingdom, deposing and killing Osroes' nominee Parthamasiris, even though Parthamasiris had submitted to him, no doubt hoping that this ploy would lead to recognition. Parthamasiris' fate galvanized neighbouring rulers, who hastened to be received by the emperor and confirmed in their kingdoms. Late in the campaigning season of 114 the Romans took the city of Nisibis, which had been under the control of the Parthian client state of Adiabene, and during their march back to Syria the kingdom of Osrhoene made a formal submission. In 115 Trajan campaigned in northern Mesopotamia, reducing Parthian vassal states, and forming a new transeuphratene province which was called Mesopotamia. During the winter of 115-16 a major earthquake struck Antioch, severely damaging that city and Apamea, but while the emperor himself narrowly escaped death when the building he was in collapsed, the event did not deter him from continuing his campaigns.

In 116 the main thrust against the Parthians began. The details are unclear, but it seems that Trajan divided his forces, one army marching down through Adiabene and the other following the Euphrates south into Babylonia. The Parthian usurper Osroes was driven away and his capital at Ctesiphon captured. This was the first time that the Romans had marched down the Euphrates river valley; and from then on this became a standard route for attack by armies on both sides, be they Romans, Parthians or Sasanians. The Roman advance continued south to the Parthian vassal kingdom of Characene, which formed an alliance with Rome. Trajan is reported to have reached the Persian Gulf, but whatever his intended next move, his plans were cut short by rebellions to his rear. Pro-Parthian forces worked to undermine Roman influence: the powerful state of Hatra rebelled; a widespread Jewish insurrection in the Roman world spread to Mesopotamia; and in retaliation

Roman armies burned the Greek city of Seleucia on the Tigris, sacked Edessa and besieged Nisibis. Trajan's next act may have been a compromise, or it may have formed part of his original plan. A son of Osroes, Parthamaspates, was crowned king by Trajan at Ctesiphon. A Roman nominee claimed the Parthian throne, but his position was as precarious as that of earlier pretenders sponsored by the Julio-Claudian emperors. The revolts posed a serious threat to the safety of the Roman armies in the south, and in 117 Trajan began his retreat. He besieged Hatra, without success, and by the autumn his forces had withdrawn from Parthian territory altogether. Once again, the Euphrates formed the boundary of the two empires. Trajan set sail for Rome, but his health was failing and he died in Cilicia in August 117.

Although Trajan's successor Hadrian (AD 117-38) decided to forsake his predecessor's Mesopotamian conquests, Trajan's invasion produced some lasting consequences, which proved damaging to the Parthian regime. The king of Edessa had been overthrown in the anti-Roman rebellions, and Parthamaspates, who had survived Trajan's withdrawal from the Parthian kingdom but had been rejected there, is found ruling Edessa under Hadrian, implying some sort of cordial relation between Rome and this Parthian vassal state across the Euphrates. The kingdom of Characene, a former Parthian vassal state near the head of the Persian Gulf, remained supportive of Rome and outside Parthian control until it was reconquered by Vologaeses IV in AD 150/151. The pro-Roman stance of Characene between 116 and 150 fostered trade via the Gulf with India and further east, and probably contributed to the expansion of the so-called caravan trade from which cities like Palmyra profited greatly (see chapter 6). In the decades following their humiliation at the hands of Trajan the Arsacids attempted to reassert their influence, threatening the Roman east at least three times during the reign of Hadrian and his successor Antoninus Pius (AD 138-61), and culminating in an invasion of Syria and Armenia in 162 under Marcus Aurelius and Lucius Verus (AD 161-69).

In Judaea there was a popular revolt under Hadrian, known as the Bar-Kokhba war (132-35). It appears to have been based in the countryside south of Jerusalem, the Judaean hills and the desert of Judah, and centred around the person of Shim'on ben Kosibah. The reasons for the revolt are obscure; it may have been a response to legislation which interfered with Jewish religious and cultural observances (including, perhaps, a ban on circumcision), or to the foundation of a Roman colony on the site of Jerusalem c. AD 130, which received the name Aelia Capitolina (after the war Jews were forbidden to enter the city). The Romans succeeded in putting down the revolt a few years after it began, but not without serious losses. The emperor himself is thought to have commanded the war for a while. As a result of this conflict Hadrian changed the name of the province to Syria Palaestina, which looks like a deliberate attempt to dissociate the name of the province from the Jewish people.

In 148 the Parthian king Vologaeses IV succeeded to the throne. He seems to have been capable, ambitious and successful, and set about reducing the legacy of Trajan's conquests. Pro-Roman Characene was reconquered and deprived of its autonomy. He invaded Armenia in 155, but was persuaded to withdraw through Roman diplomacy rather than war. In 162 he returned, defeating a Roman army and installing his own nominee as king. He then moved on to northern Mesopotamia, where he overthrew the pro-Roman ruler of Edessa and installed a Parthian nominee. Vologaeses was now in a very

Fig. 12. Sestertius of Trajan, issued at Rome c. AD 116, commemorating 'Armenia and Mesopotamia subjected to the power of the Roman people'. BMCRE III 221-222.

strong position, and able to threaten the Roman province of Syria, which he promptly invaded. Its governor and armies were unable to stem the attack, and towards the end of the year the emperor Lucius Verus arrived and consolidated the Roman position with eight legions. Verus did not conduct the campaigns in person, but shifted his centre of command between Antioch and Laodicea during the four years of campaigns, AD 162-66, while a series of campaigns were waged on his behalf by competent generals. The Parthians were defeated on the Euphrates at Sura, and, having turned the tables, the Romans pursued a devastating war against the Parthian west. Armenia was recaptured and a Roman senator and former consul called Sohaemus, presumably a descendant of one of the eastern client rulers of the first century, was installed there as king. A Roman army then annexed northern Mesopotamia and, taking the route down the Euphrates, reached Seleucia and Ctesiphon and burned them. A new, Mesopotamian, frontier was established on the River Khabur, and Roman control now extended down the Euphrates as far as Dura Europus (a city which had been briefly annexed by Trajan).

The hostilities provoked by Vologaeses had left Rome in an even stronger position in the east rather than weakening her. The Romans had asserted their domination of the Edessene kingdom of Osrhoene and in Armenia, and direct Roman control now embraced the north-western part of Mesopotamia, perhaps including the important Mesopotamian city of Nisibis. A curious series of silver coins was produced for Mesopotamia in the names of the two emperors Aurelius and Verus and their wives, sometimes with the name and titles of the king of Osrhoene, Ma'nu, and others with the inscription 'for the Roman victory'.[7] The Mesopotamian city of Carrhae issued civic bronze coins for Aurelius and Verus, and thus for the first time asserted its position as a Greek city of the Roman world. But we do not know where or even whether Roman forces were garrisoned in Mesopotamia.

Lucius Verus died in 169, leaving Marcus Aurelius sole emperor. The governor of Syria from c. 166 was Avidius Cassius, a native of the Syrian city of Cyrrhus and one of the chief figures in the Parthian campaign. By about the time that Verus died Marcus Aurelius is thought to have raised Cassius to a higher command over the eastern provinces, while the emperor himself waged war on the empire's northern frontiers. In the spring of 175 false reports of the death of Aurelius circulated, and Cassius was proclaimed emperor by his armies. For a short time the situation was extremely grave. Cassius controlled the resources of the wealthy eastern provinces and a considerable military force. Aurelius had set out for the east when news reached him of Cassius' murder at the hands of his own officers (summer 175). Even so, the emperor thought it prudent to visit the east to reaffirm his authority in person, which aside from meting out punishments presumably involved securing the allegiance of local elites as well as that of the armies. The historian Cassius Dio adds that as a consequence 'a law was passed at this time that no one should serve as governor in the province from which he had originally come, inasmuch as the revolt of Cassius had occurred during his administration of Syria, which included his native district.'[8] Does this signify that the rebellion had some local or 'national' character? It seems unlikely. However, a native usurper might command greater loyalty among the local elites than a stranger. While not a national movement, the rebellion of Cassius could have had a local component.

The Severans

The assassination of the emperor Commodus in Rome on New Year's Eve 192 led to a civil war, in which a candidate put up by the emperor's Praetorian Guard was challenged by nominees of the armies in Britain and Gaul, the Danube, and Syria. The candidate from Syria, the governor Gaius Pescennius Niger, established control over the whole of the eastern Mediterranean from Asia Minor to Egypt, and gained a few footholds in Europe. It seems that he could also count on the support of the Parthian king Vologaeses V and his vassals, the rulers of Adiabene and Hatra. Niger's principal rival, the Danubian candidate Septimius Severus, secured Rome, and Niger's authority in the east weakened following successive defeats at Cyzicus and Nicaea in north-western Asia Minor. Egypt and Arabia went over to Severus, and there were revolts in the cities of Syria. The final confrontation came at Issus, where centuries earlier Alexander the Great had triumphed over Darius. Niger was soundly defeated and fled to his supporters in Parthian territory, but was overtaken and killed (194).

The historian Cassius Dio wrote that during this civil war the Mesopotamian kingdoms of Osrhoene and Adiabene rebelled, laying siege to Nisibis, a Roman stronghold which lay more or less equidistant between them. The statement illustrates how ignorant we are of the details of this period. Osrhoene is known to have been within the Roman orbit, whereas Adiabene is thought to have been within the Parthian. One can speculate that some diplomatic understanding between Rome and Adiabene had been achieved (and hence its apparent support for Niger), but little more. This is also the first certain indication that Roman forces were stationed as far east as Nisibis. Osrhoene and Adiabene appear to have taken advantage of the war to pursue their own designs, but later claimed that they had been fighting *against* Niger (and must therefore have switched sides). All to no avail: for Severus directed his armies against them immediately after Niger's defeat, taking the titles Parthicus Arabicus and Parthicus Adiabenicus in honour of his victories. The kingdom of Osrhoene survived, as is shown by a boundary stone of AD 195, but on a greatly reduced scale: it seems to have been restricted to the city and territory of Edessa. The rest of north-western Mesopotamia then became a province also known by the name Osrhoene.

During Severus' war against his other rival Clodius Albinus in the west (AD 196-7) the Parthians retaliated, invading Mesopotamia and besieging Nisibis. In 197 Severus returned to Syria with three newly raised legions, I, II and III *Parthica*. His second Parthian war followed the pattern established by Trajan and Lucius Verus. First he secured the north and then marched his armies down the Euphrates to sack Ctesiphon (197/198). There followed a retreat up the Tigris, with a detour to besiege, inconclusively, the Parthian vassal-state of Hatra. He launched another attack on Hatra in 199, and may have concluded a treaty with the local rulers of that city. If so, this would be the first piece of evidence we have of the gravitation of Hatra towards the Roman sphere, an action for which it was later to pay dearly. At some time during or after the conclusion of the war (199) a province called Mesopotamia was established alongside that of Osrhoene. Severus claimed to have created a 'bulwark of Syria' through the establishment of the two Mesopotamian provinces. Cassius Dio was unconvinced, and complained that it was expensive and produced very little for Rome. His objections are often quoted, but in the long term Severus'

Fig. 13. Silver denarius of Pescennius Niger. The reverse legend reads 'BONI EVENTUS' ('good luck'). BMC *299a.*

strategy was vindicated. While the 'bulwark' failed to protect the provinces of Syria from invasion in the middle of the third century, subsequently most of the fighting was concentrated in Mesopotamia, leaving Syria unharmed. However, the acquisition of Mesopotamia was seen as a major transgression by the Sasanians, who fought hard to recover it.

Following Pescennius Niger's defeat, Severus had divided the province of Syria in two: Syria Coele in the north and Syria Phoenice in the south. This seems to have been another measure aimed at curbing the power of the governor and the potential for military revolt. For the first time in Syria there was large-scale production of imperial coinage, in the form of the silver denarius. The mint is uncertain but it was probably Antioch. This may be indicative of imperial desires for the region to be more independent of supplies of this coinage from Rome; it also highlights the growing importance of the city of Antioch as something more than just a major *polis* of the eastern Mediterranean. During the second century Antioch had served as the capital city of the empire: Trajan had moved his court there during his Parthian campaign, and so had Lucius Verus. Rome, the symbolic centre of the empire, was beginning to lose its importance as the political capital. Imperial duties now involved spending time in the provinces rather than at Rome, and from the late second century it was commonplace for the emperors to accompany their troops on campaign, even if, for much of the third century, it was felt important to visit Rome as early in the reign as possible. Emperors were often created on the peripheries, by the armies, rather than at the centre, yet they still found it prudent to invest in formal recognition by the Roman Senate and a period of residence at Rome. But campaigns demanded the emperor's presence on the peripheries of the empire, with the result that certain provincial cities acquired the infrastructures necessary to serve as imperial capitals. Antioch, as a former capital of the Seleucid kingdom, had sufficient dignity (and possibly still had Seleucid palace buildings) to serve imperial needs. Initially, however, Severus punished the city. Civil war provided rival cities with opportunities to challenge each other by supporting different contenders (see chapter 7). It was a risky business, since there could be only one winner in the struggle for empire, and cities that backed the loser could be punished by the victor. Antioch was particularly vulnerable. As the chief city of Syria it was highly likely to be seized by a usurper based in the province. Consequently Severus punished Antioch for its support of Niger, demoting it to village status and annexing it to the territory of its neighbour and rival Laodicea, which had declared for Severus. In the long term, however, this demotion did nothing to inhibit Antioch's role as an imperial capital. It is possible that Laodicea, which was made a *metropolis* following Niger's defeat, took over the role of chief meeting-place for the provincial imperial cult (see chapter 9), but later shared this position in some way with Antioch after the latter was restored. We do not know exactly when Antioch was restored, but it seems to have regained full status by the beginning of the third century. Other cities were also rewarded for their support against Niger: Heliopolis, Tyre, and Sebaste in Samaria, while their pro-Niger rivals were punished. This might appear unusually vindictive, but such measures were a way of maintaining Roman hegemony and keeping subject communities in line.

In the Parthian realm a prolonged civil war began when two brothers, Vologaeses VI and Artabanus IV, opposed each other from about AD 212. Severus' son Caracalla, now sole emperor, took advantage of the situation. He deposed the kings of Osrhoene and Armenia, declaring the kingdoms annexed to the Roman empire, although a rebellion in Armenia prevented the Romans from establishing authority there. Nevertheless these acts could be seen as an attempt to consolidate Rome's position before attempting to annex more of the Parthian kingdom. In what happened next it is very difficult to distinguish genuine intent from treachery. Caracalla submitted an extraordinary request to Artabanus of Parthia: the hand of Artabanus' daughter in marriage. Any offspring from the union could potentially claim the right to rule in both empires. This attempt to combine the two civilized powers is sometimes interpreted in the light of Caracalla's apparent fascination with Alexander the Great. The marriage consciously imitated the union between Alexander and the Persian Roxane. It is impossible to know whether the request was serious, but Artabanus agreed to a meeting. If Caracalla truly had been planning to unite the two empires through intermarriage, he had by then changed his mind. Instead of welcoming them, the Romans fell upon the Parthians and massacred them. Artabanus himself escaped, and Caracalla began a campaign (216) against the Parthians. After marching through Adiabene and Media he returned to winter at Edessa, from which he presumably hoped to conduct an attack on Ctesiphon in 217. But he fell victim to a conspiracy on a journey between Edessa and neighbouring Carrhae, and was replaced by Macrinus, his praetorian prefect. The new emperor had to contend with Artabanus' retaliatory invasion of Mesopotamia, and at Nisibis the Romans suffered a resounding defeat and agreed to pay an indemnity for the damage Caracalla's campaign had caused. It was not a particularly spectacular debut for Macrinus. On the diplomatic front the emperor achieved success in Armenia by offering reparations to its Arsacid monarchy for the actions of Caracalla, but his hold on power was precarious. Macrinus' status made his suitability as emperor questionable: he was of equestrian, not senatorial, rank (the Senate, however, had acquiesced to his rule). Caracalla had been popular with the rank and file, and there were other members of the family living in Syria who could challenge his position. Caracalla's influential mother Julia Domna was still alive, and resident at Antioch where Macrinus had set up court. Her subsequent suicide may not have lessened his problems.

A rebellion was engineered by the adherents of the remaining members of the Severan house who were based at Emesa. Julia Domna's sister Julia Maesa lived there, together with her two daughters, both of whom had a son. In 218 the eldest of these boys was proclaimed emperor in opposition to Macrinus, and won the support of troops stationed at nearby Apamea. Macrinus was unable to stem the revolt, and in a battle near Antioch he was defeated and overthrown. The new emperor, Bassianus, was given the throne name Marcus Aurelius Antoninus, like Caracalla, and he appears to have posed as either the adopted or real son (through an incestuous relationship) of Caracalla. He is better known to posterity as Elagabalus or Heliogabalus, the Roman name of the Syrian deity of Emesa whose high priest he was.

Once Elagabalus' position seemed secure, he set out for Rome, choosing an overland route through Asia Minor and the Balkans. In about 219 two of the Syrian legions rebelled against him, proclaiming as emperor Verus, the governor of the province of Syria Phoenice. The details of the rebellion are extremely obscure and little is known, except that it failed and some Syrian cities were punished or rewarded for their dispositions during the rebellion. A palace assassination in AD 222 disposed of Elagabalus, and the second of Julia Maesa's grandsons, Severus Alexander, took the throne. In the east the Roman empire had reached its greatest extent. The Roman army was established in the steppe and deserts of Syria, Arabia and Mesopotamia, perhaps as far as the Tigris and certainly as far as the middle reaches of the Euphrates. However, Roman supremacy was shortly to be upset, for in the Parthian kingdom something had happened which was to change the balance of power in the Fertile Crescent.

ROME AND PERSIA

The battle at Nisibis between Macrinus and Artabanus proved to be Rome's last major confrontation with a Parthian king. Hostilities between the two great powers, however, were only one facet of a complex story of political activities, and in spite of the intermittent conflicts and aggressive campaigns over the previous two and a half centuries, Rome's relations with its eastern neighbour had generally been stable. There were regular diplomatic links between the empires, as evidenced by a document of *c.* AD 208 in which the governor of Syria Coele instructed the commander of the garrison at Dura Europus on the middle Euphrates to receive a Parthian envoy. But diplomacy might also have contributed to Parthian decline as much as Roman military aggression. Roman relations with Mesopotamian vassals of the Parthian kings had been established from the earliest days of Rome's presence in the region, and these diplomatic efforts included attempts to exploit the decentralized Parthian system of power by establishing alliances with, or trying to influence, Parthian vassals. The organization of power in the Parthian empire had always involved a certain degree of tension between the king of kings and his vassal rulers, which the Romans could turn to their advantage. But usurpers arising within the Parthian empire could also exploit this tension. Eventually one of these vassals proved strong enough to challenge the established hegemony. The vassal ruler Ardashir of Fars (Persis) brought Arsacid supremacy to an end. Allied with other Parthian vassals who were dissatisfied with Artabanus IV, Ardashir overthrew the Parthian king *c.* AD 224 and ushered in a period in which Rome was forced on to the defensive in the east.

A monumental relief beside the Sasanian road at Firuzabad in his native Persis shows the decisive battle of Hormizdegan in heroic style: Ardashir and his son Shapur are seen toppling Artabanus and his grand vizier Darbendan from their horses, whilst a Sasanian cavalryman sweeps up another Parthian and holds him prisoner (fig. 14). The Arsacid family was not destroyed, but now it was reduced to vassal status. As under the Parthians, the major offices of state remained in the hands of a few great families. That of Sasan held the kingship (Ardashir's dynasty was named after an ancestor called Sasan); that of Suren produced commanders-in-chief of the army, as they had under the Parthians. As under the Parthians, the nobles frequently exercised a strong influence over the Sasanian king, and, if he did not suit their interests, he might be deposed. The concept of royal blood remained strong, making it difficult for usurpers to establish themselves, although this was precisely Ardashir's problem: as a usurper against the Arsacids, he had to fight hard to establish his authority.

To legitimize their rule Ardashir and his immediate successors concocted an imperial identity which looked back to empires of earlier times. Ardashir's

family hailed from the same region as the Achaemenid kings, and he could claim that he was recovering his ancestral right to that empire after it had been usurped by Alexander. It is fairly clear that the Hellenistic and Parthian past was of no use to the Sasanian kings, and recollection of the past five centuries rapidly faded under Sasanian rule. The very name Iran is derived from *Eranshahr*, 'empire of the Aryans', a concept created by the Sasanians in the third century. The Achaemenids had identified themselves culturally as 'Aryans', linking themselves to myths of ancient Iranian kings, and the concept of *Eranshahr* provided an identity for the Sasanian empire and at the same time legitimized the 'Aryan' Sasanians as the rightful rulers. Iran was juxtaposed with Aneran, the non-Sasanian powers, and the Sasanian attitude towards those non-Sasanian powers was initially antagonistic. Roman sources claim that the Sasanian kings sought to recover lands which were formerly part of the Achaemenid empire, just as the Parthians are said to have done. Iranian sources are more ambiguous, although the kings might claim to be kings of 'Iran and Aneran'. Some prefer to read the 'insider's' view as evidence that the Sasanians made no claims to Roman territory beyond Mesopotamia, and that their raids on Syria were expeditions fought for glory and plunder with no intention of conquest. But claims that they wanted to recover the lands of the former Achaemenid empire concur with other aspects of Sasanian ideology, and if third-century Sasanian rulers did not intend to conquer Syria and the Near East, by the beginning of the seventh century AD when the king Khusrau II successfully annexed the region their policy had clearly changed.

Within the Sasanian state there was a tendency towards greater centralization than there had been under the Parthians, perhaps in an attempt to forestall any potential rebellions by quasi-independent vassals. The number of official titles used at court increased during the course of the third century, suggesting the evolution of a more complex bureaucracy than had prevailed under the Arsacids. Royal iconography finally abandoned Greek influences. Ardashir created a new crown for himself, and henceforth all Sasanian kings had distinctive personal crowns, rather than the Hellenistic diadem normally worn by the Parthian rulers. Ardashir also introduced a new coinage in silver, which broke entirely with earlier traditions. Unlike Roman and Parthian coins the Sasanian ones were produced from broad, thin pieces of silver, and were so different in appearance that they could never be mistaken for the issues of previous or contemporary rivals (fig. 15).

The link between Zoroastrian religion and the kingship seems to have been stronger than it had been under the Parthians. Some see this as further evidence of a state-guided sharpening of Iranian cultural and religious identity. But the impetus appears to have come from the Zoroastrian priests, particularly

Fig. 14. Drawing of the relief at Firuzabad, Iran, showing the victory of Ardashir over Artabanus IV. On the right, Ardashir topples the Parthian king from his horse.

Kartir, spiritual advisor to king Shapur I and his successors. These priests sought to influence the kings, and sometimes to initiate persecutions of non-Zoroastrians, and the political strength of Zoroastrian orthodoxy seems to have depended heavily on the religious inclinations of individual kings. In general the Sasanian rulers, like their Arsacid predecessors, appear to have been tolerant of other religions. There are hints that non-Zoroastrian religious communities were formally recognized by the state through the institution of religious leaders, each one responsible to the king for his sect.

Roman attitudes to the Sasanians were even more ambivalent than they were towards the Parthians. The Iranians could hardly be considered savage barbarians in the same sense as the Germanic foes on the northern frontiers, and Sasanian prowess at fending off Roman invasions demonstrated that they were a worthy opponent. On the one hand they were a threat to Roman interests in the east, provoking the Romans into undertaking campaigns in imitation of the razzias of Trajan, Lucius Verus and Septimius Severus, while on the other imperial rhetoric sometimes hinted that the Sasanian obstacle to Roman world-domination was accepted. A late antique metaphor for Rome and Persia as the 'Two Great Lights' implies a mutual cultural purpose. In spite of hostilities the two empires had a common interest in preserving civilization in the face of the barbarian onslaught, a task which tended to draw them closer together. Some have seen the foundation of a new Roman capital at Constantinople in the fourth century as symptomatic of a more general process of political gravitation eastwards towards Rome's rival Ctesiphon. When the Roman emperors adopted Christianity, religion was even more strongly identified with the ruling power than in Persia, and gave the Roman empire a new sense of communal identity that paralleled the less rigorous use of Zoroastrianism by Sasanian kings. For emperors and elites in late Roman times the pomp of the contemporary Sasanian court provided a model to emulate as much as the traditions of Augustus and his successors. Thus there were various cultural and ideological points of convergence between Rome and Persia, but there was little hope of one empire culturally assimilating the other.

Rome on the Defensive

Having overthrown Artabanus, Ardashir set about winning the submission of the other Parthian vassal-states. It was a difficult task. Coins struck in AD 227/228 at Seleucia on the Tigris are in the name of a Parthian king, Vologaeses VI, the rival and brother of Artabanus IV. If the date given on the coins is not a die-engraver's error, it provides tentative evidence for a possible Parthian challenger to Ardashir a few years after the fall of Artabanus. But nothing else is known. More importantly, the new regime's struggle for hegemony had dramatic repercussions on the edge of the Roman world, where vassal-kings and -states declared for or against Ardashir. Some, such as the powerful Mesopotamian state of Hatra, were opposed, and may have sought an alliance with Rome. Thus a conflict between Rome and the Sasanians was almost inevitable.

In those states that were conquered, Ardashir often installed relatives as rulers. He was unable, however, to depose the Arsacids in Armenia, and Hatra remained defiant. Northern Mesopotamia, which the Romans had occupied within living memory, was regarded as legitimate Sasanian territory and targeted almost immediately after the Parthian dynasty was overthrown. By

Fig. 15. Silver coin of Ardashir. On the obverse a bust of the king, wearing his personal crown; on the reverse, a Zoroastrian fire altar.

about AD 230 Ardashir had laid siege to Nisibis and was launching raids into Roman Mesopotamia. The emperor Severus Alexander appears to have tried negotiation and, when that failed, arrived in AD 231/232 to conduct a three-pronged attack on the Sasanian west. The outcome of this ambitious war looks inconclusive. The Romans were successful in Media, but appear to have been defeated on the Euphrates. Even so, this may be the point at which Hatra, a powerful former vassal of the Parthians, was brought into a fuller alliance with Rome. If Rome had become accustomed to victories in the east, the ambiguous outcome of Alexander's campaign suggested that it was well not to be complacent. Confrontation with Rome had not dampened Ardashir's determination, and with further Sasanian action in Mesopotamia (including, c. 240, the sack of Hatra), firm action was needed to preserve Rome's interests in her eastern-most possessions.

The young emperor Gordian III arrived in 242 to conduct a campaign. The date more or less coincides with the end of the Edessene dynasty of Osrhoene. Caracalla had deposed the dynasty and made Edessa a colony, but now – after an interval of about twenty-six years – the dynasty was restored in 239/240. The circumstances are completely unknown; whether the local dynast was exploiting Rome's weakness or whether the Romans found it expedient to have a client king in Edessa organize his own defence against the Sasanians cannot be determined. Reliance on locals is a distinct possibility, and Rome was to rely increasingly on local initiative during the decades which followed. Coins issued in the kingdom show the new king Abgar and Gordian together, implying imperial approval. But the experiment at Edessa did not last long, for by the end of 242 the colony had been restored and the royal house of Osrhoene had disappeared for good. By this time Ardashir had died and his son Shapur, joint king during Ardashir's last years, had to face Gordian's invasion alone. He was more than up to the task. Although defeated in Mesopotamia in 243, Shapur was victorious in 244 when the Roman army invaded southern Mesopotamia along the Euphrates. Gordian either died in the battle or afterwards during the Roman retreat, a victim (or so it was later claimed) of the machinations of the two brothers from the Hauran who were his Praetorian Prefects, Marcus Julius Priscus and Marcus Julius Philippus. The latter succeeded Gordian as emperor, and concluded a peace with Shapur. As under Macrinus, the Romans agreed to pay an indemnity. Other details of the agreement are unclear, as is whether the Romans made any serious territorial concessions.

Philip set off for Rome while his brother Priscus held an extraordinary command over the eastern provinces. The rule of Priscus is said to have been unpopular, and it seems to have prompted the usurpation of a certain Iotapianus, who was proclaimed emperor. The location of this rebellion cannot be pinpointed precisely, even though the usurper struck coins – the sources name Syria, or Cappadocia – and Iotapianus does not appear to have lasted long. Philip himself was overthrown in 249, but the actions of his successors in Armenia (the details are obscure) were regarded by the Sasanians as a breach of the earlier peace agreed with Philip, and provided the pretext for a fresh round of hostilities. Shapur invaded Syria in the 250s, wiping out a Roman army on the Euphrates at Barbalissus and sacking various cities, including Antioch. The exact date of this campaign has been the focus of much debate: 252, 253 or 256, or perhaps two separate campaigns in different years. While Antioch suffered no permanent damage as a consequence of these invasions,

Zeugma seems never to have recovered fully from its sack, remaining a city more in name than in extent. The same fate appears to have befallen neighbouring Doliche, the centre of a well-known cult of Jupiter. During the early 250s northern Syria seems also to have suffered from the ravages of a usurper named in the sources as Mariades or Cyriades, who appears to have had supporters at Antioch and perhaps had links with Shapur. Our evidence is too fragmentary to attempt anything other than the most tentative reconstruction of events, but it is clear that Rome's control over the east was becoming increasingly insecure.

Preoccupation with barbarian invaders elsewhere diverted imperial attentions away from the region for several years. A Persian attack on Emesa c. 252 or 253 apparently failed, and the issue of coins in the city in the name of a certain Lucius Julius Aurelius Sulpicius Uranius Antoninus (fig. 121) may be connected with this event. That some of his coins add the name Severus could indicate a connection, real or pretended, with the Severan dynasty, and he may have been a priest of the god Elagabal (the appearance of this Emesene deity on his coins is not conclusive proof). What is significant is the fact that a local notable could successfully organize some kind of defence against the Persians, and pose as emperor. In this sense Uranius Antoninus anticipates the growth of Palmyrene power two decades later.

We do not know what happened to Uranius Antoninus, and he probably did not survive the arrival of the legitimate emperor Valerian in 254. Our knowledge of events in this period remains vague. Occupation, if not reoccupation, of places like Dura Europus was maintained until c. 256, after which the Romans abandoned any claim to territory on the Euphrates below the confluence of the Khabur. Henceforth Roman and Sasanian disputes centred on Mesopotamia.

Interlude on the Middle Euphrates

During the second century the invasion route along the Euphrates to southern Mesopotamia had proved strategically important to Rome, and following the wars under Lucius Verus the Roman presence was slowly extended along the middle Euphrates until it reached as far south as Kifrin and the island of Bijan (fig. 16). Before the Roman conquests Palmyra had played some military role in this region, to support its trade links with southern Mesopotamia and the Persian Gulf. Palmyra still had some part to play in garrisoning sites here, even after regular Roman soldiers were stationed on the middle Euphrates in the later second century, but how the two forces interacted is uncertain.

For once, however, we have an extraordinarily full documentary record. Excavations at Dura Europus, a city annexed by Rome under Lucius Verus and sacked by Shapur in the mid-third century, yielded dozens of papyrus and parchment documents as well as graffiti and inscriptions, providing valuable evidence for a wide variety of activities on this part of the river. The region had strong social and economic connections with Roman Mesopotamia, as is shown by documents from Dura and a recently discovered archive from this region (see p. 143), and the presence in abundance of coins of Mesopotamian cities. A unit of regular auxiliary troops, the *cohors XX Palmyrenorum*, was its principal garrison.

Concrete evidence for the extension of Roman control along the river south of Dura came from excavations conducted by international teams in advance of the construction of the Qadisiyya dam at Haditha on the Euphrates, which

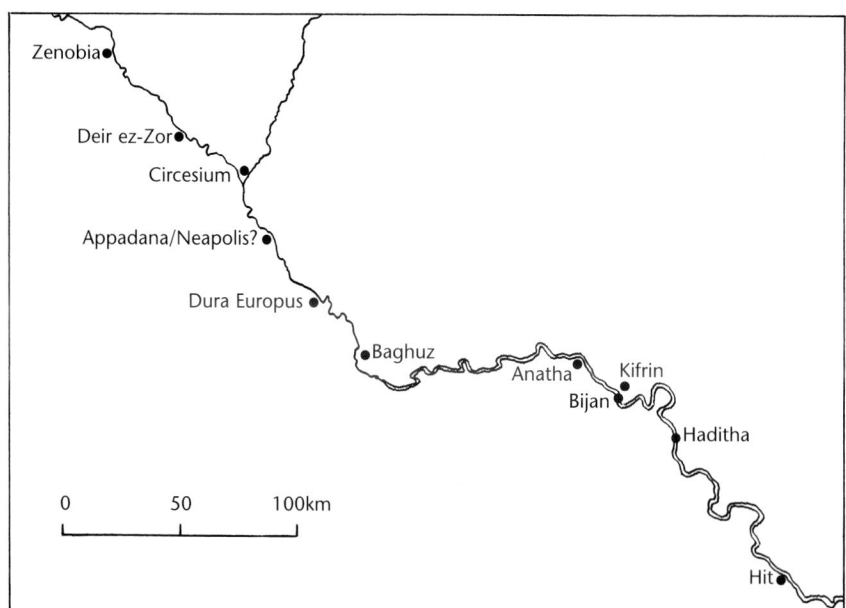

Fig. 16. Map showing sites on the middle Euphrates.

flooded part of the middle Euphrates valley in the early 1980s. Palmyrenes seem to have been prominent in the military occupation of this area, and probably controlled outposts along the river before the Roman conquest of Mesopotamia. A Palmyrene officer is known to have been in charge of Anatha ('Ana) in the Severan period, and a Palmyrene inscription refers to a Nabataean cavalryman there as early as AD 132. Archaeological sondages on the island settlement of 'Ana yielded plausible evidence of Roman presence in the form of hard-fired, red, ribbed 'brittle ware' cooking pots characteristic of Roman sites in the region, though the precise dates for this material are insecure. Much stronger archaeological evidence for the Roman presence came from the larger site of Kifrin, which lay on the east bank of the river and may have been the settlement of Bechchouphrein mentioned in papyri at Dura. A detachment of Palmyrene soldiers from Dura was perhaps stationed there, and may have occupied the heavily fortified zone (which the excavators dubbed the 'citadel') at the north-western end of the site. Structures included what appear to be administrative buildings in Parthian/Hatrene style, tombs, and a Roman bath. Graffiti and inscriptions on potsherds attest to the use of Latin, Greek and a Hatrene-style Aramaic script. Further downstream the heavily fortified island of Bijan seems to have been occupied by Palmyrenes, and the material excavated there include brittle ware pots, coins of the Severan period, and pot-sherds inscribed with Palmyrene and Latin characters, as well as a local script closely resembling that of Hatra.

The Roman occupation of the left bank of the Euphrates this far down-stream might have been linked to Roman relations with Hatra in this period. Three Latin dedications from that city attest to the presence of Roman soldiers there, between at least AD 235 and *c.* 240, when the city fell to the Sasanians. Of the coins found at Kifrin, the Roman issues are almost exclusively Severan, although there is also a small hoard of silver coins ending with issues of Gordian III, *c.* 243/244. But there is also a significant number of coins from Hatra, which is located about 150 kilometres (90 miles) away to the north-east.

Thus it is possible that the Kifrin belonged to Hatra, or it relied on Hatrene support, and that an alliance with Hatra led to a Roman presence at Kifrin. With Hatra's fall to the Sasanians *c.* 240, the Romans were forced to withdraw from the area. Documentary evidence from Dura indicates a Persian raid on the middle Euphrates did indeed take place at about this time. A Roman evacuation of Kifrin and Bijan might explain why, when Shapur invaded Syria in the 250s, the first place he mentioned in his list of conquests was the island of Anatha ('Ana), upstream of the aforementioned sites. By this time the southernmost outposts, perhaps briefly reoccupied by Gordian on his march down the Euphrates, had been abandoned by Rome.

The Romans were finally driven out of this region in about AD 256, when the Persians took Dura Europus. Dramatic and rather grisly evidence for the fall of Dura was uncovered during excavations of the city's western wall. The Persians attacked this in two spots, one at the south-western corner of the city, and the other to the north of the city's main gate. Shortly before the siege the defenders had reinforced the city walls by constructing earth embankments along the inside and outside (fig. 17). It seems that the Persians first attempted to undermine the wall north of the gate by digging a tunnel under a tower (tower number 19 on the excavators' plan; see fig. 113) and a section of wall, hoping to create a large breach. On the flat plain west of the city, however, it was difficult for the besiegers to conceal what they were doing, and the defenders dug a counter-mine to intercept the Persians. But when they broke into the Persian mine, a battle ensued underground in which the defenders were overwhelmed. In the panic those inside the city blocked the entrance to the counter-mine to prevent the Persians from entering, but did so before the wounded and the tardy on their own side had had time to escape. The Persians then set fire to the wooden props of this counter-mine, so that most of it collapsed, burying some sixteen to eighteen Roman soldiers along with their weapons, armour and coins (the latest of which dates to AD 256). Having blocked off the counter-mine to prevent any further attacks, the Persians then fired the props of their own mine. Part of the wall and the south western corner of tower 19 sank about 2.5 metres (8 ¼ feet) into the mine, but remained upright, supported by the embankment (colour plate 16). The tower caught fire, as had probably been intended, but the flames were rapidly deprived of oxygen as the interior had been sealed off by the defenders. In the southwestern corner of the city the besiegers had better luck. They built an assault ramp between towers 15 and 14 (the latter occupying the south-western angle of the fortifications). Anyone on the ramp would be exposed to missiles from tower 14, so the Persians decided to undermine the tower. This time the entrance to the mine was concealed in a ravine to the south-west and the defenders may not have known about it until it was too late. Like tower 19, tower 14 sank and remained upright, but the undermining was more extensive and probably rendered it useless to the defenders. Another, much wider mine was dug next to the assault ramp and went straight under the wall into the city. This was probably intended to enable the assailants to attack the defenders in the rear as they concentrated on beating off the Persians on the ramp. This ramp and tunnel were probably the means by which the Persians broke into the city, bringing the Roman occupation of Dura, and the city itself, to an end.

With the fall of Dura the Romans seem to have evacuated this section of the Euphrates altogether. Henceforth the southernmost military post was

Circesium, located at the confluence of the Euphrates and Khabur rivers.

Palmyra

In AD 260, during a campaign against the Persians, the emperor Valerian was defeated in Mesopotamia by Shapur and taken prisoner. The capture of Valerian was a tremendous symbolic as well as military victory for Shapur, who could now portray himself as having triumphed over three emperors (the others being Gordian III and Philip). The Persian armies then broke up into raiding parties, plundering Syria and Cappadocia. But this was the last of Shapur's successes. The Roman army regrouped under two commanders, Macrianus and Callistus (or Ballista), and forced the Sasanians to retreat. Shapur then suffered a defeat at the hands of Septimius Odaenathus of Palmyra, and withdrew from Roman territory. Nobody negotiated for the return of Valerian, who was taken as a hostage to Iran, where he remained for the rest of his life.

Fig. 17. Dura Europus, showing the western ramparts which bore the brunt of the Sasanian assault.

Macrianus and Callistus decided that their next move would be to try their luck against Valerian's son and co-ruler, Gallienus. The two sons of Macrianus, Macrianus Junior and Quietus, were proclaimed emperors. Macrianus Senior and Junior then set off for Europe to confront Gallienus, while Callistus and Quietus remained in the east. In 261 the European expedition was defeated by an army loyal to Gallienus and the two Macriani were killed. In Syria Odaenathus of Palmyra overthrew Callistus and Quietus. Gallienus had gained nominal control of the east, but he owed much to the Palmyrene leader.

In spite of the number of surviving inscriptions referring to him, the career of Odaenathus cannot be constructed with confidence. After the defeat of the Persians, the forces of Palmyra seem to have been responsible for bringing order to Syria and Mesopotamia, and Odaenathus played a key part in this process. He must have commanded a substantial militia in order to be able to take on Shapur and the usurpers Callistus and Quietus. Gallienus remained in direct command of the central portions of the Roman empire, but he was otherwise preoccupied with barbarian invasions and checking the power of an independent 'Romano-Gallic' empire in the west. There was little hope that Gallienus could protect Roman interests in the east, so he relied on others to protect those interests for him. What authority enabled Odaenathus to act as he did can hardly be established for certain on the evidence as it stands at present, but in protecting Roman interests he clearly led Palmyra to a position of eminence in the Syrian region. As the central power weakened, Palmyra took on the task of preserving the Roman empire in the east. Odaenathus remained loyal to Gallienus throughout his lifetime, but the situation seems to have changed following his death *c.* 267/268. He was succeeded by his son Vaballathus, but real power resided in the hands of Odaenathus' wife Zenobia.

Although Palmyra had achieved some sort of political supremacy, its economic standing may have been in decline. Trade links between the Persians and Romans were not as they had been between the Parthians and Romans. References to caravans from Characene and southern Mesopotamia, common in second-century inscriptions, disappear in the third century. In the Persian Gulf region where the Palmyrenes traded, Roman goods such as glass were frequently used as prestige objects for elite burials up to this time, but thereafter they are replaced by Sasanian goods. Palmyra was land-locked, having no direct outlet on the Mediterranean. The details are sketchy, but Palmyra was also involved in some sort of conflict with the nomadic Arab tribes of the Syrian and Arabian steppe, and sought to assert her authority in these remote regions. Palmyra's economic and political insecurity, caught as she was in the middle of a Roman-Persian stand-off, may have prompted the enterprise which followed.

Gallienus was succeeded in 268 by Claudius who, although he reigned for only two years, laid the foundations for the recovery of the central empire, a process which was vigorously pursued by one of his successors, Aurelian (AD 270-75). Before reducing the 'Romano-Gallic' empire, Aurelian had to turn his attention to the east where, following the death of Claudius, Palmyra had begun acting too independently for his liking.

In 270, the year of Aurelian's accession, the Palmyrenes attacked the province of Arabia, and then launched an invasion of Egypt. They also extended Palmyrene domination into Asia Minor. Vaballathus' portrait began to appear on coins minted at Antioch and Alexandria (fig. 149.2), but in deference to Aurelian the emperor's portraits were placed on the flip side to the portraits of Vaballathus. Vaballathus' images and titles avoided any references to his holding imperial power. Perhaps one of the most extraordinary assertions of

Fig. 18. Palmyra. The so-called 'Baths of Diocletian', which some have suggested was a palatial residence of Zenobia. The columns in the foreground frame a rectangular basin or impluvium, *resembling the installations found in Italian houses. The entrance to the complex from the grand colonnade is marked by re-used Egyptian granite columns (visible in the background, to the right). In the background on the left, the grand colonnade and the monumental arch.*

power to survive from this period are milestones in the names of Vaballathus, 'the most illustrious king of kings and corrector of the entire Orient', and Zenobia, 'the most illustrious queen, mother of the king of kings'.[9] Some are in Latin, the usual language of milestones, but others are unique in that they are inscribed in Greek and Palmyrene. In erecting such markers the Palmyrenes were appropriating a typical 'Roman' symbol.

The remainder of the story is well known. At its greatest extent the Palmyrene empire included Syria, Arabia, Palestine, Egypt and the eastern provinces of Asia Minor. When Zenobia found she could not negotiate with Aurelian, Vaballathus was proclaimed emperor. Coins were struck giving him imperial titles, and in the name of Zenobia as empress, without any reference to Aurelian. But Aurelian regained Antioch and Alexandria in 272, and the Palmyrene forces were unable to block his advances. Another defeat followed near Emesa, and a siege of Palmyra followed. Zenobia was captured and the city surrendered in 272. In 273, after Aurelian's departure, Palmyra rose in revolt and the emperor returned, sacking the city. Not everyone in Palmyra had accepted the dominance of the family of Odaenathus, it seems: one of the latest known Palmyrene inscriptions proclaims that a man of senatorial rank, Septimius Haddudan, 'had aided the army of Aurelian Caesar'.[10] Zenobia herself was taken to Rome for Aurelian's triumph, and granted an estate near Rome where she spent the rest of her days.

The episode of Palmyra under Zenobia illustrates how remarkably resilient was the Roman empire in circumstances which might have torn other empires asunder. It cannot be seen as a Syrian rebellion against Rome. The Palmyrene elites felt sufficiently integrated into the Roman world not to abandon their commitment to it. When the centre was weak, the elites of the periphery took matters into their own hands in an attempt to preserve the whole. The usurpation of Uranius Antoninus during a similar period of weakness two decades earlier may have been a response to the same sorts of problems. Tenuous though the centre's authority might be, circumstances had changed considerably since the Parthian invasion in 40 BC, when many local rulers had sought to escape Roman control. But it was difficult to surrender peripheral power to the centre once the crisis had passed. Far from providing a focus for 'national' sentiment in Syria, in their rebellion against Aurelian the Palmyrenes remained steadfast to the ideal of empire, even down to their claim to be acting through the legitimate authority of Vaballathus Augustus and Zenobia Augusta.

The destruction of Palmyra brought an end to one of the more distinct cultures that had evolved in Syria under the aegis of Rome (see chapter 8), and led to other groups, such as the Roman military and the Arab tribes of the steppe and desert, exercising greater influence over this region of the Syrian interior. There had been nothing new in Rome's reliance on regional powers to organize their own defence and to safeguard her interests. In previous centuries she had supported 'client' kings with their royal armies. But Palmyra's very success in this respect had proved both the city's downfall and a threat to the centre's hegemony. Nevertheless, in the centuries that followed, the emperors continued to find it expedient to rely on local configurations of power in the more marginal areas of Syria and the Near East.

The Struggle for Mesopotamia

The collapse of Palmyrene domination of the eastern provinces and the re-establishment of central Roman control more or less coincided with the death of Shapur. The Sasanian king had not attempted any further offensives against the Roman empire during the final decade of his rule. Although he had been defeated in the west by Odaenathus, he had successfully established Sasanian rule from southern Mesopotamia to north-west Pakistan, and from the Caucasus to the Persian Gulf – no mean achievement for the son of a usurper against the Arsacids. He was able to pass on to his successors a fairly stable empire, but in the west they would have to contend with the aggressions of a restored Roman empire ruled by a succession of energetic military commanders.

In the Roman world the restoration of central Roman control did not prevent provincial armies from challenging the ruling emperor. Probus, the commander of the eastern armies, usurped the empire in 276 and won; in 278 the governor of Syria Coele, Saturninus, usurped Probus and lost. Like Aurelian, Probus worked hard to restore the fortunes of the state. He eventually succumbed to a mutiny in 282 and was replaced by his Praetorian Prefect Carus, who launched a devastating attack on the Sasanian empire in 283. It was the first fully successful military action against the newly established Sasanian regime, even though Carus himself was assassinated during the campaign. The Roman invasion adopted the familiar strategy of taking the route down the Euphrates and into southern Mesopotamia, capturing Ctesiphon and forcing the Sasanian king to flee. A peace was obtained, by which the Persians recognized Roman control of northern Mesopotamia.

Rome was also to gain control over Armenia in the following years. The emperor Diocletian (AD 284-305) promoted an Arsacid called Tiridates to the Armenian throne while the Sasanians tried to impose a member of their own family. Early in the fourth century Tiridates adopted Christianity, which rapidly gained a foothold in Armenia, and which may have been in part an affirmation of identity on the part of the Armenians, placing them in opposition to the Zoroastrian Persians. Narseh, who succeeded his nephew Bahram II as king of the Sasanian empire in 293, began challenging Roman interference in the region. Initially he was successful, expelling Tiridates from Armenia and invading Mesopotamia, where he defeated Diocletian's deputy emperor Galerius in 297. The following year, however, Galerius returned with a new army and inflicted a resounding defeat on Narseh in Armenia, capturing the royal harem and following up the victory with a campaign into southern Mesopotamia, advancing as far as Ctesiphon. The humiliated Narseh sought a peace, and Diocletian stipulated that the Sasanians relinquish all claims over Armenia as well as northern Mesopotamia. The truce was to last forty years.

The late third and early fourth century saw the restoration of Roman power in Syria after decades of weakness. Little is known of the period between the fall of Palmyra and the time of Diocletian, but Diocletian's reign marks a major change to the administrative and military organization of the empire, which had important consequences for Syria and the Near East (see chapters 3, 4 and 10). Under Diocletian's collegiate system of emperors the number of imperial capitals increased, and Rome lost its importance as a centre of power as the emperors moved around and took up residence in the provinces. The city of Antioch functioned as an imperial capital for prolonged periods: Galerius was frequently in residence there from his investiture in 293 until his Persian campaigns of 296, and the senior emperor Diocletian, under whom a palace was constructed in the city, was present on several occasions, particularly between 296 and 302. Between 305 and 313 Galerius' deputy and successor Maximinus was frequently resident at Antioch, and perhaps in the south at Caesarea Maritima as well. Antioch became an imperial capital again when Constantine's son Constantius set up court there in 335.

Roman military presence in the more remote areas of the Syrian provinces expanded during this period. New military installations constructed by Diocletian and his successors, aimed at improving communications and fortifications in the steppe, may have been a response to the end of Palmyrene hegemony over the Arab nomads of these regions. Now these peoples had to be monitored and dealt with directly by Roman troops. The result was that these peoples came to be incorporated within the military structure of the empire (see below).

By 312 the dominant emperor in Diocletian's rapidly disintegrating collegiate system was Constantine, who shared the empire with Licinius and Maximinus. All three were rivals rather than colleagues. Maximinus was defeated and overthrown by Licinius (313), and Licinius himself was eventually defeated by Constantine (324). By this time the Sasanian empire had found a strong ruler in the person of Shapur II (AD 309-79). Shapur was prepared to dispute Roman control of the territories ceded by Narseh, and much of his long reign was spent trying to recover them. In 330 he invaded Armenia but was repulsed, and in the following years he harried Roman Mesopotamia. Constantine appointed his nephew Hanniballianus as ruler of Armenia, with the unusual Persian-sounding title *rex regum*, 'king of kings', which looks rather like a direct challenge to Shapur's authority. More ominous were Constantine's preparations for a major war with the Sasanians. These were supposedly provoked by Persian persecutions of Christians; and from now on there was often a religious dimension to Roman-Sasanian conflicts as the two states sought to promote their favoured faiths. However, Shapur was spared all-out war with the emperor's death in 337, which terminated whatever plans he had formulated. The succession of Constantine's three sons, Constantine II, Constans and Constantius, divided the military resources of the empire, greatly reducing the support that any one of the new emperors could draw on. Dynastic squabbles soon reduced the emperors to two, Constans and Constantius (340).

Constantius' principal residence until 350 was Antioch, from which he oversaw the protection of the east, as Shapur contested the territory gained by Galerius in 299. The emperor's policy was defensive rather than offensive. He may have erred on the side of caution, but he managed to preserve his half of the empire intact in spite of internal and external pressures. Rather than embarking on risky schemes of invasion and conquest, he sought to ensure that the eastern frontier was well maintained, keeping his armies at full strength and in good order, building or strengthening fortresses (fig. 19), and using strategic diplomacy where circumstances permitted. Compared with the aggressive policies of his colourful successor Julian, the exploits of Constantius in the east look equivocal and rather lacklustre, but to his credit Constantius managed to prevent the Persians from annexing any of Galerius' conquests, whereas Julian's campaign led to disaster.

Shapur launched raids into Mesopotamia almost immediately following Constantine the Great's death in 337, an act which led to a series of inconclusive razzias by both sides over the following years. The Persians besieged Nisibis three times between 337 and 350, but were unable to take the city. The Romans crossed the Tigris in 340 or later, invading Adiabene and perhaps capturing Nineveh in 343, and a battle was fought in the vicinity of Singara in 343 or 344, in which the Persian crown prince was killed. In 350 Constantius suddenly found himself sole surviving son of Constantine, but he was still unable to throw the full weight of the Roman army against Persia. The west was now held by the usurper Magnentius, who had overthrown and killed Constans.

Constantius was forced to turn his back on the eastern front, and left to engage Magnentius, appointing a cousin, Constantius Gallus, as Caesar in command of the eastern provinces (351). Gallus set up court at Antioch, but his rule proved very unpopular with the aristocracy of the city, who managed to undermine his authority. Once Magnentius had been dealt with, Gallus was summoned by the emperor, arrested, tried and executed (354).

In 359-60 Shapur, who had been busy dealing with problems in other parts of his empire, returned to Mesopotamia, capturing key Roman fortresses there (among them Amida, whose siege is vividly described by an eye-witness, the historian Ammianus Marcellinus). This crisis drew Constantius back east, but the emperor had little time to organize an offensive before learning of another rebellion against him in the west. In 361 Constantius turned westwards again, to challenge Gallus' brother Julian, who had been proclaimed emperor in Paris and was marching against him. On the way he contracted a violent fever and died, leaving Julian sole master of the Roman world.

Fig. 19. Roman bulwark in Mesopotamia: the great fortress of Amida (Diyarbakir) on the Tigris was constructed by Constantius II while he was Caesar under Constantine.

Julian took on Constantius' plans to wage war on the Sasanians. He arrived in Antioch in 362 and set up court there, before marching against the Persians in the spring of the following year. The Persian campaign was probably intended as a repeat of the victories of Trajan, Lucius Verus, Septimius Severus and Carus. Among those accompanying Julian was Hormizd, Shapur's brother, who had fled to the Roman empire in 324 and perhaps hoped to be made king. The attack was two-pronged, one army crossing Mesopotamia and the other marching down the Euphrates. Near Ctesiphon Julian defeated the Sasanian army, but he did not take the city itself. His army began the march north to meet the Mesopotamian division, but in another confrontation with the Sasanians the emperor was fatally wounded (June 363). He had reigned less than two years.

The retreating army now chose Jovian, the commander of the imperial guard, as Julian's successor. In exchange for an unharassed retreat he agreed to cede the strategic Mesopotamian fortress cities of Nisibis and Singara, as well as abandoning Roman influence over Armenia. The Persians finally regained much of what they had lost over half a century earlier, and most of these territories were never again to be ruled by Rome. The treaty was supposed to last for thirty years; unlike many other treaties it did not lapse with the death of either signatory. For Shapur this was fortunate, as Jovian died on the journey to Constantinople (364), and the empire then passed into the hands of a senior army officer called Valentinian, who elevated his brother Valens to share the duties of empire.

The Sasanian acquisition of Nisibis changed the balance of power in Mesopotamia. Shapur began consolidating the new frontier, settling Arab tribesmen as soldiers in the frontier regions. He also seems to have wanted to reduce certain vassal-states to direct rule. He was particularly interested in imposing direct rule over Armenia, even though this would violate the treaty of 363 (this conceded Sasanian *influence* over Armenia, but not its absorption). Valens was distracted for several years by the rebellion of Procopius (AD 365-6) and a Gothic invasion of Thrace, but Shapur's activities brought the emperor to Syria in 370. The emperor set up court at Antioch, and ruled from there for much of the rest of his reign. Summer campaigns against the Sasanians became a regular feature in the years that followed.

The Rise of the Federate Arabs

The sources for the late empire mention Arab tribes of the Syrian and Arabian steppe more frequently than the sources of preceding periods. This may in part be due to the relative abundance of late Roman sources concerned with Syria and the Near East, but this increased notice may also reflect a growing importance of nomads to Roman military and political strategies in the region. There is thought to be a link between the collapse of Palmyra and the ascendance of these groups, so that in the vast areas where once Palmyra had made alliances and fought with the nomadic groups on behalf of Rome, now Rome had to do these things without her Palmyrene intermediary. Any tribe which had an alliance with Rome was expected to protect Roman interests, particularly against attack by other Arab nomad tribes. We find the tribes being used on major military campaigns, and there are hints of some fairly substantial conflicts of interest between Rome and her allied tribes at the provincial level. In many cases the details of the arrangements are far from certain, although in modern discussions the allied tribes are usually referred to as federates. In return for state subsidies, the federate tribes organized and carried out raids on enemy territory and provided recruits for the army. One tribe appears to have been predominant throughout the entire region, and its chief received official recognition from the Romans. By the sixth century these chiefs were receiving the title of phylarch (originally used to designate a tribal chief but later employed by Rome to refer to a commander of auxiliary troops). The dominant tribe was responsible for collecting tribute for Rome from other tribes in their area of influence. These federates were not simply rough nomad militias. Their camps became fortresses, and many former nomads are thought to have adopted a more sedentary lifestyle. Nevertheless these soldiers were expected to form an important mobile element in the defence and policing of Roman territory.

We also find the Sasanians utilizing Arab tribes living on the peripheries of their empire, particularly the Lakhmid tribe from al-Hira on the southern Euphrates. Such tribes could be used against the Romans and their allies. On both sides, Roman and Sasanian, Arab tribes became institutionalized within military and political structures, and to some extent their religious leanings were shaped by the great powers. From the fourth century onwards the gradual adoption of Christianity by federate tribes helped cement a sense of identity with Rome and against Zoroastrian Persia and the pagan Arab tribes, but questions of orthodoxy and heresy sometimes led to conflict between Rome and her tribal allies. When Arab allies of the Sasanians became Christians, they tended to adopt Nestorianism, the sect prominent in the Persian empire but regarded as heretical by the Roman orthodoxy.

A political desire and military need to influence the tribes at the boundaries of the Roman and Sasanian empires may help to explain the Sasanian campaigns against the Arabs in 326, when Shapur II crossed the Euphrates in the south, beyond the frontiers of Roman Arabia and Syria, to establish his authority over the tribes in those regions. These campaigns are also thought to explain the remarkable funerary inscription in Arabic found at Namara, in Roman territory east of the Hauran. This commemorates a certain Imru' al-Qays, a 'king of (all?) the Arabs', who is considered to have been a prominent ally of the Romans. It is not certain who Imru' al-Qays was, but if he is to be identified with a Lakhmid chief of that name, it would appear that he defected to Rome some time before his epitaph was inscribed in 328/329, perhaps as a direct result of Shapur's actions against the Arabs. An alternative view is that he died while raiding Roman territory on behalf of Shapur. The reading and interpretation of this important inscription is disputed, and consequently it is difficult to fit Imru' al-Qays into any confident historical narrative.

The dominant pro-Roman tribe in the fourth century appears to have been the Tanukh, but their exact status is uncertain, and it is extremely difficult to reconstruct a history of relations between the different tribes and Rome. Occasional references to Arab or 'Saracen' allies in the sources usually neglect to tell us their tribal affiliations. The accession of Constantius II (337) was marked by a brief revolt of at least some of the federate Arabs, perhaps as a reaction against Constantius himself, who tended towards a heretical form of Christianity known as Arianism. Later, the Arian emperor Valens found himself in conflict with the Arab *foederati*, resulting in a serious rebellion or 'Saracen war' of 375-8, which was led by a certain queen Mavia (which tribe or tribes she ruled remains unclear). Religious differences may have been the cause of the troubles, although Mavia initially could have been a pagan and adopted Christianity only during the revolt. The rebellion seems to have been widespread, covering the inland areas of Phoenice, Arabia and Palaestina and even reaching Egypt. A Roman force was defeated by Mavia's warriors, and Valen's government, now hard pressed by the Goths in the Balkans, came to terms. Mavia obtained consent for an orthodox religious leader to be appointed for her people, which appears to have been her principal concern at that point. She was certainly not opposed to Roman rule in general, and sent a cavalry force to Thrace to assist Valens in his campaign against the Goths. Too late, as it transpired: Valens and a large part of the Roman army were annihilated at the battle of Adrianople (378), but in the aftermath the Saracen cavalry performed with savage efficiency by destroying a Gothic column advancing on Constantinople. In 383 there was a further Arab revolt in Syria, probably organized by the Tanukh, which Roman armies successfully subdued. The conflict may have led to the end of Tanukh hegemony over the Arab *foederati*, since from this point on we encounter the leaders of another tribe, the Salih, as the dominant figures among the Arabs of southern Syria and Transjordan.

The Divided Empire

The death of Valens left the eastern half of the empire without an emperor, and in 379 the young and inexperienced western emperors Gratian and Valentinian II appointed the capable general Theodosius to rule the east, where the situation in the Balkan provinces was now extremely grave. In the same year Shapur II died, and under one of his sons and successors, Shapur III, the Romans and Persians finally reached an agreement concerning Armenia. The kingdom was partitioned between them. Persarmenia, the Sasanian portion, was far larger than the Roman part, but Theodosius probably considered it a worthwhile compromise to secure peace. The six western satrapies of the Armenian kingdom ruled by Rome retained their traditional rulers and military forces, but the satraps had to recognize the Roman emperor rather than the Persian-appointed Armenian king as their overlord.

Contemporaries might have agreed with the judgement of modern scholars that the problems of the empire were too great to be handled by a single emperor, but the division of the Roman world between the imperial houses of Valentinian and Theodosius resulted in some complex political arrangements. Gratian was overthrown and killed by the western usurper Magnus Maximus in 383, leaving his brother Valentinian controlling Italy and the central provinces of the empire. By recognizing Maximus, Theodosius made it clear that he would not avenge Gratian, until Maximus invaded Italy in 387, forcing Valentinian to seek refuge at Theodosius' court. The eastern emperor then marched against the usurper and defeated him. Valentinian was restored, but not for long. In 392 this last remaining representative of the house of Valentinian was assassinated, and the west was usurped by the pretender Eugenius. Theodosius, who now ruled with his two sons Arcadius (appointed in 383) and Honorius (appointed in 393), withdrew a large number of troops from the eastern provinces to fight him. Although victorious, Theodosius died shortly afterwards (395), and the empire was divided between his sons. Honorius took the western half and Arcadius the east. The political and military organization of the empire had been structured along territorial lines since the late third century, but from the reigns of Valentinian I and Valens the division between east and west grew more pronounced. The weaknesses of a divided empire had become apparent under Theodosius, Gratian and Valentinian II, but after AD 395 the political and military partition became permanent. Now, under Arcadius and Honorius, the two halves evolved as separate and sometimes competing entities. One side might come to the assistance of the other, or, if an emperor had died, his counterpart in the other half of the empire might have to approve a successor, but the empire was increasingly unable to act as a single force.

Theodosius died at a particularly awkward moment. Most of the imperial field army was with him in the west, under the command of the half-barbarian commander Stilicho. Stilicho used his authority to consolidate his power and influence over Honorius and the western empire. His position was resented in the east, where Arcadius' government strenuously opposed him. From 395 relations between the two halves of the empire were often covertly and sometimes openly hostile. East and west intrigued against each other, and appeared to be on the brink of war between 405 and 408, conflict being averted only with Stilicho's murder. To easterners the western empire came to seem more and more like a foreign power, to be dealt with almost in the same manner as the Sasanians or barbarian federations. The increasing instability and decline of the western empire saw to it being treated as a kind of junior partner by the eastern emperors, who enjoyed greater political stability and continuity than their western counterparts. Several times the eastern emperors intervened in the western succession, and western emperors found it prudent to secure recognition from Constantinople. As before, the division of the empire also reduced the amount of manpower that either half could harness to solve a military problem, but now an expedient solution to barbarian threats was to encourage the enemy to attack the other half instead.

The reigns of Arcadius (383-408) and his son Theodosius II (402-50) were relatively free from conflict with Persia. No major confrontation occurred until the conflict in Mesopotamia of 421-2, and that too was quickly settled. The prolonged hostilities that characterized Roman-Sasanian relations in the fourth century were succeeded in the fifth by a greater degree of co-operation. Relations between Arcadius and Theodosius II and the Sasanian rulers appear to have been good, at least down to the 420s. The frontiers of both empires were under pressure from the barbarians, and both sides appear to have recognized that the survival of the two empires was necessary to prevent civilization from being destroyed.

One joint strategy (if it can be called such) involved the protection of the 'Caspian Gates', a remote pass in the Caucasus Mountains. Although the Sasanians controlled the pass, its defence was expensive and difficult, and the Romans were aware that the barbarians beyond the pass threatened Roman as well as Persian lands. The importance of an effective defence was made patently clear when in 395 the Huns managed to break through the Caucasus and moved on to ravage Armenia, Cappadocia and Syria, reaching major cities like Edessa, Antioch and even Ctesiphon. As early as the first century the Romans had shown an interest in protecting this pass against the formidable Sarmatian barbarians beyond. Nero had planned an expedition there, and the Parthian king Vologaeses had proposed some sort of Roman-Parthian co-operation in defending the pass, which Vespasian had rejected. In the third century Philip the Arab agreed to pay Shapur I some sort of subsidy, and Rome intermittently recognized the need for financial assistance thereafter. After Jovian's treaty, and the permanent division of Armenia between the two great powers, Roman access to the region was curtailed and the burden of defence fell heavily on the Sasanians. Nevertheless it would appear that the Sasanian rulers were keen to seek Roman financial assistance, and at some point either towards the end of the fourth or beginning of the fifth century the Romans accepted that they should pay a subsidy (or at least were prepared to discuss payment). In regarding protection of the Caspian Gates as a joint effort, Rome recognized the Sasanian empire as a colleague in the defence against barbarism, meaning that refusal to pay for these defences could be viewed by the Sasanians as a serious negation of Rome's obligations in the partnership. However it is unclear to what extent there was any formal agreement for regular payments in the long term, and complaints lodged by the Persians make it plain that fifth century emperors often chose to ignore the matter, perhaps because they did not consider it an obligation.

The Sasanian ruler most likely to have been responsible for improved relations between Persia and Rome is Yazdgard I (399-420). He seems to have courted minority groups in his empire, such as Christians and Jews, in an attempt to subdue the power of the Persian nobility and the Zoroastrian priesthood, and sought to maintain frequent diplomatic links with the Roman world in order to avert crises. But this relaxed atmosphere did not survive his death in 420, and, if war was infrequent, suspicion and mistrust reigned at both courts in subsequent years. Persian persecution of Christians and Roman refusals to pay for the Caucasus defences contributed to further conflicts in 421-2 and 440 or 441. But rather than framing their disputes solely in terms of battles over territory, the two superpowers seem to have been drawn into conflict increasingly over ideological and financial matters. The Caucasus defences provided one pretext; religion provided another. Persian Christians could view the Roman empire as a refuge, and their flight from persecution was a potential affront to the majesty of the Sasanian king. As a Christian empire Rome could claim that an attack on believers was also an assault on the dignity of the empire and its faith. Squabbles over land continued, but most attacks look more like punitive plundering expeditions than serious attempts to annex territory. The arena was very much the same. Mesopotamia, Septimius Severus' 'bulwark of Syria', was still the stage for military conflict, and the Christianity of the Armenians remained a potential problem for the Sasanians. Syria, Arabia and Palestine, however, were not exempt from attack, as pro-Sasanian Arabs, led by the Lakhmid tribe from al-Hira, were not averse to leading raids against the Syrian provinces. These Arab warriors were to remain faithful clients of the Sasanians throughout the fifth and sixth centuries.

Even Arab allies of Rome could prove troublesome. We find Arab tribes, perhaps under the leadership of the tribe of the Salih, fighting against Roman forces in the region of Damascus in 452 or 453. During the reign of the emperor Leo (457-74) an Arab called Amorcesus (probably a Hellenized form of the Arab name Imru' al-Qays) emerged as a powerful figure in the Hijaz, taking control of an island called Iotabe which was a lucrative trading post at the entrance to the Gulf of Aqaba. In seizing Iotabe and ejecting the Roman customs officers stationed there Amorcesus seems to have been acting entirely in his own interests. At the time Leo was heavily involved in actions against the Vandals in north Africa, a costly project which absorbed a considerable amount of Roman manpower. In spite of his actions Amorcesus managed to gain legitimate status as an ally of the Romans and was appointed 'phylarch of the Saracens around Petra' by the emperor, and even received the courtesy of an official visit to Constantinople at public expense. For the Romans, who had far more serious matters to deal with elsewhere, appeasement and assimilation were expedient ways of coping with disturbances on the desert peripheries.

By the third quarter of the fifth century the western Roman empire was in serious decline. The dominance achieved there by barbarian commanders was seen in Constantinople as a plausible reason for its disintegration, and Leo was determined to ensure the same did not happen in the east. The eastern army was heavily infiltrated by Arian Germanic barbarians, whose power Leo sought to curb by promoting various Isaurians (from southern Asia Minor) and by treacherously killing the most powerful of the Gothic officers. Among those Isaurians who profited was the general Tarasis, who became an increasingly important figure during Leo's unsettled government. Tarasis adopted the name

Zeno, married Leo's daughter Ariadne, and eventually succeeded to the throne (474). His chaotic reign began badly. The new emperor found that he was far from popular, having earned the hostility of Leo's wife Verina, who was anxious to have him removed in favour of her brother Basiliscus. When Basiliscus usurped the throne in 475 Zeno was forced to leave the capital in disgrace, but he made a remarkable comeback the following year when the general Illus, another Isaurian sent by the usurper to capture the fugitive, switched sides and returned with Zeno to depose Basiliscus. However, relations between the restored Emperor and his new ally degenerated, and Verina exploited this to her advantage. Illus was made *magister militum per orientem* and Verina was put under his guard, but the two became co-conspirators and at Tarsus in 484 they elevated a general called Leontius to the rank of Augustus, in opposition to Zeno. Their notable supporters included such unlikely allies as Pamprepius, an Egyptian Neoplatonist, and Calendio, the patriarch of Antioch. The rebels then occupied Antioch, but Edessa and Chalcis refused to accept the official portraits of the usurper. Zeno's forces subsequently ejected them and their supporters from Antioch and drove them into the mountains of Isauria. Verina died there shortly afterwards, but Illus and Leontius were besieged in their Isaurian stronghold until their capture and execution in 488.

The situation in the Persian realm was scarcely better than in the Roman empire. During the third quarter of the fifth century the Sasanians were under intense pressure from the Hephthalite Huns who threatened their north-eastern frontier. Just as the Gothic barbarians had acquired power in the Roman empire, so the Hephthalites gained ascendancy in the Sasanian. In 476 King Peroz was captured by them and forced to come to some very disadvantageous terms to secure his release. In 484 came an even greater disaster: Peroz and his army were wiped out by the barbarians, and various members of the royal family fought to obtain Hephthalite support in their bids for the throne during the final decades of the fifth century. The kings were short of money to pay their Hunnic allies, and in desperation turned to the Romans for financial aid.

By now, however, the Romans were in no mood to provide help. Illus and Leontius had sought Persian backing with a large quantity of gold, and the first Persian request for more funds from Zeno was particularly ill timed, reaching the emperor while he was still fighting the rebels. Financing a precarious Sasanian monarchy propped up by rapacious Hephthalite sponsors was hardly a promising investment, and the Romans quickly found a permanent pretext for refusing any more Sasanian requests for cash. It concerned the Mesopotamian city of Nisibis, which had been ceded to the Sasanians after Julian's death in 363. Now the Romans claimed that the treaty of 363 had stipulated that Nisibis was to remain in Persian hands for a mere 120 years, so that in 483 it should have been returned to Rome. There is no evidence that this was so, but it was a ploy adopted by both Zeno and his successor Anastasius (491-518) in the face of repeated Sasanian demands for help, and a policy which prompted a war between 502 and 506. A peace treaty resolved the matter, in which Rome agreed to pay some money in return for Persian assurances that Roman fortresses in Mesopotamia would be left unmolested. Nisibis, however, remained in Persian hands, and in about 505-507 Anastasius ordered the construction of the fortress of Dara on a site nearby, as part of a general programme aimed at improving defences and infrastructure in the eastern provinces. Dara provided the Persians with a new grievance – it was built in flagrant contravention of a treaty agreed between Theodosius II and Bahram V in 422, in which both sides had promised not to build any more fortresses in the frontier regions. It would seem that the Romans had decided that their cash-strapped neighbours could best be deterred from plundering raids by an improved system of defences.

The Rise of the Ghassanids

The western empire finally came apart in the 470s, and with this the succession of western emperors ended. The west's collapse put the eastern empire under even greater pressures in the sixth century, as its emperors diverted resources to lengthy campaigns aimed at recovering the lost western provinces. The best troops and commanders were required for these campaigns. To fight wars on several different fronts was impossible, and in the Syrian region some contingency was required to hold the Sasanians and their Lakhmid allies at bay. Now the 'Saracen' *foederati* became an important element of Roman defences in the east.

The Salih, who had replaced the Tanukh as the dominant tribe among the *foederati*, seem to have declined in importance in the later fifth century. Two other Arab tribes emerged as powerful forces on the fringes of the Roman east: the Kindites from central Arabia and the Ghassanids. These lay outside Roman control in the late fifth and early sixth centuries, and raids on Palestine and Syria may have been orchestrated by the Kindites. Details are sketchy, and little is known of relations between the Arab tribes and Rome during the first decades of the sixth century, although Anastasius allowed the Ghassanids to settle in Roman territory and arranged a treaty with the Kindites. The Kindites seem to have been in competition with the Lakhmids, although the latter eventually prevailed and reasserted themselves as the dominant group. With Kindite power broken and Lakhmid power restored, the Romans sought to find a suitable Arab tribal leader to keep the Lakhmid ruler al-Mundhir in check. They were looking west, and needed security in the east. In particular they needed a commander who could weld the loyalty of the tribes and their leaders together and liaise more efficiently with the Roman commanders. A kind of 'phylarch of phylarchs' was necessary if Roman forces were to respond adequately to the Lakhmid and Persian threats. Such a commander would be expected to accompany regular Roman troops on campaign as well as conducting independent operations. They found a likely candidate in the person of al-Harith of the tribe of Ghassan.

The Ghassanids had been operating on the fringes of Roman Syria and Arabia since at least the fifth century. They had controlled the island of Iotabe when the Romans recaptured it, and it is possible that Amorcesus, who seized the island during the reign of Leo, was a chief of the Ghassan. Initially the tribe would have been subordinate to the Salih, but by the early sixth century the Ghassanids seem to have replaced the Salihids as the dominant tribe, and were soon recognized by the Romans as *foederati*.

Al-Harith was given his command in 529, and proved himself a valuable ally of the Romans over the next four decades. Already during the Roman suppression of a Samaritan revolt in Palestine in 529 he had played an important supporting role. Al-Harith was more than a match for the Lakhmid al-Mundhir, sacking al-Hira and, later, defeating and killing him in battle near Chalcis. But the Romans found the independence of their Arab allies disconcerting, and

Fig. 20. The interior of Sergiopolis (Resafa), a city founded in AD 431 at the site of an important shrine for Christian pilgrims: the tomb of the martyr Sergius. In the sixth century Sergiopolis became a major religious centre for the Ghassanids.

often sought to restrain them, leading to a great deal of mistrust on both sides.

The Ghassanid presence extended roughly from Damascus to the Hijaz, with the Hauran and Golan as their heartlands, but they were to be encountered over an even wider area than this. A church-like structure outside the city walls at Sergiopolis (a major centre of pilgrimage for the Ghassanids and other Arab tribes) bears an inscription naming one of the tribe's rulers. It has been taken to be some sort of Ghassanid official residence, but this function is disputed. The Ghassanid phylarch may have used it as a temporary audience chamber and a means of asserting his authority over the Arab tribes making the pilgrimage to Sergiopolis. An important centre of the Ghassanid confederacy was at Gabitha (al-Jabiya) in the Golan, but this may have alternated as a seasonal centre with the palatial complex at Qasr al-Abyad (Khirbet al-Bayda) east of the Jebel Says. No one place served as the Ghassanid capital, and their diffused social and political organization was reflected in their use of a variety of fortified centres spread over a wide area of the Syrian hinterland.

Justinian and his Successors

In the sixth and seventh centuries the Roman empire underwent a major transformation. It expanded, over-reached itself, and in the early seventh century collapsed almost entirely. The west was reconquered (and much of it rapidly lost again) at the expense of security in the east, particularly on the Danube and in Syria and Mesopotamia. Roman culture became more heavily Christianized, breaking with many classical traditions of the past. Religious dissent became increasingly unacceptable; the emperor represented orthodoxy and his views were not to be challenged. Syria was a hotbed of divergent religious views, and thus important sections of its population were viewed as heretics. Many cities appear to have declined in wealth and importance, and the Arab *foederati* were able to exercise a greater degree of influence over the frontier regions.

Disasters, both natural and man-made, feature prominently in the history of the first half of the sixth century. Bad harvests, disease and plagues of locusts receive attention in the sources, as do a series of devastating earthquakes. In 526 Antioch was destroyed, and two years later further quakes hit the city, also causing serious damage to the neighbouring cities of Laodicea and Seleucia. Antioch was renamed Theoupolis, City of God, in the hope, perhaps, that the divine patron would protect it better in future. In the mid-fifth century more earthquakes struck the region, particularly affecting the cities of the Phoenician coast, Palestine and Arabia.

The man-made disasters were chiefly caused by the Sasanians and their Arab allies. After the treaty of 506, peace with Persia endured until the end of the reign of Anastasius' successor Justin I (AD 518-27). The catalyst for the war seems to have been religious: the Persians attempted to impose Zoroastrianism in the north-western regions of their empire, and a Persian vassal, the Christian king of Iberia, appealed to the Romans. The Sasanians struck first, opening the war on the south-eastern shore of the Black Sea and in Mesopotamia. By 529 they were targeting Syria as well. Justin's nephew and successor Justinian inherited the war, but it was a conflict he was anxious to conclude as quickly and efficiently as possible.

The new emperor was immensely ambitious. He intended to unite the Mediterranean under a single ruler by restoring the Roman empire to something approaching its former glory. Perhaps he feared that the diminished eastern Roman empire would become a satellite of the larger Sasanian realm if something were not done to improve the empire's dignity and extend its economic base. He was more interested in conquering the west, however, than in pursuing military activities in the east, where he adopted a policy of bribery and conciliation to maintain the peace while his armies waged war in north Africa and Europe. An important element of this plan was the appointment of al-Harith the Ghassanid. For the first time since the third century Syria was bearing the brunt of Persian hostilities, in which the Lakhmids played a major role. A young general, Belisarius, was placed in command of the Roman army. He rapidly distinguished himself, but the war in the east dragged on for several years and was interrupted only with the death of the Sasanian king Kavad. Kavad was succeeded by his youngest son Khusrau I (531). The new king needed to consolidate his position and agreed to an 'endless peace' with Justinian in 532. The peace was just what Justinian wanted, and among other concessions he agreed to pay a huge sum of gold for the Caucasus defences. Finally he was able to turn his full attention to the west.

Justinian's successes in the west during the 530s suggested to contemporaries that the Roman empire was reviving, although the reconquest may have strained the truncated empire's resources to their limits. For the next decade most of the military might of the empire was concentrated in the west. Khusrau had spent this period reorganizing the administrative structure of his empire, and once his affairs were in order he decided that the time was right to initiate hostilities on Justinian's eastern front. There were the usual grievances: non-payment of the Caucasus subsidy and the continued garrisoning of Dara. A squabble between the Ghassanids and Lakhmids over grazing rights in Palmyrene provided a pretext. The Sasanian king then accused Justinian of trying to subvert the Lakhmids. Justinian, tied down with obligations elsewhere, tried to negotiate with the Sasanians, but to no avail. In March 540 Khusrau took an army up the Euphrates valley and moved quickly into Syria. He was the first Persian king to have done so since Shapur I, three centuries earlier. Sura fell, Hierapolis paid a ransom, and then Beroea was sacked when its inhabitants were unable to raise the money demanded by the king for their safety. In June Khusrau and his army reached Antioch. The Roman forces fled the city, and when the Antiochenes refused to pay a ransom, the great *metropolis* was devastated and large numbers of its citizens were taken prisoner. The king also visited other places in northern Syria, including Daphne, Seleucia and Apamea, extorting money where he could. But he made no plans to annex what he had conquered; the aim seems to have been merely to acquire booty to alleviate his financial difficulties at home (the Hephthalites still demanded tribute). Justinian offered a bribe, and Khusrau retreated, forcing protection money from cities such as Chalcis on the way. On the way he laid siege to Dara until the inhabitants paid him off. The captured Antiochenes were deported to Ctesiphon and installed in a settlement nearby called 'Khusrau's Better-than-Antioch'.

The emperor had little option but to retaliate. Belisarius and al-Harith invaded Mesopotamia, using a large number of troops drawn from Syria. The Romans laid siege to Nisibis but failed to capture it. The threat of a Lakhmid attack on Syria alarmed the commanders of the Syrian troops, and when plague broke out among the soldiers Belisarius was forced to withdraw his sick and rebellious army. A Persian army returned in 542, obtaining a large ransom from Sergiopolis before retreating. The weaknesses in the Roman military structure of the east were becoming apparent: in the cities, which were key points for the defence of the provinces, the inhabitants displayed a worrying tendency to surrender to the invader rather than fight, attempting to arrange ransoms contrary to the wishes of the military commanders and the imperial government; and regional commanders preferred not to operate for prolonged periods away from their provinces. These were problems which the Romans were unable to correct before the Syrian provinces collapsed in the face of a new enemy in the seventh century.

Plague and war dominated life on the eastern frontier over the following years, during which neither the Romans nor the Sasanians managed to achieve any decisive victory. Meanwhile the Ghassanids and Lakhmids waged a war of their own. Rome's abilities to maintain control over its Arab allies were limited: during Belisarius' campaign in Mesopotamia, al-Harith had taken his warriors across the Euphrates, but it proved impossible to monitor or regulate what he was doing. Eventually Khusrau found himself contemplating a war on two fronts when the Hephthalites renewed hostilities in the Sasanian east, and he sought to bring his conflict with the Romans to an end. In 561 the two sides agreed to a fifty-year peace. The Persians finally recognized the Roman right to the fortress of Dara, but insisted that no new forts be built in the frontier regions. In addition the Saracen allies of both empires were to abide by the treaty.

The greatness of Justinian cannot be denied, and his achievements were many. His policies in Syria, however, were difficult to reverse if anything went seriously wrong. Although he inherited a treasury surplus, his ambitious projects may have exhausted it. It was claimed that Justinian was responsible for cancelling pay owed to eastern frontier troops (the *limitanei*) and demobilizing them. If there is any substance to the claim, it may have taken place after the 'endless peace' of 532, when Justinian turned his attention fully to the west. Although the demobilization is unlikely to have been universal, the absence of Justinian's later bronze coinage in Palestine and Arabia, and the abandonment of many forts there during the sixth century, has been taken by some scholars as evidence for a diminution in the empire's forces in these regions, which were also where reliance on *foederati* was most intense. It is perhaps significant that the historian Procopius, who wrote an account of Justinian's building programmes, does not credit many fortifications in Arabia to this emperor. The phylarch system was cheaper to maintain than fortresses and garrisons, but the antagonism between the Ghassanids and Justinian's successors undermined it.

Justinian's methods of conciliation and subsidies were not those of his nephew and successor Justin II (565-78). To him Justinian's bribes were expensive and a sign of Roman weakness. With the benefit of hindsight the policies which he adopted might seem foolish, but at the time he probably wished to check the slide into reliance on Arab *foederati* on the eastern frontier. The Romans had been able to deal with potentially rebellious barbarian allies before by using treachery and violence. Justin refused to send subsidies to various federate Arab tribes, and they subsequently deserted to the Lakhmids and began raiding Ghassanid territory. The Ghassanid leader, al-Mundhir, the son of al-Harith, defeated the Lakhmids and asked the emperor for more funds to continue the war and press his advantage. Justin refused. In 572 he cut off Ghassanid subsidies and plotted to kill al-Mundhir. The story goes that he sent two letters, one addressed to the *magister militum per orientem*, instructing him to invite al-Mundhir to a conference and then to arrest and execute the Arab leader, and a second addressed to al-Mundhir himself, which contained the invitation. Somehow the letters were transposed and al-Mundhir received the

Fig. 21. The fortress of Zenobia on the Euphrates, the defences of which are attributed to Justinian. Note the high citadel on the left.

instructions for his betrayal. The story may be fiction but something clearly happened to estrange al-Mundhir from the Roman cause. However, the cutting of finance to the allies, who expected payment for their services, could be viewed by the Ghassanids as sufficient betrayal in itself.

An Armenian rebellion against the Persians in 571 triggered a further round of hostilities with Persia, culminating in another Sasanian invasion of Syria. The Armenians appealed to the Christian emperor for assistance. Justin responded by refusing to pay the annual subsidy to Persia in accordance with the treaty of 561 and threatening to attack Khusrau if the interests of the Armenian Christians were not respected. A Roman expedition ended in disaster: the army failed to capture Nisibis, and was chased by a Persian force to Dara, where it was forced to surrender at the end of 573. Another Persian army moved on to northern Syria, looting and devastating, and sacking Apamea. The Ghassanids refused to lend assistance to the Roman cause. Once again the Roman defences of Syria had demonstrated how decrepit they were.

The loss of Dara was a major blow to Justin's confidence. Since the reign of Anastasius it had replaced Nisibis (which had been ceded to Persia by Jovian) as Rome's principal bastion in eastern Mesopotamia. Its capture was said to have initiated the emperor's final descent into lunacy. Within a couple of years he was unable to govern at all, and his wife Sophia ran the empire along with a deputy emperor, Tiberius. To calm him in moments of extreme madness, the chamberlains were reputed to have threatened him with the return of the former Ghassanid phylarch by saying 'Al-Harith will come!'.

All the while the Roman position on the eastern frontier was deteriorating. Khusrau estimated that he had the advantage and would not settle for a comprehensive peace. The Ghassanids and Lakhmids were busy fighting a war of their own, but Roman initiatives managed to bring the Arab tribe back under imperial supervision, and in 575 an agreement was reached. Years passed, and the war dragged on. Tiberius concentrated his efforts on building up an army which would strike some sort of decisive blow and enable him to negotiate with the Persians from a position of strength. In 578, the year of Justin's death, he appointed the capable general Maurice as *magister militum per orientem*.

Maurice's successes in Armenia and Mesopotamia brought Tiberius to within a hair's breadth of achieving his aim, but the death of Khusrau wrecked his plans. The new king, Hormizd IV, refused to accept peace under Tiberius' terms, and the conflict continued. Maurice and the Ghassanids invaded Persian Mesopotamia and inflicted a defeat on Hormizd in 581. The campaign, however, met with only limited success, and Maurice began to suspect that the fidelity of the *foederati* lay elsewhere than with Rome. He was convinced that it was time to reassess the value of the Ghassanid confederacy to Constantinople.

The Ghassanid leader, al-Mundhir, was accused of treachery. This time he was captured and exiled. The Ghassanids then demanded the return of some of al-Mundhir's property at Bostra, and when the Roman commander refused they defeated his forces and killed him. Revolts forced Tiberius to recognize al-Mundhir's brother, and then his son Nu'man, as successive phylarchs, but they seem to have been unable to maintain authority over the Ghassanid confederation, which now began to disintegrate.

Tiberius, who by now was on his death-bed, arranged for Maurice to succeed him (582). There was little love lost between the Ghassanids and the new emperor, and the Ghassanid confederation's position worsened. With the decline of the tribe of Ghassan went security along the eastern frontier. There were also some serious religious differences to contend with. Constantinople regarded the monophysite Ghassanids as heretical. It is possible that in this confused period the orthodox Salih found themselves in favour once more, but by now they were weaker and less influential than the Ghassan, so any exercise of Roman power through them would be correspondingly diminished.

The Roman empire, which was under intense military pressure on virtually every front, was also in serious financial difficulty. War with Persia continued, although both empires appear to have reached something of a stalemate. Both were quite capable of launching punitive raids deep into each other's territories, but neither achieved much in the way of lasting successes. Then, quite unexpectedly, a curious chain of events brought hostilities to a close. A Persian general, Bahram Chobin, rebelled against Hormizd (589). The latter was already unpopular with the nobility, and news that Bahram was advancing on Ctesiphon with an army led to the king's overthrow. His son Khusrau II was elevated in his place. Bahram, however, refused to come to terms with Khusrau, and the new king was forced to flee. He headed westwards, to the Roman empire. At Circesium Khusrau despatched an embassy to the emperor. Bahram also sent a mission. Both proposed generous terms to Maurice, the surrender of fortresses and relieving payment for the Caucasus. Maurice decided that Khusrau's offer was the more advantageous. If he sponsored a takeover in Sasanid Persia, it would undoubtedly offer him a chance to influence the resulting government. Bahram's rule was unstable, particularly since he was not of Sasanian royal blood, and key fortresses such as Nisibis declared for Khusrau. Early in 591 Khusrau set out for Persia with a Roman army. Bahram was defeated in a series of engagements and was eventually killed.

As a result of this victory two decades of fighting ended. Mesopotamian fortresses captured by the Persians, including Dara, were returned to Roman control, and the king also relinquished claims over Armenia. In such ways Khusrau acknowledged Maurice's help in restoring him to his throne; nonetheless he was a strong-minded and independent ruler, and by no means a puppet of the Romans. Furthermore, the extraordinary circumstances of his elevation did not endear him to all members of the Persian nobility.

In spite of frequent periods of warfare, the relationship between Romans and Sasanians in the fifth and sixth centuries was far better than it had been in the days of Ardashir and Shapur I. When the Sasanian king Peroz had been captured by the Hephthalites in 476, Zeno reputedly helped to pay part of the ransom. In the early sixth century Kavad, in an attempt to secure the throne for his youngest son Khusrau, had proposed that the emperor Justin adopt him. The proposal was rejected in the belief that it would give Khusrau a legitimate claim to both empires. The very contemplation of such an adoption, however, indicates how far relations had changed since the third century. In a certain way the association between Rome and Persia in the sixth century resembled those of the two halves of the Roman empire in the fifth: although neither side trusted the other entirely, both sides could sometimes view the other as a possible source of political (and even military) support in times of difficulty. Political bonds between both empires developed as the sixth century progressed, but hostilities between the empires would also indirectly undermine both powers.

Persian Ascendancy

Khusrau was determined to curb Lakhmid power, especially after the conversion of their leader Nu'man to Christianity. He imprisoned Nu'man in 602, and then appointed the leader of another tribe, the Tayy, as ruler of the pro-Persian Arabs in the south-west. The experiment was not a success, and with the decay of the Lakhmid state, stability in this border zone of the Sasanian empire came to an end. An independent tribe, the Bakr, gained ascendancy in the region, and in 604 the Bakr and their allies defeated the Sasanians and pro-Persian Arabs at the battle of Dhu-Qar. Although it did not erase Sasanian control in the area, the defeat was humiliating for the Persians, and must have weakened their authority there.

The Romans were also having problems with their former allies, the Ghassanids. Even though the tribe was no longer pre-eminent, it was still a powerful force whose independence could cause the Roman government embarrassment. When the Ghassanids took it upon themselves to raid Persian territory, Maurice had to reassure an angry Khusrau that he had not incited them. Both the Romans and the Persians had soured relations with their principal Arab allies in the Near East, inadvertently weakening their own position along the edge of the Arabian desert, a region which, at the time, can hardly have seemed a major threat to the security of either empire.

In 602 the Roman army in the Balkans revolted and set up the centurion Phocas as emperor. Maurice was overthrown and executed, and Phocas embarked on a hapless reign in which the political and administrative errors of his predecessors finally bore fruit. Some of the problems can be ascribed to events beyond the emperor's control, but in many cases the catastrophes were aggravated by his own actions. Relations with Persia were predictably negative. Khusrau refused to acknowledge the murderer of his imperial sponsor Maurice, imprisoning Phocas' ambassador. The usurper's attempts to convert the Jews to Christianity had a particularly disastrous effect on cities in Syria, many of which had a large Jewish population. Antiochene Jews rioted and started killing Christians, and Christians had responded in kind. Soon Phocas was faced with grave military crises on the northern and eastern frontiers. In the Balkans he was unable to stem the invasions of Slavs and Avars. Narses, the commander of the eastern armies, raised a rebellion in Mesopotamia in 603, but rapidly lost ground when forces loyal to Phocas attacked him. Besieged in Edessa, Narses allegedly decided to seek assistance from Persia. But Khusrau seems to have required little prompting from a desperate Roman rebel to launch a major invasion of Mesopotamia, and Narses reportedly withdrew to Hierapolis as the Persians advanced. From Mesopotamia the Sasanians moved in to occupy Armenia and central Asia Minor. By 606 the provinces of Syria were under threat. This time the Persians did not enter simply as raiders. This time they intended to stay.

Another rebellion against Phocas began in north Africa, spread to Egypt, and from there gathered momentum across the empire. In 610 the rebels deposed and killed Phocas in Constantinople and replaced him with their own nominee, Heraclius. The new emperor ruled an empire in deep crisis. Now more than ever the Roman world looked as if would become a satellite of the Sasanian empire. In about 611 the Persian general Shahrbaraz took Antioch, then Damascus in 613, and Jerusalem in the following year. There is little indication of any organized resistance by the population, except in Jerusalem, where the Christians staged a rebellion, massacring Persians and Jews. Shahrbaraz laid siege to the Holy City and sacked it. Now the Christians found themselves the victims. Large numbers of them were killed, the Church of the Holy Sepulchre was burned to the ground, and the relics of the Crucifixion were taken to Ctesiphon. Jews from the neighbourhood of Jerusalem joined the Persians in exacting retribution upon the Christian population. It was easy for Christians to accuse the Jews of being Persian collaborators, and rejoicing at the Christian empire's imminent demise. Some Jews, however, shared a Christian opinion that the world was about to end with the apparent collapse of the Roman empire. For some, then, identity with the Roman world ran deeper than religion. However, it may well be the case that many of the inhabitants did not have cause to regret the end of Roman political and religious control. The social and religious tensions caused by orthodox Christian rule (see chapter 9) could have made rule by a pagan king preferable to Constantinople in certain quarters.

Very little is known about Syria and the Near East under Persian control. The period is too short to be recognized easily in the archaeological record, and most of our information has to be gleaned from literary sources. The Persians do not seem to have devastated Syrian towns and cities, and preferred to negotiate a peaceful surrender wherever possible. Only in those places where they encountered resistance did they practise more destructive policies. By supporting religious minorities such as Jews or non-orthodox Christians such as Nestorians and monophysites they appear to have been exercising a policy of divide and rule, breaking the political and cultural power that orthodox

Christians had over Syrian society.

The destruction of Jerusalem and the capture of the relics was a disastrous blow to Roman confidence. The provinces of Syria had been lost, and they were to be recovered by the Romans only for a brief period of about eight years before being lost again through conquest from an unexpected quarter. Although short, Sasanian dominion over the region produced a political and military discontinuity which was difficult for the Romans to redress.

Heraclius and the Persian Wars

By 619 the Persians had taken Egypt. This, combined with the destruction and pillaging of the Holy City, and the Slav and Avar conquests in the Balkans, suggested to some contemporaries that the empire was suffering divine retribution for some misdemeanour, and was on the brink of total collapse. To restore order and recover the lost provinces would be an immense undertaking, requiring some drastic new strategy. Heraclius first set about the vital tasks of strengthening his power base and replenishing the treasury. Finally, in the spring of 622, he set out from Constantinople with a large host. The Romans managed to outmanoeuvre the forces of Shahrbaraz in Asia Minor, inflicting the first of a series of defeats on their Sasanian adversary. Over the next five years the armies of both empires engaged in a bitter struggle, in which Heraclius led his soldiers against the Persians in person. Partly through battle, partly through negotiation and partly through subterfuge Heraclius managed not only to retain what was left of the empire but also to inflict resounding defeats on the Persians in their own territory. At Nineveh in 627 the Romans achieved a decisive victory over the Sasanian army and advanced on Ctesiphon unopposed. Khusrau fled his palace and Heraclius burned it. The king's refusal to accept terms exasperated the nobility and military commanders, who wanted an end to the war which was sapping the strength of the kingdom. A plot was formed, and Khusrau was replaced by his more pliable son Kavad II.

Heraclius wanted to revive the *status quo*, not to destroy the Sasanian empire. The struggle to gain control of the Fertile Crescent had been won by the Romans, but their weakened empire was in no position to secure what was theirs by right of conquest. Kavad agreed to a peace, ceding all of the captured territories, and returning the holy relics captured in Jerusalem. So it was in 628 that Syria and the Near East were returned to the Roman empire and the Christian world. Heraclius had achieved a brilliant victory. For nearly two decades many of the eastern provinces had been under Persian control, and from near-defeat the empire had recovered and prevailed. It was to be Rome's last victory over Persia. The weakened Sasanian kingdom began to dissipate into anarchy, and, like its Parthian predecessor four centuries earlier, would soon be toppled by a foe more injurious to Roman interests. But at the time no one could have predicted that within a decade the Roman east would be lost to the empire forever.

PART II

ORGANIZING SPACE AND TIME

3 POLITICAL ENTITIES

Space and time can be viewed as socially constructed dimensions, which all states and empires exploit to their advantage by imposing new institutions and altering old ones. Whether the disunited collection of independent political entities encountered in Syria immediately prior to the Roman annexation had any identity as 'Syria' is debatable, but the empire transcended their differences by providing an overarching system of governance, imposing an institution called Syria on the entire region. It was to a governor of Syria that the inhabitants looked to settle local disputes and to whose office their communities paid taxes. A communal institution called Syria was the entity around which the cities of the region organized worship of the emperor. To ensure regular reckoning and payment of taxes time itself had to be rationalized and organized in new ways, as did space in the form of land to be measured and recorded. The movement of goods as taxes in kind stimulated the production of commodities and integrated diverse regions of Europe and the Mediterranean. The communications infrastructure of empire shrank space and the time needed to cover distance. Empire and province had a profound effect on the way in which people in the region lived their lives.

The rapid expansion of Roman power in the first century BC was followed by a period of consolidation as the empire's rulers struggled to impose various forms of unity over an enormous geographical area. The 'universal' censuses of Augustus, such as the one conducted in Syria in AD 6 and recalled rather inaccurately in the Gospel of St Luke, attempted to create an inventory of people and their land. It became important not only to list different subject peoples, but also to describe the regions, provinces and spaces they inhabited. This interest in peoples and places had a practical purpose, because Rome found local knowledge crucial to the organization and domination of her empire. Military strength alone would not ensure continued Roman hegemony in the provinces. Compromise between the centralizing and universalizing tendencies of that empire (achieved, among other things, through a hierarchical system of power and coercion centred on Rome and the emperors, a network of long-distance trade and a common system of symbols) and the particularizing tendencies of the subject communities (generated through local knowledge) was inevitable. In the final analysis, the structure of Roman power owed a great deal to the geography of human societies. The self-organizing capacities of subject peoples (the kingdoms, tribes and city states) provided the practical framework for Roman rule. The Romans did not in general dismantle existing power structures when they annexed a region, and where possible preferred to exercise control through the social institutions that they found already in place. They favoured centralized, strongly hierarchical organizations, and rewarded such societies, with the consequence that the Roman empire was an environment friendly to their growth and multiplication. In Syria a network of cities and kingdoms predated Roman rule and provided a ready-made power structure, which was manipulated and augmented over time. It was these political entities which gave form to the province of Syria, and it is to these that we now turn.

PROVINCES AND PRINCIPALITIES

Roman rule has justifiably been characterized as 'government without bureaucracy'.[11] The empire can be seen as a project in which the local elites conspired. They drew honours and privileges by conniving with the centre of power, employing its symbols to their own ends, and reciprocating by giving Rome their support. Occasionally the strategy did not work. The Jewish revolt has been seen as the result of a conflict between the desires of Rome and the local elites which it backed (in this case the priestly families) and those of a broad mass of lower classes. In this case the strategy failed because the elites did not command the respect of the people. In general, however, the project seems to have functioned well. It enabled Rome to rule by deploying the minimal number of officials – perhaps no more than 350 senior officers for the entire empire *c.* AD 200. It was an extreme economy of government.

Roman Syria was therefore a collection of self-regulating political entities of various sizes and types, usually ruled by local elites, all of which were loosely managed by a small number of officials appointed by the emperors. From the second century, during their Parthian and Persian campaigns, the emperors themselves were intermittently present in the region, and Antioch's role as a temporary imperial capital became increasingly less temporary in the third and fourth centuries. Normally, however, the highest representative of Roman authority was the governor. Under the republic the governors had been of senatorial rank, appointed on a yearly basis (with exceptions for certain individuals like Gabinius or Crassus), and chosen by lot in the senate. From the time of Augustus Syria was considered an 'imperial' province, meaning, essentially, that its governors were appointed and dismissed by the emperor without any length of tenure being specified. The governor, who was a senator and former consul, was assisted by a tiny group of officers of lower rank: the senatorial legates, each of whom commanded a legion, and a financial officer (*procurator*) appointed by the emperor. The representatives of Rome were therefore few, and their ability to control the provincials rested on good relations with provincial elites or, if that failed, military coercion. These two options were the true limits of empire, where Rome's imperial opportunism succeeded or broke down. The two great Jewish rebellions illustrate how difficult it was for Rome to rule without the consent of the population, and yet the overall stability of the empire for so many centuries, even in times of crisis, suggests that the system was remarkably successful. Bringing the provincial elites into the hierarchy of power was therefore an essential tool of Roman government. Strongly class-divided societies were rewarded and reinforced by giving the provincial elites honours and gifts like autonomy in local affairs, property rights, or (in the early empire) Roman citizenship. Under Hadrian the class differences were enshrined in law, with the upper classes receiving much more favourable treatment than their social inferiors. In the late empire class differences became even more pronounced, and the wealthiest grandees were able to exercise considerable influence over their communities (p. 263). A regulated hierarchy of social relations and opportunities, from lower classes through the mediating institutions of the elites to the governor, was what gave the province its conceptual shape and integrity.

One might expect the governors to have been men of initiative, considering the distance from Rome (and, later, Constantinople) and the difficulties of communicating over such long distances, but it is remarkable how often we see the emperors intervening or arbitrating in affairs of the province. It is also remarkable how often we observe governors writing to emperors and expecting them to make decisions on matters which we might suppose them to have solved by themselves. However, it is clear that some did take important decisions without consultation, although they might run the risk of imperial displeasure if their actions contradicted the emperor's desires. They were effectively the emperor's proxies, functioning as on-the-spot observers and advisors and, in the early empire, commanding part of his imperial army. They were expected by the emperor to implement imperial decisions made on the basis of their reports. To the modern mind this seems a remarkably inefficient way to run an empire, given the time and distances involved, but if nothing else it shows us how concepts of time and space are constituted differently in different societies. Sending a report to Rome and waiting for a reply before acting was a normal way of exercising power. That power could be exercised at a distance in this way may be the reason why Tiberius did not object to the fact that one of his governors of Syria, appointed for eleven years, never set foot in the province, and left direct management in the hands of a deputy.

Aside from reporting to the emperor, the governors were expected to safeguard the province (which could mean making immediate decisions to prevent crisis), to authorize civic embassies to Rome or the emperors, to supervise the cities and to keep an eye on 'client' rulers. They exercised a judicial function, travelling around the province via a regular route and sequence of cities, judging cases among the provincials (although some of these might be referred to the emperor). Senators were not professional bureaucrats or civil servants, and remained essentially amateurs. They were not expected to formulate new provincial policies or initiate new forms of administration, but to deal with matters through accepted channels according to time-honoured methods. As aristocrats the emperors had to treat them with the respect due to their rank. When, as occasionally happened, emperors appointed relatives and trusted assistants to extraordinary commands, such as proconsular *imperium* (which gave them the same legal rights as emperors to interfere in provinces on the state's behalf), the hierarchy of power might be disrupted. Though on the two occasions when Augustus' trusted colleague Agrippa was present with *imperium* in the east, or when Augustus' grandson Gaius Caesar held the same powers there, no serious conflicts between the holders of *imperium* and the provincial governors ensued, the appointment by Tiberius of his nephew Germanicus in AD 17 was less fortunate. The hierarchy of power in this case was perhaps unclear; as governor Piso was supposed to implement Germanicus' decisions, but Tiberius also seems to have appointed Piso to his post in order to restrain the headstrong Germanicus. The two quarrelled publicly, and their disagreement over the treatment of the Parthian hostage Vonones ended with the captive's attempt to take matters into his own hands and his subsequent violent death. When Germanicus died at Antioch in AD 19, the blame fell on the unfortunate governor. Piso, who had left Syria, now returned to try to reclaim the province, an action for which he was accused of trying to foment a civil war. He was conducted to Italy to stand trial and, presuming his case to be hopeless, committed suicide.

As the province of Syria was subdivided, new governorships were created. A number of these new posts were for individuals of lesser rank than ex-consuls, and included equestrians (the rank below senator). The details of these developments will be outlined in the following section.

The Provinces of Syria

Provincia meant both a sphere of command and a territory where command was exercised. The status of the governor was normally determined by the importance of his command, although emperors seem to have been able to make exceptions in their appointments. For an imperial governor of the early empire, the bigger the army under his control, the higher his rank had to be. Provinces with legions required governors of senatorial status, and provinces with more than one legion required ex-consuls. The early Roman governors of Syria were therefore extremely distinguished and high-ranking men with large armies at their disposal, and consequently they represented a potential threat to the power of the emperors. Under Tiberius, Piso was accused of rebellion; Nerva reputedly considered choosing the governor of Syria as his successor, fearing that he might usurp the empire; Avidius Cassius, even if he held some greater command over the east (p. 47), still seems to have retained his post as governor when he rebelled (or that is what inscriptions suggest); and Pescennius Niger had stood a good chance of gaining supreme control in the civil wars of AD 193-4. Septimius Severus' decision to divide the province of Syria in two (fig. 23) is seen as a response to this. He limited the power of the Syrian governor by creating two commands, Syria Coele (the northern half) and Syria Phoenice, reducing the number of legions available to the governor of Syria to two by placing the third in Syria Phoenice. For the rulers of the early empire, the need to rely on deputies in the provinces and the dangers constituted by a concentration of power in the hands of these deputies presented an insoluble problem. Aside from the military threat, the fact that governors could arbitrate in the affairs of local elites meant that they became a potential focus of regional political power as well.

The early province of Syria under Augustus was not tidy (fig. 22.1). To a rationalizing mind it looks difficult to control, and indeed it is unlikely to have been the product of a strictly rational strategy. It was simply a contingent expression of what the Romans' imperial opportunism was able to acquire at the time without stretching resources beyond their limits. The province extended from the broad plain of 'Flat' Cilicia in the north to Judaea in the south, but much of the region was not directly controlled by the governor, being subject to 'client' rulers 'friendly' to Rome (see below). The most heavily urbanized areas tended to be the ones under direct control. Client states isolated Syria from other provinces: those in mountainous 'Rough' Cilicia, the Amanus, and Commagene separated Syria from the rest of Asia Minor, while Judaea and the Nabataean realm divided Syria from Egypt in the south. Within the areas controlled by client rulers there were pockets subject to direct control, for example, the city state of Gaza or the cities of the Decapolis. In the more remote regions it may have been difficult for Rome to exercise any control at all. The Romans

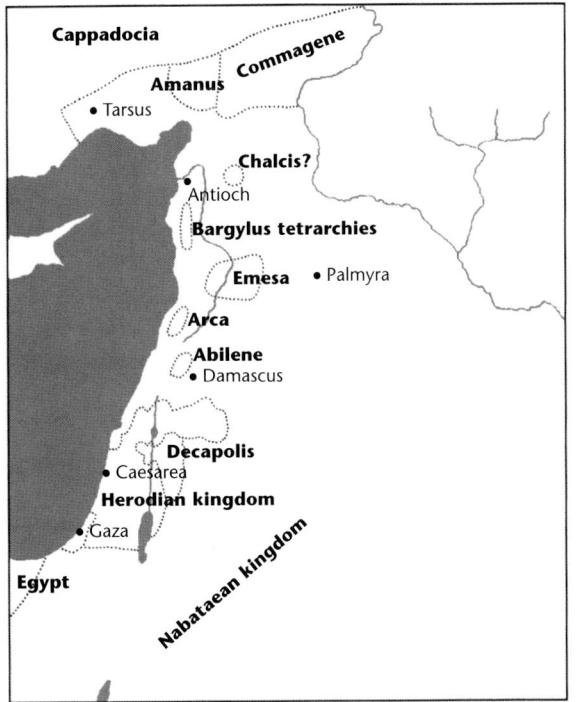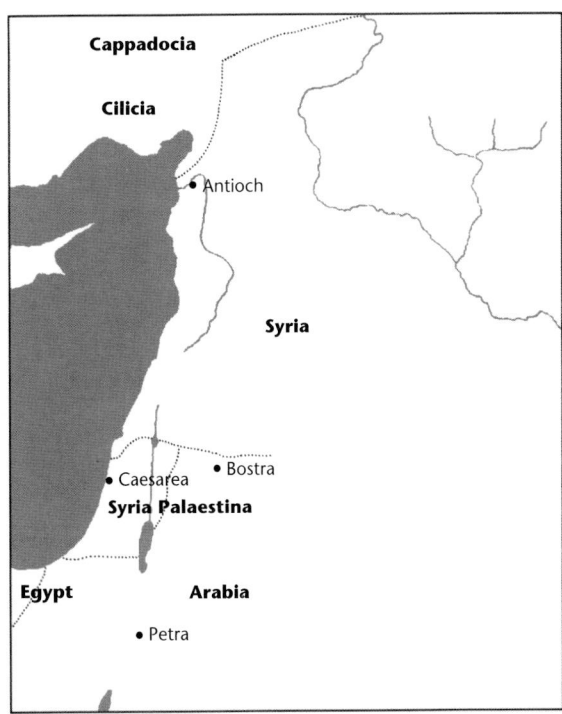

Fig. 22. The provinces of Syria during the early empire. Approximate boundaries.
22.1 Under Augustus.
22.2 Under Hadrian.

clearly favoured the Greek-style city state as a political institution, but they were forced to deal with other sorts of political entity: client states large and small; autonomous, non-civic communities; small tribal federations; temple-estates and perhaps areas of small village communities which were not subordinate to any city. Many of these are only just visible in the documentary sources. Another category, also only just visible, comprised the imperial estates, owned by the emperor and overseen by imperial officials. These lands could be used by the emperors to raise revenues, either by exacting cash rents from tenants or, perhaps more importantly, by producing foodstuffs to meet the state's obligations to the army and other employees. There was one such estate in the lava-flows of Trachonitis, the *saltus Bataneos*; another in the Euphrates region called Eragizenon; and in the north the Bab el-Hawa estate (first mentioned in the fourth century, but probably earlier in origin). The Babatha archive, a collection of private documents from the region of the Dead Sea, mentions an imperial estate in Zoar, at the southern end of the Dead Sea. The Euphrates archive (see chapter 5) contains documents referring to a village called Beth Phouraia as a village 'of the lord' (emperor). Imperial estates would seem to have been numerous and varied considerably in scale. One must also envisage large private estates with tenant farmers, often owned by wealthy city-dwellers, even though there is very little certain evidence for them. These are perhaps difficult to spot because they could have been divided up into many different parcels of land in different locations.

During the first century AD the number of client states was reduced, most being annexed to Syria. In AD 6 Judaea was made a kind of subsidiary province, garrisoned with auxiliaries and governed by a military prefect of equestrian rank (a similar arrangement may have operated in the Decapolis). His duties were similar to those of the Syrian governor, but on a much reduced scale, and he did not command regular legionary troops; hence he could be of lower status than his senatorial counterpart. It is noteworthy that among the Judaean prefect's responsibilities was the appointment of the Jewish high priests, a function which the kings of Judaea had previously performed. The prefects seem to have relied heavily on the governor of Syria in the frequent moments of social and political crisis encountered there during the first century. After a period of reversion to royal rule under Claudius, Judaea was again restored as a subsidiary province, governed by a civilian procurator, until the Jewish revolt of AD 66-74. From 70, as a direct consequence of this war, Judaea had a permanent legionary garrison. A single legion required that the governor be of higher, senatorial rank, a former praetor who could function in a double role as commander of both the province and the legion. The creation of a fully fledged province called Judaea was a response to the crisis of Roman rule engendered by the revolt, aimed at greater control of the subject population.

The Nabataean kingdom was annexed to Syria only briefly, before being constituted as a separate province called Arabia (AD 106). It is not clear why it was felt necessary to create a separate province, but Nabataea's remoteness from the centre of power in Syria may have been an important factor. If Rome believed that the solution to the problem of policing Judaea was to elevate it to the rank of a province separate from the Syrian command, similar considerations may have prevailed in the state's treatment of Arabia. In any case keeping the region as a single province when there were so many legions in it would have given the Syrian governor far too much military power. The new province's governor was an ex-praetor who also acted as commander of the single legion placed there, as was the case in Judaea. Initially the Romans appear to have occupied the whole of the former Nabataean kingdom, as evidenced by the graffiti left by Roman auxiliary soldiers at Medain Salih in the Hijaz, and the military presence in this southern region, even if intermittent rather than permanent, seems to have continued into the third century. The Arabian province also extended west into the Negev and Sinai. In remote desert regions there may not have been a clearly defined frontier. But further north a distinction between Arabia and its neighbours Syria and Judaea had to be properly delineated. This resulted in the break-up of some former political entities. The Decapolis cities of Philadelphia and Gerasa were attached to the new province, as was (probably) Adraa. Bostra lay in the very north of the province; the border with Syria was about 15 kilometres (9¼ miles) further. What the initial arrangements were further west are unclear; Gadara, Pella and Capitolias may have been given to Judaea, but it is uncertain whether some of the other cities belonged to Syria, Judaea or Arabia.

Under Trajan or Hadrian Judaea received a second legion, and its status was raised to that of a province governed by a former consul, with the same arrangement as Syria (the governor having legionary legates serving under him). It was renamed Syria Palaestina by 139, four years after the end of the Bar-Kokhba war (fig. 22.2). As we saw in chapter 2, this measure was probably a direct response to that conflict, but in general these arrangements look like attempts to strengthen direct control over the south, concomitant with the gradual extension of Roman military power in the region.

The next important development in the extension of Roman provincial power was the division of Syria into two provinces under Septimius Severus: Syria Coele and Syria Phoenice (fig. 23). The former contained two legions and

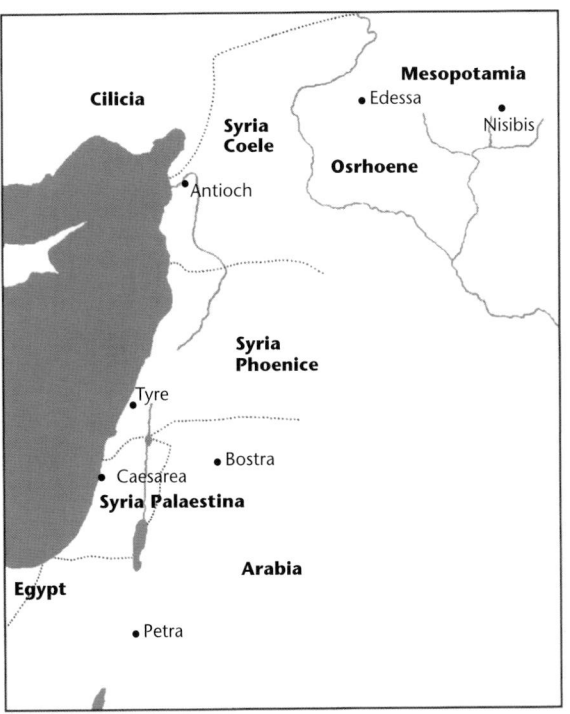

Fig. 23. The provinces of Syria under Septimius Severus. Approximate boundaries.

continued to be governed by former consuls, the latter had but one, the *legio III Gallica*, and was governed by lower-status officials of ex-praetor rank. From the evidence available it would appear that the boundary between the two new Syrian provinces ran from the coast near the ports of Paltus and Balanea-Leucas, inland north of the headquarters of the *legio III Gallica* at Raphanea, and south of Arethusa on the Orontes. Palmyra lay in the province of Syria Phoenice, but further inland, Dura Europus on the right bank of the Euphrates was in Syria Coele. Adjustments were also made in the south between Syria Phoenice and Arabia. Arabia was extended northwards to include northern Batanaea, Auranitis and Trachonitis (on these names, see p. 157). Namara, a site in the steppe east of the Hauran, seems to have been in Arabia rather than Syria Phoenice. After Severus' conquests in Mesopotamia and the creation of new provinces there, the role of the Syrian governors was less crucial for the defence of the east against the Parthians (although invasions up the Euphrates valley would remain a problem). The Mesopotamian province of Osrhoene, created in 194 or 195, was a small entity governed by a procurator of equestrian rank, but its neighbour Mesopotamia, created in or shortly after 197, had two legions. However, instead of being governed by a former consul, it had an equestrian prefect, like Egypt. During the third century more and more posts in government traditionally reserved for senators came to be usurped by equestrians; among them, the governorship of Arabia, which shifted from a senatorial to an equestrian appointment in the second half of the third century. The governors of Syria Coele and Syria Phoenice appear to have been senators down to the reforms of Diocletian, and then these posts too were filled by equestrians (although Constantine later restored some governorships to senatorial *consulares*).

At the end of the third century Diocletian, deciding that the empire's problems were too complex to be solved by a single ruler, created the tetrarchic system where two senior emperors (Augusti) ruled with two junior Caesars. These four were assisted by equestrian civil administrators in the persons of the Praetorian Prefects. In the third and early fourth centuries Praetorian Prefects were administrative and military deputies or 'grand viziers' and travelled with the emperors, but by the reign of Constantine command of the armies had been transferred to other officials, the *magistri militum*. By the sole reign of Constantius II (AD 350-361) the Prefects each administered a portion of the empire called a prefecture, in which they were responsible for estimating and collecting taxes, acting as supreme judges, recruiting troops, and providing supplies and salaries for state employees. By the end of the fourth century there were four of these regional prefectures in the empire; the provinces of Syria, Arabia and Palaestina lay in the eastern one, which was administered from Constantinople. Another of Diocletian's initiatives was to divide up the old provinces into smaller ones. The adjustments made in Syria and the Near East are clear enough, although the date of the changes is not always certain, and most of the new provinces there were probably created after Diocletian. At some point probably towards the end of the third century the old province of Arabia was broken up. The northern part retained the name Arabia, but the southern part was added to Syria Palaestina. Syria Palaestina itself was subsequently divided into three provinces, probably after the middle of the fourth century: Palaestina Prima, Secunda and Tertia. In the late fourth century Syria Phoenice was divided into coastal and inland provinces, which occur in the sources under various names: Phoenice Prima/Paralia and Phoenice Libani/Augusta Libanensis. Syria Coele was also divided at some point: first the regions along the Euphrates became a province called Euphratensis, and by *c.* 400 the remainder had been divided into Syria Prima, with its capital at Antioch, and Syria Secunda (or Syria Salutaris), with its capital at Apamea. Under Justinian yet another province, called Theodorias, was created on the coast, incorporating the cities of Laodicea, Gabala, Paltus and Balanea (fig. 24.1-2).

In many of these provinces the governors no longer had control over the armies as they had done in the past. Instead military power was in the hands of a *dux* and the *magister militum* (see chapter 10). The governors of Diocletian's new provinces of Syria, Arabia and Palaestina were now of equestrian rather than senatorial class and their functions were primarily administrative and judicial (but, as noted above, some offices were later returned to men of senatorial status). In Diocletian's scheme governors were subordinate to an intermediate rank of imperial official called a vicar. Vicars were appointed by the emperors and acted as deputies to the Praetorian Prefects, supervising groups of provinces within each prefecture known as dioceses. The diocese in which the Syrian and Near Eastern provinces were located was called Oriens, which

Fig. 24. The provinces of Syria in the late empire. Approximate boundaries. 24.1 Under Constantius II. 24.2 Under Justinian.

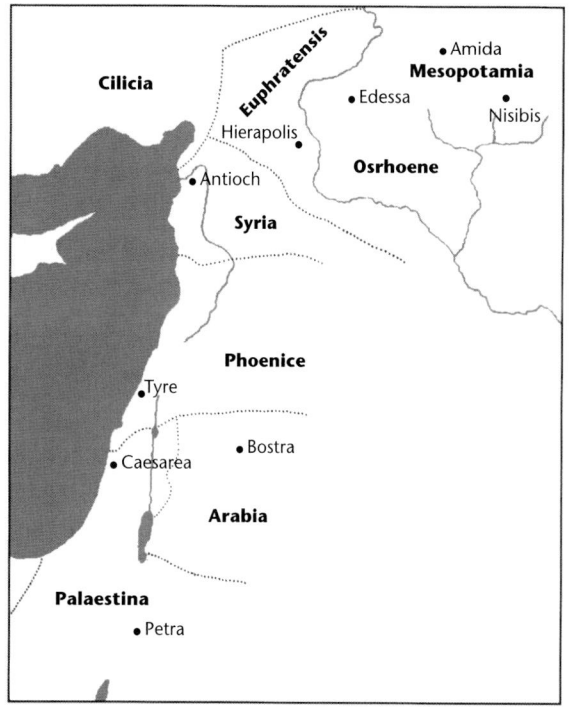

initially included the whole of the east from Cilicia and Isauria to Egypt and Libya (although the latter two regions were detached from Oriens under Valens). During the fourth century we find that the supervisor of Oriens had a special title, *comes Orientis*, rather than *vicarius*. His position seems to have declined in the fifth and sixth centuries, so that by the time of Justinian the *comes Orientis* was merely the governor of Syria Prima. The evolution of the late Roman system of civil administration is extremely complex, but it seems to have been fairly flexible, leaving emperors free to reduce, distribute, abolish or restore offices and alter hierarchies as they saw fit.

FRIENDLY KINGS

'Client' or 'friendly' kings and rulers existed at the social and political limits of the empire. They might not occupy its geographical limits, but they ruled societies and communities which the Roman state would otherwise have found difficult to govern directly. For the most part such client states comprised tribal and village communities where the structures of social power were diffuse, being distributed among many small centres. From the point of view of the Roman government they could be considered 'backward' in that they had not developed the strongly centralized, class-divided societies with a system of autonomous elite governments characteristic of those areas where the city states were supreme. Nevertheless the ruler of a client state was himself an elite member of provincial society, often outranking the wealthiest elites of the cities. He might not always bear the title of king, being a 'tetrarch' or 'ethnarch' or holding some other title, but he controlled considerable resources and his assets would outstrip those of most other provincial elites. Client rulers had their own armies which would have been much larger than any forces the cities could provide. There was also a marked difference in the relations enjoyed by these rulers with the centre of power. Other provincial elites could petition the emperor or participate in embassies, but the links of client rulers with the emperors were personal. Emperors endorsed their right to rule, and sons or relatives needed imperial consent in order to succeed to the throne. When Aretas IV seized the Nabataean kingdom without Augustus' consent in 9 BC, the emperor was furious, and only complex negotiations and fortuitous political circumstances allowed Aretas to keep his throne. A number of client rulers in the early empire would have been familiar faces in the capital, having been raised and educated there, growing up alongside their peers in the imperial house, as the Herodian Agrippa I and Antiochus IV of Commagene did with Caligula.

Though client states could be regarded in some ways as being outside the Roman empire (for example, they may not have paid regular tribute to Rome), they were clearly integral to Roman power in the provinces. They were allies of Rome, and expected to safeguard Roman interests, both by policing their principalities and using their armies to support Roman military action in the east. This meant that they were not independent actors on the political stage. Their titles and powers were decided by the emperors. The prudent ruler sought the counsel of the governor and emperor on all sorts of matters, and was prepared to travel to Rome to plead his case at court. But these friends of Rome seem to have been able to act independently to some degree. The movements of kings were not confined to their territories; in fact, the fragmentary nature of some kingdoms, which consisted of several discontinuous holdings, meant that movement outside their lands was necessary for them to perform their tasks. Their mobility, coupled with their high rank and personal relations with the emperor, was a potential threat to the governor's authority. Under Claudius, the governor of Syria happened upon a meeting of kings at Tiberias: from Judaea, Chalcis, Emesa, Commagene, Armenia Minor and Pontus. Considering such a gathering of powerful men dangerous for Rome, the governor told them to disperse. Agrippa I of Judaea was affronted at this challenge to his dignity, and used his influence with Claudius to have the governor removed. Client rulers were not simple puppets of Rome, and the web of power relations was partly woven by them. Many (but not all) of them were natives of the regions that they ruled, and sought to uphold the rights of their peoples. The Herodian kings were able to champion Jewish rights in cities outside their control by appealing to the governor of Syria. Conversely the king's subjects could circumvent the client's authority in certain circumstances by petitioning the emperor directly. Following the death of Herod in 4 BC, the kingdom was divided between Herod's sons; but popular appeal to the emperor saw one of these, Archelaus, deposed in AD 6. In AD 17 the kings of the Amanus and Commagene died and the citizens petitioned Augustus' successor Tiberius for direct rule by Rome (a request which was duly granted, both regions being annexed to Syria). Nonetheless such appeals could be a dangerous move when contrary to the wishes of the client. The city of Gadara asked Augustus for independence from Herod's rule, but when the emperor refused the request, the desperate petitioners committed suicide rather than be forced to throw themselves on Herod's mercy.

Relations between the client rulers were complex, forming an eastern dynastic network of peers. They were in regular communication with one another, and with states beyond the boundaries of the empire. Dynastic intermarriage led to tangled genealogies, and complicated social relations which were not always congenial. Governors and emperors were prepared to act as arbitrators when disputes arose. Sometimes hostilities broke out, but, as in the case of city states, Rome would not tolerate war between client rulers unless it happened to suit Roman interests. In 9 BC Herod was permitted to attack Nabataean territory, partly because the Nabataeans had supported bandits in Trachonitis, an area which Herod controlled, and partly as punishment meted out to the Nabataeans for refusing to agree to the settlement proposed by the Roman governor. But Herod may have interpreted Roman sanction too freely; at any rate his invasion led to a rebuke from Augustus, who had been moved by the plea of the Nabataean chief minister.

With their great wealth the kings could afford to be great builders. The contribution of Herod to the monumentalization of Syrian cities is well known, and other rulers are likely to have done the same. Through their gifts and donations to Greek cities outside their kingdoms these rulers were promoting the 'international' or Hellenizing culture of the Roman world, and contributing to the emerging hierarchy of cities in the eastern empire (see below). Many of these rulers also worked hard to establish or develop city states within their own principalities, just as the Seleucids had done, giving them dynastic names or, being mindful of their positions within the Roman hierarchy of power, naming them after members of the imperial family.

Ultimately all of the major client states of the first century AD were annexed and placed under direct rule. The process looks deliberate and purposeful: passage from indirect rule by friendly king to direct rule by provincial governors. In the absence of any ancient account detailing the motives for annexing most of these kingdoms one is forced to speculate. Friendly kings are seen as a tool of imperial policy, ruling 'backward' areas, 'civilizing' them (for instance, by encouraging the growth of cities and towns in the areas they ruled) and preparing them for full incorporation into the empire. Regarded in this way, the annexation of a kingdom was a sign of its success rather than an indication that its ruler had been incompetent. But this supposes a clear strategy on the part of emperors. There are some vague indications that certain emperors, such as Tiberius and Vespasian, preferred direct rule, but that others, such as Caligula and Claudius, favoured kings. Overall Rome seems to have preferred direct rule over cities, perhaps because city territories tended to be smaller and their resources divided among a number of great civic families, meaning that they were weaker and easier to dominate than the major client states. The process of imposing direct rule looks complete by the early second century, after the annexation of Nabataea in 106. And yet with the eastward extension of Rome into Mesopotamia in the second century, the kingdom of Osrhoene emerged as an important client state. In the late Roman empire indirect rule in Syria and the Near East (through Arab phylarchs) emerges once again. We might question whether there was any clear strategy at work here, other than the attempt, where possible, to impose greater direct control. These developments and reversions seem to chart the long-term ebb and flow of Roman power and military infrastructures on the social and political limits of its empire. Indirect rule was always an expedient, though perhaps less desirable, way of running these peripheries.

Aside from the major client states, we also catch occasional glimpses of other, smaller or less powerful non-civic communities, particularly in northern Syria during the first centuries BC and AD. These are thought to be a product of the instability of the late Seleucid period, when nomads moved in and began to encroach upon the settled regions and weakened the authority of the cities there. An inscription from Apamea honouring a second-century AD civic notable, Lucius Julius Agrippa, describes him as the descendant of a tetrarch called Dexandros, first high priest of the provincial imperial cult under Augustus. His tetrarchy was presumably in the vicinity of Apamea, and it is noteworthy that such non-civic communities could be found interspersed between the great Hellenistic foundations of northern Syria. Many of these communities seem to have been small tribal states – for example many of those mentioned in his description of Syria by Pliny the Elder, who ended one of his lists of Syrian peoples with a dismissive 'plus seventeen tetrarchies divided into kingdoms and bearing barbarian names'.[12] Some tribal centres became towns bearing the tribal name; other tribal names may be the origin of modern names for places and peoples. The Gindareni presumably gave their name to the village of Gindarus, near Antioch, the Gabeni are thought to be connected with the Ghab, the modern name for the broad marshy valley through which the Orontes flows between the Ansariyeh mountains and Apamea, and it is likely that the tribal capital of the Mariamnitai was the city of Mariamme (modern Miryamin). The Rhambei or Rabbeans inhabited the steppe east of the Orontes and north of Palmyra as far as the Euphrates and perhaps even across the river. Chalcis ad Belum was possibly their political centre, although their core territory seems to have been along the Euphrates. There is some evidence to suggest that Chalcis ad Belum was not under direct Roman rule as part of the province of Syria until AD 92, though admittedly its interpretation is open to debate: coins from Chalcis issued in AD 117 bear what may be a date, 'year 25'. This would produce an era beginning in AD 92. The city also bore the name 'Flavia', indicating that it had received some sort of privilege from Vespasian or his sons (perhaps Domitian, AD 81-96). In itself this does not certainly signify the end of a dynasty of local rulers, but the clearest parallel case is the Commagenian city of Samosata, which began a new era after the dynasty of Commagene was abolished in AD 72, and was also named Flavia.

Because the major client states were important players on the political scene during the first centuries BC and AD, it is worth examining each one separately, before moving on to the other important element of political geography in Syria and the Near East: the city-state. Late Roman examples of powerful non-civic communities in the region have already been mentioned in chapter 2. The federate Arabs of the fourth, fifth and sixth centuries evidently commanded substantial armed forces under the command of a single tribal leader, although they did not develop significant urban capitals. Those states east of the Euphrates with which Rome had important relations will not be considered in detail here, but they deserve a mention. The Parthian vassal kingdom of Osrhoene occupied a crucial corridor in the Fertile Crescent, and with the arrival of Rome on the Euphrates, it found itself caught between the two empires. Like Armenia it became the object of fierce political rivalry, and only with the Mesopotamian conquests under Marcus Aurelius and Lucius Verus did Osrhoene align fully with Rome. Culturally, however, it remained relatively independent of the Graeco-Roman world (at least until its absorption into the Roman province of Osrhoene in the third century), with its capital Edessa being an important centre for Syriac literature (see chapter 8). With the weakening of the Arsacid state in the later second century other Parthian vassals deeper inside the Parthian realm, such as Hatra and Adiabene, came under Roman influence, although the Sasanians put an end to the westward gravitation of their political ambitions.

Commagene

In the first century AD Commagene was reckoned to be among the wealthiest of the client kingdoms. It had gained independence from the Seleucids towards the middle of the second century BC, and its dynasts, who were Iranian by descent, had married into the Seleucid royal house. Antiochus I (c. 70-36 BC) had allied with Rome against Tigranes in 69 BC in order to achieve independence from the short-lived Armenian empire. The complexity of late Republican politics required some deft manoeuvring on Antiochus' part. The Parthian king Orodes II was his son-in-law, but when the Parthians invaded in 51 following the defeat of Crassus, Antiochus dutifully informed the Romans. Nevertheless the position of his kingdom on the Euphrates bend, sandwiched between Rome and the Parthians, left him balancing on a diplomatic tightrope. Rome accused him of collaborating with Pacorus in 40-38 BC and he was besieged in his capital city, Samosata. A huge bribe seems to have convinced the besiegers of his loyalty, and Antiochus retained his kingdom, dying shortly afterwards.

Fig. 25. The tumulus at the top of Mount Nemrut, where Antiochus I is presumed to have been buried. Around it are installations for his cult, including two terraces with gigantic seated figures of Antiochus and the gods. This picture shows the east terrace, with statues of (from left to right): Apollo-Mithras-Helios-Hermes; Tyche; Zeus-Oromasdes (Ahuramazda); Antiochus; and Heracles-Artagnes-Ares.

The history of the dynasty after the battle of Actium is obscure. In AD 17 King Antiochus III died and Commagene was annexed to the province of Syria. Caligula restored the kingdom in 37 or 38 to Antiochus III's son, Antiochus IV, who had Roman citizenship and seems to have been a personal friend of the emperor. Not long after, in circumstances not entirely clear, he was deposed, but restored a few years later by Claudius. His domain extended beyond the boundaries of Commagene proper. He acquired part of Armenia, and held several cities in Cilicia. Antiochus issued coins bearing portraits of himself and his family at several different mints in Cilicia, Lycaonia and Commagene, suggesting that he controlled a large, rambling and fragmented kingdom. In the far west of Cilicia he established the city of Iotape, named after his queen, and, in honour of the emperors under whom he ruled, he founded Germanicopolis, Claudiopolis and Neronias. In Commagene itself the ancient city of Marash was renamed Germanicia Caesarea. He was prominent among the client rulers who supported Vespasian's rebellion against Vitellius in AD 69, but three years later he was accused of collaborating with the Parthians and deposed. His sons, after an abortive attempt to organize resistance, fled to the Parthians, but after Antiochus was allowed to go into retirement in Greece the Parthian king negotiated a safe reunion of the family. Antiochus' descendants became prominent figures in the Roman aristocracy; the monument to his grandson Philopappus, senator and consul, still stands on the Hill of the Muses at Athens.

Emesa

The kingdom of Emesa was located in central Syria on the upper reaches of the Orontes river. It was a significant political force in Syria during the final years of the Seleucid kingdom and in the early years of the Roman province. Like other friendly kings, the rulers of Emesa provided military support for Roman armies. The origins of the kingdom, however, remain unclear. There are occasional references in the sources to a 'phylarch of the Arabs' and the 'Emisenoi', based at Arethusa, in the first century BC. These hint at a tribal, perhaps mainly nomadic people, with a chieftain and some sort of capital in the upper Orontes valley. A tomb inscription from Arethusa is dated using an era 'of liberty' which begins in 31/30 BC, suggesting that if this was the first capital of the kingdom, it was no longer so after the battle of Actium and had become a city state independent of the Emisenoi. A city called Emesa (modern Homs) is not mentioned in any early sources which refer to the kingdom. This may mean that there was no city there at the time, although recent excavation on the tell at Homs indicates a history of settlement activity going back to the Bronze Age. It is quite uncertain what Emesa was like in the first centuries BC and AD. Speculation about the origin and development of the city seems futile until the evidence from excavations there is properly assessed.

Most of the rulers were called Samsigeramus, Iamblichus or Azizus, but reconstructing the history of the dynasty is no easy task. Unlike the dynasts of the other major client states described here, those of Emesa did not issue coins, reducing the evidence for their rule to a few inscriptions and brief mentions in the sources. A Samsigeramus, active during the early days of the province, was an influential figure in the twilight of the Seleucid dynasty and was regarded as a reliable Roman ally, but two of his successors were deposed and executed at the time of Actium (one by Antony, the second by Octavian). By the first century AD, however, the ruling family had acquired Roman citizenship. The last ruler that we know of is Sohaemus, who provided the Romans with stout military assistance during the Jewish revolt and during the Roman annexation of the kingdom of Commagene. The end of the dynasty is as obscure as its origins. No source mentions the kingdom after the invasion of Commagene in AD 72. The city of Emesa did not issue civic coins (a sign of an independent city state) until the reign of Antoninus Pius (AD 138-61). A funerary monument from Emesa, now demolished, once bore an inscription naming a Gaius Julius Samsigeramus who is presumed to have been a member of the royal house, but it makes no mention of the kingship. This inscription bears a date corresponding to AD 78/79; thus it is presumed (but by no means proved) that the dynasty no longer ruled at this date. However, other inscriptions referring to members of the same family likewise omit royal titles, making it probable that the kingdom had indeed come to an end by the end of Vespasian's reign.

Like the descendants of the rulers of Commagene, the royal house of Emesa may have furnished Rome with senators, but no certain links exist between the rulers of the first century and prominent figures from Emesa such as the empress Julia Domna and her sons Caracalla and Geta, the emperor Elagabalus or the usurper Uranius Antoninus. The senator called Sohaemus who was appointed by Marcus Aurelius to the throne of Armenia (p. 47) *may* have been a descendant, but even that is not certain. The kings may have been high priests of the chief deity of Emesa, Elagabal, but we do not know for sure that this was their traditional role. One hypothesis posits Arethusa as the original tribal capital, with Emesa and Elagabal coming to provide a religious focus for the kingdom later, perhaps only towards the end of the first century BC. The influence of Emesa saw to the kingdom's eventual polarization around the centre of the cult, and the loss of Arethusa (as punishment for supporting Antony before Actium?) only accelerated the process.

The Ituraeans

The Ituraeans appear in the sources as unruly inhabitants of the mountains of Lebanon and the Antilebanon. With the waning of Seleucid control they became a serious threat to inland cities like Damascus and those of the coast, and by the time of Pompey's annexation they controlled the coastal cities from Orthosia to Byblus and perhaps Berytus. They also occupied the region of Mount Hermon and parts of northern Galilee and Transjordan. The two main Ituraean principalities were Chalcis and Arca; however, there also appear to have been other Ituraean non-civic communities and tetrarchies in the mountains, independent of these two larger states. Very little is known of Arca from the written sources, but it may have been a rival of Chalcis rather than an ally. Its capital, Arca (modern Tell Arqa), was renamed Caesarea under Augustus, and was still known as 'Caesarea of the Ituraeans'[13] in the third century AD, long after the dissolution of the dynasty. It may have been ceded to the Emesene dynasty in the first century AD; we know that Caligula gave some Ituraean territory to a certain Sohaemus, who is thought to have been one of the Emisenoi. In 53 it was given to the Herodian Agrippa II. The other main Ituraean principality, Chalcis, was ruled by a dynasty whose rulers perhaps functioned as high priests of Heliopolis (a cult centre later incorporated into the territory of Berytus). Its capital, Chalcis, may have been at Majdel Aanjar (the former Gerrha) in the Bekaa valley, but the location is by no means confirmed. Before 64 BC Chalcis had under its ruler Ptolemy expanded east to surround Damascus, annexing large areas to the south of the city, and coming into conflict with its neighbour, the kingdom of the Nabataeans. Ptolemy retained his domain by bribing Pompey with a large sum of money, although the Roman general trimmed some of the Ituraean ruler's territories. Yet this slight does not appear to have been a serious setback, and Ptolemy went on to reign for more than two decades, dying during the Parthian invasion under Pacorus (*c.* 40 BC). The dynasty enjoyed very mixed fortunes thereafter. Ptolemy's son Lysanias was executed by Antony and his tetrarchy was given to Cleopatra, who leased it to a certain Zenodorus (probably, but not certainly, a relative of Lysanias). After Actium Zenodorus was allowed to rule as tetrarch, striking coins with his own portrait and that of Octavian, but he seems to have lost favour with the emperor and his tetrarchy was slowly reduced in size, his lands being given to more favoured states such as the coastal cities and the kingdom of Herod of Judaea. On his death in 20 BC he ruled only the southern Bekaa, the region of Mount Hermon at the southern end of the Antilebanon range, and the Golan, and even these territories were subsequently granted to Herod. The later history of Chalcis is difficult to determine; the sources mention Herodian dynasts ruling 'Chalcis', but it is not always certain whether Ituraean Chalcis is meant. As we have seen above, Chalcis ad Belum in northern Syria could have been under the control of dynasts as late as AD 92. The brother of Agrippa I, Herod 'of Chalcis', who ruled from 41 to 48, struck coins, but if he ruled the Bekaa valley his coins have so far not been recorded there. His son Aristobulus was made king of the Roman client state Armenia Minor by Nero, yet the historian Josephus mentions an Aristobulus 'of Chalcis' who helped the Romans annex Commagene in AD 72. The last days of Ituraean Chalcis languish in almost total obscurity.

A smaller tetrarchy called Abilene, based in the Antilebanon mountains, was ruled by a certain Lysanias under Tiberius; he may have been a descendant of the dynasts of Chalcis. In AD 37 Abilene was given to the Herodian king Agrippa I, but thereafter the tetrarchy disappears from history.

The Ituraeans seem to have resisted foreign domination and appear in the sources as aggressive conquerors of their weaker neighbours or, more nega-tively, as 'robbers'. Both the neighbouring client states and the Romans seem in general to have been hostile and heavily biased against them. Their remote villages and strongholds in the high mountains may have made it difficult for Rome to impose control, and in the initial years of the first century AD the Ituraean communities of Mount Lebanon were still sufficiently independent and threatening for Roman military activity to be directed against them.

Judaea and the Herodian dynasty

The rise of the Judaean kingdom coincided with the decline of the Seleucids, particularly following the Seleucid loss of Iran and Babylonia to the Parthians. In 129 BC the Hasmonaean family under John Hyrcanus established a dynasty independent of Seleucid rule, but adhering closely to the model of Seleucid kingship. Earlier rulers had achieved a degree of independence yet generally maintained close relations with the Seleucid court. Hyrcanus' son and succes-sor Alexander Jannaeus (103-76 BC) had expanded the kingdom east of the Jordan, capturing several of the Decapolis cities. He conquered Galilee and extended his rule to all of the coastal cities as far south as Raphia. Only Ascalon remained independent. Thus the kingdom of Judaea had incorporated most of the cities of the south. Pompey removed these conquests from the kingdom, re-establishing the settle-ments as independent cities and reduc-ing the kingdom to the districts of Judaea, Samaria, Galilee and Peraea. He deprived Alexander's son Hyrcanus II (63-40 BC) of the kingship but allowed him to rule as high priest. Disputes over Hasmonaean succession clouded the early years of the Roman province, and eventually led to the Romans searching for an alternative. The governor of Idumaea, Antipater, was very successful at furthering his own career as the Hasmonaean dynasty declined, and managed to convince the Romans of his fidelity and utility. Roman influence saw Antipater (died 43 BC) and his sons Herod and Phasael being promoted to powerful positions. Herod's advancement appeared to have been crippled by the Parthian invasion in 40 BC, in which Phasael committed suicide and the Parthians captured Hyrcanus II, replacing him with another member of the Hasmonaean dynasty, Antigonus. But the Roman response was to appoint

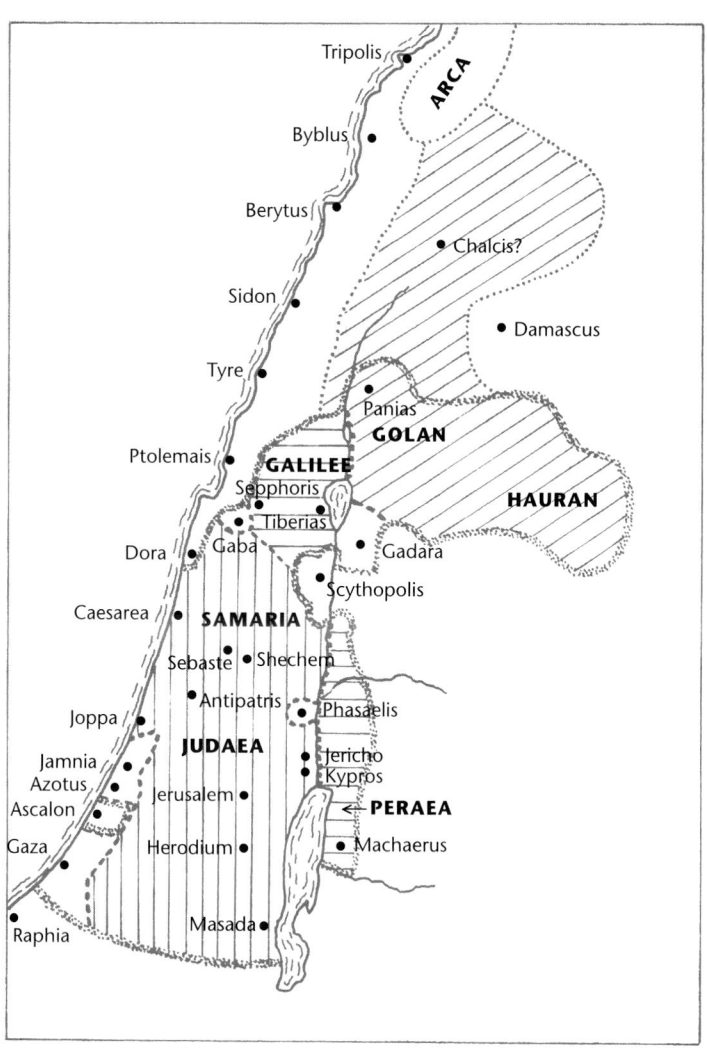

Herod as king. During the Parthian withdrawal Herod successfully reduced Antigonus and, with Roman assistance, overthrew him. After Actium he persuaded Octavian that he would prove a faithful ally, and was confirmed as king. Over the years he managed to serve his own and Roman interests with considerable skill, and acquired many of the cities that had been freed from the Hasmonaeans by Pompey.

The dynasty of Herod figured prominently in the royal politics of Syria during the first century AD, and, thanks to the writings of the Jewish historian Josephus, we know far more about this dynasty than any other. The Romans gave Herod and his descendants considerable responsibilities, and in general these rulers demonstrated their competence and loyalty. Herod himself was an excellent administrator and an exemplary friendly king. Although a Jew, he was also an enthusiastic supporter of Hellenism and a dutiful king to his pagan subjects. He was surrounded by Greek speakers at court, and made Jerusalem the centre for his isolympic games in 27 BC. His gifts of buildings to the cities of Syria, and not least the foundation of his own Greek city of Caesarea on the coast of his kingdom, confirms his support for the Hellenized elite culture of the empire. Nevertheless he and his successors actively supported the cause of Judaism. Herod built the great Second Temple in Jerusalem, and his descendants Agrippa I and Herod of Chalcis petitioned the emperor to confirm the rights of Jews in the eastern cities. However, Roman support for Herod may not have been matched by popular support: his fortress-palaces, Masada and Machaerus on opposite sides of the Dead Sea; and Herodium, where he was buried, were away from the main concentrations of the population, and were designed to be command centres in the event of a popular uprising as much as 'pleasure-domes' in the country.

Only three Herodian dynasts ruled Judaea itself: Herod, his son Archelaus and grandson Agrippa I. Herod divided his kingdom in his will between three sons, and Augustus refused all of them the title of king. Archelaus, appointed as ethnarch of Judaea, proved unable to handle delicate religious and political situations diplomatically. Augustus deposed him in AD 6 and annexed Judaea to the province of Syria. A second son, Antipas, ruled the tetrarchy of Galilee and Peraea, two regions physically separated from one another by the Decapolis cities. He too had an extremely difficult time. The countryside of Galilee was rife with millenarian activists. He arrested and executed the prophet John the Baptist, and it was quite by chance that another potential troublemaker from Galilee, Jesus of Nazareth, was arrested and executed in Judaea under the Roman prefect Pontius Pilate, rather than in his homeland. Antipas appears to have been capable and dedicated, but his private life provoked a scandal, and unhappily led to conflicts with the Nabataeans when he disowned his Nabataean wife in favour of his niece Herodias. He was accused of being a Parthian sympathizer, fell out with the influential governor of Syria, Lucius Vitellius, and was deposed by Caligula. The third son, Philip, ruled Batanaea, Trachonitis, Auranitis and the southern Hauran. He was sufficiently far removed from the troubles in Judaea and Galilee to keep his throne to the end of his life (AD 33/34).

A grandson of Herod, Agrippa I, was remarkably successful. Educated at Rome, he was a personal friend of Caligula and Claudius. His career up to the death of Tiberius was distinctly chequered, but he was saved from obscurity by Caligula, who appointed him Philip's successor and in addition gave him

Fig. 26. The Herodian kingdom. The stippled border shows the kingdom of Herod the Great; the diagonal shading the approximate extent of the principality of Chalcis. The southern part of Chalcis (the Golan and Hauran) was given to Herod, and the diagonal shading within the boundaries of Herod the Great's kingdom shows the territories inherited by his son Philip. Horizontal shading shows the territories inherited by Antipas; vertical shading those inherited by Archelaus. Ascalon was a free city, independent of Herod's kingdom; other cities, such as Gaza, Gaba and Gadara were annexed to the province after Herod's death. Azotus, Jamnia and Phasaelis were inherited by Herod's sister Salome.

Ituraean Abilene. He was also granted the title of king. In 39 he received Antipas' former tetrarchies, and in 41 Claudius entrusted him with the kingship of Judaea, which since the fall of Archelaus had been under direct Roman rule. Like Herod he was a benefactor of Greek cities and a champion of Jewish rights, although his reign was relatively short; when he died in 44 his large kingdom was annexed. Agrippa's brother Herod was made king of 'Chalcis', which may mean that he inherited the remnants of the Ituraean kingdom. Herod also acquired the right to appoint Jewish high priests, a right inherited by his successor, his nephew Agrippa II. This second Agrippa's kingdom was disparate and rambling, and large portions of it seem to have consisted of former Ituraean territory. He later exchanged Chalcis for territories in Lebanon and the Antilebanon, and also gained Philip's kingdom, Caesarea/Arca 'of the Ituraeans', and parts of Galilee and Peraea. He negotiated with the Jews at the outbreak of the rebellion in AD 66, but proved his loyalty to Rome by providing assistance in the conflicts that followed. The latter part of his long reign is less well known (mainly because Josephus' narrative ends with the collapse of the Jewish revolt), and he died during the reign of Domitian, *c.* AD 94.

Nabataea

The Nabataeans were sufficiently remote to have retained a fair degree of independence from the Hellenistic powers that controlled the region after Alexander the Great, though in theory at least they may have been vassals of the Ptolemies and Seleucids. Like the Hasmonaeans and other dynasts, they profited from the weakening of the Seleucid kingdom in the later second century BC. The Nabataean heartlands were the southern part of Transjordan, the Negev and Hijaz, but by the early first century BC they ruled a broad swathe of land east of the Jordan, and the kingdom stretched from the Sinai to Damascus, incorporating the rich farmland of the Hauran. Their history during the Hellenistic period is difficult to reconstruct from the scattered references, but like the Palmyrenes they seem to have profited from long-distance trade. Much of the kingdom consisted of dry steppe and desert where nomadism was the normal way of life, but careful water management, and the annexation of regions where dry farming was possible, enabled some of the population to settle, and the Nabataeans appear to have become increasingly sedentary during the Roman period. Their capital was Petra, but apart from Bostra in the north, and some towns in Transjordan, the Negev, and a few settlements in the southern part of the kingdom, Nabataea was not urbanized. The kingdom initially remained independent after 64 BC, but it rapidly became an ally of Rome, partly in opposition to its enemy to the west, the Ptolemaic kingdom of Egypt. Yet the Nabataeans continued to be remote from the centre of power, and survived the political turmoil of the Roman republic in spite of conflicts with Judaea and the political machinations of Herod.

The wealth of the Nabataean kingdom is thought to have derived initially from the so-called 'caravan' trade with India via the Red Sea and the 'incense routes' from south Arabia, in which the Nabataeans acted as escorts and middlemen for exotic goods bound for the Mediterranean ports (although evidence for Nabataean merchants in south Arabia remains elusive). Petra was the main city on trade routes from southern Arabia to the Mediterranean, and through Transjordan. The presence of Indian pottery in excavations at Petra confirms the existence of trade with the east, but not its intensity. Nabataean involvement in this trade is thought to have waned with the development of alternative trade routes via Egypt or through Palmyra to the Persian Gulf, and Rome may have encouraged the use of these alternative routes after the disastrous military expedition to south Arabia led by Aelius Gallus, prefect of Egypt, in 25 BC, in which the empire tried to appropriate the Arabian overland network, without success. The failure was blamed on the Nabataean guides. Other sources of income than the 'caravan' trade are believed to account for the prosperity of the kingdom in the first century AD. One suggestion is that the increasingly sedentary lifestyle of the Nabataean population and its exploitation of hydraulic techniques for irrigation led to a boom in agriculture.

The Nabataean kingdom evolved a distinct cultural identity, writing in its own script, issuing royal coinages in both silver and bronze (other major Roman client states in the region issued only bronze), developing its own architectural styles (see chapter 8) and producing a distinctive fine ware pottery ('eggshell ware', the distribution and use of which seems to have been confined almost exclusively to the kingdom). The geographer Strabo portrays the Nabataeans as a prosperous and civilized society with minimal class divisions. His account may be romanticized, but archaeology attests to his claim that Nabataea could boast a highly developed culture. The site which became the Nabataean capital, Petra, advanced considerably under King Obodas III (c. 30-9 BC) and his successor Aretas IV (9 BC – c. AD 40). It was remote, being located on the edge of the high southern part of the Transjordan plateau, but the surrounding lands were sufficiently fertile to support the city. Although springs provided water for Petra, this supply had to be augmented by reservoirs and cisterns. The city is most famous for its huge funerary monuments, cut from the rocky cliff faces around its urban centre. The grandest of these appear to have served the cults of deceased Nabataean kings, prompting scholars to suggest that the city developed from a site sacred to the ruling dynasty. By the end of the first century AD it had acquired the accoutrements of a 'Graeco-Roman' city: a theatre, monumental temples and other public buildings, and a paved main street. From the positions of the few private houses so far uncovered, there appears to have been little in the way of formal planning outside the city centre – perhaps further evidence of the light social control exercised by the rulers.

The reign of Aretas IV was the heyday of the Nabataean kingdom. Whether the Nabataeans reoccupied Damascus during his reign, as some have suggested, is uncertain. The evidence includes mention in the New Testament (II Corinthians 11.32) of the 'ethnarch of Aretas the king' in Damascus. Such a reoccupation could have occurred in the troubled times following the death of the Herodian Philip and the clashes between his brother Antipas and Aretas IV. Occupation of a city without Roman consent may be one of the reasons why Tiberius instructed the Syrian governor Lucius Vitellius to attack Aretas in 37. Vitellius was prevented from doing so by the emperor's death in the same year, and Aretas survived a few more years before being succeeded by his son Malichus II (c. 40-70). We know little about Malichus, who makes his final appearance sending military assistance, like other client rulers, to the Romans during the Jewish war. Rabbel II, the last Nabataean king, succeeded in the same year (AD 70). Epigraphic evidence suggests he may have favoured the northern city of Bostra over Petra. If this is so, his choice may have had something to do with the waning of southern trade routes and the increasing

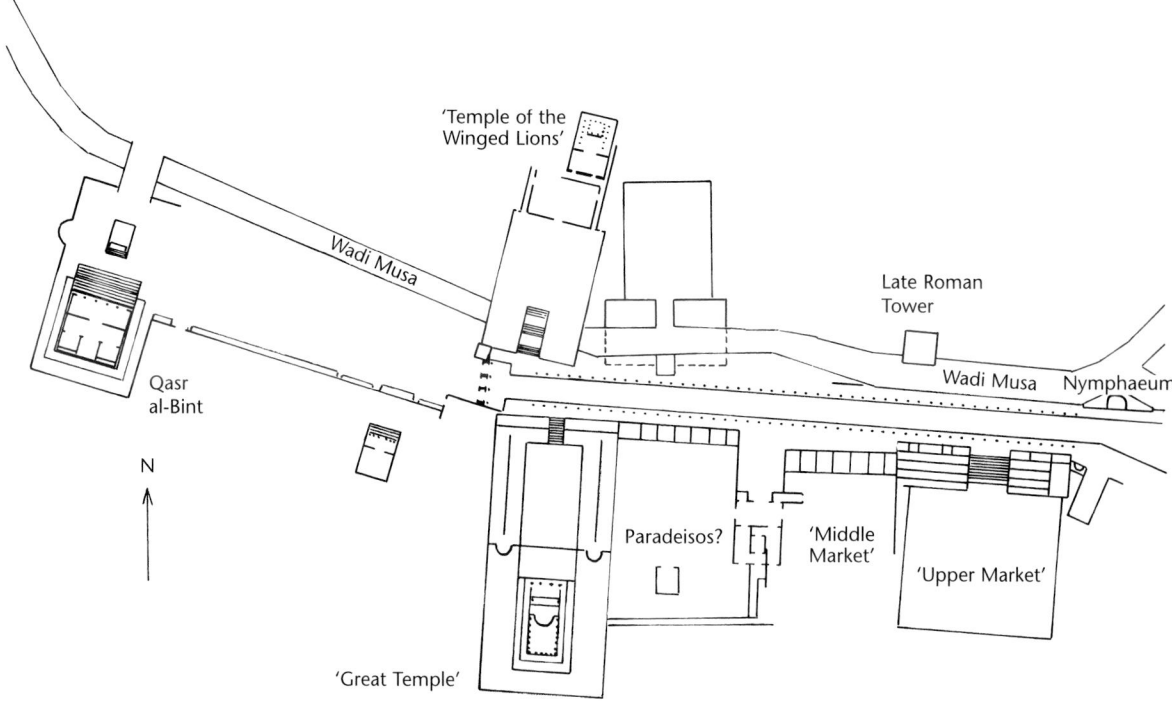

'Temple of the Winged Lions'

Wadi Musa

Late Roman Tower

Wadi Musa   Nymphaeum

Qasr al-Bint

N

Paradeisos?   'Middle Market'

'Upper Market'

'Great Temple'

Fig. 27. General plan of the centre of Petra.

emphasis on agricultural wealth – Bostra lay on the southern edge of the rich agricultural plain of the Hauran, and during the course of the first century AD is thought to have developed as a major centre for the northern part of the kingdom. But Bostra was not simply an agricultural town. It too was a centre for long-distance trade, located as it was at the head of an inland route from central Arabia up the Wadi Sirhan, running through the oasis of Azraq (situated some 80 kilometres (50 miles) south-east of Bostra).

In AD 106 the kingdom was annexed. The collection of documents from the western side of the Dead Sea known as the Babatha archive spans the period of the annexation and shows how rapidly Roman institutions penetrated daily life (see chapters 5 and 8). That Nabataean distinctiveness declined after the Roman take-over suggests that the ruling dynasty played a large part in generating and organizing Nabataean identity over such a wide area.

THE CITIES OF SYRIA AND THE NEAR EAST

The distinction between Roman rule through indirect control of client rulers and direct control of the cities is to some degree misleading. Both forms of rule were indirect, because Rome was unable to dominate her empire through intensive direct government. There were simply too few state representatives to perform such a task, so she resorted to a form of control using local political entities, great and small. Local governments were expected to maintain order in the areas under their jurisdiction, arrange for the collection of taxes, and oversee the production and distribution of foodstuffs in their territories. Of all forms of local government, the Romans had a marked preference for the city state, and in the eastern Mediterranean the model for this was the Greek *polis*. Effectively the *polis* was the definition of a city. By declaring the cities of Syria 'free', Pompey linked the notion of the Greek-style city state with Roman rule in the new province from the very beginning. Cities in particular were fundamental to the structure of Roman power and the fabric of provincial space.

A city was a settlement that was recognized by the government as having civic status. It was an institutional concept, not a physical distinction, and therefore civic status did not necessarily have anything to do with settlement size or monumentality. Cities were both large and small. Some were wealthy, and others were comparatively poor. Some villages were as large, and therefore probably as rich, as some cities, and some villages had monuments of the sort one might expect to find in a city. So villages or towns might resemble cities, even if they did not have the same status. This means that a settlement could be city-like (for example, the late Roman 'town' of Androna in the north Syrian steppe, with its circuit walls, barracks, bath building, numerous churches and other monumental structures, and imported limestone and Proconnesian marble elements) without officially being one (Androna seems to have remained a *kome* – a 'village'). Villages might have elaborate systems of self-government and magistracies that resembled those of the cities (though admittedly the evidence for this is debated – see chapter 5). Some small cities had village-sized territories, and some were nothing more than villages that had been raised to civic status. Smaller cities, although constitutionally independent, might depend economically on larger ones. This means that the resources on which a larger city could draw might include the territories of any smaller and economically weaker neighbours. Consequently a city might be easy to define in constitutional and legal terms, but more difficult to distinguish in other ways. A certain degree of monumentality, and a particular set of buildings might be expected (see chapter 7), and these no doubt helped persuade inhabitants and visitors alike that a place deserved its civic status, but that status did not depend on them. Certain acts, such as the issue of civic coins, were confined to settlements that had the status of a *polis*. The right to celebrate Greek festivals was also restricted to cities. Documentary evidence (inscriptions, civic coins and so on) allows us to determine which settlements were cities, but generally these tell us little about what sort of places they were. As we shall see below, size clearly did matter: it helped determine a city's position within a hierarchy, and that position brought benefits.

A Macedonian New World?

Beroea; Chalcis; Pella; Axius; Pieria: Cities, rivers, regions. With such names Hellenistic rulers and colonists appropriated features of the Syrian landscape. The names were not arbitrary signifiers, devoid of any ideological content. They were those of places in Macedonia or Greece, the homelands of the conquerors. In renaming it, the conquerors took over the Syrian landscape and its history.

A sceptic might ask whether this renaming had any impact on the original inhabitants of the land. The question underestimates the power of names, and the ability of new names to subvert and suppress indigenous knowledge. Renaming is a colonial act of 'symbolic violence' aimed at the landscape, 'the moment when the [cultural] space is shaped and reorientated by the gaze of the foreigner'.[14] If new names become the 'official' nomenclature, this forces indigenous names to persist through subversion and, potentially, the creation of an alternative landscape.

The names were Greek or Macedonian, but they did not attempt to distinguish the new from the original. Syrian Beroea was not distinguished from the Macedonian city of the same name by being named 'New Beroea' or such like. The two cities were, perhaps, parallel places, both equally cities which were inhabited by Beroeans, without the need for a distinction. There were sometimes broad similarities in the physical situations of the 'parallel' cities and places. When a group of Thessalian cavalry was settled on the strategic site next to the Orontes river in the late fourth century BC, did naming their settlement Larissa derive from nostalgic sentiment for the Larissa next to the River Peneios in their homeland, or was the landscape itself imagined as a kind of parallel Thessaly? Questions like this may be impossible to answer, and it is in any case unclear whether the colonists or the kings were responsible for the new names. The impact of the Macedonian renaming was predominantly psychological, having little or no effect on the physical environment, but there is no reason to suppose that it was superficial.

Macedonian colonialism was strongest in the north of Syria, where it was greatly reinforced by Seleucus I, who promoted and maintained a city-based culture there; as yet there is limited evidence for settlements in the south at the beginning of the Hellenistic period. It is likely that the renaming of cities using Macedonian place names belongs to the generation before Seleucus I, when Antigonus the One-Eyed controlled northern Syria. The Seleucid foundations broke with this earlier tradition by being given dynastic names, providing a clear identity with the empire (chapter 1). Unlike the 'parallel' cities of the earlier period, these dynastic cities did have qualifying epithets – Apamea on the Axius (Orontes), or Laodicea by the Sea. When the Seleucids drove the Ptolemies out of Phoenicia and the south, they acquired the coastal and inland settlements of the Lebanon range and Palestine, giving dynastic names to some of these. The Ptolemies had also given dynastic names to cities there, but the character of these settlements in the third century for the most part eludes us. Not all settlements with Seleucid or Ptolemaic dynastic names had civic status, and some may have been nothing more than forts. But the renaming, whether Macedonian, Ptolemaic or Seleucid, was a consequence of violence and conquest.

Once suitably transformed, the conquerors' history and myths could be applied to the landscape. The springs west of Antioch became Daphne, named after the daughter of the Arcadian river-god Ladon, who was the unwilling target of Apollo's advances, and, on praying for help, was transformed into a bay tree. In such ways a Greek past could be created for a place, and Syria made a part of Greece (see chapter 8).

Many of these names and 'histories' persisted throughout the Hellenistic and Roman periods, and were abandoned only after the Muslim conquest. This implies that they were intimately bound up with the Greek culture of the region, and shows us how Rome drew on that Greek culture during the seven centuries of her rule in Syria and the Near East. The fact that these names and legends were often abandoned under the caliphs is no indication of the hollowness of the Greek tradition in the region during the Roman period, but rather of an important cultural discontinuity at its end, when the old traditions no longer served as a source of legitimacy.

Pecking-orders

Urban development in the Hellenistic period provided the framework for civic evolution in the Roman era. Some cities were clearly more favoured within the Roman imperial system than others, such that by the heyday of the monumental city in the second century AD the network of Syrian cities comprised a fairly well-defined hierarchy, with certain centres often receiving benefits at the expense of their neighbours. This hierarchy emerged after the fragmented patchwork of Syrian states was incorporated into the empire in the first century BC. No doubt a hierarchy of cities had existed under the Seleucids, particularly in the north of Syria, but the decline of Seleucid control had led to the division of political power among many different centres. With the Roman annexation the cities became part of a single imperial system in which rewards and advancements were centrally regulated, and there was no opportunity for a city to aggrandize itself through conquest (though it might do so through trade). Competition was accepted, but only through the mediating influence of Roman authority. Titles and honours were sought from the emperors. The honours were not necessarily empty gestures, for favoured cities could also gain greater economic advantages than their less-favoured neighbours. Imperial indulgences included the right to hold celebrations of the imperial cult or Greek cultural festivals, and gifts which might range from buildings to regular donations of corn (fig. 74), or tax concessions. Famous cities attracted wealthy patrons, eager to be seen as conspicuous benefactors donating buildings or endowing cultural events. Small cities, on the other hand, were vulnerable. In physical appearance they might be difficult to distinguish from large villages, and were in danger of reverting to village status if they were unable to perform the civic tasks Rome expected of them.

While one may question whether Rome regarded its provinces as having capitals (because governors did not reside continuously in any one city and were expected to undertake regular tours of their province during their period of office), certain provincial cities tended to come out on top, and remained there for the entire period of Roman rule. So even if one should avoid calling Antioch the capital of the Roman province of Syria, there can be little doubt that it was from the very beginning the most favoured city of that province. As the province of Syria was subdivided, so other cities emerged in first place in their respective provinces: Tyre in Syria Phoenice, Caesarea in Syria Palaestina, Damascus in Libanensis, Apamea in Syria Secunda. But Antioch managed to remain in the lead by adopting a new role, that of *imperial* capital. As we have seen in chapter 2, from the second century onwards emperors used the city as a base when campaigning in the east, and during the late third and fourth centuries the rulers were often in prolonged residence there.

From the very beginning of Roman rule Antioch had held the title *metropolis*, 'mother city'. The term was originally used to describe a city which had sent out colonists, and had therefore mothered new cities. Tyre, as the founder of Phoenician colonies like Carthage, could regard itself as *metropolis* in this respect. Under Roman rule *metropolis* became a title bestowed by the emperor, and to be one was to be a member of a highly exclusive club of cities. But if the title had an administrative meaning in the early years of the province, it is difficult to discern one. Coins show that in the late first century Tyre also became an official *metropolis*, then, by the reign of Hadrian, Samosata and Damascus had acquired the title. There seems to be some connection between the use of *metropolis* and a city's role as a centre for the imperial cult (on which, see chapter 9). Consequently the use of the title *metropolis* in the second century seems to provide an indication of which cities were pre-eminent in the region. Even so, the absence of the title is not always a reliable guide to the *unimportance* of a city. In Arabia, Petra used the title from or not long after the annexation of Arabia in 106, but Bostra, which was equally important in the province, did not acquire it until the third century. Likewise the major city of Caesarea Maritima did not acquire the title until the reign of Severus Alexander (AD 222-35).

These 'front-line' positions might be disputed. The most successful challenger to Antioch's position was its rival Laodicea ad Mare, which after the civil war and Septimius Severus' defeat of Pescennius Niger in AD 194 was rewarded for its support of the victor by being promoted to *metropolis*. As was mentioned in chapter 2, Antioch was demoted to village status and placed in the territory of Laodicea. Its dignity was restored shortly afterwards, but Laodicea managed to retain its new title. A similar situation occurred in the new province of Syria Phoenice, where Berytus disputed Tyre's pre-eminent position. However, Berytus backed the wrong contender (Niger), and after Severus' victory Tyre's position was strengthened. But a couple of decades later, under Elagabalus (218-22), Tyre supported a rebellion and (if the evidence of the coins is to be believed) lost its title to its other major rival, Sidon, which had evidently remained loyal. As with Antioch, Tyre's disgrace did not last long, and it was soon returned to its former status.

The presence of the title *metropolis* would seem to be a useful index of a city's position in the provincial hierarchy, but this is not always so. Elagabalus gave the title to his native city of Emesa, but coins issued there by the usurper Uranius Antoninus (*c*. AD 253-4) suggest that the title was subsequently lost, and Seleucia Pieria was also a *metropolis* by the reign of Severus Alexander. It is hard to see how these cities fitted into any official hierarchy, although they may be evidence of attempts to challenge that hierarchy by appeals to particular emperors. In the fourth century the title came to be used to describe the chief city of the province, whose bishop had jurisdiction over all the other bishops in his province. This new definition is well illustrated by an episode in the fifth century. Once again, it was the product of rivalries between cities. Following the 'Robber Council' of Ephesus in 449 (on which, see chapter 9), the emperor Theodosius II was petitioned by Bishop Eustathius of Berytus for the right to consecrate bishops in the coastal cities of the province which lay to the north of his see. Theodosius granted Berytus 'metropolitan dignity' equal to that of Tyre, explaining: 'Let [Tyre] be "mother of the province" by the kindness of our ancestors, and let [Berytus] (be) by ours, and let each enjoy similar rank.'[15] A little while later Photius, bishop of Tyre, complained to Theodosius' successor Marcian. The emperor ruled that Berytus' promotion was irregular and had effectively divided the province in two. But he could not overturn the rescript of Theodosius so easily. The problem was resolved by allowing Berytus to retain the title *metropolis* but stripping it of any administrative meaning, and restoring to Tyre its full rights as the 'true *metropolis*'.

This episode illustrates how a city of the first rank could have its position challenged by a contender. The position of Tyre could be disputed by Berytus or Sidon, and that of Antioch by Laodicea. In these cases the differences in size and wealth between contenders were perhaps not all that great, except that the honours given to the first-rank cities brought greater benefits. But in general it seems that once a city had achieved pre-eminence, it was very difficult for a contender to wrest it away successfully and permanently. The imperial system achieved stability through ancestral privileges rather than other mechanisms such as economic impetus.

Titles provide us with one means of reconstructing the hierarchy of Syrian and Near Eastern cities. But they depend very heavily on accidents of survival: issues of civic coins or inscriptions which bear the titles, or the occasional mention of a city in a papyrus. It is also instructive to look at the extent of the physical remains at the various sites, to see how well they correlate with other sorts of evidence. One approach to city ranking is to examine the sizes of the areas enclosed by the cities' walls (fig. 28). The largest, Antioch, was gigantic compared to most other cities. However, Antioch was not alone among the 'super-cities' of the province. The defended areas of Antioch's sister cities of the Tetrapolis, Laodicea, Seleucia and Apamea, were almost as impressive. These four foundations all enclosed areas substantially larger than the other cities, and this is perhaps why only a city like Laodicea could seriously challenge Antioch's position in the hierarchy of honours. It also illustrates the absurdity of the Severan demotion of Antioch to a village of Laodicea, and why that position could not be maintained for more than a couple of years at the most. The other cities shown in fig. 28 are all 'monumentalized', having an array of public buildings and colonnades, and may represent a middle-range type, albeit significantly smaller than the Tetrapolis centres. Palmyra's early walls enclosed an area much larger than the others (see fig. 97), but its inhabited area was on a scale comparable to the others and its later walls enclosed an area similar in size to the middle-range cities (colour plate 12). The defended areas of cities like Berytus, Sidon and Tyre are likely to have been of similar proportions, although at present their circuits cannot be traced with any confidence. Each one of these was a potential competitor of the other. However, there were certainly cities much smaller than these, such as Laodicea ad Libanum in the Orontes valley (fig. 29), which were no bigger than some of the larger villages known.

One problem with this type of analysis is that not all of the areas enclosed by the city walls were necessarily built up, and therefore the defended area does not give any indication of the populousness of a city. Fortifications sometimes had to incorporate strategically weak points, or provide a link between an acropolis and the settlement, leaving large empty areas in between. Antioch's walls enclosed the high ridge of Mount Silpius which overlooked the city, and it is unlikely that the steep western slope which lay within the city fortifications was much settled. Nor does this sort of analysis give any impression of the extent of extra-mural settlement, or changes in the extent of intra-mural settlement over time. By the fifth and sixth centuries Caesarea was enlarged to about twice the size shown on the plan. At Palmyra the defended area was reduced in size between the first and fourth centuries, although much of the area encompassed by the early walls was probably open rather than heavily built up.

Another, complementary approach is to examine expenditure on public monuments. The fragmentary nature of our knowledge precludes any detailed analysis of this sort, but a measure of monumentalization could perhaps be determined by the length of a city's main colonnaded street, where it is known or can be estimated. This of course does not take into account the fact that

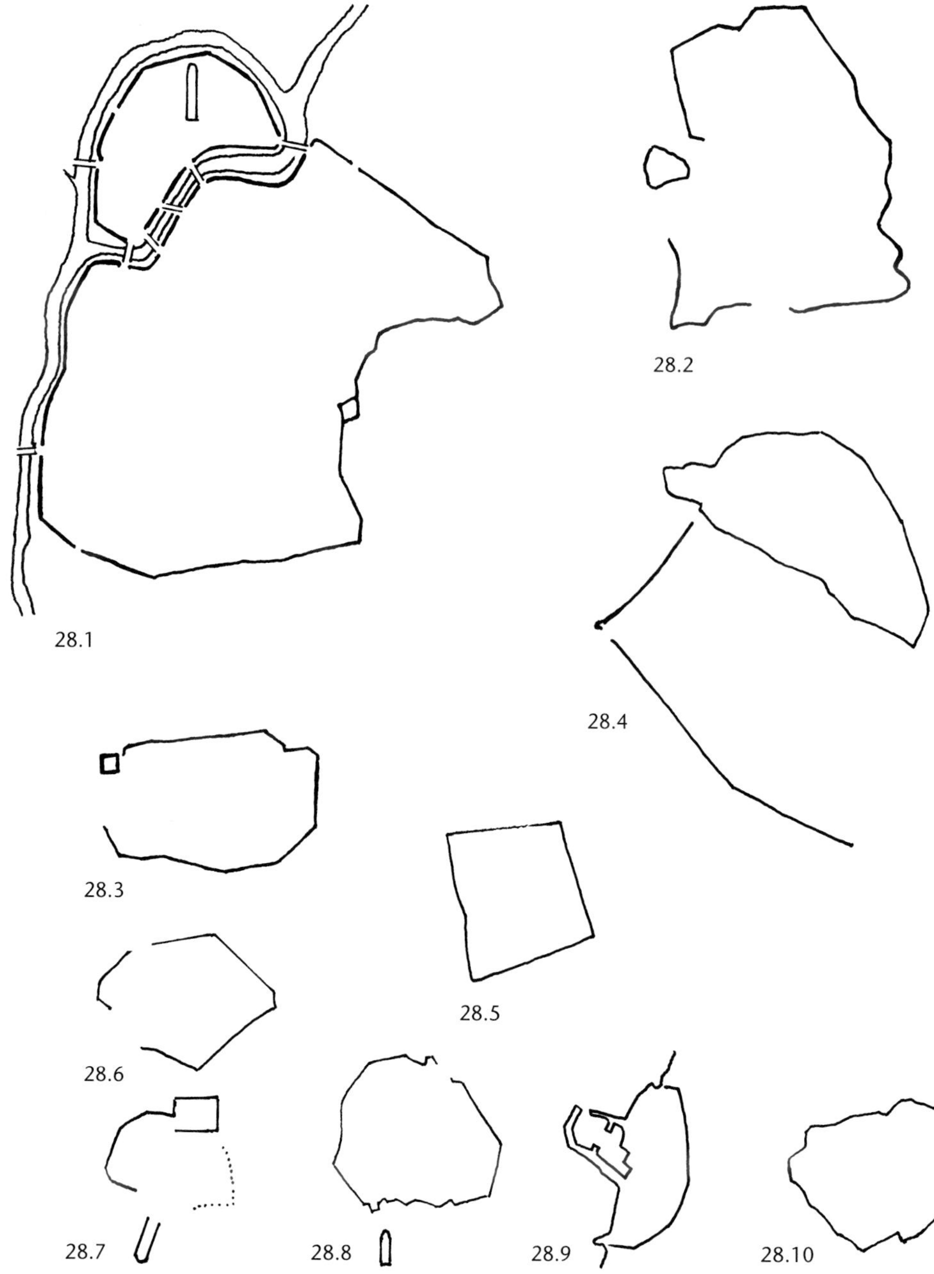

28.2

28.1

28.4

*Fig. 28. The defended
areas of Syrian and
Near Eastern cities,
to the same scale
(1 cm = 500 m).
28.1. Antioch.
28.2. Apamea.
28.3. Damascus.
28.4. Palmyra.
28.5. Philippopolis.
28.6. Heliopolis.
28.7. Bostra.
28.8. Gerasa.
28.9. Caesarea.
28.10. Sebaste.*

28.3

28.5

28.6

28.7   28.8   28.9   28.10

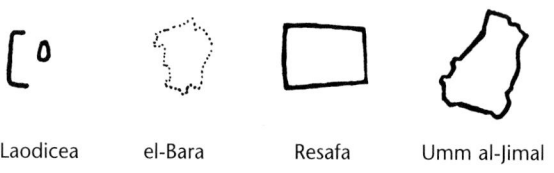

Laodicea   el-Bara   Resafa   Umm al-Jimal

*Fig. 29. The city of Laodicea ad Libanum (Tell Nebi
Mend), with its acropolis and lower city wall,
compared to some late Roman sites: from left to right,
the village of Kapropera (el-Bara), the city of
Sergiopolis (Resafa), and the village of Umm al-Jimal
(ancient name uncertain). Scale: 1 cm = 500 m.*

most of the cities listed had more than one colonnaded street, or that the coastal cities, which are not represented in this list, had colonnades of expensive imported stone. Nor does it allow for the fact that certain cities, such as Dura Europus (fig. 113), had no colonnaded streets at all. Nevertheless it does give some impression of relative wealth, and the ranking is not unexpected (fig. 30). The distribution does not form a steep curve, which we might expect from a very strongly differentiated hierarchy. Once again the Tetrapolis cities emerge as the clear leaders, with Antioch having the longest monumental street (though Apamea's was wider). The middle-range cities all have colonnades of roughly similar lengths, although Petra's is perhaps rather shorter than might be expected. The very smallest cities may not have had colonnaded thoroughfares.

Fig. 30. The length (in metres) of the main colonnaded streets in some cities of Syria and the Near East.

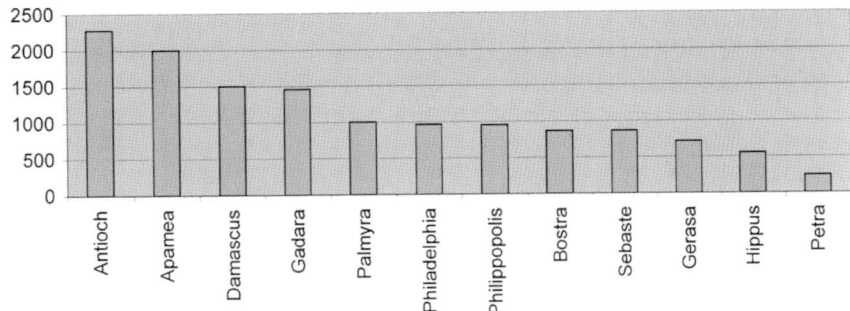

The large number of middle-range cities suggests that many Syrian cities of the early empire, most of which had been established long before Roman rule, were successful. The smaller ones, which might be termed the 'losers' in the struggle, are for the most part very imperfectly known. Laodicea ad Libanum maintained its civic status throughout the period of Roman rule, but it remained small (fig. 29). Many of the settlements which achieved independent city status under Rome were probably villages which had been dependent on the larger cities during the Hellenistic period, and few of these new cities were as successful as their older neighbours. The Hellenistic kings would perhaps have been reluctant to promote small settlements with restricted hinterlands to the status of city, whereas the Romans were content to do so, suggesting that the Roman interest in urban development differed somewhat from that of the Seleucids or Ptolemies.

Access to resources was a key factor in sustaining the urban hierarchy. The large and middle-range cities are spaced widely apart, and are confined to agriculturally rich areas (Palmyra being the notable exception). Few were less than a day's travel from their neighbours (see fig. 43). Their hinterlands were extensive and the cities could support large populations, using the foodstuffs and materials produced there either for their own consumption or for exchange with other cities. Unless they were deprived of their lands for some political misdemeanour, this greater access to resources ensured that they remained ahead of their smaller neighbours. Small cities are found either in the drier steppe, where agricultural resources were much poorer, or on more fertile lands but in close proximity to other cities. By the late Roman period there were concentrations of small cities in fertile regions of the northern Hauran, along the Orontes valley and the coast, and in Palestine. Many of these are unlikely to have possessed large territories, and consequently the reserves on which they could draw were much more restricted.

All attempts to estimate the populations of the cities are little more than guesswork, based on general measurements of scale such as those outlined above. Compared to modern cities, however, they were small. The largest, Antioch, perhaps had as many as 250,000 inhabitants. Other Tetrapolis cities could have contained around 50,000-100,000 (the Augustan census in Syria recorded 125,000 citizens in Apamea and its territory in AD 6). The middle-range cities may have had populations of 20,000 or less, and the smaller ones may not have contained more than 5000. The larger villages could boast population figures comparable to those of the minor cities. The village of Umm al-Jimal at its height in the sixth century is thought to have housed between 6000 and 8000 people.

Urbanization: Instrument of Empire?

The fact that a *polis* could not make itself enabled Rome to manipulate the political geography of Syria, by confirming some centres as cities but denying this power to other settlements. It is clear from documentary sources that emperors saw the growth and multiplication of cities as a measure of success. Even so, there is not much evidence for direct imperial involvement in urbanization in Syria and the Near East during the early empire. In any case it is not always easy to discern whose initiative led to the foundation, refoundation or elevation of smaller settlements to city status. The number of cities increased under Roman rule as villages were raised to cities, or old city settlements which had fallen on hard times were resettled and developed, yet when it comes to deciding whether emperors were proactive in pursuing a policy of urbanization by creating new urban centres, or merely reactive, supporting their autonomous multiplication by responding to petitions from the inhabitants, the evidence is often ambiguous. There were very few new foundations that can be directly attributed to imperial initiative. The clearest example is Philippopolis, founded in the Hauran *c.* 244, presumably on the orders of the emperor Philip (244-9), at a site which is thought to have been his birthplace. Late Roman fortresses in the regions most likely to be attacked by the Sasanians were sometimes granted city status, which might reflect imperial interests. But for some scholars, the claim that the emperors had a long-term policy or strategy of urbanization in Syria is pushing the evidence further than it will allow. At the very least, the proliferation of cities under Rome can be attributed to the imperial preference for this form of local government. In that sense the growth of urbanism was regulated and supported by Rome, and the emperors were proponents of urbanism.

Some modern claims concerning Roman urbanization strategies are even harder to substantiate. For example, there is little to suggest that the Roman colonies in Syria had any special strategic purpose (see chapter 7). With the notable exception of Berytus, all other colonies in the region seem to have lost any Latin character that they possessed as the descendants of the legionary veterans became assimilated into the local population. While in other less urbanized parts of the Roman world colonies could be regarded as instruments of urbanization, this is clearly not the case for Syria and the Near East.

Nor was the Roman record entirely one of successes. Some Syrian cities declined. Dura Europus was completely abandoned in the mid-third century, and Zeugma, which also suffered destruction during the same invasion by the Sasanians, was clearly a different sort of urban centre in AD 350 from the one it had been in 250. If some of the sources are to be believed, Emesa went into decline in the late Roman period, although this decline (if it occurred at all) was probably shortlived (see p. 115). But these failures were to some degree compensated for by the creation of new cities. However, the new cities of the later empire were for the most part small and may have contributed to increasing political fragmentation in the region rather than cohesion (though such fragmentation could have suited the Roman authorities, if they found a divide-and-

Fig. 31. The cities of northern Syria.

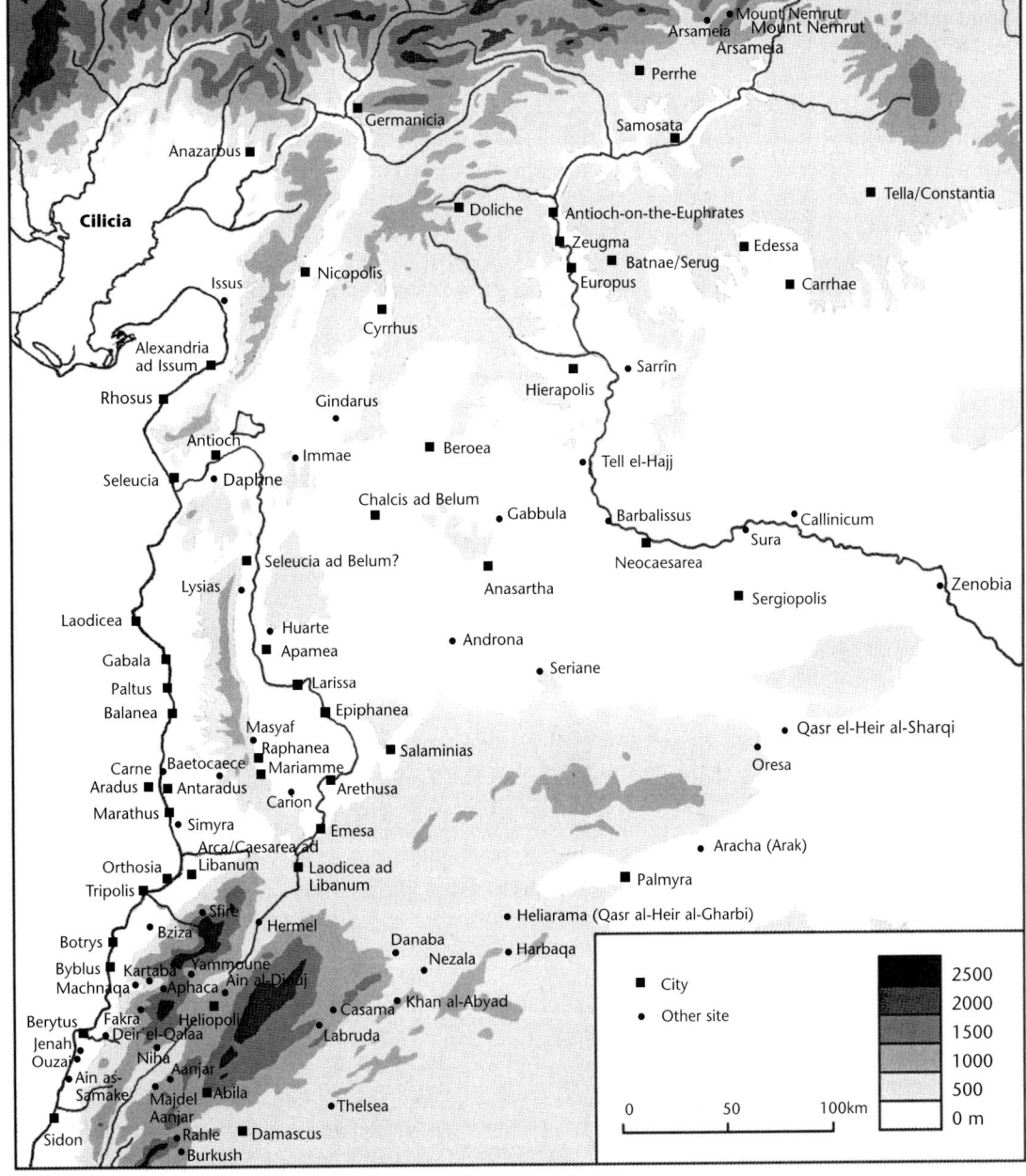

rule strategy useful). Again, the ambitions of locals, desirous of seeing their village elevated to city status, and a government willing to acquiesce to their demands, may have been the driving force behind the spread of some of these later cities.

The Progress of Urbanism

Different conceptions and features of the ancient city are examined in chapter 7. Before that it is necessary to provide a brief introduction to the cities of Syria and the Near East during the period of Roman rule. Here we confine ourselves to 'greater Syria' in the geographical sense, even though this was not always coterminous with the Roman provinces of Syria. It should be recalled that in its early years the Syrian province included eastern Cilicia, with great cities like Tarsus, Anazarbus and Aegeae. These were removed from Syria under Vespasian, and are not included in this brief survey. ,

The Pompeian annexation brought northern Syria, the Phoenician coast and the inland enclave of the Decapolis under direct Roman administration. It is probably no coincidence that these areas happened to be the most urbanized parts of Syria. The majority of cities in the north were Macedonian or Seleucid foundations, the most famous of these being the four cities of the Tetrapolis (Antioch, Seleucia, Apamea and Laodicea). All four had been founded by Seleucus I between 301 and 299 BC. On the coast, at the foot of the Amanus range, he dedicated the city of Seleucia in Pieria (in honour of himself); further south, a natural harbour proved a suitable site for the foundation of Laodicea (named for his mother Laodice). Inland, at points controlling the Orontes river and routes into the Syrian interior, he founded Antioch (named after his father Antiochus) and, further up river, the well-fortified Macedonian colony called Pella was refounded as Apamea (for Seleucus' Persian wife Apama). The Tetrapolis centres were conceived as large cities from the time of their foundation, although Antioch (modern Antakya) emerged as the biggest by the mid-second century BC. As the Seleucid empire declined and other royal cities in Asia Minor and Babylonia were lost, Antioch became the focus for royal power. Its situation, at the bottle-neck of a fertile though swampy inland plain, with a mild Mediterranean climate and a navigable passage along the Orontes to the sea, made it a suitable capital. Close to Antioch was the suburb of Daphne (modern Harbiye), with its grove sacred to Apollo and Artemis, which in the Roman period was renowned for its pleasant climate, wealthy patrons and lavish villas.

The city of Seleucia in Pieria (a now-abandoned site near the modern village of Çevlik) lay on a site where streams from the mountains above flow into the sea. The mountain behind the city was called Pieria after the mountainous region in Macedonia, and from this Seleucia derived its epithet. The coast around the mouth of the Orontes was exposed and unsuitable for anchoring large ships, so Seleucia was provided with an artificial harbour. The city itself occupied a large area spread over several natural terraces on a slope facing towards the sea. Under the Romans it became an important base for the Syrian fleet, and for emperors visiting Syria it was often the first port of call.

The other Tetrapolis port, Laodicea (Latakia), was also provided with an artificial harbour. In the Roman period its lighthouse was probably its most famous monument, being depicted on the city's coins together with the personification of the fortune (*Tyche*) of Laodicea (fig. 93.1). The city remains an important

Fig. 32. General plan of the city of Apamea. The city's Roman walls were constructed on the foundations of the earlier Seleucid defences, maintaining the size and form of the city through Roman times.

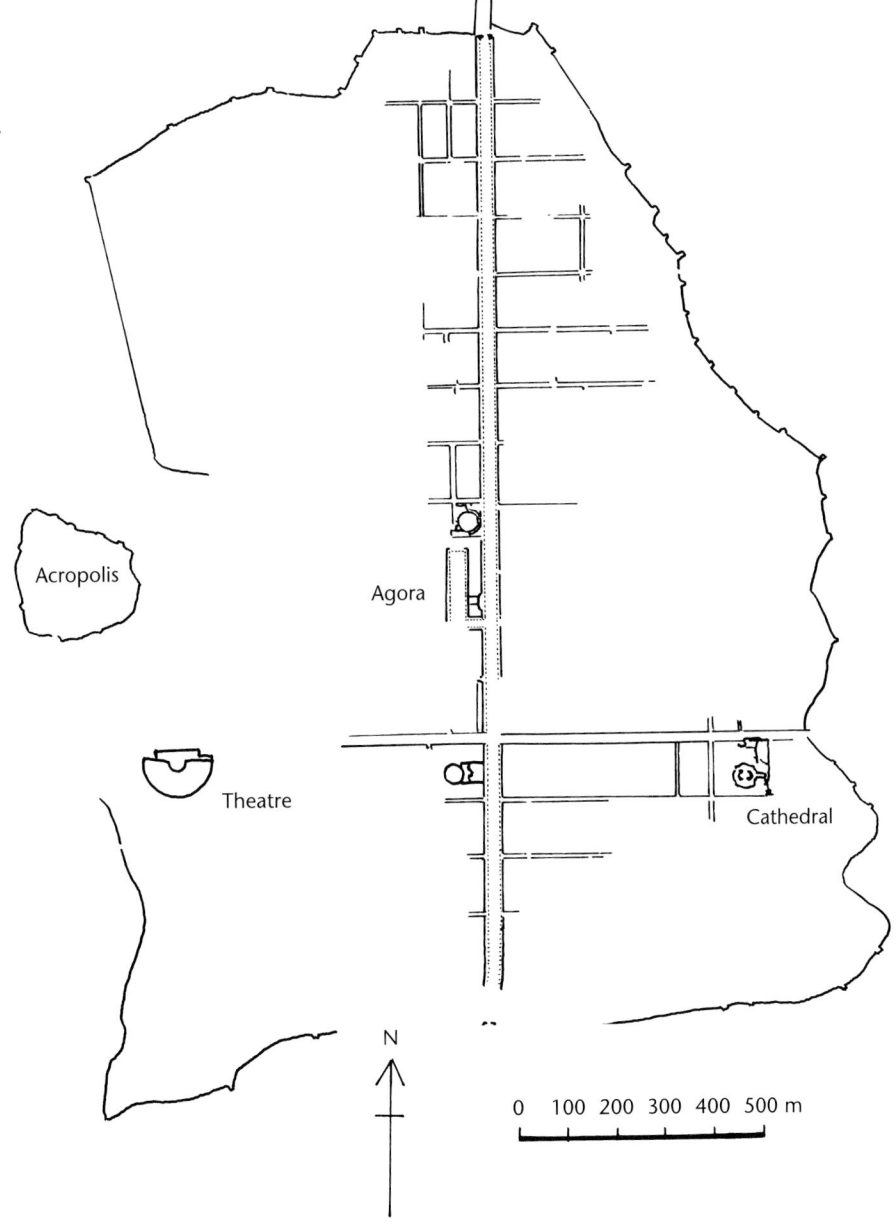

Acropolis

Agora

Theatre

Cathedral

N

0 100 200 300 400 500 m

Mediterranean port to this day, and consequently its archaeology is the least known among the sister cities, being covered by the modern town. To the south of Laodicea were three small coastal ports: Gabala (Jebleh), Paltus (Arab al-Mulk) and Balanea (renamed Leucas under Claudius, the modern Banias). The fourth Tetrapolis city lay inland, beyond the Bargylus range of mountains, overlooking the marshy valley of the Ghab through which the Orontes flows. Apamea (Qalaat al-Mudiq) occupied a plateau on the eastern side of this valley, which according to Strabo earned it the nickname *Cherronesos* ('Peninsula'). Under the Seleucids it was a major arsenal and military training centre, but its *floruit* was in the Roman period, as its extensive and monumental ruins testify.

Most of the other settlements with city status in the Orontes valley are known by little more than name and a few references in ancient sources. Their status during the early years of the province is not always clear. The Thessalian colony of Larissa (Shaizar) issued coins in the early first century BC, by which time it had presumably achieved city status. Further upstream were Epiphanea (Hama), and then two centres associated with the tribe of the Emisenoi, Arethusa (ar-Rastan) and Emesa (Homs). As we have seen, Arethusa seems to have gained its independence from Emesa under Octavian/Augustus, but Emesa remained under the control of the local dynasty for almost another century. Above Emesa lay Laodicea ad Libanum (Tell Nebi Mend), which appears in some Roman sources as 'Scabiosa', an epithet meaning rough or scabby; one suggestion is that this has to do with malarial conditions prevailing there in ancient times. Mariamme (Miryamin) is listed as a city by Pliny the Elder, and features in late Roman lists, although it did not issue coins and little is known of it in Roman times. Another settlement in the Orontes valley, Seleucia ad Belum or Seleucobelus (a site not securely located, but thought to be in the vicinity of Apamea) may also have had civic status at this time; it certainly did in the late Roman period.

North and east of the Tetrapolis region was a broad arc of fertile land stretching to the Euphrates. Part of this belonged to the kingdom of Commagene at the time of Pompey, but there were also a number of settlements outside the kingdom which appear to have enjoyed the rank of city under the Seleucids and continued to do so under the Romans. Immediately north of Antioch lay Nicopolis of Seleucis (Islahiye), an obscure city in the valley of the Kara Su, which issued coins in the second and third centuries AD, but not before. Its neighbour, Gindarus (Jandaris), never issued coins. The geographer Strabo described the latter place as a *polis* in the first century BC, but five centuries later Theodoret, bishop of Cyrrhus, describes it as a village in the territory of Antioch, although it had a bishop in the fourth century.

The city of Cyrrhus itself was a Hellenistic foundation which occupied a now abandoned site called Nabi Huri, on a hillside overlooking the Sabun Suyu, a tributary of the River 'Afrin. It may have been a pre-Macedonian settlement. Chalcis (Nabi Iss, medieval Qinnesrin) and Beroea (Aleppo) certainly were, as attested by their large tells. The medieval street plan of Aleppo is thought to preserve a rectilinear grid laid out in Hellenistic times at the foot of the tell. Hierapolis (Mambij), the 'Holy City', was a name given by the Seleucids to an important cult centre which seems to have been called Mambog or Mabbug by Aramaic speakers. The site has scarcely been explored, but literary sources make it clear that Hierapolis remained important in the Roman period, both as a cult centre and as a mustering-place for legions preparing to invade Mesopotamia. The only other city in Roman territory of the Pompeian period this far east is Europus (Carchemish) on the Euphrates.

Another important group of urban centres of the time of Pompey comprised the Phoenician city states of the coast. The most significant northern Phoenician city was Aradus. It occupied a low offshore island, about 10 metres (33 feet) above sea level at its highest point. Aradus had a long tradition of independence, having gained autonomy from the Seleucids as early as 259 BC, and was in the Hellenistic period a major commercial centre as well as possessing a

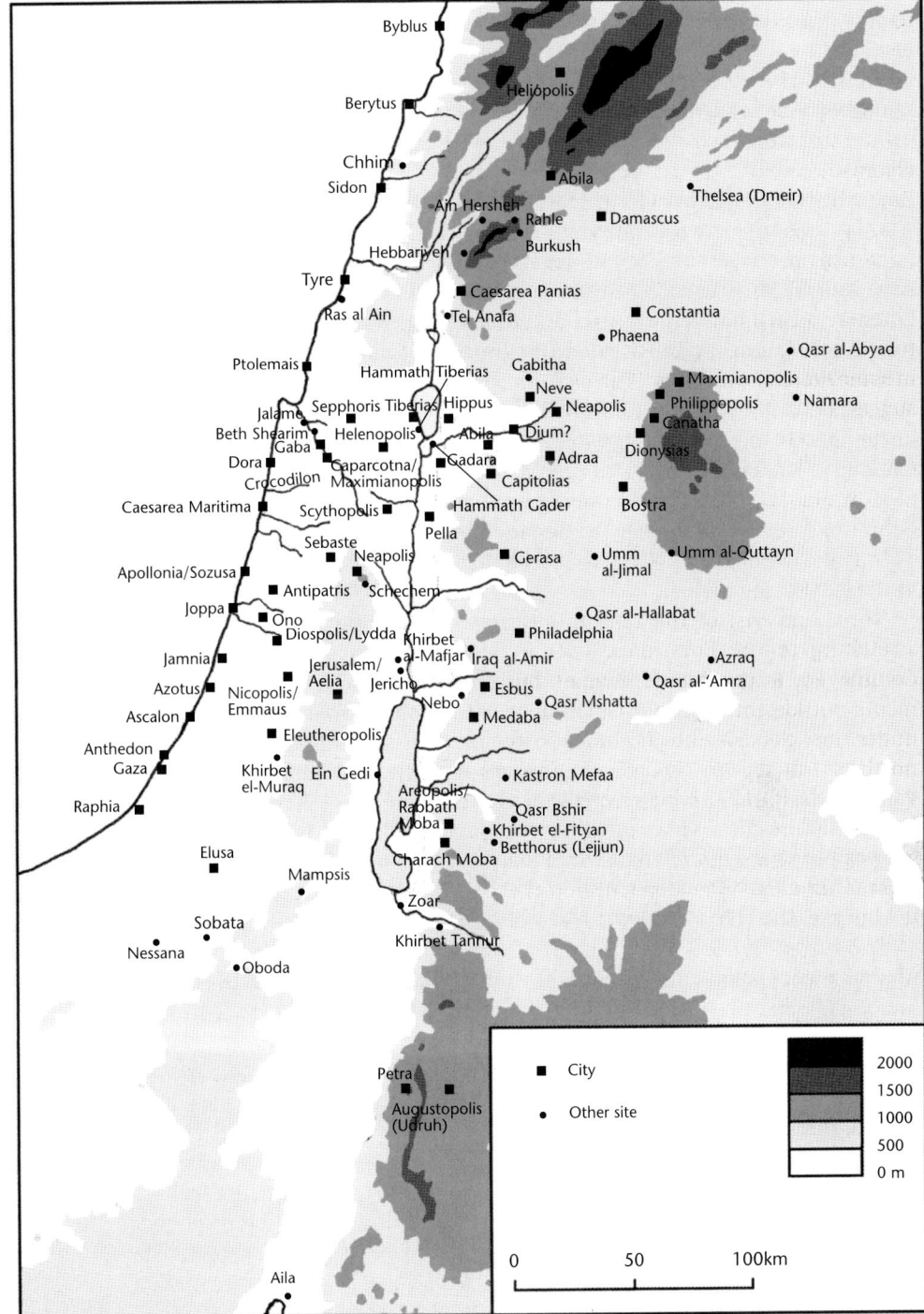

Fig 33 The cities of southern Syria, Palestine/Judaea, and Arabia. Some places mentioned as cities in late Roman lists (for example, Phaena) have not been labelled as such here.

formidable fleet. At the time of the Roman annexation it appears to have dominated the smaller coastal cities of Marathus, Balanea, Paltus and Gabala, but these regained their independence in the decades that followed. By the second century AD a mainland dependency of Aradus, called Antaradus (Tartus), had become the major centre for the region, and by the late Roman period had eclipsed Aradus itself.

Further south lay the little city of Orthosia (Ard Artusi), whose remains have yet to be explored, and Tripolis (modern Tripoli), a Phoenician city which the sources claim was founded under Persian rule by the three cities of Tyre, Sidon and Aradus (hence its Greek name). It was located on a broad, low promontory with a well-protected harbour on its southern side. The small city of Botrys (Batroun) was situated on the coast just south of the high cliffs of Cape Theoprosopon (modern Ras Chekka), and further along the coast was the ancient port of Byblus (Jbeil). Although an important power in the Bronze Age, Byblus appears to have been relatively unimportant by the Hellenistic period. It clearly revived under Roman rule, and acquired the regular trappings of a monumental coastal city in the second century.

Berytus was a minor Phoenician city which grew in importance under Seleucid domination. Its development was arrested in the 140s BC when it was sacked during a Seleucid civil war and little is known about the site until veterans from two Roman legions were settled there under Augustus. The Augustan arrangement gave Berytus an immense territory, which included a large part of the Lebanon range and the Massyas (Bekaa) valley. Of all the cities in Syria, Berytus was regarded as the most 'Roman' in character. The original legionary settlers no doubt established its Roman quality, but from the third century AD it became an important centre for the study of Roman law, which probably helped to preserve its Latin features in later centuries.

Sidon had been one of the major cities of Phoenicia in the Achaemenid and Hellenistic periods. It was situated on a low promontory, with harbours to the north and south. Its architectural remains suggest that it remained a city of some note in the Roman period, but it seems to have been overshadowed by its neighbours Berytus and Tyre. Sidon's territory is thought to have been large, extending over the Lebanon range as far as Mount Hermon.

The city of Tyre had once been an island offshore like Aradus. Alexander the Great had built a causeway out to the island to besiege it in 331 BC, and in the centuries that followed the shallows around the causeway had silted up, transforming Tyre into a peninsula. By the Roman period the area of the causeway was broad enough to accommodate the city's hippodrome (fig. 113). It too had an extensive hinterland, stretching east to the Huleh valley. With Severus' division of the province of Syria Tyre became the chief city of Syria Phoenice, and, from the fourth century, of Phoenice Paralia or Prima.

The Phoenician city of Akko had been renamed Ptolemais under the Ptolemies. In the mid- to later second century BC the city featured as a southern capital and an occasional residence for Seleucid kings. It became a Roman colony in the reign of Claudius, and like Berytus legionary veterans were settled there (see chapter 7).

Many of the cities further south had fallen under the influence of the Hasmonaeans of Judaea by the time of the Roman annexation. The only coastal port of note to maintain its independence was Ascalon. Pompey and his successors restored the 'freedom' of the subject cities, but not all of them managed to survive as city states after the first century BC. Those that did included Dora (Tel Dor), Gaba (Tel Shush), Samaria (refounded by Herod as Sebaste), Strato's Tower (refounded by Herod as Caesarea), Gaza, Anthedon (Blakhiyeh) and Raphia (Tel Rafah). To commemorate their restoration they sometimes adopted the names of those governors who had honoured them, thereby advertising Roman approbation of their civic status. The inland settlement of Samaria adopted the name Gabinia after Aulus Gabinius, governor 57-55 BC, and further north Gaba became Philippia after Marcius Philippus, who was the first senatorially appointed governor of Syria in 59 BC. Their independent status was shortlived, as most of them were given to Herod (under whom a number of Pompey's 'free' cities appear to have been reduced to administrative dependencies, and were not revived as cities after his death). They were inherited by Herod's successors, except for Gaza, which was attached to Syria, forming part of a tiny enclave in the south along with Raphia and the free city of Ascalon until the annexation of Judaea in AD 6.

The only other urbanized area of note under direct Roman control at the time of Pompey was the Decapolis. Though the name, 'Ten Cities', implies some institutional arrangement, it was never an official league or alliance of cities. The term was used to describe an enclave of highly Hellenized city states, a part of the province of Syria and therefore (in theory at least) directly administered by Rome, but which in the early years of the province was entirely surrounded by the Nabataean, Herodian and Ituraean client states. Our sources, where they bother to mention the Decapolis cities separately, do not agree which made up the ten. Pliny the Elder lists the Decapolis cities as Damascus, Canatha (Qanawat), Scythopolis (Beth Shean), Pella (Tabaqat el-Fahil: colour plate 20), Gadara (Umm Qais), Hippus (Qalaat el-Husn), Dium (Tell Ashari?), Philadelphia ('Amman), Gerasa (Jerash), and an unknown city called Raphana; but he acknowledged that 'not all persons give the same cities in their lists'. Raphana may be Capitolias (Beit Ras), a city south of Abila (Tell Abil) which issued coins in the second century using an era beginning in AD 98. To this list must be added Abila itself, not mentioned by Pliny, but using a civic dating era beginning with Pompey's annexation (on the use of city eras, see chapter 4). An inscription of AD 133/134 calls it 'Abila of the Decapolis'. Pompey restored a number of these cities to independence after a period of Hasmonaean domination, as is evidenced by the use of 'Pompeian' dating eras at Abila, Canatha, Dium, Gadara (fig. 37), Gerasa, Hippus, Scythopolis, Pella and Philadelphia. By the second century AD some of these cities were advertising their Greek origins by claiming Hellenistic kings as founders. Capitolias and Gerasa claimed Alexander the Great, while Abila avowed both Alexander and Seleucus (fig. 119). By intermittently using its old dynastic name Antiochia during the Roman period Gerasa also linked itself with the Seleucids. Other cities aligned themselves more fully with Roman rule. Though clearly very Hellenized and called by its native poet Meleager (second to first centuries BC) 'Attica in the land of the Assyrians', the city of Gadara, located on a high promontory overlooking the sea of Galilee and Yarmuk valley, adopted the name Pompeia. Canatha's early history is obscure, but the city is called Gabinia on its coins minted during the second and third centuries AD, presumably after Aulus Gabinius. Pella took the additional name Philippia, probably referring to Marcius Philippus as benefactor. Not all of these Decapolis cities maintained their independence from the kingdoms around them in the decades following the Roman annexation.

Gadara, Hippus and Canatha were given to Herod, and Philadelphia was possibly under Nabataean rule for part of the first century BC. Many of the cities were attached to the new province of Arabia in AD 106, but during the second and third centuries the civic coins of Abila, Dium, Gadara, Pella, Philadelphia and Scythopolis proclaim these cities to be 'of Coele Syria'. This may not be a reference to the Roman administrative province, but to a 'province' of the imperial cult (see chapter 9). Following the creation of the three provinces of Palestine in the late Roman period Philadelphia, Gerasa and Canatha remained in Arabia while the rest of the Decapolis cities were given to Palaestina Secunda.

Damascus had a chequered history in the late Hellenistic and early Roman periods. The city occupied level ground east of the Antilebanon range, in what would have been dry steppe, were it not for the Chrysoroas river (Barada), which flows from the mountains to form an oasis. Like its Phoenician neighbours to the west Damascus probably had a very large territory. The city was subject to the Nabataeans in the early first century BC, but later fell to Tigranes. Coins with Cleopatra's portrait were issued here and Damascus is therefore presumed to have been among those cities given to her by Antony. It may have returned temporarily to Nabataean rule in the first century AD (see above), but by the reign of Nero (54-68) it was back under Roman control. Coins of Hadrian indicate that it acquired the title *metropolis* in the first half of the second century, and that of *colonia* by the reign of Severus Alexander (222-35). In the fourth century it was the chief city of the province of Libanensis.

As client kingdoms gave way to direct Roman control, other cities were brought into the province. Commagene, annexed in AD 72, occupied a prime position on routes to Melitene, Anatolia, Syria and Mesopotamia, but it was evidently not heavily urbanized under its kings and remained that way under Roman rule. Inscriptions of the reign of Septimius Severus on a bridge over the River Chabinas (fig. 11) near the Commagenian royal sanctuary at Arsameia-on-the-Nymphaeus (Eski Kahta) mention 'four cities' of Commagene. The identity of the four is uncertain, but it presumably included the former royal city, Samosata (Samsat). Other possible contenders are Doliche (Dülük), Germanicia (Marash), and perhaps Perrhe (Pirin), or Antioch-on-the-Euphrates, also known as Urima (site uncertain, but north of Zeugma). Samosata was located on the Euphrates between the confluence of the Nymphaeus (Kahta river) and Singas (Göksu river). Its acropolis consisted of a large tell, on the western side of which stood the lower city, surrounded by a fortified wall. Excavations revealed a large residence on the tell, which may have been a palace, with gilded column capitals, frescoes, mosaics and sculpture. The plan of the city remains uncertain, and although a legionary base existed at or near the site, its location is unknown. Zeugma, 'the Bridge' (modern Belkis), was probably founded by Seleucus I, and occupied the site of an important Euphrates crossing. It originally consisted of two settlements, one on each bank, called Seleucia and Apamea (fig. 3), but only Seleucia seems to have survived as a city into the Roman period. Zeugma, as it became known, may have been detached from the kingdom of Commagene in the first century BC or at the time of the kingdom's annexation under Tiberius, and in the first century AD it is recorded as a legionary base. Rescue excavations at the end of the twentieth century (aimed at recording and salvaging before a third of the site was inundated by the Birecik Dam) revealed that the city prospered in the

Fig. 34.1. Coin of Zeugma of the reign of Philip I (AD 244-9), showing a temple on a tall hill. BMC 29.

34.2. The same hill dominates the site of Zeugma.

first two and a half centuries of our era, but never fully recovered from its sack by Shapur in the 250s.

The city of Emesa is thought to have been annexed to the empire in the second half of the first century, along with the kingdom of the same name. Its subsequent history is very uncertain. The city first issued coins during the reign of Antoninus Pius (AD 138-61), although virtually nothing else is known of the settlement at that date. Emesa was best known for its temple of the god Elagabal, which contemporaries marvelled at, but all trace of this has completely disappeared. It may never have been a large city during Roman rule. In the fourth century the Antiochene writer Libanius noted that it had declined, and was 'no longer a city',[16] although it continued to behave like one, sending ambassadors and crowns to emperors. In spite of his gloomy description Emesa quite clearly retained its city status, and it managed to gain metropolitan autonomy from its rival, the provincial *metropolis* Damascus, in the fifth century. The sixth-century *Life of St Simeon the Fool* gives us a vivid glimpse into contemporary life there.

In the Ituraean heartlands cities were few, perhaps reflecting a preference for a more diffused social structure of villages. Only the chief centres gained full civic status. Arca minted coins (a sign that it had become a *polis*) under Antoninus Pius (AD 138-61), presumably following the end of dynastic rule there. Its territory seems to have extended into the mountains of Lebanon above Orthosia and Tripolis. Abila was a city in the late Roman period but it is not known when it acquired this status. The only settlement in the Massyas (Bekaa) valley to achieve city status was Heliopolis; Chalcis did not. During the Roman period Heliopolis acquired several monumental public buildings, including a theatre and walls, and there can be no doubt that it was a respectable city as well as a cult centre. Yet in spite of the richness of its monumental remains, there are many things about Heliopolis that remain enigmatic, not least the question of when it acquired civic status. Strabo does not mention it, although he does state that a large part of the Massyas was given to Berytus when it became a colony. Before that Heliopolis is thought to have been a religious centre for the kingdom of Chalcis, and coins of the Ituraean ruler Lysanias call him high priest, perhaps indicating a hereditary role for the dynasts. For the next two centuries it was dependent on Berytus, as evidenced by the number of Latin inscriptions from the site (see chapter 7). The city first began issuing coins under Septimius Severus. These show that it was a colony, and that its name was *Colonia Julia*. This is peculiar, because cities normally adopted the family name of the emperor who granted them colonial status, and therefore, if Septimius Severus had been responsible, we would expect the city to have been *Colonia Septimia*. Of republican generals and emperors who had founded colonies before, the most likely candidate for a *Colonia Julia* is Augustus, the emperor who founded a colony at Berytus. Yet the jurist Ulpian, who came from Tyre, clearly states that Septimius Severus made Heliopolis a colony. But Ulpian says nothing about its elevation to civic status, and the coins remain the only certain date for its constitution as a city. Some of these coins have colonial designs on them, and among these are military standards inscribed with the numbers and names of two legions: *V Macedonica* and *VIII Gallica*, the legions whose veterans were settled by Augustus in Berytus. The most satisfactory solution to the matter is that Heliopolis was incorporated into the territory of Berytus at the end of the first century BC, and formed a *pagus*, a country district of Roman colonists, settled in the territory of Berytus rather than in the city itself (a *pagus Augustus* is known from inscriptions at Niha, on the western side of the Bekaa). Then at the end of the second century the town was detached from the territory of Berytus by Septimius Severus and constituted as an independent city with colonial status, but for some reason Heliopolis chose to refer to its original founder, Augustus, and not to adopt the name *Septimia*. The case of Heliopolis illustrates just how little we know about the progress of urbanism, even for some of the better-known sites.

The main centres of Herod's kingdom were Jerusalem, the administrative capital of Judaea, Sepphoris, the capital of Galilee, and Shechem, the capital of Samaria. Samaria refounded by Herod as Sebaste and named in honour of Augustus ('Sebastos' being the Greek equivalent of 'Augustus'), was a pagan city, colonized by non-Jewish veterans from the royal army. The site was (and still is) dominated by a great temple to Augustus. Herod's other principal foundation was Strato's Tower, refounded with the name Caesarea. To distinguish it from numerous other Caesareas in the Roman world it is commonly referred to as Caesarea Maritima. Anthedon (Blakhiyeh), a small town on the coast near Gaza, was refounded by Herod as Agrippias (after Augustus' lieutenant Agrippa), and Antipatris, named after his father Antipater, was founded at the site of Biblical Apheq on the edge of the coastal plain east of the modern city of Tel Aviv; but whether these two places remained cities for the whole period before the third century, when they issued coins, is unclear. Herod's sons also contributed to the urbanization of the regions which they ruled, Antipas through the foundation of Tiberias (named after Tiberius) on the western side of the Sea of Galilee, and Philip through Caesarea Philippi or Caesarea Panias (Banias) at the southern foot of Mount Hermon.

Exactly when Palmyra became a city is a matter that has yet to be resolved, as the extent and nature of the Hellenistic settlement is poorly known. There is also the problem of defining what is meant by the word 'city' in this context. Should it refer exclusively to a Greek-style settlement? By the beginning of the first century AD Palmyra could be described in Greek as a *polis*, and its tribes were electing officials who were termed 'treasurers', but it is only in the second half of the first century that the standard constitutional trappings of a Greek-style city can be more clearly observed. The process of its absorption into the Roman empire cannot be traced with confidence. Mark Antony's cavalry raid on the city in 41 BC suggests that it was still independent at that date. It is generally supposed that incorporation occurred between the reigns of Tiberius and Claudius. The territory controlled by Palmyra was vast: its boundaries to the west with Apamea and Emesa are known through inscribed boundary stones, but to the east and south its borders are hardly defined at all. On the Euphrates the boundary of Palmyra is likely to have been coterminous with the Roman empire, and there was a Palmyrene military presence as far south along the river as the island of Anatha.

The number of cities under direct rule increased in the first and second centuries. Raphanea (Rafniye), the headquarters of the *legio III Gallica* on the western side of the Orontes valley, issued coins under Elagabalus (AD 218-22)

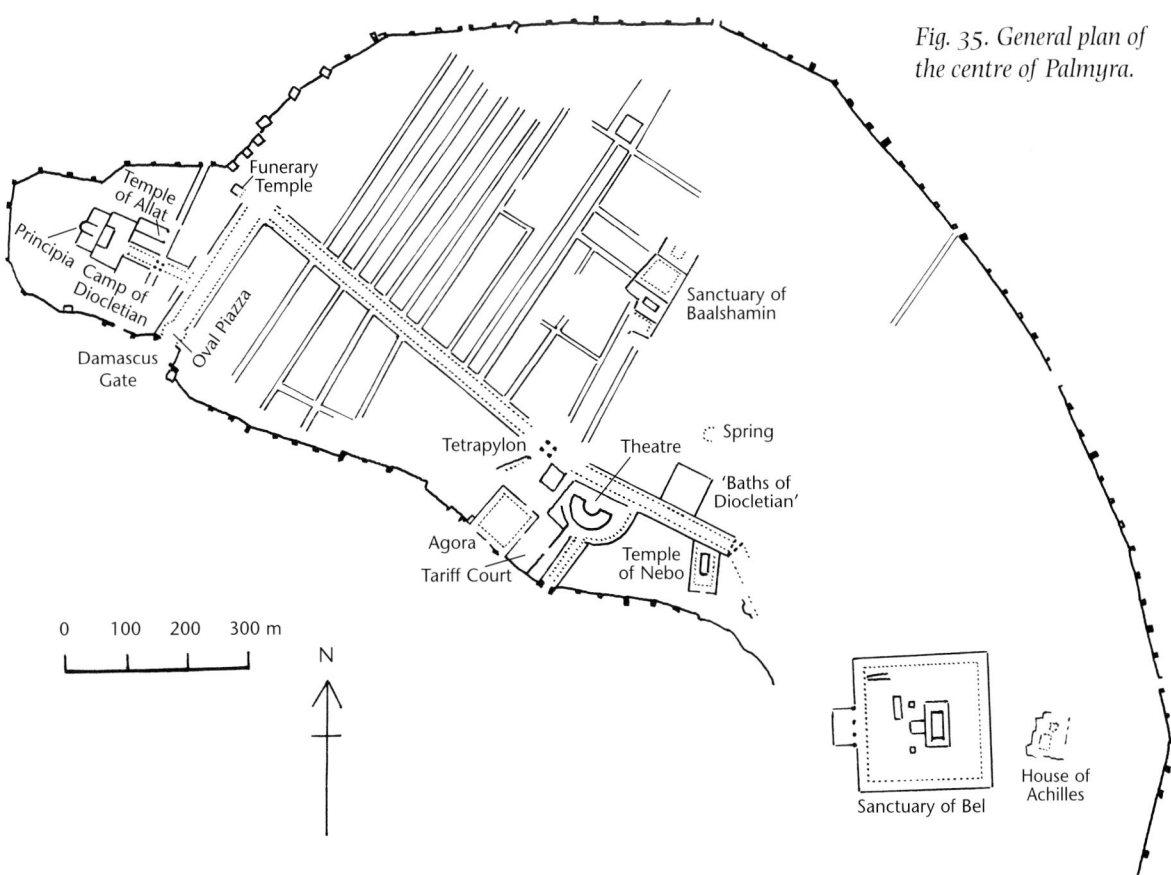

Fig. 35. General plan of the centre of Palmyra.

and had presumably grown from a fortress into a city, though very little is known about the site. Roman conquests in Mesopotamia and along the Euphrates during the later second century brought into the Roman empire cities that had formerly been under Parthian control, such as Dura Europus, and before long new cities were appearing in those regions as well. Among them was the village of Appadana, just north of Dura, which recently-discovered documents from the Euphrates region (see chapter 5) suggest became a city called Neapolis before the mid-third century.

The lava-lands of the south remained relatively underdeveloped during the first century AD. Neither the Ptolemies nor the Seleucids had attempted to found cities in the region, and for a long time the only city in the area was Canatha (modern Qanawat), on the western side of Auranitis (Jebel al-'Arab). The Herodian dynasts had settled colonists in the region when it was under their rule, but these settlements did not achieve full civic status, except for Caesarea Philippi in the south-west. Dionysias (Suweyda), a village near Canatha, became a city in the Antonine period. In the third century the emperor Philip (AD 244-9) founded Philippopolis (Shahba) on the north-western edge of Auranitis on a site presumed to be his birthplace; more will be said about this important site later (see chapter 7).

The founding or refounding of cities continued in the south after the dissolution of the kingdoms there. Sepphoris is encountered as Neronias Irenopolis under Nero (AD 54-68), but thereafter the city reverted to its original name. Vespasian, who had been governor of Judaea during the first Jewish War, created a new city called Neapolis (modern Nablus) at a village close to Samaritan Shechem, and this emperor or one of his sons refounded the coastal settlement of Joppa (Jaffa). Herod's Caesarea gained colonial status from Vespasian, although in this case no veterans were settled there and the indigenous inhabitants received Roman citizenship. Jerusalem, which had been sacked under Vespasian, was refounded by Hadrian as *colonia* Aelia Capitolina and peopled with non-Jewish colonists. Hadrian is also thought to have been responsible for renaming Sepphoris Diocaesarea, for this latter pagan name appears on its coins issued under Hadrian's successor Antoninus Pius (Sepphoris issued no coins under Hadrian). Sepphoris and Tiberias had been strongly Jewish settlements since Herodian times, and if the renaming of Sepphoris was an attempt to reduce Jewish influence in Galilee, there is no evidence that it did so. Galilee became the focus of Judaism after the destruction of the Temple at Jerusalem, and by the fourth century Diocaesarea and Tiberias were important Jewish centres. The Severan period saw foundations on the western fringes of Judaea: Severus established the cities of Diospolis (at the site of Biblical Lod) and Eleutheropolis (Bet Guvrin), and Nicopolis was founded under Elagabalus on the site of Emmaus.

Bostra (Bosra) and Petra were the two most important centres of the Nabataean kingdom and remained pre-eminent after the Roman annexation. Bostra became the chief city of the province of Arabia, and was the headquarters of Arabia's only legion, the *III Cyrenaica*. The emperor Philip is thought to have been one of its patrons; coins issued during his reign indicate that the city had become a *metropolis*, and its principal Greek festival, the *Actia Dousaria*, appears to date from this time. Smaller settlements were also granted civic status following the Roman annexation. These included Adraa (modern Deraa, the Biblical Edrei), on the Yarmuk river west of Bostra, and a group of settle-

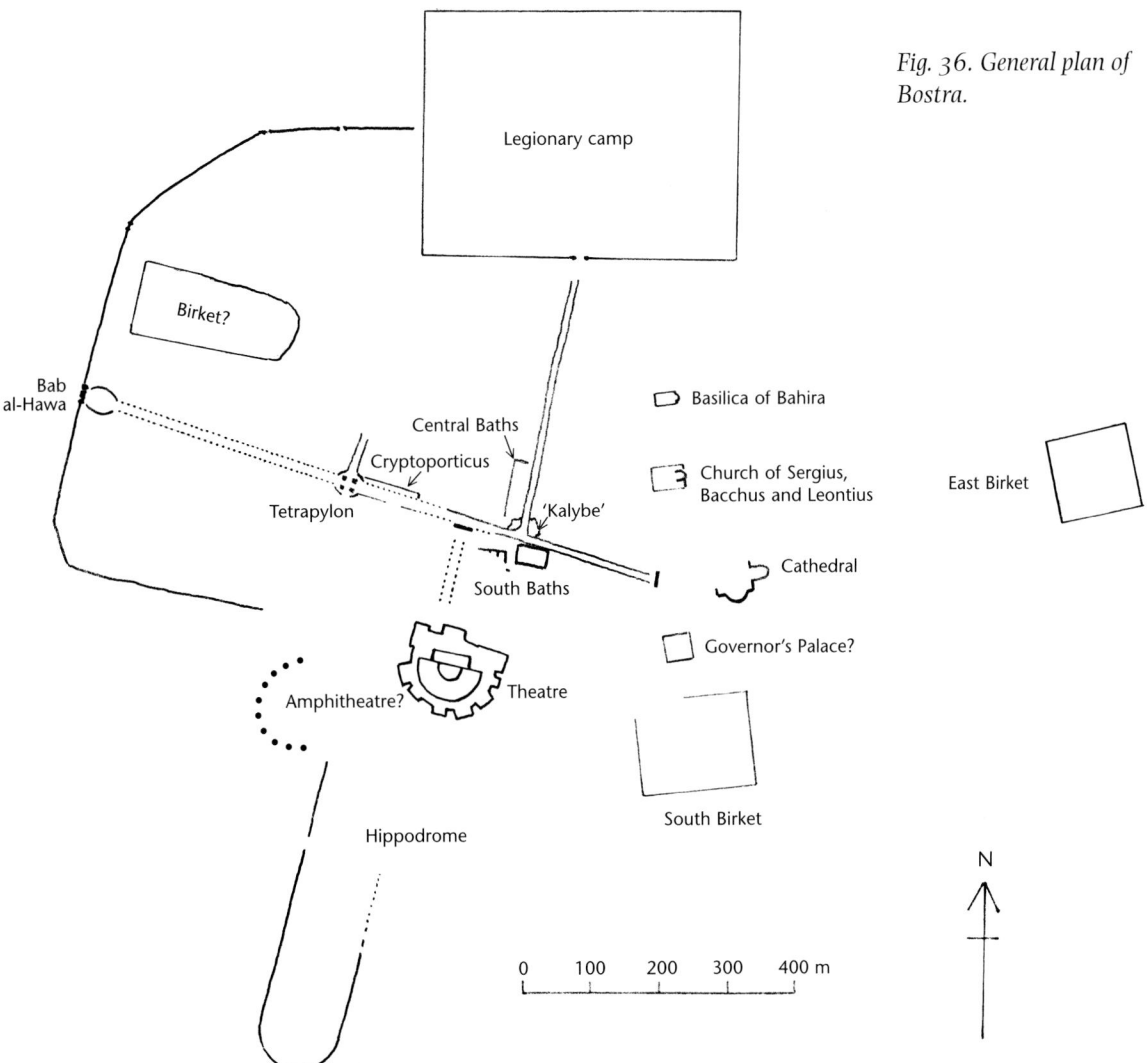

Fig. 36. General plan of Bostra.

ments located on the eastern side of the Dead Sea, along the main Roman north-south artery, the *via nova Traiana*: Esbus (Heshban, the Biblical Heshbon), Medaba (Madaba), Rabbath Moba or Areopolis (Rabbah), and Charach Moba (Kerak).

The process of urbanization, or at least of elevation of settlements to city status and the division of the landscape into city territories, continued in the late Roman period. Before the middle of the third century AD coins are a good indicator (and sometimes the only indicator) that a place had civic status. With the extinction of civic coinage in the mid-third century (see chapter 6) examination of the process becomes more difficult. Lists of cities survive, often made for official purposes such as church councils, but these do not always agree with one another, and sometimes it is not clear whether every place listed really did have city status. Inscriptions and papyri provide proof, but they depend very heavily on chance finds. Little is known of what becoming a city in Syria and the Near East during the last three centuries of Roman rule entailed. It would seem that many of those places which gained civic status were relatively small places, villages and fortresses, and that the grant was not accompanied by any substantial rebuilding (with the exception, perhaps, of fortifications). Some of them may have served military purposes, or acted as refuges for rural populations during times of trouble. The problem of distinguishing between cities and other sorts of settlement is one to which we will return in chapter 5. Some of the villages elevated to city status already had monumental buildings, and they do not appear to have acquired any of the structures typical of the older cities, such as colonnaded streets or theatres (although some, such as Sergiopolis, gained substantial fortifications, if they did not already possess them). Otherwise change in status seems to have been the most significant transformation for these new cities.

The fragmentary nature of our record means that we cannot be certain that the first known mention of a place as a city is any indication of the date of its elevation, and therefore some cities thought to be late Roman may have acquired city status in earlier times. The use of imperial names is highly suggestive, unless the cities in question were refoundations of existing cities. Diocletian must have been responsible for approving two cities named Maximianopolis after his imperial colleague. One was located on the northern edge of Auranitis at the former village of the Sakkaioi (modern Shaqqa), and the other in Palestine at Caparcotna or Legio, the headquarters of the *legio VI Ferrata*. Constantine founded Constantia (Buraq) in the lava-lands on the northern edge of Trachonitis. It is difficult to see any overall plan in the pattern of foundations, which look more like random imperial responses to local petitions. Those in regions contested by the Sasanians, however, are likely to have had strategic value to the state. On the Euphrates the fortress of Neocaesarea (Dibsi Faraj) became a city, probably in the fourth century. Its neighbour Sergiopolis (Resafa), a famous centre of pilgrimage on account of its patron saint Sergius, gained civic status in the fifth. In this case the renown and sanctity of the site must have been an important consideration. It is harder to discern why in the sixth century several small settlements inland acquired city status, such as Salaminias (Salemiya), east of Apamea, or Anasartha (Khanazir), renamed Theodoropolis by Justinian. Some of these little cities in the steppe were perhaps located in territories which had formerly been dependent on Palmyra and, after that city's fall in the third century, they had gained a greater degree of independence. An increase in the settled population of this steppe zone during the late Roman period was probably also a factor (see chapter 5). Religious concerns may also have influenced grants. Constantine made Antaradus a city; and by this time Aradus itself was in serious decline. He is supposed to have done so because the inhabitants of Antaradus had adopted Christianity while those on the island remained resolutely pagan, and was therefore responding to competition between two rival sections of the same settlement, but he may also have been prompted by the relative size and importance of the mainland settlement by this period.

Other late Roman elevations were perhaps the result of competition between villages, which again reflected a system of favoured winners and losers. In the lava-lands Neapolis (Sheikh Miskin) had become a city by the fourth century, and in late Roman civil and ecclesiastical lists we find Phaena (Mismiye) and Neve (Nawa) treated as cities as well. Together with Maximianopolis and Constantia they formed a group of civic foundations all located in the northern part of the Hauran region, and most probably had relatively small territories. There is no evidence that any were conceived as foundations on the same scale as neighbouring Philippopolis, created in the third century.

In the provinces of Palestine there were also new cities. Some, like Jamnia and Apollonia (renamed Sozusa), were among those given city status by Pompey but which had subsequently lost it; others, such as Ono, near Diospolis, or Helenopolis (named after Constantine's mother Helena) in Galilee, were new. Some ports gained independent status from their cities: that of Ascalon became Diocletianopolis, and Constantine separated the port of Gaza from the city, giving it the name Constantia. Azotus, another of Pompey's cities which had declined and later recovered, was apparently divided into two cities, with one being designated Azotus 'by the Sea'. In the south of Palestine the town of Elusa (Halutza) had by the late Roman period acquired city status, as perhaps had nearby Mampsis (identified with the site of Kurnub). Again, most were unlikely to have acquired very extensive territories with their grants.

Thus the number of political entities modelled on the Greek *polis* increased significantly under Roman rule. But many of the later foundations must have been little more than 'glorified villages'.[17] It is unlikely that they possessed very large agricultural hinterlands, and therefore they cannot have been expected to grow to a large size. The later phases of the urbanizing process were perhaps more quantitative than qualitative. The old cities which existed at the beginning of Roman rule had been given huge territories, and the 'urbanization' which followed consisted of assigning large territories to the new foundations in the more remote areas or, where this was not possible, elevating villages to civic status with little change to the size of their hinterlands.

4 TIME AND MOTION

THE MEASURE OF TIME

Marking the Years

By introducing their own era, beginning in 312 BC, the Seleucids had imposed a new reckoning of time on the regions that they ruled. The Seleucid era has been seen as one of the tools used by the Seleucids to create a sense of identity for their empire, and as a system of reckoning it was remarkably successful. Its official character is suggested by a Jewish name for it, the 'era of contracts'. When Antiochus III wrested Phoenicia and the south from the Ptolemies at the beginning of the second century BC, the cities there also adopted the Seleucid era, although one vestige of Ptolemaic rule remained: these cities tended to use a Ptolemaic symbol, shaped like the Latin letter 'L', to designate the word 'year'. However, complete standardization had not been achieved under the Seleucids. Different regions of their empire employed different methods for reckoning the calendar, with the result that new year's day fell at different times of the year in different places. Nonetheless, by the early Roman period the beginning of the Seleucid year in Syria had been fixed, falling on 1 October. In the fifth century it was shifted to 1 September to coincide with the tax year (see below), although rather confusingly Syriac and Arab writers seem to have continued reckoning from 1 October. The Seleucid era persisted into medieval times; some treaties signed between Muslims and Crusaders used it, and its religious inertness perhaps made it agreeable to both sides. Of the various attempts by ancient and modern regimes to introduce a universal era, the Seleucid was one of the more successful.

Initially all cities ruled by the Seleucids were supposed to use the era, but with the decline of Seleucid power many cities asserted their independence by declaring individual eras of 'autonomy'. These civic eras might be revised from time to time, beginning with a new year one, and all the villages and towns in the territory of the city tended to use the era of their city (see chapter 7). The Romans made no attempt to impose any new universal system on the province of Syria, although dating by the regnal year of an emperor was common practice, and the Roman method of dating by consuls was used for government documents (and sometimes private ones). A system of reckoning from the foundation of Rome was not in general use because the age of the city was disputed (the most favoured dates were 753 or 752 BC). Consequently the cities and other states were free to employ their own civic eras or continue with the Seleucid system. Following the Roman annexation a number of Syrian cities adopted what are often referred to as 'Pompeian' eras, but these were all individual civic eras, not a universal Roman one. One city (perhaps Gadara) initially called hers 'year one of Rome' (fig. 37), but it remained an era of the Gadarenes (or of some other city), not of Syria. Honours granted to the individual cities by republican generals, governors and emperors provided the impetus to initiate new civic eras. At Antioch, for example, Pompey's visit led to the city abandoning the Seleucid era in favour of a new system. A few years later Julius Caesar's visit and honours encouraged the citizens to adopt a 'Julian' era, which remained the city's principal dating system in the Roman period. But during the Parthian occupation of the city in 41/40 BC the Antiochenes briefly reverted to the Seleucid system (an anti-Roman comment?). After the battle of Actium (31 BC) some cities experimented with the victory of Augustus as a new year one, but during the first century AD they abandoned this 'Actian' era. Only in Arabia was a provincial era initiated, beginning with the creation of the province in AD 106. Such provincial eras were quite rare in the Roman world, and there is no evidence that one existed for the provinces of Syria or Palestine. The Arabian era would suggest that Rome wanted to create a significant break with the Nabataean tradition that had preceded it, and it perhaps contributed towards a post-Nabataean identity for the new province. Indeed, so successful was the Arabian era that it survived the province, not only in those parts of the province of Arabia that were later incorporated into the provinces of Palaestina, but also after the Muslim conquest (see below).

Fig. 37. Anonymous bronze coin minted in 64-63 BC, attributed (with reservations) to Gadara. The obverse bears a bust of Heracles; the reverse, the ram of a galley. The Greek inscription above reads LA ΡΩΜΗΣ, *'Year one of Rome'.*

The city eras persisted into late Roman times, suggesting that the sense of civic identity which they helped to generate remained strong. That of Sidon is known in the fourth century and probably continued later, and Tyre's is attested in the late sixth. The eras of Berytus and Gerasa are found still in use in the early seventh century. Use of the era of Aradus may have declined with the city: there is epigraphic evidence to suggest that the city of Mariamme, which had once been in the territory of Aradus and had continued to use its era thereafter, had adopted the Seleucid era by the sixth century. Some systems continued even later – the provincial era of Arabia, for example, is found still operating under the Umayyads, as are the eras of Gadara and Gaza. But, as usual, our evidence depends entirely on accidents of survival.

The late Roman period witnessed the development of new, more universal methods of dating. A cycle of indictions, based on the system of censuses (see chapter 6), became a common way of keeping time over short periods. From the reign of Constantine, each tax cycle lasted fifteen years. Within each cycle the individual indiction years were counted from one to fifteen, beginning with the new tax year in September, when the Praetorian Prefects announced their budgets. After that there was a new census, and a new cycle, beginning again with indiction year one. The system was useless for dating outside the fifteen-year cycle, because the cycles themselves were not numbered. Reference to some other system of dating was needed; otherwise 'indiction ten' was indistinguishable from all the other indiction tens that had occurred every fifteen years before it. It was common practice to use a local era alongside references to an indiction. Thus a mosaic from the floor of a church at 'Ain as-Samakeh south of Berytus is conveniently dated year 661 (the civic era of Berytus), indiction fifteen (the last year of the tax cycle). In this case the mosaic can be dated very closely: year 661 of Berytus ran from 1 October AD 580 to 30 September 581, and indiction fifteen ran from 1 September 581 to 31 August 582, meaning that the mosaic can have been laid only in September 581. But references to other dating systems are sometimes lacking, meaning that without corroborative evidence an exact date cannot be obtained.

The indiction system became popular because it was no doubt easier to remember than the cumbersome Roman system of dating by consuls. It was more meaningful to the individual too: everyone's affairs could be related to tax payments. In the sixth century its popularity was further ensured by Justinian, who abandoned the consular dating system and insisted that all official documents be dated by the indiction instead. People became so accustomed to using it that the indiction system continued in the region after the Muslim conquest (various late seventh-century papyri from Nessana in the Negev use it, sometimes in conjunction with the Muslim Hijra years, and an Umayyad period mosaic at Umm er-Rasas is dated to AD 718, during the second indiction). An imperial dating system had transcended the empire.

The late Roman period also saw a greater interest in universal eras. Christian teaching provided a moment of creation and a universal history for humanity. There were various attempts to generate a framework, by relating past events to a Christian scheme. The key points were the Creation, Incarnation, Nativity and Passion, but there was only a vague general agreement between experts over the precise dates of these events. (A sixth-century scholar at Rome, Dionysius Exiguus, was responsible for the system of BC and AD which is used today, by calculating that the Nativity occurred 753 years after the founding of Rome.) But while these schemes might be used by historians, they were not generally employed in everyday contexts, at least not during the time period covered by this book.

Marking the Months

The Seleucids had adopted the Babylonian lunisolar calendar, merely substituting Macedonian month names for their Babylonian equivalents. The months followed phases of the moon, with extra months added at fixed intervals over a period of nineteen years in order to realign the lunar year with the solar one. However, it is not known whether all the cities ruled by the Seleucids adopted this calendar. What is certain is that by the first century BC many Syrian cities were using calendars that operated independent of any general Seleucid system, so that each of these cities tended to have its own method of reckoning months and the cycles of festivals and religious observances. Calendars could be based on either lunar or solar months, with extra days or months inserted at the end of a cycle to adjust the calendrical year to the solar year. Thanks to the influence of the Ptolemies and Seleucids, the Macedonian month names were popular among the cities, but they were by no means universal.

Some of these Syrian civic calendars are preserved in medieval copies of ancient *hemerologia*, tables listing days of the months according to a variety of different reckonings. Where they can be tested against surviving dated inscriptions, they seem to be correct and suggest that these calendars could have existed as early as the first century AD. What they demonstrate is that the Julian reform of the calendar, initiated by Julius Caesar in 45 BC and continued by Augustus, had a strong influence over these local systems, even if it did not fully replace them. If the Julian calendar was in use in Syria during the first century AD, it was perhaps introduced under Augustus. The birthday of Augustus (23 September) was the date which some communities used to mark the beginning of their year. It is possible that 23 September was the new year for observances of the imperial cult (which was certainly introduced to Syria by Augustus – see chapter 9), and thus this date remained significant in the east long after Augustus. Some scholars have suggested that 23 September was also the beginning of the fiscal year, and that this was later 'rationalized' by shifting it to 1 September, which became the beginning of the indiction year as well as the late Roman and Byzantine new year's day. It is in the organization of the year, rather than in the marking of years, that the impact of Rome can be most fully appreciated.

Although Roman month names were not in general use until the sixth century, some cycles were evidently coterminous with Julian months, such as those at Antioch, Seleucia and Sidon (fig. 38). Other calendars had months which did not correspond to Julian ones, but in general they seem to have followed a 365-day Julian system. Tyre and Heliopolis did so by having seven months of thirty days and five of thirty-one days; Gaza, Ascalon and Arabia followed the Alexandrian system of twelve months of thirty days plus five 'epagomenal' days. The key point here is that Roman rule had brought about a revolution in the reckoning of time, even in those places where communities maintained traditional names for the months and even when the beginning of the year was different. Antioch's calendar began on 1 October (until the second half of the fifth century, when it was changed to 1 September to coincide with the indiction year), Tyre's new year was on 19 October, and Gaza and Ascalon followed Alexandria by beginning on 29 August. Sidon may have followed the Julian calendar by celebrating its new year on 1 January.

Many cities called their months by Macedonian names, but this did not mean that the calendar employed was the same in every city. At Antioch the Macedonian month of Panemos corresponded to July. At Sidon Panemos corresponded to September, and Artemisios fell in July. At Gaza Panemos lasted for thirty days, beginning on 25 June, and at Ascalon Panemos was the same length but began on 25 July. The potential confusion arising from these individual arrangements is staggering, the equivalent of having March in London corresponding to May in Manchester, but the idea of imposing a universal time on the cities does not seem to have been attempted, even where the calendars followed the Julian years. As in many other respects, when it came to managing their internal affairs the autonomy of the cities was respected.

Fig. 38. Names of the months at Antioch, Seleucia and Sidon, and their correspondence to the Julian calendar.

JULIAN	ANTIOCHENE	SELEUCIAN	SIDONIAN
JANUARY	Audynaios	Aphy (Audynaios?)	Dios
FEBRUARY	Peritios	(...)	Apellaios
MARCH	Dystros	Itoinios	Audynaios
APRIL	Xanthikos	Anthisterios	Peritios
MAY	Artemisios	Artemisios	Dystros
JUNE	Daisios	Herakleios	Xanthikos
JULY	Panemos	Nenealios	Artemisios
AUGUST	Loos	Hadoni(o)s (Adonis?)	Daisios
SEPTEMBER	Gorpaios	Apilios (Apellaios?)	Panemos
OCTOBER	Hyperberetaios	Koronios	Loos
NOVEMBER	Dios	Pantheios	Gorpaios
DECEMBER	Apellaios	Sandis (Xanthikos?)	Hyperberetaios

However, not all cities used the Macedonian month names, as can be seen from the practices at Seleucia and Heliopolis. The Seleucian month names were Greek in origin (although some forms given in the *hemerologia* seem corrupt), but Heliopolis used Semitic names (fig. 39). This does not rule out the use of Greek or Macedonian month names alongside the Semitic ones at Heliopolis, especially since the calendar employed a system of months similar to that found at Tyre, where Macedonian names were used. The epigraphic evidence from Palmyra shows Macedonian months (written in Greek) corresponding to local ones (written in Aramaic). There the local names were based on the Babylonian calendar, and are similar to those used at Heliopolis, but the exact form of the calendar used is more uncertain. The Jews are known to have maintained a calendar based on the Babylonian one, and Josephus provides a concordance between its Semitic names and the Macedonian months. As we have seen, Arabia had its own provincial calendar 'of the Arabs'. Its year began on the spring equinox (22 March). The Macedonian names for the months were used, but Nabataean inscriptions show that these had their Nabataean equivalents. Clearly the calendars could be bilingual, even if in most cases the framework on which the months rested had a single structure, that of the Julian 365-day solar year.

HELIOPOLITAN	PALMYRENE	JEWISH
Ag	Tishri	Tishri
Thisrin	Kanun	Marcheswan
Gelon	Kislul	Kislev
Chanoun	Tebet	Tebet
Sobath	Shebat	Shebet
Adar	Adar	Adar
Neisan	Nisan	Nisan
Iar	Iyar	Ijar
Ezer	Siwan	Siwan
Thamiza	Quenian	Tammuz
Ab	Ab	Ab
Iloul	Elul	Elul

Fig. 39. The Heliopolitan, Palmyrene and Jewish months. It is not known when the Heliopolitan new year began; the names are listed here as they appear in the Hemerologion Florentinum. *The* Hemerologion *has the Heliopolitan month of Ab beginning on 23 September (Augustus' birthday). This makes a plausible new year. The first month of the Palmyrene year appears to have been Tishri, which inscriptions correlate with the Macedonian month Hyperberetaios. The Jewish calendar is that given by Josephus. According to him Tishri corresponded with Hyperberetaios, which he equates with September.*

In Syria and the Near East the reckoning of time shows a mix of Semitic, Greek, Macedonian and Roman elements. While the Julian system of a 365-day year seems to have affected most of the local calendars, one cannot rule out the possibility that lunisolar calendars, with intercalary months added to the year at certain intervals, remained in use in some places. The Jews certainly employed such a system. The use of Semitic calendars at Heliopolis and Palmyra does not appear to have been entirely independent of Greek or Roman influences, but presumably the retention of Semitic names represents a conscious choice, marking them as different from those using purely Macedonian ones.

From the fourth century the Antiochene civic calendar became the official calendar of the Antiochene patriarchate. This gave it greater authority than other civic calendars; once again, the chief city of Syria asserted its pre-eminence in the pecking-order of cities. Its new year coincided with the official Seleucid one (1 October), so that it too could be seen as a calendar 'of the Greeks'.

As for the Julian calendar itself, with its elaborate system of kalends, nones and ides, this was employed by the military and for official government documents, but never ousted the local systems (which simply numbered the days of each month). In the fourth century the Julian calendar is found in a simplified form, with days counted from the first of the month, as is the practice today. This 'Byzantine' form was based on the Julian, except that it began with the new fiscal year on 1 September. Following the loss of Syria and Egypt in the seventh century, this system became the standard calendar in the remaining portions of the Roman empire.

REDUCING DISTANCE: TRANSPORT AND COMMUNICATIONS

In order to govern such a vast empire Rome needed a reliable communications network. The construction of roads, ports and canals by the Roman army is a guide to the development of the military structure in Syria and the Near East, and an indicator of the advance of Roman imperial power. The government's purpose in building the roads is thought to have been primarily strategic, allowing for speedy communications and movement of troops. In the desert they connected forts, water sources and other strategically important features. But these features also made civilian travel relatively easy and unexceptional in the Roman world, for both wealthy and poorer persons, and in doing so they shrank the distances between different locations. Bandits and robbers were a problem (see chapter 10), but they did not prevent regular movement of people, goods and ideas by land or water.

Roman roads possessed an ideological quality, in that they were highly visible reminders of empire, even in remote places. Bridges, causeways and cuttings overcame obstacles of nature, symbolizing Rome's technological mastery of the environment. Milestones, supposedly planted to serve the useful function of recording distance, were most commonly employed to advertise the names and titles of emperors under whom construction or repair of the road was undertaken. In this sense the milestones had a propaganda value for those using the roads (even if travellers could not make sense of their terse Latin abbreviations, they were an unmistakable assertion of imperial power), and for travellers the encounters with soldiers and public servants along the way will have served as a reminder of Rome's presence.

Three principal types of road were constructed in the region. The most elaborate form was that found in cities and towns, or in difficult passages such as marshy or rocky terrain (fig. 41). In these cases the surfaces were paved with large stone slabs. In the late Roman period there was a preference in some cities for a surface of rectangular cobbles, laid in rows diagonal to the kerbs, and sometimes set directly over the earlier paving. Drains, often placed centrally, were usually substantial, to cope with the torrential rains of winter. Most roads between cities were either paved with gravel, or had dirt surfaces. Gravel-paved roads were generally between 4 and 7 metres wide (13 and 23 feet) and were not dissimilar in construction to Roman roads in Italy. Their upper surfaces consisted of a layer of clayey soil mixed with gravel, which lay over a layer of

small, densely-packed stones about 20 centimetres (8 inches) thick. Sometimes a bed of flat stones formed the foundation. Along both edges of this structure ran a retaining line of stones, and a third line ran along the centre of the road. Repairs were frequently necessary; if the surfaces broke up and exposed the stone bedding, the road could become almost unusable. Milestone inscriptions indicate that the second-century road across the lava-flows of Trachonitis was repaired twice in three decades. The third and simplest form of road had only a dirt surface. Dirt tracks were especially common in the steppe or desert, and included some major highways such as the so-called 'Strata Diocletiana' (see chapter 10). This road had forts, waystations and milestones along its length, but no specially prepared surface. Stones were cleared to the sides of the track to form low retaining walls. Because of their simple construction, such roads are often not very visible nowadays at ground level, but can be seen easily from the air.

To deal with other problems of terrain, the Romans constructed bridges, cut through rocky spurs, or raised causeways (fig. 11; fig. 40). A causeway in the marshy Plain of Antioch was raised 2 metres (6½ feet) above the surrounding plain, and was over 6 metres (20 feet) wide with retaining walls pierced by drainage arches. The builders of the Trachonitis road maintained a fairly level surface across the uneven lava-flows by levelling or raising causeways as topography required.

The elaborate road system created by the Romans in Syria and the Near East cannot be described in detail here. The main routes included the road along the coast, running from Antioch in the north to Raphia in the south and thence to Pelusium in Egypt, and which connected the major ports. Another route ran

Fig. 40. Roman bridge over the Sabun Suyu, a tributary of the 'Afrin, at Cyrrhus.

through the Orontes valley to Emesa and from there branched to Heliopolis and Damascus, finally reaching Bostra. Other important roads connected the coast with the Euphrates via Antioch, to Samosata, Zeugma or Hierapolis, and led across the steppe from Emesa or Damascus via Palmyra. The principal ones were those of the official network for the *cursus publicus*, the imperial postal system, but there were plenty of minor roads and tracks used primarily by locals. The development of this system is important in that it tells us a great deal about the evolution of the provinces in terms of their military organization, and the growth in overland communications. The slow but steady advance of Rome into the Syrian steppe and the remoter reaches of the hinterland during the second and third centuries can be detected through the construction of roads and defensive structures in these regions.

However, observing these developments is a difficult task. In general roads are not easily dated unless accompanied by inscriptions on milestones (which seem to have been confined to the official network), and the date of even some of the more famous and conspicuous stretches of Roman road still surviving in Syria can be a subject for debate (fig. 41). Those in the desert are easier to trace than those in areas which are still densely populated, where all vestiges have often disappeared, and the bias is therefore in favour of roads in remote places. Nevertheless a tolerably good plan of the overall network can be reconstructed. What is more problematic is to determine when different stretches were built, and what motives prompted their construction. Both questions are crucial to any deeper understanding of the Roman road network, yet often the answers to them rely on the slenderest support. A milestone from Arak in the steppe east of Palmyra shows that a road was being constructed there under Vespasian, which is the pivotal evidence on which turns the notion that this was when the entire stretch of road from Palmyra to Sura on the Euphrates was built, as part of a Roman strategy to extend control further south along the right bank of the Euphrates river. In other cases milestones record repairs but give us no indication of the date of the original construction. The fashion for erecting milestones alongside the roads in the name of an emperor did not follow any strict logic. Some roads were lined with many milestones, and others appear to have had none at all. Sometimes there are clusters of milestones in the same place, as if the first had started a trend and during later repair works the builders had felt the need to compete by erecting their own commemorative monument. In certain places the milestones or their inscriptions may have been made of a material which has not survived. For example, certain roads across the Negev have stone markers, but these are completely blank. Once thought to be 'anepigraphic' Nabataean imitations of Roman stones, it now seems clear that they are Roman and originally bore painted inscriptions.

The history of Roman road building in Syria and the Near East therefore relies very heavily on milestone epigraphy. There are many roads which must belong to the period of Roman rule, but which by themselves cannot be dated. It would appear that the main period of construction occurred in the second and third centuries, after which much of the activity revolved around maintenance. The evidence peaks in certain reigns, particularly those of Trajan (AD 98-117), Marcus Aurelius and Lucius Verus (AD 161-9), Septimius Severus and Caracalla (AD 193-217), and Diocletian (AD 284-305), which would seem to indicate a correlation between road building and major campaigns (these rulers all conducted wars against the Parthians and Sasanians). But during the fourth century the practice of erecting inscribed stones along roads died out, and we know comparatively little about road building or road maintenance after this. The carefully constructed paved surfaces of some undated roads are thought to be more suitable for pack animals than wheeled vehicles. There is some evidence to suggest that the former were a much commoner form of transport than the latter in late Roman times, and this preference was perhaps dictated by a deteriorating road network. In the seventh century a western pilgrim expressed surprised at the absence of carts in the Near East, which may indicate that the old gravel-paved roads which formerly supported such traffic had fallen into disrepair.

The fate of many roads after, or even during the late Roman period is unclear. Some roads, such as the Damascus – Bostra route through Trachonitis which bypasses completely the important settlement of Dionysias (Suweyda), can only have served Roman military interests and after the end of Roman rule fell into disuse. The stone bedding was frequently removed from other stretches of metalled roads which were still in use, not so much for building material but because if the roads were in a state of bad repair their rough stony surfaces were more harmful to animals' feet than a dirt track. A badly maintained gravel-paved road was worse than no road at all.

Augustus had established the imperial post system, the *cursus publicus*. The Achaemenid Persians and Hellenistic kings had also created such communication networks, but the system of paved roads accompanying the *cursus publicus* is a uniquely Roman feature. Apart from the roads themselves, the system had

Fig. 41. Roman road, of uncertain date, crossing a saddle between the Jebel Barisha and Jebel Halaqa between Antioch and Beroea. Stone-paved roads provided a solid, durable surface over rough terrain, and could prove more long lasting than their gravel-paved counterparts.

waystations where those on official government business could obtain food, lodging and, if necessary, fresh horses and carriages. Such inns and hostels were maintained at the expense of local communities. Officials with an imperial permit were housed for free, but private individuals had to pay for services. From the third century the system was also designed to help supply provisions to the army: taxes collected in kind could be delivered to specified depots within the system. The arrangement sounds efficient, but was not particularly so (see chapter 6). The system did, however, make journeys for both officials and ordinary people far less arduous and dangerous than they might otherwise have been. Inns in remote places provided safety from bandits and could sometimes supply welcome meals for hungry travellers, although officials on business would expect priority treatment. Maps like the Peutinger Table (fig. 42), which were probably based on information taken from military maps and itineraries, provided travellers with information about the distances covered and places ahead. The ability to *plan* a journey greatly reduced the contingencies of travel, even if perennial hazards like banditry remained.

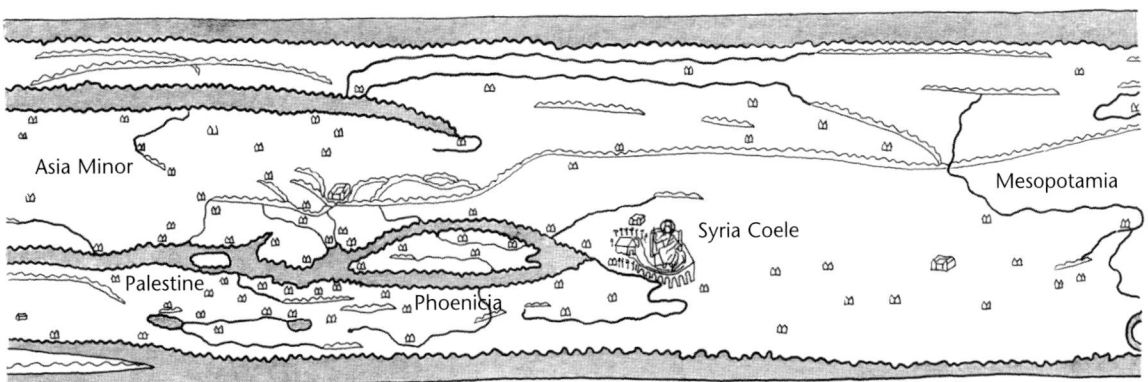

Fig. 42. Drawing of the Syrian section of the Peutinger Table, simplified to omit roads and place names but showing icons for cities and road stations. The map survives in a single medieval copy of an original believed to date to the fourth century, but based on earlier maps, perhaps of the second century. It was probably designed for civilian rather than military use, since no emphasis is given to forts. The personification of Antioch, supplied with water via aqueducts arising in the famous grove of Daphne, dominates this eastern section of the map.

We have very little information about the speed of travel by land, and it is difficult to generalize from the fragments available to us. Much will have depended on the physical condition of the people travelling, the state of the roads, the weather, the time of year and hours of daylight, and the urgency of the journey. Accounts of more recent centuries, by travellers journeying under similar conditions, help to give us some idea of the time required. In the late nineteenth century Aleppo was about three days' travelling from the Mediterranean coast. A similar pace can be observed in a papyrus archive from Egypt of an official called Theophanes, whose itinerary from Egypt to Antioch during the civil war between Constantine and Licinius (*c.* 317-23) has survived. Theophanes did not travel light. He took with him an assortment of clothes, cooking and dining utensils, materials for washing, plus mattresses and other gear for sleeping. All of this, as well as provisions purchased during the journey, were no doubt carried by the large number of servants who accompanied him, and by animals requisitioned from the *cursus publicus*. His daily accounts show that the trip along the entire coast of the Near East, from Pelusium in Egypt to Antioch, lasted eighteen days (fig. 43). The journey back took the same time. The pace must have been fairly brisk, although lengthened by breaks or business in some of the cities *en route*. His journey also demonstrates that the major coastal cities were conveniently located about a day's journey from each other. No doubt they provided the best facilities for travellers. There were probably many people making regular long-distance journeys of this sort, travelling between the main centres of the Near Eastern provinces and beyond.

Wheeled transport need not have been faster than journeying on foot. The travellers described in the second-century Pseudo-Clementina *Homily* XIII.1.1 went by carriage from Antaradus to Laodicea. In one day they covered the distance between Balanea and Gabala, and by the second day had reached Laodicea. They took two days to cover the distance travelled by Theophanes in a single day, but perhaps haste was not one of their foremost concerns. Travel by sea might be considerably faster, weather permitting; the Acts (27.1-3) has St Paul travelling in a ship from Caesarea to Sidon on an overnight voyage. The same journey by land took Theophanes three days.

Sea traffic increased dramatically during the Roman period, as attested by the large number of shipwrecks all around the Mediterranean. Most Syrian ports predated Roman rule, but the increasing quantities of imports and exports demanded an infrastructure capable of accommodating the ships involved in this trade, and not all of the old ports were suitable. Many parts of the Syrian coast lack natural harbours, and artificial ones had long served some coastal cities. The sites were not always well chosen, and construction of a harbour could initiate an intermittent war with the forces of nature in order to keep the port serviceable. The great artificial basin at Seleucia Pieria, constructed under Seleucus I, required frequent dredging to prevent it from silting up. Because the city was an important base for the Roman fleet the inhabitants could expect military assistance in such operations. The *Descriptio Totius Orbis* attributes harbour works at Seleucia to Constantius II, presumably as part of his programme for supplying and maintaining the military infrastructure of the east rather than for the benefit of the local economy. The best-known harbour of the Roman period is that built by Herod for his new city of Caesarea, founded at the site of the Hellenistic settlement called Strato's Tower. A local tyrant had constructed a harbour in the late second century BC, which served as the innermost of the three basins of Herod's new harbour. This triple 'Harbour of Sebastos' (Augustus), as it was called, was a vast structure on which no expense was spared. The basins were protected by two immense breakwaters, the shorter, northern one being about 240 metres (262 yards) long and between 50 and 60 metres (55 and 65 yards) wide (for a simplified plan, see fig. 28.10). The southern breakwater, which curved northwards, was about 500 metres (547 yards) long and 70 metres (77 yards) wide, supporting vaulted chambers and a broad quay. The entrance channel between the breakwaters was about 100 metres (109 yards) long and 20-30 metres (22-33 yards) wide, and marked by two towers, the largest of which is thought to have functioned as a lighthouse. A nearby shipwreck contemporary with the harbour's construction contained wooden beams and volcanic ash, and it has been argued that the ash was pozzolana from the Bay of Naples, imported to produce Roman hydraulic concrete (which sets underwater) for Herod's breakwaters. The core of the breakwaters was constructed of huge blocks, some as large as 125 cubic metres (4414 cubic feet), composed of this hydraulic concrete mixed with rubble. The blocks were formed by pouring the concrete into submerged wooden moulds which may themselves have been made using imported materials shipped from Europe. This immense substructure was overlain with stone blocks and given additional protection from the sea in the form of a berm of rough stones. Despite the care that went into its construction, keeping Caesarea's port in good working order proved an arduous task, as silting and seismic activity took their toll. By the third century the harbour was in bad shape, and it underwent extensive repairs during the reign of Anastasius. But by the seventh century the once magnificent haven had largely silted up and the city was in decline.

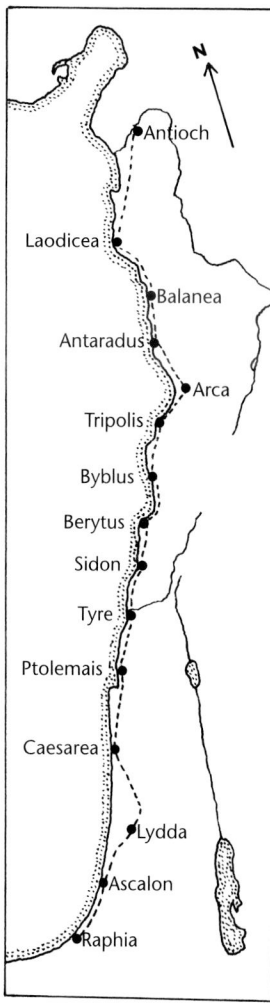

Fig. 43. The outward journey of Theophanes, c. 317-23, showing the places where he stopped for the night. Berytus lay more or less equidistant in travelling time from Ascalon and Antioch (six to seven days).

Heavy goods could sometimes be moved inland by water, where navigable rivers permitted. The level of the water in a river could be artificially raised by constructing weirs or other structures which could impede the flow of the river without blocking it completely. In this way quite small rivers could carry light traffic, but movement inland from the Mediterranean by water was hampered by the fact that few rivers breach the mountain chains along the coast. The

Fig. 44. Rock-cut sea wall at Botrys (Batroun), a small coastal city between Tripolis and Byblus.

Orontes is the most obvious and the most navigable; Strabo claimed that the voyage from Seleucia Pieria up the Orontes to Antioch could be completed in a day. Improvements included cutting a canal at some point before the second century in order to bypass a shallow section of the river and to allow vessels with a deeper draft to pass up river to the Syrian *metropolis*, and further canal work to improve navigability (and drainage?) up river of Antioch may have been carried out by the army together with some of the Antiochenes during the Flavian period. These operations would have helped to reduce transport costs by allowing military supplies to pass by water inland as far as the northernmost bend of the river, some distance east of Antioch. Small boats could certainly travel even further up the Orontes beyond Epiphanea (Hama), perhaps as far as Emesa. A shipwright is attested from an inscription at Derkush, about 50 kilometres (30 miles) upstream from Antioch (presumably he built river-going vessels rather than sea-going ones). We know rather less about transport on other rivers. The Lycus, near Laodicea, may have been navigable sufficiently far inland to serve the Bdama pass into the Orontes valley, and the Eleutherus (Nahr al-Kabir) was probably navigable along its lower reaches. In a similar manner the Leontes (Litani) could have served the hinterland of Tyre, and was perhaps a route into the Bekaa valley. The vast Euphrates, which provided access to the Persian Gulf, was navigable up river at least as far as Zeugma, and small vessels could go further north to Samosata, perhaps as far as the mouth of the gorge in the Kurdish Taurus, where rapids would have made further travel very difficult. Palmyrene and Durene merchants brought goods up the Euphrates by boat, and the river served as an artery of supply during Roman campaigns against the Parthians and Sasanians. Strabo also mentions goods transport on the Jordan, which he claimed was undertaken 'by Aradians especially'.[18] The importance of riverine transport to civilians and the military has yet to be assessed, but, as on land, the Roman empire is likely to have left its prominent signature.

PART III

PRODUCTION AND CONSUMPTION

5 EXPLOITING THE AVAILABLE

ANTAGONISM AND SYMBIOSIS

That production in antiquity was predominantly based on agriculture is hardly controversial. The majority of people worked on the land, and the primary 'industry' of the Roman empire was farming. Some modern analysts have emphasized the countryside as *the* place of production, to be contrasted with the towns and cities, which were centres of consumption. Both sides had an interest in the other – the consumers in the city needed agricultural produce and the farmers needed markets in which to sell surpluses, but behind it lay a power struggle between urban centres and the countryside. The countryside might be exploited by absentee landlords resident in the cities, or country-based landlords might exploit the dependency of the urban populations. This antagonism between city interests and country interests helped shape the ancient city and its hinterland.

Such analyses present a strict dichotomy, between city and country, or between city and village, which is likely greatly to oversimplify the complex processes of production and consumption in Roman Syria and the Near East. For a start, there is the question of whether the distinction between cities and villages is a useful one in this particular instance. The term 'village' is itself inadequate for the task of describing the wide variety of settlements encountered, from small agglomerations of rural buildings to 'towns' of several thousand inhabitants. A city might be distinguished from a village in legal terms, but as we have already seen (chapter 3), not all cities were equal, and nor were all villages. The main distinction between a city and a village was legal and institutional, and hierarchical in that a city had villages for dependencies and villagers in city territories were expected to contribute to the expenses of the city. But large villages acted as economic and religious centres for the surrounding countryside, just as cities did. They had communal funds and common land, and magistrates and officials, some of whom were responsible for distributing the tax burden of the community. In some regions there is little evidence to suggest that the villages were legally subordinate to any city. In such places there may have been hierarchies of settlements, with leading villages acting as markets or centres of redistribution for other villages, although the evidence for this is debated. A subordinate settlement might gain political independence from a city by being elevated to civic status, but in economic terms small cities probably differed little from larger villages. In the late second century the village of Dionysias (Suweyda) acquired city status, and archaeological investigations there have demonstrated that it acquired monumental buildings, with a carefully planned civic centre, but Dionysias had a small territory and can hardly have been an important economic competitor with its neighbour Canatha. Indeed, Dionysias had formerly been a village in the territory of Canatha, and Canatha may have continued to dominate the new city economically. Villages were *potential* cities, if the right conditions prevailed, but in many cases they did not challenge the existing economic order. Conversely there were settlements that ought to have been cities even if they did not possess that status legally. We have seen how Heliopolis appears to have been dependent on Berytus until the late second century (chapter 3). However, it had acquired monumental structures that could compete with anything in Berytus, and some are likely to have exceeded anything found in Berytus, before its 'independence'. It probably attracted wealthy benefactors, and had typical civic monuments like walls and a theatre (admittedly the date of these features is unclear and they may post-date Heliopolis' dependent status). It therefore *resembled* a city, even if constitutionally it was not one, and treating Heliopolis as if it were a village would probably not reflect its economic importance in the Bekaa valley. The dichotomy, if such there is, contrasts the smaller settlements with the larger ones, the latter lying at the point where agricultural subsistence ceases and where large-scale consumption and redistribution of surpluses begins. For the purposes of this chapter, then, settlements which had civic status and the larger villages which might be characterized as 'towns' will be considered together in contrast to the 'countryside'.

Cities are the products of social processes, the result of debates by country-dwellers and city-dwellers about whose needs these settlements are meant to serve. They can serve the needs of a predominantly agricultural population, or they can shape the country to their own needs. For the French historian Fernand Braudel the town 'has to dominate an empire, however tiny, in order to exist',[19] but the relationship might sometimes be described as more symbiotic than one of dominance and submission. However, this symbiosis between city and country was unlikely to have been a happy and democratic marriage of urban and rural populations. In antiquity control of production and distribution of food was the surest way to power, and that control could be achieved by urban or rural elites through social institutions like the city state.

A popular urban model for antiquity is the 'consumer city' promoted (with some reservations) by scholars such as Moses Finley and A. H. M. Jones, who were building on the ideas of sociologists like Max Weber. The argument in favour of this model runs roughly as follows: in the Roman world the value-systems were governed by those who lived in towns and cities. For the elite inhabitants of these centres, agriculture was the proper source of wealth, not manufacture and commerce. The countryside was therefore where production was located, and it was dominated by city-based landlords, who absorbed the agricultural produce. Society was urban and elitist, and the city unproductive. The ancient 'consumer city' was intended as a contrast to a medieval mode of productive towns, but like the dichotomy of city/village, that of consumer/producer for the ancient city and its hinterland oversimplifies the complexity of relationships suggested by the evidence derived from archaeology.

Archaeology reveals clear evidence for production in the heart of the major cities. Iron slag and hammer scale (detritus from the forging of iron objects) reveal evidence of smelting and smithing, loom weights hint at textile production, and there is widespread evidence for glass manufacture. The coastal cities of Syria and the Near East sometimes yield quantities of murex shells used in dyeing (see below), and important dye-works have been found at the coastal cities of Dora and Gaza. Kilns can indicate not only the production of pottery; the types of container being made suggest the manufacture of other products as well. The second-century AD *macellum* or food market off the monumental *cardo* at Gerasa was enlarged in the late Roman period, becoming in the sixth century what its excavators describe as a 'closed industrial area' rather than a market, containing a dye-works and a lime kiln, as well as storage and stables. Production in the cities was most likely organized according to guilds, for which there is evidence from inscriptions. The obsession with recording occupations on tombstones (see chapter 8) means that funerary epigraphy is an unusual but valuable source of information about various forms of manufacture in the cities, particularly of occupations which leave little trace in the archaeological record.

While most urban excavations invalidate the strict consumer city model, it is less easy to quantify the scale of production in cities relative to agricultural production. However, it seems likely that cities provided an organizational framework for all forms of production within their territories, whether or not these were exploitative of the country dwellers, and if so, cities were an integral part of rural productive schemes. Raw materials for production in the cities are often likely to have originated in the countryside (see below), so production in the two locations was intimately linked. Cities might organize the packaging of products in distinct containers for export, or simply for redistribution within the city territory. There is some evidence in Jewish sources of the second and third centuries for the cities setting the market prices of goods in their territories, so that these goods could not be bought or sold in violation of these prices. The fact that cities seem to have been the principal institutions responsible for organizing the export of goods from their territories (whether or not the individual exporters were private entrepreneurs rather than public contractors), and that these exports were sometimes on a large scale, means that those cities were exploiting their hinterlands for purposes other than direct consumption. Taxation in kind may account for a growth in production and export of various commodities at some centres rather than independent economic growth (see chapter 6), but in general a command economy does not explain the complexity of the archaeological evidence for exports. Generalizations are difficult from the varied textual and material data available, but year by year the archaeological support for an elaborate economic interrelationship between city and country is growing.

Practical and social considerations placed limitations on the productivity of cities. Although pottery kilns are not unknown on or close to urban sites, large centres of production required a fair amount of space. A number of prominent industries were considered obnoxious and dangerous if confined within urban centres. Strabo's description of the smell emitted by the vats of the profitable purple industry at Tyre, which 'makes the city unpleasant to live in',[20] is well known. In the late first or early second century Rabbi Akiba prevented a tannery being set up west of Jerusalem because the prevailing wind came from that direction. A late Byzantine document, the *Legal Manual* of Constantinus Harmenopolus, preserves the decrees of a prefect recorded by a certain Julianus 'the Architect' of Ascalon, in which explicit restrictions on the siting of industries are laid down. It is not certain how universal these regulations were, but they concur with other sources of information about the offensive nature of certain industries. Cheese-makers and manufacturers of *garum* [fish sauce] 'do no small damage to those nearby. For the smell from them is extremely unpleasant, and obnoxious at a large distance. Hence such trades-men must not live at all in either city or village. But if there is need for them for the necessities of towns and villages, they must be three stades [c. 600 metres (656 yards)] distant.'[21] Similarly glass-makers, iron-workers and bronze-casters 'must not carry out those operations in the cities proper. Or if there is a neces-sary reason that they should inhabit cities and carry on these occupations in them, they must work in remote and sparsely populated parts of cities. For the danger to buildings from the fire is considerable; and so likewise is the constant bodily harm to persons.' Any processes involving furnaces and fumes were considered a potential danger, and whilst makers of plaster of Paris, quicklime, dyes, olive oil, and any processes involving fumigation, such as rush-weaving and wool-cleaning, were allowed to set up in cities, Julianus states the distances and positions that were legally permissible. If these kinds of restrictions existed everywhere and were enforced, it would seem that many industries were better off located outside the cities, although archaeological evidence suggests that the regulations might sometimes have been ignored.

In the countryside the dominant social and economic unit appears to have been the village, rather than the villa estates characteristic of many parts of the Roman west, and the importance of the village in Roman Syria and the Near East cannot be over-emphasized. Indeed, the region has with good reason been characterized by scholars as a land of villages; and by stressing the rural, we seem to be according prominence to this form of settlement over that of the city. Sometimes Syrians themselves appear to have done so as well: rather than identifying themselves with a city of origin as was normal, some Syrians abroad might prefer to be identified with their home village instead. This is an interesting phenomenon, and is indicative of the social importance of the Syrian village in relation to the city.

Were villagers for the most part landowners, or were they tenants on private estates owned by wealthy city-dwellers? The answer to this question is crucial to our understanding of the relationship between the city and the countryside, but it is not yet resolved. Conditions are likely to have varied from city to city and village to village. Opulent rural villas are known, such as those at Çekmece or Yakto near Antioch, those at Jenah and Ouzai south of Berytus, or the forti-fied 'manor' at Khirbet el-Muraq in Judaea. Some of these may well have been country retreats for the civic aristocracy; others may have served rural grandees. If the wealth of the Roman empire was predominantly agricultural, the wealthy must have owned large rural estates, making these villas a mater-ial manifestation of a particular form of social organization and exploitation. The third-century villa at Yakto provides us with a glimpse of such places, albeit incomplete. The excavated area included a court containing an orna-mental pool surrounded by a colonnade, probably used as a fish-pond. There were exhedras on two of the three sides exposed in excavation, and a small private bath. The Çekmece villa also had a pool surrounded by a colonnaded portico and an adjoining private bath. Both villas were provided with sumptuous mosaics. Another mosaic pavement, this time from Antioch itself, shows a large fortified building which may be intended to represent an aristocratic rural residence (fig. 45.2); note, however, that village houses in the region sometimes had towers and high walls surrounding their courtyards (fig. 45.1; see also p. 306). Whether large estates were common, or whether the elites tended to hold

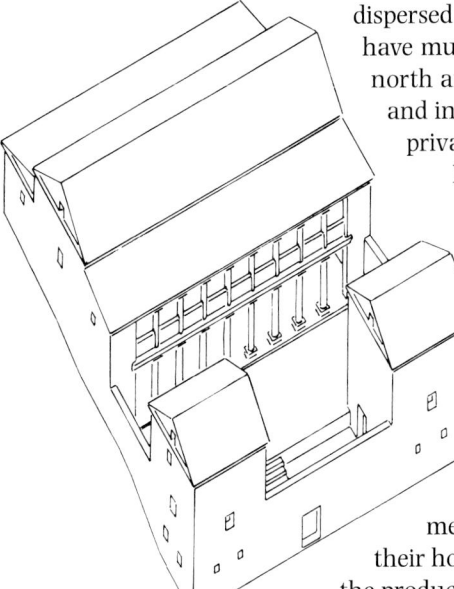

Fig. 45.1. Late Roman house at Dalloza in the Jebel Zawiye with two towers. After G. Tchalenko, Villages antiques de la Syrie du nord, *vol. II, plate xxii.*

Fig 45.2. Topographical border of a fifth-century-AD mosaic pavement from a building at Antioch, showing what may be either a rural villa or a house similar to that in fig. 45.1. The owner's name, Alexandrenos, is given.

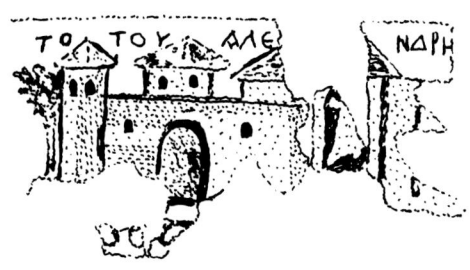

dispersed properties in different villages, is not clear. In those places where we have much information about villages (mainly the limestone massif of the north and the Hauran) large estates do not appear to have been the norm, and instead free peasants seem to have worked their own lands. But large private estates are possible in other areas.

Private individuals were not the only owners of estates. Apart from those owned by the emperors, there were those owned by the church, which was also a major landowner in the late Roman period. Monasteries were centres of production as well as consumption, with the larger ecclesiastical estates often selling or exporting their considerable surpluses. The monks themselves were active forces for development in marginal areas, farming in the wilderness and interacting with the nomads there. The economic dependence of groups of nomads on a monastery might even motivate these people to settle in the vicinity. In some cases private landowners might encourage the establishment of a monastery on an unproductive and uncultivated part of their holdings, doing their duty to the Lord and at the same time increasing the productivity of their estates.

A. H. M. Jones saw the process of urbanization as antagonistic to the interests of country-dwellers, because the wealthy landowners who lived in the cities were slowly able to eliminate 'peasant proprietorship' through the creation of large private estates, leaving the country-dwellers as poor tenants or working marginal lands.[22] As time went by, things became worse. In Jones's view, and that of Finley, life in the countryside in late antiquity was harsh, with the peasantry crushed by the burdens of taxes and other obligations in cash and kind. The blame was largely placed on state demands to supply the army, the *annona*. The consequences were serious indeed. Over-taxation led to a decline of productivity in the countryside, which led to the empire's decline.

While the sources make it clear that there were large estates in the hands of urban elites, and villagers who were tenant farmers, ancient writers do not always concur with the gloomy views of Finley and Jones. The fourth-century Antiochene author Libanius claimed that the villages of the Antiochene hinterland 'had little need for the town, thanks to exchange among themselves'.[23] Archaeological studies of that hinterland – of which more below – have stressed the growing prosperity of the countryside at a time when it was supposed to have been declining. It was once thought that this Antiochene hinterland could be explained as exceptional, but studies of other rural landscapes of Syria demonstrate that it was not unusual, and that this growth can be observed in the ruins of settlements in the basaltic zone to the south-east, or in the Hauran. In fact, the evidence from almost every part of Syria in late antiquity suggests a growing population, and an increase in the amount of land put under the plough. Whether this overall spread of agricultural production represents *per capita* growth, so that the lot of ordinary farmers improved, is more difficult to answer, but there is some evidence to suggest that it does (see below).

If such growth can be discerned, does this mean that urbanization improved the lot of villagers rather than making life harsher? To what extent were the cities involved in the process whereby sedentary lifestyles spread into areas formerly inhabited by nomads? As suggested in chapter 3, there may be a relation between agricultural growth in the steppe and the spread of urbanism there. Cities, of course, depended on their agricultural hinterlands, so we should not necessarily expect altruistic motives from city-based elites with respect to country-dwellers, but it was in the interests of the civic centres to develop their resources. Wealthier cities were probably able to indulge in more costly and elaborate projects aimed at encouraging agricultural growth. An important area where they could help rural development was in matters of water supply. Villages did not have the resources and manpower for large hydraulic projects; by constructing aqueducts, *qanats* and dams, cities could provide water for lands that needed irrigating. The building of a dam on the lake of Homs (Emesa) and the irrigation projects associated with it are thought by some to have coincided with Emesa's consolidation as a city, perhaps as late as the first century AD. Canatha in the Hauran seems to have been responsible for providing water to villages in its large territory, and other civic schemes elsewhere could have supplied the hinterlands (see below). Cities also provided markets, a religious focus and an administrative centre for dependent villages. With good reason some scholars consider that the 'urbanization of Roman Syria may be described overall as due fundamentally to the economic requirements of the villages and to the religious needs of their inhabitants.'[24]

The fact that in many areas a rise and fall in the level of rural occupation can be seen to coincide with the growth and subsequent decline of the cities implies a high degree of dependency of villages on urban centres. Villages relied not only on urban markets but also on the elaborate social, organizational and religious infrastructure that cities could provide. As cities shrank, so did markets and the organization of the infrastructure, and village life receded from the marginal zones.

The Spread of Sedentarization

In the midst of all this uncertainty one rural trend is absolutely clear. During the period of Roman rule the settled rural population increased enormously in Syria and the Near East. Good land was densely settled, and marginal lands such as the dry steppe or stony highlands were occupied more intensively than at any time before. This growth is most striking in late antiquity, and the trend in Syria seems to be part of an empire-wide phenomenon. Far from exhausting its resources, the Roman empire appears to have encouraged more efficient exploitation.

Literary sources suggest that there was little or no settlement in the steppe during the first century BC. The inhabitants are characterized as 'Arabs', meaning that they were tent-dwellers or bandits, whose lifestyle was the antithesis of that of the civilized, city-based peoples. At the time of Pompey these nomadic peoples had encroached on many of the city territories, and in some cases had taken them over. Under Roman rule, however, the nomad presence retreated from the cities. Even so, the process seems to have been a slow one, because the Orontes valley and neighbouring regions still contained non-civic communities under Augustus. Rome may have encouraged the spread of settled agricultural populations through legislation. Roman laws passed in the first and second centuries allowed peasants to own uncultivated land if they developed it, and this probably led to the spread of farming in marginal areas or regions where nomadism had previously been rife. It may explain the regular field systems noted in many areas, particularly in the limestone massif of northern Syria, in the Orontes valley and in the steppe to the east of these two regions. Rather than being centuriated plots for army veterans, these fields may well have belonged to peasant farmers. Roman state surveyors were perhaps employed to lay out the fields in regular-sized plots in order to make it easier for the authorities to assess tax on the land. From the fourth century the number of settlements rose dramatically, and this fact, coupled with the accelerated pace of development in marginal areas, is seen by some as a consequence of the reorganization of the imperial tax system under Diocletian, and the payment of taxes in kind. This system, aimed mainly at supplying the military, stimulated agriculture in late antiquity rather than depressing it with excessive demands. In addition, the Roman state might have purchased for cash any additional surpluses that the farmers produced which might not otherwise have found a ready market locally. It is thought that in late Roman times the border troops, the *limitanei*, cultivated their own lands and provided at least some of their own food from their fields. A rescript issued by Constantine offered tax incentives, grants of cash, draft animals and seed grain to military veterans who were prepared to farm deserted lands. In the steppe the growth of a system of forts (see chapter 10) was accompanied by irrigation systems which were probably developed by the garrisons. According to this model, it is a symbiotic relationship between the military and the countryside, rather than purely between city and country, which accounts for some of the development.

However, it is likely that cities were an important part of the process. If there was any long-term strategy on the part of the Roman state regarding agricultural production, it may have been as follows: the principal aim was to increase the state's tax base, and to supply the army. Cities provided a suitable focal point for the collection of agricultural produce and taxes within their hinterlands, so direct rule was established over cities and the sedentarized countryside, while areas characterized by nomadism were left to client rulers. These client rulers were expected to encourage sedentary lifestyles, and the mark of a kingdom's success was its incorporation into the empire (see chapter 2). Seen in this way, the spread of urbanization was dependent on the spread of sedentarization, and urbanism was a mark of agricultural success.

Dating the spread of sedentarization is difficult. Much depends on dated inscriptions from sites and surface finds of ceramic fine wares, and the dates they provide may not coincide with the earliest phase of settlement in a given region. But the broad trends just cited are traceable. Increasing settlement in the steppe would have extended the area over which direct Roman rule (or self-regulating government on behalf of Rome) was imposed, since it was much easier to regulate sedentary farmers than nomad communities. It is not always clear whether the spread of sedentarization forced nomads further into marginal areas, or whether it was the nomads themselves who were settling down. The interplay between sedentary peoples and nomads is another complex topic which cannot be reduced to the dichotomies of antagonism and symbiosis (see below).

There are, however, alternative ways of viewing some of the evidence for growth. Farmers will have used a variety of subsistence strategies, diversifying when life became difficult, and focusing on one or two strategies when surpluses allowed. So by itself, the observation that *more land* was being used is not evidence of great agricultural success. It could signify the opposite. Fortunately other sorts of evidence are available which allow us to suggest which model is more appropriate.

Village Life

We should not conclude that this world of villages was a thoroughly parochial one. There is plenty of evidence for interaction between villagers and Roman officials, and the involvement of villagers in a wider world. For some people at least, life was not confined within the limits of the village. Imported fine ware pottery on rural sites speaks of economic interaction, but not necessarily of an extended network of social interaction. However, the number of papyrus and parchment document finds from the region is slowly increasing and these texts, which often come from rural contexts and concern villagers, provide us with good evidence for social activities and movement of people. Some of the best-known ones are from fairly marginal economic zones on the peripheries of our area, but there is no reason to suppose that social relations in these regions were atypical. We see villagers petitioning the Roman authorities, or travelling to appear in court before the governor in one of the cities. The archives also provide evidence of different languages in use: the same archive may contain documents in two or three languages, and in some cases a single document may contain more than one language.

The Babatha archive, found in 1961 in a cave in the Judaean desert, contains a series of documents dated to between AD 94 and 132 written in Aramaic, Nabataean and Greek, which formed the private archive of a Jewish woman called Babatha, from the village of Maoza in Arabia. They are extremely important for yielding a great deal of information about village life, legal procedures and Nabataean and Roman provincial administration, and for providing us with a glimpse of the transition from the Nabataean kingdom to the province of Arabia and of the way in which Roman legal institutions permeated daily life after the Roman annexation in AD 106. As the documents reveal, Babatha's personal life was complicated: she was married first to a Maozene Jew by whom she had a son, and then to a Jew from Ein Gedi, who took her as his second wife.

Fig. 46. 'Dead Cities': the ruins of the late Roman village of Baqirha in the limestone massif of northern Syria.

Both husbands died, leaving her with difficult legal matters to pursue. After the first husband's death male guardians were appointed for her son; they held the son's inheritance and from them Babatha received payments for the boy's maintenance. She contested the guardianship, and the amount paid, but lost. After her second husband's death Babatha found herself in competition over property with his other wife, and she also found herself in litigation with Julia Crispina, a Roman citizen and possibly the daughter of a Roman consul, who acted on behalf of other members of her husband's family. Babatha was caught in the Roman offensive during the Bar-Kokhba war, at Ein Gedi; her skeleton may be among those found in a cave where a group of people had taken refuge. It was in this cave complex that her archive was discovered, stowed away along with other documents and belongings of the refugees.

The Babatha archive shows that the village of Maoza, which was located somewhere at the south-eastern end of the Dead Sea, had a registry, which if normal would imply an elaborate administrative network in the Nabataean kingdom. The registry continued to operate when Maoza, which lay in the territory of Petra, was incorporated into the Roman province of Arabia. We have Babatha's declaration of property during a census taken in AD 127, in which her land is listed, giving its area (calculated by the quantity of barley that could be sown in it), and its tax liability in dates and, 'for crown tax', in money. On private properties irrigation rights were outlined in detail: two documents make it clear that each landowner had a regular time assigned for tapping the nearby wadi channel. We see the villagers freely buying and selling land, giving it as gifts, or declaring it as security against a loan. Women could own land, and Babatha herself had substantial properties in Maoza. Crops were clearly sold for cash. Babatha's second husband borrowed money at 1 percent interest per month from a Roman centurion, and it was possible for him to speculate on future crops on a leased date grove by purchasing them a year in advance. None of this suggests a heavily oppressed peasantry, or a particularly primitive economy.

Another important set of documents is the mid-third-century Euphrates archive, also known as the Mesopotamia papyri. It is not known exactly where these documents come from (they were purchased on the antiquities market by a collector), but they appear to be connected with a village called Beth Phouraia, which was an imperial estate on the Euphrates up river from Dura Europus, and they mention several other places which lay along the middle stretch of the Euphrates river. The archive contains five petitions in Greek, written by professional scribes. Two of these are signed in Syriac by the petitioner, Aurelius Abidsautas, who was a councillor of a place called Neapolis (thought to be a newly created city at Appadana near Beth Phouraia). There are two legal documents entirely in Syriac, again written by professional scribes; two private letters in Greek; and several private documents, all in Greek but several with subscriptions in Syriac. One petition, dated 28 August 245, concerns a property dispute between two groups of villagers, and is addressed to Julius Priscus, the brother of the emperor Philip (AD 244-9). Four villagers from Beth Phouraia travelled to Antioch to put their case to Priscus, but had to wait eight months to see him. Other petitions, all brought before Roman officials, concern a dispute over a vineyard and lost revenues from it, acts of physical violence, and a murder. The private documents include sales contracts (slaves, a boat), loans of money, and the lease of land together with houses and a courtyard.

Although they come from a city, the parchments and papyri found at Dura Europus furnish us with additional information about village life in the same region as the Euphrates archive. The city was sacked by the Sasanians in the middle of the third century (see chapter 2) and excavations at the site produced a wealth of documentary material from both military and civilian contexts. Most came from a military archive housed in the Temple of Azzanathkona, and concern the activities of soldiers. The Dura documents are perhaps better known for the information they provide about life and languages in the city (there are texts in Syriac, Palmyrene, Parthian and Middle Persian as well as Greek and Latin) and the workings of the Roman army (see chapter 10), but a few of them also highlight the importance of soldiers and army veterans in the countryside. One papyrus deed of sale in Greek, found near the city's synagogue, records the purchase by a veteran soldier of a vineyard in a village on the Khabur river. The individual may have been adding to lands assigned to him by the state on his retirement from military service (the text mentions that he owned adjoining properties). It is worth noting that this document stipulates that as owner of the land the buyer must meet his obligations (imperial taxes) and village services (liturgies). Such a sale was technically a civilian affair but the deed was drawn up in the winter quarters of the veteran's old unit. The witnesses were soldiers, all but one of them signing in Latin, and it is likely that the unit was stationed in the Khabur region. Another document, this time on parchment, records that a second veteran witnessed the divorce of a probable civilian couple in the village of Ossa (location uncertain, but perhaps near the confluence of the Khabur and Euphrates). A third document is a marriage contract of a veteran and a soldier's widow at a place called Qatna (probably on the Khabur), written in Greek. It seems clear that ex-soldiers became prominent figures in the rural communities where they settled, and that villagers along the middle Euphrates had regular dealings with the Dura's registry.

From the late Roman period we have the recently discovered archive found in a church in Petra which had been destroyed by fire. This collection, which contains documents from the first half of the sixth century until the reign of Maurice (AD 582-602), appears to have belonged to a certain Theodore, son of Obodianus, who was archdeacon. The documents seem to deal more with comparatively wealthy landowners than peasant farmers, and the land itself may often have been leased or farmed by less wealthy individuals. We see what appears to be an attempt by three brothers to diversify farming strategies by cultivating different sorts of land in several different geographical areas, in the manner described above (p. 140). Even so, given the total amount of land recorded for them, they can scarcely be classed as smallholders eking out a living at the margins. Land was measured not only in the official late Roman units called *iugera* but also by the traditional method, in terms of grain needed to sow it, just as in the Babatha archive. The Petra archive also shows how the landowners had properties in the territories of other cities, and private land straddling the boundaries of two cities, Petra and Augustopolis (Udhruh?).

A further late Roman collection of papyrus documents was found in the village of Nessana in the Negev. The site lies in a marginal environment which receives about 10 centimetres (4 inches) of rainfall annually. It was established by the Nabataeans, but flourished in late Roman times, when it was subordinate to the city of Elusa. Most of the documents come from a room attached to a small church in a Roman fort, where they had been discarded or carelessly stored away during the declining years of the settlement, more than half a century after the Muslim conquest. Most of the texts are badly damaged, and appear to be from a variety of sources. Many are personal or financial in nature: a marriage contract, divorces, loans, documents concerned with inheritances and divisions of property, and other legal contracts. There are texts connected with a sixth-century military unit, which appears to have been a camel corps, personal documents associated with church officials, fragments of Virgil's *Aeneid* and Biblical texts together with commentaries which probably formed part of a small teaching library from a monastic school, and a set of writings in Arabic and Greek dating after the Muslim conquest. As in other cases these papyri illustrate the fact that the villagers were well connected with a wider world. The village seems to have had a caravanserai for merchants. Itinerant tradesmen, who appear to have travelled in a caravan, visited the village, buying goods (particularly animals) to sell elsewhere, and the villagers enjoyed fish brought from the Mediterranean. Growers of dates stockpiled produce and sold it to Egyptian dealers, who traded in the Negev as well as Egypt.

SYRIAN LANDSCAPES

While much work remains to be done on the Syrian countryside, a number of important regional studies help to define the ways in which different zones developed.

The 'Dead Cities'

The north-western corner of Syria is characterized by fertile plains framed by broad stretches of limestone hills which are less favourable to agriculture. Yet it is the rather unpromising upland environment of this limestone massif that contains some of the most remarkably well-preserved examples of ancient rural landscapes found anywhere in the Roman world. Not only do entire villages survive, but often so do their field systems, burial grounds and rural outbuildings. In spite of the popular sobriquet these ruins, although dead, are not those of cities, but of villages in the territories of cities like Antioch, Apamea, Chalcis, Cyrrhus and Beroea. There are more than 700 settlements, ranging from modest hamlets containing a few buildings to large agglomerations with numerous communal oil presses, churches and monasteries. Some, such as Serjilla in the Jebel Zawiye or Babisqa in the Jebel Barisha, possessed bath buildings. The majority of larger settlements are to be found on the edges of the limestone hills, close to or on the more fertile lowlands, with convenient access to roads or rivers, but small villages are scattered across the region. Most of the surviving buildings belong to the fourth, fifth and sixth centuries, when occupation and cultivation of the limestone massif was at its most intense. The reason why these villages have survived so well is that much of the land on which they stand is marginal – it was densely occupied in the late Roman and very early Islamic periods, but more sparsely inhabited thereafter and virtually abandoned from the ninth or tenth century. Consequently the ruined buildings were not used as quarries for building material, simply because there were no later inhabitants in the region to plunder them. Many structures still stand to full height, lacking only their upper floors, roofs, doors and shutters.

Although not particularly fertile compared to the lowlands around it, the highland region enjoys a mild climate. It averages between 500 and 600 metres (1640 and 1970 feet) above sea level, and nowhere rises much beyond 800 metres (2625 feet). Rainfall provides most of the necessary water for agriculture, and the few types of water installation used there in antiquity consist predominantly of cisterns. There are two principal stretches of limestone hills: the Jebel Zawiye in the south; and in the north a series of ranges, the most important of which are the Jebel A'la, Jebel Barisha, and the northernmost mass, the Jebel Halaqa and Jebel Semaan (named after St Simeon Stylites, whose martyrium is located here).

Fig. 47. North Syrian landscape: contrast of the fertile plain with the limestone massif. In the middle distance is the late Roman monastery at Breij.

The region may have been fairly sparsely populated before the Roman annexation, with development beginning only in the late first or early second century AD. Archaeological excavation in the limestone massif has been very limited, so our understanding is drawn mostly from surface surveys, and in general these have been restricted to studies of structural remains. In many cases it seems that the houses of this early phase of development were demolished and the materials used in later periods of construction, effectively obliterating evidence of earlier settlement. Fortunately a local habit of inscribing buildings with their year of dedication or construction according to one of the local city eras (see chapter 4; fig. 90.1) allows us to date this early phase even when the materials have been reused, and quantitative analysis provides us with broad trends. Using data from inscriptions (particularly those from tombs), a significant period of development between c. AD 110 and 250 can be identified. The settlement of Me'ez in the Jebel Barisha seems to have been one of the first centres of any significance, though other buildings of the second and third centuries are known from other regions of the limestone massif. Some of the pagan temples of the region, such as that at Burj Baqirha (see frontispiece), may have had dependent villages (though this is not certain), and thus the religious centres may have been important for the agricultural development of their immediate surroundings during this first phase. In the period after 250 there is little evidence for development, but from c. 330 to 550 the limestone massif witnessed a significant increase in population and occupation. Building activity reached a peak c. 450–80. Pressure on agricultural land increased, and between 330 and 550 the amount of land available per head of population (based on a count of the number of rooms in houses in selected villages relative to the extent of the village territory, where this could be determined) dropped dramatically. One estimate puts the fifth-to-sixth-century population of the Jebel Barisha at 21,000 (100 people per square kilometre) and that of the Jebel A'la at 8500 (53 per square kilometre). These estimates are based on the number of surviving houses. The figures may not be all that reliable, but they give us some impression of relative densities of population

Fig. 48. The limestone massif of northern Syria.

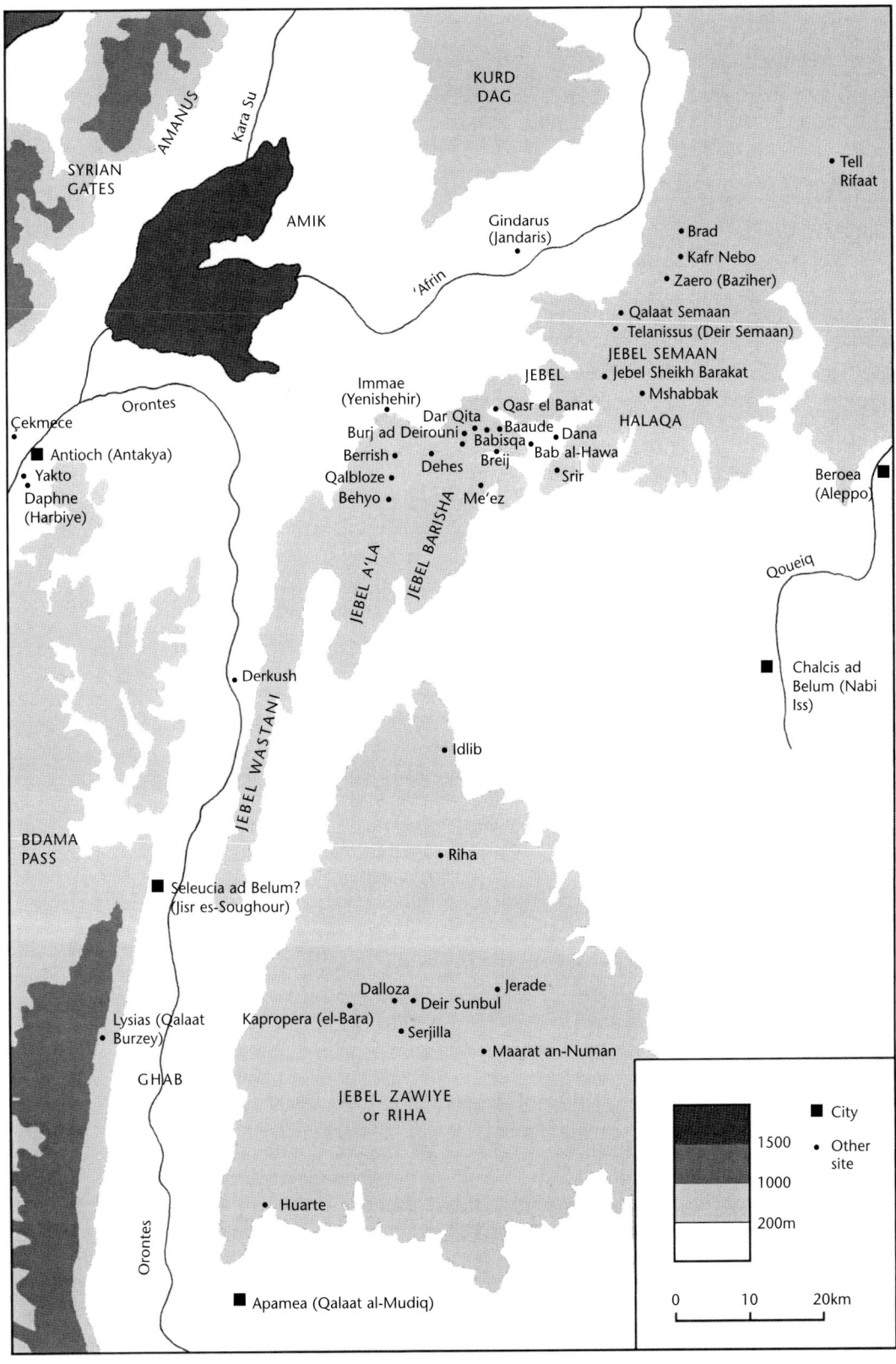

when occupation of the region was at its height. However, this growth does not seem to have brought about impoverishment, or at least, not before 550. The largest number of high-quality buildings belong to the period closer to 550, suggesting that until the mid-sixth century the land was able to support its inhabitants, and that intensive farming of the region brought prosperity to them.

But who were the inhabitants? Independent communities of rural peasants? Tenant farmers or estate workers, subordinate to absentee urban landlords? Or were the larger buildings the country residences of wealthy estate owners? The Dead Cities have long attracted the interests of travellers and archaeologists, and the landscape of the limestone massif has been read in very different ways over the years. When first described in detail by the Marquis de Vogüé in the nineteenth century, many of the buildings were seen as genteel farmsteads and villas inhabited by a rural bourgeoisie. A more thorough survey was published in 1953 by Georges Tchalenko. He saw the villages as servicing the great cities and, in the late Roman period, participating in large-scale overseas export of olive oil. Impetus for rural development therefore came from the cities, or the demands of state-controlled redistributive systems of taxation in kind. He proposed that the development of the more marginal hill country was due to investment in olive oil production, and that the oil produced in the limestone massif was often destined for foreign markets. As olive trees take a long time to mature, olive culture was an expensive long-term investment that would have been best undertaken by wealthy estate owners, or encouraged by the Roman state through tax incentives offered to less wealthy individuals, rather than on the initiative of an independent rural peasantry. At the same time there was plenty of evidence for the villagers raising livestock and growing other sorts of crops – grain, wine, fruit, much of which was probably destined for local consumption. His thesis was an attractive one. At the time that Tchalenko's ideas were formulated the gloomy model of a depressed late antique country-side proposed by Finley and Jones was gaining ground, making the Dead Cities appear anomalous in their apparent prosperity. Placing them at the heart of an important oil industry was one way of explaining why they were different. The intensification of settlement, particularly in the fifth and sixth centuries, could be seen as a response to events taking place elsewhere in the Roman empire. In the fifth century the Vandals had conquered the major oil-exporting provinces of north Africa. Northern Syria was able to take advantage by developing its own oil-exporting industry to replace what the empire had lost, and consequently the limestone massif prospered when in other areas the countryside was in decline.

Support for the thesis appeared to come from the analysis of pottery in the western Mediterranean. A major amphora type, Late Roman 1 (see chapter 6), is common in southern France, Italy and north Africa, and is often thought to be connected with this oil industry. It is also found widely in the eastern Mediterranean. The date range of the exports, from the fourth to sixth century, seemed to fit conveniently with the date range of standing buildings in the limestone massif. The region of Antioch is considered to have been a major centre for production of Late Roman Amphora 1 (LRA 1) – although this connection remains to be proved and it was also produced in Rhodes, Cilicia and Cyprus. No LRA 1 kiln sites have been identified in the Dead Cities, and thus a direct connection between agricultural development in the limestone massif and LRA 1 exports cannot be proved. But the amphoras could have been produced at kilns on the coast or near the cities, and the oil transported from the limestone massif in temporary forms of packaging such as animal skins. Furthermore, some features of the LRA 1 suggest that oil could have been only one of the products being exported – pitch linings in some of the amphoras indicate that another was wine. Wine exports would help to solve the puzzle of the massive quantities of LRA 1 imported to Carthage between AD 450 and 550. Carthage was a major centre of oil production, so why would it need to import foreign oil? If in this case the LRA 1 was carrying wine, the 'carrying coals to Newcastle' conundrum is negated. Even so, a connection between the Dead Cities and exports of wine and oil in LRA 1 has yet to be demonstrated, but this is one archaeological problem which might suddenly be solved, one way or the other, by fresh evidence.

Several recent studies of the Dead Cities have stressed local consumption over exports. While the overall number of presses in the villages is considerable (over 500 have been identified), in some cases old surveys confused the rectangular cuttings in the bedrock, which were used for crushing olives, grapes or fruits using stone rollers, with presses, and this has produced an artificially high estimate of the number of presses per household. Another question concerns the quantity and quality of the oil produced in the presses. One view holds that the majority of presses can hardly have been used for oil production on a scale sufficient to support the theory of export. Most have no installation for a second refinement (although this could have been done by using a hand-held strainer) and in many cases the pulp was produced by a crude technique using stone rollers (unless these rollers were normally used for grapes or other crops). While each press itself is likely to have been protected by a roof, these installations were commonly open on one or more sides, which exposed them to bad weather and wind-blown detritus. Communal use of the presses by the villagers is unlikely to have made the quality any better. According to this argument, it would seem that the products of these presses were destined for local use, or, at most, markets in neighbouring towns or cities. Enclosed presses are much rarer, and tend to be larger, well-built installations. These would have produced much better quality oil, and may well be the equipment of wealthy landowners or communities whose products were destined for export. Even these tend to lack any fixed means for providing a second refinement, but there are reasons to think that their products were destined for uses other than local consumption. Once again, the discovery of a connection between the export of LRA 1 and oil production in the Dead Cities would completely alter our picture of production and consumption in the region.

Some buildings have been tentatively identified as public structures associated with the storage and perhaps marketing of oil: a rare type of building, which Tchalenko called an *andron*, may be a public utility. These buildings are usually situated at the centre or entrance of the village, and are without the substantial walls and courtyards characteristic of houses (fig. 49). In those at Baude in the Jebel Barisha and Berrish in the Jebel A'la the lower storey consists of an undercroft for storage or a press; above is a single large room. The upper floor could have been a meeting-place for traders or producers of goods – rather like a medieval European market-hall. But this hypothesis is far from certain. The only *andron* to be identified as such by an inscription is at Me'ez, and the precise layout of this building, which is unpublished, is unclear. It is also early; the inscription is dated to AD 129, and it may have been a banqueting-hall for a pagan cult. The best known *andron* is the so-called 'café' at Serjilla, which stands at the centre of the village, next to the bath house (the two public buildings may have formed a single complex, but again this is not certain).

Apart from olive oil, Tchalenko recognized the importance of other types of agricultural product in the limestone massif (wine, grain, fruit and livestock). A few inscriptions mention a variety of crops other than olives, but these are too few to

Fig. 49. The 'café' at Serjilla, which some have interpreted as a commercial depot at the centre of the village.

support any general argument for agricultural diversity in the limestone massif. There is, however, plenty of material evidence. New studies have concentrated on this evidence, proposing that the surrounding cities were sufficiently numerous and large enough to consume all of the surpluses of the limestone massif, and that it is unnecessary to invoke export as an explanation. Oil production, while important, was clearly more significant in some regions of the limestone massif than in others: some villages had few or no oil presses (or at least, none is identifiable today), whereas in other villages the number of presses is enormous (for instance, at Behyo, where thirty-seven presses have been identified). Viewed by region (see fig. 51), the number of presses indicates that olive cultivation was most intense in the Jebel Barisha and Jebel A'la, among those Dead Cities closest to Antioch. The more easterly ranges of the Jebel Semaan and Halaqa have fewer presses, but there the villages have a large number of stone feeding troughs or mangers, which can be seen as evidence of a greater concentration on the raising of livestock. The southernmost region, the Jebel

Fig. 50. The ambiguity of architectural remains: these buildings in the northern part of the village of Baaude in the Jebel Barisha are arranged in a row and have porticoed façades reminiscent of classical stoas. Some believe them to be 'market halls' or shops in a commercial centre; others consider them houses, but there is no clear evidence for courtyard walls between individual properties.

Zawiye, has fewer presses and mangers and is something of a puzzle: it has some of the best agricultural land, and some of the biggest settlements, including the large village of el-Bara. Perhaps agriculture was mainly given over to products that leave little or no trace in the archaeological record, such as grain or fruit trees. Rectangular and elongated strip fields found in the Jebel Zawiye are suitable for such crops and lend some weight to the hypothesis that these were the major products.

The limestone massif was an environment which was not devoted to a single crop, but to many forms of agricultural exploitation, with regional preferences or specializations. The Dead Cities may have been mainly communities of free farmers rather than estates inhabited by tenants. One estate is known from epigraphy, Zaero (modern Baziher) in the Jebel Semaan, but its ruins are in a very poor state of preservation and it is difficult to discern whether it was different from other villages presumed to be independent. The landscape contains very few buildings that could be classified as villa-estates or grand houses, such as we might expect had there been great patrons or estate owners living on the land, though the question of absentee landlords remains. It is likely, however, that estates were to be located in the more fertile lowlands rather than the marginal limestone hills, and the Dead Cities represent the efforts of individuals who moved into these hills after the plains had come under full cultivation.

The villages lack any formal planning. There are no regular streets or grids. The majority of surviving buildings are houses, although the purpose of some house-like structures remains ambiguous (fig. 50). These substantial, stone-built dwellings are a measure of success: prosperous local smallholders profited from selling surpluses, and were able to invest their profits in expensive housing. Houses can also be differentiated: the quality of wall construction varies and some buildings have exceptional decoration on them. These differences are likely to reflect differences in wealth and status, and a possible hierarchy among the villagers.

Fig. 51. Presses and mangers or feeding troughs in the Dead Cities. After G. Tate, Les campagnes de la Syrie du nord, du IIe au VIIe siècle, *vol. I, Paris, 1992, p. 254.*

	JEBELS SEMAAN AND HALAQA	JEBELS BARISHA AND A'LA	JEBEL ZAWIYE
NUMBER OF PRESSES	61	157	36
NUMBER OF ROOMS WITH MANGERS	281	183	40

After houses, the commonest buildings are churches. They are not found in every settlement, but they are extremely common (the limestone massif as a whole contains something like 1200). Villages frequently contain two, and sometimes three. Monasteries are also found in the limestone hills, and their lands were probably worked by monks. Even so, there is little to suggest that they were involved in large-scale olive oil production. Monasteries with large territories, such as Qasr el Brad in the Jebel Semaan or Qasr el Banat in the Jebel Halaqa have a single, small installation for pressing olives. But they may have been producing and marketing other kinds of goods.

One distinct building type found in villages, attached to houses, or free-standing in the countryside, is the tower. Some of the towers had flat roofs, others may have had pointed ones — it is not always clear from what survives (colour plate 26). Rather than being mainly defensive, the towers were perhaps used for surveillance of villages and their fields. Additionally they may have served as habitations or as stores. The presence of latrines in some and machicolations (a tower in the village of Jerade tower has both) suggests habitation and defence (fig. 52).

Many other buildings labelled in earlier surveys as 'inns', 'androns' and 'stoas' may prove on closer inspection to be houses. It is hard to make a distinction between a building given over wholly to economic or public functions (such as is implied by the term 'market-hall') and one mixing economic activities with residential functions (as most of the houses do) given the present state of the evidence, but public utilities would seem to be rare. Where some scholars have looked at the ruins of certain villages and seen in these evidence of regional centres for collection and redistribution, others have seen only individual peasant dwellings. It is difficult to distinguish inns from farms, but one large early sixth-century building at Kafr Nebo in the Jebel Semaan looks very much like an inn. It contains a large number of stables (identifiable by their mangers) on the ground floor, but even so it may be nothing more than a group of houses. The functions of unique buildings, such as the three-storey 'Residence' at Deir Semaan, are enigmatic. Deir Semaan probably catered to pilgrims visiting the martyrium of St Simeon, and such structures may have been 'hotels'. One mid-sixth-century building at Babisqa in the Jebel Barisha bears an inscription which describes it in Greek as a stoa, and its general appearance resembles that of a classical stoa. The ground floor consists of a portico fronting five rooms of similar proportions; the second floor has a veranda and rooms which may have been for habitation. The whole looks like an elongated version of the typical house structure and the notion that it was given over to commercial use is by no means secure, although it too might have tended to the needs of pilgrims travelling to the sanctuary of St Simeon.

Fig. 52. Tower at Jerade in the Jebel Zawiye, which still stands about 20 metres (65 feet) high.

The archaeological evidence points to a wealth of agricultural activities, based around mixed farming, with significant surpluses sold for profit. The claim by Libanius that the villages of the city's hinterland thrived by selling and buying among themselves, and that they had little need of the city, may apply in part to the Dead Cities, but there is reason to think that these settlements relied on city markets as well. Markets in the Roman world were certainly not confined to cities, but permits to hold them in the countryside were regulated by the authorities, to prevent those in villages or on private estates competing with urban ones. If the villages themselves had markets, these were most likely held in the open air. Spaces in villages which were formerly described as 'agoras' now seem doubtful. Excavations in one, at Dehes, have revealed that what was thought to be an open space was in fact divided up by walls to form courtyards for three separate houses.

The Dead Cities suggest a symbiotic relationship between city and country in which the rural inhabitants fared well. The villagers were able to benefit from large markets provided by the major cities like Antioch, Apamea, Chalcis and Beroea, selling their surpluses in these regional markets, or perhaps exporting them overseas. The rise and fall in prosperity of these marginal areas seems to be linked to the growth and decline of the great cities. We have less information about settlement on the richer plains surrounding the limestone massif, but it was perhaps here, rather than in the marginal environment of the Dead Cities, that large estates, given to monoculture and exports, were located. A recent survey in the Amik plain, the broad and once marshy zone north-east of Antioch, makes it clear that these lowlands were intensively settled in the Roman period, as might be expected. The remains here are much less spectacular than those of the highlands because of continuous habitation in the region and pilfering of sites for building materials, but they provide a good deal of information about settlement in the lowlands, even if they do not as yet supply evidence for the types of agricultural activities practised. Besides demonstrating that there was an increase in the number of Roman sites all over the plain when compared with earlier periods, the results of the survey suggest a significant relationship, or even dependency, between lowland rural settlements and the neighbouring 'towns' and cities. There are particularly strong concentrations in the valley of the Kara Su to the north, along the eastern half of the plain, and in the south-west, close to Antioch. Some of the sites in the south-west are identified as wealthy villas on the outskirts of the city, but most other sites appear to be agricultural. With the establishment of Antioch and large villages like Immae (Yenishehir) and the road networks between them, smaller rural settlements seem to have gravitated out of the central part of the plain and towards these centres. The colonization of the limestone highlands may be an indirect consequence of more intense exploitation of the lowlands by the cities, as smallholders were squeezed out by large estates and had to look elsewhere. Until more information about lowland settlement in the region is available, such comparisons only invite speculation.

Chalcidice and the Eastern Steppe: Desert and Sown

The land east of the Orontes and the Jebel Zawiye gradually shades away from fertile fields to arid steppe as one moves towards the Euphrates. Chalcidice, named for the ancient city of Chalcis ad Belum (Nabi Iss), is a broad region extending east of Chalcis in the north-west and Salaminias (Salemiya) in the south-west, between the Lake of Jabbul in the north and the Jebel Balas in the south. The western regions are suitable for growing vines, olive trees and cereal crops, but agriculture becomes progressively more difficult as one moves east.

An American expedition at the turn of the twentieth century was the first to describe the ruins here in any detail. Later, the Jesuit fathers Antoine Poidebard and René Mouterde explored the region between 1934 and 1942 and interpreted the ruins there as a product of Roman imperial organization. Like Tchalenko, they saw this rural environment being altered by outside concerns, but whereas Tchalenko posited an elaborate economic system for the limestone massif, Mouterde and Poidebard stressed the military organization of Chalcidice. In their study, Le limes de Chalcis, Chalcidice was presented as a frontier zone, which, although arid, possessed a complex military and economic network, and formed an important part of the Syrian limes. The limes, they suggested, was not a linear boundary or no-man's-land, but a frontier zone of habitations, roads and forts. Mouterde and Poidebard believed that many of the ruins were those of Roman military installations. Much of the reconnaissance was done by air and through the interpretation of aerial photographs, but they also concentrated on field work (particularly the recording of inscriptions) and

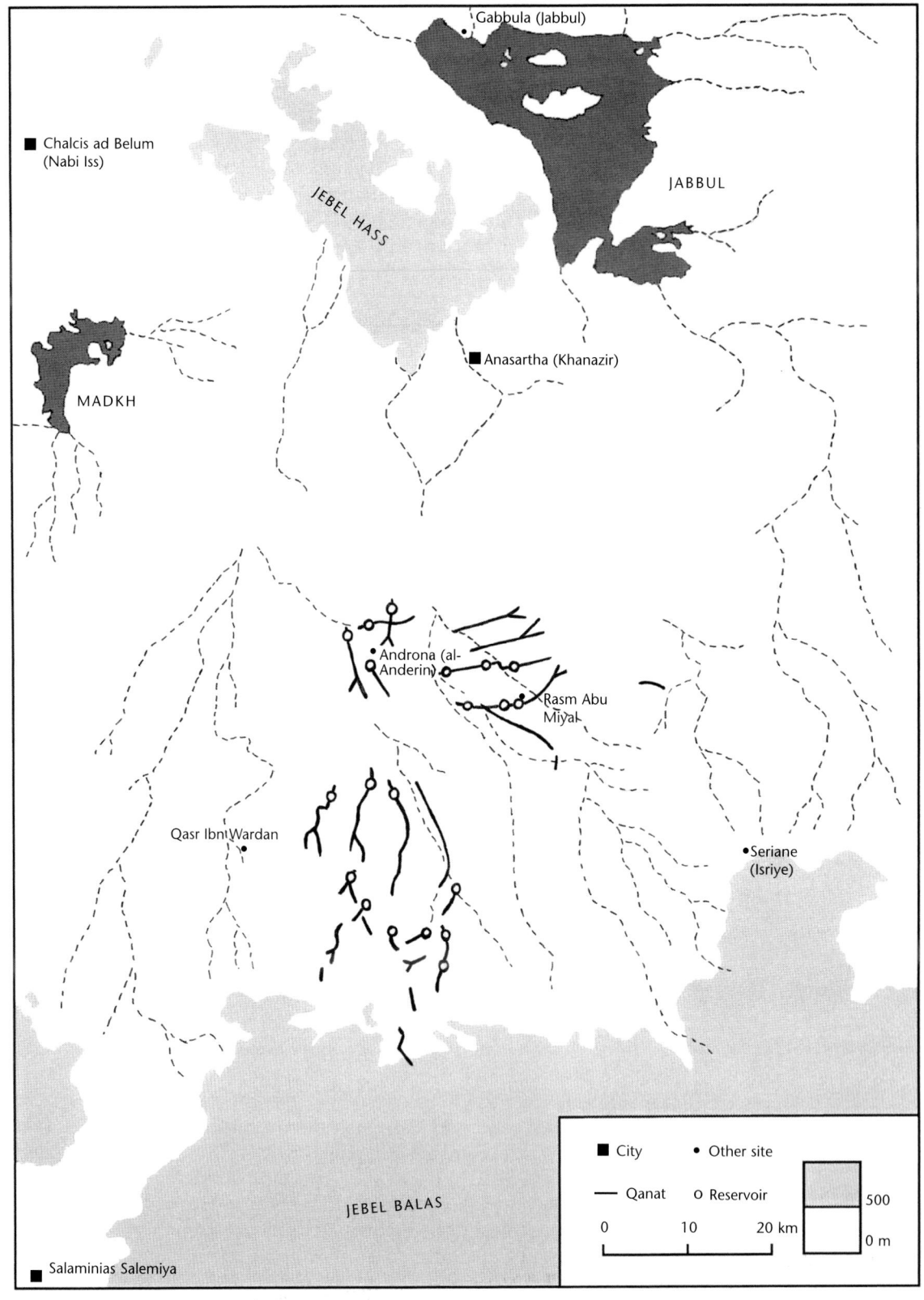

Gabbula (Jabbul)

Chalcis ad Belum
(Nabi Iss)

JEBEL HASS

JABBUL

Anasartha (Khanazir)

MADKH

Androna (al-
Anderin)

Rasm Abu
Miyal

Qasr Ibn Wardan

Seriane
(Isriye)

JEBEL BALAS

Salaminias Salemiya

■ City	● Other site
— Qanat	O Reservoir

0   10   20 km

500

0 m

Fig. 53. Map of Chalcidice and the eastern steppe zone, with qanats and other water installations marked. After B. Geyer, 'Des fermes byzantines aux palais omayyades, ou l'ingénieuse mise en valeur des plaines steppiques de Chalcidique', in L. Nordiguian, J.-F. Salles (eds), Aux origines de l'archéologie aérienne. A. Poidebard (1878-1955), Beirut, 2000, pp. 109-22.

attempted to date sites through the study of surface scatters of pottery. However, pottery chronologies were not well refined at the time, and uncertainty about the date of many sites remained. The inscriptions were almost all late Roman in date (fourth - sixth century). Nevertheless, Mouterde and Poidebard considered that the *limes* system was developed in the early empire.

New research has enabled the settlements to be more closely dated, and raised questions about the history and nature of agricultural exploitation of the steppe. There is little evidence of any grand military organization. As with the limestone massif, the more arid regions of Chalcidice do not appear to have been developed in the early empire. Some of the regular field systems noted in the western parts and in the north in the Jebel Hass may be due to Roman planning in the second or third centuries, but otherwise the region was during the early empire an area of semi-nomadic communities which were probably engaged in raising livestock. There is the well-known third-century temple in the eastern part of the region, at Isriye, indicative of a community with the funds, organizational capacity and manpower to build a monumental structure of this sort, but otherwise this site seems to have become of real military importance only under Diocletian. Some Roman military presence can be detected along routes of communication, and in larger settlements of late Roman times (see below), but many of Poidebard's 'forts' appear to be late Roman farms (or, in some cases, Umayyad and Abbasid). Thus Chalcidice owes little to Roman military organization and much to a growing population in late Roman times, just like the Dead Cities.

The late Roman settlements appear to have developed independently of any centralized strategy. Exploitation depended on careful water management, either drawing water from distant sources or relying on rainfall and run-off from the mountains. The region around al-Anderin (ancient Androna) is particularly notable for its heavy use of hydraulic *qanat* technology (see p. 164). The *qanat* tunnels can run for long distances, sometimes more than 10 kilometres (6¼ miles), and often supply large communal basins or reservoirs. The primary purpose of most of this water was to irrigate fields, but *qanats* were also used to supply the large settlement that developed at Androna. This seems to be a particularly good example of a countryside developing in symbiosis with an emerging urban centre. In more remote and drier regions further east such water sources were not available or too difficult to exploit, but cereal crops could be cultivated by locating farms in those places most likely to receive moisture, such as alongside the beds of wadis. Such farms are recognizable by their large, walled enclosures which defined the boundaries of cultivatable land. There are also farms and enclosures away from the wadis, but these tend to enclose smaller areas and were probably used for livestock. In any case, it is likely that even those farms situated in the wadis practised mixed farming of animals and cereals.

Late Roman occupation of the region includes an additional feature: a few large administrative and military complexes which appear to have served the surrounding regions. Like large villages, such elaborate structures were possible only with the support of a developed agricultural infrastructure. The most famous of these is Qasr Ibn Wardan: a complex of three free-standing structures, identified as a 'palace', church and barrack building (fig. 54). The palace is dated by epigraphy to AD 564, and the whole complex would appear to have been constructed in the mid-sixth century. In technique it resembles the archi-

tecture of Constantinople, with complex vaults and domes of baked brick which are unparalleled in the area. The foundations are of basalt, superimposed with walls alternating bands of brick and basalt. The arches and domes are of brick only. The dimensions of the bricks at Qasr Ibn Wardan are of a standard size, resembling those used at Constantinople for the so-called Palace of Justinian and for Hagia Sophia, and it is possible that some materials were imported. However, regional parallels have been recognized: the barracks of nearby Androna, dated AD 558, use the same basic construction technique of basalt and brick, and the ruins of the episcopal palace at Bostra are similar in design to the palace at Qasr Ibn Wardan. The design is also paralleled further afield, by the Umayyad palace at Mshatta in Jordan. These links with other Syrian buildings suggest that, in spite of its Constantinopolitan appearance, Qasr Ibn Wardan was designed by Syrian architects.

The evidence from Chalcidice and the eastern steppe, for a significant increase in exploitation, and thus of population, in the late Roman period, and for reliance on mixed farming, including raising livestock, helps to put the ruins of the limestone massif in perspective. The development of small cities in the eastern steppe went hand-in-hand with the increase in rural settlement. It is likely that the systems of *qanats* required social organization on a scale greater than that of individual villages, or even groups of villages. The developments were of benefit to both city and country. However, there is also evidence for the existence of large estates, and such estates are also an important feature of the Umayyad period. These estates could have possessed organizational capacities similar to those of the small cities of the region, and point to a third element in the relationship between city and country. By the Umayyad period the existence of several large estates and palaces in the region may be an indication that the initiative had passed away from the cities to the rural elites.

Fig. 54.1. Qasr Ibn Wardan, with the church (on the left) and the 'palace' (on the right). It was presumably the residence of an important official or landowner, but nothing is known of its owners.

Fig 54.2. Reconstruction of the north elevation of the church at Qasr Ibn Wardan. After H. C. Butler, Publications of the Princeton University Archaeological Expedition to Syria, II. B. Part 1, plate 1.

Palmyrene

Drier still was the territory of Palmyra. However, Palmyra itself should not be characterized as a 'desert city', for its territory contained numerous small watering places and villages. It is likely that livestock raising was the chief concern, given the problems of irrigating some of the land in this region. These villages seem to have been dependent on, and were probably encouraged by, the city – they appear with the growth of Palmyra and disappear with its fall. Pack animals used for transport and the caravan trade were probably raised there, as, perhaps, were war horses used by Palmyra's powerful militias. Palmyra itself is likely to have been founded by a confederation of nomads who came together and settled at the oasis, and the maintenance of good relations with the tribes of the countryside was absolutely necessary for the city's success in long-distance trade. One explanation for the sudden end of a distinctive Palmyrene culture in the city after its capture by Aurelian in the third century is that a large proportion of its population simply abandoned urban life and returned to a more nomadic existence in the countryside. Unlike Chalcidice and the limestone massif, Palmyrene's development was arrested early on.

The Hauran

The strongest evidence for the notion of village independence comes from the basalt region which lies in the south of the modern Syrian Arab Republic and northern Jordan. The landscape here varies greatly from one district to another and in antiquity the districts bore distinct names, just as they do today (fig. 55). Auranitis was the name given to the uplands (the modern Jebel Druze or, as it is now officially called, Jebel al-'Arab). In the mountainous central part of Auranitis the altitude and cold climate may have discouraged settlement, but this desolate zone was ringed with villages. Winter temperatures in Auranitis were not suited to olives, and both textual and archaeological evidence suggests that viticulture was an important activity, perhaps accompanied by the growing of fruit trees. The northern part of Auranitis around Shaqqa (Maximianopolis), Hayyat and Hit has some of the best conditions for agriculture, and this may explain why two cities (Philippopolis and Maximianopolis) developed here. The rough lava-flows extending north-west of Auranitis were known in antiquity as Trachonitis (modern Leja). The landscape here is rugged and desert-like, except for the pockets of fertile land in the depressions. The more important settlements tended to be located on the edge of the larger depressions, or at the very edges of the Leja flows, close to land better suited for farming. To the west of Auranitis lies the broad plain of Batanaea (the Nuqra), which shades off into Gaulanitis (the Golan) further to the west. Although not well watered, Batanaea was developed in the Roman period and probably concentrated on the production of grain. Villages were often situated on rocky outcrops so as not to take up agricultural land.

The inhospitable terrain of Trachonitis made it difficult to administer, and in the first century BC the region is presented in our sources as a refuge for bandits. King Herod was granted control of it, and he and his successors placed colonies around the region and encouraged agriculture. It is worth noting, however, epigraphic evidence suggesting that there were villages in Trachonitis in pre-Roman times, so the wholesale characterization of the inhabitants as robbers hiding in caves may be inaccurate. By the late first century AD we hear no more about the bandits of Trachonitis, and from then on the region was characterized by village settlements. Nevertheless the Romans saw fit to build a road across the region, and inscriptions attest the presence of military personnel, which may indicate that the forces of coercion were still required.

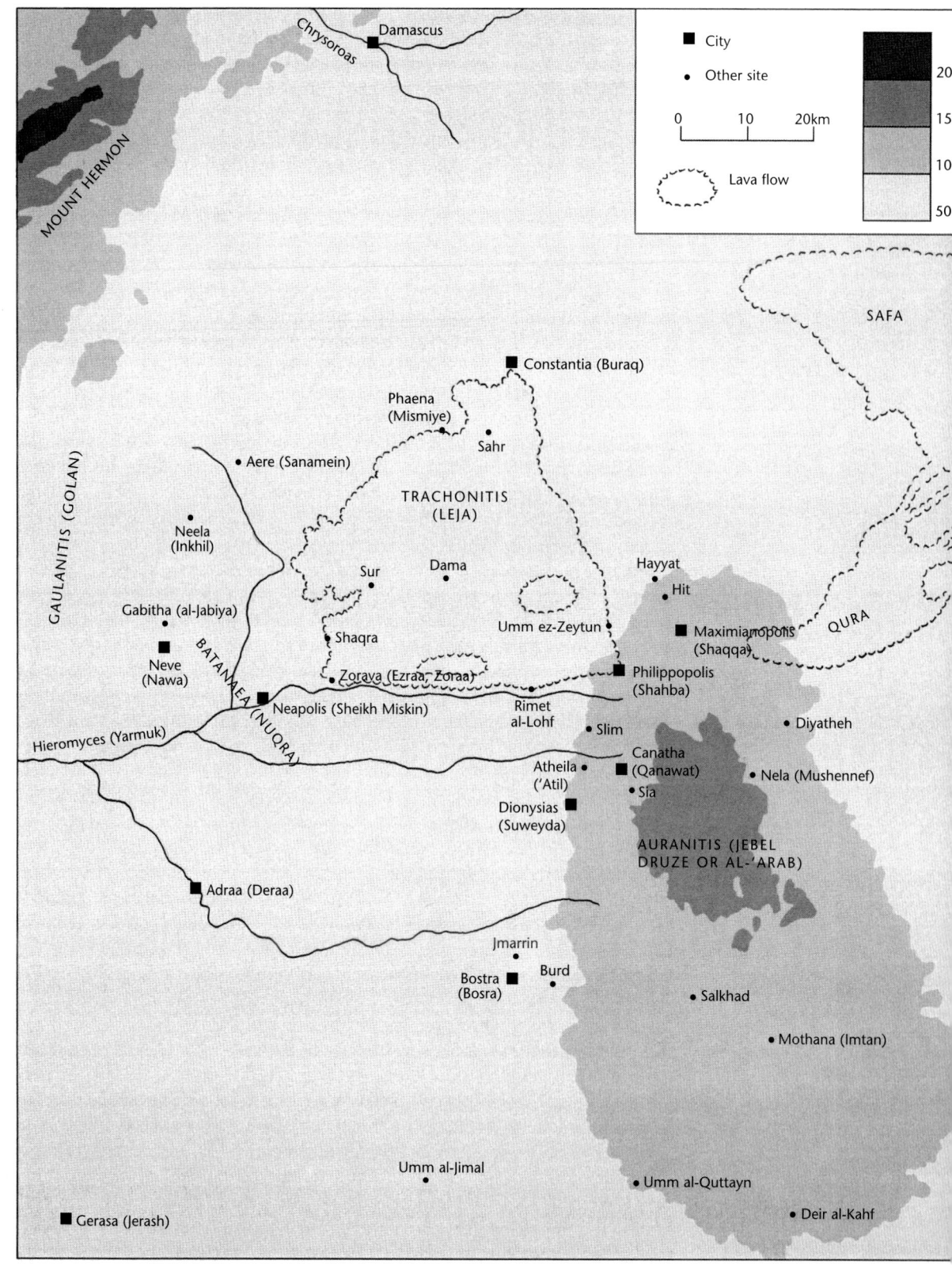

Fig. 55. The Hauran.

At the time of Pompey the only city in the region was Canatha (Qanawat), which appears to have controlled a large section of the southern part of Auranitis and the northern part of Batanaea. In the early empire other parts of Batanaea are likely to have been included in the territories of the cities to the south, in particular Adraa (Deraa) and Bostra (Bosra). To the north of Canatha lay a large number of villages which do not appear to have been subject to any city in either early or late Roman times, and it is from here, in the northern part of Auranitis, and in Trachonitis, that some of our best evidence for village life comes, although recent studies have also looked in detail at other areas of the Hauran. Parts of Trachonitis and Batanaea may have been given over to large imperial and private estates, and there is some evidence for small ecclesiastical domains in the late Roman period, but it would seem that the village was the dominant social unit in all areas throughout the Roman era. There are strong similarities with the Dead Cities of the north. The villages have no formal plans, no roads or streets, and contain irregular open spaces between buildings. House plans resemble those of the limestone massif – the ground floor being reserved for economic activities, and upper for living – but there are notable differences (see chapter 8). Like their modern counterparts in the Hauran, the outskirts of the ancient villages were ringed with small enclosed gardens and plantations, the larger open fields lying beyond these. There is evidence from the inscriptions, particularly from northern Auranitis and Trachonitis, that the village inhabitants formed a commune with common funds for public works, and that land could also be owned communally. There may also have been village assemblies in special buildings set aside for this purpose, though none has been securely identified and some would question the existence of such structures.

Overall, the agricultural development of the Hauran between the first century BC and the seventh century AD was a success, and ancient field systems cover practically the whole region. Dated inscriptions suggest two main phases of building, one lasting from the late third or early fourth century until the early fifth, and a second from the first half of the sixth to the early seventh. Inscriptions also mention hydraulic projects but it seems that these were intended to supply village reservoirs rather than to irrigate fields. As in the Dead Cities, the agriculture of the entire region looks as if it relied mainly on precipitation. In late Roman times the villages may have come under pressure from nomadic tribes from the desert regions to the east of the Hauran, but the epigraphic evidence of the first to third century AD hints at a possible symbiotic relationship between villagers and nomads, and in some cases the inhabitants may have been members of a nomadic tribe that had adopted a sedentary life (some scholars have questioned these interpretations, however, positing a more antagonistic relationship between the villagers and the nomads to the east).

Much information about the Hauran derives from inscriptions, and again those of northern Auranitis and Trachonitis are particularly important. Many are undated, and thus rather difficult to fit into a detailed chronological framework. Many are also no longer *in situ*, having been reused in other structures. A large number, however, name officials, buildings and settlements, and in doing so provide a wealth of evidence for the character of local administration and village institutions. There is a bewildering variety of officers whose titles suggest very specific functions. Some have seen this as evidence of a complex, almost city-like system of autonomous village government, with elected officials and colleges of magistrates performing specific tasks. This might appear to suggest a top-down approach, with Rome encouraging the agricultural and civic development of a backward region of Syria (often using centurions as administrators in the early empire), as part of a general strategy of urbanization. Others have raised doubts. A few of the titles may be inexact or inconsistent Greek translations of traditional titles for more general offices such as a village chief or head man. Most of the officials are named on building inscriptions, and hence their function may have been to supervise construction, or provide for a religious or public building in some other way. Some may have been temporary posts, specifically for the purpose of erecting a building, and so these people cannot really be seen as village administrators. Some of the titles occur almost exclusively in the Hauran and Arabia, and are perhaps peculiar to the region. There is some evidence for a shift in the titles being used in the building inscriptions between the early and late empire, with old ones dropping out of use and new ones being introduced. Some old ones, such as *episkopos* ('overseer'), continued, but the meaning was changed (in the case of *episkopos*, it also signified 'bishop' from the fourth century). This alternative view plays down the notion of any complex village bureaucracy, and with it any planned imperial strategy for the region. Whatever the case, the epigraphic evidence from the Hauran provides us with extremely important, if only partial, evidence about social organization, religious duties, land management and ownership of common land, both sacred and secular, among the villages.

As in the steppe east of Chalcis, some of the villages of the Hauran achieved city status. This has been seen as possible evidence for an imperial policy of urbanization, with the region passing from lawless banditry to a land of settled villages and thence to a landscape organized into city states. Opponents of this view object that the geographical distribution of the cities is peculiar and very uneven, if there were a policy of urbanizing the region: four (Canatha, Dionysias, Philippopolis and Maximianopolis) are concentrated in the north-western part of Auranitis, and one (Constantia) is located at the northern edge of Trachonitis. One explanation for this configuration is that imperial estates occupied large parts of Batanaea, and perhaps Trachonitis. Cities would not be developed on imperial property. Another explanation is economic: the first four of these were situated on or close to some of the best agricultural lands and water supplies of the region.

Apart from settlements with the status of village or city, we also encounter those with the title *metrokomia*, 'mother-village'. The title is found in Batanaea and Trachonitis. To give a village a purely honorary title (as was perhaps sometimes the case for cities with the title *metropolis*) would be unusual; that it designates some administrative function would seem more likely. The term might indicate that *metrokomiai* were the top rank in a hierarchy of villages, but there is no clear evidence that other villages were subordinate to the known *metrokomiai*. One ingenious solution is that the term was granted as an intermediate stage in the process of urbanization, so that a village became a *metrokomia* before acquiring city status. However, there is as yet no evidence that any *metrokomiai* became cities (unless one counts the evidence from late Roman civic and ecclesiastical lists that Phaena in Trachonitis eventually did – see p. 120). Therefore it is possible that the term designated a settlement that could *not* become a city. A recent suggestion is that *metrokomiai* were, in the context of the Hauran at least, settlements located on imperial estates. An inscription from Sanamein mentions such an estate, and the known *metroko-*

miai are located in the vicinity. There was no question of settlements on imperial estates attaining city status, so the term *metrokomia* could be viewed as a kind of substitute title for large villages that might have attained city status had they lain outside the estates. A number of the *metrokomiai* had bishops in the fourth century, suggesting that they were places of some importance, and this fact may explain why late Roman ecclesiastical lists placed Phaena among the cities. Such reasoning adheres to the view that there was a general trend towards urbanization which specific circumstances denied to these settlements, and that as elsewhere urbanization and rural development were linked.

RURAL RESOURCES AND THEIR EXPLOITATION

Water

The distribution of natural water supplies throughout the region is very uneven, and water, more than any other resource, has shaped the pattern of settlement. Below an annual average of 250 millimetres (10 inches) of rainfall, farming becomes very difficult without irrigation, but livestock raising is possible in the steppe zone, which is characterized by about 150-250 millimetres of annual rainfall (fig. 56). A limited amount of arable farming in this steppe zone is possible through judicious use of what little water there is, and occasional rains can be used to sow one-off crops. Beyond this zone, in the true desert, wells are necessary to support life, and only seasonal presence of flocks is possible. This is the zone of camel herders and nomads.

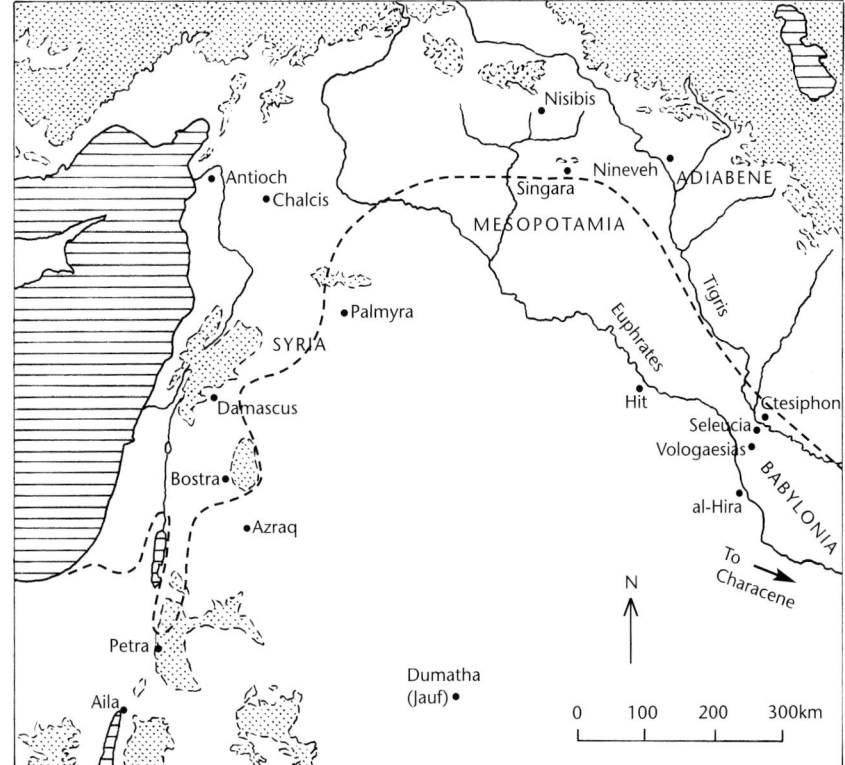

Fig. 56. Desert, steppe and sown: approximate limits of desert, steppe and regions where dry farming is possible. The land to the north of the broken line receives 200 millimetres or more of rainfall annually; the regions to the south receive less.

Water could be transported from a source to a place where it was needed, but this often required considerable effort and investment. Many of the more elaborate installations were likely to have been organized by cities or by the Roman state, because they would seem to be beyond the capabilities of villages. With large projects, such as aqueducts, dams or canals, the involvement of the military is often apparent (fig. 190). The Roman army possessed both the technological skills and the manpower to carry out such jobs efficiently; if necessary, it could also coerce locals into assisting. But military involvement need not mean that the project was intended solely for military purposes, and it may have been undertaken for the public good at the behest of governors or other Roman officials, or commissioned and paid for by local authorities.

Aqueducts are the best-known and most conspicuous form of hydraulic installation of the Roman period, and are closely associated with 'consumer' cities. Where at all possible, the aqueduct ran below ground, following the contours of the terrain, since this was generally cheaper than raising the channel on masonry supports such as arches. Only when the terrain left no other option were arches and bridges contemplated. Because gravity was the sole source of power conducting the water, the source normally had to be higher than the city itself. In the case of the aqueduct which supplied the coastal port of Tyre the source was at more or less the same level as the city, about 5 kilometres (3 miles) to the south, on the coast at Ras al-Ain. The solution was to build large, high-walled tanks around the points where water emerged from the ground. These artificially raised the level of the source and created a sufficient head of water to supply the aqueduct, which then ran on arches for its entire length, extending alongside the main road into Tyre on its final approach. The tanks and a section of the aqueduct at Ras al-Ain still function, although the water is now drawn from the aqueduct for irrigation of surrounding fields (fig. 57).

Fig. 57. Aqueduct at Ras al-Ain, south of Tyre. The concrete channel is modern, but sits on top of Roman arches.

The main purpose of aqueducts is thought to have been to supply baths, hence their association with particularly 'Roman' and city-oriented ways. But they also supplied small reservoirs, fountains, nymphaea (see p. 249) and public latrines. Private houses and workshops might also tap the supply (presumably for a fee, which went towards maintenance). The main aqueduct channel needed regular cleaning to remove lime deposits and blockages, and so it had to be large enough for someone to crawl in, and often was large enough to stand in. Inside the city terracotta pipes were commonly used to distribute supplies, but lead pipes have also been found in urban contexts (for example, at Berytus). Because they appropriated water sources, often in locations distant from the destination, and were very wasteful (all unused water poured directly into the city drains), the social symbolism of aqueducts seems particularly appropriate to the subject of relations between the city and country. Aqueducts appear to present us with a good example of the consumer city parasitizing the countryside and consuming its vital resources, giving nothing in return. However, it seems that rights to tap water along the course of an aqueduct could be negotiated. Research at Caesarea shows that the aqueducts which supplied the city were tapped to supply lesser settlements and rural needs. Thus, even if the city benefited most from the construction of aqueducts, rural communities along their routes also stood to gain.

Other projects sought to conserve and regulate water supplies. Although dams are an important way of managing water in many parts of the world today, they were not a major feature of water management in the Roman empire. Large dams seem to be a feature only of the drier provinces, and several good examples are known from Syria and Jordan. One of the finest is the dam at Harbaqa, near Palmyra (fig. 58). It is probably a Palmyrene work of the late first or second century, but the dam and its irrigation system were utilized again in the eighth century by the Umayyads. It blocks the Wadi el-Barda and is 345 metres (377 yards) long and about 20 metres (65 feet) tall, constructed of rubble and mortar, and faced with limestone cladding. During the winter season rainfall collected behind the dam, forming a lake (which today has largely silted up) that could be used throughout the year. Outlets at the base of the barrage controlled the flow of water from the lake, which fed into a reservoir downstream. From the reservoir water was drawn off in conduits to feed the valley into which the wadi originally flowed. Dams such as these created oases in the dry zones, greatly increasing the agricultural productivity of the steppe

Fig. 58. The Harbaqa dam near Palmyra. It was presumably an important road station on the routes between Palmyra, Damascus and Emesa.

and providing water for travellers, traders and their animals. Elsewhere, on rivers and streams, the dams were often linked to canals and aqueducts. At Caesarea the Crocodilon river was dammed to feed the low-level aqueduct and a system of water mills. Still functioning is the masonry dam of rubble and mortar on the Orontes at Homs (Emesa). The date of the original phase of construction, and of successive works, is unclear, but it is assumed to be Roman in origin. In this case the purpose was to increase the capacity of a natural lake into which the Orontes flowed and to regulate the river. Canals drew water off from the lake to supply the fields of the valley downstream, and to supply the gardens of Emesa. The older works suggest a structure between 5 and 7 metres (16 and 23 feet) high and up to 2 kilometres (1¼ miles) in length, and before alterations in the 1930s this dam retained some 90 million cubic metres

(19,800 million UK gallons) of water. By regulating the flow of the Orontes, the dam may well have helped to increase the area of cultivatable land downstream by allowing marshlands to be drained.

Like aqueducts and dams, canals required the mobilization of considerable manpower and expertise. The canalization projects around Antioch under Vespasian, which involved soldiers and inhabitants of the city, have already been mentioned (p. 133). One seems to have been to supply city fulling-mills, but other work may have been for water transport, making the Orontes and its tributaries in the Antioch region more navigable and at the same time helping to improve drainage off the marshy Amik plain north of the city. Some projects were perhaps prompted purely by military requirements, but civic needs may have inspired others. The best-preserved evidence for such work is at Seleucia Pieria. The city's artificial port was in danger of silting up, and as a preventative measure under Vespasian soldiers dug a tunnel 1300 metres (1420 yards) long through a mountain spur to divert a seasonal stream away from the harbour (fig. 59). The work is impressive, and in some places the tunnel runs 50 metres (55 yards) below the surface, but in principle it was little different from the *qanats* and aqueduct channels found elsewhere, which ran for many kilometres underground. Such projects illustrate how Roman technology could transform the forces of nature.

A *qanat* or chain well consists of a gently sloping tunnel, dug into a hill or mountain to tap an underground water source. The tunnel then drew water downhill from this source and delivered it to an outlet, often in the form of a large basin or a canal. Above ground its course was marked by the presence of vertical shafts, spaced at regular intervals. These acted as ventilation and access points but also for extracting spoil when the tunnel was being dug. *Qanats* are particularly common in the steppe, and there is an impressive example at Palmyra, built to supply the Efqa spring which was an important source of water on the south-western side of the city. As we have seen (fig. 53), some qanats run for more than 10 kilometres (6¼ miles), and are impressive feats of engineering which were probably achieved through a high degree of social co-ordination.

Fig. 59. *Seleucia Pieria, the so-called 'Titus Tunnel', which diverted a seasonal stream through a hillside. Shafts were dug at intervals to provide access from above.*

Less grand, but perhaps more conspicuous at the source, were irrigation schemes which drew water off directly from the rivers. Large water wheels called noriahs still survive on the Orontes river today; these are powered by the flow of the river. Containers are attached to the wheel and used to lift the water up into the channel of a small aqueduct, which irrigates fields and gardens in the vicinity. Noriahs were common in medieval times, but the only certain evidence for their existence in the Roman period is from Apamea, where a fifth-century mosaic depicts one in operation (fig. 60).

Unless supported by a nearby town or city, smaller communities could not afford elaborate installations for water. Even in cities simple time-honoured means of supply were used, particularly wells and rock-cut cisterns, and it was not uncommon for urban dwellings to be supplied by one or two such installa-

Fig. 60. The wheel of a noriah on its stepped stone plinth, depicted on a mosaic from the portico of the cardo maximus at Apamea, dated AD 469.

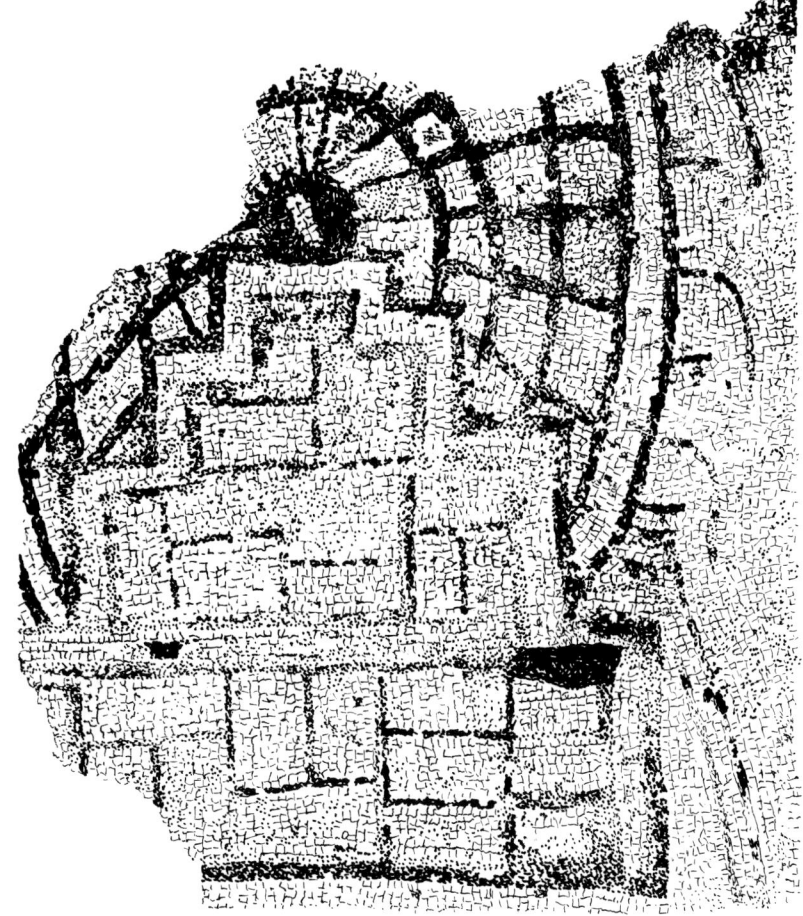

tions. Cisterns are typically bell- or bottle-shaped, with a narrow neck to slow evaporation, the mouth often being covered with stone slabs. Communities in the highlands had to find simple solutions for their everyday needs. In the limestone massif of northern Syria there are very few springs even in the lowland areas, and none at all on the hills. The agriculture practised depended on rainfall, but water storage was essential for human and animal requirements, and there are hundreds of small cisterns, about 1 metre (3¼ feet) deep. In such an environment it is perhaps surprising to find bath buildings like those at Brad, Babisqa and Serjilla, but these too were supplied by cisterns and, unlike their city counterparts, were probably frugal in their use of water. Large communal reservoirs, with roofs supported by pillars or vaults, are found in both cities and villages all over Syria and the Near East. Good examples are to be seen at Canatha (Qanawat) and Umm el-Jimal in the Hauran, but the most impressive are those at Sergiopolis in the north-eastern steppe (Resafa: fig. 61). These immense underground vaulted chambers were sufficiently impressive to receive a mention by the historian Procopius. The largest of the three is estimated to have contained more than 15,000 cubic metres (3,300 UK gallons) of water, enough to see a substantial population through the dry season and perhaps an indication that the city was sometimes expected to receive refugees from the surrounding countryside during Sasanian attacks.

Communal wells or birkets (cisterns open to the sky) also served villages and cities alike. Birkets in the highlands and remote places were fed by rainwater channelled into them (fig. 62). Evaporation usually emptied them by the end of the summer. In the lowlands and cities they were sometimes fed by aqueducts, and remained full all year round. The grandest examples are those at Bostra (fig. 36), the largest of which is about 150 by 120 metres (164 by 130 yards) and 8 metres (26 feet) deep, but there are also good examples at Gerasa, where a double birket to the north of the city measures about 88 by 43 metres (96 by 47 yards) and is 3 metres (10 feet) deep.

In remote and drier parts of the steppe and semi-desert where there was a complete lack of springs and perennial water channels, rainwater required very careful management. The development of villages in places like the Negev suggests that such inhospitable environments were capable of producing significant agricultural surpluses if the right strategies for water collection and storage were pursued. Barrages were built blocking wadi beds, and channels directed water to cisterns or to fields where they could provide moisture for the soil. When rains come, even the desert can prove productive.

Fig. 61. One of the great cisterns at Resafa. Procopius ascribes their construction to the emperor Justinian, but they are probably earlier, perhaps belonging to the reign of Anastasius (AD 491-517).

Agriculture and Livestock

Grain was the staple of the ancient diet, and much agricultural land in Syria would have been turned over to its cultivation. The surpluses produced by smallholders and great estates found ready markets in the cities, and additional surpluses could find markets abroad. Some arrangements for export may have been reciprocal, where grain-rich cities sold their surpluses to other cities in exchange for different sorts of produce. A city might be rewarded with a gift of grain by an emperor or a wealthy citizen (fig. 74). Such gifts might have helped alleviate a real need, bring the cost of grain down, or allow the city to sell its own surplus elsewhere. There is some textual evidence to suggest that wheat from the Syrian region was regarded as superior to Egyptian wheat, and was more expensive, but this did not prevent coastal cities from importing Egyptian produce.

The degree to which Mediterranean coastal cities depended economically on one another is a topic of debate, but it should have been possible for famines in one area to be alleviated by imports from another. Widespread crop failures in the early empire, such as happened in Syria and Egypt between AD 44 and 47, probably encouraged the larger cities to attempt to secure supplies. Arrangements, however, may have been *ad hoc* and not very reliable, and sometimes it was not possible to find alternative sources. Famines and shortages were frequent occurrences, and cities might attempt to stockpile grain, although such practices were not always undertaken for humanitarian reasons. As noted at the beginning of this chapter, control of the food supply was a route to social power, but crises placed a strain on distribution systems. Elites could profit by importing or stockpiling and selling the grain at inflated prices during a regional or local famine; conversely the authorities could intervene to fix low prices even when supplies were running out. Precisely this sort of crisis

Fig. 62. The birket at the village of Nela or Nelkomia (modern Mushennef) in Auranitis, which lies behind a religious sanctuary with a small basalt temple dated to AD 171 (centre).

occurred under Constantius II, when the Caesar Gallus came into conflict with the great landowners and councillors of Antioch, who refused to lower prices when a shortage occurred. A violent riot ensued, in which Gallus fled the city and the Syrian governor was lynched by an angry mob. Between 381 and 384 there was another shortage of grain in Syria. The *comes Orientis* tried to regulate prices to prevent starvation, but bakers and suppliers refused to produce any bread at the recommended tariff.

As well as providing surpluses for cities, supplying the army of Syria would have been a major task for Syrian farmers. Sixty thousand soldiers would consume 22,000 tonnes of wheat a year, assuming a kilo (2¼ lb) per person per day. These quantities had either to be acquired directly through tax in kind or purchased by the state in exchange for cash. While supplies could be transported long distances from their places of production, much of the food supply for the army would have been provided locally. This probably explains the location of legionary bases in fertile areas of farmland such as Commagene, the Orontes valley, or Bostra. It is also highly likely that imperial estates were heavily involved in supplying the army. During campaigns, when large numbers of additional soldiers were concentrated in Syria, grain was sometimes imported from neighbouring provinces as well. Without extra supplies, too many troops in one place are likely to have caused food shortages. This may have been the cause of the famine under Gallus, who was preparing for a campaign; a similar event occurred in AD 362, when Julian came into conflict with the Antiochene landowners over grain prices after they had been driven up by the presence of troops preparing for his Persian war. In these cases the balance of production and consumption was disrupted.

Modern surveys have revealed traces of ancient field systems in many areas of Syria, particularly in the more arid regions east of the Orontes and in the north around the Jebel Semaan, and in the Hauran. These have often survived because little or no farming has occurred in the region since Roman or Umayyad times, whereas the ancient field boundaries of the richer and more fertile lands are easily confused with more recent ones. However, property boundaries are notoriously conservative, which sometimes allows us to use modern alignments as evidence for ancient arrangements. Even so, dating any ancient field system is no easy task. The field systems around Antioch appear to be an extension of the city's cadastral plan, suggesting that these were developed under the Seleucids. In other fertile lowland areas much older traditional field boundaries may have survived into the Roman period. This much is implied by the very ancient tradition of measuring land by grain needed to sow it, a practice recorded in the Babatha and Petra archives.

To date, some of the most detailed studies of field systems have been undertaken in the Hauran. The fields there range from regular, formally aligned systems in long strips, to irregular patterns which perhaps predate the Roman annexation. A Roman road running from Sia to Dionysias (Suweyda) cuts across such irregular fields (fig. 63), as does another from Sia to Canatha (Qanawat). The latter road diverges from its course slightly to avoid some tombs of the first century AD, providing a *terminus post quem* for its construction. This suggests that in the vicinity of Canatha, Dionysias and Sia these irregular fields are first century AD or earlier. Field systems west of Bostra (Bosra), in the vicinity of the modern village of Burd, align with the mid-second-century Roman road running from Bostra to Mothana (Imtan) and presumably belong to the same period. These fields are laid out in a highly regular rectilinear pattern and are perhaps the product of Roman land surveys following the Roman absorption of Nabataea in AD 106. Similar regular patterns are known around Mothana itself. Here the evidence points to development under Roman rule, probably on land that had not previously been cultivated, and possibly in connection with Roman military settlement. It is quite likely, given what we know about settlement patterns in Syria as a whole, that many of the regular field systems found in the marginal and drier inland areas were created in the Roman period. Not all need have been connected with the requirements of the military (although some may be the result of state relocations of peasants dispossessed by settlement of army veterans). As stated earlier in this chapter, in the second century the Roman state introduced laws designed to encourage the utilization of uncultivated lands, and it is possible that the planning and layout of field systems in these marginal zones belongs to that time, as landless peasants moved in and began cultivating regions which had previously been sparsely settled. Many systems may have been established prior to the reign of Diocletian (AD 284-305), because the well-known land surveys of his reign, and other, later surveys of the fourth century, appear in the main to have confirmed existing boundaries rather than creating new ones.

Inland, in the plains of the Hauran and around Chalcis, fields for grain were probably predominant. Olives and grapes were valuable crops, and land planted with olive trees or vines was reckoned at a much higher rate of tax than land for grain. However, olives and grapes can grow in more marginal conditions, in stony highland areas where arable farming is more difficult. The presence or absence of wine or oil presses (see below), and their density in

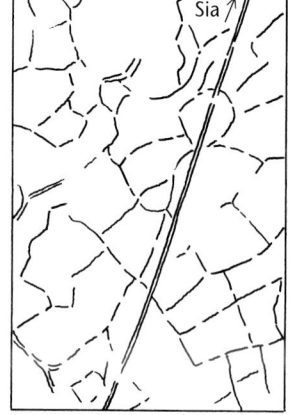

Fig. 63. Roman road from Sia to Dionysias, cutting across older field systems. After P. Gentelle, 'Éléments pour une histoire des paysages et du peuplement du Djebel Hawran septentrional, en Syrie du sud', in J.-M. Dentzer (ed.), Hauran I, Paris, 1985, p. 39.

different regions of Syria, helps to confirm the importance of these crops in the local economy. Some field systems also seem better suited to them. Ancient sources describe the inland hills of Auranitis as being covered in grape vines, and, as mentioned earlier, the climate is unsuitable for olives. An abundance of presses attests to the importance of wine in the local economy. The remains of ancient terraces there show that land was parcelled into elongated plots by long walls running perpendicular to the terraces, from the top of the slopes to the bottom; in other words, the individual properties were divided into fairly narrow steps running down the hillsides, rather than each cultivator having a terrace. Such fields were best suited to plants like vines rather than being put to the plough.

The slender, strip-like field systems common in some areas, such as the limestone massif of north-western Syria, may have been particularly well suited to fruit trees, but this observation is based on modern analogies; in the plains of Batanaea such fields were probably intended for grain, and the vine terraces of Auranitis described above are divided into elongated plots (of course, it is possible to raise trees or vines together with grain in the same field). Nevertheless, fruit was of sufficient significance to be mentioned in the literary sources: Syria is noted as a producer of pistachios, pears, apples and figs by Roman writers, which suggests that these were exported. Once dried, figs and dates could be easily shipped to other parts of the Roman world, as could raisins, gathered from wild vines around Laodicea and Antioch. A small, carrot-shaped amphora produced at Berytus and perhaps in Palestine may have been a container for exporting dates (fig. 73.2). Walnuts are among the products known to have been carried in amphorae like the late Roman Palestinian bag-shaped type (see chapter 6), and while such crops could have been destined for local or regional consumption, export too is possible. Walnut trees could produce a crop on higher slopes than olives or figs, and they were perhaps harvested in the coastal mountains. The Peutinger Table (see p. 131) places between Raphanea and Emesa a location called Carion, perhaps derived from the Greek Karyon, 'chestnut' or, more probably in this context, 'walnut'. But foreign fruits may also have been imported to the region; at any rate, the documents from Masada show Herod importing apples from Cumae in Italy.

Through irrigation projects of the sort described earlier the amount of agricultural land could be extended, but in drier regions livestock raising became increasingly significant. It is likely to have been the dominant economy of the marginal steppe zone. Drought or minor fluctuations in climate could have devastating effects on these communities, and it was better for them to pursue a flexible farming strategy, concentrating on livestock and adopting a variety of other approaches as conditions permitted. This subject seems to take us far away from a world of cities, buildings and elites, into the worlds of pastoralists, nomads and people living on the peripheries of 'Graeco-Roman' society, who invested their cash surpluses in animals rather than in durable buildings. And yet pastoralists did not exist in isolation from town and city; nomad economies relied on sedentary populations for materials and foodstuffs, and they were dependent on markets for milk, wool and meat.

Raising flocks of animals need not have been an entirely separate occupation from that of arable farming. The finds of mangers in the houses of the Dead Cities and the Hauran suggest that animals were part of the sedentary economy too. Draught animals were needed for cultivating fields, and there is evidence from the limestone massif and the Hauran of cattle raising. But it is difficult to assess the economic importance of raising of livestock on farms compared to the practices of pastoralism and transhumance, because the evidence for the various modes cannot be quantified either in absolute or relative terms.

Different methods of livestock raising – sedentary farming, pastoralism, or long-distance transhumance – could potentially compete for land. Transhumant livestock herders will have moved into the drier areas during the winter months when grazing was better, and brought their flocks closer to the settled regions during the summer months. Legal arrangements were sometimes necessary between farmers and pastoralists, particularly over grazing rights. These agreements are occasionally mentioned in the papyrus and parchment archives, and might even be of concern to the cities. The tariff from Palmyra (chapter 6) makes a distinction between Palmyrenes grazing flocks in Palmyrene territory, who do not have to pay for the privilege, and those from outside Palmyrene territory, who do. Routes of transhumance, pastures and peoples are likely to have been carefully regulated by the civic authorities of the region, and major movements of flocks and people were probably of interest to the imperial authorities as well.

It is difficult to generalize about the status of nomads, or even to draw a strict distinction between them and settled farmers. The peoples of the steppe, who built no permanent settlements, qualify as true nomads, but sometimes the line between transhumant pastoralists and sedentary peoples is blurred. Some nomads and sedentary farmers may form part of a single community in the eyes of the inhabitants, one group remaining in the village to cultivate crops and the other taking the animals to seasonal pastures.

Animal bones from excavations suggest that sheep and goats supplied the meat of preference in the region, and these animals are well suited to pastoral and transhumant herders. Pork consumption was generally low, as was beef. Religious taboos may account in part for the relative dearth of pig bones. Apart from Jewish prohibitions, other communities also abstained from pork. The his-

Fig. 64. The underlying continuities of rural life: modern nomad family and flock, near Urfa (ancient Edessa) in Mesopotamia.

torian Herodian wrote that Elagabalus would not touch pigs 'by Phoenician law'[25] (whatever that meant). However, most of the animal bone evidence is drawn from Israeli sites only, and further study may reveal differences between different regions, and perhaps between city and country. Pork consumption is noted in some of the more Hellenized towns and cities (one is reminded of the Gadarene swine of Mark 5 and Luke 8, for example), and consumption of this meat may have been a sign of high status and 'Hellenization'. However, it may also have been a sign of 'Romanization'. Italy is unique among the regions of the Roman Mediterranean for its very high consumption of pork, and the Italian preference for this meat is mirrored in some Roman colonies in the western and eastern Mediterranean. The evidence from Berytus indicates that pork was an important element of the diet there, right down to the Muslim conquest in the seventh century AD. Does this indicate Italian-style dietary preferences among the colonists, and its maintenance in succeeding centuries? Further analysis will no doubt provide evidence for regional or local preferences, and it will be interesting to see if the analysis of faunal remains reveals further evidence for diets conforming to religious taboos. After all, food and dietary preferences are an important aspect of social identities.

There is plenty of material evidence for agricultural activity even in those places where field systems do not survive and where excavations have not yet been undertaken. The presence of livestock is signified by stone water troughs or mangers. The main Mediterranean crops – grain, olives and grapes – all needed processing, and the stone installations often survive when all other traces of agricultural activities have disappeared. Corn grinders and querns are commonly made of rough volcanic basalt, and vary in size and complexity from small, hand-operated devices suitable for domestic use to large rotary mills turned by animals or a couple of people (fig. 65). More elaborate equipment included water mills, employed where running water was available. Olives and grapes tended to require special installations and processing them was always a communal activity; it is estimated that eight or nine people would normally be needed to operate the mills and presses necessary for making olive

Fig. 65. Basalt mill for processing grain on a large scale.

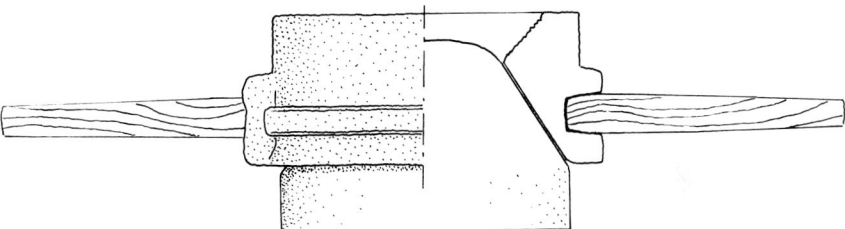

oil, and most of the presses associated with wine production are clearly designed for teamwork.

So many remains of olive mills and presses survive that it is worth describing some of the more prominent types (fig. 66). In the first stage of processing the harvested fruits were crushed to a pulp in stone mills. These might consist of large basins in which simple stone rollers were levered over the fruits using crowbars, or more elaborate rotary mills. The circular stone basins in which the rotary mill wheels were turned are a common sight throughout the Mediterranean, and the same technology was used in the recent past in northern Europe for other types of fruit, such as apples. The mill wheels are stone, fixed to a wooden central axis and turned using a wooden beam, operated by humans or animals (fig. 66.1). Some basins, however, lack any sort of installation for a central axis, and these may have housed cylindrical rollers that could be spun around. Next the pulp, consisting of the crushed olives, their stones, oil and water, was pressed to produce the crude oil. Layers of pulp were placed in flat baskets or panniers, and these were then stacked one atop the other to form a pile that would be squeezed under pressure. The first pressing produced the finest-quality oil; after the pulp had been mixed with water, a second pressing produced a lower quality. Further pressings might obtain more oil, but each time the quality decreased. The residue could be used as fertilizer or animal fodder, or, because it burns easily, for lighting fires or fuelling kilns.

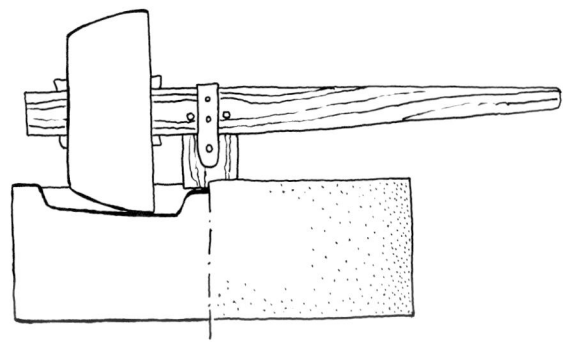

A wide variety of methods for pressing was available in antiquity. Many were variants on the lever press, where the pressure was applied using a wooden beam. This would be slotted into a support at one end and pressure brought to bear at the other. The main variants of the lever press are defined by the mechanism whereby pressure was applied. In some cases winches or ratchets were used to draw the beam down; these could be held in place by counterweights or by being fixed to upright posts or heavy stone blocks on the floor. Others used a screw, held in a heavy stone weight, to draw down the beam (fig. 66.2).

The oil produced by this process was unfit for consumption, regardless of whether it was the first or a subsequent pressing, and contained a mixture of oil, pieces of olive and water. This mixture was allowed to drain into a receptacle set in the floor of the press. Here it settled: the water and detritus sank to the bottom and the lighter oil separated to the top. This could then be ladled off by hand, or more water could be poured in to raise the level of the oil, which might then pour over a sluice into another tank. This first refinement was followed by a second. The oil had to be filtered to remove any remaining impurities, which could be achieved either by straining it into a portable container or basin or by using a variation on the first process of refining. Permanent installations for this second refining process consist of a basin or a series of basins, through which the oil flowed, the idea being that as the oil passed through each basin more of the impurities would sink to the bottom. Water often had to be added to assist the flow and separation.

Fig. 66. Devices for processing olives. After O. Callot, Huileries antiques de Syrie du nord, *Paris, 1984.*

66.1. (Above) Mill for crushing fruits.
66.2. (Below) Screw press, similar to that shown in fig. 67. The beam was drawn down by a screw held in place by a large cylindrical stone weight, bringing pressure to bear on the stack of containers.

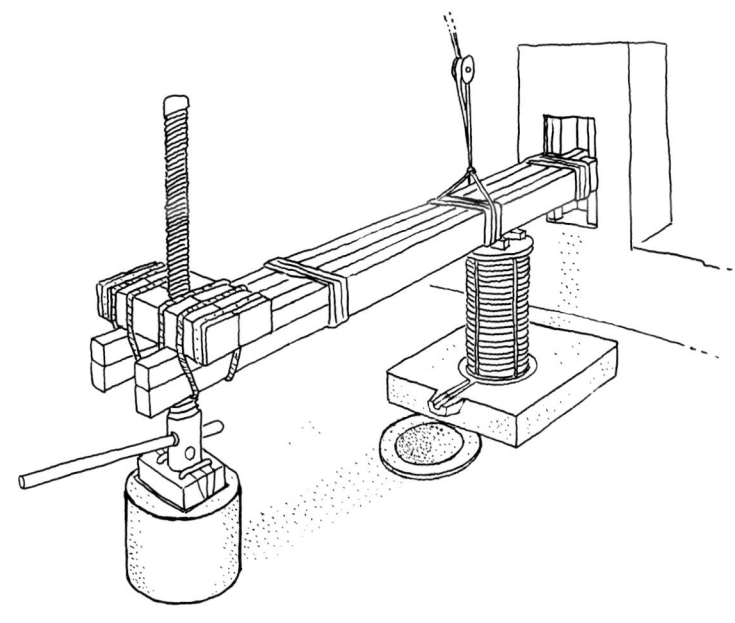

Grapes did not necessarily need pressing, since they could be crushed by treading, although additional juice could be extracted from the grape pulp using a press. Installations identified as presses for grapes have a waterproofed treading floor, which slopes down towards a reservoir. Some also contain the remains of screw or lever presses. The grape juice flowed into the reservoir where it was left to ferment, or else was transferred to pitch-lined jars or casks for fermentation. After this it was transferred to amphoras to mature. However, it was common for fermentation to continue in the amphoras, and these often have small holes in their necks to prevent a build-up of gases that might otherwise have caused the pots to explode. The same press could perhaps be used to produce both olive oil and wine (as asserted by no less an authority than Cato the Elder, author of *On Agriculture*), but one wonders what the quality of such products would be like. Specialized installations seem more likely.

Because oil and wine tended to be packaged in ceramic containers, we are able to trace the movement of these agricultural products far more precisely

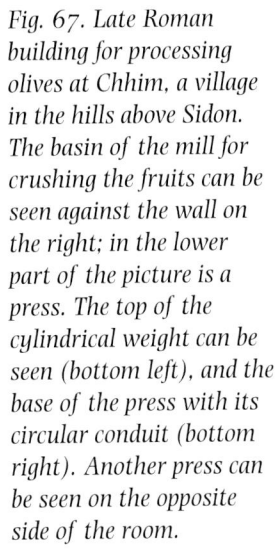

Fig. 67. Late Roman building for processing olives at Chhim, a village in the hills above Sidon. The basin of the mill for crushing the fruits can be seen against the wall on the right; in the lower part of the picture is a press. The top of the cylindrical weight can be seen (bottom left), and the base of the press with its circular conduit (bottom right). Another press can be seen on the opposite side of the room.

than we can grain, and more can be deduced about the trade in these goods. Syrian olive oil receives little notice in the sources, but certain areas of Syria and the Near East are celebrated for the popularity or excellence of their wines: the Orontes valley around Apamea; Berytus; the coast of Palestine around Ascalon and Gaza; and Sharon, Carmel and Diospolis-Lydda. There are, however, some difficulties in marrying the information derived from the texts with that derived from archaeology. The texts suggest that Laodicean wine was particularly favoured abroad. According to Strabo, who was writing in the time of Augustus, it was exported in large quantities to Alexandria in Egypt, but the container in which it was shipped has yet to be identified. The amphora of Berytus has been identified, but it does not appear to have been widely exported. Sometimes, though, the texts and the archaeological finds agree. Gregory of Tours in his *History of the Franks* mentions wine from Gaza, indicating that this product was making its way as far as western Europe into the sixth century. Archaeological evidence confirms a widening market for Gazan wine in the fifth and sixth centuries, and the presence of Gazan amphoras in Gaul confirms Gregory's statement. The movement of goods in amphoras is examined in more detail in chapter 6.

Regional or Local Products

Specialized products, which tended to be non-essentials, are mentioned in textual sources but are often difficult to identify in the archaeological record. These include various perfumes and unguents. Styrax, a gum from a tree resembling a quince, was used in the preparation of medicines and perfumes. Pliny identified the northern coast, on Mount Casius, and Gabala and Marathus, as sources for styrax resin. Balsam was produced in various parts of Palestine, along with papyrus, which grew in the Jordan valley. The most famous specialized product of the Syrian region was purple, a highly expensive dye for which the Phoenician cities were particularly renowned (although this commodity was also produced in other parts of the Mediterranean). Various sea creatures were used, producing colours ranging from purple to brownish-red, but the best quality was extracted from a sea snail, the murex. The product was extremely expensive: while the price edict of Diocletian quotes a maximum price of 175 denarii for a pound of best-quality Tarentine wool, it quotes 50,000 denarii for the same quantity of purple-dyed wool – at a time when a skilled labourer was to receive a maximum daily wage of about 50 denarii. The tremendous value of murex purple permitted a labour-intensive industry, employing fishermen and dyers and the processing of thousands of tonnes of shellfish. Murex fishermen seem to have been organized into guilds according to the ports in or from which they worked, and murex fishing is recorded as the sole occupation on a number of epitaphs. To obtain purple from the murex required mortally wounding it. When stressed or dying the animal produces a secretion which turns purple when exposed to the sun and oxygen. It was a smelly and unpleasant process. The murex snails, fished from the sea, had their shells broken and were left to die in shallow vats, or their dye-producing gland was removed and put in the vat, and salt was added. Over a period of about three days the liquid would become coloured through photochemical action with the sun and air. The resulting mix of fluid and rotting murex was then transferred to heated vats where it was processed for a period of about nine days before straining. Thousands of snails were needed to make a few grams of dye (one estimate suggests 12,000 snails were needed to make enough dye for the border of a single garment), and the industry produced huge quantities of waste in the form of broken shells. A hill on the southern edge of Sidon, into which the city's ancient theatre was built, is formed of crushed murex shells; a testimony to only one of many major purple dye-works along the coast.

Building Materials and Techniques

Most of the surviving buildings of Roman Syria are constructed of local materials, predominantly the abundantly available limestone and basalt. In the Euphrates region a local gypsum was employed, and on the Lebanese coast soft local tufas were occasionally used for foundations and sandstone served as a low-quality substitute for limestone. While stone quarried in one region of Syria might be exported to another, the convenient use of local materials contributed to the persistence of local building techniques over the centuries.

Marbles and granites, which had to be imported, were employed most commonly by cities on the coast (see chapter 6).

Classic Roman building techniques, such as *opus reticulatum* (a decorative facing for rubble and mortar walls using small squared stones laid in diagonal rows), often encountered in Italy, are rarely found in the region, and where used they may have been chosen deliberately as a statement about the Roman affiliations of their builders. The few examples of *opus reticulatum* belong to the early Roman period, and most are associated with client kingdoms: for example, a wall at Samosata, a tomb at Emesa, Herod's third palace at Jericho, and a wall of Herodian date at Caesarea Panias. Another classic Roman building technique, using rubble and mortar faced with brick, is also rare. It is occasionally seen in layers alternating with bands of ashlar masonry. By itself mortar and rubble construction was used for domes and vaults, usually on top of ashlar walls and piers. It is found, for example, in the baths at Dura Europus, Bostra and Philippopolis, and in the domes of late Roman churches. Baked brick was often employed in baths in hypocaust construction, although stone could be used, even for the pillars which supported the hypocaust floors. In the late Roman period baked brick was employed extensively at sites in the steppe, such as Androna (al-Andarin) and Qasr Ibn Wardan, and especially along the Euphrates, at places like Sergiopolis (Resafa), Sura and Barbalissus (Meskene). Some of the brick was probably made locally, but there is good evidence for imports as well (see chapter 6).

An abundance of suitable limestone enabled architects to maintain the tradition of ashlar architecture when in many other parts of the Roman world mortar and brick had become more common. Sometimes we find limestone ashlars used even in those places where mortar would normally be expected, as in the well-preserved dome and vaults in the west baths of Gerasa. This tradition continued throughout the period of Roman rule in Syria: the fifth- and sixth- century houses of the limestone massif of northern Syria, or those of the Hauran, are generally devoid of mortar, bricks or vaults. Dry masonry was the norm, using large blocks, and spanning gaps with a post-and-lintel technique. Grander buildings employed the arch (frequently used for the interior arcades of basilical churches) and the semi-dome (for apses). Limestone was a versatile building material, although it varies greatly in quality from one region to another. It is easy to cut or saw, and limestone surfaces will take elaborate carving and drilling. In some places the deposits are badly fractured, which greatly limits the size of stones that can be quarried; this is not so in other places which have particularly excellent stone (fig. 68).

The basalt regions of the Hauran and Golan, Emesa and north-east of Chalcis are characterized by the use of this dark volcanic stone. It was difficult to cut evenly; buildings constructed of it tend to be made of small, uneven blocks. Nevertheless

Fig. 68. The so-called Hajjar al-Hiblah, the 'Stone of the Pregnant Woman', lies in the quarry south of the temple of Jupiter at Heliopolis, at the foot of the nearby Sheikh Abdullah hill. It is 20 metres long (65 feet), and over 4 metres (13 feet) square, and would have weighed over 1000 tonnes if completed. Although destined for the podium of the Temple of Jupiter, it was never detached from the bedrock.

some monumental buildings, fortifications and houses were formed of finely squared basalt ashlars. Colonnades employed basalt columns and capitals, and the sculptors of the Hauran were able to produce some remarkable basalt reliefs and statues. More commonly buildings were constructed of roughly squared, dry stones, or walls built of wedge-shaped blocks were laid to form an outer and inner face, the void between being filled with rubble. Corners, doorways, windows and occasionally foundations consisted of dry dressed ashlars, and the rubble cores were sometimes bonded with clay or mortar (fig. 69). In the Hauran flat roofs and floors of upper storeys were frequently formed of basalt slabs, laid not on wooden beams but on corbels or stone arches springing from the interior walls of the buildings (this would seem to suggest that there was little or no supply of adequate timber for building in the region). The strength of basalt meant that it was better suited than limestone to corbelling. Even so, only fairly narrow spaces could be roofed in this way. For wider spans, supporting arches were necessary. The problem of roofing the two second-century temples at the village of 'Atil in Auranitis was solved using such transverse arches and roofing slabs, although here the roofs were pitched, as was normal for classical-style temples (fig. 70). One might have expected a city like Philippopolis to have used imported timber, but the surviving buildings suggest that this was not the case, and they too frequently used either roofing slabs or, less commonly, vaults of mortar and rubble. One of the finest examples of basalt roofing is to be found in the elaborate public complex known as the 'Kaisariyeh' at Maximianopolis (Shaqqa). This building employs transverse arches extensively to support the roofing slabs (most of which are only a couple of metres long). The arches span the roofs of two long halls which meet in a large apartment, thought to have been roofed with a dome. The piers for the high arches in one of the halls were strengthened by the use of exterior buttresses, thus minimizing the penetration of the piers into the interior of the building. However, not all of the basalt regions were utterly devoid of wood, even if it had to be imported. At the late Roman village of Umm al-Jimal, 30 kilometres (18½ miles) south of Bostra, there is evidence for the northern nave of the Double Church being roofed with timber, even if the aisles were corbelled in stone.

On the coast the soft, coarse sandstone of petrified dunes was used for a variety of purposes – walls, arches, vaults and columns. It is a poor building material, having very rough surfaces, and is often found rendered with a plaster surface in imitation of limestone or marble. It was probably a material of expediency rather than choice, although some monumental structures were erected using it. The colonnade next to the hippodrome at Tyre utilized this porous sandstone, as did the nearby aqueduct and the monumental arch spanning the main road into the city. In the latter case limestone was also employed for decorative elements.

Where there are stone buildings, quarries are usually never far away. However, not all of the stone was destined for local consumption, and there is growing evidence for regional trade in certain stones in the Syrian region.

Fig. 69. Umm al-Jimal: basalt wall in a private house, consisting of two stone facings, the void between being filled with rubble and clay.

Fig. 70. The northern temple at 'Atil, the ancient village of Atheila, near Dionysias (Suweyda). Note the interior arch, which supported the pitched roof. The elaborately decorated doorway with its flanking niches is ancient, but the blocking of the entrance using pieces of the temple is modern.

Sometimes it was the physical properties of the stones that were the attraction; in other cases stones were desired for their colours and appearance. Hard basalt was a preferred stone for doors of tombs, and these were often carved in imitation of wooden doors. Presumably there were centres of production located in the basalt areas, and those living in other regions could order them from the quarries. Some large basalt grain mills found on Cyprus have been traced to a source in Galilee, near Tiberias. Lava grist from Trachonitis was probably used in road-building; this material served as the penultimate layer on Roman roads in Arabia. Limestone columns were brought into Bostra, where they were set up in the basalt theatre (colour plate 17), or alternating with basalt columns along the main street – a contrast of white and black which presumably reflects an aesthetic choice. The Bekaa valley and the region south-west of Damascus contain extensive deposits of Miocene conglomerate. Some of this is stained with iron oxide, producing an attractive pattern of white inclusions set in a pinkish matrix. There must have been quarries for such conglomerates somewhere in the region, as the stone is encountered in the form of columns and pilasters in the Bekaa and the coastal cities of Lebanon.

Mud brick was the predominant building material in the dry steppe. It was also used in the regions further west, and is sometimes found in the coastal cities where stone buildings were the norm. Mud brick walls were usually, but not always, built on foundations of rubble masonry. This is the common pattern among private houses at Dura Europus, where walls built entirely of stone are rare. There the door jambs were of stone, and the entrances often had moulded lintels or arches. Roofs of buildings at Dura were flat and probably supported by wooden beams overlain with wattle and daub. Mud brick was not confined to small or domestic structures, and at least parts of some defensive circuits were made of this material (for instance, at Sura on the Euphrates).

Timber

The mountains, particularly the Amanus, the Bargylus and Lebanon provided ample supplies of wood: pine, oak, larch, fir, spruce, juniper, cypress and cedar.

Little survives today, although these forests once extended far inland. The now barren Jebel Muntar near Palmyra was referred to as the 'Mount of Terebinths'. It is unclear whether exploitation in the Roman period led to serious deforestation, but the need for fuel for baths in towns and cities is likely to have had environmental consequences as much as the need for building materials. A lack of good wood is implied by the frequency with which stone was employed for lintels over doors and windows of private houses. Stone lintels crack easily, and the builders had to resort to constructing relieving arches to distribute the weight either side of the door or window. These might be proper arches with keystones or simple corbelling, leaving a gap of only a couple of centimetres above the lintel.

A remarkable series of some 200 Latin inscriptions cut into the faces of exposed rock outcrops across the Lebanon range provides us with evidence of an attempt by the Roman state to manage forest resources, perhaps in some sustainable way. These inscriptions, which all belong to the reign of Hadrian, carry a variety of formulas. Some seem to indicate a rotational system of harvesting and planting, or management of particular species: 'Under the Emperor Hadrian Augustus, the limit of the forests. Four species [of tree reserved]. The others for private individuals.' In this case the four types of forbidden tree were probably those destined for naval shipyards, such as cedar and juniper, and perhaps oak and spruce. It is by no means clear whether the vast areas demarcated by the inscriptions indicate an imperial estate or whether some arrangement was made by the Roman state with the pre-existing villages (and perhaps cities like Berytus) over the cutting of timber. The degree of imperial control may have varied from one location to another. While this looks very much like imperial recognition of a conservation problem, it cannot be seen as any sort of serious environmental programme, and merely reserved certain species of tree for exploitation when necessary by imperial agents. But it does suggest that where the use of timber resources was concerned there were potential points of conflict between the needs of the Roman state and those of villagers and even city-dwellers.

Natural Mineral Resources

Although many varieties of mineral deposits are known in Syria, it is far from certain that all were exploited in antiquity. Some clues are provided by place-names, such as settlements called Chalcis (*chalcos* means 'copper' in Greek), which could be taken to suggest (but not to prove) the presence of copper deposits nearby. Ancient copper mines are certainly known from the Syrian region, but currently little can be said about their character or extent of production. Commagene is described in inscriptions from around the Roman empire as the country 'where iron grows',[26] and the Taurus range is particularly rich in iron, but the importance of Commagenian iron remains to be proved. Otherwise, there are few good iron ore deposits in Syria, though there are many poor ones. Argentiferous galena is to be found on Mount Casius, but there were better silver-producing lead ores in other parts of the Roman east. There were gold deposits in Arabia, and Strabo mentions that the Nabataeans produced some silver and gold themselves, but imported copper and iron. It was once thought that the hills above Byblus yielded deposits of tin, but this myth appears to have developed from a misinterpretation of prospectors' reports of the early twentieth century. Stibnite (antimony ore) occurs in the Amanus.

Pliny mentions that orpiment, a yellow sulphur compound of arsenic ore used by painters, was found in Syria.

The small, strongly saline lakes of the Syrian interior, like the Madkh and Jabbul, were a useful source of salt, which was also collected near Palmyra. Salt features prominently in the Palmyra tariff (p. 193). Further south, the Dead Sea, in addition to producing salt, provided bitumen and sulphur. There were bituminous springs at Hit, an important crossing place on the Euphrates in Parthian and later Persian territory, and bitumen deposits in the southern Bekaa may have been exploited. Quicklime, used mainly for mortar, was produced by burning limestone; Theophrastus (fourth - third century BC) singles out Syria and Phoenicia as important sources for this, and there are indications that this industry continued throughout the Roman period. It is difficult to draw any general conclusions from the information available to us. The list of mineral products mentioned in the sources is extensive; and the list of mineral deposits in Syria and the Near East that *might* have been exploited is long; but we are some way from understanding the intensity of that exploitation, or how it was organized.

CITY AND COUNTRY

Overall, when the cities prospered and developed, the countryside did the same. The city is likely to have been an important institution for organizing production and distribution of agricultural produce and other materials from its territories. The increase in the settled rural population in all areas of Syria and the Near East during the Roman period, and its expansion into marginal agricultural zones, is striking. Some of this expansion could be achieved only through large-scale projects aimed at altering the environment: draining marshes, building dams, aqueducts and *qanats*, and the planning and laying out of new field systems. The manpower needed for these projects required considerable organization and expense. Some regions, such as the limestone massif, the Hauran and Palestine, witnessed tremendous growth in the Roman period, from being economic backwaters to major centres of agricultural production. In the late Roman period some of the larger settlements in these marginal areas became cities, and agricultural development was clearly a prerequisite for urbanization. The cities which had existed prior to the Roman annexation were best served by stable rural populations, and this was best achieved by making provision for the villages. Both the cities and the Roman state were acting in their own interests by stimulating the primary mode of production. When civic life declined, growth in the countryside came to an end.

6 PORTABLE ANTIQUITIES

MEDITERRANEAN TRADE

Archaeology has revolutionized our understanding of trade in the Roman Mediterranean. Long-distance trade by sea was nothing new, but the scale of the exchanges was notably different from what had gone before. The scope of economic contacts was increased by imperial demands for goods, which were then redistributed to the populace at Rome, or to state servants (and in particular the army), and also by individuals or groups operating independently of state concerns. Foodstuffs, textiles and raw materials such as marble or metals probably formed the bulk of the cargoes transported, but other kinds of goods were also moved along with these. The state exacted surpluses as tax in kind as well as money, and cities also appear to have been able to market their specialized products overseas, exchanging them for goods produced in other coastal cities. A growing trend towards regional specialization in certain parts of the empire led to increased levels of production of particular types of goods over time. Ports clearly had an advantage over communities inland, being better positioned to market their surpluses abroad, but regional distributions of goods can be detected in land-locked areas as well. Mediterranean products also made it to inland areas, but these appear in the main to have been 'luxury' goods rather than bulk foodstuffs. However, it is apparent that even bulk

Fig. 71. The agora at Palmyra. In such spaces cities regulated exchange and prices of goods.

products could be transported inland along major trade routes where there was a demand for them.

The Roman economy has not always been viewed as dynamic. In the 1950s the historian A. H. M. Jones felt able to observe, in connection with the economic life of Roman towns: 'It was only products of a rather superior kind which commanded a wider market and were manufactured on a large scale. The *terra sigillata* of the Principate, an ornamental ware used in better-class households, was, for instance exported to all the western provinces from its original place of manufacture in northern Italy; but even in this case provincial factories were soon established which could undercut the Italian product by saving transport costs.'[27] His view was shared by another influential historian, Moses Finley. Long-distance trade, they argued, was limited because of the high cost of transport. In the Roman world only those who owned land could be considered wealthy, and land was certainly the only form of *respectable* wealth. Rich and powerful people did not sully their hands with trade. Agriculture was the dominant mode of production in the Roman world, and its produce was consumed locally. Cities parasitized their hinterlands, being centres of consumption rather than production, and supported by rents and taxes (see chapter 5). They were also the centres of social power, for this was where the landowners lived. Regional trade did exist, but on a small scale because of the poor transport infrastructure; there was little need to move basics around the Mediterranean because these basics were produced almost everywhere. The only long-distance trade was in luxury goods.

Finley and Jones were reacting to works such as Michael Rostovtzeff's *The Social and Economic History of the Roman Empire*, which viewed the Roman economy with a distinctly modern eye, and emphasized the importance of trade in staples such as grain, wine and oil. They were dealing with the same material as Rostovtzeff (mainly texts and inscriptions, supported by some archaeological evidence), but they read that material in a quite different way. Far from being integrated, the economy of the Roman world was a rather primitive structure, with little overall organization, so that the empire could scarcely be considered an economic unit. That such diverse readings of the evidence could be possible is a reflection of its very fragmentary nature.

While this 'primitivist' view (which has also suffered from caricature from the pens of its opponents) no longer holds, its influence is still felt. Yet archaeological evidence accumulated over the last three decades or so, particularly from the study of pottery, has rendered such a limited view of the Roman economy untenable. It is quite clear that there was widespread movement of goods all over the Mediterranean and beyond, and on a considerable scale. This was not limited to luxuries; indeed, most of it seems to have been the movement of staples. 'Luxuries' such as the *terra sigillata* pots mentioned by Jones were transported only because there were established routes for more mundane goods. The amount of trade, its complexity and its nature mark the Roman imperial economy as something quite different from preceding and succeeding periods. What remains debatable is the degree to which much of this movement of goods was prompted by the demands of the state (taxes in kind to supply Rome and state servants, like the army) and how much was in the hands of private traders and entrepreneurs who were exploiting the existence of a market economy and freedom of movement afforded by the *pax romana*. Those influenced by Finley and Jones prefer not to emphasize the role of private traders, while others see them as an important factor in the movement of goods.

The existence of a class of traders conducting private transactions on a significant scale, unconnected with state demands, is implied by Roman legal texts dealing with exchanges between individuals. There is also evidence that aristocrats did not consider it beneath their dignity to profit from involvement in long-distance trade, and were prepared to take risks by investing in this business rather than in agriculture. In fact, state demands and private enterprise may have been interlinked. The transport of bulky, perishable goods destined for state use required an infrastructure to move it around. Instead of a merchant navy to deal with its fiscal cargoes, the state relied on private contractors, and it is clear that these ships commonly carried private cargoes along with the state ones, even if the state frowned on such practices. Fiscal cargoes were exempt from port taxes, and so, it seems, were any private loads carried in the same vessels, making these ships particularly attractive for entrepreneurs who could not be certain that their goods would be sold at the first port of call. The 'hijacking' of state-contracted ships for private interests could even lead to deviations from the regular route to offload private cargoes, or, worse still, selling the fiscal load *en route*. But the establishment of important shipping routes across the Mediterranean, whether or not they were mainly for state cargoes or also plied by private companies, allowed markets for secondary and tertiary cargoes like *terra sigillata* to develop along these routes. In addition, Mediterranean ports appear to have developed a complex network of economic interdependence, exchanging their respective specialized produce with one another and creating subsidiary shipping lanes which could also be exploited by entrepreneurs.

The state too was involved in producing and selling things on the open market. The trade in marble seems to have developed as a commercial concern under imperial supervision (see below). In this case it would appear that state-owned quarries marketed their products over wide areas of the Roman world. The objects they made were often prefabricated in the quarry before shipping, and some quarries mass-produced particular classes of object. Prefabricated designs could have contributed to 'Romanizing' or 'Hellenizing' styles. The movement and distribution of foodstuffs like fish sauce and Greek-style wines (implied by particular shapes of amphora) also played a part in creating more homogeneous cultural practices, by affecting and altering local preferences in eating and drinking habits, or catering to changes in those habits. So part of the standardization of culture observable in the Roman period rested on elaborate commercial links and institutions, both public and private, establishing overseas branches to market their products. This standardizing tendency did not come from the centre (Rome), but through interchanges between the provinces under the auspices of Rome. Was there anything special about the Roman world that could have increased this interchange? Roman suppression of piracy may have been a factor, as was perhaps political peace across the Mediterranean, although it is evident that political hostilities did not always inhibit regional and long-distance economic exchanges.

With such active trade links between different parts of the Mediterranean, one would have expected a universal currency to facilitate trade. Perversely, as we shall see, for the first three centuries of Roman rule in Syria, the region maintained local and regional currencies, precisely at the time a fully international currency might have been most useful (see p. 212). Local coinage looks insular and parochial, but the goods traded speak of a broader network, linking Syria and the Near East to a wider Mediterranean world. Even when the currency became more homogeneous in late Roman times, there are distinct regional differences (see p. 214).

Transport

That huge quantities of foodstuffs and other goods could be transported long-distance implies that transport costs were relatively low. Emphasis is often placed on the contrast between water transport (cheap) and land transport (expensive). The distribution of imported goods, which are common at coastal sites and less so inland, and the construction of canals such as those in the plain of Antioch (p. 133), would seem to confirm the distinction, but doubts remain about the significance of this contrast between land and water transport. We have no specific information about the cost of either, and in general we are forced to resort to analogies with more recent times. Various ratios of the cost of sea to land transport have been proposed, varying from land transport being more than twenty-five times more expensive than sea to more than sixty times. There is unequivocal evidence that large, heavy loads were transported overland, which could be seen as an indication that carriage by road was not prohibitively costly, and that the Roman land transport infrastructure was better developed than was the case with many of the proposed analogues. If so, the transport of some 188 Egyptian granite columns into the Bekaa valley to the courtyards and propylaea of the Temple of Jupiter at Heliopolis, while still an extraordinary physical feat, may have been less of a financial feat than might be supposed. We simply do not know. The same might also be noted for the granite columns at Palmyra which, although much fewer in number, nonetheless represent enormous physical outlay. Columns count as 'luxury' or prestige goods which people would have been prepared to spend money on, but the same can hardly be said for brick and tile imported to inland sites. Wear and tear on vehicles, and the entropic forces of friction and physics, no doubt made land transport more costly and less desirable than water transport, but their costs relative to each other in Syria and the Near East are unknown. Land transport must have been responsible for the widespread distribution of certain forms of amphora produced and marketed in the Syrian interior. As in the case of brick and tile the value-to-weight ratio of these 'cargoes' of wine and oil cannot have been very great, and implies that costs were not prohibitive.

In this context it might be worth re-evaluating the role of roads within the Roman economy. As noted in chapter 4, these are considered to have been constructed for strategic purposes, allowing armies and officials of the imperial postal service to move around swiftly, and for transporting military supplies. Their economic importance outside of state and army concerns is considered less significant because of the assumed high cost of land transport. Even so, roads were presumably designed to make land transport as efficient as possible, and thus reduce effort and expense. Some road construction and repair seems to have been undertaken by civilians rather than soldiers, which might imply that this activity was in their own interests, but it may have been at the behest of the Roman state rather than for the civilians themselves. It would certainly seem that by late Roman times the state obliged civilians to maintain roads and bridges. The economic effects of a good road network may well have been incidental to state concerns, but the ways in which the road system could have been in the economic interests of the Syrian cities rather than simply being a burden on their resources has scarcely been explored.

Caravans: a Minor Diversion

No discussion of economic activities in Roman Syria can omit reference to the so-called 'caravan trade' in luxury goods from outside the empire. Although it is well known from numerous texts and inscriptions, archaeological evidence for this trade remains meagre compared to the evidence for Mediterranean trade. This is no doubt because of the nature of the goods imported: copper, various exotic woods, pepper, cotton cloth, indigo, exotic herbs and spices, cochineal, and Chinese silk and furs, among other things. The best evidence relating to Syria is for trade with India and Sri Lanka, either from the Persian Gulf, through Parthian Babylonia and up the Euphrates, or from Arabia and the Red Sea via Petra and Bostra. The quantities of goods shipped were no doubt much smaller than those in the Mediterranean, but they were evidently profitable, so much so that it appears that an import tax of 25 per cent could be levied on goods entering the Roman empire from the east (see below). The importance of other caravan routes is difficult to assess, as currently there is very little material evidence. One appears to have come from central Arabia, up the Wadi Sirhan to Bostra, and others, the so-called 'silk routes' from central Asia, may have served the cities of the north, like Beroea and Antioch, via Iran, Babylonia and Mesopotamia. These overland routes to central Asia are thought to have been especially profitable to the Parthians, who as the middlemen in this trade took pains to see that direct contact between Rome and China was kept to a minimum.

While very profitable for those involved in it, the 'caravan trade' was probably a relatively minor element of the economy of Syria. It attracted the attention of Rostovtzeff, who exaggerated the importance of this commerce for the urban economies of the region. The rise and demise of routes for long-distance trade in luxury goods is still sometimes invoked as an explanation for the growth and decline of cities, but the extent to which the cities of Syria and the Near East as a whole profited is unclear. Palmyra and Petra derived much wealth from this enterprise, but the model of these 'caravan cities' should not be extrapolated to the other cities of the region, as if Syria were some sort of free-trade zone for the transit of commodities. Even Palmyra and Petra drew on the agricultural produce of hinterlands which were more promising in antiquity than they appear today; the caravan trade simply produced additional wealth.

Palmyra was the 'caravan city' *par excellence*, and provides us with some of the clearest evidence for the way in which this long-distance trade in luxuries was organized. Here we see, contrary to the views of Finley and Jones, wealthy people indulging in trade activities, and Palmyra may not have been exceptional in this respect. Public inscriptions set up in the city by merchants thank powerful and influential individuals who paid for or acted as protectors of the caravans. These caravan-chiefs need not have travelled with the caravan itself, but they arranged safe passage through the steppe. Caravanserais and camel-riding militias provided support for merchants in the vast area controlled by the city, and good relations with the nomadic tribes of the region will have been essential. The Palmyrenes financed trade with India, and most of their activities were directed towards the Persian Gulf. Palmyrene merchants are known to have been active in several cities in Parthian Babylonia, or at Spasinu Charax, the capital of the kingdom of Characene, which operated with a fair degree of independence from the Parthians, particularly between AD 117 and 150. Whether the Palmyrene merchants commonly travelled to India or left that section of the route to others remains unclear. They perhaps had ships on the Euphrates, and some certainly owned or hired ships to sail to the trading port of Barbaricum on one of the mouths of the Indus. A sarcophagus fragment from Palmyra shows a man standing next to a ship; this is thought to represent a merchant and his vessel employed in this trade. A Palmyrene-style tomb on Kharg island in the Persian Gulf provides some additional support for the presence of Palmyrenes on this leg of the journey. The periodic military conflicts between Rome and the Parthians conceal a generally tolerant attitude towards international trade, even though Characene's friendly disposition towards Rome had been established as a result of Trajan's aggressions against the Arsacid realm. Indeed, although Characene's role in trade with India and Palmyra remains enigmatic, the relationship between Palmyra and Characene appears to have been strong. A caravan inscription from Palmyra honours a Palmyrene merchant called Yarhai who was satrap of the Thilouanoi (Bahrain) governing on behalf of the king of Characene, who seems to have exercised control of the western side of the Gulf during this period. It is presumably as a result of these contacts that Roman glass and fine wares were introduced into (and, in the case of fine wares, imitated in) the Gulf region. Among the non-commercial activities of these Palmyrene merchants we find one dedicating a temple to the Roman imperial cult at Vologaesias, a city in Parthian territory near Babylon, founded by Vologaeses I (c. AD 52-80). Such activities would be unthinkable in the highly antagonistic political atmosphere a century or so later, under Sasanian rule.

Fig. 72. Drawing of a fragment of Chinese silk from the tomb of Elahbel at Palmyra, decorated with dragons in a roundel.

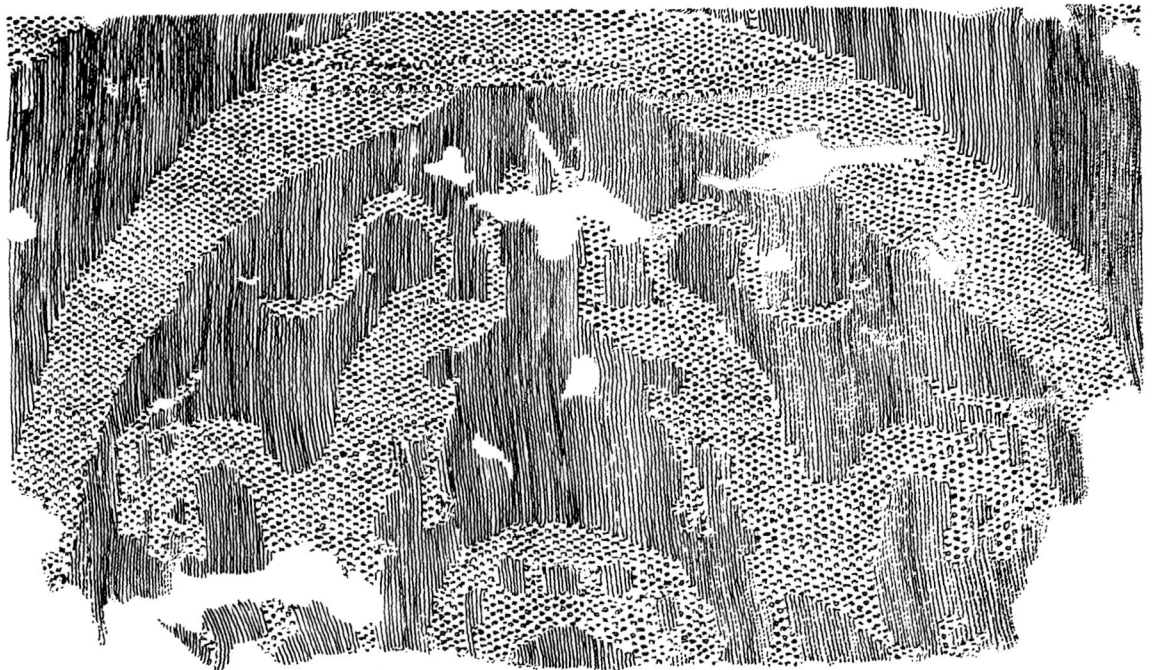

The Palmyrenes also worked on the sea route from the Red Sea to India. Palmyrene inscriptions refer to a guild of ship-owners and merchants who had a base at Coptos on the Nile, together with their caravans, and archaeological evidence has recently been found attesting the presence of Palmyrenes at the Egyptian port of Berenice on the Red Sea coast.

Although the inscriptions from Palmyra give little hint of the kinds of luxury goods imported through the caravan trade, fragments of Indian cotton and Chinese silk have been recovered from tombs. Official Roman supervision and organization of all of this Palmyrene activity is nowhere explicitly evident, although the Roman upper classes would have been the main beneficiaries and the empire received revenues from taxes on these foreign imports.

In the late Roman period trade across the borders with Sasanian Persia was very strictly regulated, with merchants having to keep to a specified route and market city to do business. This was partly for security, to prevent spies entering the empire, and to stop secrets and supplies reaching the enemy, but the restrictions could also be used as a political and economic weapon, depriving potentially hostile peoples beyond the frontier of goods by temporarily cutting off all trade. The anonymous but probably Syrian author of the fourth-century *Descriptio Totius Orbis* (Description of the Whole World) remarks that Mesopotamian merchants were forbidden to sell bronze or iron to the Persians. (The Sasanians were able to exercise a similar policy against the Romans, monopolizing all overland and seaborne trade to the east, much to the chagrin of the emperors.)

The Circulation of Commodities

Our main concern here, however, is not trade outside the empire, but Syria and the Near East's participation in Mediterranean trade. The role of Syrians within the Roman empire, as merchants at Delos, Rhodes and Brundisium (Brindisi), or in Spain and Gaul, is well known from epigraphic and literary evidence. Traders and bankers from Berytus were established at Puteoli and Rome, and that Puteoli even had a temple to Jupiter Damascenus suggests a significant Syrian community there. Sporadic epigraphic evidence points to the presence of Syrian merchants all over the Roman world. These texts provide important evidence for the presence and activities of individuals, and for the sorts of goods in which they traded, but in order to gain some idea of the impact of exports from, and imports to, Syria, we have to turn to other sources. The archaeological evidence is significant in that it can be quantified (even if this quantification is relative rather than absolute), and helps to offset conclusions drawn from what are often incidental asides in literature, or chance finds of inscriptions. It cannot provide the whole picture, because much of what was moved around has perished without trace. Grain was shipped either in sacks or loose in compartments of boats. Had shipments of liquids been made predominantly in barrels rather than in amphoras, we would have very little evidence for the movement of goods such as oil, wine and fish sauce. However, even if certain goods have themselves perished without trace, their movement is sometimes possible to detect. As has been pointed out above, major cargoes of perishables were often accompanied by minor loads of other goods. Established trade routes opened up overseas markets for entrepreneurs and producers, and some of what they exported, such as ceramic cooking pots, or table ware, survives in the archaeological record. The frequency with which such pottery occurs, even on fairly remote rural sites, suggests that the markets for secondary cargoes were huge and profitable, even if individual items were cheap. A distribution of such secondary or tertiary cargoes far from the place of production is likely to indicate movement of more important cargoes of which no trace survives, such as grain. As the evidence accumulates, it becomes increasingly possible to suggest trade routes based on the various forms of ceramic evidence.

What is also remarkable is the movement of materials which might be expected to have been more conveniently produced locally, such as roof tiles or bricks. Regional or local specialization led to the development of major centres for the production and export of such products. Syrian consumers in coastal cities might choose to be interred in a sarcophagus of local limestone, but during the second and third centuries imported alternatives also existed, ranging from relatively humble clay coffins to elaborate and extremely heavy marble sarcophagi.

Even if the cities themselves consumed more than they produced, they nonetheless acted as a channel for the movement of goods between their territories and the outside world. Trade allowed coastal cities to grow larger than they could if they had to rely solely on their agricultural hinterlands, but it also permitted the countryside to benefit from that trade. As noted in chapter 5, there is growing evidence that cities managed the distribution of goods within their territories as well as production. If this is so, the city state becomes a key element in the organization of production and distribution of commodities in Syria and the Near East.

The coastal cities had been importing goods from other parts of the Mediterranean long before the Roman annexation. Hellenistic pottery finds from the port of Berytus show links with western Asia Minor, particularly Pergamum, extending through the third and second centuries BC, and from the Ptolemaic to Seleucid period of control of the city. Attica was a source of pottery imports in the third century BC, and ceramics from what is today Tunisia, and from Campania in Italy, occur in second-century deposits. Traders and cities may have been able to operate with a degree of independence from regional politics and the clashes between the Hellenistic kingdoms. Nevertheless political changes could make a major difference. Berytus became a Roman colony in the reign of Augustus, and this event appears to coincide with an influx of western foodstuffs transported in amphoras, such as fish sauce (produced mainly in southern Spain). The first half of the first century AD saw many imports from Italy and the western Mediterranean: Italian *terra sigillata*, amphoras and glass, but these declined rapidly after about AD 50. Whether this was the consequence of a special relationship between the first generation of new colonists and Italy, or was part of a more general movement of Italian goods to Syria, has yet to be determined.

Integration into the Roman empire does seem to have greatly increased the scale and scope of imports to Syria. The Syrians were presumably paying for these goods, though at present it is difficult to see what they produced in exchange during the early empire. Laodicean wine was clearly one product, exported during the first century BC and AD, although, as pointed out in the preceding chapter, the container for this wine remains uncertain. One broadly distributed product from the region was packaged in small, carrot-shaped amphoras with a wide mouth (fig. 73.2). These are very common on military sites in Britain, Gaul and Germany, and were made in Berytus and probably in Palestine as well. The contents are uncertain; fish or fish sauce is a possibility, or perhaps dates. Another amphora, contents unknown, which was produced either in the very north-western part of Syria or in Cilicia is a small type known as the Pompeii 5 amphora (fig. 73.1). As its name suggests, it was exported to the west, but only in small quantities. Aside from these there is at present not much material evidence for Syrian exports before the fourth century (except for the fine ware called Eastern Sigillata A; see p. 200).

The later empire appears to have been a boom time for exports from the east, particularly as the western empire began to disintegrate in the fifth century. Eastern exports from Syria and Palestine found important markets in the west after supplies there were disrupted during the barbarian invasions and settlements, such as the Vandal conquest of north Africa. This eastern take-over is quite dramatic. In Italy, north Africa, Gaul and Spain imports of eastern amphoras increased greatly between the mid-fifth and mid-sixth century, and these often constitute more than half of the amphora fragments recovered from sites in this period. Opportunities for export from Syria and Palestine to the west may have arisen with the growth of Constantinople. Even if the eastern capital did not import large quantities of Syrian foodstuffs, it may have commanded the products of the Aegean, which could no longer be directed westwards, leaving a gap in the market to be exploited by other producers. Attempts by the Roman authorities to control exports in the western Mediterranean could also have worked to the east's advantage. Wine produced in areas of the west still under Roman control, such as southern Italy, was not sold to the Vandals, and during the fifth and sixth centuries the latter seem to have done a particularly brisk trade with the Syrian region. At Carthage three quarters of the amphoras dating to this period are eastern, mostly Late Roman I (see below), a type of container for wine or oil which comes from eastern Cilicia and Cyprus and perhaps northern Syria. The fact that this trade was conducted with Rome's enemies, the Vandals, Ostrogoths and Visigoths, gives the impression that private interests were at work in this case; at least, it is harder to imagine this export being organized by the Roman state. This trade continued after Vandal power was broken with Justinian's reconquest of Carthage, although the decline after the middle of the sixth century may be explained as a consequence of Justinian's attempts to re-establish state control of production in the west. However, places in the west that were lost to the Romans, such as southern Gaul, maintained connections with eastern producers.

Taxation may also have been an important stimulus for export, as cities traded in order to accumulate cash to pay their taxes. Taxation in kind will also have stimulated production (see below). The Diocletianic changes to the tax system may have provided such a stimulus, and institutions other than the Roman state and the cities are likely to have played a role in the production and consumption of goods. The Christian church was a major economic player in the late empire. It inherited large tracts of land from donors, and there is ceramic evidence for its being involved in the production of staples like wine and olive oil. Foodstuffs from ecclesiastical estates were distributed to the poor, or sold to raise money for the church. In addition to institutions such as the state or church, private individuals with large estates might trade or even donate produce on a large scale, give gifts to other wealthy persons, and receive

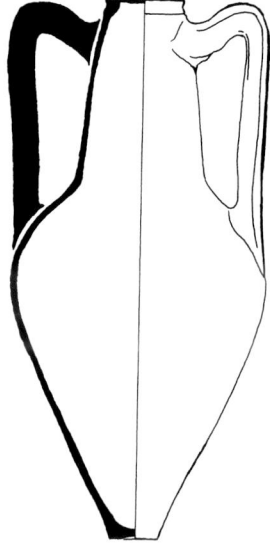

Fig. 73. Two amphora forms of the early empire in which goods were exported from the region (not to the same scale).

73.1. The Pompeii 5 amphora (first to mid-second century), a small vessel produced in eastern Cilicia and perhaps Syria.

73.2. The 'carrot amphora', a small container from Berytus and the south, perhaps for packaging fish or dates.

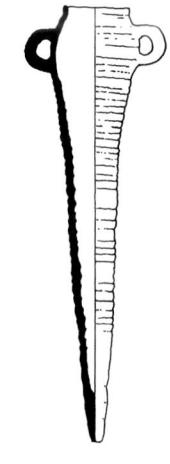

gifts of produce in return. Economic integration allowed for many modes of production and distribution.

TAXES AND STATE BURDENS

The Early Empire

The Roman state's survival depended on its ability to extract tribute from the people it ruled. That said, it is by no means clear how communities paid taxes in the early empire, or in what form. There seems to have been no attempt to create a standardized system. The great organizing and rationalizing force that was the Roman state appears to have dealt with the crucial matter of its incomes in a somewhat haphazard fashion. As with political systems, so too with taxation: the Romans annexed the traditional financial systems of the states they conquered and did little to change them. There is a belief that in the late republic, and especially under Augustus, money taxes became almost universal, and that the main tax-coin was the silver denarius. Large quantities of denarii were therefore being moved around the empire with great efficiency as the public paid taxes to Rome and Rome paid her employees. This model of taxation, which is still debated, has overshadowed evidence suggesting that communities in the early empire also paid taxes in kind. As early as the time of Caesar we find Sidon paying an annual sum of grain; this foodstuff probably went to the army and for distribution elsewhere. The Babatha archive shows Babatha registering her date-palm grove in a Roman census of AD 127; the tax to be paid was calculated in both money and dates. To some extent state demands may have been tempered by feasibility: what a community could reasonably produce was given as tribute. So in some places the state probably exacted payment in cash and in others in kind (there is also evidence for mixed payments).

The impression is that the system in the early empire was disorganized, inefficient and contingent (but this also made it flexible), despite some attempts by emperors to systematize procedures. Censuses do not appear to have been regular and much of the coinage in use in Syria and neighbouring provinces was unsuitable for making direct monetary payments to Rome (see below). Communities may have opted to pay in whatever they could produce as a surplus (for example, textiles or dates), and if so, tax in kind was somewhat of an expedient measure, but no doubt useful if the materials could be redistributed efficiently. Taxation may have provided an incentive for some cities and regions to specialize in particular products, either as tax or as exports to raise capital to pay tax. Whether tax was paid in cash or kind, the Roman tax system might therefore have encouraged increased production and trade.

Methods of assessment differed from one region to another, with no apparent logic behind the system. As Roman power expanded in the eastern Mediterranean, the different, traditional tax systems of various communities and regions were incorporated into the fiscal system without much alteration, and Rome then accepted whatever cities and provinces could offer. The state did its best with what ensued; if it needed cash but accepted tax in kind, it sold the foodstuffs and other materials on the open market to raise the sums required. Even when the state had stipulated that a community's tax should be paid in money, it might have had to accept some payment in foodstuffs. At other times it was easier for communities to pay in cash than in kind, and they might seek to commute their tribute to coin. The notion of taxation in kind and its accompanying mechanisms for redistribution originated in the attempts by emperors to supply the city of Rome and to safeguard against famine there, as well as to provide supplies to state servants and the army. This system, known as the *annona*, developed in the first and second centuries. Little effort, however, was made to secure supplies of staples to other cities, although some communities were rewarded for their loyalty during times of rebellion or instability by being granted regular supplies of grain. Laodicea seems to have received such a grant under Septimius Severus, and Sidon under Elagabalus (fig. 74). Such supplies presumably allowed these cities to profit in times of plenty by selling grain on to other communities. In times of shortage cities might petition a governor or Roman official in charge of a province or region which produced a surplus to provide aid; but there seems to have been a hierarchy or pecking-order to respect, and important cities were likely to be placed at the front of the queue. However, a lack of state interest in supply to the cities does not mean that the cities themselves did not make regular arrangements with each other for supplies.

Under the republic tax collection was farmed out to private contractors, the *publicani*. In early imperial times there is a shift to state employees, who were responsible for overseeing collection through the convenient bureaucratic machinery of the cities, but there is also evidence for continued use of private contractors. Once again, there is no impression of a completely rationalized system at work. There are hints of a possible attempt to systematize by standardizing units of tax according to Roman coin denominations, but the evidence for this is patchy and it may have had little impact on the sorts of coins being produced in places like Syria. The civic tariff of Palmyra quotes a letter from a Roman governor of *c.* AD 69 stating that taxes should be reckoned in denarii, and this governor quotes in turn a letter from Tiberius' nephew Germanicus, who had earlier stipulated reckoning in 'Italian *asses*'. As Italian *asses* did not circulate in Syria, these must have been notional units of account rather than physical coins.

The burden of collecting tax fell heavily on the cities, probably because the state recognized them as centres responsible for organizing local production and redistribution. City councils had to elect officials from among their members to collect the tax. Responsibility for all assessments, and for payment of any tax assessed but not collected, fell upon these officials. The main forms of direct taxation in the early empire were the *tributum soli* (land tax) and *tributum capitis* (poll tax), which were assessed through a census, collected by the local authorities and then handed over to imperial officials. Land tax was based on what the land produced, and was assessed according to what the land was used for and its location, whether meadow, pasture, arable, vineyard, woodland, mountain or plain and so on, together with the number of slaves working it and any other assets. However, the exact manner in which this tax was assessed may have differed from region to region. According to Appian (second century AD), in Syria the land tax was 1 per cent of the capital valuation, which might represent 5-10 per cent of the land's annual production (it is unclear how Appian arrived at this figure, or whether it had any general application at all). This figure is not particularly high, but other calculations of tribute in kind result in figures as high as 20 per cent of the crop from the land

Fig. 74. Civic bronze coin of Sidon of the reign of Elagabalus (AD 218-22) showing a corn measure and bearing the inscription 'aeternu[m] benefi[cium]', suggesting a regular grant of grain in perpetuity. BMC 274.

assessed, which is considerable. In any case it was of paramount importance for tax-payers to ensure that their property boundaries, and hence what they were liable for, were well defined. Only Italy was exempt from land tax, although the extension of *ius italicum* to some Roman colonies abroad, such as Berytus, meant that their lands were considered 'Italian'. The *Digest of Roman Law*, published under Justinian, cites the late second/early third-century lawyer Ulpian, who states that in Syria males aged between fourteen and sixty-five, and females from twelve to sixty-five, were liable for *tributum capitis*. How this tax was related to land tax assessments remains obscure. *Tributum capitis* was presumably paid in money, and may not have been particularly burdensome.

Because the tax assessment was a proportion of the total assessment for land and persons, estimates of these had to be obtained through censuses. The first proper census of Syria was performed under the governor Publius Sulpicius Quirinius in AD 6, when all the inhabitants were to declare their property in terms of money. This was the census somewhat inaccurately recorded in the Gospel of St Luke: 'there went out a decree from Caesar Augustus, that all the world should be taxed. And this taxing was first made when Cyrenius [Quirinius] was governor of Syria.'[28] The historian Tacitus wrote that the inhabitants thought that the taxes imposed as a result were too high and appealed for a reduction in AD 17. It is not known how frequently censuses were conducted thereafter.

The two regular forms of direct taxation sometimes had to be supplemented by additional demands, suggesting that the rather simple system was inadequate for coping with fluctuations in state spending. Among these irregular taxes was a demand by the emperors for gold, either as bullion or in the form of crowns. Originally these seem to have been offered by various communities of the empire on extraordinary occasions, such as an imperial victory, but by the late second century, if not before, the *aurum coronarium* (crown gold) was institutionalized as a form of tax on the cities.

The most important indirect tax was the *portorium*, a tax on the value of goods in transit. This was levied at harbours and at points within and on the boundaries of provinces, on goods both entering and leaving. The eastern frontier of the Roman empire seems to have had an extraordinarily high tax on goods crossing the border from the Parthian kingdom, which in turn suggests that the profit on imports from that direction was high. A mid-second-century inscription from the console of a column at Palmyra describes a certain Marcus Aemilius Marcianus Asclepiades, senator of Antioch, as a *tetartones*, presumably an official who extracted a 'fourth', a 25 per cent duty, on the value of goods entering the Roman empire. This is the highest level of duty known; in other places it was considerably lower (2 or 2½ per cent). Customs stations were located in ports or at fixed sites on roads, where travellers had to declare what they were carrying with them. They were taxed on whatever was deemed inessential for travel (this may have been at the official's discretion, and these individuals appear not to have been noted for their honesty). The employees seem to have been imperial rather than city officials. In Philostratus' *Life of Apollonius of Tyana* (early third century) the holy man and his companion have a misunderstanding with a customs official stationed at Zeugma (an important crossing-point into Parthian Mesopotamia), partly due to Apollonius' spiritual pomposity and partly to the official's greed and stupidity: 'When they were about to cross into Mesopotamia, the tax-collector stationed at Zeugma took them to the registry and asked them if they had anything to declare. "Prudence", replied Apollonius, "Justice, Virtue, Temperance, Courage, Perseverance", stringing together a lot of nouns in the feminine gender. Immediately the official, with an eye to his own profit, said, "Well then, make me a list of your slaves." "I cannot", retorted Apollonius: "it is not my slaves I am declaring, but my mistresses."'[29]

Other indirect taxes included sales taxes (usually quite low), taxes on craftsmen, on the purchase of slaves, on pastures, markets, the inheritance of Roman citizens, and on slaves buying their freedom. There were also other obligations placed upon the city and the citizens: providing recruits for the army; or lodgings for officials, soldiers and employees of the postal service, and fodder and stabling for their animals. While not exactly a form of taxation, their demands did cost the inhabitants time and money, and often the loss of beasts of burden or wagons, requisitioned for state requirements (see chapter 10). Locals could hardly resist such demands; the best they could hope for was that a high state official, or the emperor, would write a letter outlining what was an acceptable demand and what was not, so that this could be posted in a public place for all to take note.

The Late Empire

The chaotic tax system of the early empire came under considerable strain in the third century. The unstable political climate, accompanied, perhaps, by some disruption of long-distance trade, the decline of Italy and the city of Rome as a focal point for political and military power, and a period of high inflation coupled with the end of local coinages, required new strategies. It was the emperor Diocletian (AD 284-305) who formally reorganized the increasingly unworkable and irregular tax base of the empire. The belief that his system represents a change from heavy reliance on money tax to a system of taxation in kind is debatable, but the changes which he introduced were far-reaching, and remained the basis of the imperial tax system of the late Roman empire. One of his most important innovations was the creation of a flexible tax rate, so that the state did not have to rely on a fixed annual income supplemented by arbitrary demands to meet costs. The Praetorian Prefects were charged with estimating annual budgets for their respective parts of the empire, which were published in September every year. As a result, the rate of taxation now varied every year according to expected state expenditure (exceptional needs were still met by exceptional tax demands, *superindictiones*). Land was assessed according to an abstract unit of value, the *iugum* or *zugon*, rather than in units of currency. So instead of valuing land tax at a fixed rate, how much would be extracted from every *iugum* depended on the rate of tax for that year. The way in which the *iugum* was defined appears to have varied from one region to another, but it does appear to have been an attempt at standardization. A late Roman text, the *Syro-Roman Lawbook*, shows the area of the *iugum* varying according to crop, quality of crop and quality of land. Thus it distinguishes between two sorts of olive trees and three classes of arable land (the third class thought to include pasturage and wasteland). Whether such rules applied throughout Syria is unknown, and other definitions seem to have been applied in different regions of the empire. The tax reform required a reorganization and reassessment of land, and in Syria and the Near East boundary stones of this period, set up by cadastral surveyors, have been found at many locations. A number of them are dated. All dates correspond to AD 297, the year of the tax reform, and many name the censors involved. In rural areas people and animals were also assessed according to an abstract unit, the *caput* (although use of this unit may not have been universal). How many people and animals made up a *caput* is unclear, as is the precise relationship of the two modes of taxation to one another, although the *iugum* and *caput* appear to have been considered equal in value. In this way this poll tax, where it was used, could be assessed either in money or in kind. The age limits on liable persons in Syria presumably remained the same as under the early empire, because they are cited in Justinian's *Digest*. The new system also standardized cycles of annual requisitions (*indictiones*). These cycles originally lasted five years, but from the time of Constantine became fifteen-year periods (see chapter 4).

As before, responsibility for collection of tax fell on city officials, who also had to arrange for its delivery to an agreed point, such as a fort, a military station along a main road (where it could be used by soldiers and officials in transit), or a port abroad. Responsibility extended not only to gathering the tax and keeping accounts, but also to overseeing and paying for the transport and storage of these goods until they reached the right depot or the state servants for whom they were intended. Later adjustments and changes to the system cannot be described here, but there are signs that by the sixth century tax collection was being organized by the rich and powerful grandees of the cities, rather than by councillors. The system of delivery of any taxes in kind probably remained inefficient, but some have linked the overall improvements to the tax system in late Roman times with the increasingly intensive settlement and cultivation of the countryside, as the state became more adept at extracting taxes in kind. Nevertheless it would seem that by the sixth century taxes had predominantly reverted to cash, so increased agricultural production may have been aimed at the market, to raise tax money, rather than serving the needs of the state directly.

Civic Taxes

Cities also exacted municipal taxes for their own use, and gained money or foodstuffs by renting municipal properties. While this money did not go to the imperial treasuries (at least not until the late empire: see p. 263), emperors might take an interest in civic finances, and cities could not introduce new taxes without imperial permission. We are fortunate to possess an extraordinary document from Palmyra, listing in both Greek and Palmyrene script the taxes due on goods within the city's territory. The Palmyra tariff, dated to AD 137, fixed in stone the exactions to be levied on a range of goods, because previously disputes had arisen between the tax collectors and merchants. The law is not concerned with the luxury items of the caravan trade, but with everyday goods being imported or exported, and services provided in the city itself. It lists dues on slaves, dried produce, wheat, wine, purple-dyed fleece, unguents, olive oil, animal fat, animal skins, salt and salt fish, horses, livestock and animals for slaughter, fodder and unloaded pack camels. There were sales taxes on prostitutes and tradesmen, and a hefty charge for the use of Palmyra's main water sources, presumably levied on caravan merchants watering their animals. Animals brought from outside to graze on Palmyrene lands were taxed, and the tax collector could insist that they be branded for identification.

The most luxurious things mentioned are bronze statues (presumably imported from centres of production elsewhere), to be taxed at half their value by weight. The tariff shows that imperial officials took a significant interest in civic taxes: several governors and high-ranking Roman officials are mentioned, or their rulings quoted, including Germanicus, who stipulated that taxes were to be reckoned in Italian currency, probably in an attempt to create some standard form of accounting amidst a multitude of local currencies (on these, see below). It also clarifies how bulk loads were transported: by wagon, camel or donkey. The tariff provides us with a fascinating glimpse of the sorts of essentials being traded in the interior of Syria during the second century AD.

As time went by, imperial controls on civic finances tightened. In the late Roman period civic incomes were allotted to specific areas of expenditure and could not be transferred to other areas, leaving the cities with a predictable but inflexible system (see p. 264).

Taxation, imperial and civic, is likely to have been important in determining patterns of production, imports, exports, distribution, consumption and monetization. No overall study of these patterns has yet been attempted for the Syrian region, and it is unlikely that one will be attempted in the near future. What follows is a brief examination of various categories of manufactured materials that were imported to and exported from Syria and the Near East, and the monetary networks of the region.

POTTERY

For a long time the study of Roman pottery in the eastern Mediterranean meant the study of fine wares, a category of pottery made from finely refined clays and used for presenting food and drink. Some types were traded long-distance, or had a wide regional distribution; others were made for local consumption. But these wares, which comprise just a fraction of the pottery found on Syrian sites, present us with only part of the story of pottery production and consumption. Less well developed is the study of more utilitarian ceramics ('coarse wares'). These have great potential, because they too were traded, often in substantial quantities, and their distribution provides a key to understanding the trading networks of the Roman world in considerable detail. It is not surprising to find transport amphoras being moved about; it was their contents that were desired, rather than the amphoras themselves, and of all the types of coarse ware pots amphoras are among the most studied forms. Common sense would suggest that cheap coarse ware items like cooking pots or bowls ought to have been made locally, with only containers like amphoras and the higher-status, displayable table wares being imported. It is all the more startling, then, to find abundant evidence at coastal sites for imported ceramics of all sorts: cooking pots, bricks and tiles, storage jars and clay coffins. Sometimes most of the pottery found at a site was imported, with very little being produced locally. In Berytus even the cheap and common loom weights used in the city's textile workshops were imported from a specialized production centre, probably in neighbouring Sidon. This does not mean that local industries did not exist in the cities but it should not be assumed that the majority of coarse wares found at a site will always be local. Inland sites tend to exhibit less variety in their ceramic finds than coastal ones, but even in the interior of Syria the coarse ware pots were often produced centrally and marketed over wide areas. North central Syria and the Euphrates looks as if it had its own market, with sites like Resafa and the tells around Aleppo producing plenty of finds of imported 'Late Roman C' fine wares from western Asia Minor, coarse 'brittle ware' (see p. 56), and amphoras made in a whitish-green coloured fabric from an uncertain source in the north Syrian region. The evidence from sites far from the Mediterranean, such as Dura Europus on the Euphrates, suggests a strong orientation towards Mesopotamia and the Parthian realm, but there are some imported Roman wares at Dura, including fine wares which came to the site before the Romans had taken the city from the Parthians. The late Roman site of Dibsi Faraj (Neocaesarea?), also on the Euphrates, produced significant quantities of fine wares imported from the Mediterranean, including Late Roman C and African Red Slip from Tunisia. Amphoras imported from the Mediterranean are known from these sites, and from Kifrin further down river, but these do not seem to have been brought to the sites in any great quantity.

Some production centres for Syrian pottery have been identified, but we still do not know exactly where some of the more common amphoras and other ceramics were made (although the general regions are often known), a problem which renders any detailed discussion of how and why the trade developed as it did a somewhat speculative exercise. Local wares may imitate imports, compounding the problems of identification. Nevertheless, some broad sketches are possible. It would seem that in the early empire most cities had a ceramic industry (although certain potteries may have served more than one city), and that these cities often produced their own distinctive type of amphora (although some of the trends were regional rather than city-specific). Some cities exported widely, but other amphora types appear to have been confined to the territory of their respective cities. The distributions of certain amphoras which were not widely exported sometimes appear to coincide with their respective city territories. These cases may well reflect the importance of the city as an institution for organizing production, redistribution and consumption within its territory, rather than hinting at patriotic locals preferring home-made products.

Different forms of cooking wares and table wares are likely to reflect different culinary habits and dietary preferences. There is some evidence from the early empire to suggest that Roman soldiers, who were often alien to the parts of the empire in which they were stationed, preferred to use ceramics which resembled those of their homelands. Local imitation of Italian-style casseroles in Berytus may reflect more western culinary habits in the colony. Other ceramic distributions may be linked to native dietary and culinary preferences, or to expressions of identity. The distinctive and well-known Nabataean red fine ware made at Petra is more or less confined to the kingdom and does not seem to have been exported in any quantity (although it is found on Palestinian sites). The tradition developed some time after 100 BC, but it ended with the Roman annexation of Nabataea. This hard-fired, thin-walled 'eggshell ware' is found in some quantity at Bostra, but it was not made there, and instead was imported from the main centres of production in Petra. However, it does not occur commonly north of Bostra, even in those places where there was a Nabataean presence (such as the cult centre of Sia near Canatha), so its distribution is not coterminous with Nabataean rule, although its association with Nabataean culture is clear.

The Roman annexation of the Nabataean kingdom had a clear effect on pottery production, and in other cases where production centres are known and pottery typologies can be dated we can sometimes see the impact of Rome. The Beirut amphora type appears with or shortly after the Roman annexation (see below) and disappears with the Muslim conquest. It would seem therefore to be one of the consequences of Roman control of the city, and perhaps the result of a particular pattern of exploitation in the city's territory, although the Beirut amphoras were only rarely exported. Not all coastal cities show such marked changes coinciding with the Roman period. The Tyrian pottery industry, which aside from making amphoras also produced closed vessels like jugs and mould-made items such as lamps and masks, represented an unbroken tradition stretching back to the Iron Age. In the early third century this industry appears to have ceased, although Tyre continued to produce lamps, unguentaria and figurines. It revived again in the seventh century, following the Roman loss of the Syrian provinces.

The following brief survey of ceramics begins with the coarse wares, and in particular the vessels used for transport, because these provide a wealth of evidence for regional and empire-wide trade. It should of course be borne in mind that there were other types of containers than those in ceramic, particularly sacks and barrels, but neither these nor their contents survive in sufficient quantities to tell us much about the movement of goods.

Amphoras

These were two-handled jars, often with wide bodies, used for transport and storage. There were small ones, usually with flat bases, which were suitable for use at the table, but the greatest interest lies in the large containers, often with a body tapering to a pointed or rounded base, which were used for transport. The earliest-known examples are the so-called Canaanite jars of the Bronze Age from coastal Syria, Phoenicia and Palestine, but during the eighth and seventh centuries BC the form spread and was adapted throughout the Mediterranean. By the Roman period it was a major means of packaging, mainly for liquids such as wine, oil and fish sauce, but sometimes other sorts of produce: fruit, nuts, whole olives, small fish such as sardines, oysters, and even mineral products. As noted above, cities had their own very distinct amphora shapes, but in the Roman period the shape and size could also be used to advertise the type of product the amphora contained. Regional preferences are, however, apparent, and in many cases the traditions seem to have been maintained for centuries. Eastern Cilicia (and perhaps Antioch) preferred small containers such as the Late Roman Amphora 1 (see below), which was probably the descendant of an earlier small container, the Pompeii 5 amphora (first to second century: fig. 73.1). Further south, Ras al-Bassit (and perhaps Laodicea) produced round-bodied, 'globular' amphoras, and the coastal kilns between Marathus and Berytus made amphoras with a tapering, carrot-shaped body. These all have handles attached to the neck in the Greek tradition, but below Beirut some much older conventions were maintained. Sidon seems to have ceased producing amphoras under the Seleucids, but Tyre made its containers in cylindrical or cigar-shaped forms, with little or no neck and ring handles attached to the body. A similar practice may be noted at Ascalon and Gaza, where there was also a preference for cigar-shaped vessels with ring handles. These seem to be consciously archaic forms in a pre-Greek amphora tradition.

The fact that amphoras can be associated with particular cities or regions means that they are useful indicators of the scale and nature of local, regional and long-distance trade in the Roman world. The patterns of imports and exports changed as tastes and social relations changed. The ceramic material from King Herod's palace at Masada shows that he was importing Italian wines in the second half of the first century BC, and Italian products of the period are also known at other sites, so Herod may have been taking advantage of existing or newly developing commercial links rather than being a trend-setter. Even so, the consumption of Italian wine could be taken as a political and cultural statement. From the second century AD the cities of the Syrian coast began receiving quantities of foodstuffs (oil, fish sauce) in amphoras from southern Spain and Lusitania. These products were exported widely to the Roman world and are also a reflection of particular tastes. Amphoras from Sinope on the Black Sea are common in the late second to mid-third century, and are found again in the fifth and sixth centuries. Whatever these amphoras contained (fish sauce?), it was commonly consumed in the Syrian region, and imports of foodstuffs from the Black Sea are known from inland sites in Jordan as well as in the coastal cities. Italian wine was popular again in the Severan period. Common fourth-century imports from far afield are Tunisian, south Spanish and Lusitanian fish sauce amphoras, but western Mediterranean imports are generally absent from the mid-fifth century. By this time the Syrian region had become a major exporter of goods (see below).

Not every amphora type stood at the centre of a wide overseas distribution network. Some seem to have been used for goods consumed almost entirely within the territory of the city which produced them. The Beirut amphora has already been mentioned in this respect. A creation of the Roman period, it did not survive the Muslim conquest in the seventh century. It does not appear to have been produced for export on any scale, and presumably served the needs of Berytus and its territory. Prior to its introduction the city imported or used amphoras predominantly from Tyre and another source, perhaps Sidon. The date of the Beirut amphora's introduction is not certain: it may be Augustan (in which case it could be linked to the foundation of the colony), or earlier (perhaps following the Roman annexation by Pompey). The main product carried in it seems to have been wine. A few of the first-century AD amphoras are stamped 'COL. BER.', which could mean that these contained wine produced on communal land belonging to the colony rather than on private estates. In the second century a larger version of the amphora was produced. This was sometimes exported, to Cyprus and Egypt in particular, and occasionally even further afield (one complete example was found in Britain, at Ringmer in Sussex), but this development did not survive the century. Beirut amphoras predominated in the city during the first and second centuries, being much commoner than imported ones, but by the fourth century imported amphoras began to take over. If the wine of Berytus was famous, as some sources suggest, there is precious little evidence for its export in any quantity – at least not in the Beirut amphora.

As noted earlier, there is little evidence for exports in amphoras from Syria and the Near East before the fourth century. However, from the time of Constantine onwards there is a notable change, beginning with exports from one part of the Syrian region to another, and to Egypt, and spreading westwards in the fifth century. Cilicia (and perhaps Antioch) and Palestine in particular were major exporting regions, and the markets came to be dominated by a narrow variety of amphora forms. Some of these late Roman amphoras have crosses and Christian names painted on them, perhaps indicating their origin on ecclesiastical estates. There is also evidence for standard capacities being used, with amphoras being produced in a range of sizes. As mentioned earlier, one problem hindering amphora studies is that often we do not know exactly where they come from or what they contained. A case in point is a common eastern amphora type, Late Roman Amphora 1 (fig. 75.1), produced from the late fourth or early fifth to the mid-seventh century. It was exported in large quantities, first to Phoenicia, Palestine and Egypt, and from the fifth century to the west. LRA 1 is heavily represented at Carthage, but also at Rome and Marseilles. It occurs too in western Asia Minor, in Greece, on the lower Danube, in Italy, southern Gaul, north-eastern Spain, and south-west Britain. It is perhaps better thought of as a regional type rather than being specific to a certain city. Kiln sites have been discovered in eastern Cilicia and Cyprus, but it is not yet clear whether the form was associated with Antioch as some have proposed. What LRA 1 contained is uncertain; most probably oil or wine, or perhaps both products were exported in these containers. Whatever the case, LRA 1 was clearly at the centre of a major distribution network, but until the places of production can be identified more confidently the connection between this amphora type and the economy of Roman Syria is a matter for speculation (see chapter 5). Its demise seems to coincide with the Muslim conquest, so a connection with Roman state taxation in kind is not impossible, although the fact that LRA 1 was commonly traded with Vandalic Carthage (see above, p. 188) might speak of private enterprise rather than state interests.

Another important late Roman amphora is a cigar-shaped vessel from southern Palestine, associated with Gaza and Ascalon (Late Roman Amphora 4: fig. 75.3). This was a continuation of the traditional pre-Greek-style amphoras mentioned above. In Palestine these containers, which were called 'Gazans' by contemporaries, were used for a variety of purposes, although the ones exported mainly contained wine, and perhaps fish or oil. The Gaza and

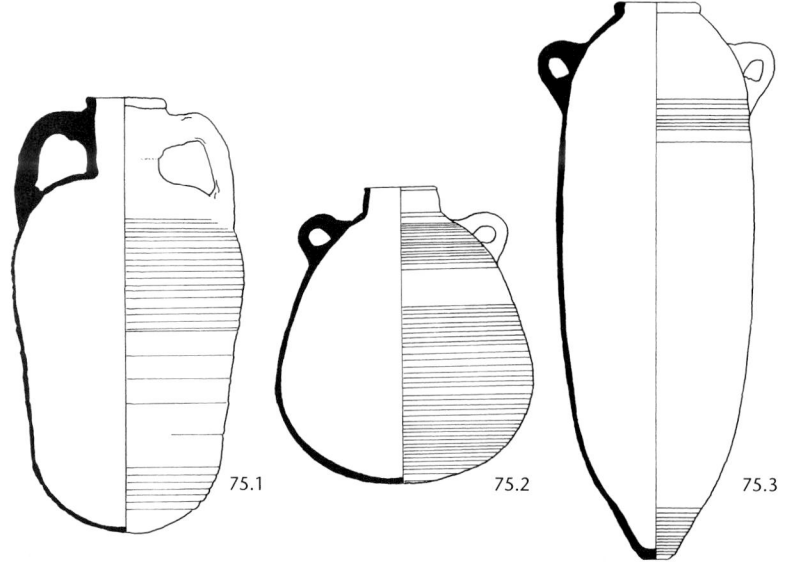

75.1   75.2   75.3

Fig. 75. Common late Roman amphora types from the Syrian region (not to the same scale).

75.1. Late Roman 1, from Cilicia, Cyprus and perhaps northern Syria.

75.2. Late Roman 5, Palestinian bag-shaped amphora.

75.3. Late Roman 4, associated with Gaza and Ascalon.

Ascalon region was a major producer of wine in late antiquity, as evidenced by the numerous presses found there. Gazan wine was heavily exported to the western Mediterranean from the late fourth or early fifth century onwards, but the evidence from excavations in Beirut suggests that Gaza and Ascalon initially exploited markets much closer to home, with a major rise in regional exports to the Syrian coast in the fourth century. This would match the comment in the *Descriptio Totius Orbis*, a text believed to date to the reign of Constantius II (AD 337-61), that Ascalon and Gaza 'export excellent wine to the whole region of Egypt and Syria'.[30] On the strength of the Beirut evidence this regional market was in decline in the sixth century, perhaps indicating that the Gaza/Ascalon industry lost interest in trade with Syria as it directed its trade further afield.

Distinct from the Gazan containers are bag-shaped Palestinian amphoras (fig. 75.2), which, like LRA 1, have a 'corrugated' surface to their bodies. They too were a continuation and development of an earlier regional amphora tradition, most likely connected with the many local wine industries of Palestine. They were probably made at a number of centres in Palestine and Arabia, and most are thought to have held wine, although in the Golan there are large numbers of olive presses in the countryside, so the main product there would seem to have been oil. Their distribution is mainly within Palestine and coastal Syria, but they were also transported to other parts of the Mediterranean, particularly in the sixth and seventh centuries, although not in the same quantities as LRA 1 or the Gazan LRA 4.

Amphoras have been compared to modern jerry cans or oil drums, part of a use-once process from production to consumption. As containers they could of course be recycled, but there are hints that after emptying many were discarded in specialized dumps. The practice of re-using, and even patching up empty amphoras seems to have been more common in late than in early Roman times, but in the late period discard was still common. At Caesarea in the late Roman period a new residential area was laid out on a thick levelling dump, consisting only of broken amphoras. Broken pottery and refuse was commonly used in levelling layers for the construction of buildings. Whether or not discarded amphoras were deliberately collected and sold as building aggregate is uncertain, but some evidence points that way.

Other Coarse Wares

Coarse ware pots, such as vessels for cooking or preparing food or for storage, were also traded. Unlike the amphoras, they were goods in themselves rather than containers for staple foodstuffs, and probably travelled on the back of trade in other cargoes, though it is not always clear what these other cargoes were. Italian cooking wares, made from a strongly fire-resistant volcanic clay, were imported to the Syrian region from Campania in the first half of the second century AD, but Campanian amphoras were not. Jugs, small jars, cooking pots, casseroles, basins and storage jars might be produced locally, but there is often a heavy reliance on imports. Sometimes imported coarse ware pots predominate over locally produced ones, which is rather astonishing if trade in the Roman economy were as limited as some have suggested.

Bowls used for grinding and mixing food (*mortaria*) are a typical coarse ware form of the Roman period, although similar vessels had been used for the same purposes in earlier times. A source at Ras al-Bassit near Laodicea specialized in producing them, along with basins and large storage jars. The *mortaria*, in a dark brown ware roughened with volcanic grits, with a channel on the rim for pouring, are often stamped with the makers' names. They are widely distributed in Syria during the late Roman period, and were exported to other parts of the Roman empire, some examples even reaching north-western Europe.

Bulky ceramic products, such as large basins, storage jars (*dolia*), roof tiles, bricks and clay sarcophagi were traded regionally. As noted above, the degree to which a site relied on imported wares was likely to have been influenced by its position in the trading network, and how easy it was to transport the goods there. Berytus, like most coastal cities, depended almost entirely on imported tile rather than making its own. Remote inland sites may have had to rely more on local ceramic building materials, but this is by no means the rule. There is some uncertainty as to whether batches of tiles or bricks formed the principal cargoes or whether they moved with other goods. Centres which produced ceramic building materials may have functioned like quarries (see below), producing and shipping on commission. Eastern Cilicia was an important source of clay sarcophagi, roof tiles and large basins for Syria between the first and third centuries AD, and the products of this centre dominate the ceramic building materials of the Syrian coast: at Seleucia, Ras al-Bassit, Ras Ibn Hani, Marathus, Berytus and Tyre. The sarcophagi are found widely in the coastal regions of Syria and Palestine, and Cyprus.

Dolia, large storage jars with thick walls, were possibly used for transporting wine as an alternative to amphoras. A first-century BC shipwreck from near Caesarea had *dolia* in the hold. As the ship had come from Italy, it is thought that the *dolia* may have contained Italian wine. The use of these containers for transporting liquids seems to have been an Augustan innovation, but did not survive the early imperial period. Otherwise these large jars found useful employment on farms and in domestic contexts.

Fine Wares

Fine wares, like cooking pots, must have travelled with more valuable cargoes – staples like grain, wine and olive oil. Thus the pots, while not highly significant goods in themselves, are an indication of the movement of other goods. The fine wares are also fairly well documented and datable, and some of them enjoyed a very wide distribution.

Most Syrian cities did not produce their own fine wares, and instead relied on imports. The shapes often imitate those of more expensive metal vessels. The potteries may have been at rural locations rather than in the cities themselves, but currently many of the production sites for east Mediterranean fine wares are unknown. A major fine ware industry for the glossed ware known as Eastern Sigillata A (ESA) was located somewhere in northern Syria or eastern Cilicia. Production of this ware began in the second century BC and the pots rapidly became common in Syria and the Near East. Output remained high for more than two centuries, but by the second century AD the industry was in decline. Although the ESA tradition commenced before the important sigillata fine wares of Italy started production, the Italian industry of the first century BC became very influential, and from the late first century BC onwards ESA imitates the forms of Italian red-gloss sigillata wares, sometimes adding Italian-style makers' stamps, but in Greek rather than Latin. ESA was widely exported to other parts of the eastern Mediterranean basin and to the west, suggesting

76.1. *Early Roman mould made volute lamp with decorated discus. After R. Mikati,* The AUB Beirut Souk Excavations 1994-95: The Terracotta Lamps, *unpublished MA thesis, American University of Beirut, 1998.*

76.1. *Early Roman mould made volute lamp with decorated discus.*

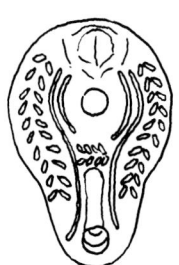

76.2. *Late Roman moulded slipper-shaped lamp, fourth - fifth century AD.*

Cilician or Syrian exports of more important cargoes to the same destinations (for instance, Leptis Magna, Carthage, Rome). No other significant Syrian (if indeed ESA is Syrian) export industry for fine wares has been identified. In the late Roman period all of the major fine wares were imported: the classes called Late Roman C and Late Roman D, Cypriot Sigillata and a little Egyptian Red Slip. African Red Slip wares from Tunisia are common on Syrian and Near Eastern sites, implying the import of other goods from Africa to our region. That at least a part of this trade was civilian rather than connected with military supply is implied by the fact that this trade continues after the eastern and western Mediterranean began to go separate political ways. But the commonest late Roman fine ware in the region, Late Roman C, which is associated with Phocaea in western Asia Minor, has a strong connection with military sites.

Other ceramic products made from refined clays include lamps, which were produced in stone or plaster moulds. It was easy to create new moulds from existing lamps, and in this way identical designs could have been replicated at more than one centre. The common form in the early Roman period is the round-bodied discus type with volutes on either side of the spout, which often carries a motif in relief in the central discus (fig. 76.1). This form gave way to the slipper lamps of late Roman and early Islamic times (fig. 76.2). Small flasks with long, narrow necks (unguentaria) were made to contain aromatic oils, unguents and perfumes. Tyre was an important centre of production and regional export for these vessels during the early empire. Glass forms overtook clay unguentaria by the second century, but clay forms continued to be produced at some centres. A major centre for imports of clay unguentaria to Syria in the fifth and sixth centuries was Ephesus. A much rarer type of small container encountered in late Roman times is the so-called 'pilgrim flask', a mould-made vessel with a flat-sided body and a pair of handles and usually bearing religious motifs in relief. It held oil or water which had been blessed and was probably produced for sale to visitors to holy sites.

GLASS

The technique of blowing translucent glass vessels was reputedly developed in the Syrian region in the later first century BC, but it spread so rapidly in the Mediterranean that glass vessels appear at many different sites at roughly the same time, between the end of the first century BC and the beginning of the first century AD. Glass objects had been manufactured in the region since the middle of the second millennium BC, but all previous methods of manufacture had involved melting and fusing glass in moulds or forming them around a core. Common vessels were small, core-formed bottles and mould-made bowls. Blown glass, on the other hand, extended the number of possible forms and decorative techniques, allowing glass to become a substitute for a variety of vessels of other materials. Not only that, but over time glass also became a relatively *cheap* substitute for vessels of other materials.

Manufacture involved two processes. In the first, the raw materials were melted in large furnaces, producing blocks of glass (cullet). The potential scale of this operation is apparent from the huge block of melted glass found at Beth Shearim in Palestine. This was a slab 3.4 metres (11 feet) long, 1.95 metres (6½ feet) wide and 45 centimetres (1½ feet) thick, corresponding to the size of the furnace; it weighed almost 9 tonnes, but was presumably abandoned because the composition of the glass produced was wrong, making it unusable. When successfully melted and cooled, such huge slabs could then be broken up into blocks for remelting and blowing, which was the second part of the glass-making process. Production of cullet and production of vessels did not usually take place in the same location. There is ample evidence for the transportation of cullet to secondary production centres where the vessels were blown. The site of Jalame, about 10 kilometres (6¼ miles) south-east of modern Haifa and not far from Beth Shearim, was evidently such a place, and the large furnace at the site was for remelting cullet before working it, or simply for gathering heat-softened chunks of glass on the end of a blowpipe and heating them in the furnace until they were sufficiently viscous to blow into vessels. Glass-blowing workshops were to be found in both cities and at locations in the countryside, and can be identified by quantities of broken or melted glass and – most telling of all – moils (the glass left over on the ends of the workers' blow pipes) and pieces of collapsed glass vessels. Although a specialized craft, glass-blowing was by no means a rare one. Because of the sheer size of the operations and the danger of fires, the furnaces for the large-scale production of cullet were more likely to be located in the countryside, or away from built-up areas, but glass-blowing was sufficiently inoffensive for workers to set up shop in urban environments. The production of glass linked city and country.

Early glass vessels often imitated more expensive ones in stone or metal. Once glass-blowing had developed, there was little further change to the basic range and function of forms, and nothing characteristically 'Syrian' about most of those produced in the region. Currently no detailed chronological typology like that of pottery is available, although some forms and types are characteristic of particular periods and are easily dated. By the beginning of the first century AD glass-workers were blowing glass into moulds to make more elaborate shapes and to produce relief designs on the surfaces, but most workshops did not go to such lengths when producing the cheap, transparent or green glass vessels for everyday use, and the basic forms of these did not change much over the centuries. Like pottery, glass was traded, although in most cases the places of manufacture are extremely difficult to determine. Unlike pottery, broken glass vessels could be recycled, so that raw materials from multiple places of origin ended up being mixed together. Some cast bowls of the second and first centuries BC were produced in Syria or Palestine and exported to other parts of the Mediterranean. A group of strongly coloured mould-blown vessels bear makers' names, often describing these people as Sidonian. 'Sidonian' vessels are known from various parts of the Roman world, but none is known from secure contexts in the Syrian region. Strongly coloured glass is typical of Italy in the early empire, so these objects may be the work of Sidonian glass workers established in Italy and not representative products of Sidon itself. In the late Roman period small mould-blown bottles and pitchers were produced in the Syrian region, decorated with religious motifs. Like the ceramic 'pilgrim flasks' they may have held holy oils and waters.

MARBLE

The trade in decorative stones is one of the most improbable consequences of the Roman empire. That hundreds of tonnes should be quarried, roughed into prefabricated and standardized shapes, and then shipped hundreds or even thousands of kilometres across the Roman world seems an unlikely undertaking, but such was the prestige of exotic stones in the empire that the unlikely became commonplace. Columns, capitals and bases, architectural mouldings, sarcophagi and even statues were mass-produced and shipped to clients all over the eastern and western Mediterranean. It is doubtful, however, whether this unusual trade would have developed without imperial impetus. Decorative stones of the type which the Romans called *marmor* were quarried and shipped to Rome under the Julio-Claudian and Flavian emperors for use in imperial building projects, the object being to enhance both the prestige of the capital city and its imperial benefactors. In order to secure the supply, and to exploit these stones on a large scale, the emperors took control of many of the quarries producing them. In this way imported stones, with their distinctive and attractive colours and patterns, or their fine surfaces and polishes, became symbolic of the centre of power. They could be obtained only at great effort and expense, and they were clearly associated with imperial supremacy. Cities and individuals in the provinces sought to obtain these symbols to enhance their own prestige, and by the late first or early second century the demand for such stones was strong enough to engender a viable distribution network to supply clients and communities outside Rome. The imperial supply system began providing stone commercially for other cities of the empire. What is most remarkable is not that it was possible to extract and move such quantities of stone, but that a social need for such quantities made it acceptable to do so on a regular basis.

The System

Our understanding of the marble trade owes much to the pioneering work of John Ward-Perkins, who was able to demonstrate the scale and importance of Roman exploitation. Only the general outlines of this trade's development and mode of operation are known, and some elements of the basic model are disputed. Nevertheless there is general agreement about the existence of an organized system and the importance of this for the spread of 'Graeco-Roman' architectural styles and building types in the eastern Mediterranean. Major quarries appear to have come under imperial ownership during the first century, although some were opened up for large-scale exploitation only in the second, when the demand was increasing. The manner in which the imperial quarries were exploited is not entirely clear. They seem to have been run by imperial officials, who leased out parts of the quarries to private contractors. It remains possible, however, that certain centres of production remained independent of imperial control. Most of the quarries were close to the sea, enabling their products to be shipped easily, and the shapes and designs of the individual items were often roughed out prior to shipping to lighten the load (quarries located far from the sea appear to have gone to greater lengths to finish off their products before moving them, presumably to cut down on transport costs). The physical characteristics of the stones often dictated what sort of objects could be produced, and the dimensions of the flawless blocks that could be quarried limited the sizes and shapes of those objects. In this way a high degree of uniformity in the end product was established right at the outset.

The distribution of products from individual quarries shows that each quarry had preferred areas to which exports were directed. Apart from the city of Rome, the overall bias in the use of decorative stones is clearly towards cities of the eastern Mediterranean (where the majority of quarries were located), but finds are known as far west as Britain, albeit in small quantities. Marble sarcophagi are one of the commonest forms of monumental stone object to be mass-produced and exported by quarries (see below), and trade in these is better understood than for some other classes of object. Their distribution resembles that of ceramic fine wares in that there are clusters of the same types of sarcophagi in certain regions, suggesting that these regions were targeted intensively by particular quarries. It is not clear whether sarcophagi, like fine pottery, travelled with other cargoes, but their bulk and weight presumably formed the major element of a ship's freight. The quarries probably employed agents at targeted centres overseas, who took orders, perhaps stockpiled popular products, and who employed sculptors familiar with the qualities of the stones to finish the products for clients. These sculptors may sometimes have travelled from the quarry to the overseas agency, but it is more likely that they were permanently established overseas. As noted above, the fully fledged system of trade in decorative stones did not develop until the late first or early second century, perhaps in connection with the massive building projects at Rome under Domitian (AD 81-96), Trajan (98-117) and Hadrian (117-38). Whilst there is some limited evidence that individuals other than emperors may have been able to acquire some stone during the early phase of imperial exploitation under the Julio-Claudian emperors, it was only afterwards that a sophisticated commercial system developed. Now the quarries produced ready-made items for sale. From the early second century the trade was characterized by massive exploitation of particular sorts of stone hailing from a limited number of centres, and widespread use of these stones by communities all over the eastern Mediterranean.

Syria and the Common Vocabulary of Stone

The ancient concept of 'marble' embraced a rather broader category of rocks than the modern geological notion of marble, and covers all sorts of decorative stones that could be given a polished finish. While a wide variety of these stones has been found on Syrian and Near Eastern sites, the products of certain quarries are particularly prominent there (fig. 77). In its combination of imported stones, particularly granites, Syria resembles the southern coast of Asia Minor, and Egypt, more than it does Greece or Italy.

Syria was a major importer of decorative stones, having no significant supplies of its own. Some quarries produced local limestones and gypsum which could be polished so that they resembled marble, but otherwise all decorative marbles were imported or, if unavailable or too expensive, imitated in some less costly medium. Prior to the widespread availability of decorative coloured stones, a common option was to paint wall plaster in imitation of marble veneers. This is what King Herod did when building his elaborate 'hanging' palace on the precipitous northern spur of the rock of Masada in Judaea. Although Herod took advantage of the possibilities of long-distance trade to import other prestige goods, he reigned too early to benefit from the main phase of trade in marbles. Otherwise, no doubt, the walls of his palace would have been faced with imported veneers, and the limestone columns and Corinthian and Ionic capitals, cut by Jewish masons, would have been prefabricated marble ones (this is not to imply that he was unable to acquire any high status materials, as he did have *opus sectile* floors mixing local and imported stones in his palaces). Even after they became widely available, decorative stones might prove too expensive for some projects. At Majdel Aanjar in the Bekaa valley a locally-occurring conglomerate (see p. 177) was used for the columns and pilasters of a large temple of the second century AD. The stone is of a rather rough quality, but from a distance its mottled pink colour vaguely resembles that of Egyptian granite. The building may have been trying to compete in a modest way with the great religious complex at nearby Heliopolis. The design and decoration of this temple was similar to the so-called 'Temple of Bacchus' at Heliopolis; the use of this pinkish conglomerate may be a conscious imitation, in cheaper local materials, of the genuine Egyptian red granite used in the courtyard of the Temple of Jupiter Heliopolitanus.

Movement of huge, heavy stone objects was greatly facilitated by water transport, and therefore import of decorative stones was commoner at sites on the Syrian coast than at sites inland (colour plate 18). This is no doubt a contributing factor to the general observation by modern scholars that the coastal

Fig. 77. Sources of the principal decorative stones exported to the Syrian region.

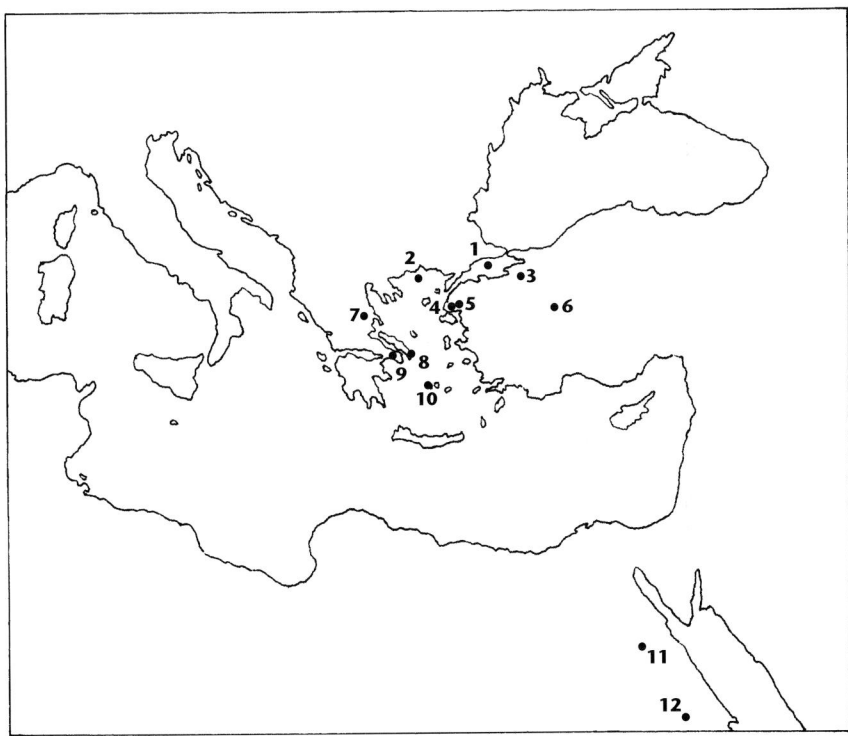

1. *Proconnesus (white marble)*
2. *Thasos (white marble)*
3. *Bithynia (breccia corallina)*
4. *Assos* (lapis sarcophagus)
5. *Troad (grey granite)*
6. *Docimium (pavonazzetto)*
7. *Thessaly (green breccia = verde antico)*
8. *Carystus (green-veined marble = cipollino)*
9. *Mount Pentelikon (white marble)*
10. *Paros (white marble)*
11. *Mons Porhyrites (purple porphyry)*
12. *Syene (Aswan, pink granite)*

cities were more thoroughly Hellenized than those of the interior. *Opus sectile* floors laid with coloured marbles, cemeteries populated with imported sarcophagi, or colonnades of *cipollino*, grey or red granites, are a notable feature of Syrian and Palestinian coastal cities, while local limestones proliferated in high-status buildings at inland centres. Nevertheless, it was clearly felt to be important for cities inland to have at least some decorative stones, and the inhabitants must have expended considerable effort in obtaining them: large columns of Egyptian red granite are found at Heliopolis, Gerasa, Philadelphia (Amman), and even as far inland as Palmyra. A common architectural vocabulary, based around imports of the same stones and forms, linked the cities of the Syrian hinterland to those of the coast.

One of the most important centres of marble production and export was the island of Proconnesus in the Sea of Marmara, which yielded a fine white marble with faint bands of grey. The entire island is made of this marble, and thus it was easy to extract and ship. Proconnesian marble was used for a variety of purposes, mainly for architectural elements such as column capitals and bases, entablatures and pilasters, but the quarry also specialized in sarcophagi. The island's exploitation probably increased in the fourth century with the foundation of Constantinople, but the quarry was being worked intensively and its products widely distributed overseas long before this. Proconnesian marble is very common in the Syrian region.

Geology determined what stones were preferred for columns. In Syria and the Near East the favoured imported types were granites and a green-banded marble from Carystus in Euboea which resembles the layers of an onion and since the Renaissance has been called *cipollino*. The main sources of granite in the eastern Mediterranean were quarries in the Troad of north-western Asia Minor (producing grey granites) and Egypt (producing both red and grey). Most of the grey granite found in the Syrian region is thought to be Troadic rather than Egyptian (which it seems was used almost exclusively for imperial projects). Other quarries in western Asia Minor provided grey granite columns, but in smaller quantities. Columns appear to have been produced in standard sizes, although it seems that quarries could make special sizes (such as very large columns over 12 metres (40 feet) high) to order. Unlike most other objects which were merely roughed out before leaving the quarries, columns were shipped in an almost-finished state, with projecting collars to protect their ends. These collars could then be dressed into torus mouldings on arrival.

Many quarries produced blocks of stone for use in wall veneers and *opus sectile* floors, which were sawn into suitable panels at the destination. There is some evidence to support the view that these blocks were cut to standard sizes, to minimize waste. Veneers were widely employed in both public and private buildings, giving them the appearance of being made of solid marble, and are commonly found in the cities of the coast. Small quantities were relatively easy to transport overland, which may explain the modest use of *opus sectile* flooring in places like Palmyra. Coloured limestone sometimes sufficed as a substitute when the real thing was too expensive or too difficult to find, or it might be used in combination with limited quantities of marble. The sixth-century *opus sectile* floor found in the so-called House of the Consoles at Apamea used mainly limestone, slate and ceramic (materials commonly employed in mosaic) in imitation of more expensive decorative stones.

Mass-production of architectural elements by the main quarries leads us to wonder whether the design and decoration of buildings was limited by what the customers or builders could obtain from the quarries, or whether the quarries were tailoring their products in response to popular demand. It is noteworthy that the inspiration for the styles tended to derive from the place where the quarry was located rather than from overseas. Thus the Attic quarries exported capitals of a type characteristic of Roman Athens. The Proconnesian quarries are thought to have been influenced by the tastes and styles of late second- and early third-century Asia Minor, and their influence helped to make these designs part of an interprovincial architectural vocabulary which we now associate with early imperial 'Graeco-Roman' architecture. An element typical of Asia Minor is the pilaster decorated with floral scrolls, inhabited by small human figures; very similar 'peopled scrolls' are found at Caesarea and Scythopolis, at Leptis Magna in Africa, and sites in Asia Minor. Such a degree of similarity might not be expected from local sculptors working in the different cities, but is easily explained if the quarries directed the decoration according to standardized patterns. The fact that in the Syrian region grey granite columns tend to occur in conjunction with Proconnesian capitals, entablatures and column bases (for example, at Tyre, Caesarea, Gadara), whereas Egyptian granite columns more commonly employ local limestone elements, hints at a possible co-ordination between the Troadic and Proconnesian quarries, the former supplying columns and the latter the other elements.

It seems likely that the quarries disseminated the styles, which were adopted by communities overseas. In the case of sarcophagus designs, when it came to deciding which types to market in Syria the quarry at Proconnesus may have been influenced by local preferences, yet the types preferred were actually inspired by sarcophagus designs popular in Asia Minor (see below). Even if the styles were the result of a two-way process of dialogue between quarries and customers, the resulting range of 'off-the-shelf' designs was limited, rather like the products available in modern do-it-yourself stores, and this would have forced architects and builders to work with standard sizes, colours and types. Proconnesian architectural elements found in Berytus were carved with instructions for assembly, probably at the quarry. In the late empire quarries on the islands of Thasos and Proconnesus were producing ready-made 'kits' for churches, including columns, chancel screens, altars and other fittings. The marble trade contributed to architectural uniformity, and there are growing indications that it may have contributed to artistic uniformity as well. There is good evidence for statues being mass-produced, either being finished in the quarry or shipped in a roughed-out state for completion at the destination. (This does not rule out the production of unique pieces to order, but the sculptors employed are likely to have been those familiar with the working properties of the marble. Therefore the style of unique pieces is likely to have conformed to the typical products of a quarry.) Generic busts could be shipped with the features of the faces roughed out; an appropriately skilled craftsman could subsequently turn them into individual portraits. Certain quarries specialized in particular sorts of statue, so that poses or the types of figure were to some extent predetermined and limited. As with architectural elements the kind of stone might determine the size, type or pose of the statue. Purple porphyry from Egypt was deemed particularly appropriate for imperial figures (an excellent if headless example, probably of Hadrian, is to be found re-employed in the so-called 'Byzantine esplanade' at Caesarea). Although desirable and expensive, a considerable quantity of the sculptural 'high art' of the Roman world was mass-produced; it was the provincial art that was often more truly original. It is perhaps not surprising that the purely classical-style sculptures are commoner on coastal sites and local styles in local materials more characteristic of the interior. As with architecture, the difficulties and cost of land transport provided greater incentive to 'do it yourself' inland, rather than import the elements ready-made. Sometimes those sculptures that were imported to the cities of the hinterland might provide a curious juxtaposition with local work. The sanctuary of the goddess Allat at Palmyra contained an imported marble statue of Athena (a goddess assimilated to Allat), a copy of a fifth-century BC Greek masterpiece by the sculptor Pheidias. It must have provided a strong

Fig. 78. The Tyre necropolis. Imported marble and local limestone sarcophagi are placed side by side among and on tombs.

stylistic contrast with the Palmyrene limestone sculptures of the sanctuary (fig. 140). It was no doubt a prestige object, but its purely classical form does not necessarily prove that Palmyrenes preferred classical art over native art – prestige objects of this sort were simply not available in local styles and forms.

However, the prestige of objects in marble did encourage their imitation in cheaper local stones, and the craftsmen employed by the overseas agents of the major quarries may have been prepared to work for clients using local materials. Limestone imitations of Proconnesian sarcophagi sometimes resemble the originals to an astonishing degree. Such imitations in local stones strongly suggest that these craftsmen employed by the quarries were permanently established at importing centres, rather than travelling with shipments to finish them wherever they were sent. Through imitation, successful quarries disseminated their styles over a much wider area, influenced products made in local materials and potentially increased demand for the real thing.

Sarcophagi provide the clearest evidence for the theory of mass-production and stockpiling. The Syrians had always tended to bury rather than cremate their dead, and an increasing trend towards burial rather than cremation in the Roman world in the second century led to a growth in the demand for

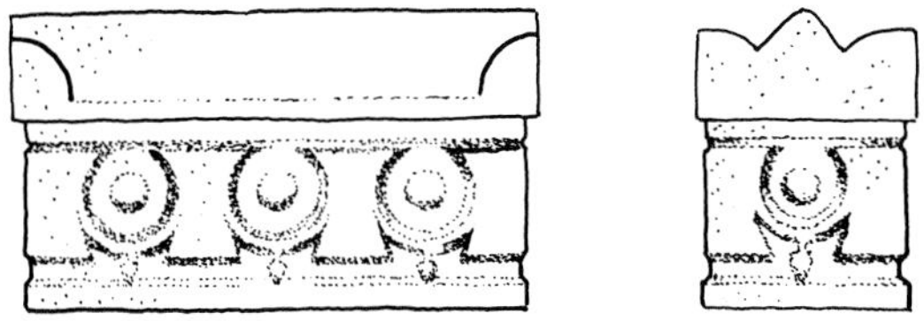

79.1

79.2

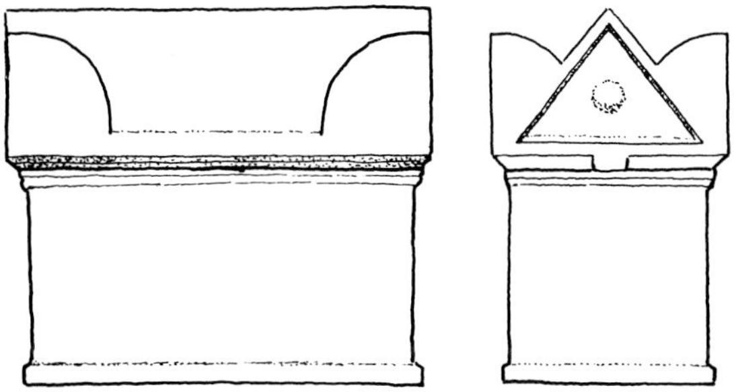

79.3

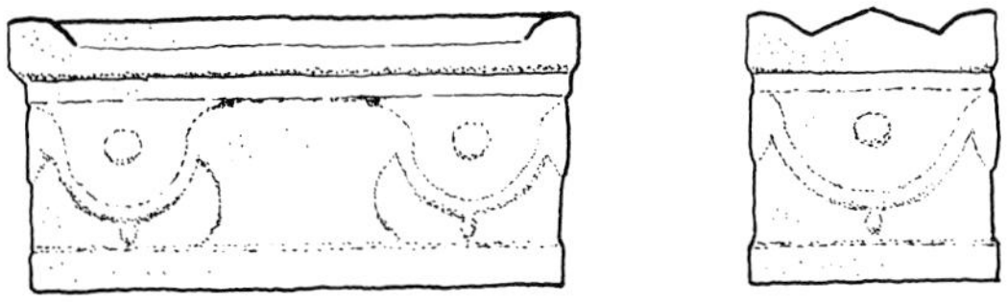

79.4

Fig. 79. Typical imported sarcophagus forms.
79.1. Proconnesian garland sarcophagus in quarry state, side and end views.
79.2. Garland sarcophagus after reliefs have been added in situ.
79.3. Proconnesian pedimental gable sarcophagus, side and end views. The boss in the pediment was often worked into a decorative motif.
79.4. Sarcophagus of lapis sarcophagus, side and end views.

sarcophagi. The Phoenician cities of the coast had imported marble sarcophagi in the Persian and Hellenistic periods, as finds from Sidon show, and the Roman trade in these objects may represent a continuation of the tradition. Most quarries shipped their sarcophagi in what is called a 'quarry state', that is, with the surfaces roughly dressed with a claw chisel and the areas for relief designs blocked out. As a result, standardization at the quarry often dictated how the decoration on the surfaces of the finished sarcophagus would look. The standard form for marble sarcophagi was a rectangular box closed with a lid, the latter normally having a pitched roof and *acroteria* at the corners. The sarcophagus thus resembled a house or a temple; a similitude not lost on some people, who had the sloping sides of the lids sculpted in imitation of roof tiles. The *acroteria* also helped to strengthen and protect the corners of the lid. Only after it had been placed in the tomb or cemetery would the surfaces of the sarcophagus be finished, and normally only those sides exposed to view would be completed. Sometimes they were lined with a second sarcophagus made of lead sheets, although lead sarcophagi were also used for independent burials. Lids were secured with metal clamps, but finds show that they were frequently tampered with, not necessarily to rob the contents, but to reuse the sarcophagi at a later date. Sometimes they were used for multiple burials over a period of time, perhaps by the same family; at other times old sarcophagi were appropriated illegally by strangers. A number of inscriptions on the sarcophagi naming the deceased are crudely carved compared to the care lavished on the decoration, and suggest that the occupants named were not their original owners.

The Tyre necropolis gives us a good idea of the trade in these objects. The excavated part of the cemetery lies on the peninsula of Tyre, surrounding the main road and aqueduct approaching the city. The majority of imported sarcophagi there come from Proconnesus, but Tyrians evidently had a number of choices when selecting sources and designs. Quarries might specialize in more than one design, but each was peculiar to the quarry producing it. The Proconnesian quarries manufactured three main types, but of these only two forms were marketed in the Syrian region: the so-called 'garland sarcophagus' and the 'pedimental gable' type (fig. 79). Garland sarcophagi seem to have been common in the necropoleis of coastal cities in Syria and Palestine, and they were shipped in their quarry state from Proconnesus to destinations all over the eastern Mediterranean and to Italy. When decorated they were usually sculpted with putti or ox-heads supporting garlands, with gorgoneions in the fields (fig. 79.2). At Tyre most people were content to leave them in their quarry state, or at the most covered the sarcophagus with a smooth layer of plaster; only occasionally was a sculptor employed to decorate them. The rarity of decorated ones at Tyre led Ward-Perkins to suggest that no suitable workshop for finishing them was regularly available in the city, and that perhaps the main centre for importing and decorating them was located in another coastal city. Finished garland sarcophagi are known from Laodicea, Tripolis, Byblus and Berytus, and also from Antioch, Apamea and Arethusa, but it is impossible to quantify the ratio of finished to quarry state pieces at these places without systematic exploration of their cemeteries, and it is not clear which of the cities could have served as the main regional centre for such imports. The chronology of the sarcophagi is also difficult to establish. Because they were reused, inscriptions and contents are not necessarily an accurate guide. The garland design is thought to have developed in the marble quarries of Asia Minor in the first half of the second century; the precise date of its adoption by the Proconnesian quarry is uncertain. It was certainly being produced in the second half of the second century and through the third, though perhaps no later than this. The pedimental gable type appears to have been produced for the Syrian market, and may be an example of a quarry catering to local tastes. However, there is no clear evidence for prototypes of the pedimental gable type in local stones, so the inspiration may have been foreign to Tyre. The decoration on the pedimental gable sarcophagi is fairly minimal, and mainly restricted to gorgoneions or rosettes and mouldings in the pediments. The type began in the second century but continued into the late Roman period, though once again the dating is insecure.

Another common class of sarcophagus was produced in a rough, dark volcanic stone, the source of which was identified by Ward-Perkins at Assos, in north-western Asia Minor. This was known in antiquity as *lapis sarcophagus*, 'flesh-eating stone', which Pliny the Elder in the first century referred to as capable of consuming corpses in forty days, 'except for teeth'.[31] From the second to third century sarcophagi were exported to Syria, Greece, Egypt and Italy. Their quarry state seems to have been their finished state; the stone was so rough that it was hardly worth trying to dress them any further. Their surfaces are decorated with stylized garlands and a panel which could receive an inscription (fig. 79.4). To the modern eye they do not look aesthetically pleasing, but they were perhaps appreciated for their other well-known property.

Much less common is a class of Attic sarcophagi in Pentelic marble from Athens. Again, these are dated to the second and third centuries. The very fine white marble of which they were made was highly prized, and the products of the Attic quarries are thought to have been considerably more expensive than those of Proconnesus. The faces of the sarcophagi are usually decorated with elaborate figured panels, which were prepared in shallow relief at the quarry before being transported. The lids were either gabled like those of the Proconnesian sarcophagi or sculpted in imitation of funerary couches, bearing reclining figures of the deceased. The faces of these figures were left unfinished; accurate likenesses of the clients would be added when the sarcophagus was in position, though in the case of the Tyre examples this was not always done and the heads remain in their quarry state. The location of the sarcophagus in the tomb or cemetery, and the angles from which it could be viewed, tended to dictate how many sides would be carved in deeper relief and polished.

It is important to emphasize that not all sarcophagi in the Tyre necropolis were imported. Large numbers were made of local limestone. These were sometimes of a simple 'shoe-box' design with a flat lid, but more commonly they had pitched lids with *acroteria* at the corners, and therefore resemble the general form of the two main Proconnesian types. The commonest have no decoration, although they often bear traces of a plaster or stucco coating. Some have an altar carved in high relief at one end to receive offerings. However, the local limestone sarcophagi also imitate specific imported types. What is perhaps most remarkable is that garland sarcophagi were imitated in their quarry state as well as their finished form, suggesting that even in their unfinished condition the originals were highly prestigious. At any rate, the popularity of the garland type among the imitations attests to the influence of Proconnesian designs.

The marble trade had a profound effect upon the material culture of Syria and the Near East. Cities could acquire prefabricated elements for buildings, or, if they could not afford these, they might be able to have competent copies made in local materials. Temples and other public buildings could be decorated with sculpture, either mass-produced or specially commissioned. Individuals could have statues and portraits produced by craftsmen skilled in classical styles, and they could be buried in imported sarcophagi. The uniformity of this cultural material speaks of a desire for regularity, but it should be noted that this desire was mainly that of the elites who could afford to pay for such expensive objects, and who had the most to gain by aligning themselves with the 'international' overlay culture of the Roman Mediterranean. This is a topic which will be readdressed in the chapters that follow.

TEXTILES

Textile production appears to have been very important in many Syrian and Near Eastern cities. The product, unfortunately, is less durable than the other classes of object discussed, and apart from a few fragments of fabric from the drier regions and sites like Dura Europus, Palmyra and the Euphrates fortress of Zenobia, most information has to be gathered from written sources. These hint at a large-scale trade in textiles, and at the fact that there were major centres of textile production which manufactured goods for a wide market. Linen, which could be woven into fine, cool and light garments, was exported from Syria to the west. The *Descriptio Totius Orbis* mentions cities which 'export linen to all the world': Scythopolis, Laodicea, Byblus, Tyre and Berytus. The author neglects to mention Antioch as a centre of linen production, and yet Antiochene linen is recorded in other sources as a material for cheap and probably low-quality clothing. It was also exported in quantity, so much so that even a 'primitivist' like A. H. M. Jones, noting that cheap clothes called 'unbleached Antiochenes' were available at Rome in the fourth century, conceded the possibility 'that in large towns at any rate the cheapest clothing was imported from the large centres of production'.[32] Cheap products, shipped in bulk, suggest that transport costs for such items were low – unless these linens were exported solely as tax in kind. Egyptian papyri record weavers producing garments to be exported for military use. These weavers functioned independently of the state factories established, probably by Diocletian, to supply the army, and the fact that they did so suggests that the state did not rely entirely on its own workers for supplies of textiles.

The Edict on Maximum Prices published in AD 301 by the emperor

Diocletian lists prices for types of garment according to place of manufacture. From it we learn that Damascus, for example, produced woollens, linen mattresses and pillows, and it concurs with the *Descriptio Totius Orbis* that Laodicea, Byblus and Scythopolis were important for linens. That the cities were listed in an edict published empire-wide suggests their products were familiar to more than strictly local consumers. These were 'international' products. They seem to have been distinguished according to quality, but perhaps also by design or cut, because the list distinguishes 'imitation' products (for example, Alexandrian linens imitating those of Tarsus). As with marble sculptures and architectural elements, widespread trade in particular designs of clothing will have led to standardized styles.

From Syria there is also some documentary evidence for textiles and traders who dealt in clothes. Nebuchelus, the owner of a house at Dura Europus, and perhaps a textile manufacturer, left a number of graffiti scratched into the plaster of the walls recording commercial transactions. One recorded a large mixed load of goods which travelled up the Euphrates north to Appadana. It included short cloaks, 'dalmatic' cloaks, damaged boys' clothes, girls' clothes and other textile items.

The textile industry exported and supplied ready-to-wear garments at a variety of prices, suitable for all classes. Expensive clothes seem to have been produced only in a few centres, particularly Scythopolis, Byblus and Laodicea, and in the latter part of the sixth century a silk industry was established at Antioch, Berytus and Tyre to serve the requirements of the ruling elites. This is not to say that all textile goods were imported from regional or distant centres of production. Cheaper textiles, such as the fragments of woollen tapestry, and goat's hair carpet or saddle cloth found at Dura Europus, could have been produced locally.

COINAGE

Historians generally assume that the Roman empire was a single monetary system, with a commonly accepted currency. This standardization is thought to have been due to the tax demands of the Roman state, which coincidentally facilitated regional and long-distance trade. As the Roman empire expanded, it imposed its coinage on conquered regions, and was thus able to bring those regions into a monetary economy centred on Italy. Taxes in coin flowed out of tax-producing provinces to the centre (Rome), and were then redistributed to tax-consuming provinces, particularly those where large armies were stationed. A single monetary system greatly facilitated trade, enabling tax-producing provinces to engage in overseas exports to win money with which to pay taxes. In this way, taxation stimulated trade, and the monetary system provided an ideal environment for these activities.

However, in reality things may not have been quite so simple. The main tax coin of the early empire is presumed to have been the silver denarius, but a variety of silver and bronze coinages were issued in the Roman provinces, and these did not circulate widely. How these coinages worked in relation to the denarius is not always clear. For the first three centuries of Roman rule small change in the east was provided mainly in the form of local, Greek-style city coinages. These were a continuation of a long-standing tradition whereby

Greek cities had issued their own coinages, a custom which the Romans respected. Not every city issued its own money, and those that did not, or those which issued coins only rarely, seem to have made do with the coinages of neighbouring cities. Exactly how they acquired the coinages of their neighbours is not certain. All of this raises questions about the ways in which communities paid money taxes.

We have no definite knowledge of how coins were put into circulation. Clearly the Roman state did not simply give newly minted money away for free. An obvious route by which coins could enter circulation, and the one most frequently invoked, is as payment for services. The Roman state needed to pay its employees, particularly its armies. While it is highly likely that the bulk of imperial coinage was produced with such considerations in mind, a single explanation of this sort is likely to oversimplify the motives for striking coins, particularly when it comes to the question of civic issues. Local city coinages are likely to have been produced to meet local needs. At any rate, by producing coinage themselves the cities did not have to rely entirely on coinage sent from Rome. (But, at the same time, it is hard to see how Rome could have controlled the amount of money in circulation.) Some eastern cities might also have commissioned other mints to produce the coin for them, including major mints like Rome. It is now known that certain issues of provincial bronze and silver were made at Rome and sent to Syria and other eastern provinces. The possibility that local communities could buy coin direct from a mint provides an alternative route for coinage entering circulation.

It is difficult to assess the extent to which the Syrian economy was fully monetized, but what evidence there is suggests that the use of coinage was widespread, in the countryside as well as in the cities. Inscriptions and papyri provide clear evidence of cash transactions for all sorts of exchanges and in different sections of society. Many of these are for relatively large amounts or costly items, but some provide us with a glimpse of prices for everyday expenses. A third-century account from the *mithraeum* at Dura Europus lists the prices of materials required for a ritual banquet: 'Meat, 1(9) denarii [...]; sauce, 1 denarius; paper, 1 obol [?]; water, 1 denarius; wood, 1 denarius; jar of wine, 28 denarii 11 obols [?]; total: 51 denarii, 11 obols [?].'[33] Other documents, such as those from the Babatha archive and the archive from the Euphrates (see p. 142) suggest that coinage was in common use in the villages of first- and second-century Nabataea and Arabia, and the Euphrates region during the third century.

Finds of coins from sites also suggest a high degree of monetization. There are two basic categories of find: hoards, which were deliberately concealed and tend to contain valuable coins; and site finds, the product of casual loss or discard, which are largely composed of low-value bronzes. Thus site finds can tell us very little about the circulation of silver or gold coins, and securely provenanced hoards of bronzes are comparatively rare, at least in the early empire. Apart from the site of Dura Europus, destroyed by the Persians in the mid-third century, few Syrian sites have yielded significant numbers of silver coins. This does not mean, however, that a reconstruction of the monetary economy of Roman Syria is beyond us; on the contrary, although much remains to be done, the general outline is becoming clearer as more finds are analysed.

Roman Imperial Coinage

In general, the bronze coinage issued at Rome did not circulate, although it is clear that some special coinages were struck at Rome for issue in Syria. But the regular issues of sestertii, dupondii and asses of the sort commonly found in the western empire are mostly rare or absent, and the region relied heavily on locally produced currencies in bronze. In this respect the pattern of base metal coin use in Syria resembles, in broad terms, that observed in neighbouring Asia Minor. It is clear from hoards and site finds that silver denarii and gold aurei did circulate in Syria and the Near East, but the date of their introduction is problematic. A few mixed hoards combining local Tyrian tetradrachms (shekels) and republican denarii or Augustan denarii are known, hinting that these Roman imperial coins circulated in Phoenicia and Judaea during the late first century BC and under the Julio-Claudian emperors, but there is no clear evidence of their circulation in the north until the second century. The statement by Tacitus, that during the initial stages of Vespasian's rebellion against Vitellius (AD 69) gold and silver coinages were struck at Antioch (*Histories* 2.82), is supported by surviving issues of aurei and denarii which can be attributed to that mint. This suggests that aurei and denarii were circulating in the north from the Flavian period onwards, but what happened there under the Julio-Claudians is unknown. If AD 69 does indeed mark the introduction of Roman imperial coinages in precious metal to northern Syria, this change may be related to developments in provincial silver issues (see below).

By the second century denarii and aurei were regularly being hoarded with local silver currencies, and inscriptions and papyri indicate their presence (at least as units of account) from the Flavian period. Most of these denarii were produced at Rome, and the only significant production of aurei and denarii in Syria occurred under the usurper Pescennius Niger (AD 193-4) and during the early years of Septimius Severus' reign. In the third century, under Gordian III (AD 238-44), Antioch became a mint for imperial silver 'radiates' or *antoniniani*, and under Trebonianus Gallus (AD 251-3) *antoniniani* became the only sort of silver coin to be produced in Syria. Some have seen this as a response to the Sasanian invasions of the mid-third century and the need to supply armies with imperial coins, though why the change should have been prompted at this juncture and not during earlier crises is unclear. A number of factors may have contributed to the change (see below).

Provincial Issues

It remains to discuss the other kinds of coins that circulated in Syria and the Near East during the early empire. These were a continuation of late Hellenistic coinages. The Seleucids had struck royal coinages in silver and bronze, principally at Antioch but also at other mints such as Damascus, Tyre and Ptolemais. Independence from the Seleucid empire had resulted in many cities striking their own bronze civic issues, sometimes dated from the year of their autonomy. A few of these cities also struck civic silver coinages, most notably Laodicea, Aradus and Tyre. That their issues were regular is confirmed by the dates which the coins bear, and the number of dies used and the number of hoards known confirm that many issues were fairly substantial. A possible context for these remarkable silver coinages is the frequent warfare of the late Hellenistic and late republican periods, with cities being obliged through alliances with one Roman supremo or another to make cash contributions to

80.1

80.2

Fig. 80. Provincial silver coinages of Roman Syria.

80.1. 'Posthumous Philip' tetradrachm of Aulus Gabinius, 57-55 BC. Head of Philip Philadelphus / Seated figure of Zeus of Daphne, monogram of Gabinius before.
80.2. Tyrian didrachm or half-shekel. Head of Melqart / Eagle on thunderbolt.

their military efforts. A recent study has shown that production at Laodicea and Aradus was higher in 65-63 BC than before or after, and relates this to Pompey's presence in Syria.

Initially the Roman annexation had little effect on the types of currencies being issued. The principal unit of silver coinage issued in Syria was the tetradrachm, a large coin of about 15 grams (½ oz). However, in addition to tetradrachms, a half-unit (the didrachm) was commonly issued by mints in Phoenicia, particularly Tyre. That the didrachm was hardly struck at all in the north may well be significant, suggesting different regional needs. One obvious use for the didrachm in the south is the Jewish Temple-tax, which was set at one half-shekel (equivalent to one didrachm) per person. For the first few years of the new province the north relied on old Seleucid silver coins, but under the governor Aulus Gabinius (57-55 BC) Antioch began striking tetradrachms once again (fig. 80.1). These could be considered the first 'official' coins of the province of Syria. Gabinius is viewed as having a certain degree of financial acumen, but whether he was personally responsible for reviving the Antiochene tetradrachm is another matter. The choice of designs is interesting: the coins retained the portrait, name and titles of the Seleucid king Philip Philadelphus (93-83 BC). Gabinius' authority is confined to his name in the form of a small and cryptic monogram on the reverse, making it unclear whether the coins were the product of Gabinius' initiative. Hoards show that genuine coins of Philip were in widespread use in the north, and the choice of types may have been prompted by the desire to make the new coins acceptable to the population. A political statement could also be construed: Philip, who ruled before the invasion of Tigranes, was the last Seleucid king whom the Romans viewed as legitimate, and the new coinage was making a statement about legitimacy. The first Roman coinages of Asia and Egypt likewise imitate pre-Roman issues and denominations.

These 'posthumous Philip' tetradrachms continued to be struck at Antioch down to the end of the first century BC, many of them dated according to the Caesarean era of Antioch and using a monogram of the city's name in place of that of Gabinius. Elsewhere regular minting of silver ceased at all cities with the exception of Tyre, which continued to strike its distinctive tetradrachms and didrachms with traditional designs (fig. 80.2). Unlike the posthumous Philips, the Tyrian coins bear the inscription 'of Tyre, sacred and inviolate', clearly identifying them with their city of issue rather than a ruler, living or dead. Hoards show that the two types of coinage did not circulate together: the posthumous Philips circulated in the north, and the Tyrian coins in Phoenicia and the south. The alloys used were different too: Tyrian silver was considerably finer than its northern counterpart. Thus there is reason to view the region being divided into two quite separate systems as far as the circulation of provincial silver was concerned.

These provincial silver coinages must have been expensive to produce. We do not know for certain whether they were financed by the Roman state, but if they were used to pay taxes it is likely that the state would have had an interest in them. The choice of types for the posthumous Philips can be read as evidence that this was a kind of imperial coinage for the province of Syria, but the Tyrian coinage does not fit this mould so easily. To characterize all of the provincial silver of Syria and the Near East as 'imperial' is to wield an assumption rather than to describe its nature.

80.3

80.4

80.3. Antiochene tetradrachm of Vespasian (AD 69-79), with a 'Tyrian' eagle reverse type. BMC Phoenicia, Provincial, 3.
80.4. Tetradrachm of Caracalla (AD 198-217) from Tyre; the murex shell between the eagle's legs on the reverse identifies the mint. BMC Phoenicia, provincial, 36.

From about 5 BC the Antiochene tetradrachm bore the imperial portrait. Tyrian silver, however, continued to carry traditional designs, with no hint that Tyre was part of the Roman empire. The two patterns of circulation, and the degree of 'Romanization' of their designs, parallels rather neatly the political and military situation of the Julio-Claudian period: the north, characterized by a strong military presence, with its possible 'imperial' coinage; and the south, characterized by a much lesser military presence, with a silver coinage making no reference to Roman power at all.

81.1

A major change to the silver came under Nero. Antioch began striking tetradrachms which combined the imperial portrait with reverse designs typical of Tyre. A few hoards show these new Antiochene coins circulating in the south alongside Tyrian silver, and by AD 69 or 70 Tyre had ceased production altogether. The change is quite dramatic: Antiochene silver, which was less pure, replaced the Tyrian, but adopted Tyrian designs, which remained standard for Syrian tetradrachms thereafter (fig. 80.3). Whatever special needs had been served by having two separate systems for provincial silver would henceforth have to make do with one, consisting only of Antiochene tetradrachms. The coincidence of the fall of Jerusalem to Titus and the end of Tyrian coinage has led some to suggest that Tyrian silver was produced specifically for Jewish needs (or that it was not produced in Tyre at all, but at Jerusalem), but hoard evidence from a variety of sites in Phoenicia supports a broader interpretation of their purpose.

81.2

Later hoards are important for showing not only the adoption of a single system for silver, but also the complete elimination of Tyrian silver and any northern issues prior to the new coinage of Nero. Once again, this fits quite neatly with the observations made by scholars about the changes made to the eastern provinces under Vespasian and the greater integration of Syria and the Near East into the military system of the empire during this period (on these, see pp. 43-44 and 221-222). The coincidence of the two processes might suggest that they are related, as might the striking of aurei and denarii at Antioch. Some change to the system of coin use had clearly taken place, although without more evidence from finds it will be hard to elucidate the precise nature of this change.

81.3

Apart from a reduction in silver content under Trajan, hoard evidence shows that during the period from Nero to Septimius Severus there were no major changes to the pattern of provincial silver in circulation. The main mint remained at Antioch, although there is evidence to suggest that during this period some mints outside Syria were used to strike Syrian tetradrachms – particularly Rome and Alexandria in Egypt. This phenomenon, of a mint in one region being used to produce provincial silver coinage for another, has been noted for other eastern provinces. It could mean that provincials were able to apply to mints outside Syria to produce their coinage; alternatively it may have been one method of dealing with the movement of tax surpluses from one province to another, although if so such movement was intermittent and it is hard to discern any overall plan in the pattern of minting.

The sole reign of Caracalla (211-17) witnessed another debasement of the tetradrachm, and also saw this denomination being produced at many mints in the Syrian region (fig. 80.4). Output of these debased issues was high until Elagabalus (218-22), under whom production ceased. As had happened in the years following Nero's debasement, the earlier, purer issues began to disappear

Fig. 81. Some Syrian and Near Eastern provincial bronze currencies.

81.1. SC bronze of Claudius (AD 41-54) from Antioch. BMC 181.

81.2. Civic bronze coin of Trebonianus Gallus and Volusian (AD 251-3) from Antioch, showing the Tyche of Antioch in a portable shrine. BMC 656.

81.3. Civic bronze coin of Philip I (AD 244-9) from Damascus. Bust of Tyche in portable shrine; either side, female figures supporting shrines, each of which contains a bird. BMC 26.

81.4. Civic bronze coin of Tyre, dated year 289 of the city (AD 153/4), showing the head of the city-goddess on the obverse and a galley on the reverse. The inscription reads 'of Tyre, sacred, metropolis, 289'. BMC 326.

81.5. Bronze coin issued in Judaea in regnal year 5 of Nero (AD 58-9), with a palm branch and wreath, and the inscription 'year 5 of Caesar Nero'. Such coins lack imperial portraits in deference to Jewish sensitivity about images.

from circulation. Production at Antioch was revived in the reign of Gordian III (238-44), and continued on a grand scale under Philip (244-9) and Trajan Decius (249-51). Why the Antiochene tetradrachm was discontinued under Trebonianus Gallus (251-3) is not known. The very last issues of this Greek-style silver coinage were produced at Emesa under the usurper Uranius Antoninus (c. AD 253-4).

The changes to the coinage may relate in some way to changes in the system of taxation. If denarii were introduced to northern Syria c. AD 69, it may be no coincidence that during this period the tax law of Palmyra shows the Syrian governor Mucianus (AD 68-9) confirming that taxes should be reckoned in denarii. The withdrawals of pre-Neronian and pre-Severan provincial tetradrachms find a parallel in the empire-wide withdrawals of pre-Neronian and (to a lesser extent) pre-Severan denarii at precisely the same periods. The coincidences are surely significant, but more evidence is needed before we can discuss confidently the reasons why the silver coinage was manipulated in this way – and by whom it was manipulated.

Antioch was also the centre of production for a major series of bronze coins with an imperial portrait on the obverse and the letters 'SC' in a wreath on the reverse (fig. 81.1). This SC coinage began under Augustus and was struck for most emperors down to Philip I (244-9). During the first century the inscriptions were in Latin, but under Trajan (98-117) the language switched to Greek. The first-century issues seem to have circulated widely in Syria, and were

81.4   81.5

perhaps intended to be some sort of 'imperial' bronze coinage. However, the second century saw a diminution in the area supplied with SC coins. By the reigns of Marcus Aurelius and Lucius Verus (161-9) they were mainly confined to northern Syria. From the sole reign of Commodus (commencing in 180) to the sole reign of Caracalla (commencing in 211) no SC bronzes were issued at all. They were then revived and struck in large numbers, particularly under Macrinus (217-18) and Elagabalus (218-22), but thereafter they were eclipsed by a new Antiochene city coinage in bronze (fig. 81.2). The SC coinage may have been the casualty of an increasing trend towards local production at city mints, but until its distribution is better known the interaction between the SC bronzes and civic coins will remain poorly understood.

It is impossible to generalize about the civic bronze coinages produced by the cities of Syria and the Near East, except to emphasize that most of the issues were intermittent and that what distinguishes them from the SC coins is that they are inscribed in the name of the civic community. The inscriptions are normally in Greek and in the genitive plural – that is, 'of the Antiochenes', 'of the Damascenes' and so on – which suggests that they were viewed as belonging in some way to the citizens named. They can thus be seen as a sort of register of Syrian civic communities, although not every Syrian city issued its own coins. Nor is the number of coins produced an indication of the importance of the community: the great city of Apamea ceased issuing civic coinage in the reign of Claudius (AD 41-54), while the small coastal community of Balanea continued to issue its own coins down to Gordian III (AD 238-44). Civic bronzes were struck in a wide range of sizes and weights, and it seems that there was no attempt by the Roman government to impose any order on the denominations being issued. It is not at all clear whether the coins were intended to be the equivalents of Roman bronze denominations or Greek ones – some certainly bear Greek value marks, whereas clear Roman value marks are absent.

Syrian civic coinages were slow to adopt the imperial portrait, which did not become common until the later first century. Tyre did not begin placing emperor's heads on its bronze coins until the city became a colony under Septimius Severus (AD 193-211). Aside from imperial portraits, the designs tend to stress specific local identities: deities of the city, and scenes related to the foundation or origin of the community. Consequently there is an enormous variety of images, each one a recognizable sign of communal identity to its issuers, though sometimes less intelligible to us today. Nevertheless, a wealth of information resides in the iconography of civic coinages (figs. 81; 153; 155; 175). An increasing interest in visibly non-Greek deities can be noted from the early second century, which has some relevance for the survival of non-Greek identities under Roman rule (see chapter 8).

Even if some of the types appear to be non-classical, the history of civic coinage coincides with the heyday of the classical city in the Hellenistic and Roman east – from its increasing autonomy under the Seleucids and Ptolemies to the decline of monumental building by local elites in the third century. Issues of civic coins can be viewed as monuments themselves: they projected self-images of the community, and it is likely that they were paid for by the civic elites, in the same way that local notables often paid for buildings and other expenses of their city. Increasing reluctance among the elites to make financial contributions (see p. 261) may have led to the decline of civic coinages. The inflation of the mid- and later third century may also have played its part, rendering bronze coinage uneconomical to produce, although if so it is curious that third-century communities tended to persist in issuing large bronzes when they could have issued small ones more economically. The end of provincial coinages may well be linked to changes in the nature of the classical city. Once again, it is a topic that deserves further investigation.

Civic bronze coins do not appear to have been struck to supply armies, although cities may well have capitalized on the presence of large numbers of Roman troops passing through their territories on campaigns by making the soldiers exchange their silver and gold coins for local small change. Money-changers licenced by each city exchanged foreign coin and silver or gold for the city's own currency. They charged a fee for doing so, and some of this fee went to the city treasury, although the sums acquired cannot have been very great. In any case cities need not always have issued coins for purely economic motives. Often several decades would pass between successive issues; sometimes so long that a city's coinage degenerated into almost completely worn bronze discs through protracted use. Some cities may have struck coins simply as a means of asserting their sovereignty, and providing their citizens with small change embossed with symbols of local pride. Site finds suggest that city coinages had a limited circulation (see below), which may mean that the designs were addressed primarily to insiders rather than those from outside the civic community. Thus they were a reminder rather than an advertisement intended to promote the city's symbols abroad.

While civic bronze coins were issued in the names of citizen bodies, they were not always produced in the cities where they were issued. Sometimes civic coins were made centrally in a workshop, and the same obverse die (the stamp used to produce the 'heads' side of the coin with the imperial portrait) could be used for the issues of more than one city. Perhaps, like the quarries discussed above, these workshops operated as commercial entities, producing coins for clients more cheaply and efficiently than the latter could make coins themselves. There is no clear evidence for the existence of workshops in the Roman east prior to the late second century, and in Syria the only certain one was centred on Antioch, which during the third century struck coins on behalf of Seleucia, Cyrrhus, Hierapolis, Zeugma, Samosata, Laodicea and Philippopolis in Arabia. While this could be viewed as evidence for greater standardization imposed by the state, it is clear that many cities – including some of those listed above – continued to produce their own more eccentric coinages locally, so any standardization was limited in scope.

Overall the circulation of civic bronze coins appears to have been much more restricted than that of the SC or precious-metal coinages. Exactly how restricted has yet to be determined, but it is possible that certain civic bronzes were legal tender only in the city which issued them. Someone embarking on a ship at Caesarea with a purse full of Caesarean coins may not have been able to use those coins at Sidon or Berytus, for example. This may seem extremely inconvenient to us, but in an environment where hundreds of cities issued coins with thousands of different designs some sort of regulation would have been necessary to determine which coins were legitimate and which were not.

Trade does not seem to have suffered from having such complex arrangements for currency. Inter-regional trade involved the movement of cargoes, and not necessarily money. The *Digest of Roman Law* cites a contract of the second century, where a trader borrowed money in Berytus to buy a cargo to sell in Italy. The loan was approved on condition that the trader sell his cargo in Brundisium (Brindisi), use the Italian currency acquired from selling the cargo there to buy another cargo, sail back to Berytus and sell the second cargo and finally repay the loan. Merchants involved in regular regional and long-distance trade may have maintained credit in local currencies with bankers in the cities where they normally did business. This does not mean that coins such as denarii and aurei did not sometimes move about in trade; it merely illustrates how such trade could function without the movement of coinage.

Production of Syrian provincial coinage came to an abrupt end in the third century. No city in the region issued coins later than the joint reigns of Valerian and Gallienus (AD 253-60). Civic bronzes may have continued to circulate later, but we have very little evidence at our disposal. Thus, within about a decade the nature of coinage produced in the region had changed dramatically: provincial tetradrachms had ceased by *c.* 253-254, and civic bronzes a few years later. Only one sort of coinage was now being produced and used on any scale: the radiate or *antoninianus*, which was nominally a silver coin but by now contained only about 2 per cent silver. Production of this coinage at Antioch had begun under Gordian III, and greatly increased under Trebonianus Gallus, at about the time that tetradrachm production at Antioch came to an end. State intervention is possible, although as noted above, other problems characteristic of the third century, such as a change in the nature of the classical city and high inflation, may have had an important part to play in the demise of Roman provincial coinage.

Late Roman and Byzantine Issues

The end of this complex Roman provincial coinage led to greater uniformity of currency. Or at least, the coinage *appears* uniform, but the distribution still shows strong regional patterns, as if the coinage did not move around very much after its initial injection into a locality. Mints producing coins only of the sort produced at Rome (aurei and *antoniniani*) opened up in the east, lending a vague degree of homogeneity to the coinage of the empire. Reforms were attempted, particularly under Aurelian (AD 270-75) and Diocletian (AD 284-305), but the distribution of these new coins was patchy, and it is often unclear to us exactly how new issues were supposed to relate to the old. In Syria and the Near East regional supply was provided mainly by an imperial mint at Antioch, with some subsidiary mints active in the late third century. There were far fewer mints for coinage in the Roman east than there had been before, but output was on a far greater scale than the local civic mints had been able to achieve. Antioch's products did not enjoy exclusive dominance in the Syrian provinces, and coins also came in quantity from Cyzicus in Asia Minor and Alexandria in Egypt and, after its foundation in the 320s, Constantinople. The designs of fourth- and fifth-century coins in gold, silver and bronze were standardized, with major types being struck simultaneously at most mints, whose products were distinguished by abbreviated mint names in small letters on the reverse of the coins. The designs were changed at regular intervals, and in the case of base-metal issues the changes sometimes seem to have been accompanied by demonetization of the preceding issue. However, the degree to which the central government was able to control coin use in the various communities of the empire seems to have varied. In some places old coins continued to circulate, or poor supply of currency was supported by imitations or 'forgeries' on a grand scale. These irregular patterns in what was supposed to be a universal currency look like local responses to specific conditions. By the mid-fifth century the system appears to have been in disarray. Silver, which had once been the backbone of the precious-metal coinage, was issued in quantity only in the second half of the fourth and first quarter of the fifth centuries, and its distribution within the empire may have been very irregular. A standard value was maintained in the gold coinage, which remained remarkably stable from the fourth century onwards, but the fifth-century bronze coinage was composed almost entirely of small pieces (nummi) of about 12 millimetres in diameter. The exchange rate between the gold and bronze seems to have varied with no attempt to fix their relative values, the number of bronzes to every gold *solidus* being measured in thousands. The bronzes probably circulated by the bagful, by weight, rather than as individual coins. There seems to have been little attempt to control the quality of this material: hoards often contain imitations, blank discs, old Hellenistic and Roman provincial issues, or late fourth century coins – anything that was the right size. It seems that nobody looked very carefully at the bronze coins they were using. The later fifth-century bronze coins are much rarer than those of the late fourth to mid-fifth century, but this does not signify a shrinking of the monetary economy between *c.* 450 and 498, because large numbers of late fourth- and early fifth-century coins remained in circulation.

In AD 498 the emperor Anastasius undertook a reform of the bronze coinage, introducing new, larger coins, clearly marked with units of value. The largest of these was the follis, valued at forty of the small nummi. The introduction of this new bronze coinage marks the beginning of what numismatists have dubbed 'Byzantine' coinage, as opposed to 'late Roman'. In 512 Anastasius made further adjustments, increasing the sizes and weights of the denominations. This coinage continued without significant change under Anastasius' successors until AD 538, when Justinian increased sizes and weights yet again. Thereafter, however, weights and sizes declined. By the mid-seventh century Byzantine bronze coinage looked rather shabby, and the coins were often made from irregular fragments of metal, including pieces cut from bronze plate, or sometimes even struck on top of old Byzantine or Roman coins. Like its late Roman predecessor, this 'Byzantine' coinage was uniform in appearance, but not in distribution. In the first half of the sixth century some of the coastal cities of Phoenicia seem to have opted out of the post-512 system of Anastasius, using only his coins of 498-512, whereas other regions adopted both. In Egypt an entirely separate system of denominations was used, and these issues seem also to have gained some currency in Palestine alongside the regular denominations. And in most places the small late fourth- and fifth-century coins continued to circulate. Nor did the end of Roman rule in the seventh century see the end of 'Byzantine' coinage. Old issues remained in use, and for reasons that are quite obscure, Syria under Muslim control imported large quantities of bronze coins of Constans II (AD 641-68). It may be the case that local communities, used to handling Byzantine coinage, continued to acquire coins from Constantinople, and that the Muslims tolerated this. The Umayyads themselves imitated seventh-century Byzantine coinage, even to the extent of copying Christian crosses and symbols of Roman sovereignty. This 'Arab-Byzantine' coinage was produced at a number of mints in Syria and Palestine at the end of the seventh century (fig. 82), and in this respect it resembles the old Roman provincial coinage, perhaps revealing once again the underlying regional variations which had always existed, even when the coinage *appeared* to be uniform.

Fig. 82. Late seventh-century 'Arab-Byzantine' fals (follis) struck at Heliopolis (Baalbek). The obverse shows two emperors carrying crosses. The figure on the right holds a globe topped by a cross, and another cross is placed between the crowns (topped by crosses) of the two figures. The reverse bears a large value mark, M (= 40 nummi), standard to the Byzantine follis, and the mint name either side in Greek, Helioupole, and beneath in Arabic, Baalbak.

THE ECONOMY OF ROMAN SYRIA AND THE NEAR EAST

In chapter 1 it was noted that Syria was somewhat loosely integrated into the political and military structures of the Roman empire in the Julio-Claudian period, and that a process of greater integration began only under the Flavians. The evidence for Mediterranean trade provides an interesting contrast to these observations. Economic links between Syria and Italy were established well before, so connections with the centre of power were forged in various different ways. However, archaeological evidence for Syrian and Near Eastern exports during the early empire remains limited, so it is not entirely clear how the region fits into a model whereby the provinces raised tax money through export in this period. With its large armies, the region was probably a tax-consumer, but its agricultural wealth should also have made it a tax-producer. Was the region comparatively self-sufficient in the early empire? How were imports paid for? Export of goods that leave little trace in the archaeological record, such as grain, remains a possibility, and the westward movement of

Eastern Sigillata A fine ware pottery may be connected with such trade. But it is only after the various administrative and fiscal reforms under Diocletian and Constantine that we can detect an upsurge in Syrian and Palestinian exports. This may be connected with the foundation of Constantinople and the need for foodstuffs in the new capital, but a link has yet to be demonstrated. Diocletian's interest in reforming the tax system, and with taxation in kind, probably provided an important stimulus for agriculture and exports in general. The cities were in all probability fundamental to the new economic system, as they had been in the old. The development of regional trade between the Syrian cities and also with Egypt during the fourth century seems to coincide with a major phase of building in many of these cities, concentrating not on public structures but on large private residences, a likely sign that the civic elites were prospering. The fifth century witnessed a general boom in Mediterranean trade, with all corners of the sea exporting and importing goods. Continued agricultural expansion in Syria and the Near East corresponds with the expansion in trade westwards and throughout the empire of Syrian and Palestinian wine, oil and perhaps fish sauce during the course of the century.

Much of the long-distance trade taking place was between Syria and other provinces rather than Rome or Constantinople, and some of the commodities traded between communities helped establish a more uniform culture in the eastern Mediterranean. The pattern of trade was as much about interaction between the different regions of the periphery of the empire as it was about exchange between centre and periphery. Whether the exchanges were the result of a 'free market' or 'free trade' in the Roman empire is still debated, but the complexity of the exchanges makes it highly likely that private interests were an important factor in the movement of goods.

The existence of a major provincial coinage in silver raises questions about the nature of money taxes in Syria. If taxes were collected only in denarii and aurei, it is hard to see how money taxes could have been collected in northern Syria under the Julio-Claudians, and it is unclear why large numbers of tetradrachms continued to be minted long afterwards. (The problem is not unique to Syria; major provincial silver coinages were also produced in neighbouring Cappadocia and Egypt.) If taxes were collected in tetradrachms, are we to assume that these sums were spent in the province or regions where they circulated? The possibility that they were transferred to Rome, melted down and recoined as denarii for distribution elsewhere cannot be overlooked, but where we have evidence, through trace element analysis of denarii, this suggests that recycling of provincial silver was not a universal practice. Denarii of Vespasian, for example, were produced from discrete sources of metal, whose trace element profiles do not match those of contemporary silver coins struck in the eastern provinces. The provincial coinages also raise questions about the nature and extent of monetary exchanges accompanying trade. While long-distance trade could be undertaken with denarii or aurei, it is not clear why provincials persisted in making and using coins which were unsuitable for these purposes. Perhaps the market, although far from being underdeveloped and primitive, was not quite as unbounded and 'free' as is sometimes claimed.

PART IV

THE CONSTRUCTION OF COMMUNITIES

7 PUBLIC VALUES

Some of the most conspicuous ruins in the cities of Roman Syria and the Near East are also among the most homogeneous: the colonnaded streets, the theatres, agoras, arches and nymphaea. They suggest a culture which was equally homogeneous, but these buildings may reflect the aspirations and desires of a small sector of the population. In chapter 3 we looked at city states as part of the framework of Roman rule in the Syrian region; in chapters 5 and 6 we considered the importance of the city for the organization of production and the management of consumption; here we look at the urban spaces and the social and political forces that shaped them.

The monumental phase is characteristic of the early empire. While there was some monumental architecture in Syria before and after, there were no phases of construction on quite such a comprehensive scale, encompassing all of the major public spaces, or with quite the same intentions. In spite of their scale and spectacular nature we have only a general idea about what went on in these very public cities – the processions and religious festivals, the civic meetings and public acclamations. The theatrical appearance of the monuments was accompanied by a certain theatricality in public life.

THE THEATRE OF THE PUBLIC

Cities are artefacts created by the societies which use them, and therefore urban development ought to track changing ideals; in this case the ideals of the civic elites whose values dominated city life. The popular image of the Graeco-Roman city is one of monumental public buildings: fortified walls, colonnaded streets, temples, agoras, basilicas and hippodromes, aqueducts and baths. Between the first and third centuries AD most Syrian cities acquired the 'set' of such classical public buildings, so that in their architecture the Syrian cities came to resemble not only one another but also cities in other parts of the Roman east. The monumental structures were not imposed by Rome, and some were not even particularly Roman in inspiration; instead most were built by local elites, at their own expense, over several decades. The buildings reflect the shared values inculcated in the elites of the Syrian cities through a common system of education (see chapter 8).

Piecemeal construction should not disguise the determination with which the model or ideal was pursued by these elites. But what was that ideal, and what did they think they were achieving by investing in extremely elaborate stone structures? It is easy enough for us to see this pursuit as beneficial: the goal being the city as order and amenity, and as a magnificent cultural, political and religious focus for its rural hinterland. Some motives behind the public city, however, may have been less altruistic.

'Public' implies something useful to the community as a whole, and yet public buildings and spaces may benefit certain sections of the population more than others, and may even work to exclude or marginalize certain sectors of the population. In public spaces the individual can be made highly visible, and can be controlled by prohibiting or enforcing certain activities and movements. Monumental settings constrain behaviour, prompting the citizens to act in certain appropriate ways, and the monumental space is defined by what activities are expected to occur in it.

To enter or live in the city is to accept certain restrictions, and to acquiesce to the laws and traditions governing its spaces. The city often makes demands, social and financial, on those who belong there. The citizen of a modern city can live fairly anonymously, but anonymity was not so easy in the smaller, close-knit communities of the past. To be a fully qualified member of civic society often required participation in public events which helped to affirm communal identities and the social order, and required contributions, financial and otherwise, in support of the community. The citizen's worth and self-esteem was gauged by public activity; his peers, superiors (both natural and supernatural) and inferiors constituted the audience. Pageants and ceremonies conducted in grand architectural settings could assert the superior status of the elite participants, and for the largely uneducated lower classes religious processions, festivals and other events in the civic calendar provided a sense of belonging and structure to their world.

The transformation of most, if not all, of the public spaces of a city into monumental settings is a defining moment in the history of the 'Graeco-Roman' or 'classical city' in the Syrian region. The monumental city was an instrument through which the elites expressed their status and their importance to the community. It set in stone their position in the social hierarchy and their adherence to a particular way of life. The classical city of Syria was a ceremonial space celebrating the ideals, permanency and power of the civic elites.

THE PURSUIT OF ATTENTION

A model for the Syrian cities was the Greek *polis*. The *polis* was the communal property of its citizens, and an institution in which they could lead the good life. The economic ideal of the *polis*, dating back to the time of the autonomous city states of archaic and classical Greece, was self-sufficiency. At that time cities had supported themselves on revenues from rents and taxes, and any other resources which they controlled. From the late fourth century BC cities began to lose their autonomy, and external domination by Hellenistic kingdoms and, later, the Roman empire, diverted revenues from the city to the central government. The result was that the cities could no longer support themselves on revenues alone, and had to turn increasingly to benefactions from wealthy members of their communities. The classical city had always demanded participation of its citizens, but now the generous support of its elites was also embedded in the idea of a city.

The ideal of the self-sufficient city continued to thrive under Roman rule. To the Roman government this ideal was certainly convenient, and to be encouraged, to minimize any burden on imperial finances. The city was to maintain peace, order and prosperity for Rome and for itself, and to cover its expenses as well as paying taxes to Rome. Its citizens and its lands should provide for its upkeep: paying or providing labour for public works, covering salaries of teachers, rhetors, doctors and others on the public payroll, the costs of fuel and heating for the baths, of sending embassies to the provincial governor or emperor, of holding festivals and public banquets, and of maintaining and subsidizing the market, among other things. Some money was obtained through tolls and taxes on goods entering the city territory, special poll taxes on foreign residents, rents from public land and civic estates bequeathed by generous individuals (some of these lands might lie in the territory of another city, or even in a different province), or exchange rates on foreign currency, to name but a few sources of revenue. However, these revenues were insufficient to cover the expensive and ambitious building programmes of the first to third centuries. These were funded mainly by rich citizens.

The classical city had always been a communal project, a public stage where private individuals could be seen participating in the ideal. When restrictions on the political life of the city were few, political activities were attractive to rich citizens, advancing their power as well as their honour and prestige. But the Hellenistic kings and Roman emperors did not encourage the civic elites to continue in this vein. Cities were to be self-governing within their territories, yet were not expected to involve themselves in interstate political affairs without imperial sanction. With opportunities for power curtailed, the elites turned to less risky demonstrations of their status. In a state like the Roman empire civic architecture was a relatively safe arena in which to compete for glory with one's peers. These demonstrations of elite power turned inwards, focusing on the city itself.

Government and Citizenship

To be a citizen was an honour, and inspired patriotism. Not all of the people living in the city belonged to the citizen body (*demos*). Large sections of the population might be excluded, particularly resident foreigners, freed slaves and country peasants. The citizen body was divided into tribes, which might be based along genuine lines of kinship or, in the case of new foundations or tribes added to the existing citizen body, might be artificial creations. Traditionally the governing body of the city was divided between the popular assembly (*ecclesia*) and the council (*boule*), although it must be admitted that for our region we have very little evidence for the former institution. The *boule* was normally composed of the wealthier citizens, who had membership for life. There was also a tendency for members of the *boule* to be drawn from a small number of powerful families within the city. However, in the larger cities the number of councillors might run into hundreds, which allowed some of the less wealthy individuals entry into this important element of civic government. Magistrates, elected annually by popular vote or by the boule, proposed projects for approval by the councillors. If the city had an assembly, approved projects were put to the popular vote. In this way a hereditary elite dominated the decision-making process, but the assembly still played an important role in local politics with its right to veto and its enthusiastic acclamations of candidates for magistracies, particular proposals or those responsible for them. Whatever the system, the burden for the magistrates was often high, since they were expected to finance their activities from their own resources while in office – paying for a building project, or financing a civic festival, for example. Some money might be available from the civic treasury, but in general magistrates were obliged to draw on their own resources.

A city might also benefit from voluntary donations offered by wealthy individuals who were not holding office, but who acted out of their love for the city and for the prominent public profiles such acts could provide. Generosity gave them greater status and honour, and demonstrated their deep involvement in the high culture of the Greek city. Public opinion was important: it conferred honour on the individual through approval and acclamation. Nobody appreciated parsimony from the elite, and in these communities, where public life was transparent, everybody knew the details. Magistrates, particularly the less wealthy ones, might negotiate with the public in an attempt to avoid outlays that were damaging to their personal finances, but shame would prevent them from reneging on their obligations altogether. The donor or magistrate aimed at achieving something that would endure in the public consciousness, and this did not always require the construction of a physical monument. The nymphaeum or colonnaded portico petrified the act of generosity to serve as a permanent reminder, but benefactors and magistrates might instead choose to pay for grain distributions to citizens, or finance the import of foodstuffs from abroad to keep prices low in times of shortage. Collective recollection of the generous act was their monument. The financial obligations of office could be a serious burden, or even ruining, and the ambitions of the city might exceed the abilities of local donors to pay for everything. In the search for rich benefactors a city might turn to members of the imperial family, or a 'client' king, persuading them to hold office *in absentia*, or taking advantage of their generosity. Even those who were without full civic rights, such as foreigners or women and children of the rich families, might hold office, or a wealthy temple might cover expenses, with its god or goddess effectively serving as benefactor.

Benefactors had the opportunity to immortalize their acts by setting up inscriptions on their buildings, explaining who they were and what they had achieved. The concept of a 'monument' included monumental writing as well, and inscriptions could help to immortalize the generous act. An inscription of the early second century AD, thought to have been placed in a bath house at Apamea, outlines the liberality of a certain Lucius Julius Agrippa. This was probably typical of the activities expected of the wealthy citizen. It tells us that Agrippa, who was descended from Dexandros, the first high priest of the provincial imperial cult under Augustus, and whose ancestor's name was inscribed on bronze tablets on the Capitoline hill in Rome as a friend and ally of the Romans, performed his duties as a magistrate and as a donor to the city, that he was a priest, that he was overseer of the markets and that he spent a noteworthy sum of money in this post, that he was civic secretary, an officer of the peace and the official civic grain distributor, that he financed part of an aqueduct and built the baths with a basilica and a stoa (presumably a section of the northern part of Apamea's grand colonnade: fig. 83), decorating the baths with bronze statues. The text tells us why we are supposed to be impressed by him – because of his contributions to the civic life of Apamea (even though, as the inscription relates, he was officially exempt from such obligations), and because of his ancestry, which confirms ancient family ties

Fig. 83. The northern end of Apamea's grand colonnade, part of which was built by Lucius Julius Agrippa after an earthquake in AD 115, showing the eastern portico and the façade of the shops (on the left) that lay behind the columned frontage.

with Rome. Aside from bearing inscriptions, monumental buildings set up by such elite figures could also be fitted with statues – of the donor, or other worthy and honourable individuals, or, depending on the setting, mythical figures or deities. The monuments with their honorific statues and inscriptions not only celebrated the donors and various worthies; they also reminded other wealthy citizens what was expected of them.

All citizens, even the poorer ones, were expected to contribute to civic life, by providing funds for small-scale civic expenditures or physical labour on civic estates and building projects, particularly on essentials like the building or repair of city walls. A canal constructed at Antioch in AD 73-4 was undertaken by citizens, organized by their city blocks. Owners of properties might also be responsible for providing street lighting at night. But the participation of humble citizens is likely to have been very much subordinated to the demands, desires and tastes of the elites.

Problems and Solutions

This self-financing system was not without problems. Where building projects were concerned, there was sometimes little interest in building structures that nobody could see, such as underground aqueducts. Over-ambitious projects might never be completed. Governors could intervene to see that civic funds were channelled into essential infrastructure works rather than grand public edifices, but competition between cities to have the most admirable buildings, or peer competition between the great families within a city, could leave urban centres with superfluous monuments. By the late first or early second century the erection of public buildings using civic funds had to be sanctioned by the emperor, and during the second century emperors began appointing curators to oversee civic finances. Imperial supervision may have helped to homogenize the urban landscapes, by approving the erection of buildings and styles deemed suitable. Buildings erected with private funds were another matter, but from the early second century there were attempts to ensure that pledges to build were fulfilled, if not by the original donor, then by his heirs.

As we have seen in chapter 3, the original classical cities of Syria were colonies. The Seleucid kings had founded and promoted cities – Antioch, Seleucia, Laodicea, Apamea, Zeugma – but from the moment of their foundation these cities had been dependent on the king. They were not truly independent states. Whatever the elites of these cities were doing in the third and second centuries BC, they do not appear to have been investing in monumental buildings on any grand scale – or at any rate very little survives to attest to monumental buildings. It would seem that the Seleucid city was designed as a central place for administering the villages and countryside which formed its territory, providing services such as markets and a focus for cult activity, and that few of these functions required the erection of monumental structures. However, archaeology may change this picture. Excavations at Apamea have revealed a large, two-storey colonnaded portico extending outside the northern gate of the city, dated to the late second century BC. Monumental structures clearly were possible, but because our knowledge of Seleucid cities is so limited we cannot say how typical the Apamea portico was. The southern half of the Near East, which was dominated by the Ptolemies of Egypt until the beginning of the second century BC, is likewise poorly understood. Some monumental buildings are known (fig. 7), but, as in the north, there is little in the way of monumental *civic* buildings. For the moment it would appear that the Hellenistic cities of Syria, although populous and prosperous, were not places where the elite placed a great and monumental emphasis on public life, although further investigations may alter our views.

Substantial public buildings began to appear in cities in the first century BC. A phase of monumental enlargement of religious sanctuaries, starting in the first century BC to first century AD, was followed in the later first and second century AD by a phase in which monumental buildings were extended to most of the public spaces of cities in the region. Restructuring and refurbishing continued in the second century, but by the end of that century there are signs that the drive towards monumentalization was slowing down. This cannot be simply because the cities had now acquired the 'full set' of monumental structures, because peer polity rivalry demanded regular improvements to the civic form: wider and grander colonnades, more magnificent religious sanctuaries, additional theatres and so on. There are signs that the elites were turning to other ways of expressing civic ideals.

Regular festivals incorporating athletic, literary and musical competitions were, like public buildings, a matter of intense civic pride, and an alternative way of demonstrating one's munificence was to endow such an event. International 'sacred' festivals, drawing competitors from all over the Greek world, needed imperial consent. They were organized to fit into a regular concourse for the convenience of professional athletes and artists who did the rounds of these events. There were also local festivals, although these were obviously not as desirable and prestigious. (Gladiatorial combats and wild beast hunts were features associated with celebrations of the imperial cult or with the Roman army, and were not normally combined with the activities of the Greek civic festivals.) We know of only two cities in the Near East which had Greek festivals during the Hellenistic period: Sidon and Tyre. In the first century BC Herod had given his foundation at Caesarea a festival, the *Sebasteia*. Precisely when later festivals were created is not always clear; our main sources of information are civic coins and inscriptions, so we are at the mercy of the material.

For example, we know from textual sources that Antioch had various festivals, including an Olympic Games established under Commodus, but Antioch's coinage never once refers to any of them. On third-century coins of other cities references to festivals are commonplace. It is assumed that coins celebrate only the more prestigious 'sacred' games, rather than local ones, and faulty though it is, the evidence does point to a considerable increase in the number of cities holding such festivals from the late second and third centuries. In other words, the rise in civic festivals appears to correspond to the decline in building activity. Third-century civic coins record a 'Sacred Capitoline Games' at Laodicea, a *Helia Pythia* at Emesa, a 'Sacred Capitoline Oecumenical Iselastic Games' at Heliopolis (fig. 84), a *Sebasmia* at Damascus (which by the mid-third century was the *Olympia Sebasmia*), an *Actia Dousaria* at Bostra, and an 'Iselastic Oecumenical Isolympic Games' at Gaza, to name some of them, and show that Tyre's Hellenistic *Heracleia* had become the *Actia Heracleia*, in honour of the battle of Actium. These festivals were a celebration of Greekness (though sometimes honouring 'Roman' events like Actium), and it may be of some cultural significance that cities like Palmyra and those in the southern part of the province of Arabia do not appear to have held them.

It is not clear why civic building projects became rare in the third century. One explanation assumes that endowing a festival was cheaper than paying for buildings, and that the choice reflects an impoverished elite or a reluctance on the part of the rich to continue the levels of funding seen in the second century. Whatever the case, the end of the monumentalizing phase seems to mark an important change in the nature of the cities of Roman Syria (see end of chapter).

Fig. 84. Reverse of a bronze coin of Heliopolis, reign of Valerian (AD 253-60). Three prize crowns containing victor's palm branches are arranged in a row; beneath, the inscription 'Sacred Capitoline Oecumenical Iselastic Games', which advertises the fact that the competitions were international and that the victor had the right to a triumphal entry in his home city. BMC 27.

The Dangers of Political Expression

Civil wars provided cities with rare opportunities for independent political expression. Support by a city for one imperial contender or another might be dictated as much by the disposition of a rival city as by any other consideration. Such declarations could be extremely hazardous for the civic elites, but in the long term they rarely affected the position of the cities in the pecking-order. When Antioch supported Pescennius Niger in 193, its rival Laodicea was quick to adhere to the cause of Septimius Severus. Sacked by the troops of Pescennius, Laodicea was elevated in honours when Septimius Severus eventually proved victorious, at the expense (temporarily) of Antioch. A similar rivalry may be noted between Berytus and Tyre in the same conflict. Sidon won honours under Elagabalus, presumably for having stayed faithful to him during a military rebellion by the *legio III Gallica*. It was awarded with the title 'Loyal' and promoted to a colony and *metropolis*, whereas its rival Tyre, which had been implicated in the revolt, temporarily lost colonial and metropolitan status.

The Roman Colonies: an Alternative to the Greek Polis?

Roman colonies were originally designed to accommodate soldiers retiring from the legions. Colonial foundations on the site of existing cities need not have benefited the original inhabitants, who might be dispossessed of land and rights in favour of army veterans or, at the very least, would have to compete with the newcomers over such things. The major phase of veteran settlement outside Italy belongs to the time of Julius Caesar and Augustus. In the western empire, where cities were rare or absent before the Roman conquests, colonies have been viewed as tools of the Roman state, little islands of *Romanitas* or urbanization implanted in a sea of 'foreign' habits. But how different were the Syrian colonies from neighbouring cities? A degree of cultural allegiance with Rome can be discerned among the early, 'true' colonies inhabited by veteran soldiers: Latin is commonly used as a public language, and the two chief civic magistrates are called duovirs, a characteristic of the Latin west. Their civic coinages tended to use Latin rather than Greek, accompanied by specific colonial symbols (fig. 85). The first colony to be founded in Syria was Berytus, under Augustus. This was settled by veterans from two Roman legions, the *legio V Macedonica* and *legio VIII Gallica*, and was granted *ius italicum*, meaning that for tax purposes its land was considered Italian (Italy being exempt from land tax). It is not clear what happened to the indigenous population of Berytus. During the following two centuries three other colonies were founded in the region: Ptolemais (under Claudius), Caesarea Maritima (under Vespasian), and Jerusalem (using the name Aelia Capitolina, under Hadrian). Ptolemais seems to have had veteran settlement and perhaps *ius italicum*, but Caesarea probably had neither, although the city's inhabitants appear to have been exempted from the poll tax. Caesarea was therefore an early example of a city acquiring colonial status as an honour, and it stands in the vanguard of a new trend in granting colonial status to cities that had won imperial approval, rather than as a way of rewarding retired soldiers. Aelia Capitolina seems to have been one of the last 'true' Roman colonies ever founded, with settlers brought in from elsewhere after the original population had been driven out. The *legio X Fretensis* was based there, and its veterans may have been settled in the city. But little is otherwise known of the colony.

It was once thought that the colonial settlement in Berytus involved replanning the city, but what can be discerned of the urban plan seems to be an extension of an earlier Hellenistic and Iron Age city layout. It is not yet certain whether the city had axial main streets rather than a main north - south thoroughfare leading to and from the city's harbour. Evidence for two forums and a western-style capitol are tenuous in the extreme, but like many other Syrian cities Berytus had a large monumental bath building, several other baths, a nymphaeum and a hippodrome, and literary sources mention a theatre. It acquired vast territories at the time of the colony's foundation, stretching over the Lebanon range to the eastern side of the valley of Massyas (Bekaa), which may have been a deliberate attempt to make the city the economic equal of its powerful neighbours, Sidon and Tyre. The veteran soldiers appear to have been Latin-speaking, with Roman citizenship. They were enrolled in the Roman tribe Fabia, and their descendants formed the civic elite. Veterans were also settled in the countryside. At Niha on the western edge of the Bekaa valley there was a country district of colonists, called the *pagus Augustus*. Heliopolis, with its great temples, seems also to have been a sort of rural colonial settlement in the territory of Berytus, until it achieved independent city status under Septimius Severus (see chapter 3). The widespread use of Latin inscriptions in the Berytus countryside, even in fairly remote locations such as Yammoune, a temple site also in the western Bekaa, suggests that for a while at least Latin was the dominant language in Berytian society and permeated the entire territory. The use of Latin has been employed to help determine the extent of the territory of Berytus (see p. 235). Finds of imported goods from Italy suggest strong Italian connections for the first generation of colonists (see p. 187); but thereafter this trade drops off. The colonial images on coins of Berytus (fig. 85) resemble those

Fig. 85. Colonial symbol: a priest ploughs the first furrow to delineate the city walls according to Etruscan rite – a symbolic representation of the foundation of a new Roman colony. This image comes from the reverse of a bronze coin of Berytus issued under Augustus. The historical reality of the scene can be doubted; Berytus was already a city at the time of the foundation and there is no evidence that any major alterations to the urban plan occurred at the time. BMC 54.

issued by other colonies in the Roman world. Inscriptions attest to the cults of Roman deities, some of which would have been quite exotic in this context, such as Proserpina or the obscure goddess Mater Matuta. These imply some sort of transmission of Roman or Italian identity into the local cultural environment (the female dedicant to Mater Matuta is a Roman citizen with a mixed Greek and Semitic name). But these dedications should also be set against others, to Jupiter Heliopolitanus, to Jupiter Baalmarcod (the 'Lord of Dances' whose sanctuary lay in the hills above Berytus), and to Atargatis, the Syrian Goddess, which suggest the survival of local cults or the import of regional ones. The strict colonial character of the early coins becomes diluted in the second and third centuries with the appearance of 'local' types referring to city deities and pre-Roman myths connected with the origins of Berytus, and by late Roman times Greek had replaced Latin as the main language of inscriptions. But the Latin character of Berytus remained in late antiquity: the city was a centre for the study of Latin literature and, from the third century at least, Roman law. It had produced the eminent Latin grammarian and specialist in Latin literature, Marcus Valerius Probus, in the first century AD. By the fourth century it was drawing large numbers of students from all over the Roman world, who came to study Roman literature and law in the schools established there; this was the principal cultural legacy which the Augustan foundation bequeathed to late antiquity. Of the four early colonies, Berytus is the only one where veteran settlement can be seen to have had a major and long-term impact on civic culture, but in terms of its architecture and urban plan it may not have been significantly different from its neighbours.

Fig. 86. The Niha valley (the pagus Augustus), with the Bekaa and the Antilebanon beyond. The temple of Hadaranes (see p. 359) can be seen among the trees in the middle distance.

The second phase of colonial grants begins with Septimius Severus, and it coincides with the proliferation of civic festivals and imperial grants of other city titles. These colonies were not created for veteran settlers. *Colonia* was now a coveted epithet, like *metropolis*, and was one more reward that emperors could use to manipulate the hierarchy of Syrian cities. The Severan emperors gave colonial status to Laodicea, Antioch, Seleucia, Emesa, Heliopolis, Palmyra, Damascus, Arca, Sidon, Tyre, Sebaste, Bostra and Petra; probably also to Dura Europus. Some, such as Laodicea, were granted *ius italicum*; others, such as Antioch, were not. But this extraordinary number of cities elevated to colonies under the Severans is not a phenomenon found in neighbouring regions of the eastern Mediterranean, except in Mesopotamia. By the reign of Philip, Neapolis and Philippopolis had also acquired colonial status. It is not absolutely clear whether Philippopolis had this status from its foundation (*c.* AD 244); an inscription dated 'year one' of the city does not mention it, and the issue of civic coins which bear the title were struck no earlier than AD 246/7 (the date of Philip's son's elevation to the rank of co-emperor). With the end of civic coinages and a decline in the 'epigraphic habit', our evidence for colonial grants becomes scarce. There is some evidence that Gaza, Ascalon, Gerasa and perhaps Gadara also became colonies at some point in the third century, although when is not known. However, it is fairly clear that grants of colonial status ceased in the late empire, and the existing colonies rarely continued to advertise the title. Whatever advantages there had been in having colonial status no longer adhered in the fourth century and beyond.

There is a fairly strong correlation between imperial interests and grants of colonial status in this second phase. Emesa, Arca and Philippopolis were all home towns of emperors or places with which they had strong connections (Caracalla and Elagabalus with Emesa, Severus Alexander with Arca, and Philip with Philippopolis), and were hardly in the first rank of cities. Laodicea, Sidon and Tyre were rewarded for their support of an emperor during a time of crisis or rebellion. Heliopolis is thought to have gained both civic and colonial status from Septimius Severus as a consequence of Berytus having supported his rival, Pescennius Niger. The punishment meted out to Berytus was the loss of territory to a new rival city. Similar motives are thought to have prompted Severus' grants to Laodicea, Tyre and Sebaste in Samaria. Others cities granted colonial status, such as Antioch, Damascus, Bostra and Petra, were among the first cities of their respective provinces, and in rewarding them with colonial status the emperors may have been responding to the pressures of peer polity rivalry.

Whereas the old colonies adopted some Latin features, these new colonies do not seem to have changed their character as the result of grants of colonial status, suggesting that *colonia* was just one of several titles which a city might hope to acquire. Some opted to use Latin on their coins, but others continued to use Greek. Where Latin was employed it was not always used with confidence. Laodicea's coinage compromised by using Latin letters to write in Greek. Thus the use of Latin, which had formerly been a distinguishing mark of colonies, did not necessarily signify fluency or competency in the language in these later colonies. The use of colonial symbols was likewise irregular. Some of the new colonies alternated images of priests ploughing the first furrow (fig. 85) or military standards with traditional civic designs, but others ignored colonial designs altogether. A figure of the satyr Marsyas (fig. 87) is found on coins

*Fig. 87. Reverse of a coin of Berytus issued under Elagabalus (*AD 218-22*), showing the figure of the satyr Marsyas in a monumental setting. The architectural backdrop strongly suggests that the figure is a statue, but the nature of the monument cannot easily be determined. It looks like a tetrapylon with a curved court behind, but some have read these as the vault and supports of a monumental arch.* BMC *194.*

issued by many, but not all, colonies in the region during the third century. This is thought to recall a statue of Marsyas that stood in the forum in Rome, providing an iconographic link with the centre of power. It is not clear whether the images on coins represent the statue at Rome, a reproduction at different colonies, or whether the image is purely symbolic. The precise meaning of this image is lost, and it is not found on the early coinages of the 'true' colonies. Nevertheless the use of Latin and colonial symbols suggests that many of the new colonies aspired to special connections with Rome.

The colony of Philippopolis, founded *c.* AD 244 at the north-western end of Auranitis, might seem to provide an example of Roman influences in a late colonial foundation. The city probably enjoyed imperial patronage, if only briefly, as the birthplace of the emperor Philip I (AD 244-9). It conforms more or less to the 'ideal' Graeco-Roman city: roughly rectangular in plan, and with colonnaded axial main streets meeting in a tetrapylon. It contained various monumental buildings typical of such cities: a bath house, a theatre and a piazza. There are traces of imported veneers in the bath building, but otherwise the stonework is mainly local basalt. However, a survey conducted at the turn of the twentieth century emphasized the Roman nature of elements such as the bath building, supplied by an aqueduct drawing water from a source to the east, and the use of rubble and mortar domes and vaults in construction. It was suggested that Philip might have employed western architects for his new city.

Other elements of Philippopolis seem less 'Roman'. The monumental piazza on the western side of the city presumably functioned as the city's administrative and economic heart, but the buildings that surrounded it were not typical of forums or agoras elsewhere. The large building on the eastern side might have been a basilica, but its function, like that of the other buildings in the piazza, remains enigmatic. The tall structure on the western side seems to have been a monumental setting for statuary, presumably of the imperial family, and was perhaps a sanctuary of the imperial cult. It is sometimes called a *kalybé*, but is rather different from a class of religious structures which are referred to

Fig. 88. A general view of the site of Philippopolis in northern Auranitis. The city is situated at the foot of a volcanic cone (visible on the left).

Fig. 89. The so-called 'Philippeion' at Philippopolis. Brackets for statues of the emperor's father Julius Marinus stand proud either side of a large doorway (the small entrance is a modern feature). The equally austere interior contains large niches for statues and a staircase allowing access to the roof. This building was probably Marinus's mausoleum and like an adjacent structure contained statues of the emperor and his family. The rectangular piazza onto which these buildings faced is interpreted as a forum or agora.

by that name (see chapter 9). Structures probably for display like that at Philippopolis are known in other cities of the Hauran, for example Bostra. On the southern side was a square building, the so-called 'Philippeion', which housed statue groups of Philip and his family (fig. 89) and was presumably a mausoleum for Philip's father. Nearby, on the northern side of the decumanus, was a temple-like building with a six-columned portico and an apse at the rear. Rather than being a good example of the influence of Rome, the whole city would seem to be a successful imitation, using mainly local materials and perhaps employing expertise drawn from a wider area, of the great cities found in other parts of the Near East, combined with more local elements.

In general terms, it would seem that most colonies were not distinct, monumentally or culturally, from the neighbouring Greek cities. If the 'true' colonies differed significantly from other cities immediately after their foundation and veteran settlement, these differences did not persist. Only Berytus retained any traces of its Latin character into the late Roman period.

THE CITY DEFINED

The problems of distinguishing a city from other sorts of settlement have been mentioned in chapter 5. Civic status had to be recognized by the Roman state, which used the administrative apparatus of the city to maintain order and to collect tribute. Each city had a territory, which was as much a part of the *polis* as its urban area, incorporating the city's agricultural resources, rural shrines and temples and subordinate villages. These territories were rigorously defined, although it is often difficult to follow their boundaries now. Some clues are available to us. Occasionally we are lucky enough to find explicit boundary stones between cities, such as that between Emesa and Palmyra, found at Qasr el-Heir el-Gharbi (ancient Heliarama?), but such chance finds are rare, and other approaches have to be adopted to define city territories. Many Syrian cities had their own system of dating (see chapter 4), and each era was exclusive to the territory of the city which used it and would not be employed by a neighbouring city, suggesting that the civic eras were often important facets of communal identities. The use of city eras within the territory of a city can help to define the extent of that territory, if there are enough dated inscriptions *in situ*, and provided that neighbouring cities used eras which were sufficiently different. Dated buildings from the villages of northern Syria define the boundary between the territories of Antioch and Apamea (fig. 90.1). In the case of Berytus, the territory has been fixed largely through the use of Latin inscriptions (fig. 90.2). Berytus, as a Roman colony, adopted the use of Latin for monumental public writing, which made it distinct from its neighbours Sidon and Byblus. This does not mean that Greek was never employed, but that what

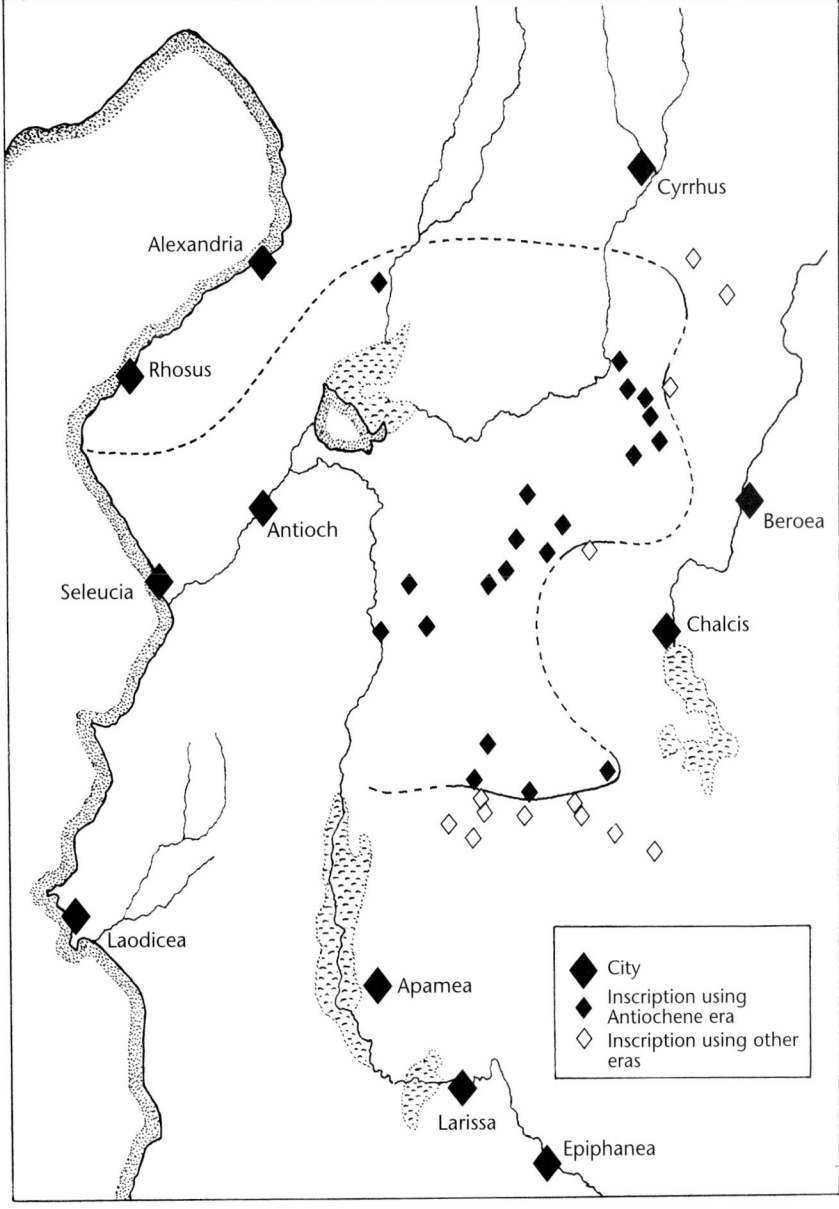

Fig. 90.1. Boundary between the territories of Antioch, Apamea and other cities, according to dated inscriptions from the villages of northern Syria.

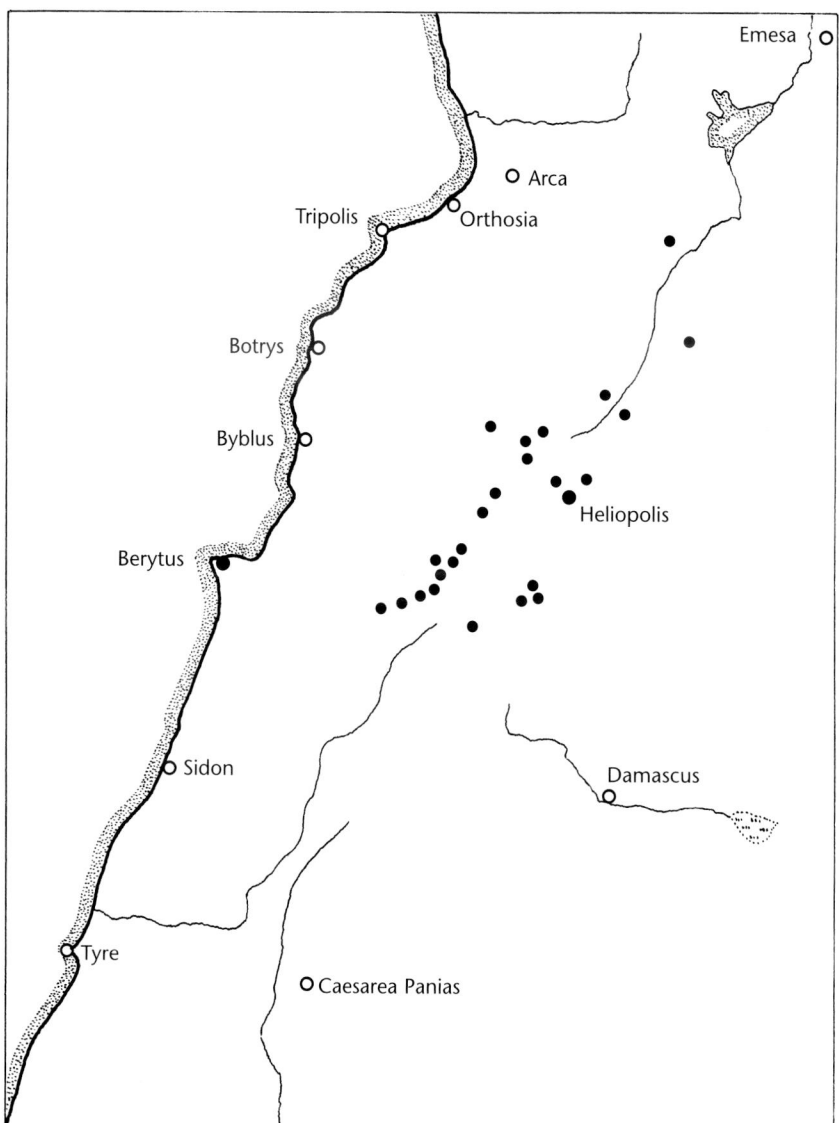

Fig. 90.2. Distribution of Latin inscriptions (small black dots) in the Bekaa valley, believed to delineate the territory of Berytus there. Heliopolis achieved independent city status only under Septimius Severus (AD 193-211), and prior to that time it appears to have been in the territory of Berytus.

makes Berytus distinct is its use of Latin. Although Berytus had its own civic era, the Latin tradition tended not to employ it, and it is known mainly through Greek coins issued before the colony was established, and inscriptions dating from the late Roman period (when Greek returned to common use in Berytus as a language for inscriptions). Other possible methods for defining territories, whose potential as yet lies largely untried, include distributions of city coinages and locally-produced amphoras, which may in some cases conform to civic territories (see chapter 6).

THE CITY IMAGINED

A common symbolic definition of the city in Syria was expressed by the image of the city Tyche, the 'fortune' or guardian spirit of the city. Most of these

Fig. 91. Late fourth-century AD silver statuette of the Tyche of Antioch, from the treasure found on the Esquiline hill in Rome in 1793. It was one of four figures personifying the main cities of the Roman world: Rome, Constantinople, Antioch and Alexandria; all were perhaps originally fittings for a chair.

imitated an original model, which was the one commissioned by Seleucus Nicator for his new foundation at Antioch. The colossal bronze statue showed a female personification of the city, dressed in a veil and heavy drapery, wearing the walls and towers of the city on her head. She was seated on a rock, supposed to represent Mount Silpius, the steep slope of which dominates the city, and held in her hand corn ears, a symbol of the fruitfulness of her territories. At her feet swam a naked male figure, representing the River Orontes. The statue combined significant natural and man-made features with a divine image. That the walls should be selected as the architectural feature defining the city may indicate how few other monumental structures Seleucid Antioch possessed, but the image of the city defences was itself a powerful sign of civic autonomy. The Tyche frequently appears on Antiochene coins, and seems to have been recognizable throughout the Roman world as a symbol of Antioch. Various copies of the statue are known in a variety of media and sizes (fig. 91), and sometimes they occur in conjunction with personifications of the three other great cities of the Roman world: Rome, Constantinople and Alexandria.

Other Syrian cities adopted this image, but sometimes changed the details to provide local references: on coins of Laodicea the river god holds up an image of the city's famous lighthouse, or, if the coins show only the head of Tyche, the lighthouse is depicted within the city walls on her head (fig. 93.1). Another variant, commonly used by coastal cities, and especially those of the south, was a standing city Tyche wearing the short dress of an Amazon, with one breast exposed. The most famous 'Amazonian' city Tyche is that of Caesarea, known not only from coins but also from a marble statue found in the city and from an inlaid bronze cup of late Roman times. She also wore the city walls on her head, but carried a sword in a scabbard over her shoulder, and held a sceptre or ship's rudder in one hand and a small bust (an image of the emperor or the city's founder, King Herod?) in the other (fig. 93.2). A relief found at Dura Europus in the so-called 'Temple of the Gaddé', which belongs to the final years of Parthian rule, shows three figures: one is the dedicant, making an offering before a male figure labelled in Palmyrene as the Gad (Tyche) of Dura; the other is the city's founder, Seleucus Nicator, crowning the Gad (fig. 92).

These images represented the spirits or fortunes of their respective cities and were worshipped as such. Apamea's temple to its Tyche lay close to the heart of the city, between the agora and the colonnaded *cardo* (see p. 244), and civic coin issues from various mints depict temples to their respective city Tyches. An inscription from Balanea records a certain Antiochus who constructed a temple and set up a statue of Tyche, presumably on behalf of the city. (Villages too might have such buildings, it would seem: a *Tychaion* was consecrated at Aere (Sanamein) in the Hauran by a Roman centurion in AD 191.) A city Tyche was the symbol of the city, but not necessarily of its inhabitants, who might be considered to have a separate, collective Tyche of their own (fig. 93.3).

ICONS OF CIVIC FORM

Competition between the elites of a city was not the only factor contributing to the drive towards monumentalization: rivalry between different cities was also important; and both of these factors are likely to have been responsible for architectural homogeneity through the imitation of influential models and

Fig. 92. Drawing of a relief made from Palmyrene limestone found in the 'Temple of the Gaddé' at Dura Europus. It shows Hairan, son of Maliku (on the left, wearing a Palmyrene priest's hat and holding a palm branch), making an offering on an altar before the Gad of Dura, who is crowned by Seleucus I (on the right, holding a spear and wreath). The Gad resembles Zeus; he holds a sceptre and ears or a sheaf of corn, and is seated between two eagles. The three Palmyrene inscriptions underneath the figures read (from left to right): 'Image of Hairan bar Maliku bar Nasor'; 'The Gad of Dura, made by Hairan bar Maliku bar Nasor. In the month of Nisan, year 470 (AD 159)'; 'Seleucus Nicator'. Seleucus had his own cult and priesthood at Dura. Another relief from the same temple showed Hairan before the female Gad of Palmyra.

Fig. 93.1. Reverse of a silver tetradrachm of Hadrian (AD 117-38) from Laodicea ad Mare, dated year 172 of the city (AD 124/125) and showing a bust of the Tyche of Laodicea wearing a mural crown. Her tresses are adorned with bunches of grapes (a reference to Laodicean wine?) and the city walls on her head encompass other monuments, most notably the city's famous lighthouse, which can just be discerned at the rear.

Fig. 93.2. Reverse of a civic bronze coin of Caesarea of the reign of Trajan (AD 98-117), showing the city-goddess in a temple, holding a sceptre and portrait bust and armed with a short sword. The small male figure at her feet is thought to represent Herod's great harbour of Sebastos. BMC 41.

Fig. 93.3. Reverse of a civic bronze coin of Antioch, of Severus Alexander (AD 222-35). The Tyche of Antioch is shown seated at the centre, with a small male figure

representing the River Orontes swimming at her feet. The standing figure on the left-hand side is another Tyche, thought to represent the fortune of the citizens of Antioch. The identity of the standing male figure on the right is less certain. He wears military dress and crowns the Tyche of Antioch with a wreath; he may be the emperor, but equally he may be the city's founder, Seleucus Nicator (see fig. 92 for a parallel). BMC 483.

styles. In order to keep up with rival cities some existing schemes were upgraded, although not all were completed. But the citizens – or at least those elites whose writings have come down to us – took pride in the beauty and utility of their civic monuments, those iconic buildings which helped to define their self-constructed communities modelled on the ideal of the Greek *polis*.

The great monuments of the city were often visible from afar, competing with nature for domination of the skyline. Among these landmark symbols of civic identity the walls would have been prominent, but in many cases the pre-eminent structures were temples, which were frequently placed on podiums or at high points within the city. In his *Description of the World* the late Roman poet Avienus described the great temple of Elagabal at Emesa as 'higher than the peaks of Lebanon, ... with which it jealously competes'.[34] In the monumental *polis* of the first to third century the holy and the public were given precedence over private interests.

The approach to the city, however, is likely to have been peppered with a curious mix of the public and private, monumental and humble, in contrast to the emphasis on public interests within the city walls. The roads leading to the city gates were lined with tombs, the dead being relegated to their own residence, the necropolis, situated outside the walls to keep the urban space free of the pollution of death (though note the arrangement at Palmyra: fig. 97). Large public structures for entertainment (such as hippodromes and amphitheatres), judged too big to place within the city walls, were often located in the same areas, perhaps partly motivated by a similar desire to keep the city clean of death and human bloodshed as well as concern for the damage that riots (which often started in such places) might cause if the buildings lay inside. Outside the walls we might expect to find the hovels and lean-tos of the destitute, dumps for refuse, places for displaying the bodies of executed criminals, and industrial areas. Monumental gates might mark the approach, leading on to colonnaded streets and a suite of architectural forms which symbolize the 'classical' or 'Graeco-Roman' city.

Fig. 94. The Hadrianic arch at Gerasa, built in AD 129-30. It was a symbolic entrance, for it stands over 450 metres (1/4 mile) south of Gerasa's city walls, next to the hippodrome.

The magnificence of the monumental city gave it the aspect of a vast palace, and it is possible that some of the inspiration for the monumental city derived from palaces. The great Hellenistic palaces had included public buildings and courts, religious sanctuaries and banqueting halls, and those at Antioch, Alexandria and Pergamum are acknowledged as having a strong influence over early Roman imperial architecture – particularly in the palaces at Rome, but also in the private dwellings of the elites, their tomb architecture, in public buildings such as the façades of theatres, monumental portals and gateways, porticos, banqueting halls and basilicas. Are the monumental cities, with their interlinked complexes and separate buildings for specific functions, their open spaces, arches, tetrapylons and porticos, attempting to create palatial-style public spaces, in the same way that the great palaces came to assume public as well as residential functions? A recent study of Hellenistic palaces concludes that one of the distinctive features of these complexes was that they 'gradually took upon themselves many of the functions of the polis'.[35] With the decline of Hellenistic royal power in the first century BC, perhaps the cities took it upon themselves to 'palatialize'. It is perhaps no coincidence that client kings like Herod (a notable builder of elaborate palaces) were prominent donors in the initial phase of this civic palatialization.

The Urban Plan

The plan is as much an icon of civic form as the buildings within it. Distinctions are sometimes drawn between planned cities and those that grow 'organically', but however irregular or accidental-looking a city plan might appear, its form is usually dictated by the organized structure of old property boundaries, social and political topographies, and a contest of private and public desires. In these contests power – which is concentrated in the hands of those who control the urban land – is crucial in negotiating the design of the city. A city founded on virgin ground, or appropriated from a disenfranchised population, can be planned anew. However, few cities were founded in the Syrian provinces during the centuries of Roman rule. Most either existed already or were elevated from village to city status. In their plans the cities of Roman Syria were largely inherited ones, reflecting the strategies of those that had gone before. To understand the urban plans of the Roman cities we have to examine the schemes of the Hellenistic dynasties of the Seleucids and Ptolemies.

The regular grid-like plans of many Hellenistic cities are said to be 'Hippodamian', and this form is usually seen as evidence of Greek influence. And yet there is nothing peculiarly Greek about the grid. Although we know relatively little about the ideas of the fifth-century BC urban theorist and planner Hippodamus of Miletus, one thing we do know is that the grid was not his idea and that it had existed for centuries before him. Some have looked instead to non-Greek traditions to explain the origins of the 'chequer-board' pattern of streets and blocks found in the Roman cities of Syria. Yet, as the most premeditated of plans, the grid hardly requires the support of any tradition. It can be seen as the very antithesis of tradition: making little concession to what has gone before, the grid either begins with no tradition or obliterates it. As the architect Spiro Kostof has noted, the grid is 'by far the commonest pattern for planned cities in history. It is universal both geographically and chronologically'.[36] The motivation that produces the grid may be very different from one place to another. It allows colonists to be given regular and equal parcels of land. The pattern of rectilinear streets also permits easy surveillance. The Hellenistic Seleucid cities of Syria – for example, Antioch, Seleucia, Apamea and Cyrrhus – were all dominated by a high acropolis which served as a military garrison. The panoptic effect of the grid and its military citadel may be unintended, but they serve to remind us that the strategic positioning of an acropolis, and perhaps the layout of the streets, do not necessarily represent the interests of the citizens. The urban plan may be a reflection of the movement of the heavens: we use the Roman terms *cardo* (north - south axis) and *decumanus* (east - west boundary line) to describe the axial streets of a Graeco-Roman city. The imposition of a grid on what was previously a more irregular layout may reflect social ideals, engendering a sense of improvement, of creating greater order. The design has multiple intentions and meanings: religious, strategic, social and practical.

Where the details are known, the Seleucid cities appear to have been designed with two axial main streets, so that at places like Apamea, Laodicea and Cyrrhus one could almost talk in terms of the cities having a *decumanus maximus* and *cardo maximus* – except that these are Roman terms and perhaps a little inappropriate for the Hellenistic period. At Antioch, Laodicea and Apamea the dimensions of the city blocks are strikingly similar, indicating that one could have provided a model for the others or, more probably, that they were the product of the same planners. The correspondence in alignment of Antioch's city blocks with field systems around the city indicates that the two were planned together, and both were probably intended for colonists. But not all Syrian city grids were Hellenistic in origin. Before the conquests of Alexander Berytus consisted of a settlement on and close to its Bronze Age tell, and there is evidence to suggest that the lower city was laid out on a grid, or at least using a rectilinear pattern, and that the expansion of the city under the Seleucids merely extended this existing plan. This in turn dictated the layout of the early Roman city (see above).

Some plans seem to have been dominated by a single main street crossing the city along its longest axis. Smaller streets led off the main one at right angles, but none of these seems to have formed major transverse axes. Examples include Hippus (Qalaat el-Husn), Gadara (Umm Qais), Philadelphia (Amman), Capitolias (Beit Ras), and perhaps Abila (Tel Abil). In the cases of Hippus, Gadara and Capitolias the city itself occupied an elevated acropolis. The location of these examples in the south has been taken as a possible indication that this is a Ptolemaic design, although a similar single main street was employed in Herodian Sebaste. It is of course possible that this plan predates Herod, or that Herod was influenced by Ptolemaic models.

Other cities are dominated by a single main street, but this does not cross the city from one side to the other. Instead the street ends at a monumental arch, which gives on to a large religious sanctuary. This design is vividly apparent at Bostra and Petra, and so it has been viewed as a 'Nabataean' city plan, although precise dates for the final forms of these layouts remain unclear. The emphasis is on a processional way, leading to the cities' main cult complex. At Bostra the colonnaded 'decumanus' leads from the western gate to a sacred precinct at the eastern end of the city (fig. 95). At Petra the main colonnaded street leads to the religious sanctuary of the Qasr al-Bint (fig. 96). In these cases the design is driven by the need to accommodate a particular form of religious and social activity.

Regional traditions are therefore apparent in this most elementary icon of civic form, and in the majority of cases the Roman phases are enlargements or improvements on what already existed. The notable exceptions are some villages which achieved city status in the early Roman period, such as Philippopolis, discussed above, or its neighbour Dionysias (see p. 135). But local topography also constrained the plans of cities regardless of traditions: Philadelphia's streets followed valleys, and the urban layout of Canatha must have been dictated in a large part by the irregularities of the terrain.

Dionysias (see p. 135).

Walls: the City Circumscribed

More than any other structure, the walls and their towers defined the city. As noted above, each city Tyche wore a mural crown; only rarely were any of the monuments within represented (fig. 93.1). This emphasis on walls is not surprising. They were a sign of civic autonomy. Walls helped demonstrate that the settlement was a city and provided a clear boundary between the urban core and its territory. It seems that not every city possessed them from the outset, although they might strive to acquire these costly structures. The imperial authorities did not always approve of cities having walls, and sometimes insisted that they be demolished – a sure sign that these edifices signified, in a very real way, the autonomy of the community. Although the wall was usually built of local materials (preferably stone rather than mud brick), it was the largest and

Fig. 95. Bostra. The Nabataean arch, standing at the end of the main thoroughfare. The capitals on the engaged columns are typically Nabataean.

Fig. 96. Petra. The Qasr al-Bint sanctuary with its great temple, which lies at the end of the city's main street.

most expensive public monument a city could possess, and was probably beyond the financial resources of some of the smaller cities. Walls often enclosed areas greater than their built-up areas, either to allow for expansion, to create protection for gardens or to take advantage of the most easily defensible natural features. In most cases the Roman-period defences followed the earlier ones, helping to preserve the urban layouts described above. The walls of Apamea are about 7 kilometres (4⅓ miles) long, encompassing the plateau on which the city sits. Sondages there confirm that the Roman-period defences were constructed on Hellenistic foundations. At Palmyra, however, the circuit of city walls underwent several modifications, resulting in dramatic changes to the size and scope of the defended area. The fortifications were originally conceived on a grand scale (fig. 97), although their height may have been relatively modest. Constructed of mud brick on a stone foundation, the extensive southern rampart probably stood 2 metres (6½ feet) high. The northern rampart is less well preserved (a simple embankment of clay and mortar was all that archaeologists could detect). These defences are perhaps of the first century BC and were probably in use when Aurelian took the city. The smaller circuit of dressed stone (colour plate 12), often reusing building materials from tombs and other structures, is sometimes dated to the reign of Zenobia, although it is most commonly associated with Diocletian, who stationed a legion there (see chapter 10). This later wall enclosed only the monumental zone of Palmyra, and was defined on its southern edge by a wadi which had formerly run through the city. It also changed the focus of the city somewhat: the great sanctuary of Bel

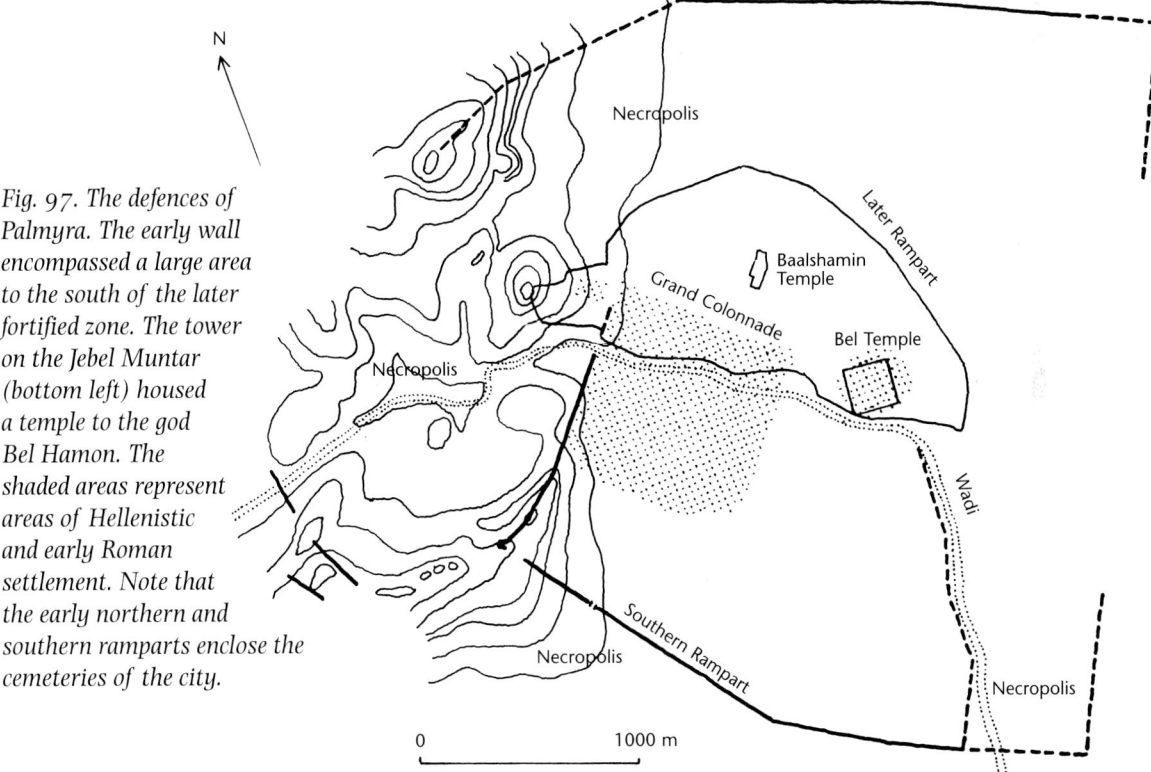

Fig. 97. The defences of Palmyra. The early wall encompassed a large area to the south of the later fortified zone. The tower on the Jebel Muntar (bottom left) housed a temple to the god Bel Hamon. The shaded areas represent areas of Hellenistic and early Roman settlement. Note that the early northern and southern ramparts enclose the cemeteries of the city.

now faced away from the main part of the defended area, and one cannot help wondering whether the layout of the new defences helped to marginalize what had once been a significant part of ancient Palmyra to the south.

The Streets

Streets, as the basic unit of urbanism, are easily taken for granted, but without them there would be no city. Because they provide access they are important public spaces, but because of their very public nature they can also be used to constrain the movement and behaviour of the inhabitants. Everyone has to use them, and therefore they are perfect places for political displays, providing a stage on which the activities and rituals of the community are acted out. The

Fig. 98. The broad main street at Apamea.

main streets of the Graeco-Roman cities could be used for religious processions and civic ceremonies, a purpose suggested by the prominent position and orientation of many important temples and sanctuaries with regard to the thoroughfares. Their builders clearly had more than mere circulation in mind.

A prominent feature of cities in Roman Syria is a long colonnaded street. It may be perfectly straight, as at Apamea (fig. 98); or an articulation of several straight sections, with the changes in direction being both marked and concealed by monumental structures such as tetrapylons, as at Palmyra (fig. 35). The expenditure and effort lavished on these streets suggests that they were very important to the civic elites who built them. They were often constructed in sections over several decades, as is evident from the rebuilding of the *cardo* at Apamea following the great earthquake in northern Syria under Trajan (AD

115). The citizens began erecting their new monumental colonnade, which was aligned precisely north - south, immediately after the earthquake. The task was enormous, as the road, which crosses the plateau of Apamea, extended for 2 kilometres (1¼ miles), and the street itself was to be nearly 21 metres (69 feet) wide, with 7-metre (23-foot) wide porticos behind. Various styles of column and architrave were employed in the different sections of colonnade, marking the successive phases of building. Construction appears to have begun at the northern end with Lucius Julius Agrippa's contribution (fig. 83). Fifty years later work was still under way, when two brothers of another important family, the Appii, dedicated statues of Antoninus Pius, Marcus Aurelius and Lucius Verus on a section of spiral fluted colonnade opposite the east entrance to the agora (fig. 99). The city's nymphaeum to the south has features which the excavators date to the same period or slightly later. This, together with other epigraphic evidence, indicates that the elites of Apamea invested in the rebuilding of their *cardo* for about a century.

In spite of the effort that went into their construction, a number of these main streets were periodically redesigned and enlarged, presumably to keep up with building schemes in other cities. The original Seleucid street at Antioch, 13 metres (42½ feet) across, was altered round about the time of Augustus to include rows of shops. While this widened the entire ensemble to 27.5 metres (90 feet), the street itself was narrower than its Seleucid predecessor. By the early second century it had been provided with 9-metre (29½-foot) wide colonnades plus shops, extending the scheme to 36 metres (118 feet), but the street itself remained fairly modest at 9 metres (29½ feet). By the end of the first century AD Gerasa had been equipped with an Ionic colonnaded *cardo*, 15 metres (49¼ feet) wide (including sidewalks), but during the second century the main, southern section of this street was widened to nearly 20 metres (65½ feet) and given larger Corinthian columns. The old Ionic columns were re-employed in monumental cross-streets.

Palmyra's grand colonnade is one of the most famous, but it is also one of the least well integrated into the monumental urban landscape. A number of major monuments face away from the colonnade rather than on to it. Most of these are oriented towards the wadi to the south-west of the monumental zone (fig. 35). These include the Damascus Gate and its monumental street with an oval piazza, the Tariff Court, and the sanctuary of the god Nebo. The focus appears to be on the Hellenistic settlement, which lay to the south of the wadi and the monumental zone, outside the later city walls (fig. 97). The grand colonnade stretched for about 1200 metres (¾ mile), from the Sanctuary of Bel, located to the south-east, to meet a monumental street leading from the Damascus Gate on the north-western side. A number of tombs occupied this latter area, indicating that this was formerly the edge of the city. The street leading from the Damascus Gate was under construction in the early second century, and the initial phase of the grand colonnade may have begun at the north-western end

Fig. 99. Spiral fluted columns opposite the entrance to Apamea's agora.

at about this time. This section of the grand colonnade is also the longest (500 metres/546 yards), and it points directly at the entrance to the great sanctuary of Bel on the other side of the city. However, extending it in this direction would have meant demolishing important buildings, most notably the first-century AD temple of Nebo. As a result, the grand colonnade was forced to skirt around this area, changing direction twice in order to reach the Bel sanctuary (colour plate 12). A tetrapylon marks the first change in alignment, and the point where another monumental colonnaded street coming from the south met the grand colonnade. If the theatre is earlier than the colonnade, as has been proposed, the second section of the street may have been guided by its alignment. Even this arrangement meant cutting through the northern edge of the sanctuary of Nebo, which suggests that the street's builders were influential enough to negotiate such alterations to sacred space. Immediately beyond the Nebo sanctuary the street was free to turn south-east to meet the propylaea of the Bel sanctuary. This is the widest part of the grand colonnade, but how it met with the Bel sanctuary is still unclear as this section seems not to have been completed. The dating of the whole colonnade remains fragile; dedicatory inscriptions on statue brackets attached to the columns are often the only clue, but these were sometimes added at a later date than the colonnades themselves. The unfinished state of many columns, particularly evident on their bases, where often only the guidelines for the mouldings have been marked out, suggests that many features of the street date to the third century.

In all of the cities that had them, the colonnades normally supported a roof, providing covered walkways or a portico in front of shops which lay at the back (fig. 83). Some columns were set on podiums, while others were placed directly on a stylobate. A noteworthy characteristic of the Palmyrene colonnades is the stone brackets jutting out from the columns (fig. 100); they once supported statues of local and imperial dignitaries. These devices were occasionally employed elsewhere, such as on the spiral fluted colonnade at Apamea, but only at Palmyra do they proliferate.

The origins of these grand colonnaded streets remain speculative. They are

Fig. 100. Part of the grand colonnade at Palmyra. Note the brackets for statues, located half way up each column.

a feature of cities in southern Asia Minor as well as Syria, so a local origin may not be the solution. The dating of many of them remains imprecise. It used to be thought that the earliest monumental street in Syria was the one at Antioch, paid for by King Herod, but, as noted above, excavations at the north gate of Apamea have brought to light a late second, or early first-century BC precursor to the colonnaded *cardo* that was rebuilt in the second century AD, suggesting that some cities could have acquired such structures under the Seleucids. In overall appearance the civic colonnades are similar to the stoas which bordered the agoras of classical Greek and Hellenistic cities, and indeed this is what inscriptions call them. This suggests a possible origin, for stoas too had colonnaded porticos and shops or booths at the back. Like stoas, the street porticos are seen as practical solutions to the climate, affording shade to pedestrians in hot weather and shelter from the rain. Porticoed shops extended the marketplace into the main thoroughfares, prompting the suggestion that an oriental souk or bazaar is the underlying model. These functional explanations are valid, but they do not explain why the streets took such costly and elaborate forms, or why certain features were rather impractical or in some cases apparently pointless. In late Roman times there was a trend for paving porticos with mosaics, yet the frequent repairs and repavings suggest that these floors were not always well suited to everyday traffic. Some colonnaded streets did not link the main public buildings of the city: at Sebaste the temples, theatre and agora are all located at higher elevations some distance away from the colonnade, which skirts around them at the bottom of the steep slope to the south. One stretch of colonnade at Gerasa, close to the quadrifons (see below), supported only an architrave. There was no roof and no building behind it, as if the colonnade were purely ornamental. The same seems to have been the case with the main colonnades at Philadelphia (Amman). One rather radical suggestion is that in such cases the street itself was roofed. Another, less radical, is that the colonnades were erected first, with the intention of constructing buildings behind it later. However, rather than the columns being merely a practical, if decorative, support for something else (roofs, porticos), might it not be the case that the colonnade itself had an important symbolic function?

The street is a space where public and private interests struggle for control. The public strategy is to keep it open, to provide access; the private strategy is to appropriate it for one's own use. On a main thoroughfare all façades, whether public or private, are given a modicum of public presence by virtue of their position. The colonnade, however, is a screen that denies a presence to private buildings and activities. The grand colonnaded street creates a public space along its entire length, hiding private interests behind the architectural curtain of columns. In this way, rather than functioning merely as an extended economic zone of shops and markets, the colonnaded street also becomes a medium for ceremonial assertions of power by a highly co-ordinated social hierarchy. It is one extreme version of the public strategy overcoming private ones. Not that the ideal was necessarily always observed in everyday life; the cities were likely to gain from renting space in the porticos to vendors, and their wares might obstruct the walkways or even spill into the street itself. But such impediments could be cleared away on festival days.

Visual continuities were provided by the repetitive patterns of the columns, which sometimes concealed irregularities behind them. The presence of significant buildings might be marked by changes in ornament, changes in column size or the use of different coloured stone, or by projecting porticos (colour plate 3). The streets were made eventful through the use of special monuments: arches, votive columns, tetrapylons, tetrakionions, nymphaea. These monuments, particularly the arches and tetrapylons, divided the street into enclosed units or vistas. They also concealed, or made features of, awkward changes in street alignment.

Arches provided symbolic gateways and boundaries, outside the city, at its entrance, or within the city. City gates of the first century BC and first century AD seem more designed for defence, usually having one entrance and projecting towers either side, but some had decorative façades. From the late first or early second century structures modelled on the Roman triumphal arch, with columned façades and a large central entrance flanked by two smaller ones, were employed for a variety of purposes. The form, and the date of its introduction, suggest that it could have been inspired by similar structures in Italy. Some of these structures were true commemorative arches. They could celebrate Roman domination (an arch in honour of Trajan was erected at Dura Europus during Rome's brief occupation of the city in the early second century); or a city could erect one in honour of an emperor as a symbol of loyalty to the regime. The form, however, had other uses. An arch could be inserted into the city walls, forming a gateway, and might be flanked by defensive towers (as at Gadara), or not (as at Gerasa). It could demarcate the boundary between a sanctuary and the rest of the city (as at Bostra and Petra). In the countryside freestanding arches might mark the boundary of a province or city territory, or of imperial or large private estates. (However, arches are not always what they

Fig. 101. Tetrakionion at Palmyra (heavily restored; the columns are not originals), which stands in a circular piazza marking the junction of another street with the grand colonnade.

seem: the so-called Bab el-Hawa, 'Gate of the Winds', appears to be an arch spanning the road between Antioch and Beroea in a gap between the Jebel Barisha and Jebel Halaqa. It was once thought to have been connected with the estate of a certain Hormisdas mentioned in a nearby inscription; but the 'arch' has now been identified as part of a destroyed church.)

Other arches spanned the main street. Probably the best known of such arches is that at Palmyra, which accommodates a change in the grand colonnade's direction. Its plan is V-shaped, with two monumental triple-arched façades meeting in the western corner (colour plate 13).

Major junctions or crossroads within the city were often marked by a class of monuments called *tetrapyla*, 'four gates'. There are two main forms of tetrapylon: the *quadrifons* or 'four fronts' (specimens can be seen at Laodicea and Gerasa; there was also one employed at the junction of the axial streets found within the camp of Diocletian at Palmyra); and the *tetrakionion* or 'four columns'. The latter was often located in a circular piazza (examples can be found at Palmyra, Bostra, Gerasa), although a tetrakionion at Antipatris in Palestine marked the junction of the city's *cardo* with its agora.

Junctions of side streets with the principal colonnaded avenue were sometimes marked with arches, punctuating the porticos. Various examples can be seen at Apamea and Palmyra. The 'Gate of the Lantern' at Bostra is an unusually elaborate example, with its triple arched façade, and resembles the triumphal arch-like structures that spanned the main streets in other cities (fig. 102).

The main thoroughfare normally hosted the city's nymphaeum (fig. 103). The term was originally applied to sanctuaries of the nymphs, set up around water sources. Civic nymphaea were artificial sources, and usually formed the terminal point of an aqueduct. An ornamental pool was backed by an elaborate architectural wall (often decorated with niches and statuary) through which the conduit poured its waters. The structures were often roofed or provided with a semi-dome, and given a columned façade and pediment. A retaining wall in front of the pool usually contained channels or waterspouts from which people could collect water for their homes. The excess simply poured into the city's drains. At Apamea a public latrine lay directly behind the nymphaeum, no doubt located to take full advantage of the water supply. The building of a nymphaeum presupposes the city's appropriation of some adequate water source. Nymphaea were ostentatious monuments and, although expensive to build, they could provide their donors with an excellent opportunity for self-advertisement.

Water from the nymphaeum, sewage from public latrines, and water from rooftops was carried away in substantial drainage channels, located either along the edges of the thoroughfare or down its centre. Although the climate of the region is dry and warm for much of the year, rainfall can be torrential and without drains the streets could easily have flooded. Stone inspection covers gave access to these for cleaning and maintenance. The

Fig. 102. The so-called 'Gate of the Lantern' at Bostra. This marks the junction of another major colonnaded street, leading to the theatre, with the decumanus.

Fig. 103. The nymphaeum at Gerasa.

only significant exception to these arrangements seems to have been at Palmyra, where the main street of the grand colonnade seems never to have been paved (the earth surface may have been kinder to camels' feet). Perhaps the city's location in the dry steppe made drainage installations of this sort unnecessary.

The excavations and reconstruction at Gerasa provide us with a particularly good collection of street monuments (fig. 104). Two Hadrianic arches of similar plan and decoration marked the southern entrance to the city: one lies to the south of the city walls, in the necropolis and next to the southern edge of Gerasa's hippodrome (fig. 94). The other, in the southern city wall, may be a little earlier in date. After passing through the latter gate one reached the entrance to the sanctuary of Zeus and the oval piazza (see below), and, crossing the piazza, gained access to the main *cardo* through another arch. A short distance along this first section of the street, four large columns on the left broke the monotony of the portico to announce the presence of Gerasa's *macellum*. Beyond this, a tetrakionion marked the intersection of the *cardo* with the southern decumanus. Further along the *cardo*, again on the left, one reached the monumental heart of the city, with the entrance to the late Roman cathedral, the nymphaeum and the entrance to the great sanctuary of Artemis. Another street, leading from the eastern part of the city, joined the *cardo* opposite the entrance to the Temple of Artemis. In design this latter street looks like a processional way leading west to the sanctuary, ending in an elaborate architectural piazza just before the *cardo*. The *cardo* itself continues north to a quadrifons which marks the junction with the city's north decumanus, and from here the street leads to the city's northern gate, dated to Trajan's reign.

It is important to stress the fact that colonnades continued to be erected long after construction of many other typically 'classical' buildings had ceased, and must have remained important to the ideal of a city in late Roman times. The substantial colonnaded *cardo* in Jerusalem, which was 22 metres (72 feet) wide, is considered to be a creation of the sixth century, improving on the earlier Roman street, which lacked columns. Recent work at Apamea has revealed the

Fig. 104. Plan of Gerasa.

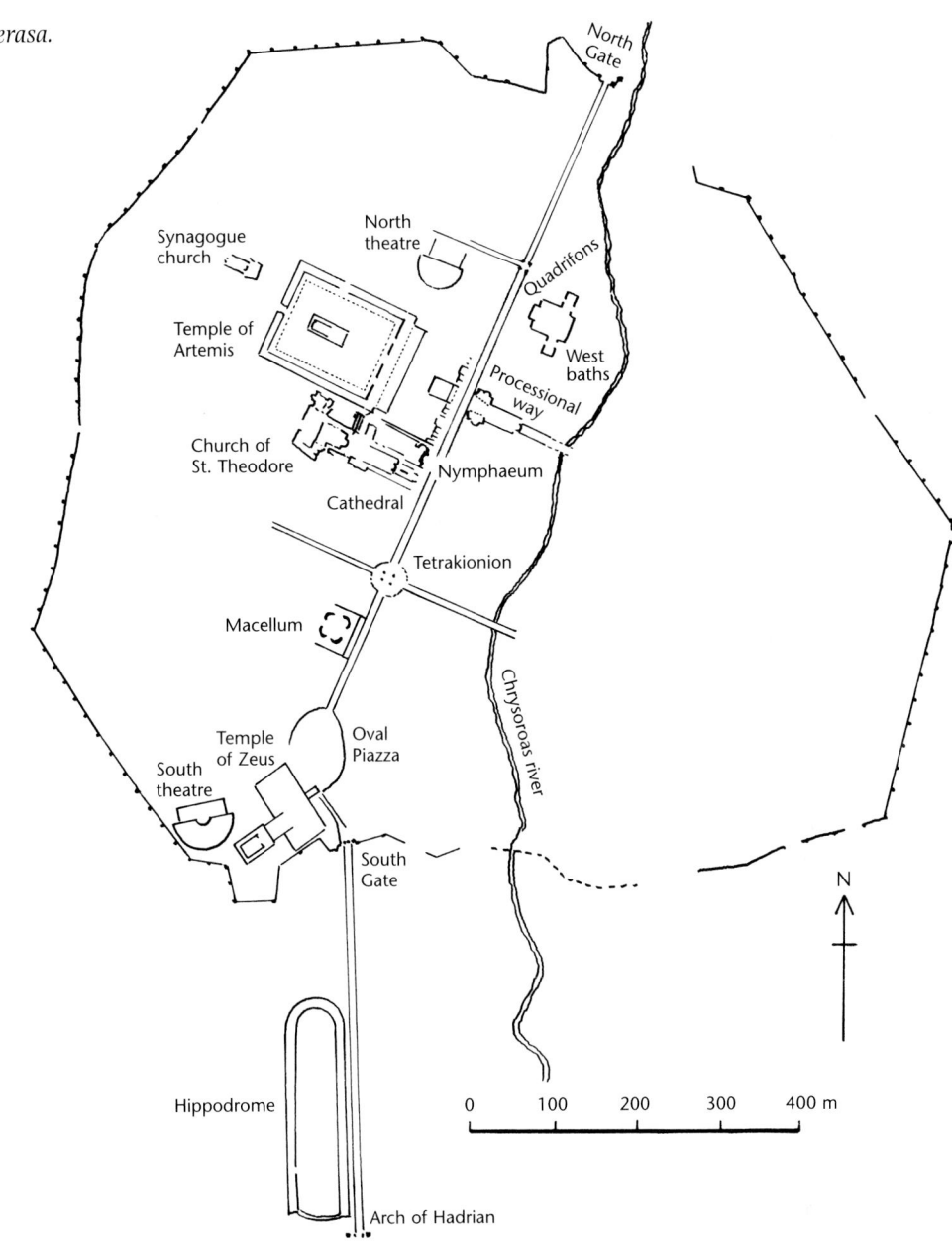

foundations of a Justinianic tetrakionion erected on the *cardo*. A major thoroughfare in Berytus had a late Roman phase, combining columns and capitals from different sources. These late creations might sometimes reuse old materials, but were attempts to maintain the grandeur of the public street.

Open Spaces

At the centre of the ideal Graeco-Roman city, preferably at or near the junction of the main streets, lay the agora or forum, the marketplace and principal public space of the city. Typically it would be an open area surrounded by colonnades fronting shops, and by civic buildings and temples, where administrative and commercial business was carried out. The position of such spaces within the Syrian cities varied, and in some cities there might be more than one. Apamea's Antonine agora was an elongated rectangular space, 45 by 150 metres (50 by 164 yards), west of the city's *cardo*, directly behind the temple to the city Tyche. For such a large city it was comparatively small, and the shops of Apamea's huge porticos may have compensated. At Sebaste in Samaria a rectangular colonnaded agora was placed about 100 metres (109 yards) away from the main street, on a slope to the north. The so-called forum at Antipatris, however, lay directly on the city's *cardo maximus*. The large agora at Philadelphia, identi-fied as such by an inscription, was trapezoidal in shape, forming a monumental ensemble in the heart of the city along with the theatre and the odeum. Palmyra's monumental agora was positioned south of the grand colonnade, and now lies up against the late Roman city wall, and at Damascus the agora is thought to have occupied an area in the north-eastern corner of the city, close to the northern gate (the modern Bab Touma) (fig. 105). Locations close to the city wall may have had a practical purpose, allowing animals to be corralled outside the urban area, near to the market but not within the city itself and without blocking the main thoroughfares when they were herded in for sale or slaughter.

Palmyra's agora is among the best preserved. It is a rectangular space, approximately 70 by 50 metres (76 by 54 yards), demarcated by a high wall

Fig. 105. Plan of Damascus. Note the position of the agora, relative to the main streets and the principal sanctuary.

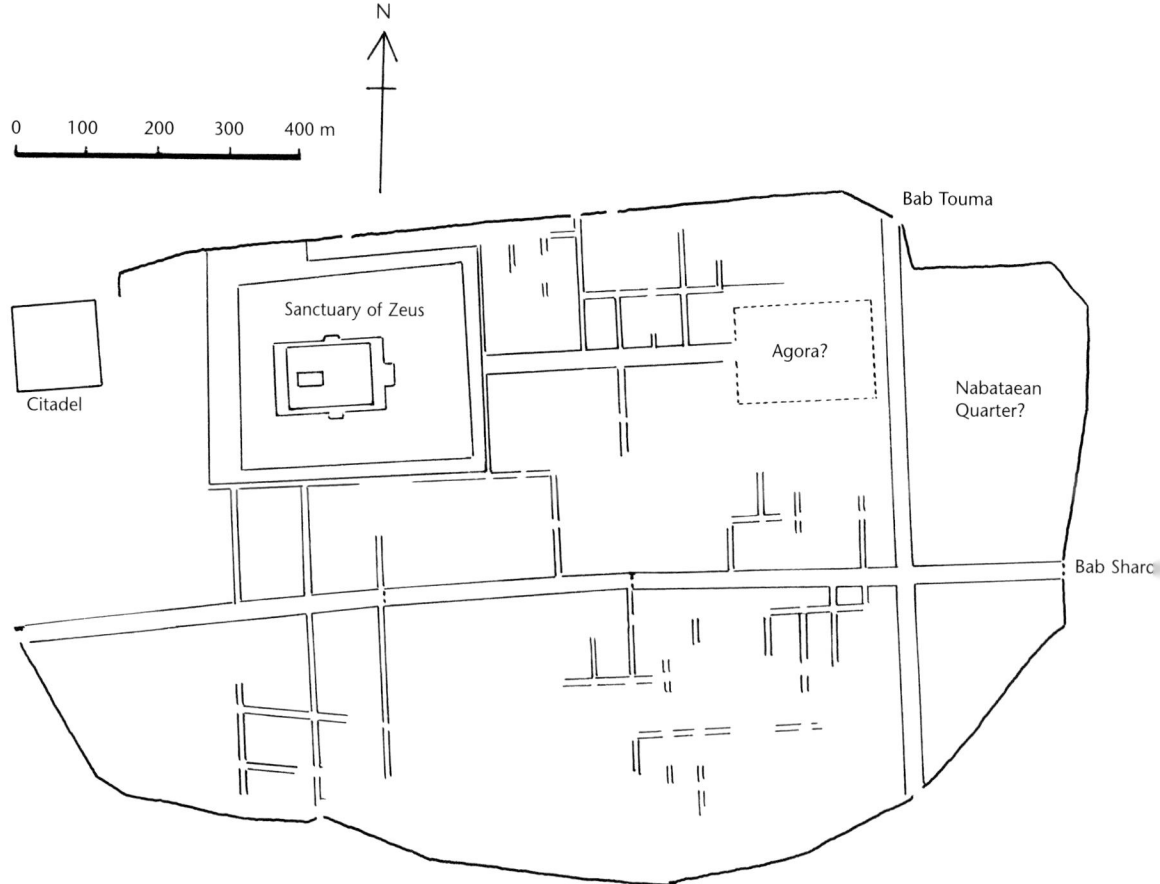

fronted by colonnades. The columns bore statue brackets honouring Roman and Palmyrene officials, merchants, caravan leaders, military officers and senators. In the south-western corner is a rectangular room opening off the portico which served as either a ritual banquet hall or perhaps a bouleterion. At the back of the room is a niche, probably for the statue of a deity, and an altar.

South of the agora, and sharing a wall with it, was a long rectangular enclosure now known as the Tariff Court. It was originally entered through a massive porticoed vestibule on the south-western side, but with the construction of the later defensive wall this imposing entrance was blocked off. A direct link with the agora was provided by three monumental doors and eight windows piercing the common wall between them. It was from the entrance to this complex that the famous Palmyra tariff was recovered in the nineteenth century, and whence the space earned its name. The court lacked porticos, and it is perhaps through the monumental entrance that animals were led and civic taxes collected.

Sometimes the purely commercial activities such as the buying and selling of foodstuffs were given separate spaces. A good example of a market pavilion or *macellum* of this sort is to be found at Gerasa, lying just off the main *cardo*. The structure is rectangular, about 65 by 50 metres (71 by 54 yards). Booths flank the main entrance at the back of the colonnaded portico, and the main open space is octagonal, surrounded by a colonnade and with exhedras on four sides.

Open spaces provided opportunities for elaborate display, such as the monumental setting for sculpture on the western side of the agora at Philippopolis (above, p. 233), but they could also be used to provide a change of environment within the urban framework. At Petra a series of courts or open spaces lie to the west of the city's main street. Three of these used to be interpreted as markets, an upper, middle and lower, but exploration of the lower market revealed a large pool with a pavilion at its centre. The current interpretation of this space is that this was a *paradeisos*, a park or garden in the heart of the city, probably connected with a palace complex. Gardens and parks were often associated with palaces, and there was a tradition of granting the public access to such spaces – at least for special occasions.

Other open public areas are more enigmatic. Oval spaces, fringed by colonnades, are known at Palmyra, Bostra and Gerasa. In all three cases they are located close to one of the city gates, at the beginning of a colonnaded street. Gerasa's is the largest and best-known of these oval piazzas (fig. 106). It is more than 90 metres (98 yards) long by 80 metres (87 yards) wide and surrounded by an Ionic portico. A limestone podium nearly 10 metres (33 feet) square originally stood at the centre and probably supported a statue. The piazza's form is in fact irregular: the eastern colonnade is not a perfect curve and to the south the space is truncated slightly by the terrace of the city's sanctuary of Zeus. Nor is the pavement level, as it rises slightly to the north. While it is large enough to have served as a market or public meeting place, it does not appear to have functioned as one. A macellum stood a short distance to the north, along the main colonnaded street (see above). Some think that the piazza's function may have been primarily aesthetic: it provided a suitably impressive open space before the sanctuary of Zeus and disguised a change of direction in the city's main street (fig. 104). Its pavement covered a broad natural depression in the terrain, and this correction of topography may also have helped to

influence its size and shape. A similar function may be posited for the much smaller and more regular example at Bostra, which also helped to disguise the fact that the city's western gate and the main street were not perfectly aligned. The oval piazza at Palmyra stood just within the Damascus Gate in the south-western corner of the late city wall. The piazza, which is about 40 metres (43 yards) wide, does not help to correct any misalignment. The street that led from it is at more or less a right angle to the grand colonnade, and much shorter, but somewhat wider. Some sort of functional link between the gateways and the open spaces behind them is quite possible, and that link is reinforced by the discovery of a paved open area inside the Damascus Gate in Aelia Capitolina (Jerusalem), which is depicted on the mosaic map from Medaba (see chapter 8). This too, however, may have helped to disguise the angles of the streets that met it. Whether these spaces were erected purely for aesthetic reasons and optical effects or whether they also had some practical purpose remains uncertain.

Chief among the enclosed public spaces, often adjacent to the main open public space of the city, was the basilica. This was a covered public hall, a Roman adaptation of the Greek stoa. The earliest attested in our region is the Caesareum, built at Antioch under Julius Caesar, but nothing of this structure has been uncovered. The basilica at Sebaste is typical of such buildings. It is probably Severan, but is thought to have replaced an earlier structure, perhaps also of the first century BC. Measuring about 68 metres by 33 metres (74 by 36 yards), it was a rectangular building divided into a nave and two aisles by two rows of columns, with an apsidal platform containing seats at the eastern end of the nave. Basilicas functioned as courts of justice, offices for magistrates and

Fig. 106. The oval piazza at Gerasa, seen from the Temple of Zeus. The great altar in the sanctuary of Zeus lies in the foreground. Beyond the piazza the cardo leads northwards; the macellum complex can be seen to the left of it, and beyond that, in the distance, the great Temple of Artemis.

places for commerce, but the term came to signify any large public hall with a roof. In late antiquity its meaning became more specific when the common basilical plan was adopted for Christian churches, and basilical halls erected during pagan times were sometimes converted into churches in the late Roman period. This is what appears to have happened to the elaborate complex called the 'Seraya' or 'Seraglio' at Canatha. Two second- to third-century basilica structures, variously identified as meeting halls, a *praetorium*, or temples, were arranged around a colonnaded court so that the whole complex resembled an L. The larger of the two structures had a complex history, probably beginning in the third century AD when it consisted of a long colonnaded courtyard entered through a portico on the northern side. An apse and two flanking chambers were subsequently built at the southern end, though for what purpose is unknown. In the fourth or fifth centuries the court-yard was divided in two by a tall and elaborately decorated wall pierced by three doorways. The southern section was roofed and converted into a church, with the altar and a semi-circular bank of seats for the

Fig. 107. The 'Seraya' at Canatha. The dividing wall which partitioned the courtyard.

clergy being placed on the eastern side. To the north, the remaining unroofed part of the colonnaded courtyard was retained as a forecourt, and the smaller of the two 'basilicas' lay to the west of this. It too had an entrance porch on the north and an apse on the south, and like its larger counterpart was converted into a church and reoriented with an apse built on the east and a new entrance on the west. A third-century basilica hall at Bostra was likewise converted into a church, but as the building was already oriented east - west such drastic changes were not necessary.

Entertainment and Assemblies

The spectacles of mimes and pantomimes, athletic and artistic competitions, chariot races and animal hunts did much more than entertain. In the theatres, stadia and hippodromes grand festivals celebrated the city, Greek culture, or Rome and the emperors. The buildings in which such events took place were also places in which the social order of the *polis* was affirmed. They were where officials like provincial governors hoped to win acclamations, and where the masses could demonstrate their approval or disapproval. Special seats were reserved in them for the prominent members of civic society, or for guild members, and means of entry to the buildings, as well as seating, was often divided according to class.

Monumental theatres do not appear to have existed in Syria in Hellenistic times, even in the Macedonian foundations like Antioch or Laodicea, although a Hellenistic period stadium (running track) is known at Marathus. The lack of Hellenistic theatre buildings is surely of some cultural significance, but caution

Fig. 108. The basalt west theatre at Gadara, which could accommodate 3000 spectators.

is required: those theatres partially cut into the hillsides in 'Hellenistic' fashion, such as at Seleucia Pieria or Apamea, may have had Hellenistic antecedents. However, there is as yet no evidence for them. Theatres could take up a lot of space within the urban fabric, and they are not uncommonly relegated to a peripheral position, particularly if the local landscape incorporated a slope which could usefully accommodate such a building. In general there is thought to have been a correlation between theatre size and the population of a city, although some cities seem to have unusually large ones in proportion to their urban area. Apamea's is the largest known in Syria, with a cavea 139 metres (152 yards) in diameter, and is positioned on a slope on the western edge of the city. Free-standing theatres, built on level ground and with the cavea raised on vaults and arches in the 'Roman' tradition, were often only slightly smaller. The well-preserved example at Bostra had a cavea 102 metres (111 yards) across (colour plate 17), and the small coastal city of Gabala's was 90 metres (98 yards; fig. 109). The theatre at Philippopolis is one of the more modest examples at 40 metres (44 yards).

Odeum is a term usually reserved for a smaller, theatre-like building, which was commonly roofed over. These were used for events like poetry recitals, or they could serve as a bouleterion (chamber for council meetings). In some places, such as Dionysias (Suweyda) or Philadelphia (Amman), the distinction between theatre and odeum was made clear by having two distinct structures, one large and one small. At Palmyra a small building close to the Tariff Court and the theatre contains a semi-circular tier of seating, and is thought to be the city's council chamber. But in other places the distinction is not so clear. A

Fig. 109. The theatre at Gabala, a port city south of Laodicea. The building could seat about 7000.

theatre could serve as a bouleterion and also accommodate the people's assembly, and small theatre-like buildings were sometimes attached to temple complexes. At Dura Europus a small, theatre-like structure in the Temple of Artemis may have served as a council chamber, but was probably also used for religious functions (Fig. 110). The unusual case of the theatre-like building inside the so-called Petra Great Temple is examined in chapter 9. Less unusual, but instructive nonetheless, is the north theatre complex at Gerasa (colour plate 19), the history of which demonstrates how ambiguous the distinction between theatre and odeum might be. The original building was an odeum, constructed in the reigns of Marcus Aurelius and Lucius Verus (AD 161-9). The seats were inscribed with the abbreviated names of the voting tribes represented on the city council. In the reign of Severus Alexander (AD 222-35) the cavea was enlarged, doubling its capacity. But this transition from odeum to theatre does not appear to have been very successful, as external buildings had begun to encroach on it by the middle of the third century, and by the fifth it had ceased to function altogether.

Other theatre-like buildings may have been constructed for more specific purposes, such as Gerasa's so-called festival theatre, built outside the city walls next to the reservoirs and probably used during the aquatic Maiuma festival. A similar function has been suggested for the curious rectangular 'arena' at Tyre (fig. 111). It is surrounded by cisterns and water pipes, and one suggestion is that the arena could be flooded for the Maiuma. However, the building does not show signs of adequate waterproofing, so it is difficult to see how this could have been achieved.

Theatres could accommodate gladiatorial shows and wild-beast hunts, but some cities had amphitheatres constructed for the purpose. An early multi-purpose building, more like a stadium than an amphitheatre in shape, has been identified as the 'amphitheatre' which, according to Josephus, King Herod built at Caesarea, although a later oval arena was constructed outside Caesarea's walls. More common than amphitheatres are hippodromes for chariot racing, but in general only the more important cities had them. Some cities, such as Caesarea and Bostra, possessed a theatre, amphitheatre and hippodrome, in keeping with their pre-eminent positions in the provincial hierarchy. Others were endowed with more than one building of the same type: Gadara had two theatres within less than 200 metres (219 yards) of each other; Gerasa had three. Given that the populations of the cities were not always very great compared to the capacity of these structures, we might wonder whether some of them were superfluous. Many no doubt reflected the importance of the festivals that their cities hosted. Cities that were centres for the imperial cult, or those that celebrated major international festivals, would draw crowds and pilgrims from much further afield than the city and its hinterland. But we may suppose that civic benefactions sometimes led to the construction or enlargement of buildings which were unnecessary. The north theatre at Gerasa is a case in point.

Bath buildings were not always so visible within the urban landscape (they were appreciated for their interior rather than their exterior), and yet they were among the commonest public buildings of the Roman east, being found in villages as well as cities. Even in places like Kifrin on the middle Euphrates, where the Roman presence may have lasted less than two decades, we find a Roman bath, probably constructed for use by soldiers. The plans and features of these baths in Syria are typical of such buildings all over the empire. There may have been a trend towards a greater emphasis on sweat rooms at the expense of pools in late antiquity, but it is difficult to be sure whether this is a cultural change or a consequence of ease of access to available water resources. Many baths built in the early empire remained in operation into late Roman times, and even beyond. Provisions for plunge pools

Fig. 110. A small, theatre-like structure, part of a complex added in Roman times to the Parthian period Temple of Artemis at Dura Europus.

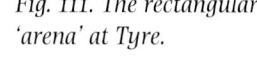

Fig. 111. The rectangular 'arena' at Tyre.

Fig. 112. One of a pair of domed caldaria (hot rooms) of the so-called South Baths at Bostra. The walls are of masonry but the dome is made of rubble and mortar. The baths were constructed in the second century but extensively remodelled and enlarged in the early third.

and hot water immersion are common in city baths, whose water supplies were assured by aqueducts. In those places where water was scarcer (the marginal zones, which were more densely occupied in late Roman times than earlier) architects had to adopt designs that were more sparing with water supplies. The beautifully preserved example from the village of Serjilla, a simple but monumental bath house dated to AD 473 (colour plate 25), had only modest water installations, and seems to have relied more heavily on sweat rooms, rather like Turkish baths. There were no aqueducts supplying the villages of the limestone massif, and water was obtained from a large cistern adjacent to the bath building.

The buildings of the monumental public city were a reminder of who controlled it, and who had the right to compete for attention in its society. Monuments gave their builders, as individuals, a place in the collective memory of the community which they helped to construct, and affirmed their importance in the social hierarchy. The monumental architecture of the Syrian cities was propagandistic in that it glorified not only the city but its builders too, and demonstrated their commitment to the elite cultural ideal of the Greek *polis*, a society in which all citizens were expected to perform their public duties. That the architecture could also be used to glorify the emperors was an added attraction, linking the donors and their city to the highest source of honour and power. With its emphasis on monumental public amenities the Graeco-Roman city might seem to express collective will and collective ideals, but it was really an environment celebrating the aspirations and social power of a relatively small proportion of the population. Yet excavation in Syria and the Near East has brought to light other notions of the ancient city which deviate from the public ideal, and which were the product of different social circumstances. We might therefore question whether the monuments represent *the* Roman city, or merely one of several alternatives.

ALTERNATIVES

Dura Europus

Dura Europus was founded by Seleucus I. It was planned on a grid pattern, and like other Seleucid foundations had a prominent citadel, in this case on the side closest to the Euphrates (into which part of the citadel collapsed in the first century BC). The defences utilized the natural topography of the site, following a cliff overlooking the river and bordered to the north and south by deep wadis, so that only one side, which faced the desert, had to rely solely on man-made fortifications (fig. 17). The Seleucid city had an open agora at its centre, which by the time of the Roman occupation had become almost completely filled with shops (fig. 113). The Romans appear to have turned the north-western part of the city into a military camp, a process which presumably involved dispossessing the inhabitants who lived there. A large palatial structure, with rooms arranged around two colonnaded courts, was built on the northern side of the city, overlooking the river. It is thought to have been the administrative centre for a Roman military official called the *dux ripae* (see chapter 10). Dura had no theatre, although an amphitheatre had been constructed over earlier buildings by AD 216, in connection with the Roman military camp established in the northern part of the city. There were no colonnaded streets (apart from one built along the main street of the Roman camp), but one feature of the Roman

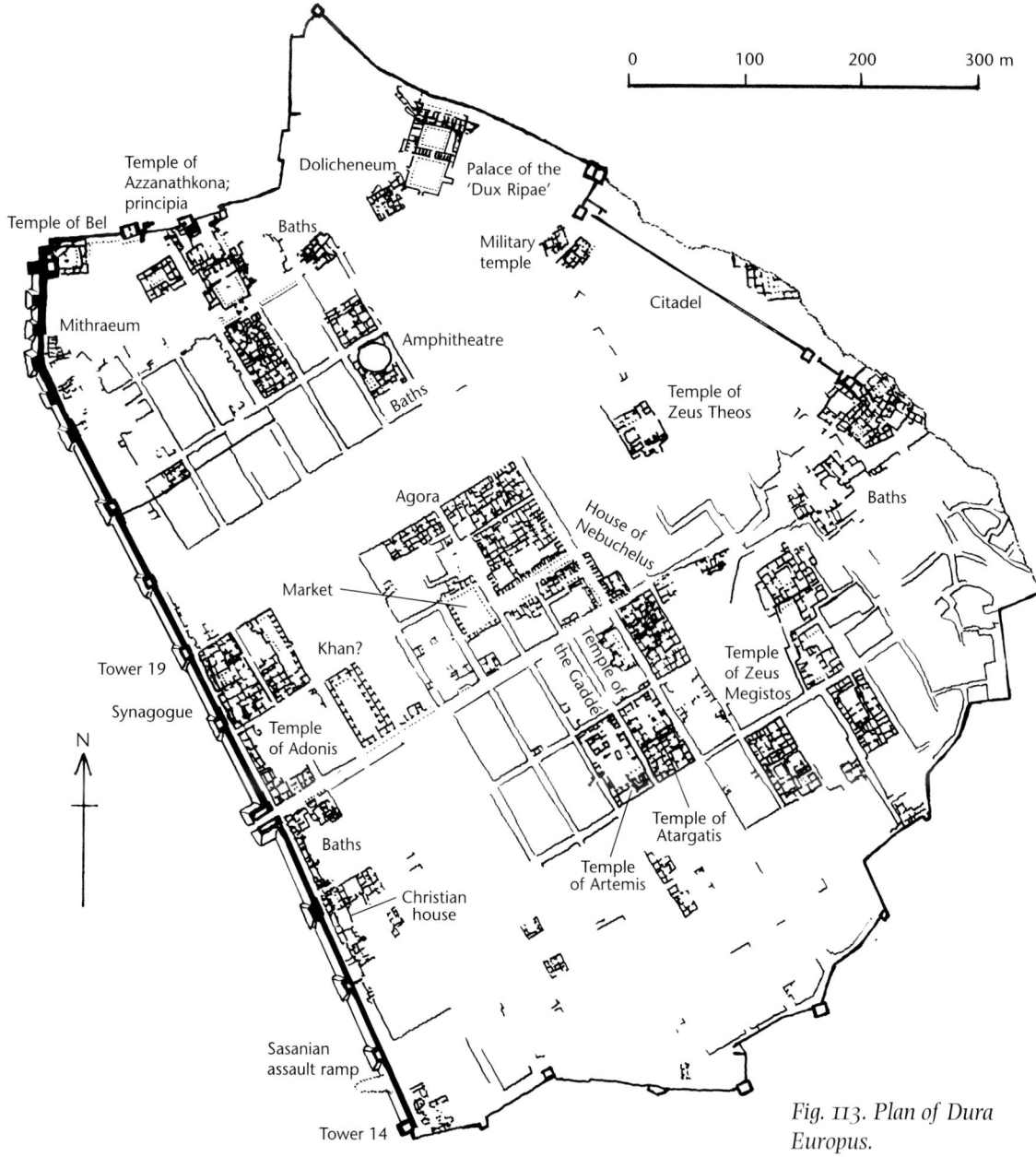

Fig. 113. Plan of Dura Europus.

period was the erection by locals of short colonnades in front of their shops or around an open market in what remained of the Seleucid agora. Occupation by Rome did not lead to the construction of major public buildings (though bath houses were a Roman addition). By the time of the Sasanian sack in *c.* AD 256 the entire city of Dura was filled with buildings, mainly houses, and there were few open spaces within its walls.

Why did Dura Europus fail to acquire monumental buildings of the sort outlined in the preceding pages? Because it was not incorporated into the Roman empire until the 160s? This was the heyday of the monumental phase elsewhere. Because it was a small commercial 'frontier' city? Because it was 'Oriental'? Something might be made of its social structure, which seems to have been rather heterogeneous. Dura had a Greek constitution, but it is possible that the councillors did not acquire the dominant role that they did elsewhere, and that the social hierarchy of the city was too fragmented for one group to achieve dominance. This was perhaps a city in which private strategies overcame the public. Without the relevant organizational capacities and a common driving force the Durenes constructed a city that served the needs of the individuals and groups within it rather than a monumental public one which exalted the ideals of a small group of highly educated councillors. In this way Dura perhaps retained the spirit and character of a Seleucid city of Syria into Roman times. The struggle for ownership of public space did not end there.

The Late Antique

Studies of the late Roman empire often draw a distinction between cities of the fourth, fifth and sixth centuries and those of the early empire. There are good reasons for doing so, because a discontinuity in civic life between the early and late Roman periods can be detected across the empire. Construction of civic monuments by local notables declined dramatically in the third century. In the eastern provinces, production of civic coinage declined and died out at about the same time. Contemporary with these developments was a disruption of long-distance trade. Some blame can be placed on the specific political and economic circumstances of the third century, but that is not the whole story. The Roman state itself seems – wittingly or unwittingly – to have contributed to a major cultural shift that eroded the old civic ideals of self-government.

Though gradual, the evolution of the Syrian cities away from the Greek model of the *polis* is difficult to trace in detail. Many factors seem relevant to the slow degradation of the old civic ideals and the emergence of new senses of community. The pace and nature of change varied from place to place, but some general explanations for the change can be advanced.

The decline of the traditional forms of civic government was an important factor in the transformation, and this process began long before the fourth century. In the second century the Roman state, mindful that competition could result in over-ambitious or superfluous projects, sought to control civic expenditure by appointing officials to oversee city finances. This may have curtailed the enthusiasms of civic elites, giving them fewer opportunities for self-advertisement. In addition there are signs that the old mode of civic finance through competition by civic elites and magistrates had become unsustainable by the later second or early third century. Providing for the cities had always been a burden on councillors, but wealthy citizens were becoming less and less enthusiastic about undertaking expensive projects, and both the poorer and some of the richer councillors now sought to escape their obligations. Certain citizens were legally exempt from holding office – in particular, senators, army veterans, civil servants and athletes – and others might try, however fraudulently, to join their ranks. Teachers and doctors were also exempt, but their number per city was limited by law. A conflict arose between the Roman authorities (who wanted the old system maintained) and the citizens (who were reluctant to hold office). The provincial governor might become involved, proposing candidates for the offices himself. The state recognized the problem, and legal rulings by emperors in the second and third centuries often increased the obligations, or changed the rules of eligibility to include people who had previously been exempt, in an attempt to maintain the fabric of civic life. When, in the early third century, a native of Byblus resident in neighbouring Berytus sought a ruling from the emperor Caracalla about his obligations, Caracalla overturned established procedure by stipulating that he was eligible in both cities. But increasing the obligations (and consequently the chances of punishment for defaulting) without increasing the honours hardly provided incentives. The onerous responsibilities of the civic elites to the empire included collecting taxes, recruiting for the army, and maintaining the roads and the public postal service. They paid for civic festivals and kept the baths running, and bought foodstuffs for the city. Building or repairing monuments still figured among the list of duties, but it was clearly an alternative that was turned to less frequently by the mid-third century. Opportunities for escape from these costly or tiresome obligations were seized upon. Imperial civil servants were exempt from their civic obligations, and many sons of the councillors went to study Roman law in centres like Berytus in order to gain entry to the civil service. This leakage of councillors from the cities was viewed as undesirable by the imperial government, which took various steps to curtail it, to the extent of introducing restrictions on their movements outside the city.

During the fourth and fifth centuries the political power of the *boule* declined in some of the major cities, as the very people who had gained exemption from their obligations – natives who had acquired senatorial rank, and imperial officials – began to exercise their influence informally. A developing system of patronage, where powerful individuals offered 'protection' to weaker groups and individuals, subverted the traditional power structure of the city. These grandees used their connections to sway governors and other powerful figures, further disrupting the framework of self-government, and the Roman state seems to have acquiesced or even encouraged this development. The state accorded the grandees more and more political rights in their home cities, but they often had no specific spheres of responsibility in civic government. Their place in the administration was informal and ill-defined, but by the later fifth and sixth centuries these informal groupings, rather than the councils, appear to have been accepted by the state as the representatives of the cities. The presence among the grandees of other dignitaries such as bishops enhanced the standing of these informal groups. Gradually the Roman state introduced new offices to replace the traditional magistracies. These functionaries were usually locals and might be chosen by the councils, but they were not responsible to the councils. Instead they looked to the provincial governors, and over time the selection of officials devolved to the grandees, the bishops and Roman administrators instead of the councillors. By the early sixth century Anastasius appears to have taken measures to deprive the city councils of some of their important functions, including the collection of taxes, leaving them with various other unrewarding obligations. Between the third and sixth centuries the city councils sank from being the driving force of civic life to being an adjunct to it.

In one sense, nothing had changed, in that civic government still rested with the wealthy, but in other significant ways it had. The number of grandees was much smaller, and these very powerful people were more resistant to state coercion than the old councils had been. Because the grandees had no specified duties or obligations, there was no requirement for them to maintain their cities in the old manner. The drive towards monumentality could be maintained as long as civic power and wealth remained with the competing elites who were investing in a communal ideal, but it seems that the late Roman grandees did not necessarily share that ideal. Wealth was more often lavished on private residences, enhancing the status and dignity of the individual, rather than the community. Although public appearances were still important, some high-ranking officials did not have to appear in public if it was thought that the occasion would impinge on their high status. There are also signs that the imperial government was beginning to find cities and their councils less crucial to the fabric of power. As the responsibilities of councils declined, new arrangements had to be found for running the cities and the raising of state revenues. For their part, the grandees who constituted the government did not need a monumental city to bolster their identity and prestige: they did their most important business out of the public eye, behind closed doors, in the reception rooms of one of the high officials.

During the early empire the cities had funded themselves by traditional means: civic liturgies; revenues from civic estates; and local taxes, customs duties, various endowments and the interest on them. The civic estates were an important source of income, and their revenues, like other civic taxes, were administered by the city council. Nevertheless emperors were concerned that cities spend their revenues in an appropriate manner, and even in the early empire permission from the emperor or provincial governor often had to be secured before undertaking important works with civic funds. In the fourth century many of these estates were appropriated by the Roman state, which claimed two thirds of the revenue from them. These revenues might be spent on the relevant cities, but control of the money lay in the hands of the state, not the city councils. Other sources of civic income were treated in the same way. This seems to be an attempt by the state to regulate civic spending more carefully by taking the matter into its own hands. It would appear that any building projects undertaken by the cities using the third of the revenue that was left still had to be approved by the provincial governor, whose priorities might differ from those of the city councillors. Governors might spend money on new buildings, but equally they might show little interest in completing a building initiated by the previous holder of their office (although completed buildings presented current governors with opportunities for self-advertisement by having their names inscribed on them, regardless of who initiated the project). Constraints of this sort no doubt circumscribed civic pretensions to monumentalize, even though money from the provincial treasury was also available for approved civic building programmes (however, there may have been a tendency for state money to be directed towards provincial capitals at the expense of other cities). In the later fifth century it was decreed that the third due to the city was to be given to its civic *curator* or 'Father of the City', one of the new classes of officials, who was appointed to administer civic finances. New regulations evolved, which specified the areas of expenditure on which various civic revenues could be spent. For example, some revenues could be used only for restoring existing structures. This fairly inflexible system gave the cities greater control over their spending without increasing the revenue. Various other attempts to supervise the collection of civic revenues were instituted in the sixth century, but these seem to have been piecemeal and it is impossible to generalize from the evidence available.

The Greek civic festivals, which had been an important element of civic pride, died out during the course of the fourth century, along with gladiatorial shows. This left mimes, pantomimes and chariot races as the main forms of entertainment. These shows tended to be concentrated in the provincial capitals and larger cities, with the provincial governor presiding. They provided the masses with an opportunity for making their grievances and feelings public, and in this way provided a sort of replacement for the old people's assembly of the *polis*. Because of the highly political nature of these assemblies, during the fifth century the Roman state took over responsibility for public entertainment, and what had formerly been a celebration of civic identity became an assertion of imperial rule. Even the few surviving great festivals, such as the games given by the Syriarch (originally the president of the imperial cult) or the Olympic Games of Antioch, were transferred to the care of imperial officials in the fifth century. All shows began with praise of God, and acclamations of the emperor, the governor and other officials, including the bishop. Complaints against emperors or officials were duly noted and sent to Constantinople. For an emperor, acclamations by the people became as important as those by the army, if not more so. The contracting organizations or factions that supplied the performers became state institutions, and their personnel became state employees. The two main organizations, named after the colours of popular circus teams, were the Blues and the Greens, and these had branches in most of the cities. In the theatres and hippodromes the two factions led the acclamations and formed the principal focus of civic politics for ordinary civilians. These factions evolved into powerful political forces in the empire, like the Church or army. They had no consistent political positions, but they could be manipulated by emperors, usurpers and grandees, and provided a potential source of opposition to established rule. Yet they could not be controlled, and were a cause of increasing civil unrest and violence during the sixth century. At the beginning of the seventh century opposition from the factions helped to bring down the emperors Maurice and Phocas. Supporters of the Blues in one city felt identity with Blues supporters in the other cities, creating empire-wide allegiance to the faction rather than a sense of identity with a *polis*. This does not mean, however, that individuals no longer identified with their cities, but the factions were important institutions competing with civic allegiances.

Physical evidence for the transformation is easy to find. Monumental centres remained, and were repaired, remodelled, or built anew, but most investment was spent on city walls, roads and churches, and occasionally on colonnaded streets. Baths and aqueducts were maintained and sometimes new ones were constructed. Donations of public buildings by wealthy individuals were not unknown, but increasingly the church came to benefit at the expense of the city. Individuals sought to win the approbation of heaven, surrounded as they

Fig. 114. The hippodrome at Tyre. A building adjacent to it on the western side contained a bath and belonged to the Blue faction; it may have been a 'club' house. Another similar building on the eastern side is thought to have belonged to the Greens.

Fig. 115. Late Roman reuse of civic space: a public latrine, blocking the monumental entrance to the agora of Apamea. Communal seating once ran around the walls, above the channel which carried away waste.

were by evidence that not even the greatest monuments could assure the benefactor a permanent place in the memory of the community. Some of the old monuments and public spaces became irrelevant, and were put to entirely different uses (fig. 115). Theatres and hippodromes often remained important, and some of the new cities of the period had theatres (for instance, Elusa), but council chambers and agoras might go out of use, and Christianity encouraged the abandonment and sometimes the destruction of temples.

Even the remodelling and reworking of public monuments suggest a discontinuity in collective memory between the monumental public city of the early empire and the late Roman city. Superfluous features were pulled apart and used to repair public and private buildings. At Apamea memory of the second-century benefactor Lucius Julius Agrippa was dishonoured in late Roman times when the inscription describing his benefactions was re-employed as a lintel for a window in the wall of his portico. The same went for another dedication to Julius Agrippa, the base of which was found reused as a kerb stone in the *cardo*, following repairs to the stylobate at an uncertain date. The monument donated by the benefactor might prove 'more lasting than bronze', as Horace put it in his epitaph to his third book of *Odes*, but there was clearly no guarantee that posterity would remember the builder, who had not reckoned on a future change in society.

Private spaces within the city became more monumental as wealthy elites invested in sumptuous town houses. Eloquent testimony to this trend was unearthed in Berytus, where from the fourth century large residences with *opus sectile* and mosaic floors began to replace the smaller dwellings and workshops of earlier times. Equally striking is the use of mosaic pavement for public spaces (which might be inscribed with the name of the donor), as if décor once appropriate to interiors were appropriating the streets. Private interests began to encroach on public spaces, particularly in the second half of the sixth century and beginning of the seventh, suggesting no formal control of the civic form and an abandonment of the classical ideal. Even public structures began to deform the earlier schemes. In the later sixth century a church was built in Apamea's *cardo*. At Scythopolis old colonnades came to be occupied by small shops and workshops. In some cities abandoned areas were converted into gardens and began to take on a rural aspect. All cities and their monuments suffer decay, but without formal instructions for upkeep or interventions by an organized civic authority or the imperial government, inhabitants found their own solutions. Regional diversity began to emerge once more from behind the homogeneous monumental façade of the Graeco-Roman city.

The mid-sixth century seems to have been a turning point. The literary sources show the late antique cities of the east as centres of Hellenism during the fifth and early sixth centuries, but it is unclear whether a formal Greek education continued to be highly desired among the elites after the mid-sixth century (see p. 276). Whether the cities 'declined', in that the populations decreased, before *c.* 600, is still debated, and it is difficult to find criteria by which one can effectively detect decline. Dated inscriptions show many buildings being erected between the later fifth and mid-sixth century, followed by fewer buildings in the second half of the sixth century. Nevertheless there is some evidence of new public buildings, and reconstruction work following earthquakes or Persian sackings, during this period. None of this, however, is an accurate gauge of urban growth or decline. In northern Syria the combined catastrophes of plagues, earthquakes, Persian invasions and mass deportations of populations are possible factors contributing to decline there, but the south was less heavily affected by some of the disasters that occurred during the course of the sixth century. In spite of this, similar patterns of urban change are found there too. At Gerasa rural-style houses came to occupy parts of the city, suggesting a dwindling population. Small buildings were constructed in the great oval piazza, and the city's hippodrome was reduced in size and the abandoned sections were given over to habitations and other private uses, before the area was deserted altogether *c.* 550.

Cities that developed in late Roman times may give us a better idea of those things society considered essential than the old urban centres, whose landscapes and points of reference were still partly dictated by the decaying monuments of the past. In north-eastern Syria, where some of the best surviving examples of late cities or large settlements may be found, the emphasis is clearly on fortifications. This accords with the account of the historian Procopius, whose work *On the Buildings* describes many of the cities and fortifications of the region, attributing them to Justinian. Procopius' attribution of so many projects to Justinian needs to be read with some scepticism, and archaeological studies indicate that instead it is earlier emperors like Theodosius II, Leo I and Anastasius who deserve the credit for many late Roman city walls in Syria.

Sergiopolis (Resafa), a major centre of annual pilgrimage for many Syrians, became a city in 431. It owed its fame to the tomb of the local Christian martyr

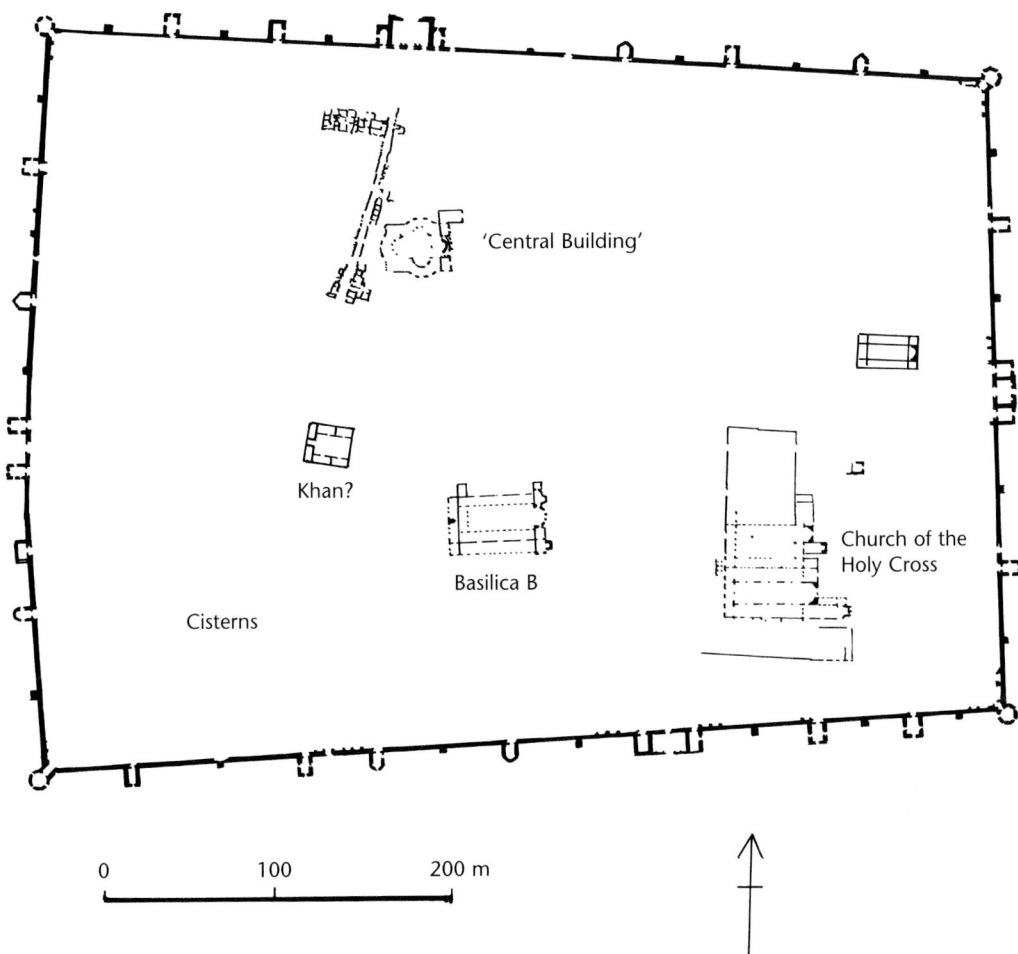

'Central Building'

Khan?

Basilica B

Church of the
Holy Cross

Cisterns

0   100   200 m

Fig. 116. Plan of the walls of Sergiopolis (Resafa).

Sergius, executed during Diocletian's reign. Where once there had been a fort for auxiliary cavalrymen a fortified city now developed. Procopius states that Resafa's walls were of mud brick until the reign of Justinian, but this claim seems improbable. The city had been renamed Anastasiopolis in honour of one of Justinian's imperial predecessors, and it is likely that Anastasius was responsible for a part, if not all, of the defences, which perhaps replaced some earlier, less substantial structure. The walls were constructed of gypsum and preserve an extraordinary array of towers: circular, rectangular, pentagonal and horse-shoe-shaped (fig. 116). They followed a slightly irregular rectangular plan of about 550 by 400 metres (600 by 437 yards), and arcaded galleries ran along their interior, supporting a walkway along the parapet. There were four gates, each located along one of the four sides, but these do not appear to have linked axial main streets. The northern gate led on to a paved street (without colonnades), but the corresponding gate in the southern wall was offset from this, lying further to the east. Deep, vaulted underground cisterns occupied the south-western corner of the city (fig. 61). There are two large basilical churches. The smaller of the two was probably built in the late fifth century, but was subsequently extended to accommodate increasing numbers of pilgrims. It may have housed the remains of the city's patron saint. The larger basilical church, which stands in the south-eastern corner of the city, was dedicated to the Holy Cross in the reign of Justinian (colour plate 27). There is also a smaller tetraconch church, similar in plan to those at Seleucia, Apamea and Bostra, which is thought to have been a martyrium to which St Sergius' remains were transferred following an earthquake which damaged the smaller basilica. The city became an important centre for the Ghassanids and, after the Muslim conquest, it was patronized by the Umayyad Caliph Hisham, who was buried in the city.

The nearby fortress of Zenobia (Halebiye), situated at the southern end of a gorge on the Euphrates, probably became a city in the sixth century, although it rarely receives mention in the sources. The settlement is thought to have been located at the site of an earlier Palmyrene fortress, and received its name from the Palmyrene queen. Although there are a few typically Palmyrene tower-tombs to the north and south, what survives of the fortress is all late Roman. It was roughly triangular in shape – 385 by 550 metres (421 by 600 yards) – with its massive gypsum defences rising to a point on a high citadel; a three-storey structure identified as a guard house or *praetorium* stands just below the citadel in the northern section of the defensive circuit. These impressive fortifications are likely to belong substantially to the reign of Justinian. There was apparently an elaborate breakwater along the river, but this has been lost. Zenobia's streets conformed to a grid pattern where the terrain permitted, and had an axial main *cardo* and *decumanus* meeting in a tetrapylon. There are traces of

Fig. 117. The walls of Zenobia, seen from the citadel, with the Euphrates beyond.

short colonnaded porticos, an open square identified as a forum, a large bath building containing a palaestra, and a suite of buildings identified as an episcopal complex. Thus the monuments of Zenobia lent it the appearance of one of the great cities of earlier times, and in many respects it was more monumental than its more important neighbour and *metropolis*, Sergiopolis. In spite of its buildings and bishop, some scholars have suggested that Zenobia never achieved full city status. The archaeological evidence seems to refute this, but if so, it would suggest that the physical distinction between settlements with and without civic status was even more blurred in late Roman times than it had been previously, and that the icons of civic form – walls, axial streets and so on – were no longer the preserve of places legally constituted as cities.

The end of the ancient city in Syria and the Near East cannot be attributed to the Muslim conquest. The cities had already changed by the first half of the seventh century. Change was brought about from within, as the Roman state tried to regulate the political structure on which it relied so heavily for the collection of tribute and the maintenance of order. The councillors once provided the dynamic for the *polis*, and emperors still regarded it as the duty of councillors to provide for their cities, but their influence in civic affairs was increasingly overtaken by others whose responsibilities were less clearly defined. The imperial government found an alternative to councils in the wealthiest and most socially prominent residents, who might be persuaded to step in and assist in the running of their cities. But while the role of the grandees has been seen as an important factor in the revitalization of cities observed in the second half of the fifth century and running into the first half of the sixth, the very power of these individuals could constitute a challenge to imperial control. Furthermore, certain cities prospered or developed in the fifth and sixth centuries for reasons that had little to do with the old pecking-order of provincial cities. The presence of Christian shrines was sometimes a factor. Sites in Palestine received imperial support and benefactions because of their religious significance. The tendency to divide up the provinces into smaller units led to more cities gaining prominence as administrative centres. Provincial governors controlled much of what remained of civic finances and were often generous to the cities in which they resided. But the idea of controlled, monumental spaces gave way to what might be termed the anarchy of user sovereignty, just as the relationship between power and public performance or activity was severed when civic government passed to the grandees who operated out of the public eye. By the time of the Muslim conquest the classical city was already dead.

The excess of visibility generated by the classical moment of the Graeco-Roman city was the product of a climate peculiar to the Roman empire, in which the ideals of the Greek *polis* and the needs of the Roman government converged. Its manifestation in Syria was particularly spectacular, and is a demonstration of how useful Greek ideals were to the rule of both the local elites and Rome. As we will see, those ideals spilled over into other areas of social life as well.

8 IMPURE GENRES

The social importance of Greek language and culture in Syria and the Near East during the period of Roman rule is undeniable. Although the greater part of the population of the Syrian region did not originate from Greece or Asia Minor, the majority of inscriptions are in Greek, mosaics and frescoes depict scenes from Greek myths, and writers from the area generally wrote in Greek on subjects which were common to the intellectual *milieu* of the empire. Greek culture, expressed in a wide variety of ways (communal life within a *polis*, literature, monumental architecture and inscriptions, religious imagery), is encountered practically everywhere. Under Rome, Syria became part of a broader Greek world. The extent to which this was the consequence of Syrians voluntarily adopting Hellenism rather than the wilful imposition of Greek culture by Rome is debated. The process of Hellenization had begun under the Seleucids and Ptolemies, but Rome's use of the Greek *polis* as a tool for domination is likely to have had a profound effect as collective identities were reorganized around the new structures. The success of Roman rule depended on the degree of assimilation of local elites, and most elites adopted a strategy of collaboration with the imperial power. In the eastern empire the culture of assimilation was Greek, so in one sense becoming Hellenized was a way of becoming Romanized for these people. A cultural heritage based on the myths and literature of Greece was a loosely binding force providing the eastern empire with a common identity and symbolism.

Yet when we turn to the material culture, not everything that we find is recognizably Graeco-Roman. The portraits of deceased Palmyrenes (fig. 118) contain numerous non-Greek elements, including short inscriptions in Palmyrene. Why did they choose to depict themselves in this way? With what culture or cultures did they identify? Which language was their mother tongue? Would they have described themselves as Syrians, Arabs, or just Palmyrenes? Or would they have considered themselves as Greek as people in Ephesus or Athens?

Some of these questions can be answered, albeit tentatively. It was possible for individuals from different cities to identify themselves as Syrian, as the funerary epitaphs of people from places as diverse as Ascalon and Nisibis demonstrate, but whether the term had any precise cultural meaning is less

Fig. 118. Palmyrene funerary portrait, inscribed 'Aqmat, daughter of Hagagu, descendant of Zebida, descendant of Ma'an. Alas!' She wears a cloak as a veil over her headdress. Late second century AD.

clear. Although Greek and Roman writers could describe certain people and their habits as 'Syrian', it is difficult for us to discern whether this means there was any universal 'Syrian' or 'oriental' culture. Strabo defined the Syrians by geography, as those 'who extend as far as the Cilicians and the Phoenicians and the Judaeans and the sea that is opposite the Aegyptian Sea and the Gulf of Issus'.[37] However, there ought to have been something characteristic of 'Syrians' other than geography for non-Syrians to ascribe this identity to them, even if Syrians did not consider themselves to share a common identity. Ascriptions by 'outsiders' are not without consequence, particularly if they are negative. In Roman literature Syrians and Syria were sometimes identified as a malignant or corrupting influence over the virtuous. Antioch, with its sundry pleasures, was frequently blamed for ruining the morals and sapping the energy of soldiers stationed there. Tacitus' description of the death of Germanicus has a sinister Syrian setting, and Juvenal's picture of Syrians as bawdy musicians and prostitutes suggests stereotypical ascription at work among the literate classes in late first- and early second-century Rome. For outsiders there were clearly ways of identifying 'Syrians', but we cannot say what the criteria were, just as insiders could use the term of themselves, but we do not know why they chose to do so.

Further uncertainty is furnished by the fact that the term 'Syrian' seems to have been interchangeable with 'Assyrian', and the two were used to describe people living on both sides of the Euphrates river, in both Mesopotamia and Syria proper. In the fifth century BC Herodotus could make a distinction between the two, but other writers did not. Lucian of Samosata (second century AD) refers to himself alternately as 'Syrian' or 'Assyrian', Philostratus (early third century AD) could call Antiochenes 'Assyrian', and the geographer Strabo associated what he knew of the Neo-Assyrian empire with 'the Syrians'. He also reminds his readers that 'Syrian' could be used in a specific sense, in terms of the geography outlined above, and in a more general sense, meaning peoples in Mesopotamia and Cappadocia as well. This seemingly indiscriminate use of the two terms would appear to emphasize both the vagueness of a general Syrian identity as well as confirming the cultural and ethnic links between what the second-century historian Appian called 'Syria this side of the Euphrates' and another Syria to the east of the same river. But the possibility that 'Syrian' had specific meaning(s) cannot simply be brushed aside.

Equally problematic is the term 'Arab', which often seems to have been used to mean 'nomad'. Whether it also meant that the people in question were speakers of Arabic is not at all certain, though the use of personal and topographical names which have close affinities with Arabic in regions identified as 'Arab' may provide a clue. The rulers of Hatra in Parthian Mesopotamia were called 'king of 'Arab' or 'king of the Arabs', and Greek sources sometimes refer rather vaguely to the region as 'Arabia'. The title may simply refer to the lifestyle of the majority of the peoples over whom the Hatrene kings ruled, but that does not preclude a more profound ethnic, linguistic or cultural interpretation of 'Arab', where the rulers considered themselves to be Arabs. However, Hatra lies outside our region. At Palmyra and in its territory there are many Arabic personal names in the inscriptions, even though place-names are Aramaic or Greek, as are the languages used for the inscriptions. The deities worshipped in Palmyrene territory and in the city include several thought to be typically Arab. It is presumed that there were large numbers of Arabic speakers among the population of Palmyra and its hinterland, but that this language was not a written one. The Palmyrenes did not call themselves Arabs; like all good citizens of a *polis*, they were known collectively by the ethnic of their city, as *Palmyrenoi*. A similar situation may have prevailed among the Nabataeans. They wrote in Aramaic, but they are thought to have spoken Arabic. While there is no clear evidence that they called themselves Arabs, after the dissolution of the kingdom Nabataea became the Roman province of Arabia; perhaps, like the region around Hatra, because of the lifestyle of many of its people, but perhaps also because the inhabitants identified with the term. At its vaguest, the term 'Arab' was perhaps a term like 'farmer' or 'merchant', indicating the manner in which the people lived, rather than an ethnic and linguistic ascription, but it is worth recalling that folk taxonomies often revolve around ascription of a particular occupation or lifestyle to an ethnic group. And it was possible for someone to identify himself or herself as an Arab together with their *polis*, as in an epitaph erected on the Aegean island of Thasos by a man who identified himself as an 'Arab' from Canatha. As with the term Syrian, there seems to have been no one context for the use of 'Arab' in the Roman world, and consequently its meaning or meanings are difficult for us to divine.

Ancient writers often defined peoples by objective criteria: language, dress and customs and, normally, the assumption that a people could be associated with a particular space or territory. In this way they came close to some modern conceptions of 'ethnicity'. This approach also allowed ancient writers to chart the survival or disappearance of peoples over time. A similar approach to culture has sometimes been used in modern times, assessing cultures and identities in terms of whether they fulfil a sort of 'shopping list' of criteria, but there are so many ways of thinking of culture and identity that we might wonder what purposes are served by conceiving of them in this limited fashion. People find varied ways of making themselves different: through language, dress, religion, art and architecture, use of domestic space, death rituals, landscape, food and traditions of dining, and attitudes to 'dirty' and 'clean' activities (to name some of the more prominent), so that no one set of criteria is likely to prove a general tool for analysis. The institutions through which identities are organized might be termed 'cultures', but individuals can belong to more than one institution (religion, city state, guild and so on) and thus can identify with more than one set of codes and symbols (on this, see below).

The three principal geographical zones of Syria and the Near East – the densely populated coastal regions, the more sparsely settled interior beyond the mountain ranges, and the steppe and desert – correspond roughly with the three zones of material culture. It is not hard to see why this should be so. The coastal region, where contacts and imports were easiest, is the most Hellenized, sharing much of its material culture with neighbouring regions of the east Mediterranean littoral. The second zone shares many forms with the first, but local styles and genres are more prominent. The presence of the Roman military also seems to have a stronger impact on the cultures of the interior. Finally, in the steppe and desert zone, the material culture retains many Graeco-Roman traits but also looks east, extending beyond the frontier of the Roman empire.

HELLENISM AS A SOURCE OF SOCIAL POWER

Greek cultural imperialism was already evident in the Hellenistic period, with the renaming of cities and Greek appropriation of other people's histories. (The Jewish historian Josephus wrote in the first century AD that the Greeks were able 'to make even the glory of the past their own'.)[38] Under Rome this process of reconfiguring memory to suit Greek tastes continued, and many manifestations of local culture appear to have been subsumed, although some cultures, most notably the Jewish, were maintained through varying degrees of resistance.

Just as the *polis* was a crucial element in the organization of administrative power in Roman Syria, so Greek culture was crucial to social power. Deprived of independent *political* expression by Rome, the elites turned to Hellenism as an expression of *cultural* independence. This was partly expressed by the civic institutions and buildings discussed in the preceding chapter, but Greek culture was also a highly literary one. From approximately the mid-first century AD to the mid-third century, the educated elites found a way of creating a common culture for themselves and at the same time distancing themselves culturally from the masses, who spoke either uneducated Greek or Semitic languages. The name given to this cultural movement or institution, which became a unifying force among Greek-speaking elites in the Roman empire, is the Second Sophistic. The term was coined by Philostratus (*c.* AD 170-249), one of its greatest proponents. The Second Sophistic tried to imitate the literary standard of Athens in the fifth and fourth centuries BC. To speak and write Atticizing Greek required a lengthy education, which ensured that only the elites could participate in the movement, and speakers of languages other than Atticizing Greek were excluded as inferiors. It was a kind of cultural club open to all who could demonstrate their *paideia*, their 'education' or 'culture', which necessarily meant Greek education and culture, particularly training in classical literature and morals. Elites of non-Greek origin could participate, as long as they adhered to the social and cultural norms of the movement, and the less well-educated could aspire to share its values. Even though they lived in the Roman empire, these elites looked to the Greek past for their cultural and intellectual life. It was a means of preserving a special identity in a world dominated by Rome. Because it was a way of life, the movement was highly influential on other forms of art apart from literature, as we will see.

The Second Sophistic cannot be considered anti-Roman, because Greek culture was highly regarded by the centre of power. The movement profited from Philhellene emperors and flourished in the prosperous environment of the empire in the late first and second centuries. Atticizing Greek was used in a variety of elite activities, from civic laws and decrees to literary, technical and philosophical works, and to public speaking, where one's performance would be judged by one's peers. Rhetoric was extremely important, not only for display of one's learning, but because the best speakers would be sent on embassies to governors or emperors where, if their performances proved suitably impressive, they could win honours and benefits for themselves and their cities. Eloquent speakers could hope to tour cities, giving speeches, for which they were rewarded with money (the second-century Syrian novelist Iamblichus, author of *A Babylonian Story*, is supposed to have gained his *paideia* for the purpose of making a living). They might win privileges such as citizenship of other cities, and could hope to enter the service of powerful Roman officials or even the emperors. At home, the sense of cultural superiority helped elites maintain administrative and economic power over the cities. Although they looked to the past as a source of authority and inspiration, the Second Sophistic's proponents were concerned mainly with preserving their cultural and political hegemony, not with conjuring up a pre-Roman fantasy world.

The colonial movement of the Hellenistic period gave many Syrian cities a legitimate Greek past, though this might not be as 'pure' as the histories of cities in Asia Minor or Greece itself. Even so, it was not only the highly Hellenized cities of the coastal regions that produced writers of the Second Sophistic. Samosata in Commagene was the home of the essayist Lucian, and two novelists are associated with Emesa: Iamblichus, mentioned above, and Heliodorus, author of *An Ethiopian Story*. Greek ancestry was not as important as Greek education. Nevertheless the Greek-speaking elites of these non-Greek cities might labour under the stigma of barbarism in the eyes of 'purer' Greeks. There are hints in his writings that Lucian, although very learned, may have failed to satisfy the highly sophisticated Greeks of Asia Minor and Greece itself, and instead found fame and fortune in the western, Latin-speaking half of the empire, particularly in Gaul. There are enough bitter statements in his satirical writings to suggest that his Syrian background was an impediment in 'old' Greece, and that his performance was not quite sufficient for his peers there to recognize him fully as one of their own. Philostratus snobbishly stated that he felt like laughing when Caracalla honoured an 'Arab', Heliodorus (who may be the novelist of that name).[39]

Hellenism can hardly be regarded as a superficial 'veneer' disguising a native substratum. It dominated the elite system of values, at least from the mid-first century AD onwards, and was an identity elites could adopt among peers and social inferiors. Hellenism's most prominent manifestations – civic architecture and coinage, and literary works – are all examples of elite culture. That the elites identified with the dominant culture of the empire should not surprise us, given the importance of status in the formation of identity. Studies of encounters between other imperial powers and local elites have shown how co-operative elites commonly adopt the traits of the external authority, sometimes leaving the majority, the 'subdominant' or 'subordinate' group, culturally or ethnically invisible. Here, however, it was ancient cultural authority of Greece rather than the contemporary political dominance of Rome that provided the inspiration.

Some scholars have suggested an even more aggressive policy on the part of Rome itself, involving the active suppression of native cultural institutions in favour of civic Hellenism. In northern Syria, the most Hellenized region, Greek is always the dominant language in the Roman period, perhaps suggesting that any suppression will have occurred in Hellenistic times, but in the south we can see cultural and linguistic changes taking place during the Roman era, and these do indeed coincide with significant political changes. The Babatha archive covers the transition from the Nabataean kingdom to the Roman province of Arabia. This shows that Nabataean was the dominant language until the Roman annexation, and thereafter the dominant language was Greek (although a number of the post-annexation documents are in Aramaic). In Judaea the papyrus documents show that Aramaic remained in common use in Judaea down to the end of the Bar Kokhba war, but thereafter Greek becomes predominant in what was the new province of Syria Palaestina. At Palmyra the deliberate use of Aramaic script for monumental inscriptions in a Hellenizing civic environment was a distinct cultural practice that remained vigorous right down to the fall of the city to Aurelian in 272. A few documents can be dated to the period immediately after the fall, but within a generation everything that was distinctive about Palmyrene civic culture seems to have vanished. There is something to be said for the view that this was the result of deliberate suppression and the 'political imposition of Hellenism', rather than evidence for the frail nature of Palmyrene culture.[40] After centuries of Palmyrene control on behalf of Rome, the steppe now came to be occupied by regular Roman troops, and Semitic inscriptions in the steppe, in Palmyrene, Safaitic and the Thamudic scripts of northern Arabia, all appear to decline and disappear following Palmyra's defeat.

The case of Judaea in the first and second centuries, where we have an unusually full record, illustrates some of the complex tensions that might be produced when imperial Hellenism met a local non-Greek culture. The Greek cities had welcomed Pompey as a liberator from Hasmonaean rule, and the Romans had generally supported the development of *poleis* in the region. The positions taken within Jewish society with regard to Hellenism varied greatly, and it was difficult in the context of the Roman empire to avoid or reject it altogether without opposing Roman rule. The distinction was in large part class-based, with the wealthier Jews tending to be more receptive to Hellenism. Herod was a great Hellenizer and founder of cities (although Greek cities also petitioned the emperor for their right to freedom and autonomy from the kingdom). He instituted Greek festivals, in which Hellenized Jews competed, but at the same time other Jews sought to maintain clearer cultural boundaries by criticizing or rejecting various aspects of Hellenism, which sometimes brought them into conflict with the authorities. The problems in first-century Judaea cannot be reduced to the simple opposition of Judaism and Hellenism, but imperial support for Hellenizing elements of the population, and Greek support for Rome, exacerbated the situation. In Caesarea under Nero a debate over sovereignty led to rioting, the Jews claiming the city was Jewish because the founder was a Jew, and the pagans pointing to its Greek pagan monuments as evidence that it belonged to them. The Hellenizing Nero ruled in favour of the pagans, which led to further rioting which preceded the Jewish revolt. Hostilities between Jews and gentiles spread, leading to wholesale massacres. In the Jewish revolt the groups opposed to Graeco-Roman influence created an independent Jewish state, minting coins with Palaeo-Hebrew inscriptions and non-Greek designs (fig. 181.1), and using their own era. Their successes against the Roman state encouraged most of the Jewish elites to throw in their lot with the rebels, although the *polis* of Sepphoris, whose population appears to have been mainly Jewish, opposed the revolt, issuing coins calling itself Irenopolis ('Peace-city') Neronias Sepphoris, leaving no doubt about where its sympathies lay. The Roman destruction of the Temple, the focus of Jewish worship, and the transfer of the Temple-tax to Capitoline Jupiter, was a manifest act of physical and symbolic violence on the part of the state against the Jewish faith. Galilee then became the centre of Judaism, but during the second century its main cities, Sepphoris and Tiberias, issued Greek coins with Hellenized pagan images. In the opposition between the heavily Hellenized cities and a predominantly Jewish countryside during the first centuries BC and AD we appear to have a classic case of dominance and resistance, but the interplay and conflicts between Hellenism, Roman imperialism, Judaism and local paganism were extremely complex. On the positive side, aspects of Jewish culture and religion could be expressed in terms comprehensible to Hellenism, and Greek literature could influence Jewish. The great first-century historian Josephus used Greek to describe Jewish history and culture to an educated, non-Jewish audience. The wall paintings of the third-century synagogue at Dura Europus are an interesting blend of Judaism and Hellenism, as are the mosaics from several late Roman synagogues (see below). But we might wonder how strong Greek influence in Judaism would have been if Judaea and Palestine had not been part of the Roman empire.

Consequently it is difficult to disentangle the adoption of Greek cultural traits from Hellenistic and Roman imperialism. However, some see Hellenism as a more deep-seated cultural force, which bound peoples of diverse origins together, even in late Roman times, after many of the traditional expressions of Hellenism (Greek cultural festivals, monumental buildings) had declined or disappeared. Greek elite culture was closely connected with pagan cult, so that by the fourth century Hellenism had come to be equated with pagan beliefs, and because of this there was much less imperial support for Greek cultural and intellectual life in a Christian empire. Greek-speaking Christian inhabitants of the empire came to call themselves *Rhomaioi* rather than Hellenes. In spite of this, a literary education and reference to pagan myths remained the mark of a cultured person in Christian times and, because the church did not offer a schooling in grammar and rhetoric, elite education was still provided by 'Hellenes'. The mosaics of Medaba, mostly of the sixth century, include images of Aphrodite and Adonis, Achilles and Heracles, and a procession of Dionysiac revellers, and the sixth-century mosaics from Sarrîn in Osrhoene in Mesopotamia depict figures from Greek myths. Such images could perhaps be read as allegories for Christian themes and morals (descriptions of paintings and sculpture had long been used to illustrate moral virtues), and pagan imagery could be deployed in public speech by learned Christians, evidently divested of any religious meaning. In his World Chronicle the sixth-century Antiochene writer John Malalas set himself the task of integrating Biblical events, Greek myth and Persian, Greek and Roman history into a continuous narrative, where Greek myth was reinterpreted and incorporated into a new, 'Byzantine' view of the past. Hellenism could provide a symbolic framework in early and late Roman times, bonding diverse elements of Syrian culture together, and allowing Syrians of different backgrounds to recognize and interpret those facets of culture which were not their own, but this symbolic framework was largely constructed in the service of power. When Roman rule came to an end in the seventh century, the loss of most of these Greek cultural traits was rapid, as the inhabitants aligned with different symbols of power. Indeed, there are signs that Hellenism was already in decline within the Roman world by the later sixth century, as Justinian and his successors introduced more and more laws against paganism, including forbidding 'Hellenes' to teach.

The benefits of a classical education are summed up in the figurative panel of an early fourth-century mosaic from Philippopolis: the personification of Euteknia (Having Fair Children) seated between Philosophia and Dikaiosyne (Righteousness). If you wanted your children to count among the beautiful people of the Roman east, you had to give them the right sort of education. The message was perhaps all the more significant here, at the northern edge of the Hauran, not far from the eastern steppe and desert where nomads had once taught themselves a south Arabian script and scribbled graffiti on rocks to pass the time (see below), seemingly oblivious of the high culture of Hellenism.

IN SEARCH OF SYRIANS AND NEAR EASTERNERS

A criticism of the interest in Hellenism is that it tends, by concentrating on literature and texts, to privilege aristocratic high culture and its traditions over the 'people without history'. In the elite environment of the early empire the people without history are indeed difficult to see, except when they are mentioned in passing or when they excited the attention of those engaged in brief characterizations of peoples and places. But people without history are not people without culture, unless we claim that their cultures were comprehensively obliterated by Hellenism. What sort of Hellenism, if any, might we credit to the people living in Mesopotamia and by the Euphrates, identified by Strabo as 'Arabian *Skenitai* (tent-dwellers), who are separated into small dynasties in places barren through their waterlessness, who cultivate either not at all or little, and are nomads having all sorts of livestock, especially camels'?[41] What traditions did they have, and what past(s) did they look to? Strabo's description is of a non-agrarian culture very different from his own, and which perhaps looked more to the east, to Mesopotamia, and south, towards the Arabian peninsula, than to the Mediterranean world. And was the public use of a Semitic language at Palmyra, and non-Greek modes of dress there, merely a veneer for an otherwise thoroughly Hellenized civic culture, or do these speak to us of a profound, non-Greek consciousness? In late antiquity a stratum of lower-class speakers of Semitic languages becomes more visible, and Christianity seems to have given country folk and non-Greek speakers a chance of social advancement which Hellenism had denied them. Various figures, even including a few bishops, were non-Greek speakers, or at least they preferred not to be seen speaking Greek. Does this fact vindicate the view that Hellenism was inextricably linked with social elitism?

The criticism that much of the evidence privileges high culture is partly true, but not wholly accurate. The Greek language and Greek cultural forms and practices penetrated beyond the high culture of the cities into rural environments as well, and in such places it is difficult to assert that in every case we are looking at the activities of an educated elite. In many instances we may be looking at cultural choices made by individuals within a Hellenizing framework of power relations, with cities acting as a focus for a corporate, Hellenized identity, but that is rather hard to argue in the case of personal letters in Greek, such as those from the Euphrates archive. The spread of cultural conformity among the elites of the Syrian region could affect the masses. However, resistance to Hellenism might be implied by the continued use of Semitic names for villages, and the persistent identification of villagers with these villages (chapter 5). But if Greek became the common language of inscriptions in the villages and at rural religious sites, does this imply a fuller and deep Hellenization of the rural populations, and the successful imposition of a dominant culture and identity at the expense of others? It is very difficult to answer such important questions, given the current limited state of the evidence.

The population of the Roman Near East was predominantly Semitic. The descendants of Macedonian settlers and other Greeks who colonized Syria are likely to have formed an important component of the ruling class in certain cities, but not in the cities which were constituted under Roman rule. In the case of Dura Europus, a Seleucid foundation, the late second-century AD annexation of the city to the Roman empire may even have changed the demographic composition of the ruling class of the city in favour of Semitic people, although it may not have affected the Hellenized nature of the corporate governing body itself. Documents show that under Parthian rule the city was controlled by a Greek-style civic elite with Greek or Macedonian names, who styled themselves *Europaioi* (Europaeans). Following the Roman annexation, and with the presence in the city of Roman soldiers, the Semitic name for the settlement, Doura ('Fortress'), starts to appear in documents, and people with Semitic names appear among the civic elite of *Europaioi*. The fact that we cannot be certain what this change means, whether it was encouraged by Rome, or whether it signifies the assertion of local culture detectable in other parts of the Euphrates region during the later second and early third centuries, illustrates some of the difficulties encountered while searching for Hellenizing and non-Hellenizing influences.

The evidence for non-Greek cultural traits varies from region to region, and across time. The north-west was highly Hellenized, and there is little evidence of any distinctive non-Greek traits there in the early empire. Some sort of communal identity among the Commagenians of the first three centuries AD might be implied by the use of the Greek term 'of the Commagenians' on royal and later civic coins of the region, but it in far from clear whether this identity was expressed in any other ways, still less that there was a distinct Commagenian culture. Across the Euphrates in Mesopotamia there are stronger indications of non-Greek cultures and identities, and in the writings of Lucian there are hints that people from the other side of the river really were 'barbarian' for most Greek-speaking elites of the Roman world. The material culture of Palmyra mixed Mesopotamian, local and Greek more visibly than some other cities. In the south Hellenism seems to have been weaker than it was in the north, at least until the second century AD. The Decapolis cities provided a Hellenized environment in the south, but even there other expressions of identity have been detected. The patterns change through the centuries. Attempts by some communities to recollect an ethnic or non-Greek cultural past could be survivals, or revivals, or even inventions, but often the nature of the evidence does not allow us to be sure. For reasons that are not at all clear, coins of the small city of Caesarea ad Libanum, at the northern edge of the Lebanon mountains, chose to identify the city with its Ituraean past, even after it became a Roman colony in the third century AD. The continuity or revival of a Phoenician identity, for which there is more evidence, will be examined below.

Any search for Syrian and Near Eastern cultures runs up against the more general problem of defining what culture is, how identities are formed, and what we intend by terms like 'Hellenization', 'Graeco-Roman' and 'non-Greek' (which imply meaning through the deployment of specific styles or languages). Are cultures to be regarded as mutually exclusive collectives, each defined by unique sets of traits, or are they muddled, 'impure' genres? We tend to celebrate cultural integrity and difference, rather than undifferentiated hybrids, but cultures often refuse to be pigeonholed so easily. Identity and culture are clearly not the same thing, so being able to distinguish one does not necessarily reveal the other. People may identify themselves with more than one culture. The individuals that constitute a particular community may assume many different identities, cultural, political, social and ethnic, even to the point of contradiction. They commonly belong to more than one institutional or corporate body (for example, city, tribe, cult). Inscriptions and literary texts include statements by individuals about their identity, but much of this evidence does not lend itself to any coherent analysis. Self-ascriptions or self-categorizations are acts of legitimation within a specific context, which means that statements of identity by a single individual can vary depending on the situation. Thus the self-ascription of an individual cannot be taken at face value; the context must also be recovered and understood. Without their contexts subjective statements of this sort are poor raw materials for objective analysis. Also we must never underestimate the role of authority in constructing identity. Imposing common ways of thinking and acting and common viewpoints are ways of limiting deviant behaviour and ensuring continuity of established social norms. Conformity and continuity may be the symptom of a rigidly controlled or even oppressive social structure. Because of this some oppositional identities may rarely be given opportunity for material expression.

Social structure is an extremely important generator of identities, individual and communal. Without identities, there are no communities, and political communities are important institutions for organizing a sense of belonging. So too are religious institutions. One of the most powerful communal forces at work in the region was the Greek-style city state, in which citizenship might be organized with or without regard to ethnicity. Citizenship required the suppression or subordination of other identities which might compete with a sense of belonging to the city. But this does not mean that a new citizen automatically lost all other identities, or that other identities might not come to the fore outside the context of civic duties. A communal past could be created to provide appropriate origins for both cities and other groupings of people, and methods of transmitting a sense of belonging could be instituted through systems of instruction, celebrations and pageantry. Links with central powers such as Rome or the emperors gave the identity of the institutional community a wider value and legitimation. For most groups there was nothing to be gained in constructing the identity of the community entirely in opposition to the dominant culture, but there were ways of affirming a regional or local distinctiveness by appealing to various other institutions that lay outside the framework of the dominant symbolic system.

If Hellenism was truly allied to social power, and widely adopted by the ruling classes of the cities, any expression by civic elites using non-Greek symbols must be significant. A clear example is that of Palmyra, where monumental inscriptions in the Palmyrene script were commonplace and a highly visible proclamation of difference from other cities. Numismatists have drawn attention to the numerous designs on civic coinage which give prominence to non-Greek deities and images, most of which coincide with the period of the Second Sophistic. Is this nothing more than the product of intellectual 'antiquarianism' and curiosity about quaint local religions, or a way for the elites to use religious institutions to subvert Hellenism? Rather than discussing the question here we

Fig. 119. Reverse of a coin of Geta (AD 208-11), from an uncertain Decapolis city (Abila?). Alexander the Great and Seleucus Nicator shake hands.

will return to it in chapter 9; instead it is worth devoting a little space at this point to how the elites of the Syrian cities used coin types to recall their different pasts, not all of which were Greek.

The designs on coins often convey to us the same sorts of information as monuments, and some would like to see coin types *as* monuments. A recurring theme is one celebrating the origins of the community, which from our point of view may be either 'mythical' or 'historical'. In Syria, as elsewhere, this might mean depicting the appropriate founder, particularly a Greek or Macedonian one, even when the city had a history extending back before the Hellenistic period. Seleucus Nicator, who founded many cities in the region, appears to have been the focus of various civic founder cults; Alexander the Great was another choice. One Decapolis city opted for both Alexander and Seleucus (fig. 119): there is no need to suppose that the image on the coin, of the founders shaking hands, reflects any real historical moment. Some see the neglect of any pre-Greek history as evidence that it had been forgotten, but it may be deliberate rejection of a known past which did not serve the interests of the Hellenized citizen community. What is interesting is that some communities *did* choose to depict a pre-Greek or non-Greek past. The Phoenician cities of Berytus, Sidon and Tyre issued types which refer to a time before the Macedonian conquest, back to the age of Aeneas, the ancestor of the Romans, and the Phoenician Dido. Given that Berytus was a centre for the study of Latin letters, such types might even be seen as a snub to Hellenism; the Roman descendants of the Trojan Aeneas were, after all, the conquerors of the Greeks. Even after the elevation of Tyre to the status of a Roman colony, we are reminded of a distant past: the Ambrosial Rocks from which the islands of Tyre formed; the discovery of the purple dye of the murex snail; Cadmus founding Thebes, or giving the alphabet to the Greeks; Dido in a galley, or founding Carthage; or her brother and enemy Pygmalion, identified as such not by a Greek or Latin inscription, but by one using Phoenician letters (fig. 120). Even if Phoenician was no longer spoken, the lettering was presumably recognizable as a symbol of Tyre's non-Greek origins. These images, of course, understand Tyre's Phoenician past in terms of Greek and Latin legend (except perhaps the image of Pygmalion, which remains unexplained), but this need come as no surprise. History is always being rewritten to serve the interests of the present. We do not have to reject these Graeco-Phoenician images as inauthentic because they are hybrid, or because they do not refer to a 'real' past. They reminded the citizens of the Phoenician cities of their difference from others, even if they used 'the powerful lens of Hellenism'.[42] The Phoenician 'historical' types on coins begin to multiply at about the time that Philo of Byblus wrote his work the *Phoenicica* (late second century). This description of Phoenician cultural institutions supposedly drew on an ancient text in the Phoenician language by a certain Sanchuniathon. Philo's work contains so many Greek elements that his veracity on this point may be doubted, but authenticity is not as important to us as the interest expressed on the part of a Greek-educated individual in the pre-Hellenic culture of his homeland. The elites of the Phoenician cities found a way to stay or become Phoenician within the framework of Rome and Hellenism. The conscious display on coins of a Phoenician past in the second and third centuries is also particularly significant, when most cities looked to a Greek or Macedonian past if they could.

Fig. 120. Coin of Gordian III (AD 238-44) from Tyre. The reverse shows Pygmalion, the brother of Dido, with a group of four stags, identified by an inscription beneath in Phoenician letters. The choice of language and design evokes a pre-Hellenic past, but although written in Phoenician characters the name Pygmalion is a Greek version of the Phoenician name Pumiathon. The use of the Greek version here suggests that Phoenician was no longer a spoken language at this date.

(Right) *Fig. 121. Coins of Uranius Antoninus, usurper in Syria, c. AD 253-4. 121.1. Gold aureus. The obverse shows Uranius wearing a laurel wreath, but the Latin inscription simply gives his names, without imperial titles.*

However, the reverse, which shows the sacred baetyl of Elagabal between two parasols, reads 'Preserver of Augustus'. It is likely that this refers to Uranius as Augustus rather than Valerian.

121.1. Gold aureus. The obverse shows Uranius wearing a laurel wreath, but the Latin inscription simply gives his names, without imperial titles. However, the reverse, which shows the sacred baetyl of Elagabal between two parasols, reads 'Preserver of Augustus'. It is likely that this refers to Uranius as Augustus rather than Valerian.

Signs of Culture

Rather than trying to define cultures by sets of unique characteristics, or 'shopping lists' of criteria to be fulfilled, an alternative approach is to view them as codes and rules for using those codes. This has the advantage of drawing together archaeological notions of material cultures with broader definitions. Cultures are about making the world meaningful in particular ways, and doing particular meaningful things, so to study culture is to study the conveyance of meaning, and cultures can be defined by the different ways they give meaning to the world. Thus cultures are distinguished not so much by the different things they produce as by the way in which the things are 'read' by both insiders and outsiders. Readings may not be identical, and therefore there is no single meaning for a thing. The code is a set of cultural signs and the rules for using those signs. Codes incorporate objective criteria: language, customs, landscape, objects and dress, controlling the way the cultural signs are received and which significations are given priority (and therefore given most meaning). Seen like this, the Second Sophistic is a culture which made itself distinct from the cultures, Hellenized and otherwise, of the masses, and which adopted a particular position within a social framework through the deployment of specific codes governing meaning. To understand the meaning of a sign is to claim expert knowledge of that culture, to be able to read its codes, the systems of signs and symbols which the culture employs. It is not a claim to be made lightly. Signs which properly belong to the realm of the aesthetic or social can have multiple meanings, and the temptation to treat them as if they were logical, with a single, denotative meaning, should be avoided. It has been suggested that the more meanings a sign has, the more powerful it is. Multiple readings permit the readers to find what is important for them about the sign. But meanings must be shared among readers for the sign to be communicable, and institutions/cultures help to create and supervise shared meanings.

The use of characteristically 'Graeco-Roman' or 'Hellenizing' things in Syria does not automatically imply *assimilation* (that is, the things had precisely the same meanings in Syria as they did elsewhere), still less a total loss of any other identity by those who adopt them. A cultural sign may be *appropriated* from one culture by another. In this case the sign is acquired, but the meaning is changed. If the Romans could manipulate Syrian cultures, Syrians might have been able to manipulate Graeco-Roman symbols. It has been suggested that such a process may be at work in the images of the third-century Syrian usurper Uranius Antoninus, who issued coins at Emesa *c.* AD 253-4 (fig. 121). Although Uranius is portrayed with imperial regalia, it is suggested that these symbols of power were not intended as a challenge to the legitimate emperor, Valerian. Instead Uranius appropriated them to emphasize his importance on a local or regional scale. This interpretation is not secure, and it may well be that Uranius intended his symbols of power to mean 'emperor', but the idea does illustrate the concept of sign appropriation rather well, and in this case it could have been a particularly hazardous form of appropriation. Misunderstanding is a symptom of sign appropriation; the fate of Uranius Antoninus is unknown, as is Valerian's reading of the imagery (the obscurity of Uranius' end could perhaps be read as evidence of Valerian's reaction).

It is also possible to combine cultural signs to create new meanings. In such cases it may be pointless to argue about whether one set of signs is a 'veneer' and the other 'real'. Consider the Temple of Bel at Palmyra (fig. 122), which is sometimes considered to be a good example of a Hellenized veneer masking an indigenous form. It has a portico of Corinthian columns and triangular pediments typical of what we understand as a 'classical' or 'Graeco-Roman' temple. The central pair of columns on the colonnades of the short north and south ends of the building are spaced slightly further apart than the rest — a symmetrical feature common in Greek and Roman temples, and framing the position of the door at one end. The formal appearance of a 'classical' temple is

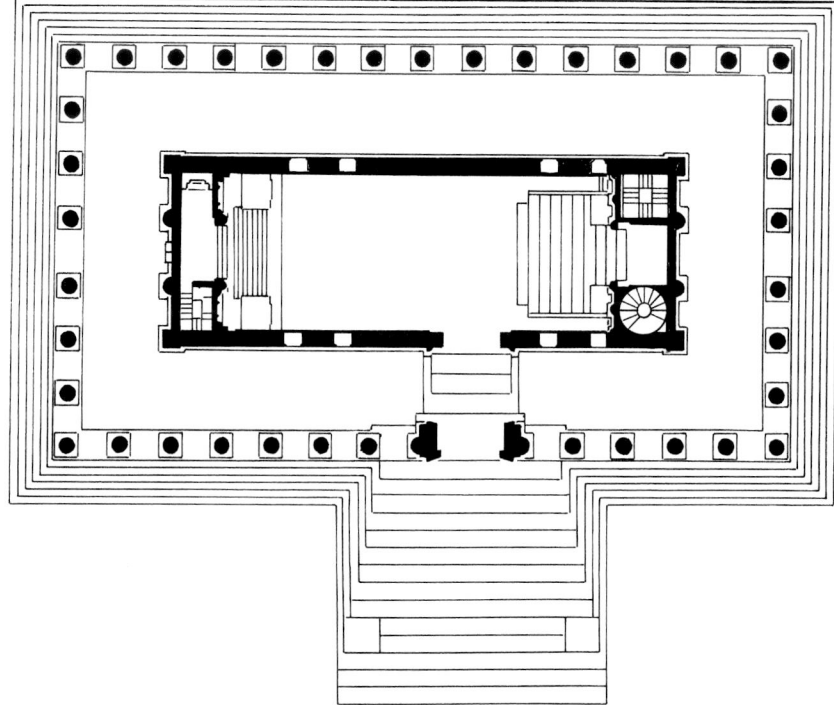

Fig. 122. The Temple of Bel at Palmyra.

122.1. Plan of the temple. The building had a complex history of construction, and originally may have been planned as a more 'conventional' temple.

122.2. View of the temple from the east. Note the 'Assyrian' merlons above the entablature, the windows in the cella walls and the engaged Ionic columns at the end of the cella, which in a conventional temple would have been free-standing, forming a portico before the cella door.

respected, and yet the door to the Temple of Bel is located at neither end, but asymmetrically in the western side. This unusual arrangement accommodated two chambers within the temple, one at the north and one at the south end, making the interior arrangement alien to the classical form. The pediments form the façade of a flat, not a pitched, roof (as would be expected in a classical temple), and four towers sprout from the corners of the cella. Finally, the roof is bounded by a row of merlons or 'crow-steps', decorative motifs which are not part of the conventional classical repertoire.

The way in which this building might have been used will be explored in chapter 9. For the moment it will suffice to consider the significance of the elements. If the intercolumnar spacing and pediments were normally important markers of the building's function, in this particular case those functions would have been better served by other forms. But function is only a part of the building's purpose. The classical form concedes the other forms, but is not negated by them. Indeed, the use of the 'Graeco-Roman' form implies profound respect for whatever symbolism it evoked. (An archetype for the basic plan has been suggested – the Hellenistic temple of Artemis at Magnesia ad Maeandrum in Asia Minor.) All the elements, including the apparently redundant plan of the colonnade and the façades, had meaning, as did the whole. Such combinations of signs can be thought of as symbolic *syncretism*. The combination is not a random hodgepodge of disparate elements, but a deliberate scheme, and with this in mind we should perhaps exercise caution before considering the classical forms to be a 'veneer', masking native forms and intentions. 'Veneer' implies something superficial and deceptive about the outward form, and something authentic and more meaningful in that which is hidden. Are the façades of such buildings a sham, a disguise for other, truer meanings? Is there something dishonest when form does not fully express function? After all, why space columns further apart to accommodate a door where none exists? Such questions suppose that the functional aspect of the object is more important than symbolic meanings.

The extreme complexity of signification is a severe hindrance to any straightforward analysis of cultures or identities in antiquity, where our knowledge of meaning is generally rather limited. Through reinterpretation, the meanings of cultural signs can alter within a culture during the course of their use. They can acquire new layers of meaning while retaining their old meanings. Obsolete signs might be revived, or new ones substituted for old ones. Through a process of transformation a typically 'Greek' image of a deity could have been understood as a 'Syrian' one, if the old sign for the deity had dropped out of use. In this case it would be wrong to see the deity as purely Greek: Greeks could regard it as Greek and Syrians as Syrian. But our problem is to differentiate between the different uses of the signs.

Language, Culture and Identity

Language itself is a system of signs, but we cannot draw a direct equation between use of a particular language and other cultural institutions, or claim that its speakers have a single identity. Several cultural groups may share a language, and bilingualism and multilingualism only complicate matters. The study of personal names, Greek, Latin and Semitic, provides clues about cultures and identities, but the evidence, derived mainly from inscriptions, has to be used with caution. It is assumed that Semitic speakers might adopt a Greek or Latin name, but that people of Greek origin (or other highly Hellenized Greek speakers) would not adopt a Semitic one. A Hellenizing environment might have stigmatized people with Semitic names, in which case it would not be too surprising to find speakers of Semitic languages choosing Greek names for their children. What is more significant is that in some regions we find people with Greek names giving their children Semitic names, which suggests that, in these regions at least, no stigma was attached. However, it is often unclear whether the use of a Greek personal name means that the individual was a Hellenized Greek speaker, or that a Semitic personal name signifies someone who was less Hellenized. It was not uncommon for an individual to have a Semitic *and* a Greek or Latin name: 'Galba, who is also called Gaulan, son of Abd al-Ga'.[43] The use of alternative names by an individual might suggest an ability to shift between alternative identities. Some of these alternatives were simple translations from one language to another: Zenobia's son Wahballat, whose name meant 'Gift of Allat' (a goddess assimilated to Athena), used both a Latin transliteration (Vaballathus) and a Greek translation (Athenodorus) on inscriptions and coins.

The study of personal names reveals that Semitic names were predominant inland, around Emesa, Palmyra, the Ituraean and Nabataean lands, the Hauran and Arabia. But they are also encountered in coastal regions. Many of these names have been identified as Arabic rather than Aramaic, although many would argue that it is extremely difficult to make a distinction when the names are rendered in non-Arabic scripts. The debate prompts the question of what language(s) these people spoke in everyday life. In regions such as Palmyrene, the Hauran and Arabia, Greek was not the only language of inscriptions (see below), and in such places Latin names are not uncommon, perhaps the result of contact with Roman soldiers instead of Hellenizing city-dwellers. In highly Hellenized regions such as the north, the coast and the Decapolis it is hardly surprising to find Greek names predominating. Semitic names become more common in these regions from the fourth century, which might reflect a greater confidence in local, non-Greek identities; but the statistics are probably skewed by the greater number of inscriptions surviving from late antiquity.

Inscriptions and texts show the predominance of Greek throughout the region. Greek was not confined to the cities, as inscriptions, papyrus and parchments from rural settings show. What then remains to be asked is whether this dominant 'public' language reflects widespread use, and whether the Greek language was a vehicle for the spread of Greek culture at the expense of others. If people were bilingual or multilingual, were they also capable of moving between cultures and identities? What proportion of the population was literate in any language, and was their choice of written language determined by the one most commonly used for administration rather than their mother tongues? Could most peasants understand Greek, or did they need an intermediary? The papyrus and parchment documents raise interesting questions about the degree of literacy outside the cities. A large proportion are legal documents and thus reflect the chief language of administration, but it is noteworthy that they may be signed by witnesses in languages and scripts other than the one used for the legal text itself, and some even show that Semitic languages could be used for legal documents. However, there are also private letters among the texts, demonstrating that Greek was in common use, even in rural contexts, and that it was not merely a language employed by highly educated civic elites. One still has to allow for a substantial proportion of the population being illiterate, particularly women (Babatha is a well-known case). In late Roman times, when the Christianized literary culture began taking a greater interest in people of humble origins, we encounter more evidence of non-Greek speakers. The Greek-speaking clergy employed translators for the benefit of the non-Greek speaking sections of their congregations. The church historian Socrates claimed that even in the highly Hellenized port city of Tyre in the fifth century there were people who could not understand Greek. This lack of Hellenization sometimes extended to more powerful figures than peasants: Theodoret wrote of a bishop from the countryside of Cyrrhus who also knew no Greek.

Was Aramaic in its various dialects the most commonly spoken language, in spite of the predominance of Greek in inscriptions? It seems likely that it was, but for some regions it is difficult to be certain. Aramaic had been important under the Achaemenids, although it would seem that during the Hellenistic period it was not in general use as a written language, in contrast to Phoenician. As usual we are at the mercy of the very limited evidence, and the picture may change with new discoveries. Written Aramaic dialects, each using a different script, developed in the early Roman empire: Nabataean, Palmyrene, Syriac, Hatrene, and these were presumably transmitted by some system of training or education. Aramaic is probably meant when Greek sources refer to the 'language of the *Syroi*', and Theodoret states that different dialects of it were spoken by the Osrhoenoi, Syroi, Euphratesioi, Palaistinoi and Phoinikes.[44] In general it is assumed that the country folk spoke Aramaic, making them distinct from the Greek speakers of the cities, but in cities the lower classes were probably also Aramaic speakers. Bilingualism or multilingualism may have been common, even among the upper classes. Rabbula, a fifth-century bishop of Edessa (died 435), who was born into a wealthy family at Chalcis ad Belum, was educated in Greek, but as bishop wrote in both languages. This is unusual, and most ancient writers, like many bilinguals today, probably felt more comfortable writing in one language (which need not have been their mother tongue).

As noted above, in the long run imperial support for Hellenism may well have counted against Semitic languages being used for administrative purposes. The Babatha archive shows how Nabataean rapidly came to be supplanted by Greek as the language of administration for the province of Arabia. The monumental inscriptions of Palmyra demonstrate that in a civic environment a dialect of Aramaic could perform at least some of the tasks normally reserved for Greek: civic decrees and laws, religious texts, epitaphs, papyrus and parchment documents. There is no evidence yet for Palmyrene as a literary language, but perhaps we should not be too surprised should that evidence turn up. Whether it would demonstrate the persistence of pre-Greek traditions, or betray a profound Hellenization of Palmyrene culture, is a matter for speculation. Nevertheless, with the fall of Palmyra, the written script dies out.

In spite of the strong political support for Hellenism, some written Aramaic forms persisted, and one in particular flourished. Palestinian Aramaic is among those attested in late Roman times, but the most extensive Aramaic writing to survive is that in Syriac. Syriac was the Aramaic dialect of Edessa in Osrhoene, which became the literary language of Aramaic-speaking

Christians over a much wider area in the late Roman period. In use from at least the early first century AD, the written language spread east into the rest of Mesopotamia and beyond, and west in late Roman times into northern Syria. That it should be nurtured in Mesopotamia may be another example of the cultural distinction detected by some scholars between Mesopotamia and the more Hellenized regions to the west. Syriac inscriptions are found in Mesopotamia during the early empire, and the Euphrates archive shows that it could also be used for legal documents, but there are no Syriac inscriptions known in Syria proper until the late fourth century. This epigraphic evidence fits with what is known of Syriac literature – only in the fifth century do we find Syriac writers from regions west of the Euphrates, and before that all were from Mesopotamia. But we would do well to remember that the inscriptions and literature chart only the spread of its use as a prestige language, and they do not imply the absence of a 'language of the *Syroi*' in northern Syria before late Roman times.

Syriac was also a language used by pagans and Manichaeans, but little of their literature survives. Spreading west, it came to be used by the populations who were bilingual in Greek and Aramaic, and hence the use of Greek style, expressions and loan words in Syriac. The church seems to have accepted Syriac (and other dialects of Aramaic) as a public language for transmitting its teachings, something that the institution of the *polis* in general had not. The use of Syriac by Syrian Christians lent it the prestige to compete with Greek as a literary language, at least in the field of religion. Even so, Greek culture had been so thoroughly imposed on the region that no native culture could develop or persist independent of its influences. The early Syriac Christian literature of the fourth century, such as the hymns of the great Mesopotamian poet Ephrem (died 373), was not very Hellenized, but Hellenizing influences can be detected in some of the few surviving Syriac works of the early empire. An early document, *The Epistle of Mara, Son of Serapion* (the context appears to be late first century, but the text itself may be later), frames arguments by drawing on Greek learning, at one point comparing the deaths of Socrates at the hands of the Athenians and Pythagoras at the hands of the Samians with puzzling references to the death of a 'wise king' among the Jews: 'For with justice did God make recompense to the wisdom of these three: for the Athenians died of famine; and the Samians were overwhelmed by the sea without remedy; and the Jews, desolate and driven from their own kingdom, are scattered throughout every country.'[45] Bardaisan of Edessa (154-222), author of various works (which unfortunately do not survive), was clearly a learned man who chose to write in Syriac, but he and his followers were strongly influenced by Greek culture, as implied by the Hellenized approach of a work on fate called the *Book of the Laws of Countries*, written by one of Bardaisan's disciples.

Later Syriac Christians drew quite heavily from Greek. For Christian intellectuals some familiarity with Greek was desirable, because the New Testament itself was written in that language. Greek philosophy, particularly that of Aristotle, was much admired, and the asceticism of some Greek philosophers could provide models for Christians. Hence the need for competent translations of Greek works. In late antiquity translations from Greek into Syriac and from Syriac into Greek were commonplace, with Syriac-speaking monks providing much of the expertise. These included translations of Syriac religious works: poetry, hagiographies, martyr narratives. There were more translations from

Greek into Syriac than the other way around, but the fact that Syriac works were translated into Greek at all is noteworthy. For some, translations into Syriac will have obviated the need for learning Greek. Greek remained the language of power, but in the north Syriac became a prestige language, and as it did so Greeks attempted to assert their cultural superiority over this barbarian literature. Just as adherents of the Second Sophistic had tried to suggest that Latin was derived from Greek (making them superior to the Romans), so the Greek speakers of the fourth and fifth centuries claimed that Greek was ancestral to Syriac (inventing, among other things, a Greek-educated son for Bardaisan, Harmonius).

While there is plenty of evidence for the use of Phoenician in Hellenistic times (in contrast to the paucity of evidence for Aramaic in this period), all the evidence suggests that by the beginning of the first century AD it had been supplanted by Greek, at least as a language for inscriptions. The latest Phoenician inscription on stone, from Aradus, belongs to the reign of Augustus, but short Phoenician inscriptions continue to appear on coins into the third century (fig. 120). It is possible that Phoenician survived as a spoken language during the first three centuries, although the implications of the coin inscriptions are against it (see caption to fig. 120) and it probably died out during this period. If a Semitic language were in daily use in the cities of Phoenicia, the most likely candidate is Aramaic.

In the south Hebrew remained in use, although it may have been deployed in specific contexts by Jews and Samaritans as an affirmation of identity, rather than a language of everyday life. Samaritans used it in their synagogue inscriptions, but it is unclear what language they spoke – it was probably Aramaic. Although the Jews seem to have spoken Aramaic in everyday life, Hebrew could still be used in synagogue inscriptions, on coins of the first and second revolts, for letters and legal texts of the Bar Kokhba revolt, and texts like the Mishnah (early third century), so at least some Jews could read and write in the language. But at the same time Greek and Aramaic were also used as written languages in a variety of contexts, including religious ones, and this perhaps gives us an inkling of the very complex multilingual environments in which the indigenous peoples of the region lived their lives.

Apart from personal names there is very little material evidence for Arabic as either a spoken or written language during our period. The earliest unequivocal evidence is an inscription in Nabataean script from Eboda in the Negev, written in the Nabataean and Arabic languages, thought to date to the second century AD. The next piece of dated evidence is the fourth-century epitaph of Imru' al-Qays, inscribed in a cursive form of Nabataean from Namara east of the Hauran (p. 65), and there are a few texts from later centuries. But recent work has uncovered texts in Thamudic and Nabataean scripts from northern Transjordan, Petra, the Hijaz, the Sinai and Egypt which are written in a language that it close to classical Arabic. Suffice to say that Arabic emerges in the region as an important written language only in the seventh century, and that before that it would appear that Arabic speakers would tend to write in Aramaic. Nevertheless the use of Arabic for monumental inscriptions is of the greatest importance for signifying the presence of a literate audience of Arabic speakers in the region.

One extraordinary epigraphic phenomenon is that of the so-called Safaitic graffiti, which consist mainly of short texts, names and genealogies scratched by tribesmen on stones littering the landscape of the basalt steppe and desert of southern Syria and north-eastern Jordan. The surviving texts number tens of thousands. Many were clearly written by nomadic herders (but there are also texts from the Hauran which were probably written by the sedentary popula-tion), and they do not appear to be aimed at any particular audience – or at any rate their informal nature does not suggest that their writers gave much thought to the convenience of the readers. It is thought that they were scratched on stones mostly for amusement, perhaps as 'free publicity for exis-tence' (to quote one sociologist's view of graffiti).[46] The script which the herders used was borrowed from south Arabia, and was quite unlike any of the other scripts used in the Syrian region. The language is similar but not identical to Arabic. The texts are difficult to date, because they rarely refer to things outside the community of Safaitic writers. The script appears to have been used from the first century BC to the fourth century AD (though such a late date is disputed). The majority of texts may belong to the first centuries BC and AD, since there are occasional references to Nabataean gods and kings (one tribesman even identifies himself as a Nabataean). What is interesting here is that we have humble herdsmen and other individuals who were to some degree literate. The number of graffiti suggests that this literacy was common among the tribes-men and the population of the region, a phenomenon so far unique in the Mediterranean world. The choice of script indicates that the writers were not much interested in communicating with their neighbours to the west and north, who were using Greek or Aramaic scripts. There are a few bilingual inscriptions combining Safaitic with Greek or Aramaic, but little to suggest that these people were greatly affected by Greek culture. The phenomenon implies that if other nomad groups in the empire had opted to use written scripts, the results might have been the same. It would be false to claim that these people were totally isolated from the outside world, however. They may represent an element of the population of the Hauran, who practised transhumance into the steppe and desert to pasture their animals, and if so they formed part of a community more firmly linked to the wider Roman sphere (the evidence for this, however, is debated). There seem to have been strong links between the tribes writing in Safaitic script and other tribes of the steppe and desert fringes. Tribes using Safaitic script were present at Palmyra and its territory, as attested by their texts. Safaitic graffiti are known further west, extending to the Lebanon region, and east, to Dura Europus. A few have even been found among the graffiti from Pompeii in Italy. The Safaitic writings suggest that among the underclass on the fringes of Roman Syria a simple training in letters was possible, outside the framework of Hellenism.

The evidence for languages is necessarily positivist, but the patterns of inscriptions and languages do invite speculation about what remained unwrit-ten. Because Semitic languages could be written in one region does not mean that it was possible in all other regions, and some languages may have been more socially appropriate to particular media and forms of communication than others. Where Semitic languages remained unwritten, speakers of those languages who wanted to write letters or erect commemorative inscriptions would have resorted to languages and idioms that were felt appropriate to those media (which basically meant Greek or Latin), whether or not they strongly identified with Hellenism or Rome. Perhaps the fact that the habit of erecting inscriptions is comparatively less common in Syria and the Near East than in neighbouring Asia Minor indicates a greater indifference among the peoples of the region to one particular Greek way of doing things. The evidence does not really permit confident assertions. The rise and demise of written languages in the historical record may track their importance as a source of social power, rather than providing evidence for or against specific modes of speech and thought in the population as a whole.

ARCHITECTURE AND ART

From language itself we might turn to the more 'secret' languages of material culture, where difference and variance could be expressed in subtle ways. Interpretation of this material culture is never a straightforward exercise. Similar designs may point to the transmission of ideas through time and space and thus to a regional tradition, or they may point to similarity of function, but be quite independent of each other. It would be quite impossible to look at all forms of material culture, so what follows concentrates on architectural decoration and style, tomb and house design (the two share some features in common), sculpture, mosaic and painting, and dress as ways of expressing identity and difference. As we will see, context and purpose (meaning whatever institutions governed deployment and reception) are important in defining the style and form, often more so than geographical location. For example, figurative mosaics of the early empire show very little local influence, and even at Palmyra, where the sculpture is so distinctive, mosaics employ classical themes.

The evidence of inscriptions and texts can always be criticized for concentrating on elite culture, but the same might be said for some of the material evidence as well. Houses filled with mosaic floors and monumental buildings and tombs are not the products of the lowest classes of societies. Like inscriptions or texts, objects can be situated within a genre (meaning, in sociological terms, 'a socially sanctioned type of communicative event'[47]), but they may depend more heavily on context for their meanings than texts do. With languages, the choices are readily apparent to us, even if the contexts are not: Greek, Latin, Aramaic and so on. If domestic architecture or tomb decoration are languages, we need to understand how they might have been read. It is not enough simply to point to the local, regional or Graeco-Roman origins of a particular form; what is more important is the meaning of the form in the period of Roman rule. The difficulties of recovering the context and understanding what meanings the material culture was trying to communicate are serious obstacles, but any approach to social identities has to grapple with such problems.

Architectural Style

The interpretation of architectural decoration and style is particularly problematic, not least because our knowledge of Hellenistic architecture, one of the likely influences on architectural style in the region, is so poor. Practically nothing is known of the decorative styles of great centres like Seleucid Antioch, and only a little more is known about Ptolemaic Alexandria. Origins and influences may speak of meanings, but we need to be sure that we have identified the right ones. Herodian palaces such as Jericho or Masada appear to blend Italian and Hellenistic styles, but the Italian style itself may be inspired by Hellenistic architecture, so the route of transmission to Judaea (Rome or Alexandria, or both?) and the meaning (deliberately Romanizing, Hellenizing, or both?) are blurred. What appear to be indigenous inventions, such as the so-called 'Syrian arch' (a pediment with an arched entablature), first encountered in the region in the Temple of Dusares at Sia, may be derived from Alexandrian prototypes. The more we know about Ptolemaic style, the less Roman some of the classical architecture of Syria and the Near East becomes. If we were to know more about Seleucid style our ideas about architecture in the region might be altered still further. In short, our comparative ignorance of Hellenistic architectural styles complicates the interpretation of classicizing architecture of Syria and the Near East in the early Roman empire.

Some features, however, are not classicizing, but these are no less problematic. Many of these motifs are derived from Mesopotamian, Achaemenid and Egyptian architecture and are presumably the result of earlier empires influencing local architectural practice. It is interesting to see the vestiges of previous imperial styles in use – for example, the bell-shaped column bases on the Temple of Baalshamin at Sia in the Hauran, which have parallels in Achaemenid buildings – but it is by no means clear what the use of such motifs meant at the time. The merlons or 'crow-steps' which adorned the parapets or façades of buildings in Palmyra (fig. 122.2), Damascus, Phoenicia and Nabataea (colour plate 22) are thought to be Mesopotamian or Assyrian in origin. When applied to classicizing temples and other structures these motifs differentiated such buildings from Roman buildings elsewhere, yet while we can point to these differences, often we cannot recover their meanings. Did they speak of an affinity between a 'Syria this side of the Euphrates' and a 'Syria' beyond? We may never know for sure. Nevertheless the continued use of these older designs is significant, as is their demise.

Up to the late first century AD there is much regional variation in the Syrian region, with buildings blending 'classical' and other motifs together. Religious and funerary monuments dominate the architectural record during the first century BC and early first century AD. In the north there is very little that can be securely dated to before c. AD 50. Early buildings from the central coast contain many decorative elements which are deemed to be non-classical, particularly the 'Assyrian' merlons. A good example of the composite building style of this period may be found at Fakra, a mountain sanctuary high above the coast between Byblus and Berytus. Apart from two temples, there is an ensemble of three structures, a *monument à colonnettes* (see chapter 9), a large altar decorated with merlons, and a tower which has been identified as a treasury (fig. 123). The decoration on the last building, which is dated by an inscription to AD 43-4, is a curious blend of different traditions, with a course of 'Assyrian' merlons, Egyptian mouldings, a Hellenistic-style Doric architrave and 'proto-Aeolic' capitals, an archaic feature which may ultimately derive from pre-Hellenistic models in Palestine. Strikingly Egyptian elements are encountered at some sites, such as a lintel with a winged sun disc found at Yammoune on the western side of the Bekaa, amid Latin dedications. Whether these designs denote earlier Ptolemaic influence or derive from Bronze Age Egyptian influences in the Lebanon mountains and the Bekaa is open to debate. Non-Greek motifs are also found in the cities: a late first- or early second-century AD Latin dedication by a freedman, Quintus Longinus Nicon, to Jupiter Heliopolitanus, found in the colony of Berytus, is decorated with merlons. All of these features

Fig. 123. Fakra. The tower, of which only the lower portion remains standing, is to the left; in the centre, a monument à colonnettes, *and on the right, a large altar decorated with merlons.*

confirm a rich blend of traditions up to the middle or late first century AD, after which architectural styles become more homogeneous. The coastal region was more open to influences from the Mediterranean than was the interior, and as the quarry system developed imports of the sort described in chapter 6 probably helped eliminate strong local variations in architectural style among the Syrian ports and their hinterlands.

Hybrids of classical and non-classical forms can also be found at many locations inland. Palmyra was one of the places where local architectural traditions survived longest. The Temple of Bel at Palmyra, dedicated in AD 32 (but probably not completed until the late first century), has already been discussed. It employed merlons, but also classical motifs such as garlands. However, the classical devices are sometimes used in unusual ways, such as the pedimented windows on the cella (fig. 122.2). A variant of the Corinthian column capital found on some of the earlier buildings at Palmyra has parallels in far-flung places such as the Seleucid city at Aï Khanoum in Afghanistan, and Gandhara, but a more likely source of reference is one of the great Hellenistic foundations, such as Antioch or Seleucia on the Tigris. The use of bands of repeated vegetal motifs, particularly vine scrolls, as frames around niches, is typically Palmyrene, but it may have been inspired by similar motifs from further east. It is likely that the decorative devices which had spread across a wide region of the east under the aegis of the Seleucid empire continued to be transmitted from the major Hellenistic cities, and Palmyra would have been equally well placed to receive influences both from Mesopotamia and the Syrian Tetrapolis. Thus stucco work became popular at Seleucia on the Tigris in the first century BC, but it was also popular in the eastern Mediterranean and its appearance at Palmyra could have been the result of influences from either direction. Palmyrene buildings are increasingly influenced by stricter classical models after *c.* AD 50, but there are also many ways in which Palmyrene architecture remained distinct, such as the heavy use of consoles for statues on colonnades and temples, and a preference for cult reliefs rather than cult statues inside the temples. Such features would have lent a very different feel to the civic environment of Palmyra when compared to its neighbours further west. But the distinctive architectural styles died with other aspects of Palmyrene culture following the fall of the city in the 270s.

Some of the decorative motifs encountered in the Hauran during the early empire have much in common with those at Palmyra, particularly the use of vine scrolls (fig. 125), which are combined with other vegetal motifs like pine cones and pomegranates. Also notable are Corinthian-inspired capitals decorated with small human busts above a band of acanthus leaves. Although these belong to the period of Nabataean rule they appear to be either indigenous to the Hauran, or in some cases influenced by Palmyra (and perhaps Mesopotamia), rather than by the Nabataean art of the south. The decorative difference between Nabataea proper and the Nabataean-ruled Hauran seems to concur with the ceramic record (Nabataean eggshell ware being comparatively rare in the Hauran – see chapter 6). However, some of the decorative styles of the Hauran may derive directly from Hellenistic models rather than being transmitted through Nabataea or Palmyra. It may be significant that the 'Assyrian' merlon, used by both Nabataean and Palmyrene architects, appears to be absent from the repertoire of the Hauran architects and stonemasons.

The overall chronology and meaning of Nabataean architecture was until recently a subject of considerable scholarly disagreement. The subject is of importance for the region as a whole, because it raises questions about the origin of designs thought to be typically 'Roman'. Early attempts at developing a chronology used the rock-cut façades of undated tombs at Petra and assumed a typology of increasing complexity, beginning with very simple designs lacking any classical style ornament and ending with the elaborate classical rock-cut façades of the 'temple tombs', which were thought to date to the period after the annexation of the kingdom. Other scholars disagreed and proposed that many complex tombs dated to Nabataean times. There was no way to date them apart from by style, and suggested dates for some of the more famous monuments such as the Khazneh (colour plate 21) or the Deir (fig. 124) ranged from the first century BC to the second century AD. Parallels for features such as the rotunda within a broken pediment found on both of these monuments were to be found in first-century BC frescoes at Pompeii, hinting at possible Roman influences – or the presence of Romans following the annexation in AD 106. The simpler forms of Nabataean tomb employed 'Assyrian' merlons (colour plate 22), sometimes with an Egyptian cavetto cornice and Hellenized cornices and door frames. Elements included decoration similar to that found in south Arabia (probably the result of the 'caravan trade') and the distinctive Nabataean capital, seen in numerous monumental buildings at Petra, Bostra, Sia and Hegra (Medain Saleh) (fig. 95). There is no need here to go into the typology of the simpler tomb types. A study of the Nabataean tombs at Hegra, many of which are inscribed with dates and the names of the stonemasons, shows that rather than undergoing an evolution, most of the supposedly early tomb types were being produced more or less contemporaneously in the first century AD, and while some forms were slightly earlier, these overlapped with later forms. Differences in designs seem to be due to individual stonemasons rather than evolving traditions. A detailed study of Ptolemaic architecture in Egypt revealed that a number of the larger 'temple-tombs' (among them the Khazneh and Deir) were inspired by third- or second-century BC Alexandrian designs, rather than Roman ones of the first and second centuries AD. These façades were perhaps derived from the Palace of the Ptolemies or other royal buildings, and belonged to the period of Nabataean rule (first century BC – first century AD), meaning that they were contemporary with the simpler designs

Fig. 124. Petra, the Deir. Its date is uncertain (first century AD?), but there is reason to believe that it was used as a triclinium for ritual banquets devoted to the cult of a deceased Nabataean king, perhaps Obodas III (30-9 BC). The rotunda set within a broken pediment is likely to have been inspired by Ptolemaic architectural styles rather than Roman ones.

from which they were supposed to have evolved. The differences in design may denote differences in status, the temple-tombs being Nabataean royal monuments or the tombs of other high-ranking officials executed in an appropriate kingly style. Their precise chronology remains uncertain, but the debate over whether many important monuments were Nabataean or Roman has now been settled, and the influence of Alexandria on the architecture of the kingdom is clear. With the Roman annexation, the distinctive Nabataean styles faded away, and with it, perhaps, another facet of Nabataean identity.

During the latter part of the first century, new buildings throughout the whole region adopted a more homogeneous 'classical' architectural style influenced by the marble quarries of Asia Minor, although Palmyra retained many distinctive elements. This homogeneous style coincides more or less closely with the heyday of the monumental Greek-style city in Syria, with the Second Sophistic, and with the development of the imperial quarry system (chapter 6). This is also the period when native culture is at its least visible. In the basalt regions the hard local stone was worked into Corinthian capitals in an effort to bring the civic architecture of these areas into line with others, although some regional elements of décor were retained. Relief work and other forms of decoration illustrate the Hellenizing drive, even in this difficult medium (fig. 125).

Identifying purely 'Roman', as opposed to 'Greek', elements in the designs of Syrian buildings is problematic, not least because Roman styles were heavily influenced by Hellenistic designs. What might appear to be the influence of Rome might be another manifestation of interaction between cities of the eastern empire. On the other hand, some features have been taken to indicate direct inspiration from the centre of power. At Heliopolis some of the limestone column capitals in the first-century Temple of Jupiter are similar in style to those found in Augustan Rome. In the courtyard of the temple, and on the cella walls of the nearby Temple of Venus (second century), the niches are decorated with shells, their keys at the top as was the common practice at Rome and in the west, rather than at the bottom as was normal in the east. Is this subtle difference a sign of the Latin origins of the *pagus* or colony? And, if so, do other elements signify older, non-Roman roots of the cults? The entablatures of the temples of Jupiter and Bacchus are decorated with a row of bull and lion protomes, appropriate animals for the deities worshipped there, and typical Achaemenid devices. What appears purely classical at a glance may be an impure mixture of classical and non-classical on a closer reading.

Architectural decoration need not have been influenced solely by architectural traditions. Some designs and patterns were common to a variety of media. The decorative architectural motifs of Palmyrene stonework are found repeated in textiles found in the city, suggesting that their symbolism was not confined to monuments. The rich decoration of 'classical' Syrian buildings such as the Temple of Bacchus at Heliopolis may owe something to local or regional woodworking traditions (colour plate 10).

Fig. 125. The entrance to the southern temple (AD 151) at 'Atil, the ancient village of Atheila, showing the richly decorated basalt stonework framing the doorway.

In the mid-third century the drive towards monumentalization of cities tailed off (chapter 7), and local styles begin to emerge again. 'Classical' styles did not die out, particularly in the coastal cities, where imports from the marble quarries could be obtained easily. However, in many places the quantity of evidence declines in line with the monumental public city. In the late Roman period churches were the dominant form of monumental building. These too could receive imperial gifts such as Proconnesian marble. The Church of the Holy Cross at Sergiopolis, and the martyrium of St Simeon Stylites acquired some marble from such sources, but how much influence Constantinople had on Syrian churches remains debatable. The capital's preference for brick stands in stark contrast to the limestone and basalt ashlars of our region. Indeed, such was the power of Syrian Christianity that the region could have disseminated architectural influence in the opposite direction, as some scholars have suggested.

It is impossible to do justice here to the variety and richness of architectural décor in late Roman Syria, and all that can be done is to draw attention to it. In the limestone lands of northern Syria the exterior decoration is usually confined to bands around doors and windows, slabs of parapets, and on arches, but it is often intricate and elaborate, with many local variations. The evolution of the decoration has been used to help date many of the buildings of the region. Designs include bands of vegetal and geometric patterns: some classical; some resembling the Palmyrene vine scrolls; and some quite new. Prominent also are discs above doorways or in the centre of column capitals, ornamented with crosses, geometric designs or vegetal motifs. The interiors of

Fig. 126. Chapel at Burj ad Deirouni in the Jebel Barisha. Note the ribbon moulding over the windows.

Fig. 127. 'Windswept' capital (seen here upside-down) at Qalaat Semaan.

churches are often heavily decorated, particularly around the chancel. A characteristic motif of the sixth century, found on church exteriors, is a ribbon-like moulding framing the tops of doors and windows and ending in scrolls (fig. 126). There is a variety of capitals, many of which are free interpretations of the classical designs, such as the 'windswept' type, which gives the appearance of acanthus foliage being blown by a strong gale (fig. 127). Another, dubbed the 'Syrian' capital, copies the plain Doric style, but adds two projecting brackets. The ornament of the region reaches its peak in buildings such as the fifth-century church at Qalbloze (fig. 185) and the complex at Qalaat Semaan (fig. 127). In the south the late Roman period is marked by a decline in the decoration of basalt. This stone was difficult to work at the best of times, and now decoration was often simplified and restrained; it includes vine scrolls, disks and simple crosses. Much of it was carved in relief rather than being incised, and even the lettering of basalt inscriptions is commonly found in relief. The progressive simplification of decoration in the Hauran stands in contrast to the elaboration found in the limestone north, or in the Euphrates region. In late antiquity the basalt and limestone environments created very different responses.

Houses of Eternity

No overall study of burial practices for the region currently exists, and generalizations over such a wide area and long period are hazardous. Once again we encounter problems with interpreting the system of symbols, and understanding the nature of the evidence and how representative it is of society in general. Are some tomb types the result of fashion rather than changes in ritual? Did the same sign or group of signs have different meanings in different places, or at different times? There are tower-tombs at Palmyra, and some towers in the Hauran *may* have been used as tombs. If this should prove to be the case, should we conclude that the tower-tombs meant the same in both places?

Some general observations about practices and forms may be made, though these are of little help in distinguishing cultural differences. Throughout the period inhumations rather than cremations were the norm, though there might be many different types of burials and tombs within a single necropolis. Most of the basic forms are encountered all over the region, and there is surprisingly little variation in tomb forms over time, even from the early to late Roman period. However, the problem of studying tomb development is exacerbated by the fact that many are difficult to date. The simplest tombs are cists or pits dug into the earth or excavated from bedrock and covered with stones laid over the top, intended to contain single inhumations. Graves of this type need not be an indicator of low status, as the rich burials from the necropolis at Emesa demonstrate. They may tell us something about elite attitudes to display among the Emesene aristocracy, but monumental tombs did exist at Emesa and much of the evidence of burials has not yet been treated in a sufficiently detailed manner for us to advance such interpretations.

Single, free-standing sarcophagi could perform a similar function to the single burials, in a more conspicuous manner. But being highly visible features of the landscape, they were also accessible – not necessarily just for plunder, but for additional burials of family members, or wholesale reuse by unrelated persons. Civic fines for illegal reuse could prevent appropriation, and inscribing the sarcophagus with phrases such as 'In vain – you cannot open it'[48] might act as a minor psychological deterrent. But the resilient sarcophagi often outlasted the descendants of the deceased, and the temptation to reuse obsolete memorials might be too great. The excavators of the necropolis at Tyre have noted how the sarcophagi were originally sealed with metal clamps holding the lid to the body. If these still remain in place, there is usually a single burial within, but broken clamps signify multiple burials or reuse. Many sarcophagi bear inscriptions with the name and occupation of the deceased, but these are sometimes much later than the sarcophagi themselves. If the lid proved too difficult to move, an expedient means of gaining entry was to cut a neat square hole in the body of the sarcophagus, which could then be sealed with stones and mortar after additional burials had taken place. This treatment of sarcophagi says something about the importance of being buried in them, though perhaps not about the inviolability of the burials themselves, but once again, there is little systematic treatment of the material evidence over the region as a whole. Like more elaborate tomb structures, free-standing sarcophagi could be the focus of rituals. At Tyre some local limestone examples have a small projecting altar in high relief at one end, presumably used for offerings (on the Tyre necropolis, see p. 209).

Grander monuments included large communal tombs.

Fig. 128. Interior of the tower-tomb of Elahbel at Palmyra. The loculi *for burials can be seen on the right-hand side, in vertical rows six deep. When occupied such burials were commonly sealed with a stone slab bearing a relief representing the deceased (see fig. 118).*

Fig. 129. Monumental tomb at Cyrrhus. Hexagonal in plan, the building dates to the second or third century. In medieval times it became the tomb of a Muslim saint.

Such a tomb might be the property of its builder and reserved only for immediate relatives, or it might remain in the family for generations. Sometimes places in a tomb, or even a whole tomb, might be rented or sold to individuals or groups who were not related to the original builders, making it hard to conclude anything about the nature of family structure from the size and capacity of these complexes. Traditions may have varied from one region to another. A common form, found in many varieties, is the hypogeum, a collective underground tomb, usually accessed by a single entrance leading to a room or several rooms containing the burials. Large, arched recesses (*arcosilia*) could accommodate sarcophagi, or might have cist graves sunk into their bases. *Loculi* were long, narrow slots designed to accommodate coffins inserted at right angles to the wall of the tomb (fig. 128). Some tombs combined *arcosilia* and *loculi*, with the *arcosilia* reserved for the founders or other privileged individuals. In certain areas one type of burial seems to predominate over the other (for instance, *loculi* in Auranitis or along the Euphrates, *arcosilia* in northern Syria). This may indicate differences in social structure or attitudes to extended family groups (more burials were possible in a tomb full of *loculi*), or taboos forbidding the burial of strangers with family members. Some sections of tombs in Palestine or in cities like Tyre and Sidon served as ossuaries, and the practice of collecting the bones of ancestors and placing them in new or rebuilt tombs is known from inscriptions. In such cases the *loculi* or *arcosilia* served as temporary burial places, the bones being collected for secondary and permanent interment after the flesh had decayed. Small, elaborately decorated limestone ossuaries for individuals were common in first to second-century AD Judaea. In the Hauran separate chambers in tombs may also have served as ossuaries. Whether the same or similar practices in different places indicate the same or similar beliefs about death is not known.

Above ground the presence of the hypogeum might be made known by some form of marker or monument. If the tomb was cut into a rock face, this marker could take the form of a relief imitating the front of a building. If it was sunk into level ground, a monument might be erected above it, such as a simple tumulus or a stele with inscriptions giving details about the deceased. Some burial markers were more elaborate, imitating architectural forms. Other hypogeum markers, particularly in northern Syria, are in fact receptacles for burials, supporting or containing sarcophagi in addition to the burials below ground. At Bostra and Maximianopolis (Shaqqa) some hypogea were covered by monuments with exhedras set into their façades, which may have contained sarcophagi or statues. The Semitic term *nephesh*, meaning breath, person, or soul, could be used to denote a grave marker or structure built in memory of the deceased, or where the spirit might reside (colour plate 7). This word was used at Palmyra to designate tower-tombs (see below). An inscription on the Nabataean period tomb of Hamrath at Suweyda (later Dionysias) translates the Nabataean *nephesh* using the Greek word *stele*, although the monument in

Fig. 130. Burial precinct in the Tyre necropolis. A Proconnesian pedimented gable sarcophagus stands alone in the foreground. Behind is a tomb containing loculi *accessed from the outside, which supports three Proconnesian garland sarcophagi and another of* lapis *sarcophagus.*

question is a large, tomb-like structure with engaged columns and a pyramidal or stepped roof. Monolithic tomb markers of this sort are numerous around Petra, and are also found in the Kidron valley in Jerusalem (for example, the 'Tomb of Absalom', the lower part of which is hewn from bedrock and the upper part of which is of ashlar masonry). Other tombs were constructed entirely above ground, without a hypogeum. Some were nothing more than blocks of *loculi*, accessed from the outside, and sometimes with sarcophagi on their flat roofs (fig. 130). Others were large mausoleums with central rooms containing *loculi* and/or sarcophagi. At Tyre there are sunken rooms of stone-built *loculi*. These had flat roofs, sometimes close to ground level, or accessed by stairs, perhaps for rituals, although some roofs carry sarcophagi. Some tombs had rooms for ritual banquets, and water installations, presumably for ritual cleansing. Recent excavations at Tyre have revealed a well-preserved example of such a room, paved with mosaics and containing a triclinium with benches veneered with imported marbles.

Funerary architecture did not have to be as practical or functional as many other classes of monument, allowing the builders of tombs to indulge in the construction of showy, fantasy structures. Some imitate temples, others comprise a massive square or rectangular chamber topped by a pyramid (fig. 131), and yet others form circular chambers surrounded by colonnades. Monumental tombs may have been influenced by famous funerary monuments of the past, such as the Egyptian pyramids or the Mausoleum at Halicarnassus, or by Hellenistic royal tombs closer to home. Regional variations are evident, which may well have their roots in social practices. Hypogea in the north sometimes have stone-cut seats either side of the entrance, perhaps in imitation of those in the vestibules of country houses of the limestone massif, where villagers could socialize. A common architectural form in the same region is the canopy tomb, with a gabled or pyramidal stone roof supported on arches or columns (fig. 132), which sometimes shelters sarcophagi. Peculiar to the Hauran, and perhaps no earlier than the fourth century, are tombs surmounted by a tower structure containing dovecotes. The best-

Fig. 131. Late Roman tomb with a pyramidal roof at el-Bara in northern Syria.

Fig. 132. Canopy tomb at the village of Dana, south of the Jebel Sheikh Barakat in northern Syria, marking the entrance to a hypogeum.

preserved example is at Rimet al-Lohf in Trachonitis, where a temple-tomb of the third century AD was later given a crudely-built additional storey containing dovecotes around the interior walls. The meaning is lost to us, but the symbolism of the doves may be Christian.

The basic classes of hypogea, temple-tombs and pyramid-tombs have no observable regional distribution in Syria, but in most places the cemeteries are not sufficiently well known for regional variants and chronological trends to be apparent. Palmyra is a particularly well-studied example, with a large number of tombs dated by inscriptions. The earliest known from the site is a hypogeum thought to date to the second or first century BC, which was later incorporated into the religious sanctuary of Baalshamin, but otherwise the hypogeum form does not become common at Palmyra until the late first century AD. At the beginning of the Christian era inhumations in burial plots were common at Palmyra, marked by free-standing gravestones cut in low relief (this type of relief was subsequently adapted for use in monumental tombs, to seal *loculi*, from the mid-first century AD). The earliest type of monumental tomb at the site is also the most prominent and distinctive: the so-called tower-tomb (colour plate 15; fig. 133). The use of the word *nephesh* to describe these edifices, and its connection with the Greek term *stele*, might suggest a connection between these gigantic markers and the humble gravestones in the minds of Palmyrenes. The towers stand up to five storeys high, excluding their roof terraces. Each storey contained *loculi* along its walls, the upper floors being accessed by staircases. The largest could accommodate several hundred burials. In the very earliest examples the *loculi* occupy only the lower levels and are accessible from the outside, but this type gave way to towers with *loculi* inside, often richly decorated with pilasters, paintings and reliefs, and busts or figures representing the deceased (fig. 128). Sculpted busts are unknown before the mid-first century AD, and are thought to be influenced by Roman funerary practices. Tower-tombs are noted along the Euphrates, at Baghuz, Dura Europus and Zenobia, and even in Mesopotamia, at Deyr Yakup, south of Edessa, suggesting links between practices at Palmyra and regions to the east. The earliest dated tower-tomb at Palmyra is the tower of Atenaten (9 BC), and the latest is the tomb of Moqimo, dated AD 128. The tower-tombs remained in use long after this, but the fashion in tomb-building had clearly moved on.

Some towers are connected to hypogea, which became fashionable as tombs in their own right from the late first century. Whether the preference for less conspicuous tombs has anything to do with differing attitudes to display is unclear, and like the tower-tombs the independent hypogea contain large numbers of *loculi*, but also *arcosilia* with sarcophagi for prominent individuals such as the founders of the tomb. The Palmyrene decorated limestone sarcophagi seem to have been another adaptation from the Mediterranean, and first appear in the middle of the second century, about the time when imported stone sarcophagi started reaching the coast. The early Palmyrene forms are peculiar. The body of the sarcophagus imitates a couch, and the lid is normally L-shaped in section, bearing an upright relief of the deceased reclining at a banquet, not a three-dimensional sculpture (banqueters in the round are a rare third-century feature). Sometimes three sarcophagi of this sort were arranged to resemble a triclinium. Among the best-known hypogea is the Tomb of the Three Brothers, Naamai, Malay and Saadai (second century). Portions of this extensive tomb were sold off, like real estate, in the later second and third centuries.

Fig. 133. Tower-tombs in the western necropolis at Palmyra.

The latest securely dated hypogeum belongs to AD 251, but they were still in use in the fourth century. Large tombs took a long time to fill up, which may explain why empty parts were sometimes sold or rented. The third and latest category of Palmyrene monumental tomb is the temple- or house-tomb, which begins to appear in the mid-second century, and sometimes reached massive proportions. Palmyrene inscriptions call these structures 'houses of eternity'. Some are indeed house-like, although this class of tomb exhibits a great deal of variety. The best-known example stands at the western end of the grand colonnade, and is precisely aligned with this street: the so-called Funerary Temple no. 86, dated to the third century (colour plate 14). This façade is clearly inspired by Graeco-Roman architecture, but other tombs seem to look to earlier Hellenistic palace architecture, much as the Nabataean rock-cut tombs of Petra do, and yet others draw on local Palmyrene designs, or combine elements from different traditions. In some cases the elites who commissioned these buildings may have drawn on expertise from outside Palmyra. The largest so far known is temple-tomb no. 36, located in the western necropolis, which was excavated in the 1980s. Although only the lowest part of the walls remain *in situ*, enough remained of the building to enable its design and decoration to be reconstructed almost in its entirety. Erected between *c.* AD 210 and 220, it was about 18 metres (60 feet) square and 12 metres (40 feet) high, and consisted of two storeys containing *loculi* and sarcophagi. Like Graeco-Roman houses it had a peristyle at its centre. It had elaborately decorated façades on all four external sides, combining local, Parthian and Hellenizing decorative elements (the latter perhaps inspired by the *scenae frons* of theatres). Some of the decorative elements are based on western designs alien to Palmyra, and may be the work of craftsmen brought from the coast. Although the grandest, it was not the latest of the temple-tombs, which continued to be constructed down to the middle of the third century.

The architecture of tombs is only a part of the ritual of death and burial. The materials recovered from them reveal evidence for distinctive practices as well as more universal traits. But here we encounter the difficulty of distinguishing between fashion or availability of certain classes of object and deeply held beliefs. The objects placed in tombs may all have had meanings, but some may not have had any particular significance in funerary rites. Tombs and sarcophagi from a variety of locations have yielded similar types of finds: jewellery, glass or ceramic unguentaria, and coins. The dry conditions at Palmyra have preserved burials in fine clothes, including Chinese silks, and burial in splendid garments may have been common practice elsewhere as well (the wealth of silk-embroidered clothes found among a jumbled mass of skeletons of adults and children in a tower-tomb at Zenobia may not be normal, however, and the bodies could be victims of a Persian massacre in the sixth or seventh century). Recent excavations in a necropolis at Heliopolis (Baalbek) revealed an undisturbed burial in a limestone sarcophagus. The body, thought to be female, had sheets of gold placed over the forehead, eyes, nose and mouth, a gold oak wreath on her head and sheet gold plaques decorated with female heads in relief on her torso. Other burials wore crude funerary masks made from gold sheets, suggesting a local practice. The tradition of placing money in the tomb, or in the mouth of the deceased, to pay the ferryman to the underworld, seems to have been widespread, which could reflect a common system of belief, but it may have been a custom that was not central to the burial ritual, given that there are also burials without coins. Burials are not normally found within the city walls, which seems to reflect a general attitude towards the separation of the living inhabitants of the city from the polluting influence of the dead, who are confined to the extra-mural necropolis (but see p. 239). In the countryside, however, tombs were sometimes located close to the living, in the courtyards of houses or in gardens, rather than being placed in a separate necropolis, perhaps indicating different attitudes towards the dead in more rural environments. Rural temples, too, are sometimes surrounded by burials.

Within the cist, *loculus* or stone sarcophagus, the body might be placed in a coffin of wood, lead or terracotta. As with marble sarcophagi, so with terracotta: they too were manufactured in particular centres (Cyprus or the Antioch/Cilicia region) and traded regionally or long-distance. The lead sarcophagi may also have been mass-produced in centralized workshops, although very little study has been done on these.

Epitaphs provided individuals with an opportunity to express their identity. This huge subject cannot be dealt with in any detail here, but it is interesting to note what sort of information was chosen. Context seems to have been influential. An epitaph might include information about the deceased's origin (what we might consider ethnicity), or their home city or village, particularly if the individual was foreign. In some cities, however, the *occupation* of the deceased is prominent: John, dealer in secondhand goods and grinder of purple; Theodorus, deacon and carpenter; George, sausage-seller and cantor at St Mary's, to name some of the many examples from the Tyre necropolis. Why record for eternity that you were a murex-fisher, or a market gardener, pastry-seller, baker, plasterer-painter, marble-worker, cheese-maker, or cabbage-seller? Rather than emphasize what ethnic group they belonged to, these epitaphs, which provide us with useful information about specialist occupations, explain what constructive role the individuals played in civic society, which suggests that the communal project of the city was very important in shaping identities, and that this tradition continued into late antiquity. Their occupation, or their membership of a guild, which fitted them into the social framework and demonstrated to others their contribution to civic life, was an important part of 'who' they were in death.

The Private Domain

A common feature of both urban and rural houses is an enclosed courtyard, around which the main units of the house are arranged. The focus of the house is introverted; homes presented blank walls to the outside world, although decoration might adorn the main entrance. In rural settings the courtyard provided not only a communal space and a source of light and air to the rooms around its sides, but also an area where the occupants could work without being subjected to the gaze of outsiders. It is in this use of domestic space for productive activities that rural dwellings may have differed from city dwellings, but it is possible to envisage courtyards or rooms in city houses being given over to production as well (for instance, to house textile looms). The courtyard also allowed the rooms around it to be subdivided into smaller dwelling units for different members of a family by providing a common and equal route of access. The simplest dwellings will have needed a space for storage and a reception/living space, with perhaps an outside area for working. The ground floor of many rural houses seems to have been given over to storage and shelter for animals; the upper floors were for living in. In this respect, too, many city dwellings may have been different.

The visual privacy of domestic space is a theme repeated in most dwellings, rural and urban, rich and poor. In the city the streets lined by private houses were quite different from the grand public thorough-fares. Here public space was relatively unimportant, the houses looked inwards towards their central courtyard, and the entrance was normally placed in such a way as to prevent the public gaze penetrating

Fig. 134. Traditional mud-brick courtyard house at Harran (ancient Carrhae in Mesopotamia). The beehive design is also common in the steppe of northern Syria, and the form appears in Neo-Assyrian palace reliefs. It may well have existed in the region in Roman times.

the dwelling. This made the house an entirely private space; it had no public role to play, in contrast to the typical Italian house with its views leading along a single axis into the heart of the building. Even in late antiquity, when the grandees began to conduct civic government in their homes, most house plans retained their seclusion from the outside world by placing the entrance away from the central axis. One notable exception is the vast house called the 'Edifice "au *triclinos*"' at Apamea, whose dimensions and decoration are such that it has been dubbed a palace, perhaps even the residence of a governor. Originally it too had an entrance offset from the main axis, but in late Roman times the complex was remodelled, reorienting the entire building around a grand axis leading directly from the street entrance, through its peristyle court, to a grand reception room with an apsidal end. The very public nature of this design sets it apart from other Apamene residences.

We know very little about humble dwellings in the cities, but there is no reason to suppose a rigid uniformity of plans, decoration and use of domestic space. In places where land was at a premium, such as the island of Aradus or the peninsula of Tyre, literary sources mention tall tower blocks. None has been identified, and it is difficult to know what they might have looked like, although they too might have consisted of a central court with wings of several storeys of apartments ranged around. The regulations about housing preserved in the text of Julianus of Ascalon (p. 137) seem to be concerned with such buildings. These regulations suggest that in Palestine flat roofs with terraces were commonplace; but imported roof tiles found in excavations at coastal cities indicate that some domestic buildings (the wealthier, Hellenized peristyle houses, perhaps) had pitched roofs. Cities and villages where flat roofs were common would have presented a rather different appearance from those where pitched, tiled roofs were the norm. Imported roof tiles of different colours could be combined to produce variegated patterns. These sorts of vari-ations may seem insignificant, but even today among the Lebanese of the coast red-tiled roofs are seen as a mark of identity and difference.

The moderately humble mud-brick houses of Dura Europus show few Hellenizing influences. Rooms were arranged around a central court, and smaller houses had only one or two sides of the court occupied by rooms. This basic house design was in use at Dura during the Parthian period, and the form is thought to derive from Mesopotamia. In many cases there was an entrance vestibule, and in many vestibules the entrance and exit were offset from one another, preventing viewers in the street looking directly into the central court beyond. The décor of the entrances, which sometimes employ gypsum mouldings, is one of the few Hellenizing features of these houses. Sometimes the courtyard had a few columns in it (again seen as a Hellenizing feature), but there were no peristyles typical of the wealthier town houses found in many of the Syrian cities. The main living or reception room opened directly on to the court and often had benches running around the walls and a hearth. The benches look as if they were influenced by the triclinium of Graeco-Roman houses. A division of living space into public and private areas (those furthest removed from the gaze of visitors) appears to be distinct. However, the layout of rooms does not indicate a strong gendered separation of space within the household. A single entrance means access was shared by men and women, and most of the rooms are accessible via each other and the central court. Furthermore, papyrus documents from Dura and elsewhere suggest how this sort of domestic space may have been used, with the court being owned communally by an extended family, and the rooms around the court being divided up among the individual family units. The partition or repartition of houses between family members means that the functions of individual rooms, and the divisions between reception and private chambers, could change over time. The interior fittings include features often found in traditional houses of the region today: niches for storage of possessions such as blankets, mattresses and water jars. Although moulded plaster cornices were frequently applied to the interior of buildings, and stucco decoration using classical motifs and perhaps even imported moulds, the inhabitants seem to have been unconcerned with demonstrating any deep affiliation with Greek culture through the regular use of figurative wall paintings or mosaics.

Regional differences are apparent everywhere, even in the grand houses of the elites. Some variations may be due to differences in climate, but it is worth noting that habitations may differ within a single community, pointing to social, economic and perhaps ethnic divisions. At Zeugma the moderately well off could perhaps not afford the space or outlay for colonnaded peristyles around the central courts of their Hellenized town houses, but they often added loggias with columns on one side. At Petra there is evidence for the gradual and haphazard transformation from a settlement of tents to stone-built houses. Courtyard houses were constructed, without any respect to a city plan, their positions and designs seemingly limited only by underlying topography. The overall appearance of Petra's domestic quarters has been likened to a petrified nomads' camp.[49] The grander ones were Hellenized by the insertion of colonnades in the courtyards, and some have stucco and wall paintings. Other, simpler dwellings at Petra were excavated from solid rock. Consisting of one or more rooms cut into the cliff faces with an open terrace in front of them, these very unHellenized houses were accessed by rock cut staircases.

Even at Palmyra, where we find some of the best examples of highly Hellenized houses, there are notable variations. The highly Hellenized houses have a central peristyle court, on to which the main reception room faces, with other rooms arranged more or less symmetrically around the axis created by the reception room and peristyle. Even so, the entrances and vestibules to the houses are offset, as at Dura, to provide greater privacy. Near to the Temple of

Fig. 135. The elaborately decorated entrance to the House of the Consoles at Apamea.

Bel is the House of Achilles, which must have been one of the grander Palmyrene residences. It had two peristyle courts and may have occupied a space of more than 1600 square metres (17,225 square feet), but its entire plan does not survive as the knoll on which it sits is badly eroded. Recent excavations in the centre of the city, to the north of the Grand Colonnade, have exposed a substantial residential complex which does not conform to the typical Graeco-Roman plan. The excavators suggest that it is a single residence, even though it is effectively partitioned in two, with a double doorway on the southern side – the smaller door giving access to the private wing of the house, and the larger to the reception rooms. Both wings have courts, and both are accessed by entrances offset from the courts. The courts have colonnades but not peristyles, and there is no axial arrangement to either wing. In its irregular layout the complex resembles the houses at Dura Europus, containing some Hellenized decorative elements but lacking the formal plan of such structures, but in its division of space it may have separated the genders more thoroughly than the Dura houses.

Several large residences have been explored at Apamea. Most seem to have been constructed in the second century, but they remained in use into at least the sixth, and they are important for giving us an impression of the private environment into which civic government retreated as the grandees who owned such residences began to dominate public life. The House of the Consoles is among the best preserved (fig. 135). It was a rectangular residence covering about 4500 square metres (48,440 square feet), with a large central peristyle court of about 2000 square metres (21,530 square feet). The entrance was offset from the court, as in houses elsewhere. Rooms close to the entrance on the west side are identified as a porter's lodge and perhaps kitchens. A large room on the southern side was probably a private dining room. A large hall, with three doors opening on to the court, dominated the eastern side. From this hall doors gave access to other rooms. It is this hall that dominates the axis of the house, and it is likely that in this space the owner conducted his affairs. Along the north side was a row of small chambers, only some of which open onto the court through small doors; these may have been private living spaces. It is likely that other living rooms and bedrooms occupied an upper floor. There are traces of painted decoration, and the floors were paved with mosaics, replaced in the sixth century by an elaborate *opus sectile* pavement. Other houses at Apamea have similar features. A characteristic of their late antique phases also emphasizes the decline of public life: private baths and latrines are established within these grand domestic spaces. The grandees may have ruled the city, but they did not need its public amenities.

The remains of country dwellings are found all over the region, but the Dead Cities of the north and the Hauran are two regions where similarities and differences can be studied in detail, using well-preserved buildings. In terms of basic plans there are no discernible differences in status between houses in the Dead Cities, although some bear elaborate decoration, much of which is similar to that employed in churches, and some are more carefully constructed than others. Houses occupied one or more sides of a walled courtyard. Most are two storeys high, the ground floor being for livestock and storage, and the upper one for living. Some, however, have sunken cellars, more appropriate for storage than for animals. The upper floors often have a veranda, accessible via an external staircase. Traditional houses of the Antioch region retain the same design and use of space (fig. 136). Their pitched roofs would have been supported by wooden beams. Beam slots on the interior walls indicate that the upper floors were generally made of wood, but some were paved with limestone slabs supported on stone arches. The rooms could be subdivided into smaller living units over time, to house extended families. Verandas might be given a decorative stone balustrade and were occasionally supported by columns which were presumably more expensive than the more normal pilasters. Entrance vestibules were sometimes provided with stone seats, allowing the occupants of the houses to socialize with or receive outsiders without letting them into the court. Properties were sometimes added to, simply by the construction of another house against the existing one (fig. 137), creating semi-

Fig. 136. Traditional village house in the countryside west of Antakya (ancient Antioch).

detached units, or by building against another wall of the courtyard. Thus the large residences, once thought to be villas of wealthy landowners, were probably communal residences for groups of farmers or extended families.

The houses of the Hauran have the same basic features as those of the north: the ground floor was reserved for storage and livestock, the upper for living. House units are arranged around one or more sides of a walled courtyard. However, the dwellings have flat rather than pitched roofs, consisting of basalt slabs laid over transverse arches and corbels (see chapter 5). Clearly there was insufficient timber, unlike in the Dead Cities. These roofs were suitable for drying grain and other produce, as is still the practice today in the villages of the region. Although the Hauran houses vary in their layouts and sizes, most have some general features in common: staircases give access to upper floors on the inside rather than the outside (stairs to the roof, however, often lay on the

Fig. 137. A pair of houses at Deir Sunbul in the Jebel Zawiye. Their verandas have gone; beam slots in the façades suggest that these were probably made of wood. More substantial verandas were made of stone. The basic design is very similar to that of the modern house in fig. 136.

outside: see colour plate 28), and the entrances to the houses are small, all of which suggest a greater desire for protection than is the case with the houses of the Dead Cities (unless these features are simply the consequence of a slightly harsher winter climate). In the simpler houses the ground floors were usually divided into two parts, a large work area at the entrance, and a smaller space at the back for animals, divided from the work area by a row of mangers. The height and layout of the mangers suggests that each was designed for a fairly tall, single animal, perhaps a cow, but also possibly a donkey or mule. Directly over the rear stable is a mezzanine floor, perhaps for storage. There might be two or more upper floors, so that some buildings resembled towers rather than houses. This house type is thought to be a traditional one which predates the Roman annexation of the region, although most surviving houses are late Roman in date, as in the Dead Cities.

There is considerable differentiation between houses in the Hauran. The humbler ones are of poor construction, and the grander ones are not only better built but also have more elaborate plans: sometimes a colonnaded portico in front, decoration around the entrance, more rooms and stables on the ground floor, verandas and more rooms on upper floors. Some contain a small court-yard close to the entrance which might merit the term *atrium*. These grand houses make their appearance in late Roman times, but they look less like the luxurious country villas of regional civic elites than the dwellings of wealthy villagers. One feature that a number of these grander houses have in common is a vaulted alcove on the ground floor, which may have served as a reception room or, in the case of local grandees, an audience chamber. This is seen as being related to the *iwan*, a type of vaulted hall found in the Parthian kingdom (although its exact origins are disputed). It is perhaps in such spaces that the rural grandees of the Hauran, like their city counterparts at Apamea, conducted their administrative affairs.

Sculpture

Sculpture, like Syrian culture in general, has been classified according to the degree of Hellenization. The three main classes are: heavily classical, providing

Fig. 138. A grand house in the metrokomia of Neela (Inkhil) in north-west Batanaea.

a common link with other eastern Mediterranean provinces and Rome; a provincial style imitating these forms; and the third group, consisting of various regional styles which sometimes used classical forms but did not copy these directly, and which often combined these with other, local or regional features. The geography of the region has an important part to play in the distribution of the first category. Many of the fine classical marble statues need not be 'Syrian' at all, and were probably imported from the quarries overseas. Consequently these mass-produced items are commonest in the coastal regions, where they served the needs of the Hellenized elites. The second class also served the needs and aspirations of the Hellenized elite through the more or less competent imitation of classical models. Such objects are found more widely distributed in the region. Examples of the third class provide the best clues about local and regional identities and are commonest at inland sites, such as Palmyra and the Hauran, but they are also found in the coastal regions. A sandstone column from Kartaba, in the mountains above Byblus, which was perhaps part of a second- or third-century funerary monument, bears a relief panel with two aediculas, one above the other, each containing the busts of a man and a woman, carved in provincial style (fig. 139). The males, one of whom has the Semitic name Abidallathos, are dressed in the Graeco-Roman manner (although one wears a cylindrical hat), while the females are dressed in conical headdresses over which large veils are draped. Although this sculpture contains numerous Hellenized elements, the portraits have features in common with sculptures from places like Palmyra, at a site just 18 kilometres (11 miles) from the coast.

The chronology and meaning of much surviving Syrian sculpture is difficult to establish because most of it has been divorced from its original context. Almost all is of stone. Nothing is known of wooden sculpture, apart from the fact that it existed. While there is some evidence for production of bronze sculptures in local styles, there may have been major production centres overseas, just as there were centres for marble statuary. At Palmyra fragments of bronze statues have been found, some of which are from classical-style figures, but a

Fig. 139. Stele from Kartaba (see text). Height of original: 1.97 metres (6 feet 5½ inches).

life-size pair of bronze feet wearing Parthian-style slippers found in the agora suggests non-classical influences at work as well. The Palmyra Tariff mentions duties on imported bronze statues, implying that bringing such items into the city from elsewhere was fairly commonplace, and a large number of the statues attached to the consoles of columns at Palmyra may have been of bronze. At Apamea in the early second century, an inscription records that the wealthy benefactor Lucius Julius Agrippa decorated a bath house with bronze statues of figures from Greek myths, such as the satyr Marsyas, and Theseus and the Minotaur. It was no doubt a way of demonstrating his *paideia*, but we do not know whether the statues were produced locally under his inspiration and supervision, or if he was able to order the groups from a pattern-book provided by a production centre elsewhere. Ready-made classical figures in stone could certainly be obtained from some of the marble quarries, and the elites of the coastal cities took full advantage of these. At Byblus a monumental colonnaded street ended in a piazza with a large nymphaeum; it was decorated with statues of Hygeia, Orpheus, Achilles and Penthesilea. Special orders could probably be commissioned: for example, a statue of the city's Tyche; or portrait statues, which could be shipped with the face roughed out and finished at the destination. Chemical analyses of marbles enable the sources of imported sculptures to be determined, though it is not always possible to pinpoint precisely which

Fig. 140. Lion relief from the sanctuary of Allat at Palmyra, first century AD.

quarries the pieces came from. Collections of sculpture at Caesarea Maritima and Scythopolis were imported from various quarries in Greece and Asia Minor. But such pieces could also be found at sites more remote from the Mediterranean. The temple of the goddess Allat at Palmyra had as its cult statue a fine marble figure of Athena (with whom Allat was equated). This provided a striking contrast with the monumental relief in Palmyrene style, constructed in the early first century AD from limestone ashlars and standing 3.5 metres ($11\frac{1}{2}$ feet) high, which adorned the sanctuary. This depicted a lion (the consort of Allat) holding a crouching gazelle in its paws (fig. 140). Both sculptures are equally powerful visual symbols of the divine, one in a local idiom, and the other in a style which served the desires of a Hellenizing member or members of the wealthy civic elite.

Inland, regional centres could supply similar designs in local materials. Nabataean sculptors used sandstone and limestone to produce reliefs and sculptures in both Hellenizing and indigenous idioms. Context and materials may often have dictated the style and form almost as much as the tastes of those commissioning the work. Sculptures that were displayed in art collections of private houses are likely to have been highly Hellenized, intended to demonstrate the *paideia* of their owner to visitors. Others were made as dedications or decorations for religious sanctuaries and public buildings. On buildings the content of the sculptural programme is likely to have been influenced by the type of monument; and for public buildings in

cities Hellenizing sculptures will have been especially appropriate. It is particularly unfortunate that the settings of many sculptures have been lost, such as
the extraordinary series of basalt statues from the Hauran region, where
analysis has mainly proceeded on the basis of style. In many cities there was a
strong demand for statues of individuals to be placed at the entrances to tombs.
Local or regional versions would have been cheaper than imports, and were
perhaps accessible to people other than the Hellenized elites, although like
sarcophagi the prestigious imported statues may have influenced the designs of
funerary portraits in local materials. Their presence and numbers probably
depended on whether there was convenient access to a centre of production,
either local or overseas. A number of limestone statues has been found in the
necropolis at Zeugma, and there may well have been a workshop operating in
the region, as there are competent reliefs cut into the solid rock of the tomb
walls as well (often a symbolic eagle for a male and basket for a female, rather
than busts of the deceased).

One series of sculptures which retains its context and which can be dated
closely is the remarkable set of figures and reliefs set up around the funerary
monument of Antiochus I of Commagene (c. 70-36 BC), located on the peak of
Mount Nemrut (figs 10, 25, 141). Here on a remote mountain top in the north-
eastern part of his kingdom, 2150 metres (7054 feet) above sea level, a large
tumulus was erected, framed by terraces containing sculptures on the eastern
and western sides. The sculptures on both terraces include a row of colossal
seated statues, 8 to 10 metres (26 to 33 feet) high. In these Antiochus takes his
place among the gods, who are syncretistic combinations of Greek and Iranian
deities (figs 25, 141). The king, who sports a Seleucid dynastic name (Antiochus
VIII was his grandfather), wears his ancestral Armenian-style tiara (denoting
his descent from the Persian satraps of Armenia, the Orontids) and Persian
dress (the Orontids had married into the Achaemenid family). A series of reliefs
depict his Persian and Macedonian forebears, from which we discover that
Antiochus claimed descent from Darius I and Alexander the Great. Others
show Antiochus shaking hands with various deities. One particularly well-
preserved relief is thought to symbolize the conjunction of the planets on the
day that Pompey confirmed Antiochus as king (fig. 10). The style is provincial,
but the content combines Hellenizing and Iranian elements, making a statement about Antiochus' ancestry and his identity as a descendant of the
Orontids and the Seleucid and Achaemenid royal houses, as well as alluding to
Roman consent to his rule. It is perhaps not surprising to find elite sculpture in
a provincial style at the very beginning of our period, when architectural styles
also combined elements from different cultural sources. And here we can at
least comprehend some of the reasons for the particular combinations.

The provincial basalt sculptures of the Hauran have generally lost their contexts and cannot be dated so closely, but two main phases can be distinguished.
One belongs to the period of Nabataean rule and the other follows the Roman
annexation in AD 106. As might be expected, the sculpture of the Nabataean
period displays more unique elements, while the Roman period works are more
Hellenized. The difficulties of working basalt forced the sculptors to produce
compact sculptures by removing as little of the stone as possible to produce the
image. The subject matter of the Nabataean-period sculpture includes animals
such as lions and horses, and in particular eagles (in this case thought to be a
symbol of the god Baalshamin). Representations of humans include standing

figures in Greek-style mantles, which may have been funerary or honorific in function, and a series of seated individuals, some of whom hold inscribed scrolls which indicate that these figures are of mortals rather than divinities and may also have been honorific or funerary. Without their contexts, however, the meanings of many pieces remain enigmatic. Sculptures of the Roman period include a series of Graeco-Roman divinities, in particular figures of Nike (Victory). These seem to have been used mainly as dedications in sanctuaries, where they may have stood in niches or even served as acroteria on the roofs of temples. Reliefs also attest to the importance of divinities in Graeco-Roman guise. A series of torsos in Roman military dress may be dedications to emperors or warrior deities. Also common in the Hauran are funerary stelae, often of crude style, topped with busts representing the deceased.

The characteristic limestone sculpture of Palmyra is particularly well known and well dated, and in many cases the contexts are known, or can be guessed. It too blended elements from 'classical' and other cultures, drawing on elements commonly found in the art of the Parthian realm. Palmyrene art is considered 'iconic' or 'static' rather than dynamic and narrative. The best-known examples come from Palmyra itself, but this style is also encountered at Dura Europus (fig. 92), Edessa (fig. 147) and at Hatra. Most of the surviving limestone sculptures are reliefs, which were the preferred form for stone sculptures in the region, although in Hatra free-standing limestone statues were also produced and some of the consoles on columns at Palmyra originally supported stone statues rather than bronze ones.

It appears to us as an art in which lively or narrative themes were difficult to express, although it is quite possible that its Palmyrene viewers could 'see' it as dynamic or narrative. It was also probably appreciated for its rich symbolism. Particularly characteristic was the depiction of human figures standing facing the viewer, rather than in profile. This is a notable departure from earlier traditions of relief carving in the Near East, such as the Neo-Hittite, Assyrian and Achaemenid, where figures were always shown in profile. Nor was it confined only to sculpture. Frontal figures are also found in frescoes and graffiti from the region. The origins of this type of art have long been a subject for debate, and more attention seems to have been paid to where the artistic tradition comes from than how it functioned and what it was for. Although 'frontality' is found in both eastern Syria and Mesopotamia as well as in India at roughly the same time, it is not clear whether the different traditions are connected. Frontal reliefs are found in the Parthian kingdom, but these seem to be later than the early Palmyrene examples. In Syria the emergence of the style appears to coincide very roughly with the

waning of Seleucid power. It is possible that we are looking at an indigenous art form, one which emerged with the development of a Palmyrene identity, rather than one inspired from elsewhere. Reliefs in profile ignore the viewer, but facing ones engage the audience, which may have allowed Palmyrene viewers to regard these sculptures as dynamic rather than static or hieratic. The experience is direct.

The majority of surviving Palmyrene sculptures are reliefs from sanctuaries and tombs. The earliest of these, of the late first century BC and early first century AD, were carved in low relief (fig. 142). Later sculptures have higher relief and more ambitious decoration, but the frontal mode of presentation remains the norm throughout. Even the cult images in temples like that of Bel or Baalshamin seem to have been reliefs rather than statues.

Funerary sculptures include stelae, reliefs covering *loculi*, lids for sarcophagi, and (rarely) full-length statues standing inside the tomb or attached to brackets on the walls. Many of them are labelled in Palmyrene as the 'image' or 'representation' of the deceased. They are not portraits as we understand the word, and attempts at individual likenesses seem schematic to the modern viewer. Nevertheless, in the images, the deceased lived on; tombs were important not only as houses and memorials for the dead but as the focus of ritual for the living, including banquets taken in the company of ancestors. The facing busts look out to the living, and participate as onlookers, or, in the case of certain more elaborate sculptures, attend the funerary banquets, reclining on couches. Symbolic elements accompanying some portraits include a curtain, probably signifying the point of transition from the accessible world of the living to that of the dead. On the early reliefs a deceased man is sometimes accompanied by a female mourner, characterized by gashed breast, lack of a tunic and loose hair falling about her shoulders. Reliefs also include reclining figures, which could be used to cover more than one *loculus*. The standard pattern shows a reclining male or two men, most commonly in Parthian dress, holding a cup and lying on a couch, and accompanied by a wife or attendants. The same design was used for the figures on top of sarcophagi. The men on the lids are often (but not invariably) priests, and their wives are frequently depicted as smaller, seated figures. Children are shown standing, usually in Greek dress. Between the legs of the couch, on the main body of the sarcophagus, there are

Fig. 142. First-century relief from a stone beam in the Temple of Bel. Deities carved in low relief stand above a classical egg-and-dart moulding, over a typically Palmyrene vine scroll. The row of figures looks static, but in fact there is action: on the far left a giant with snakes' bodies for feet is attacked by a rider and a dog; the row of five standing deities is perhaps meant to be involved. The figures have been identified as Shadrafa (with a serpent entwined around his lance), Atargatis? (with a bow, and a fish next to her leg), Poseidon? (a fish behind his legs), Arsu (with a round shield) and Heracles (with a club). The scene would appear to relate some myth, perhaps Palmyrene in origin.

commonly medallions bearing busts of other members of the family, living and dead. The designs do admit some variety. Occasionally the reclining male is wearing Greek dress, or a Greek cloak (himation) over Parthian dress, and occasionally the reclining figure is female, attended by female servants. Space between the legs of the couches is sometimes given over to other subjects such as standing figures of attendants, or men equipped for hunting.

The art of Dura Europus was closely allied to that of Palmyra, and some of the reliefs may have been imported from there, or at least executed by Palmyrene sculptors. There are numerous Palmyrene dedications from the city. The influence of Palmyra's art was strong, even in the period of Parthian rule, reflecting the cultural and political importance of that city along this part of the Euphrates river. At Dura roughly worked reliefs depicting a frontal Heracles were popular, and these may be an example of purely local art. Several were found in doorways, and they may have served as a device to ward off evil influences.

Much of the surviving sculpture from Syria is of first- to late-third-century date, and from the fourth century new works become rare. However, wealthy individuals collected older works and displayed them in their homes, just as earlier cultured individuals had done. Such collections were a way of advertising one's learning and culture in late antiquity. To a Christian, pagan images could be allegorical illustrations of virtues, in the same way that Philostratus had used paintings to discuss such subjects, and to intellectual pagans such as Neoplatonists these images still had spiritual meaning. Several sculpture collections are known from private residences across the Roman world, including a fifth-century villa at Antioch, where second- and third-century pieces, plus a few of the fourth century, were displayed. It is not clear whether the owners were pagan or Christian. Three sculptures are portraits: a bearded philosopher or ruler of the late second century, sometimes identified as the short-lived emperor Pertinax (AD 193); a cuirassed bust of the mid-third century portraying a young man with close-cropped hair and beard; and a porphyry head of a tetrarch. The remainder are mythological subjects, many of them good copies of famous Hellenistic originals: a statue identified as Meleager; the torso of a Bacchic figure wearing a panther skin, probably Dionysus himself; a head of Ares; a figure probably copying the statue of Apollo made by the Hellenistic sculptor Bryaxis for the temple at Daphne; heads of two satyrs and a nymph; a sleeping satyr; and a crouching Aphrodite. The mythological pieces all appear to be of Proconnesian marble, but the portrait heads seem to be from another source, perhaps the Aegean.

The early empire, then, is the source of most Syrian sculpture. Works in local styles and depicting indigenous subjects tend to be found more commonly in funerary or religious settings, whereas civic monuments, baths and elite private houses were more appropriate for highly Hellenized pieces, either imported or manufactured locally. Similar trends can be observed in two-dimensional arts, where context also constrained the messages being transmitted and the meanings given.

Mosaic and Painting

In the early Roman period mosaics display much less regional variation than sculpture. No doubt there were mosaic floors in the Hellenistic period, and excavation at Tel Anafa in the Huleh valley has yielded some fragmentary examples. Herod's Hellenizing palaces of the later first century BC had mosaic pavements, of which those on Masada are probably among the best known. Most were very simple geometric panels of black on white, perhaps inspired by contemporary mosaic work from Italy. However, the western palace on Masada yielded polychrome floors of a type that elsewhere would commonly contain figured panels (*emblemata*) at their centre. Instead they have geometric designs, which has been taken as evidence of Herod's Jewish sensitivity to images, but it is also noted that similar designs are to be found on the Hellenistic mosaics of the Greek island of Delos, so Herod may have had plenty of Greek aniconic models to draw on. A few simple polychrome designs are known from other sites, dated to the late first century BC and first century AD, but the tradition of mosaics in Syria and the Near East can only really be traced with confidence from the beginning of the second century. The rise in the grand tradition of mosaics would therefore seem to coincide roughly with the Second Sophistic and the increasing monumentalization and Hellenization of public buildings in the late first century. Mosaics became common throughout the region, and unlike much of the sculpture from Syria their contexts are generally known, so that potentially some of their meanings are easier to comprehend. In the private sphere they were the mark of wealthy residences, and in the public they were most commonly employed in baths (where they provided durable, water-proof surfaces) and, from the fourth century, for the floors of Christian basilicas. Plain mosaic floors were also employed in more workaday contexts, such as courtyards or wine presses, where their waterproof surface would have been much appreciated. In churches they were often donations, and sometimes the name of the benefactor is recorded in the mosaic, along with the date of its completion. In contrast, mosaics in private houses rarely give such details, but even so they still helped to assert the status of their owner. Decorative mosaics were expensive (though perhaps not as costly as marble *opus sectile*, to which floors with mosaics were occasionally 'upgraded'), and consequently the display of colourful mosaics in private households was one of many ways in which the elite could differentiate themselves from the lower classes of society.

This is not the place for a stylistic analysis of mosaics, nor for a study of the tradition's evolution over the centuries. In any case, the study of Syrian and Near Eastern mosaics is hampered by the problem of dating many of the earlier floors. The sites of Antioch, Apamea and Philippopolis have yielded many pavements, allowing a stylistic chronology to be constructed, but in many cases the dating is insecure. It is hoped that the recent spectacular discoveries at Zeugma will help to refine the framework. Mosaic design in the Syrian region can be very roughly broken down into two main periods, one extending from the second to fourth century, and the other from the fifth century onwards. The second to fourth centuries are characterized by the use of polychrome mosaics with figured *emblemata* or geometric panels surrounded by geometric and flo-ral borders. Both geometric and figurative mosaics are commonly character-ized by the heavy use of polychrome tesserae, although the figurative panels normally have a white background. In the second century each geometric band tended to utilize plain colours, but from the Severan period different-coloured tesserae employed in the bands increased the richness of the design, creating what is sometimes referred to as the 'rainbow style'. From the fifth century it became common for mosaics in public places to bear the date of their construction, which is a great aid to chronology. This is also the era of what are sometimes called 'mosaic carpets', floors which use repetitive patterns covering large surfaces.

Designs were clearly the product of choice, and it is this choice which interests us. Before the late fourth century the majority of mosaics were to be found in bath buildings and, most commonly, in wealthy private houses, which raises questions about the degree to which private patrons had a say in the designing of the floors. It seems fairly clear that there were workshops serving clients on a local or regional basis, and that the availability and proximity of these workshops would have dictated which sites were more likely to have had mosaic floors. These local workshops would have been responsible for cutting the small cubes (tesserae) from limestone, ceramic and marble, and laying them. Glass or a vitreous paste was sometimes used, though it was relatively fragile and was best employed for mosaics laid in places where people would not walk on them, such as walls or vaults. The size of the tesserae vary enormously from one mosaic to another, but are likely to reflect cost and function rather than any chronological evolution. When mosaicists did not have enough gradation of colours to attempt chiaroscuro technique, they outlined the figures with lines of tesserae in a single colour (fig. 147).

The question of choice inevitably prompts a further consideration: to what extent was that choice constrained by pattern-books? Was the process of choosing a mosaic like flipping through a catalogue of wallpaper designs? The existence of pattern-books is suggested by the fact that mosaics from different places display many similarities in their details. However, variations indicate that they might not always have been followed too closely. The Wedding of Ariadne and Dionysus is a theme found on mosaics at Zeugma and Philippopolis, but apart from the fact that the two protagonists are seated in the same manner (Dionysus to the right of Ariadne), the details and the composition are very different. If these are derived from pattern-books, the workshops were using quite different models. The workshops may have derived the designs from famous paintings or manuscript illustrations, although there is precious little evidence for illustrated manuscripts before the fifth century. The case for pattern-books remains unproved, but as we will see there can be little doubt that the figurative designs of mosaics in private houses were driven by the aspirations of the elite.

Mosaics can help to define how different parts of a room were used: which spaces were normally occupied by furniture, and which were the main areas of circulation. Like rugs and carpets, they helped to demarcate different uses of space within a house, and the degree of decoration helped define the hierarchy of different rooms. Mosaics in reception areas and bedrooms (which might serve as more private reception rooms) were given precedence and were more likely to be colourful and elaborate to impress visitors than were floors in areas of the house that would not be seen by guests. The mosaics might have been chosen to complement other decorative schemes, such as wall paintings, but in most cases the mural programmes which accompanied them do not survive. Other features might influence the layout, such as the plan and decoration of the ceiling (the painted ceilings of some Syrian tombs closely resemble geometric mosaic patterns). In one room of the so-called Constantinian Villa at Antioch the central feature was an octagonal sunken pool. Four figurative panels of hunting scenes expand out from it in the form of a Maltese cross; the bands between the panels carried representations of the seasons. The pool and the room's shape influenced the mosaic design, and in the case of the seasons the choice of subject may have been conditioned by the fact that there were four spaces to fill (seasons often occupied the corners of square or rectangular designs). This practical consideration does not exclude more symbolically significant readings of the seasons, however.

Attention is usually focused on figurative mosaics, although very many were purely geometric or contained floral motifs. Geometric patterns may have been derived from other media such as textiles or paintings, or all three media may have influenced each other. The carpet-like appearance of many geometric designs, with their repeated interwoven patterns, is very reminiscent of textile decoration, and may imitate expensive coverlets, carpets or wall hangings produced by famous regional centres of textile production, or luxury materials imported from elsewhere. Some geometric panels from floors at Zeugma resemble rugs lying on a paved surface. The geometric decoration of the vault in the Tomb of the Three Brothers at Palmyra uses repetitive patterns commonly found in mosaics (vine scroll, overlapping circles, hexagons), together with painted figurative panels common to the mosaic repertoire. Patterns found in painting and textile are also encountered in monumental relief decorations found on buildings (see above), and it is likely that woodcarving utilized the same designs. The interplay between decorative motifs in a variety of media was likely to have been complex. But not all mosaic was decorated, and some of it was more functional. Some floors were plain, and white tesserae were occasionally used to fill in irregular spaces between walls and the edges of expensive *opus sectile* floors.

The most characteristic feature of the first phase of the mosaic tradition (second to fourth centuries) is the *emblema*, and it is to these that we now turn. *Emblemata* are most commonly found in houses. In these cases there was one important constraint governing choice: the scenes had to be drawn from Greek culture. They did not always correspond exactly to scenes from myths or stories, or at least not the versions that have been passed down to us, which raises questions about the degree of constraint imposed by literary culture. But the scenes chosen were all examples of *paideia*, and the characters were often labelled so that there could be no doubt about their identity. This labelling exposes the frequent use of personifications, either by themselves or accompanying the mythical characters: Charis (Grace), Euprepeia (Comeliness), Tryphe (Luxury), Gethosyne (Joy), Bios (Life). These helped orient literate observers to the meaning of the scene or scenes, and they also hint at a rich system of allegory which is largely lost to us. That allegory is precisely what is important here, for what other meanings lie behind the simple presentation of scenes from Greek myth? Charis and Euprepeia might be attributes of the mythical figures represented, but they might also reflect the aspirations of the mosaic's owners. Did some myths have greater meaning for Syrians, and were they allegories for Syrian myths, or Syrian versions of Greek myths? The beauty contest between the Ethiopian queen Cassiopeia and the Nereids is a scene found at Apamea and Palmyra. Was this a play on the similarity between the names Cassiopeia and the Syrian Mount Casius? One intriguing suggestion is that the scene belongs to a story where the 'Syrian' Cassiopeia wins the beauty contest rather than having her country flooded by Poseidon, as in the better-known Greek version. The possibility of local readings invites new interpretations of other scenes. Was the popularity at Zeugma and Antioch of depictions of the

Fig. 143. Mosaic probably from Zeugma, late second century AD, showing a reclining female figure. At each end are squares filled by female heads.

sea goddess Tethys, mother of the rivers and wife of Oceanus, considered appropriate for cities located on the Orontes and Euphrates? Such an interpretation seems unlikely in the case of the magnificent Tethys panel from Philippopolis, however. Marine themes occur even at inland sites: Nereids and sea-deities; a marine Venus, seated in a giant scallop shell supported by two ichthyocentaurs; Poseidon in a quadriga of hippocamps. And what of Achilles on Skyros, attested at Palmyra and Zeugma, or the above-mentioned Wedding of Ariadne and Dionysus at Zeugma and Philippopolis? The power of this symbolism can be seen in the continued use of the personifications and mythical figures through the Roman period and even after the Muslim conquest (see Epilogue).

Some meanings are easily guessed from their spatial context. A mosaic from the entrance to an Antiochene house at Çekmece shows the Evil Eye attacked by an assortment of beasts and pierced by weapons. The Eye's influence is also contained by the presence of a hunchback with a huge phallus (the Lucky Hunchback was a device thought to keep bad luck at bay). The design is a blatant device aimed at diverting baleful influences away from the riches of the house and the happiness of its owners. Wealth might be displayed, but it had to be protected from the malevolent gazes or desires of others. A late Roman mosaic from a house in Berytus contained a poem about jealousy, the 'worst evil', but one that had its good side because it 'eats up the eyes and heart of the jealous'[50]. Variations on this poem are known from other contexts in the Roman world, including the collection of poetry known as the Palatine or Greek Anthology. This may have been an opportunity for the owners of the house to demonstrate their Hellenism and at the same time ward off the negative forces of envy.

Dining rooms afforded opportunities to display a variety of themes. Some were not particularly learned, though they were highly appropriate to the environment. In the House of the Buffet Supper at Antioch the mosaic for the dining room is laid out to suit a U-shaped arrangement of couches called a *stibadium*. The open space was decorated at one end with the depiction of a large bowl for mixing wine surrounded by exotic birds, and in front of that a circular medallion showing Ganymede providing a drink for the eagle of Zeus. Around the medallion, in the space that would have lain directly in front of the couches, is a band containing dishes for a banquet. Such explicit references to dining, however, are comparatively rare. In contrast there are frequent references to drinking, usually signified through Dionysiac images: satyrs and maenads, or scenes depicting Dionysus himself. Two other mosaics from the Antioch excavations portray the drinking contest between Heracles and Dionysus, and both come from dining rooms. The same theme was used to decorate a large third-century triclinium at Sepphoris in Galilee, where this theme was chosen as the central panel. It is surrounded by smaller panels, many of which are Dionysiac. One, labelled *methe* (drunkenness), shows Heracles collapsing at the end of the drinking contest. At Zeugma, *Akratos* (Unmixed Wine) pours a drink for *Euphrosyne* (Good Cheer).

Dinner parties provided the intellectually inclined with opportunities to demonstrate their learning, and the décor of the dining room was one way of stimulating intellectual conversation. Images could help to guide the subject matter of table talk, providing a framework for polite discussion and displays of rhetorical prowess by the learned. Dining-room images may owe something to the Second Sophistic technique of *ekphrasis*, or description, of art. Among the skills that were prized was the ability of the orator to conjure up a scene in the minds of those listening, and here perhaps was an alternative way of transmitting scenes rather than pattern-books or manuscript illustrations – by word of mouth. Various scenes commonly found in mosaics were those of *ekphrasis*, and favoured descriptions could have helped to make particular images popular. Hunting, a common mosaic theme and a popular aristocratic pastime, is vividly described in Second Sophistic *ekphrasis*. The popularity of such rural themes even in late antiquity could reflect the endurance of and admiration for this rhetorical skill into late Roman times as well as the popularity of the hunt. Indeed, literary epigrams on classical art continued to be composed at least as late as the sixth century.

The dinner party was also a place where performances took place in a private setting. Musical works, plays, mimes or pantomimes might be staged for the enjoyment of the guests. Such performances are vividly recalled in the depiction of female musicians on a late fourth-century mosaic from Mariamme (Miryamin). This was a large rectangular mosaic set in front of an apse in a dining room. The diners would recline in the apse and see the musicians before them. This is manifestly not a copy of a famous Hellenistic painting or some such work, because the musicians are wearing contemporary dress. There is a castanet player, an organist (the bellows powered by two erotes), a flautist, a kithara-player, a woman striking metal bowls laid out on a table and a woman with clappers. The dinner party was also the stage for what might be termed 'performance literature', where readings from poetry or Greek novels took place. Dinner parties have been posited as an important vehicle for disseminating the Greek novels characteristic of the Second Sophistic, and in this genre the dinner party itself occurs as a device where the lovers exchange their first amorous glances. The potential for liaisons in this environment may explain why themes of lovers, such as Aphrodite and Adonis, or scenes where beauty is subject to critical gaze, as in the Judgement of Paris, were considered particularly apt. Mosaic scenes from known novels are rare, but they do exist. There are representations of the lovers in the anonymous romance *Metiochos and Parthenope* known from Antioch and Zeugma, and also from Antioch an image from the novel about the Assyrian king Ninus and his beloved Semiramis. To recognize the scenes meant familiarity with these works, but they could have furnished extra meanings to the viewers about lovers separated and reunited, wanderings through exotic lands, and other stock elements found in the novels. Mosaic representations of characters and scenes from novels or Greek tragedy might suggest a sophisticated audience. However, these images do not necessarily mean that the viewers were well read in Greek literature. Mimes and pantomimes drew on scenes from plays and novels, and their popularity as stage acts and at dinner parties could betray a less refined literary origin for these images.

An ability to hold forth on allegory may explain some of the more extraordinary images, and perhaps only the sophisticated could tease out their overall meanings. One of the most elaborate of numerous high-quality mosaics of the later third and early fourth centuries from Philippopolis is a densely populated panel filled with personifications and mythical figures (fig. 144). The sky is occupied by the four winds and two putti labelled the Drosoi (Dew), emptying jars above the central figures, all of whom are connected with farming.

Triptolemos, the inventor of agriculture, stands next to Georgia (Agriculture personified); before them is Ge (Earth), surrounded by four children labelled the Karpoi (Fruits of the Earth). To the right of this group is Prometheus shaping Protoplastos, the First Man, from clay, and Hermes holding a soul. Two figures in this scene are not labelled. One, watching Prometheus, may be a nymph; the other, standing beside Hermes, may represent the union of body and soul. To the left of Ge is Aion (Eternity) holding the wheel of the heavens, and behind him stand the Four Seasons. The whole may be intended to show how Man, fashioned from clay, makes use of Earth's bounty. An Antiochene pavement shows three men reclining at a dinner party, somewhat poignantly labelled Parochemenos (Past), Enestos (Present), and Mellon (Future), presided over by the figure of Aion. Beneath the three stages of time is their label, *Chronoi*, leaving the observer with the opportunity to reflect on the differences between eternal and relative time. Such rich symbolism no doubt provided plenty of occasions for philosophical discussion.

Symbolic images need not simply have provided an opportunity for the display of learning, and sometimes they may have had profound spiritual meanings for their patrons and viewers which are very difficult for us to extract today. Rooms can have multiple functions, as is implied by the use of bedrooms as private reception areas. Moving furniture can temporarily transform a room into a different kind of space. The importance of ritual within the household can never be ignored, and many figurative panels can also be seen in a more

Fig. 144. Drawing of an elaborate figurative mosaic from Philippopolis (see text).

pious light. For example, Ge and the Karpoi provided the agricultural wealth which maintained the social standing of many elite families, and their images would have been an appropriate reminder of thanks owed. It is noteworthy that these personifications were appropriated by Christians and employed in the ritual context of the church (see below).

The fourth century saw the final flowering of the *emblema* and the adoption of the mosaic medium by Christians for paving churches. Some pagan mosaics may be a reaction to the Christianization of the empire. Excavation of the cathedral of Apamea revealed a fourth-century building underneath, its corridors paved with elaborate figurative and geometric panels. The figured panels represent Odysseus reunited with Penelope while servants dance in a circle (a scene not found in Homer); Socrates, seated Christ-like between six of the Seven Sages; and Cassiopeia and the Nereids. The excavators have suggested that this building may have belonged to the Neoplatonist school established at Apamea and that the mosaics, which are dated to roughly AD 350-75, form part of a Neoplatonic decorative programme. The mythical scenes can be seen as allegories of a quest for wisdom (as personified by 'circumspect Penelope' and the dancing servants, who perhaps symbolize education) and beauty. The prominence given to Socrates among the sages reinforces the view that Platonic philosophy was important to those who commissioned the pavements.

A late third-century mosaic from a house at Heliopolis also gives prominence to Platonic philosophy. Eight looped circles contain portraits of Socrates and the Seven Sages, surrounding a central roundel bearing an image of Calliope, the Muse of Epic. Once again Socrates is given prominence, this time by being placed directly above Calliope. The Seven Sages are accompanied by wise Greek maxims: 'know thyself', 'nothing in excess', 'moderation is best' and so on. An adjacent room bore a floor containing scenes from the life of Alexander the Great. Although damaged, the latter presents a narrative, probably inspired by literary Alexander romances. There is an annunciation scene: Olympias, the mother of Alexander, seated beside Philip of Macedon, receives an envoy of Dionysus who tells her that she will conceive through a god; next to this Olympias reclines on a couch and a servant washes the infant Alexander. The choice of annunciation may have been deliberate: a pagan appropriation of a Christian narrative for the great Hellenistic hero-king.

From the later fourth century it is Christian symbolism that dominates the mosaic medium, although references to pagan Greek culture still occur. But at the end of the fourth century the central figurative panel, the mainstay of the mythical depiction, disappears. The figures remain, but they are normally used as elements in much larger designs (the 'mosaic carpets' mentioned above). The style seems to have been driven by church mosaics, but it also dominates the tessellated floors of private houses and other buildings as well. There is an expansion of contexts in which mosaics are used, such as in the porticos of public colonnades, and the increasing variety of uses is accompanied by more regional variation. Often these are scenes inspired by daily life, rather than the mythical or personificatory images which had dominated in earlier times. The themes no longer seem so constrained by the canon of Greek literature. Devices that had once served as borders to the framed panels, such as grids and vine scrolls, now move to the central part of the mosaic. The carpets contain meanders and swastikas, fields of looped circles, grids and fleurettes. The gaps in the patterns are often filled with vases and chalices, birds, baskets and cages, and sometimes crowded with seemingly random assortments of symbols: discs, fleurettes and lozenges. Older themes are also encountered. There are Nilotic designs, with putti in boats and Egyptian buildings along riverscapes, derived from Hellenistic antecedents (fig. 145).

The use of terms like 'mosaic carpets' evokes textiles, although the relationship between the two media remains conjectural (see above). Like carpets, the later mosaics are frequently designed to be seen from more than one viewing point, even when they contain figures. The figures themselves are scattered on

Fig. 145. Border between the nave and the aisle of the church of St Stephen at Kastron Mefaa (Umm ar-Rasas, Jordan), eighth century AD. Although the mosaic was laid after the period of Roman rule, the elements are typical of the late Roman period. The nave contains a peopled vine scroll (visible to the right), surrounded by a Nilotic border with the cities of the Nile delta, putti in boats, fish and plants. The aisle (on the left) contains geometric patterns and panels with chalices and so on. Of particular interest are the topographical designs between the intercolumnar spaces, depicting Palestinian and Arabian cities. On this section we see, from the bottom upwards: Eleutheropolis, Diospolis, Caesarea, Sebaste, Neapolis and Jerusalem.

a light background, or placed in rows or registers, rather like cutouts. The motifs include Sasanian designs. A large fifth-century mosaic from Antioch, with a central motif of a phoenix, placed on a field of fleurettes, has a border pattern thought to have Sasanian origins: a repeated heraldic motif of a pair of confronted rams' heads above a pair of wings tied with a ribbon. The use of ribbons, which are sometimes shown tied around animals, seems to be inspired by Persian royal emblems. They may have been transmitted to Syria through the medium of Persian textiles, but other decorative arts, such as metalworking, could also have served to disseminate Sasanian designs. Personifications remained popular, although they often refer to the mosaic or the building in which it was laid, or to the owner. A common one is Ktisis, meaning either Foundation or Possession. Other personifications include Ananeosis (Renewal, perhaps a reference to the renovation of a building) and Megalopsychia (Magnanimity), the latter an appropriate emblem for those grandees who considered themselves to possess this virtue. In late mosaics we also encounter an interest in topographic details (fig. 145). A late-fifth century Megalopsychia mosaic from Antioch has a border showing buildings and landmarks of Antioch and Daphne. Topography reaches its most elaborate in the extraordinary mid-sixth-century floor of a church at Medaba, which is in the form of a map, with Jerusalem at its centre. The mosaic is badly damaged and its full extent is not clear, but it must once have depicted the whole of Palestine and Arabia. Cities, mountains and rivers are shown, as is the Dead Sea. Jerusalem is depicted with its main colonnaded street and principal buildings. Important geographical features likely to be of interest to Christian pilgrims are included. It has been suggested that the model was a pilgrim map, perhaps not unlike the Peutinger Table.

The inscriptions on late Roman mosaics record a variety of people of different status donating whole floors or parts of floors to public buildings. In churches it is likely that in most cases the clergy chose the designs, and that the whole ensemble was intended to be programmatic, but some designs may have been selected by lay persons, such as the representation of Mouchasos the Camel-driver from Deir el-Adas (fig. 146). The prominence given to him suggests he was the donor, although we cannot be certain. Stock elements on church mosaics include birds, vegetal motifs and vases. Scenes from the Bible are rare. This contrasts with what we know from textual sources of wall paintings, in which instructive visual lessons from the Bible figured prominently. There may have been a reluctance to place such scenes in places where people could walk on them. The floors seem to have been used as the image of the earth, God's creation, with the animals and plants, and human daily life, that it contained. Creation is emphasized in the floor of a church of the archangel Michael at Huarte near Apamea, where Adam sits amid the animals, presumably in the process of naming them (Genesis 2:19-20). Although more concerned with topographical information, the Medaba map mentioned above continues the earth-bound theme. In contrast, church walls bore images of hope and salvation, and the roof portrayed a vision of heaven. But links with the pagan past were not completely severed in these church floors: a chapel at Nebo (Khirbet el-Mukhayyat) in Jordan has a depiction of two youths with baskets of fruits flanking a bust labelled 'Ge', recalling the arrangement in the Philippopolis mosaic. Here the likely interpretation is that the floor signifies God's earth, personified together with her fruitfulness accessible to the righteous.

Indeed, the elements of the Christian vision (creation, earth's bounty, eternity) were already present in the Philippopolis mosaic. This does not necessarily signify any direct transmission, but it should alert us to the possibility of different symbols being employed to similar ends, and similar ones to different ends, in pagan and Christian contexts.

Jewish synagogues are another category of religious building where elaborate decorative mosaics were laid. There is not much evidence for their use in synagogues prior to the fourth century, but in late antiquity we encounter geometric designs resembling those used on the floors of Christian churches. These include the standard repertoire of grid patterns, looped circles, vine scrolls and animal motifs. Indeed, some have suggested that this form of decoration might have arisen from a desire to compete with the pavements laid by Christian communities. What is quite remarkable is the use of figurative, and even pagan, designs. As in churches Biblical scenes are rare, though perhaps, as in churches, scenes from the Bible decorated the walls (see below). The elaborate mosaics, probably of late fourth-century date, from the synagogue at Hammath Tiberias on the Sea of Galilee, with their inscriptions in Greek, Hebrew and Aramaic, have an interesting mix of Jewish and Hellenized elements. One large panel shows purely Jewish motifs: the Torah shrine flanked by menorahs (seven-branched candlesticks) and other ritual symbols. The other is a square containing a circular zodiac, with naked Hellenizing figures, their names in Hebrew, and a central medallion containing a figure of Helios, the Greek sun-god, in his chariot. The corners of the square have the four seasons. It would seem to point to a strongly Hellenized Jewish elite. The same designs are used about 150 years later in a synagogue at Beth Alpha, although here, while the inspiration may be Hellenic, the execution is thoroughly local. And these are not the only examples; another zodiac and Helios panel has been found at Sepphoris.

No discussion of mosaics in the region can avoid mention of a group of third-century mosaics from tombs at Edessa. Apart from representations of Orpheus, or a phoenix, the rest are remarkably non-classical in style and subject matter, with frontal portraits and Syriac inscriptions (fig. 147). Here the medium of mosaic is adapted to suit local subjects, but caution needs to exercised before viewing these as evidence that Edessenes or Mesopotamians rejected the classicizing styles. The designs may have been chosen because they were considered appropriate to a funerary context. The obvious parallel is Palmyra, where the homes of the elite were decorated in 'Graeco-Roman' style with Greek mythological mosaics, whereas in their funerary art the Palmyrenes maintained a very different, local or regional style. Something similar might be observed for some sixth-century mosaics from a tomb at Emesa which also have frontal depictions of the deceased, although this time in Greek costume. The Edessa mosaics should be compared with a group of later Mesopotamian mosaics from Sarrîn, which are very much Greek in inspiration, with mythological scenes depicting Artemis, Heracles, Aphrodite and Dionysus. They came

Fig. 146. Mouchasos the Camel-driver, mosaic from a church at Deir el-Adas in the Hauran, dated to the early Islamic period, now on display in the theatre at Bostra. Such scenes of 'daily life' are common in late antique mosaics. Mouchasos may have been the donor of this pavement.

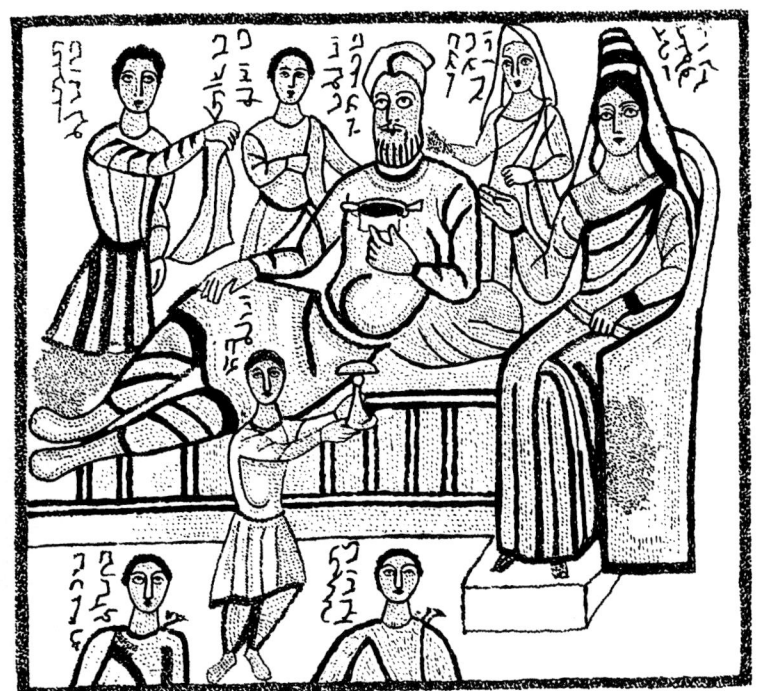

Fig. 147. Drawing of the Funerary Couch mosaic from Edessa, late Severan period. The arrangement of figures and busts closely resembles the decoration found on funerary couch sarcophagi of Palmyra.

from a peristyle, but whether the context was a private house or public building cannot be determined.

Of paintings of the Roman period, very little survives. The best evidence comes from the early Roman period, from temples and houses at Dura Europus, the Tomb of the Three Brothers at Palmyra, houses at Zeugma, a hypogeum at Masyaf, about 30 kilometres (18½ miles) south of Apamea, and a recently discovered *mithraeum* at Huarte, about 15 kilometres (9¼ miles) to the north-west of the same city. In all cases the surviving examples are unlikely to represent Syrian painting at its very best. As with sculpture, a 'provincial' style is more evident at Dura and Palmyra than in those regions closer to the coast, but the overall evidence is slender. Inland at Zeugma the content and execution is entirely Hellenic; like mosaics, paintings were a way for their owners to express their education in Greek culture, and artists skilled in the style were available. Wall paintings from a house at Petra, probably of the first century, depict fantasy architectural *trompe l'oeil* designs, likened to the Second Style of painting at Pompeii, but may draw their inspiration from nearby Alexandria rather than Italy. They too suggest that Hellenized designs were appropriate to domestic contexts.

Many of the Dura paintings come from religious structures, which may have influenced the styles. Frontal depictions are the norm, as with sculpture at Dura and Palmyra, and the figures or scenes are arranged in registers, with no attempt at perspective. When the Dura frescoes were first discovered in 1920, their frontality was thought to provide a link between the art of third-century Syria and the later Byzantine tradition. There are, however, problems with this, not least finding later examples of Syrian frontality to bridge the chronological gap between the two traditions. There may be a link, but it may be similarity of purpose (the gaze of the image connecting directly with the viewer and the room) that created the two traditions, rather than transmission from one to the other. Painted figures could serve as cult images instead of reliefs or statues. In the temple of Zeus Theos, the god was portrayed on a fresco on the rear wall of the *naos*, crowned by two victories; on either side the walls bore registers of worshippers. The formal poses of the worshippers, right hands raised in an attitude of prayer, or sprinkling incense on a burner, established these individuals, like the funerary reliefs at Palmyra, as a continual and attentive presence within the sacred space. The frescoes from the Christian chapel, although poorly executed, are rather different. A depiction of the Good Shepherd occupies the main niche above the pool which served as a font, along with Adam and Eve. The other paintings were arranged in two registers around the walls. The lower one shows a procession of women holding torches approaching a pedimented sarcophagus-like object, interpreted as the Holy Women at the Sepulchre. They also would have led the eyes of any viewers or participants in the room towards the font. Above the women is a very fragmentary set of images, of which two are identifiable: the healing of the paralytic and Christ walking on water. Separate panels showed David and Goliath and the Samaritan woman at the well. These Biblical episodes and miracles, for which the only date is a graffito of AD 232/233, furnished the worshippers with reminders of God's power. Here perhaps is an early example of the tradition for placing scenes derived from Biblical and other texts on church walls, and one wonders how much it owes to the tradition found in the nearby synagogue, whose last phase dates to about AD 245, a decade before Dura was sacked and abandoned. The magnificent frescoes of the assembly hall of this building demonstrate that the Jewish community of Dura was perfectly at home among painted images of human beings. Even the ceiling tiles were painted with figurative decoration. The west wall, containing an aedicula where the Torah was kept, is the best preserved. Biblical scenes are arranged in registers around the room: Moses and the burning bush, the Exodus and the Red Sea crossing, Elijah raising the widow's son, the sacrifice of Isaac, and Ezekiel's prophecy, to name but a few. Although evoking events of a distant past, the figures are dressed in contemporary Greek or Persian clothes. The identity of some of the scenes is disputed, and it is hard to discern any overall programme in their arrangement. The difficulty of reconciling some of the scenes with surviving texts has led to the ingenious proposition that these are the product of an oral tradition rather than one based on a canonical text or texts, providing the rabbi and others with an opportunity to expound on the scriptures and draw various meanings from the images (rather in the way that mosaic *emblemata* might have done at the Hellenized dinner party), instead of providing a simple pictorial illustration of the scriptures.

Also religious in content are the paintings from the *mithraeum* at Huarte, dated to the fourth century. Like the Dura church and synagogue, they show narrative scenes from myths: for example, the birth of Mithras, and a battle between gods and giants. Not all are obviously associated with Mithras, and the programme may have been intended to assimilate the god to other deities like Helios, Apollo and Attis. Perhaps the most remarkable scene of all is a rampart decorated with a row of hideous heads, each pierced by a yellow ray of sunlight – probably a reference to the City of Darkness and its demonic agents. Other agents of darkness have complete human forms, although at least one has two heads. They are depicted being torn apart by lions, or held in chains by horse riders. As at Dura, the figures are dressed in Greek and Persian garments.

The use of a local or regional idiom in funerary contexts has already been mentioned in conjunction with sculpture and mosaics. In some cases Hellenized and indigenous conventions could be employed alongside one another, each appropriate for the particular message being conveyed. The paintings in the Tomb of the Three Brothers at Palmyra are interesting for the way they combine the Palmyrene tradition of funerary portraits with Graeco-Roman-style narrative *emblemata* drawing on Greek myth, and with generic geometric designs seen on mosaics. The frescoes at the end of the main gallery include typically Palmyrene frontal figures and busts of the departed in both Palmyrene and Greek costume, mixed with scenes executed in a thoroughly

Hellenized style: Achilles discovered on Skyros, disguised as a woman, and Ganymede being carried up to heaven. The Achilles scene was common as a decoration for sarcophagi in the Roman world, and it also occurs on mosaic pavements in houses. Here it may be an allegory of transition, the point where Achilles chooses a glorious but short life; the theme of Ganymede stresses transition from one mode of existence to another. The paintings from the hypogeum at Masyaf are now lost; they are thought to be of the late second century. The themes were typical of funerary contexts but the treatment was purely Hellenized. On the wall were depictions of trees, an image of Narcissus, and children playing marbles. One of the sarcophagi was painted with classical figures typical of sarcophagus reliefs, associated with the Rape of Persephone. For allegorical imagery, Hellenized scenes were appropriate (however differently they might be understood); for representations of the deceased, other traditions might be employed.

Fig. 148. Stele at Arsameia on the Nymphaios in Commagene, showing Antiochus I of Commagene in Armenian and Persian royal dress, shaking hands with the Greek god Heracles. The nearby inscriptions, however, are all in Greek.

DRESSING DIFFERENTLY

The vast amount of material and textual evidence for daily life, and regional variations in that evidence, has already been alluded to in previous chapters. Through everyday activities people can make themselves different. Taboos concerning food, and variations in food preparation and presentation, traceable through animal bones and pottery, have already been mentioned (chapters 5 and 6). Attitudes to beverages could also signify difference. The dedications to a Nabataean deity, Shai al-Qaum, 'the good and rewarding god, who does not drink wine',[51] may indicate that his devotees also abstained from alcohol, or wine at least. As wine was central to the Graeco-Roman way of life, abstention would have been an important mark of cultural distinction. Likewise the treatment of the body, through acts such as male body piercing or circumcision, created markers of difference, and will have set such people apart from Hellenized ideals. The Greek and Roman notions of male beauty could cause circumcised males embarrassment in Hellenized environments like the baths or gymnasium, and some sought to disguise such physical marks through a surgical procedure called epispasm (the 'uncircumcision' of I Corinthians 7:18-19). The operation became so commonplace in Hadrianic Judaea that rabbis introduced more radical forms of circumcision which could not be easily disguised.

Clothing and dress are important signifiers of identity, being used to denote status and social role as well as gender. There are often firm rules and taboos governing what people can wear, and even subtle variations can be used as a symbol of resistance to norms. Much of the evidence for clothing comes from funerary sculpture, which presents us with a problem because the way people chose to be represented in death may not have reflected their everyday attire. It did, however, reflect the manner in which they themselves or their surviving relatives wanted the deceased to be seen for eternity (see below). Throughout the region, cult images from Commagene to Petra are found in non-Greek garb, but what was appropriate for deities need not have been so for mortals. Again, context was probably important in deciding what sort of dress was appropriate. Emperors and deities could wear military costume. Honorific, non-funerary statues for public display tend to be in Greek-style dress or wearing a toga. Gender and status might have a part to play, with male citizens emphasizing their status through Greek dress, while women sometimes used more traditional clothing (fig. 139). Client rulers were able to emphasize their cultural allegiances through the use of regular Graeco-Roman garb, but Antiochus I of Commagene chose to stress his non-Greek descent through the tall Armenian tiara and Persian-style clothing of his statues and reliefs (figs 141, 148). However, his less politically independent descendant Antiochus IV, who had grown up among the Roman nobility, was portrayed as a Hellenistic monarch, wearing the diadem. A similar diademed Hellenistic ruler portrayed on a ring from the necropolis at Emesa (fig. 149.1) would be unremarkable were it not for the prominent earring; he may be a local dynast. (Male earrings were for Pliny the Elder an 'oriental' trait and a notable mark of difference.)[52] The Ituraean rulers of Chalcis and the Herodian kings all opted for Hellenistic portraits, but whether these images are an accurate rendering of their normal appearance is unclear. Different appearances could be used for different audiences. The third-century usurper Vaballathus could be depicted with short hair, in Graeco-Roman style, on coins issued at Antioch, but some of those struck in Egypt show him with long hair (fig. 149.2). There seems little point in asking which is the 'true' portrait; both images are probably symbolic, although the Alexandrian one is a strikingly non-Roman choice in terms of social code. That it would be seen only in Egypt (because the coins did not circulate elsewhere) makes it no less extraordinary. There are numerous images of males, both mortal and divine, with long hair in Palmyrene art (most Palmyrene male portraits are short-haired, however). The use of Parthian clothes at Palmyra suggests that a Palmyrene fashion for long hair could have originated across the Euphrates, because Parthian, Hatrene and Sasanian rulers are portrayed with long hair, but it is also found among the peoples of the Syrian steppe, and among the Nabataean kings, so what statements were intended by the use of long hair for a portrait of Vaballathus are unclear to us. The meanings of other dress codes are also enigmatic, such as the loincloths found on male figures in sculpture from the Hauran of the Nabataean period. If these are to be connected with traditional bedouin dress as some scholars have suggested, it may be a statement about the comparative social prominence of nomadic groups in the region.

Palmyrene sculpture provides us with a good idea of the way in which context influenced dress. As is the case throughout the region, honorific statues normally wear togas or Greek mantles, appropriate to the civic environment. In their funerary reliefs the costumes worn by the male Palmyrene elites are Greek or Parthian rather than consciously indigenous, but parallels have been drawn between women's dress and local bedouin costume still worn in the region today. Other costumes encountered in mythological or cult scenes, such as the beam from the Temple of Bel showing a procession (fig. 159), may be indigenous. Here women are in an entirely different mode of dress from that worn in

Fig. 149.1. Signet ring from the necropolis at Emesa, depicting a ruler wearing a royal diadem. First century BC – first century AD? After H. Seyrig, Syria xxxix (1952), pl. 27, no. 6.

149.2. Alexandrian coin portrait of Vaballathus, wearing both a Hellenistic-style royal diadem and the laurel wreath of a triumphal Roman commander.

the funerary reliefs, completely veiled from head to toe, their faces hidden. The male figures in the relief wear long tunics with short sleeves, belted at the waist, which seems to be the appropriate attire for religious observances but not for other contexts. A relief from the Temple of Nebo shows male priests in similar belted tunics, with bare feet. As we do not know for certain who the people in the beam relief are, it is not possible to be sure what the costumes of the women signify, although they are probably ritual. Religious garb perhaps incorporates elements of 'Syrian' costume (see below), and thus the veils could be seen as an expression of cultural identity within a specific social context. At any rate, such clothing seems to have been unsuitable for funerary reliefs or honorific statuary.

The Palmyrene funerary reliefs and sculptures, which form the largest category of evidence for dress codes, are likely to represent the values of the civic elites, reflecting either actuality or aspirations. Some patterns may be the result of particular sculpture workshops concentrating on mass production of images with certain styles of clothing, but private demands are likely to have shaped the canons of the workshops, and in some cases the same style or hand is evident for sculptures in both Greek and Parthian modes of dress. The chronology of the portraits indicates an increasing interest in non-Greek costumes over time. Where figures appear in the early Palmyrene reliefs, they are normally shown in Greek dress, but from the mid-first century AD Parthian costume begins to make an appearance. Men might wear a pendant or torque (also found in the Hauran sculptures), finger rings (commonly worn on the little finger of the left hand) and wreaths. The male fashion for beards appears to move in concert with Roman fashion: beardless in the first century, with beards becoming more common in the second and almost universal in the third. The only exceptions are priests, who remain clean-shaven throughout the period (though former priests could apparently grow beards). Long hair is worn by figures with or without beards, and may be combined with Greek or Parthian dress. Where there are multiple figures, some may wear Parthian dress and others Greek, or individuals might mix the two, wearing a Greek mantle over a Parthian tunic and trousers. How did Palmyrene viewers interpret these different dress codes? They must have transmitted certain statements about individual identity. Did the choice of a Greek mantle for a man make a statement about cultural allegiances, to the *polis*, and/or to the Roman empire? If so, what did Parthian dress signify in this context? And what messages did mixed Greek and Parthian garb communicate?

What is called 'Parthian' dress is in fact the male clothing and hairstyles typical of Mesopotamia. It might indeed be better labelled 'Mesopotamian'. The royal statues of Hatra are dressed in the same style, and there are strong parallels with the costumes of the mosaics from Edessa (fig. 147). The 'Mesopotamian' attire consists of a short tunic with long sleeves, often embroidered with elaborate braids and strips of richly decorated material, in one or two vertical stripes. Sometimes the individual wears a long coat, open at the front, over the tunic. Loosely fitting trousers of the type worn by Antiochus I of Commagene (fig. 148) are also embroidered with stripes down them. Some sculptures depict leggings worn over the lower legs of the trousers and attached to a belt under the tunic, a form of accessory favoured by the Parthian and Sasanian nobility. This type of costume is normally accompanied by ankle-length boots, into which the trousers are tucked. A small lead tessera depicting

Fig. 150. Lead tessera of Herodian, son of Odaenathus of Palmyra, describing him as king and showing him in a Mesopotamian-style royal tiara and with his hair gathered in a bunch at the back of his head in Mesopotamian or Sasanian style. The other side (not shown) depicts him wearing a laurel wreath. After H. Seyrig, Antiquités Syriennes ii, (Paris, 1938), pp. 44-5 and pl. VI, 1.

Odaenathus' son Herodian takes the Mesopotamian theme even further, showing him dressed in the tall headdress typical of Edessene and Hatrene royalty (fig. 150). In the use of such dress, Palmyrenes appealed to identities other than Hellenism as a source of social authority.

The richness of Palmyrene female attire has attracted much comment, but there is considerable variety, making generalizations difficult. The veil worn over the head is common to funerary sculpture elsewhere, although occasionally Palmyrene women are portrayed without it. First- to mid-second-century womens' dress is fairly simple and conforms more to the forms found in other regions of the Roman world, with a veil over the head and the hair held in a diadem. Sometimes they wear jewellery, and are often shown carrying spindle and distaff – symbols of the female role in the household that would have been entirely familiar to Hellenized viewers. In the second century there is an elaboration of female costumes, with increased emphasis on jewellery: necklaces, earrings, finger rings, diadems and bracelets. The most elaborate costumes occur in the third century, where the veil is drawn over a highly decorated and jewelled turban, but other women continued to be portrayed in the simpler dress of earlier times. The combination of turban and veil may have been influenced by styles at Edessa and Hatra, where even taller headdresses are found (fig. 147).

Fig. 151. Syrian priests.

151.1. Drawing of the left-hand section of the fresco of the priest Konon and his family from the Temple of Bel at Dura, showing the offering of incense.
151.2. Drawing of the relief of the high priest Alexander from Hierapolis. Note the conical hat, belted tunic and bare feet.
151.3. Drawing of part of a relief from a tomb at the village of Babulin, 95 kilometres (60 miles) south-east of Aleppo, showing a priest called Rapsones sacrificing at an altar.

151.1

151.2

151.3

Religious dress is often conservative and at variance with everyday attire. The beardless, shaved heads of Palmyrene priests, dressed in their distinctive cylindrical hats, are well known from Palmyrene funerary sculptures. Evidently the hats alone could signify 'priest' (and the decoration perhaps signified the deity), because reliefs and sculptures show the wearers in attire appropriate to the context of the art (a toga in the case of an honorific statue), but as we have seen in the case of the beam relief from the Temple of Bel, other evidence hints that special dress (long belted tunic, bare feet) might be appropriate during religious activities. Certainly this seems to have been the case in some of the temples at Dura Europus. The dress (long tunic and tall conical hat) and pose (offering incense) found on religious reliefs and temple frescoes there, such as the late second- or third-century AD fresco of the priest Konon from the Temple of Bel (fig. 151.1), are paralleled on the late fourth-century BC coins of Mambog (Hierapolis). A basalt relief from Hierapolis of the second century AD (?) shows the high priest Alexander in similar attire, his conical cap decorated with astral symbols and his tunic belted at the waist and with a fringe of bells or pom-poms at the bottom (fig. 151.2). Two other unprovenanced reliefs of the Roman period in the Aleppo Museum depict priests in the same dress, as do reliefs now in Gaziantep Museum in what was formerly Commagene. While Dura and Hierapolis are some distance apart, there does seem to be a case for regarding these images as an example of continuity of local religious attire along the Euphrates from at least the time of Alexander. Only slightly different is the image of the priest Narkisos, son of Kasios, carved on the podium of the Temple of Hadaranes at Niha in the Bekaa valley (fig. 152). He is bearded, wears a long tunic with sleeves (which is also belted at the waist), a pectoral ornamented with relief busts of a male and female deity, and a pointed cap decorated with a crescent. The pointed cap may have been a characteristic element of Syrian costume in the Achaemenid period; at Persepolis in Iran a relief showing figures in such caps is generally thought to be a Syrian delegation visiting the Great King. Thus it is possible that elements of the costumes worn by priests and worshippers and reserved for religious activities in the Roman period were consciously 'Syrian' and had once been elements of formal dress.

Fig. 152. The priest Narkisos from the Temple of Hadaranes at Niha.

MUDDY WATERS: THE IMPURITY OF IDENTITIES

The cultures of Syria and the Near East during the Roman period are sometimes described as hybrid, drawing in particular on Greek, Roman, local and Mesopotamian influences. Yet all cultures, even the most isolated, are in some sense hybrids, so this does not define those of the Syrian region as special or unusual. One can try to tease apart the different threads of origins and influences at places like Palmyra or Petra, but the separate influences need not say anything much about what the whole meant to contemporaries. Still less do the influences help to define what is 'real' and what is 'veneer'. When looking for social identities one has to take into account all of the evidence, which is no easy task. All sorts of cultural symbols – shapes and designs of pottery, funerary rites, images of deities and so on – were manipulated by communities and individuals to express similarities with or differences from others. The same group could express difference from others in one context or field of activity (say, religion) and similarity in another (such as language or political form) without contradiction. As we have seen, the signs themselves might be open to more than one interpretation, and things that seem insignificant to us today may have generated profound feelings of distinction at the time. Even landscape creates a sense of belonging and difference.

Hellenism was a powerful influence in the region during the period of Roman rule and an important tool for constructing communities. It was certainly not simply a façade masking another reality, and nor should it be seen as an influence that somehow contaminated the cultural 'purity' of traditional identities. It did, however, have much to do with power, with social standing, and with Roman imperialism. (We should reject any attempt to provide a neo-evolutionary explanation for the success of Hellenism, whereby a superior, vigorous 'high' culture naturally overcomes or is autonomously adopted by less vigorous, 'passive' ones.) The language and writing of power was Greek (and, in certain contexts, Latin), so command of the high-status language would have endorsed the standing of those fluent in this form of symbolic capital. But the influence of Hellenism ran deeper than that. With it came a way of life and a mentality centred on the *polis*, an institution in which the elites of Syria, supported by Rome, invested a great deal. Greek cultural forms penetrated society on many levels. Hellenism may have provided a sort of symbolic *lingua franca* by incorporating different traditions into a multi-faceted unity, allowing each community to identify through its own traditions with the wider cultural community of empire. Yet incorporation or assimilation was never divorced from the realities of power. The city state, allied with the Roman empire, influenced individuals and communities in their choice of cultural performances, although it also offered some individuals, especially members of the elite, a chance to participate in a wider imperial culture.

The institutions of Roman imperialism, particularly the legal system, forced individuals and communities to interact with the dominant power on its own terms, and created new identities through organizations like the imperial cult or, from the fourth century, the state's adoption of Christianity (see chapter 9). Those who hailed from communities which had most thoroughly assimilated the dominant Graeco-Roman imperial culture might seem better positioned to attain important posts in the empire, yet there are some hints that, important though Greek culture was, loyalty to Rome need not always have been expressed and rewarded through the intermediary of Hellenism. From the second half of the first century AD wealthy Syrians began entering the Roman Senate. Most whose origins are known came from Antioch, but this strongly Hellenized city was followed by less Hellenized Palmyra, which produced at least six Roman senators. It may however be significant that Judaea, Arabia and Mesopotamia did not contribute to the senatorial class in any significant way, and that the same bias may be noted for the rather more plentiful equestrians hailing from the region. One's cultural background, it seems, probably affected one's chances of attaining high offices of state – at least in the early empire. In the Christian empire the institution of the church offered opportunities for advancement for people from a variety of backgrounds, sometimes allowing those without a classical education to circumvent the restraints imposed by imperial Hellenism.

The common use of Hellenizing or Roman symbols in the Syrian region does not necessarily mean the obliteration of other identities. The surviving material traces of languages, art and dress are all the remnants of cultural performances, within a particular context, and with a particular audience in mind: Hellenized guests at a dinner party; peers and subordinates in the civic community; participants in religious and funerary rites; advocates in legal disputes; or recipients of letters, to select some examples. Within these contexts individuals and groups made choices, selecting from the alternative signs available to create a sense of identity, and to conform to or to resist the hegemonic powers that impinged on their lives. Hellenized intellectuals might avoid making anything of their non-Hellenized origins in their writings because the genre was inappropriate for such expressions, but others of lesser social status might choose to emphasize theirs. In distant South Shields on Hadrian's Wall, a Palmyrene called Barates commissioned a funerary relief in the late second century for his British wife Regina. The imagery of the relief, showing Regina seated on a chair within an ornate aedicula is fairly normal in the repertoire of western funerary art, although the hairstyle and the spindle and distaff are typically Palmyrene. Moreover, apart from the Latin inscription, there is also a text in Palmyrene, paralleling the bilingual funerary texts in Greek and Palmyrene at Palmyra itself. Epitaphs generally suppose an audience, and the Palmyrene one hints at a desire for distinction, though we cannot know how many people in South Shields would have recognized the Palmyrene text as anything other than 'barbarian letters'. But the deployment of Palmyrene in a British context must say something for its cultural importance to Barates himself, and for the fact that it was deemed an appropriate language for such a monumental medium even in this far-flung location. Equally striking is another funerary relief from South Shields for a Mauretanian freedman called Victor, whose pose, reclining on a couch, recalls Palmyrene reliefs. So too do the small facing busts above the scene, and the vegetal scroll behind him. The designs and execution suggest a highly competent sculptor familiar with Palmyrene art, who may himself have been from Palmyra. Once again, we are presented with something 'hybrid', but in this case the non-Hellenized elements were hardly local and some of the meanings will have been apparent only to a few.

In searching for Syrians the quest is not so much to locate a multicultural society lurking behind a Hellenized façade, and nor is it to classify and arrange identities according to distinct cultures occupying contiguous regions, with well-defined boundaries between their different customs, language, art and dress, and with the individuals in each cultural group all adhering to a single identity: 'Phoenician', 'Arab', 'Syrian' and so on. As stated earlier in this chapter, identity and culture are not the same thing. Individuals and groups construct their identities by participating in cultures or social institutions to differing degrees, using various different identities to negotiate status and rights, depending on context. Those identities in Roman Syria that were more readily renegotiated and revised are difficult for us to detect, given the very fragmentary nature of our evidence. One task is to try to make sense of the reasons why particular forms were chosen: Palmyrene monumental inscriptions, self-ascriptions as 'Syrians', Egyptian cornices, imported Proconnesian sarcophagi, ritual pointed caps and so on; and why particular forms were sometimes abandoned. We are often left with impure genres of overlapping identities, deployed in situations that we cannot determine for reasons that are lost to us. We know far more about Greek or Jewish culture than we do about the others, making Hellenizing or Judaizing choices easier to recognize and explain than Palmyrene or Nabataean. Our ignorance of other identities may make them especially hard to see. Even when certain forms persist over long periods of time (as seems to have been the case with ritual dress at Hierapolis), their significance is far from certain, and it is easy for us to dismiss as insignificant meanings that we do not fully comprehend. Nor does an apparent lack of continuity indicate cultural passivity or weakness. Cultural continuity can be maintained through institutional supervision and deliberate training and instruction, but what is reproduced, and how consistently it is reproduced, will depend, among other things, on the relations of the community with outside powers, on different cultural attitudes to memory, to the primacy and authority of written texts, and the extent to which myths and tradition could be used as justification for, or altered to suit, actions in the present. The possibilities for variation are almost infinite. In the search for Syrian identities, and the ways in which people may have made themselves different or similar, historians and archaeologists have set themselves a particularly difficult exercise.

9 THE PIOUS WORLD

POLYTHEISM

Religions form another major sphere of social interaction through which people construct identities and a sense of belonging. It was also a sphere of social interaction which Hellenism respected. The Greeks may have assimilated local deities to Greek myths, but they did not suppress those local cults, or their forms of worship. This meant that local or regional cults became a channel through which local or regional identities could be affirmed. That is not to say that they did not adapt or appropriate Greek symbols, or that their adherents rejected Hellenism, or that the cults were in some sense evidence for a separate pagan Syrian culture of resistance. But at the same time we should also be wary of concluding that the metaphysical spaces consecrated to the deities (temples, shrines and altars) were seen by worshippers solely through the material remains that we ourselves observe at the sites. We should be wary too of concluding that the use of 'Graeco-Roman' architectural styles, Greek cult statues, or Greek inscriptions means that indigenous forms of piety could no longer find material or spiritual expression. The material evidence itself suggests a wide spectrum of responses and levels of interaction between Greek and native forms. We might even detect pride in these cults on the part of highly Hellenized Syrians. For example, the satirist Lucian is reverent in his treatment of the cult of the Syrian goddess Atargatis at Hierapolis, as he is with other religions of the region, and this stands in sharp contrast to his irreverent and often critical approach to the traditional Greek gods and goddesses.

Like cities, cults might seek wealthy benefactors or imperial sponsors. Dedications made by Roman soldiers and officers at the shrines of local cults may provide proof of their success at attracting these representatives of state power. At the same time major sanctuaries could become an arena for competing social identities and even competing cults, with different groups promoting their interests or 'ancestral gods' within and around the sacred space. Some irregular designs of temples and sanctuaries suggest compromises to accommodate these different interests. Whereas ethnicity or tribal affiliations might determine the composition of worshippers of certain cults, others were apparently open to a wider range of people (or they had become more open as a result of social compromises). A few of these gained international recognition, and their images, like those of the Tyche of Antioch or the figure of Roma, were icons recognized across the empire. The ways in which they gained this 'superstar' status might differ considerably: for example, Jupiter of Doliche in Commagene was adopted for private worship by Roman soldiers and spread with the army, for reasons that are quite obscure. This means that ethnic origins might have nothing to do with attachment to a highly successful cult, although in many cases Syrian soldiers and traders were responsible for disseminating Syrian cults overseas. The advance of a cult might depend on luck; emperors and other important figures were impressed by the power of the god or goddess, and became benefactors or devotees. With very successful cults there might be very little central control over the composition of worshippers, and even less over spiritual meaning. In pagan cult, there was no one authority controlling iconography, cult practice and liturgy, or architectural design. As far as we can tell, cults such as Mithraism had no equivalent of the Council of Nicaea to determine their orthodoxy. The same deity might be the subject of different, contradictory myths or the focus of different types of ritual at different shrines or cities. If worshippers did not see a god or goddess as one thing, how did this affect their sense of identity, and how does it affect our search for the 'meaning' of a deity?

Icons of Difference

A significant number of Syrian deities was recognizable through the use of highly distinctive cult images which depart from the norms of classical representations. Some of these images are traceable to pre-classical times; others were perhaps creations of the Hellenistic or Roman periods. They did not have to be exceedingly old or 'genuine' to be successful generators of difference. Their importance lies in their individuality, and the fact that the forms of many were clearly traditional and indigenous. The images are generally so distinct that there is no mistaking them for any other deity, and some scholars regard the use of these special 'icons' as affirmations of each cult's uniqueness, providing a way for indigenous peoples to assert their differences. While there were generic images of Zeus, Athena, Heracles and so on, these iconic images were defined by their specificity, and often by their identification with a place: Jupiter Heliopolitanus; Zeus Kataibates of the Cyrrhestians; Zeus Casius. The deity could be depicted in both generic and specific forms, one perhaps intended to appeal to Hellenized sensibilities, and the other denoting an indigenous origin. For example, the god might make more sense to those with a Greek education as a human figure, but be more intelligible to others as a conical stone. But the fact that we find Hellenized individuals like Lucian also taking an interest in promoting indigenous images is surely of some importance.

Fig. 153.1. Coin of Arca (Caesarea ad Libanum), of Elagabalus, dated year 530 (AD 218/219). Cult image of a goddess in an arched shrine, draped, wearing a flaring hat and with a bird-tipped sceptre. BMC 6

As was noted in the preceding chapter, non-Greek or non-generic images of deities are common on civic coins of the second and third centuries, coinciding with a growth in the number of cities issuing coins and with the development of the Second Sophistic as a cultural movement. These designs are likely to reflect the interests of the civic elites, suggesting pride in the uniqueness of the cults at a relatively high social level. Hellenism's respect for religions left the door open for expressions of identity outside the conventions of the Second Sophistic, although in the case of coin types this expression occurred within the framework of the Greek-style city state. This need not imply, however, that all of these cults were somehow created or shaped by the hegemonic forces of Hellenism; rather it betokens recognition and pride on the part of those elites that the images contributed to the uniqueness of the community, and acknowledgement of the deities as a source of social power. The explosion of non-Greek cult images on civic coins created a sacred geography of indigenous individuality only loosely linked to the religious worlds of Greece and Rome. Piety was one way for civic communities to advertise a non-Greek identity without necessarily resisting Hellenism.

Fig 153.2. Coin of Ptolemais, of Elagabalus. Shrine containing a male cult figure, holding a double axe and flanked by bulls. BMC 41.

Some of the more successful icons of cult and of place, such as Jupiter Dolichenus, Jupiter Heliopolitanus and the Syrian goddess Atargatis, gained a following far beyond the boundaries of their home cities. Their images were faithfully replicated in various media across the empire, but in each case the image referred to an original statue, associated with a particular place. The dispersal of Syrian cults outside the region is not strictly relevant here, except that as in Syria itself many used the network of cities of the empire to propagate. At the provincial level and perhaps beyond, the organization of the imperial cult (on which, see below) could have provided a model for supervising a cult over a wide area, if such supervision were deemed important. But in many cases the spread of cults may have been down to individuals or groups resident in a foreign city setting up a shrine or temple to their ancestral deity, which might develop its own rituals and operate independently of the original sanctuary.

Dedications to deities like Jupiter Heliopolitanus and Atargatis are encountered far beyond the bounds of Syria, and the cult centres are likely to have benefited from foreign patronage. For their home cities these superstar cults could attract imperial honours, bring large numbers of pilgrims and additional commerce, and advance the city in the provincial pecking-order. This is made clear by Lucian's account of the cult of a serpent god called Glycon, which in the second century was advanced by a certain Alexander from Abonuteichus in northern Asia Minor. Lucian was scathing in his account of the activities of this 'false prophet', whom he charges with inventing the Glycon cult, but in the end Alexander's efforts appear to have been successful and brought various benefits to his native city. It is possible, then, that some Syrian cults were 'discovered' or promoted by their cities with an eye to their own advantages.

Hellenized observers did indeed see the iconic images of Syrian deities as non-Greek. The historian Herodian (who is thought to have originated from Syria) specifically states that the strange cult image of Elagabal was no statue 'of the sort that Greeks and Romans put up'[53] (on this image, see below). In Lucian's work on the Syrian goddess, Syrian and Phoenician cults are presented as non-Greek, and it is emphasized that they are older, as if this link with the traditions of a distant pre-Hellenic past were a significant asset. References in inscriptions to the deities as 'ancestral' gods appeals to tradition and may suggest that many of these were originally deities connected with tribes or particular places. Perhaps it does not matter whether we can find anything 'really' pre-Hellenic or pre-Hellenistic in the scattered evidence for many of these cults, or anything demonstrating true continuity of cult across the centuries. That continuity was perceived or imagined by contemporaries is enough.

Some of these images probably drew on ancient representations deliberately. The figure of Jupiter Dolichenus, the god of Doliche in Commagene, stood on the back of a bull and held an axe; it must derive from local early Iron Age reliefs of the Neo-Hittite period which also show bearded deities in the same pose. Whether this represents continuity from the early Iron Age to Roman times or simply appropriation of an ancient effigy in the Hellenistic or Roman period, the evidence will not allow us to decide, but it is surely significant that an old and decidedly non-Greek figure was consistently reproduced as the symbol of this deity, and transmitted across the Roman world. Why he became a focus of private worship for Roman soldiers is thoroughly uncertain, but the army was clearly fundamental in spreading his very specific image. There is nothing to suggest that he was the focus of widespread worship by civilians, even in Syria.

Another grand icon was that of Jupiter Heliopolitanus. Lucian states that the cult was Egyptian (there was a Heliopolis in Egypt). Representations in bronze, stone and lead (fig. 176) found in various parts of the Roman world served as propaganda for dissemination of the cult. The image does contain

Egyptian elements, such as the mummy-like body of the figure decorated with panels and the tall hat, but these are combined with others: a whip (in Graeco-Roman iconography an attribute of the sun-god), ears of corn, and a pair of bulls. These appear to conflate a celestial deity (implied by the name Heliopolis) with an agrarian one, and the bulls and ears of corn recall images of the Aramean god Hadad, with whom Jupiter Heliopolitanus is sometimes equated. What is striking is the complete absence of representations of this figure at Heliopolis itself, even on coins of the city. Though his temple is depicted on coins, its cult statue is never shown within, as is the case with most other representations of temples on civic coinages. Was the image at Heliopolis simply too holy to permit profane gaze? A very similar cult statue is shown on coins of several cities: for example, Dium in the Decapolis (fig. 155.1), which may mean either that this type of figure was a regional form, or that the cult statue of

Fig. 154. Underside of the lintel over the entrance to the temenos at Baetocaece. An eagle carrying a herald's wand (caduceus) is flanked by two erotes holding garlands. This arrangement is also encountered at other religious sanctuaries in Syria and has been interpreted as symbolizing the sun or his messenger (the eagle), flanked by the morning and evening stars (the erotes).

Jupiter Heliopolitanus provided a model for others. The deities at Heliopolis are considered below (p. 344).

This brings us to the subject of generic rather than specific non-Greek forms for deities. These imply the existence of regional rather than purely local religious elements, and perhaps of regional identities. All the same, it might not be unduly cautious to avoid seeing these as evidence for any general Near Eastern religion, which might imply greater spiritual coherence than is actually apparent. Divine images included rectangular, conical or spherical stones (figs 155.2, 156.1-3), referred to in modern scholarship as *baetyls*, a term derived via Greek probably from the Semitic *bethel* ('house of the god'). Reliefs depicting baetyls in the form of rectangular blocks are common in Nabataea. Conical ones occur in the iconography of the coastal cities such as Seleucia, Laodicea and Sidon, as well as inland at Emesa. The use of a stone as the focus for a cult is widely attested in the region during Roman times, and naturally invites us to draw a connection between these baetyls and the black stone of the Kabaa at Mecca or, more broadly, with a Near Eastern propensity for avoiding anthropomorphic representations of the divine. But the peoples of our region did not have a

Fig. 155.1. Dium, coin of Geta, dated year 268 (c. AD 204). Cult image resembling that of Jupiter Heliopolitanus, but holding an eagle-tipped sceptre and a figure of Victory. BMC 2.

Fig 155.2. Coin of Sidon from the reign of Elagabalus (AD 218-22) showing a spherical baetyl in a portable shrine with wheels. The baetyl is draped and wears a double crown. This is thought to be a non-anthropomorphic representation of the goddess Astarte. BMC 245.

Fig 155.3. Coin of Aradus from the reign of Elagabalus (AD 218-22), dated year 587 (AD 218/219). On the left-hand side, a bull; behind which, a standard with a raised hand. On the right, a lion; behind which, a legionary vexillum; above the lion, a star. Between, a cypress tree. The whole group seems to suggest a triad of supreme god, supreme goddess and a young god of regeneration, to which Roman military symbols had accrued. BMC 383.

monopoly on representations of non-anthropomorphic deities (they occur, for example, in Asia Minor), and some baetyls were evidently meant to be understood as mountains (see below), so similar symbols might have very different meanings in different places. However, the prevalence of baetyls among the Nabataeans and the interior may indicate an 'Arab' preference for abstract, iconic visions of divinities.

A variety of other symbols may have provided a common if vague religious vocabulary. Among these are animals, real and mythical: bulls for a supreme male deity, lions or sphinxes for a major female deity (fig. 155.3). Fish and pigeons occur as symbols of important goddesses. The eagle, normally associated with Zeus, seems to have been employed as a divine messenger (it often carries the *caduceus*, the herald's wand of Hermes). It may have had various meanings: Zeus; the providence of the gods; and it is also found employed in various contexts which strongly suggest it symbolized the sun (fig. 154). Cypresses occur in association with a young deity of regeneration, and a relief on an altar from Rome shows one such tree tied at the top with a ribbon, a young Palmyrene god, Malakbel, carrying a kid, emerging (being born?) from its branches. The cypress appears on Palmyrene clay tesserae and various civic

155.1   155.2   155.3

coins (fig. 155.3). While the uses of these symbols may point to similarity of meanings, use of the same symbol at different places does not necessarily signify the same deity. Nor is there any reason to assume a single 'correct' reading of a deity or symbols.

To describe the indigenous deities of our region is beyond the scope of this chapter. All that can be done here is to provide a very brief listing of some of the better-known ones, together with their origins and some generally agreed aspects. Pious epithets were often used rather than names, as if the names themselves were too sacred to mention: Baal ('Lord'); Baalat ('Lady'); El ('God'); Allat ('Goddess'). These could function as specific labels for particular deities, but the practice hardly aids our understanding of their cults, although the epithets were sometimes made more specific: Baalshamin ('Lord of the Heavens'); or Baalmarcod ('Lord of Dances' = earthquakes?). Equations with Greek or Roman deities sometimes help to clarify possible meanings, but more often they merely underscore how little we know. The various meanings of an indigenous deity rarely produced exact equivalences with those of individuals in the Greek or Roman pantheons, so that representations of various classical gods and goddesses could be used to signify a single indigenous one, and one classical deity could symbolize several different native divinities. The more powerful an indigenous deity was felt to be, the more classical equivalents he or she might have (see below). A division has sometimes been made between an Aramean/Phoenician tradition for gods symbolizing earthly cycles of life and death, and an Arab/Babylonian preference for celestial deities, but if such tendencies can be detected in pre-Roman times, in many cases the traditions had merged by the Roman period, producing hybrid earth/celestial divinities. As with the social identities explored in the preceding chapter, the identities of the gods were equally impure genres rather than well-defined, separate 'ethnic' entities, and overlapped one another in functions and attributes without losing their individuality. Furthermore, they were not beings autonomous of their worshippers' desires.

The great Aramaean god Hadad is attested in several different locations in Roman times, although he seems to have been less popular than his female consort, Atargatis (see below). Symbols of Hadad include the thunderbolt and ears of corn, one signifying his association with storms and rains, and the other the fertility and growth of living things. More widespread was the cult of the Aramaean Baalshamin, whose attributes and functions were very similar to those of Hadad. The symbols of Atargatis included lions, ears of corn, a drum and a sceptre, suggesting a variety of meanings and associations (see below); the similarity between representations of Atargatis and of the Anatolian goddess Cybele suggests a conscious attempt to link the two through iconography as well as cult practice. Phoenician supreme gods were commonly called Baal or El, and the goddesses Baalat or Astarte. The symbolism of Astarte was complex: lions and sphinxes were creatures associated with her; her association with the planet Venus provided a link with Aphrodite (or vice-versa?); and her aspect as a warrior-goddess and a form of fortune may explain a preference for 'Amazonian' city-goddesses at Phoenician sites along the coast (see chapter 7). She was also a mother goddess, connecting her cult with that of other deities who performed this role. At various Phoenician cities there were also young gods symbolizing the cycles of nature, of annual death and regeneration: Adonis at Byblus, Eshmun at Sidon, Melqart at Tyre. Cults with probable Philistine origins include that of the god Marnas at Gaza and the goddess Derceto (who was identified with Atargatis or Astarte) at Ascalon. The Nabataean deities included three goddesses whose cults were evidently still strong at Mecca in the seventh century AD, when they were mentioned in the notorious Satanic Verses of the Qur'an: Allat, al-'Uzza and Manat. Allat ('Goddess', the female counterpart of Allah) was commonly associated with Athena; Manat was a form of destiny and could be represented as Tyche or Nemesis. Al-'Uzza, 'the Strong One', was a goddess associated with the morning star (Venus), and thus with Aphrodite, and the Egyptian Isis. Male divinities of the Nabataeans included Qaus or Qos (an Edomite deity of rains and storms who could be depicted with bulls and a thunderbolt, like Hadad), Dusares or Dushara, 'the One from the Shara' (the mountains around Petra), Shai al-Qaum, 'Companion of the Tribe', and al-Kutba, 'the Scribe'. Dusares was frequently associated with Dionysus, but he seems also to have been regarded as the head of the Nabataean pantheon, necessitating an association with Zeus. The teetotal Shai al-Qaum, 'who does not drink wine', is thought to have been a patron of nomads, soldiers and caravans, and may have been associated with Dionysus' mythical opponent Lycurgus, attested as a god in inscriptions from the Hauran. But there are problems with these identifications, for there is also evidence to support the view that Dusares, Shai al-Qaum and al-Kutba are three aspects of a single deity.

Whether sun cults were typically Syrian is debatable, although representations of Helios are common in the region. It is generally thought that the

Unconquered Sun, *Sol invictus*, established as a major Roman cult under Aurelian, was inspired by these eastern solar divinities, but it is difficult to prove a direct connection. The sun-god Shamash had a major cult centre at Hatra, and Elagabal at Emesa was also a solar deity (see below). Celestial symbolism abounds on temples in the region (colour plate 11, fig. 154), but does not necessarily mean that the temples themselves were dedicated to the sun or moon; instead it may denote the fact that the deity worshipped there had the power to influence or control natural cycles such as day and night.

Civic coins and relief sculptures often stress the particular when depicting indigenous deities such as Astarte or the sun in their native guises, as if our interest in the broader and general patterns of identity and meaning of the deities was not always shared by the people of antiquity. Religious iconography and ancient writings frequently stress the unique: Astarte appears as a spherical baetyl *only* on coins of Sidon (fig. 155.2); and a sun god called Helioseiros appears *only* on coins of Chalcis ad Belum. Dusares was a dome-shaped baetyl on coins of Adraa, explicitly labelled 'Dusares the god, of the Adraenoi', but a pillar-shaped object flanked by two smaller pillars at Bostra (and, probably, at Charach Moba, although there the baetyl is not named on coins. See fig. 156.3). Whatever was generic about these gods and goddesses, there was clearly also a desire to give them local significance. It is perhaps our own desire to find links between deities and their symbols that makes these cults seem so deeply intertwined and indistinct, and has led some to form the notion that the whole religious environment of the region was converging on monotheism (finally made manifest through the three great eastern religions of Judaism, Christianity and Islam). But these specific icons suggest otherwise, and it is certain that in the early empire Syrians still moved in a world of aboriginal gods and goddesses, of sacred springs, rivers, woods and mountains, and minor ancestral spirits who governed their lives. In late antiquity pagan intellectuals sought to bring more coherence and order, but this is probably in reaction to the triumph of Christian monotheism and is unlikely to have touched the lives of the pagan masses (see below).

Imported deities may denote the presence of foreign groups or survivals from earlier empires. Bel, a supreme cosmic deity of the Babylonian pantheon, had major cults at Apamea and Palmyra. Nebo, the son of Bel, identified with Hermes and Apollo, is found at Palmyra and Hierapolis. Cultural ties between the Euphrates regions and southern Mesopotamia, and past histories (Syria formerly being part of the Assyrian and Babylonian empires) may well explain these transmissions. Another Babylonian import was Nergal, a warrior-deity identified with Heracles. Roman soldiers brought exotic cults with them, although these are not especially common. Traces of Egyptian cults and symbols in and around the Bekaa valley are perhaps vestiges of Ptolemaic rule, but at Bostra the Egyptian Ammon was brought by the *legio III Cyrenaica*, which had previously been stationed in Egypt before being posted to Arabia. No doubt the Greek, Roman and other deities attested at Aelia Capitolina (Jerusalem) were brought by the military. Even Jupiter Dolichenus seems to have spread in Syria through the agency of soldiers and veterans. Although of eastern origin, the cult of Mithras seems to be a Roman implant; however, recent finds of Mithraic temples in a variety of locations across the region call into question the assumption that the cult was disseminated largely by the army. On the other hand we can only guess at the means by which the Anatolian god Mên came to be represented on coins of Laodicea ad Libanum, Artemis of Ephesus on coins of Neapolis in Samaria, or Diana of Perge on silver tetradrachms of the province of Arabia, and the reasons for the apparent popularity of the Egyptian Isis and Serapis in the region.

The Politics of Meaning

Most cults seem to have lacked a specific doctrine or authoritative scriptures which helped to define the manner of worship, or even what a deity signified. In many cases the most consistent feature of a cult was the image of the deity, which in the case of highly successful ones might be reproduced with considerable accuracy across the empire. However, the full meanings of a deity might not be apparent in that cult image (although images were important to meaning), and conformity of representation could sometimes disguise a wide variety of interpretations.

Fig. 156.1. The stone Elagabal in the temple at Emesa. Civic coin of Caracalla, dated year 527 of the Seleucid era, AD 215/216. The stone stands on a podium, flanked by parasols; an eagle stands in front. BMC 15.

As was noted above, basic meanings of deities are sometimes sought in the lifestyles their worshippers are supposed to have followed: those in settled regions had deities concerned with the cycles of nature, regeneration, water and the earth (all of which affected agriculture), whereas those of the nomads were astral and warrior deities. Armed gods and goddesses are common in and around Palmyra, where they are seen as a natural response to the rigours of life in the desert and the desire for protection. Meanings are also sought in patterns of representation. At Byblus and Sidon there were triads of supreme god, mother-goddess and a young god of regeneration. Iconography suggests that other places may have had similar arrangements for the chief deities in the local pantheon (fig. 155.3). So-called triads have been distinguished in many cities, although the arrangements are not always the same. At Palmyra it is thought that there was a preference for all male triads with a celestial bias: supreme god, plus sun and moon. But the number of certain triads is not large, and in a polytheistic world it is easy enough for us to find the requisite father-mother-son/daughter or chief-sun-moon combinations among the many deities worshipped at a site, particularly when the source material ranges from pre-Roman times to Christian writers of late antiquity. There is always the danger that the triads discovered by modern specialists would not have been recognized as such by the worshippers, and sceptics have seen this scholarly 'triadomania' as very much a modern predilection rather than an ancient one. Nevertheless there are some cases where the notion of a divine trinity does not appear to be inappropriate.

In late antiquity a number of sources, particularly Christian ones, describe pagan cults and explain some of their meanings. Without corroborative evidence from earlier times it is difficult to evaluate some of this material, but that does not mean that it should be dismissed outright. Ancient myths may have been preserved into the late Roman era (although there is very little certain proof of the transmission of pre-Hellenistic myths in either the early or late Roman period), and deities might bear Babylonian or Aramaean names; but once again we should be cautious about using origins to explain meanings. Myths recounted by authors writing in both the early and late Roman period *may* help to make the meanings of deities and their symbols more intelligible to us, yet it is often far from clear that many of these myths were truly of great antiquity, and some may have been relatively recent concoctions *designed* to elucidate meanings where the original signification had been lost or discarded.

Fig. 156.2. The image of Zeus Casius on a civic coin of Seleucia Pieria from the reign of Antoninus Pius (AD 138-61). The conical object is accompanied by the label 'Zeus Kasios'; an eagle perches on the roof of the shrine. BMC 47.

Fig. 156.3. Civic coin of Bostra of the reign of Trajan Decius (AD 249-51), showing a platform (motab) on which a pillar-like baetyl of Dusares stands, flanked by two smaller baetyls. The whole image is surrounded by a wreath. BMC 48.

Even the most ancient deities had to prove their value in the contemporary world. It was up to the worshippers to champion the causes of their ancestral or favoured gods. The great religious centres and sanctuaries attracted not only hordes of pilgrims, but other divinities as well. Powerful social groups could try to constrain the meanings of gods in the sanctuaries under their control for their own ends, but there could also be occasions when it was in their interests to change or add meanings, particularly when faced with pressure from another powerful group to incorporate other gods into the cult. Within the cities great families or tribal groups might have an attachment to particular deities, and arrangements such as the father-mother-son/daughter triad, rather than signifying some very antique myth, might be an invention designed to solve religious tension at a particular sanctuary. The following of a god could also be enhanced by assimilation with another. This might involve some transmutation or additional layering of meaning on the part of the god, producing a hybrid that seems irrational to us. For example, there is an inscription naming the deity of the Palestinian Mount Carmel as Zeus Carmelus Heliopolitanus, combining two site-specific entities with a generic Greek one. Note also the combination of Zeus and his father Kronos, described below p. 346. Such composite deities were the products of calculated strategies in a world where religion and politics were not separated, and where different social groups had an interest in a single spiritual focus.

Some of the best-known Syrian cults contain puzzling amalgamations: for example, that of Elagabal at Emesa, the focus of which was a conical stone. The historian Herodian describes the cult as one which attracted pilgrims from a wide area, and other writers attest to the existence of a large temple, which is depicted on civic coins of Emesa. The cult stone, which features on numerous coin types (fig. 121.1, 156.1), may have been an ancient object of veneration, but there is no reference to it or the cult prior to the Roman period. The stone was evidently not a very large object (although Herodian maintains that it was huge), as it is shown on certain coins of the emperor Elagabalus riding in a four-horse chariot and was transported to Rome during his reign. Some coins specifically name the deity ELAGABAL, and a limestone relief from Nezala (Qaryatayn), between Damascus and Palmyra, shows the same deity and is labelled in Palmyrene 'LH'GBL. This has been interpreted as Aramaic for 'God Mountain', which would suggest that the modest-sized stone somehow represented a god who was a mountain. Whether or not this interpretation is correct, an iconographic parallel can be drawn with Zeus Casius, the deity of the mountain south of Seleucia, whose cult image was a very similar conical object, probably also a stone (fig. 156.2). However, the meaning of Elagabal was evidently more complicated than this. Herodian describes Elagabal as Helios, the sun-god, and says that 'Elagabalos' was the Phoenician name (probably meaning the Aramaic name). The stone was 'conical in shape and black' and 'worshipped as though it were sent from heaven; on it there are some markings that are pointed out, which the people would like to believe are a rough picture of the sun, because that is how they see them'[54]. Civic coins of Emesa show the stone covered in heavenly symbols and accompanied by an eagle. But the civic coins also give prominence to Helios, and various inscriptions record dedications 'to the Sun God Elagabalus'. Precisely how the stone (or mountain?) came to be identified with the sun is a process that cannot now be unravelled. The theophoric name Samsigeramus borne by rulers of the Emisenoi tribe at the beginning of our period derives from the Semitic word for the sun, *shamash* or *shams*, which points to a sun cult among this tribe in the first century BC. Possibly this sun cult was grafted on to the worship of an existing local deity when the Emisenoi settled at the site; that two apparently separate spheres of divine activity (the heavens and the earth) should be fused in the image of a sacred stone might suggest a compromise between adherents of two formerly separate cults. If the cult recorded on the coins, inscriptions and texts were the product of such a social compromise, there might be no point in trying to root out one overall meaning for Elagabal, at the expense of multiple readings.

Religious syncretism (the process whereby several gods or goddesses are combined into one) is more likely to be the product of social and political pressures and compromises than an innocent and happy melding of traditions. The more worshippers a deity had, the less specific the meanings were likely to be, and the more likely the cult was to attract curious accretions. Hierapolis, the ancient Mabog or Mambog (modern Membij), was the centre of the extremely important cult of Atargatis, the 'Goddess of Syria'. Her cult, and that of her male consort, Hadad, are known at the site from the late Persian and early Hellenistic period, and are probably much older. As we have seen, both deities were Aramaean in origin. Lucian of Samosata devoted one of his works to this 'Syrian Goddess', whom he calls Hera. But he also notes that she possessed features of Athena, Aphrodite, Selene, Rhea, Artemis, Nemesis and the Fates; the processes by which such (to us) seemingly incompatible identifications were made can only be guessed. If Lucian were attempting to translate the meaning of a non-Greek goddess for the Greek reader, it is unlikely that these equations would have made specific meanings of Atargatis any more transparent, but they would convey the impression of an important and potent goddess who could accomplish many things for her followers. (As was proposed in the last chapter, the more meanings a sign has, the more powerful it is.) Hierapolis was evidently a major centre of pilgrimage and the cult enjoyed a wide following in the Roman world: Lucian states that pilgrims came from an extensive area of Mesopotamia, Syria and the eastern Mediterranean; and the emperor Nero was one of Atargatis' more prominent devotees. Wide followings were likely to result in a wide range of interpretations. That she was regarded as 'Syrian' is clear, and coins of Hierapolis regularly bear her image and the inscription 'of the Goddess of Syria, of the Hierapolitans'. Hadad (whom Lucian equates with Zeus only) appears to have become less important than Atargatis during the Roman period, but he too was considered 'Syrian', or so some coin inscriptions which show the two deities describe them: 'of the gods of Syria, of the Hierapolitans'. Coins and reliefs show the pair seated side by side on thrones, Hadad flanked by bulls and Atargatis by lions. This must be how the cult statues appeared in the temple at Hierapolis. Between them is a third image, which looks like a Roman military standard in a shrine. Lucian refers to this as *semeion*, the Greek word for an ensign or standard, and says that the 'Assyroi' have no term for it, implying that it is a late and perhaps alien addition to the cult. 'It does not have its own particular character', writes Lucian, 'but it bears the qualities of the other gods,'[55] as if somehow it symbolized divinity in general or encompassed all of the other deities present in the sanctuary. Is the presence of this object a sign of military interest in Hadad and Atargatis, or Roman 'colonization' of this native religion? Standards were indeed objects of military worship, and Hierapolis is a likely mustering-place for legions on campaign.

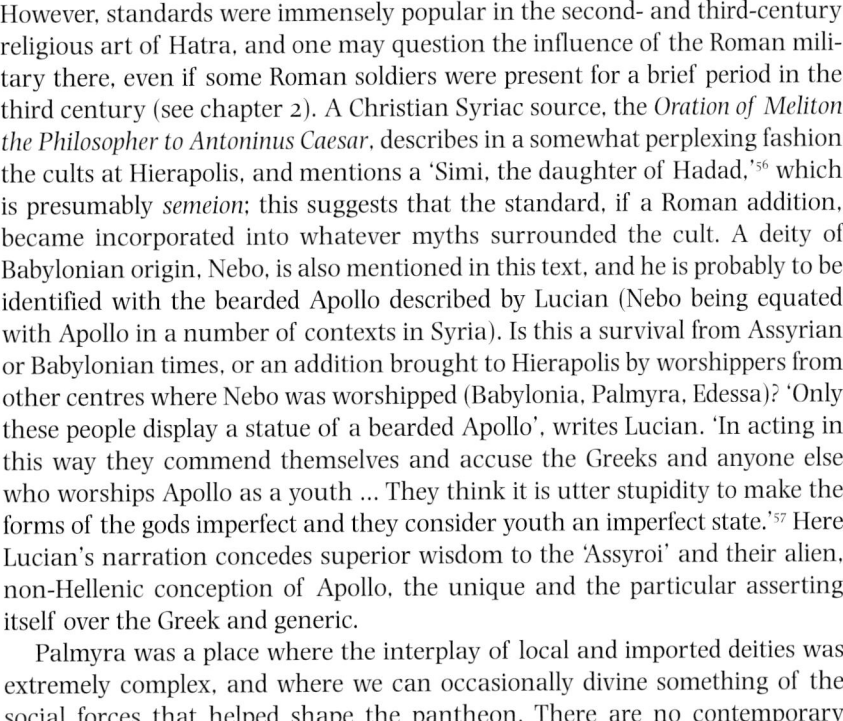

However, standards were immensely popular in the second- and third-century religious art of Hatra, and one may question the influence of the Roman military there, even if some Roman soldiers were present for a brief period in the third century (see chapter 2). A Christian Syriac source, the *Oration of Meliton the Philosopher to Antoninus Caesar*, describes in a somewhat perplexing fashion the cults at Hierapolis, and mentions a 'Simi, the daughter of Hadad,'[56] which is presumably *semeion*; this suggests that the standard, if a Roman addition, became incorporated into whatever myths surrounded the cult. A deity of Babylonian origin, Nebo, is also mentioned in this text, and he is probably to be identified with the bearded Apollo described by Lucian (Nebo being equated with Apollo in a number of contexts in Syria). Is this a survival from Assyrian or Babylonian times, or an addition brought to Hierapolis by worshippers from other centres where Nebo was worshipped (Babylonia, Palmyra, Edessa)? 'Only these people display a statue of a bearded Apollo', writes Lucian. 'In acting in this way they commend themselves and accuse the Greeks and anyone else who worships Apollo as a youth ... They think it is utter stupidity to make the forms of the gods imperfect and they consider youth an imperfect state.'[57] Here Lucian's narration concedes superior wisdom to the 'Assyroi' and their alien, non-Hellenic conception of Apollo, the unique and the particular asserting itself over the Greek and generic.

Palmyra was a place where the interplay of local and imported deities was extremely complex, and where we can occasionally divine something of the social forces that helped shape the pantheon. There are no contemporary textual sources describing the cults, and the evidence for them is in the form of temples, inscriptions, sculpture, and small clay tesserae that served as tickets to religious banquets (fig. 160). It is probably important to distinguish between those cults which had important temples and whose festivals were likely to have been major public events and those with smaller shrines or those that were the focus of private worship or dedications by individuals to an ancestral god. There is also a notable difference between deities favoured in the city and the 'cavalier gods' worshipped in the countryside. The imports are mainly found in the city: Babylonians like Bel, Nebo, Belti, Nergal and Nanai; 'Syrians' or 'Phoenicians' like Baalshamin, Bel Hamon, Astarte and Atargatis. Shadrafa (fig. 157) and Elqonera are perhaps originally Canaanite. A variety of deities characterized as Arab is found in both city and country: Allat, Shamash, Arsu and Azizu, and various spirits of rural localities. Only a few deities were purely Palmyrene; in particular Iarhibol, 'Aglibol and Malakbel. Bel seems to have been assimilated to a Palmyrene deity originally called Bol, whose name is preserved in the composites Iarhibol and 'Aglibol, and Palmyrene tribal names like Bene Zabdibol. Iarhibol was originally the god of the Efqa spring, one of the major water sources at Palmyra, but in his capacity as an associate of Bel he was also a sun-god (see below). Once again, what appear to be incompatible domains (water source, the sun) are brought together. 'Aglibol is encountered as a lunar associate of both Bel and Baalshamin. Malakbel also occurs in association

Fig. 157. Palmyrene relief, dated AD 55, showing the healing god Shadrafa. His body armour, soldier's cloak, small shield, sword and spear (here with a serpent entwined around it) are typical of Palmyrene representations of deities, who are often shown in military attire. The inscription reads 'In the month of Iyar (May), in the year 366, this stela was erected by Atenaten, son of Zabd'ateh, descendant of Toshabeb, to Shadrafa, the good god, in order that he may become patron in his sanctuary for him and the members of his house, all of them.' BM 125206.

with Bel and Baalshamin, but in different guises. Sometimes he appears as a warrior sun-god, and at other times he resembles the young gods of death, regeneration and birth found in the coastal cities. The two spheres of action could be combined: the altar found in Rome showing Malakbel as a young god emerging from a cypress tree bears another relief portraying him as Sol.

The most important city cults were those of Bel and Baalshamin, whose sanctuaries were the largest. There are also numerous dedications to an unnamed deity who is thought to be Baalshamin. Palmyra thus boasted a pantheon with two supreme deities, Bel and Baalshamin, both of whom were identified with Zeus, and both of whom had separate temples and cults. Both were rulers of the cosmos and were associated with sun- and moon-gods, although in each case these subordinate solar and lunar deities were not the same pair. The 'triad' of Bel consisted of Iarhibol (the sun) and 'Aglibol (the moon), while that of Baalshamin is believed to have employed Malakbel and 'Aglibol in the same roles (though there 'Aglibol had precedence over his solar counterpart). In his sanctuary Baalshamin was also associated with the name Durahlun, thought to be a divine name connected with the sanctuary of Rahle on Mount Hermon, and perhaps a site-specific aspect of Baalshamin. This dyarchy may seem theologically awkward to us, but in the minds of their worshippers Bel and Baalshamin were not totally incompatible, for on rare occasions they are represented together. The curious arrangement may hint at some sort of religious compromise between powerful and perhaps conflicting interests in the city.

From inscriptions it is possible to discern that certain deities were of particular interest to Palmyrene tribes or groups, who identified with them and might have an 'ancestral' claim to them (though this does not mean that each had exclusive rights to a cult). A number of tribal or collective names incorporate Bol or Bel or other deities: Bene Penabol; Bene Yedibel; Bene Taymarsu; but the full religious affiliations of these and others become clear only from the location and nature of the dedications. The Bene Maaziyan developed the Baalshamin complex, but they also had an interest in Allat (identified with Athena and Atargatis) and Durahlun. 'Aglibol and Malakbel had a sanctuary (without Baalshamin) associated with an important tribe, the Bene Komare. Meaning, symbolism and appearances were to some extent negotiable, moulded by the politics of different social groups. Iarhibol may have become a sun god in a celestial 'triad' because his sponsors were able to bring sufficient pressure to bear on the Bel cult. Every group had an interest in gaining some rights within the great sanctuaries, and association of one's gods with a major temenos would have been a powerful form of social legitimation, though it might require some adjustment to the meanings of the deities concerned.

This politics of meaning extended to classical deities as well. Representatives of Roman power perhaps played an important part in the processes, but locals could also have had a strong interest in assimilating or adding classical symbolism. The great power of a local male deity could be signified by casting him as Zeus, regardless of whether this produced incompatibilities on the local side, as in the case of Bel and Baalshamin at Palmyra, or among the variety of Greek deities symbolizing different aspects of the local deity (an inscription from Aradus combines Zeus and his father Kronos, calling this deity, which is probably a version of El, 'the most manifest of all the gods').[58] These processes probably account for many of the specific or generic epithets we encounter in

Fig. 158. The Baalshamin sanctuary at Palmyra. This was closely associated with the Bene Maaziyan, one of the main tribes or social groups at Palmyra. In the foreground, the large northern court with its colonnade. The temple itself stands beyond, and behind it is the colonnade of the southern court.

association with the name Zeus: Zeus Damascenus; Zeus Bomos ('Altar-Zeus'); Zeus Baitylos ('Baetyl-Zeus'); Zeus Megistos ('Greatest Zeus'), or Zeus Hypsistos ('Zeus the Most High'). On inscriptions and coins Jupiter Heliopolitanus was assimilated to Jupiter Capitolinus in Rome: *Iuppiter Optimus Maximus Heliopolitanus*. Was this an example of pressure applied by veteran settlers, and thus of passive acquiescence by locals to the 'Romanization' of their cult? Or was it locals appropriating the chief god of the Roman pantheon to signify the awesome power of their deity? Both readings are possible. Another deity in the same city territory, Baalmarcod, whose temple still stands at Deir el-Qalaa in the hills above Berytus, was also referred to as Iuppiter Optimus Maximus, perhaps for the same reasons. Some syncretism may have been the product of similarities between the names of Greek and indigenous deities, or between Greek and indigenous myths. These processes, however, are unlikely to have been any less innocent or devoid of social pressures or politics than those outlined above.

Experiencing the Gods

Visiting temples and sanctuaries was a key feature of pagan religious experience. Very few major cults in Syria lacked a home sanctuary (Mithraism being one of the rare 'decentred' cults with a highly distinct iconography and ritual), so pilgrimage to, and experience of, the chief temple of a cult helped to emphasize the importance of the particular over the universal. Temples were places where the superhuman, the wonderful and the strange could be experienced directly. Sacrifice was the central act of devotion, but in many cases the cult image played an important part in the reception and understanding of the divinity. The rituals and symbolism added further layers of significance, and there were priests or local wise men on hand to furnish expositions. The gods could be consulted through dreams and oracles, and showed favours to those who made vows, offered sacrifices, consecrated themselves or their children to the divinities, or demonstrated their devotion through ordeals. Deities also gave orders and instructions to mortals, as evidenced by numerous inscriptions. Their images participated in the life of the community through processions and attendance of ritual banquets. Each deity had feast days, and the major cults had grand public processions, sacrifices and feasts that helped validate the social order and identity of the community.

The painted registers in temples at Dura show offerings of incense being scattered on burners (fig. 151.1), and worshippers raising their right palms in an attitude of devotion. These poses can be found elsewhere and must have been standard (fig. 151.3). Throughout the region larger altars outside the temple proper served for the animal sacrifices. At public festivals crowds gathered in the courtyards of the great temples, sacrifices were offered and the meat divided up among the participants. Wine, too, was likely to have been distributed in quantity. The god could be honoured by a Greek civic festival, performances and distributions of gifts. The doors of the temple might open to receive the sunlight and expose the god's image to the crowd, or the effigy might be brought out among them. In processions the deity rode around in a portable shrine, carried on the shoulders of bearers or propelled on wheels like a juggernaut. Civic coins provide us with a selection of divine modes of transport (figs 81.2, 155.2). The interior of the Temple of Bel at Palmyra contains a recess at either end; the southern one has a ramp which may have housed a heavy vehicle. There are references to a portable shrine of Bel called the *phoreion*, which was made of silver. At Seleucia the privilege of bearing the symbol of Zeus Keraunios ('of the thunderbolt') went to two elected *keraunophors*, 'bearers of the thunderbolt'. The effect of carrying these images around cities and villages on festival days must have been very much like the processions in which statues of saints or the Virgin are taken through the streets in Christian religious ceremonies today. There were also organized processions *to* temples, especially if the sanctuary was located in the countryside.

Pilgrims visited temples to discover and experience, and to show their devotion. In some sanctuaries it was possible to acquire a permanent testimony to one's piety. Lucian writes that those that had made the journey to the Temple of Atargatis at Hierapolis could receive a tattoo on their neck or wrist. Not only could this mark have generated a sense of community among former pilgrims, but because such treatment of the body ran contrary to Hellenized ideals of physical beauty the tattoo was a visible reminder of a distinct religious identity.

Strange and wonderful things kept visitors coming and made a sanctuary distinct. Novelty was perhaps an important part of the religious encounter, although some of the things to be experienced do not strike the modern mind as particularly religious. Lucian describes ritual prostitution with visiting strangers in his account of the festival of Adonis at Byblus. An event celebrating the resurrection of Adonis involved women who had shaved off their hair, says Lucian; but those women who wanted to keep their hair had to pay a penance by prostituting themselves to strangers in the agora, and the money paid for their services was offered to Aphrodite. He gives no explanation for this

Fig. 159. Drawing of a stone beam from the Temple of Bel at Palmyra, showing a procession. The camel is thought to be carrying a portable shrine on its back. Note the women veiled from head to foot to the right and left.

practice, although various modern interpretations exist. Most however stress the universal over the particular and unique, emphasizing ritual prostitution as a feature of Near Eastern cults. It may have been, although explicit references to the practice in Roman Syria are not common, and some come from the pens of Christian authors whose value as witnesses may be suspect.

Some acts of devotion were organized events or rites of passage expected of initiates; others were personal and voluntary tests of faith through abstinence or self-denial, sexual or otherwise, which imparted purity to the individual. Such ordeals could demand considerable personal fortitude. At Niha on the western side of the Bekaa valley a virgin and prophetess called Hocmaea fulfilled a vow to a local god, Hadaranes, who had ordered her to abstain from eating bread for twenty years: a difficult assignment in a world where bread was a staple, but not necessarily life-threatening. More extreme were certain devotees of Atargatis who castrated themselves – a permanent, though rather drastic way of demonstrating commitment and ensuring purity. Eunuchs provided a high-profile example to others of the goddess's power to inspire devotion.

Visitors also sought guidance or instructions from the gods. The forms of oracles were as varied as the cults themselves. Borne aloft on human shoulders, the image of Jupiter Heliopolitanus impelled his bearers in this or that direction to provide answers. Baetyls hissed responses, or were seen to change shape or colour. Precious offerings were cast into pools in the hope of courting divine favours; if they were rejected, it was a bad omen. The late Roman pagan historian Zosimus recounts how the fall of Palmyra was predicted at the sanctuary of Aphrodite at Aphaca (Afqa, above Byblus) when at a festival the Palmyrene offerings of the previous year floated back to the surface of the pond into which they had been cast.

Partaking in sacred meals is a well-attested practice, although attendance at a ritual banquet was commonly by invitation only, and therefore not a major public affair. Devotees were organized into cells called *thiasoi*, 'sacred companies', each with its own dining-room in the sanctuary or elsewhere. The numerous rock-cut triclinia in and around Petra are a vivid testimony to the importance of these practices. A special building for such gatherings stood in the courtyard of the Temple of Bel, and banquets probably took place there on regular occasions, such as celebrating the consecration of a new priest. The cells helped to create a sense of identity among a small group of devotees or priests, who might be members of a single clan. At Palmyra clay tesserae were distributed for admission to such *thiasoi*. Large numbers of these tickets survive, decorated with cult images and symbols and providing us with precious information about religious life in the city (fig. 160). The sacred meals themselves may have been relatively sober and modest affairs, and the menu is likely to have been governed by religious taboos. Wine seems to have been fairly central to the proceedings, although presumably devotees of Shai al-Qaum avoided it. Some accounts for meals in the *mithraeum* at Dura survive (see p. 213), listing jars of wine, meat, fish sauce, oil and radishes, together with wood and lamp wicks for cooking and lighting, and parchment for the secretary. Detailed study of the evidence suggests that a number of invitees might take part in the proceedings of a sacred banquet along with the members of the *thiasos*, eating and drinking and possibly listening to musical performances, as well as participating in religious observances. Entry into a *thiasos* of a major cult was probably costly, and the expense of an official sacrifice and banquet might have to be defrayed by the new priest or his family.

The priests presumably had some power over the meaning of a cult and the shape of its rituals, and could demand that visitors observe certain rules for behaviour within the precinct, but they were also answerable to the faithful, as some fragmentary cases of litigation attest, and they were probably unable to control all personal acts of devotion. There may have been long-lived dynasties of priest-rulers at some centres, though there is not much proof of this, and even without a hereditary priesthood it would not be surprising to discover families attempting to keep control within the clan. Squabbles between competing groups for control of a sanctuary may underlie the dispute over the priesthood of Zeus recorded on the wall of the temple at Thelsea (Dmeir), north of Damascus, which was brought by a group of villagers before Caracalla in AD 216, and the Herodian Agrippa II seems to have been involved in a case against a certain Samsigeramus who had seized the high priesthood at Iabruda in the eastern foothills of the Antilebanon. In many instances religious offices seem to have been elected posts, which could have helped to defuse potential tensions among the contending forces (or may simply have exacerbated them!), without necessarily imparting any democracy to the process. Another legal case inscribed on the temple at Dmeir makes it clear that there was a regular turnover of *naokoroi* ('temple-wardens'). Even the high priests of Hierapolis were annually elected. It would seem, then, that many of the key functionaries in the sanctuaries were essentially amateurs rather than professional theologians – though that did not mean that they were any less devout.

Fig. 160. Palmyrene clay tessera, showing a figure standing in a tower on top of a hill. The Aramaic inscription reads 'Bel Hamon'. Rather than being a purpose-built structure, the temple of the god Bel Hamon was installed in the late first century AD in a bastion on the Jebel Muntar on the western edge of the city, and that is presumably the edifice shown here.

Fig. 161. 'Temple of Zeus' at Fakra. The temple itself is cut into a karst limestone outcrop. The rectangular temenos has a high wall with a colonnaded entrance; the interior has a portico and an altar in the middle of the court.

TEMPLES AND RITUALS

Temples were therefore an important feature of religious experience. It follows that their designs ought to tell us something about the nature of their cults. Here of course we encounter problems, for no two temples are exactly alike, which makes generalizations hazardous, and we need to distinguish between elements that were truly meaningful to the cult and those which could be the product of popular fashions and meanings unconnected with ritual. Again, meaning is often sought in the origins of the designs, which are viewed as either classical or indigenous, appealing to archetypal classical or Near Eastern forms. More than any other type of monumental building in Roman Syria the sanctuaries do indeed appear to derive from a twofold heritage: a 'Graeco-Roman' one, to which they owe their external decoration, and local traditions, which determined the layout of the interior. The result is a 'Graeco-Roman' temple enclosing a traditional shrine or shrines. Is this a victory of Hellenism over the native, is it native appropriation of a Hellenizing genre to serve indigenous cults, or once again are both readings possible?

Most major temples in Syria were located in cities, or cities had accrued around them. Public worship took place in the large courts in front of temples, rather than in the temples themselves, and the vast size of many courts anticipated the huge crowds that were expected on festival days. The gigantic scale of some sanctuaries was matched by prodigious elevations. And just as great temples dominated the civic landscape, so too the siting of temples in prominent places in the countryside appropriated the skyline for religion. Temples and sanctuaries may have been located in 'High Places' on mountains and hilltops so as to be closer to the gods, but at the same time they gave the gods and their cults a commanding position over rural society. The fertile centre of the Bekaa valley is flanked by the foothills of the Lebanon and Antilebanon ranges, both of which are punctuated at intervals by hilltop temples. From the plain these buildings would have been a prominent and highly visible reminder of this pious world (and some still are). The sacred was given additional prominence and permanence through the huge blocks of stone used to construct temples and sanctuaries (colour plate 4). This obsession with gigantism will be examined below.

Most of the temples face east and many were probably oriented towards the position of the rising sun on the most important day in the cult's calendar, so that rays of light could enter the temple and shine on the statue – at least, that is a preferred explanation for the fact that the orientations of temples vary from true east. Some, however, face west or in other directions, but this does not necessarily falsify the former explanation; it might instead suggest that the cults in question had other emphases (sunset or other celestial events).

In some cases the social dominance of sanctuaries was proprietary as well as spiritual. There is evidence for deities owning land, from which the funds for some of the ambitious building projects must have derived. Deities may have been significant landowners in villages, and in certain cases a village or a group of villages were perhaps owned by a temple (the villagers presumably paid rents to the temple). There is, though, no evidence for temples as *major* landowners, and the political position of any temple estates is much less certain. It seems that under the Seleucids Hierapolis had originally been some sort of sacred estate, but that this was subsequently constituted as a *polis*. The sanctuary of Zeus at Baetocaece in the mountains above Aradus (colour plate 4) has been seen by some as an independent political entity, but the concessions which an inscription there tells us were accorded to the sanctuary seem to be more economic and religious than political. A third- or second-century BC Seleucid king had conceded the village of Baetocaece to Zeus. Through the right of *asylia* (meaning that the sanctuary was inviolable) it had some sort of independence, it was exempt from the impositions of travelling officials, and its tax-free bimonthly fair, which had been instituted by the king, was still going strong in the third century AD. No city is mentioned in the Seleucid decree, but a letter to Augustus preserved in the same inscription is from a city (assumed to be Aradus), concerning details about the tax-free status of the fair, which suggests that by the end of the first century BC Baetocaece was not wholly independent, even if it had been before. If great sacred estates had been an integral and important part of the political landscape in Hellenistic times (and this is far from certain), it seems that this was not so by the Roman period.

Temple Design

Certain elements of the religious sanctuary (*temenos*) were common to most cults. A surrounding wall (*peribolos*) or cutting defined the limits of the sacred space. The main ritual events, the sacrifice, the burning of victims and the division of the carcass among the crowd, occurred within this area. The courtyard of the temenos might not contain any monumental buildings, but it would at the very least have an altar for these sacrifices. The temple (*naos*) was normally reserved for the priests and the cult image of the deity; it might be placed in the

Fig. 162. The northern side of the great courtyard of the Temple of Jupiter Heliopolitanus at Heliopolis (Baalbek). In the foreground, a water basin with a central fountain. Note the row of dedicatory stone altars on the steps behind. At the back is the wall of the sanctuary, with an exhedra and Aswan granite columns. Between this and the steps a colonnaded portico of Aswan granite shafts once stood (see fig. 178).

middle of the temenos, towards the rear, or projecting from the back wall. It stood on a podium, elevating it above the pavement of the sanctuary. The main entrance to the temenos (*propylon*) typically faced the temple's façade, and the altar stood between.

The sanctuaries at Dura Europus form a convenient starting-point for a brief look at the main forms, because they are the least like 'classical' temples in plan, with little or no formal axial organization. Like the famous synagogue and church in the same city, a number of the pagan temples were originally private houses, adapted and altered to suit cult requirements. They do not occupy prominent positions in the settlement, and their irregular plans and lack of symmetry are probably the result of this domestic heritage. They may be viewed as evidence of the relatively private nature of worship at Dura and the difficulties faced when negotiating for space, in marked contrast to the great public cults of other cities. They give us an impression of what small shrines for private worship in those other cities may have looked like. The Dura temples are exclusive and inward-looking, serving the needs of particular social or religious groups. For example, the so-called Temple of the Gaddé appears to have been used almost exclusively by Palmyrenes, or people connected with Palmyra. The main focus of the cult was on the Gad (Protector) of Dura, but other dedications are to the Tyche of Palmyra and deities worshipped at Palmyra, such as Malakbel, Iarhibol and Nebo. Most temples were constructed during the period of Parthian rule, with additions built under the Romans. Common features include a high peribolos wall which, like walls around private homes, shut the sanctuary off from the public space of the street. Around the interior of the peribolos was a series of rooms, many of which were chapels or dining rooms added by private benefactors. The naos was normally placed at the rear of the sanctuary, opposite the entrance. Typically it was rectangular in plan, with a single entrance in the middle of its wider side opening on to a wide vestibule or *pronaos*; beyond this was a smaller inner sanctum, which might be flanked either side by a small chapel. One feature the sanctuaries tend to share with private houses is a deliberate avoidance of strict axiality, so that the main entrance is not aligned with the entrance to the naos, preventing unauthorized viewing of the cult image from the street. Traditional features of 'classical' architecture, such as pitched roofs and colonnades, were quite uncommon. As noted above, the Dura synagogue and church house belong to the same category; they are not the secret meeting-places of persecuted cults, but typical Durene religious buildings, serving the interests of small groups.

More public cults, which could command greater resources in terms of space, manpower and money, were planned with greater monumentality and symmetricality. Topological constraints might still dictate the shape of the sanctuary, as at Sia in the Hauran, 3 kilometres (1¾ miles) east of the city of Canatha, where the rocky hilltop prevented a rigid geometrical layout of three temples which were constructed in three successive, interconnected enclosures, approached by a road 300 metres (328 yards) long running through a monumental arch. In other sanctuaries a complex history of donations, extensions and improvements might create an unusual pattern within the urban framework, as in the Baalshamin sanctuary at Palmyra (fig. 158). Rather than taking pride of place in a courtyard or at the end of a succession of courtyards, the sanctuary's temple, altar and flanking colonnades occupy a relatively small space between two larger courtyards to the north and south. The details of its earliest phase, of the late first century BC or early first century AD, are not clear, although a small courtyard with rooms arranged around it existed at the northern end, and a chapel may have occupied the site of the later temple. In the first century AD a second, much larger courtyard was laid out between the northern court and the chapel, and two *thiasoi*, one of Baalshamin and the other of Durahlun, built a banquet hall. The temple itself was built in the mid-second century, and a third court was constructed to the south of it, also in the second century. As was the case with ambitious schemes of civic monumentalization, these urban and rural sanctuaries might take decades or centuries to complete (and on some the work was never finished). The dated inscriptions from the peribolos of the temple on the Jebel Sheikh Barakat in northern Syria, between Antioch and Beroea, show that construction of this wall, which was financed by individuals, was built between AD 61 and 120. This important rural sanctuary was only about 68 metres (74 yards) square; enormous complexes like Heliopolis consumed far greater time, labour and money (see below). Even today the superhuman scale of some of these edifices is breathtaking, and must have been all the more astounding in antiquity. The monumentalization of sanctuaries seems to have begun a little earlier than other buildings in the civic landscape, starting in the late first century BC or early first century AD, and continuing down to the middle of the third century. Even quite small temples in the countryside adopted this monumentality, though on a correspondingly more modest scale. Yet as with secular building projects, we find that there is little evidence for new temple construction on a large scale in cities or the countryside after the mid-third century. The simultaneous decline in temple building and in civic architecture suggests that the two phenomena are related.

Within the courtyards there were channels and basins for water, used for ablutions and ritual cleansing (fig. 162). In the larger sanctuaries porticos ran

Fig. 163. Civic coin of Tripolis, of the reign of Caracalla (dated AD 211/212), showing a temple and, next to it, a structure which is perhaps a tower altar or a monument à colonnettes. Alternatively it may be another temple with a flat roof terrace. Note the 'Assyrian' merlons. BMC 79.

around the perimeter of the court, and the walls of the peribolos sometimes contained niches for statues or baetyls. Here too, around the edges of the court, one might expect to find rooms for banquets and small shrines to a variety of deities, and inscribed dedications on altars or altar-shaped blocks of stone. In some cases the courtyards contained more than one temple, as at Sfire in northern Lebanon (fig. 164). Just as some privileged groups or individuals could reserve places in public spaces like theatres, so positions within the courts could be reserved, or so various inscriptions on the pavements and walls at Heliopolis would suggest: 'This exhedra is reserved for the village of Elphana of the Apameans, in perpetuity'; or 'place of the copper-smiths'.[59] These places may have served as triclinia for ritual banquets or simply positions occupied during the festivals; it is interesting to note that in these cases villages and occupations, two important markers of social identity, are the defining criteria.

As stated before, the altar was the focus of ritual activity within the temenos. Many of the monumental altars were raised, probably so that the crowds could see the sacrifices. Some sanctuaries contained huge, elaborately decorated tower altars. Such buildings seem to be shown on coins of Emesa and Tripolis (fig. 163). The courtyard of the temple of Jupiter Heliopolitanus had two, both containing staircases leading to a roof terrace. Their visual prominence suggests that these towers were of extreme importance; they would have

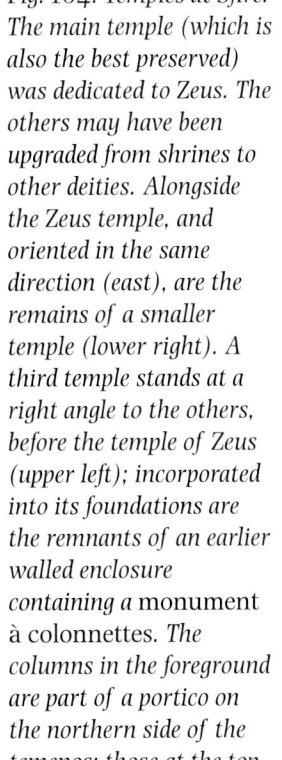

Fig. 164. Temples at Sfire. The main temple (which is also the best preserved) was dedicated to Zeus. The others may have been upgraded from shrines to other deities. Alongside the Zeus temple, and oriented in the same direction (east), are the remains of a smaller temple (lower right). A third temple stands at a right angle to the others, before the temple of Zeus (upper left); incorporated into its foundations are the remnants of an earlier walled enclosure containing a monument à colonnettes. The columns in the foreground are part of a portico on the northern side of the temenos; those at the top of the picture are part of a modern house.

dominated the courtyard, and obscured views of the temple from the main entrance. They may have functioned as artificial 'High Places' for sacrifice, although it would have been difficult to carry large animals to offer as sacrifice on to their roofs. The terrace of the larger altar may have served for ritual banquets. Courtyards also contained more modest altars for offerings of incense or oils. Another courtyard structure, particularly common in Lebanon and the Phoenician coastal region, resembles an altar but was probably not used for sacrifices (colour plate 6). A small colonnade encompassed a central edifice which in a number of cases contained niches, probably for cult images. Inscriptions on some are offerings in fulfilment of a vow, and the prominent position of some within a sanctuary makes it likely that these *monuments à colonnettes* were shrines of some sort, or a regional variation on the concept of a temple. Another suggestion is that they are a continuation of a tradition of baetyl-worship. They occur in a wide variety of sizes. A huge one stood in its own temenos at Machnaqa in Lebanon (fig. 165). At Sfire, in the northern reaches of the Lebanon range, there were several. One was found under the foundations of a later temple (fig. 164). This stood in a small walled enclosure of its own. The fact that the *monument à colonnettes* has the same orientation as the later temple suggests that the latter is an upgraded version of the former, rather than a construction intended to obliterate it. Another one stood on a hill above the main sanctuary, also within an enclosure of its own (colour plate 5). The remains of a small one, less than a metre square (3¼ feet) in plan, are to be found among the debris near the main temples. Although most *monuments à colonnettes* occur in the area of modern Lebanon they are encountered further afield, perhaps as a result of social interaction between the peoples of the coast and the interior. An excellent example is to be seen in the courtyard of the Temple of Nebo at Palmyra, which carries a relief with a row of figures, presumably divinities. Small versions or models in alabaster are known from Hatra. These objects, which retain their figures and busts of divinities and columns decorated with standards give a good impression of the overall appearance of some of the larger ones in temple courtyards.

An inscription from the sanctuary at Sia mentions a *theatron*, which in this case refers not to a theatre building but to the courtyard of the Baalshamin temple there, where banks of seats ran around the edge of the temenos (fig. 166). Since the courtyard was a place where the worshippers gathered to observe the spectacles and participate in the ceremonies, the analogy with a theatre as a place where one watches is not misplaced. At Sahr in Trachonitis a temple courtyard had seating of this sort, and next to the sanctuary was a small theatre. Earlier in date and somewhat removed in space, but probably relevant, is the theatre building in the second-century BC sanctuary of Atargatis on the island of Delos in the Aegean, where Syrian traders are likely to have worshipped. Modest in scale but probably similar in function are the rooms with banks of seats in some of the sanctuaries at Dura Europus, although the position of these, in rooms on the edges of the sanctuaries, suggests a more exclusive gathering, rather like the triclinia for the *thiasoi*. One in the temple of Artemis resembles a small theatre or odeum (fig. 110). The two Parthian-period examples in the Temple of Azzanathkona both consist of a bank of seats, bearing inscriptions, mainly the names of women. The inscriptions are probably dedications rather than denoting reserved seats because the inscriptions often take up more than a single space, and yet it is quite possible that the rooms were reserved mainly for female cult activities. Inside some

Fig. 165. Machnaqa, a sanctuary in the mountains east of Byblus. The largest structure within the spacious temenos is this monument à colonnettes, which is the biggest example known. The central part of the structure was completely solid; within its foundations are the remains of an earlier, equally solid structure, presumably of the same kind.

of the temples, too, there were ranges of steps or seats (colour plate 9). The recent discoveries within the so-called Great Temple at Petra may well be pertinent in this regard. It was originally assumed that this building was a normal peripteral temple (having a colonnaded portico running around the outside), but excavations have revealed that the columns were *inside* the building. In its first phase it seems to have been a large hall rather like a basilica. In the first century AD the intercolumnations of the interior were filled in and the rectangular space within was converted into a semicircular theatre with a stage. A large paved courtyard with porticos was laid out in front of the building. The purpose of this curious architectural ensemble remains enigmatic; if it had been a temple in its first phase, it is difficult to see how it functioned as one in the second. Another possibility is a council chamber or odeum, but an altar found in the courtyard suggests a cult function. However, it is often difficult to separate the sacred and the purely secular, and a multipurpose structure, for both civic and religious gatherings, is not impossible. Overall, these provisions for seating in the courtyards and rooms of the sanctuaries imply that ritual performances of some sort were of particular importance in certain cults.

Fig. 166. Sia: the theatron in front of the temple of Baalshamin.

If the Petra Great Temple should prove to be a cult building, it would be unlike any other temple known in the region. There are, however, many variations in the designs of temples in Syria, making appeals to any 'standard' model unrealistic. Even in the highly Hellenized regions close to the coast there are distinct traditions (see below). Other features are more widespread in Syria and Mesopotamia, yet are absent from other parts of the Roman east. Many of the basic elements of architectural decoration are 'Graeco-Roman': columns and porticos commonly use classical orders, and columns form a porch or surround the main chamber of the temple (the *cella*). The classical style undoubtedly has meaning, but we may question whether it signifies that those who visited or worshipped in such places considered the cults themselves thoroughly Hellenized or Romanized. The fact that secular buildings could be turned into temples with little alteration to their exterior intimates that outward appearances may not have been essential to the cults (fig. 160). The classical elements may be more a concession to taste and fashion than a statement about the rituals and natures of the cults themselves. Furthermore, it is not always clear whether what we perceive as 'Graeco-Roman' denotes the import of alien ideas and models rather than the continuation an older tradition. Roman influence seems apparent from the fact that many Syrian temples, like those in Italy and the western provinces, are constructed on a platform, elevating them to a dominating position on the skyline. However, the first phase of the Temple of Jupiter at Heliopolis (Baalbek), which is probably Hellenistic in date, consisted of a massive platform for a temple (see below). We know too little about temple architecture in Hellenistic Syria to dismiss the possibility of a pre-Roman tradition for the podiums. Rather than signifying adherence to Roman ways, it may indicate a more general desire to raise the holy above the level of profane, everyday life.

The façades of the temples combine classical and other elements in unusual ways, which would have created a very distinct feel to the sanctuaries. A number of temples had tall towers either side of the entrance, or at the rear of the cella (fig. 167). The Temple of Bel at Palmyra had a pair at either end. These towers commonly contain stairs leading to the roof, and in some temples, such as those of Bel and Nebo at Palmyra, they permitted access to flat roof terraces, presumably for some sort of ritual. Even temples of more normal classical appearance, such as the so-called Temple of Bacchus at Heliopolis, had interior staircases either side of the entrance, leading up to the roof. The pediments of the Bacchus temple are plain and contain a window, without the elaborate sculptural groups or reliefs commonly found in classical temples. Like the roof terraces the windows were perhaps accessed via the stairways and could have been used for cultic purposes.

Departure from the classical archetype is even more evident in the interior arrangements of Syrian temples. If any generalization about the interiors of 'Graeco-Roman' temples is possible, it was normal for those in Italy, Greece and Asia Minor to contain a cult statue, positioned close to the rear wall of the temple, and often set within an inner sanctuary or holy of holies (*adyton*). Some Syrian temples do indeed seem to imitate this pattern. Many others, however, have more elaborate structures at the back of the cella. These commonly divide the rear into three separate chapels, which are usually raised on a platform above the main floor of the cella and approached by a broad staircase. The emphasis is on the central chapel, where the cult statue or relief was probably placed. This tripartite arrangement is encountered in temples all over the region, from the Baalshamin temple at Palmyra to the Qasr al-Bint at Petra. Lucian, when describing the cult of the Syrian Goddess, uses an old-fashioned Greek term to denote this arrangement at the back of the cella: *thalamos*. There is no proof that the term was used widely in Syria in antiquity, but modern scholars have applied it to a variety of structures in Syrian temples including those corresponding to the classical adyton: rectangular chambers, apses and columned baldaquins. Some of the most elaborate arrangements are found in the temples of the Lebanon region, where the emphasis on the thalamos is particularly striking. There are sufficient similarities in most of them to suggest that the design reflects regional cult practice, even though the exteriors of many such temples are 'typically' Graeco-Roman. Good examples can be seen in the so-called Temple of Bacchus at Heliopolis and the Temple of Hadaranes at Niha, both in the Bekaa valley (fig. 168. 1 and colour plate 9). At the top of the wide staircase, the thalamos was the setting for elaborate architectural structures. Some of these structures were colonnaded; others appear to have formed more solid screens, as if to shield the flanking chapels from the gaze of those on the cella floor. Many have small windows piercing the cella wall to let light into the thalamos. It is assumed that the central part of the thalamos housed the cult statue, and that the screens imply that access to this area was probably restricted. Beneath the thalamos there is commonly a crypt, which in many cases can be entered through a door flanking the staircase or by steps descending from the raised floor of the thalamos itself. These crypts were

Fig. 167. Civic bronze coin of Abila from the reign of Elagabalus (AD 218-22), showing a temple with a tower either side of a classical colonnaded façade.

evidently intended to be accessed only from within the cella. The small temples of Ain Hersheh (colour plate 11) and Hebbariyeh at the foot of Mount Hermon have additional, larger crypts under the floors of their cellas, which are accessible from the outside, but in both cases the crypt beneath the thalamos was separate and could be entered only from within. As with the thalamos above it, access to this space was presumably carefully controlled. While the Lebanese temples share many details with one another there seems to have been no

standard plan for the interior: a detailed stone model for a thalamos found at Niha on the western side of the Bekaa valley, next to the temple of the local deity Hadaranes, has measurements in feet and other elements for a hexagonal columned baldaquin scratched on it. The model was marked with a Greek inscription 'plan of the adyton', and there can be no doubt that it was a three-dimensional architect's model for the temple. The relevant part of the Temple of Hadaranes still survives in good condition for comparison (fig. 168.1), and the measurements scratched on the model do not correspond perfectly with the dimensions of the model or the design as it was eventually built. It looks as if these measurements

Fig. 168.1. The raised thalamos of the temple of Hadaranes at Niha. Note the entrance to the crypt, half way up the stairs, on the right.

were added during discussions –between architects and priests? – over the plan. It is worth noting that the language of this discussion was Greek, although many of the monumental inscriptions at Niha were in Latin, no doubt reflecting the site's location in the territory of the colony of Berytus. Whatever the nature of worship at Niha, the design appears to have been negotiated using a non-indigenous tongue.

Other temple plans have a raised platform in the centre of the cella functioning as an altar or shrine. The fact that this plan occurs within the area ruled by the Nabataeans suggests it is a 'Nabataean' design (although some elements may derive from Egypt). The so-called Temple of the Winged Lions, north of the main colonnade at Petra, is such a building. It was originally constructed in the early first century AD, then remodelled in the mid-first, but went out of use following a fire in the early second. The cella was square and fronted by a rectangular vestibule. The focal point of the elaborate interior was a raised podium approached by steps and bearing columns, which is thought to have been either an altar or, more probably, a podium (Nabataean *motab*) for the cult image. The second-century AD temple on a hilltop at Khirbet Tannur was a rectangular edifice enclosing an earlier cube-like structure resembling a tower altar, its sacrificial function suggested by the burnt debris of offerings. The building was set within a courtyard which contained the usual elements: an altar, three banqueting triclinia and other rooms. Similar also is the Temple of Baalshamin at Sia (fig. 168.2), where a cella enclosed a smaller square

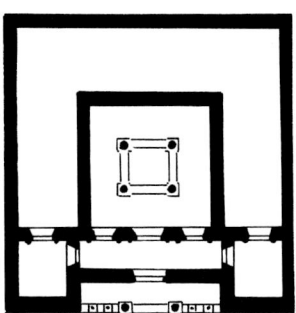

Fig. 168.2. The 'Nabataean' style plan of the late first-century BC temple of Baalshamin at Sia.

chamber, itself enclosing four columns which probably demarcated the area occupied by the cult image. It is thought that in all cases the centralized focus of the shrine or altar within the cella allowed worshippers to stand or progress around it. The basic plan has a parallel in the open-air sanctuary at Petra known as the 'High Place of Sacrifice', on the Jebel Madhbah overlooking the southern part of the city. All surviving features are carved out of living rock. The site was reached by a series of rock-cut stairways, recalling the ascents inside some of the great tower-altars and temples elsewhere. The largest feature is a court oriented north – south, 16 metres (52½ feet) long and 7 metres (23 feet) wide, with a low raised platform towards

the centre, presumably intended for offerings and perhaps cult images (or, as some have suggested, for an officiating priest to stand on). A podium is aligned with this platform, off the western side of the court. This is a raised rectangular structure of 3 by 2 metres (10 by 6½ feet) with steps on one side, surrounded by a cutting which forms a passageway. There is a slot in the top of the podium which may have accommodated a baetyl, and other cuttings around its edges may have held supports for an ornamental cover or baldaquin. This podium looks very like representations of a *motab* which was used to support baetyls, a device found on civic coins of Arabia (fig. 156.3). With the passageway around it, it resembles the temples described above. Together with the court, a tank for water and possible provisions for dining it contains all the elements present at the other temple sites. Numerous further examples of these Nabataean 'High Places' are known, and no doubt hilltop temples like Khirbet Tannur are an upgraded version of these open-air sanctuaries.

Another type of religious building with a much more limited distribution is found in the northern part of the Hauran. This consists of a large masonry façade with

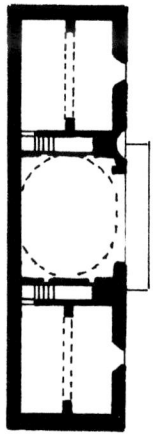

Fig. 169.1. Kalybé at Hayyat in the Hauran. Such buildings were perhaps monumental versions of smaller structures with niches designed to hold cult images, and may be a variant on the monuments à colonnettes, *many of which also contain niches.*

Fig. 169.2. Reconstruction and plan of the kalybé *at Hayyat.*

niches for statues, behind which is a room or a set of chambers that may have functioned as an assembly hall for religious rituals. A building of this kind at Umm ez-Zeytun bears an inscription dated to AD 282 which calls the building a 'sacred *kalybé*'. Similar buildings are known at Maximianopolis (Shaqqa) and nearby Hayyat (fig. 169). *Kalybé* is a Greek word meaning 'hut' or a structure made of light materials. Are these buildings, with their cult niches, a translation into stone of a portable shrine? The use of niches recalls the *monuments à colonnettes*. In modern times the term *kalybé* has been applied to a variety of monumental façades found in the region, such as the structure on the western side of the piazza at Philippopolis, designed to display statues of the imperial family, but this is misleading as it implies similarity of function. The Philippopolis '*kalybé*' may well have had a religious purpose (for example, as a sanctuary of the imperial cult), but it has little or nothing in common with the structures at Umm ez-Zeytun, Shaqqa or Hayyat, and there is no evidence that it was viewed in the same way by contemporaries.

Among the most eccentric forms of temple in the region is the Bel temple at Palmyra. The naos itself was dedicated in AD 32 (though it was perhaps not completed at the time), but the site is thought to have served as a sanctuary long before this. The vast temenos appears to have been enlarged to its present size – 210 by 205 metres (230 by 224 yards) – during the second century AD. The complex is oriented west, but the image of the deity was not aligned with the doorway of the cella or with the propylaea, as was the case in most other monumental temple complexes. The temenos was surrounded on all four sides by porticos, and the western one of these, if not all of them, must have carried

Fig. 170. Processional way leading under the west portico and sanctuary wall of the Bel temple at Palmyra. The corner pier of the colonnade, the stump of which can be seen on the right, contains a staircase to a roof terrace of the portico.

a roof terrace, as indicated by the spiral staircases contained inside the piers of the north-western and south-western corners. The monumental triple-gated propylaea stood in the middle of the western side of the temenos. A processional ramp led from the courtyard under the portico and peribolos wall in the north-eastern corner, out into the city (fig. 170). This alternative entrance may have been used to bring animals into the temenos for sacrifice. Within the courtyard was a monumental basin, a large altar and a hall for ritual banquets, identified by the large number of clay tesserae found there. The temple itself is Hellenistic in its basic design. With a Corinthian portico surrounding a rectangular cella, it originally stood on a low stepped platform in the Greek manner rather than on a podium. Following the second-century extension of the temenos the ground level was lowered a little and the stepped platform was converted into a low podium, an indication perhaps of changing fashions in external design rather than cult activity. The entrance to the cella, as noted in chapter 8, is located on the western side, and is offset towards the southern end. It is approached by a ramp rather than steps (for a plan see fig. 122.1). The

Fig. 171. Northern thalamos of the Temple of Bel, Palmyra. The central part housed a cult relief or statue; either side of this are enclosed staircases leading to the roof. Note the windows in the walls of the cella.

entrance to the cella is framed by a colossal stone door set into the colonnaded portico, a device which has parallels in Ptolemaic architecture. The deep space between the cella and the surrounding colonnade was roofed with stone panels supported by stone beams, carved in relief (figs 142, 159). Windows in the eastern and western walls of the cella are an unusual feature, and the cella is unique in having two thalamoi, one at the north and the other at the south end. The northern thalamos is considered to have been the principal shrine, containing the cult image or images, which may have been in relief form rather than free-standing (fig. 171). The southern one still retains its ramp, and for this reason it is believed to have housed a portable shrine or image of Bel which was used in processions. Quite why this arrangement was chosen is not clear. It is not known how much the present design owes to earlier temples or shrines which stood on this site, but there is evidence to suggest that construction of the cella took place in fits and starts over a period of perhaps seventy years. One

172.1

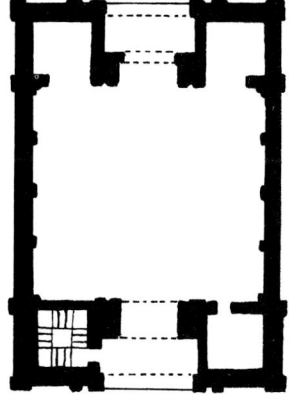

172.2

Fig. 172.1. The well-preserved 'temple' at Dmeir (ancient Thelsea).

Fig. 172.2 Plan.

proposition is that the temple was originally intended to face south, but the wadi lying immediately south of the temenos prevented monumental emphasis in that direction. There are hints that a reorientation occurred while the temple was being built. The two thalamoi which dominate the northern and southern ends appear to have been inserted, as their stone façades are not keyed into the masonry of the cella walls. If the northern thalamos were the more important, placing the entrance towards the southern end of the western side would have created more space for ritual activities before it. The unusual design may in part be the consequence of compromises made during the building's construction. As the Niha model suggests, the plans of a building could alter as the project progressed, and the double emphasis within the cella of the Bel temple may indicate more than one interest at work. As noted above, large sanctuaries could become an arena for various interest groups negotiating space for their ancestral deities, and Bel, having the most important sanctuary in the city, had to share his with other gods and goddesses. The inscription referring to the temple's dedication in AD 32 describes it as the 'Temple of the gods Bel, Iarhibol and 'Aglibol'. The stone roof panel between the cella entrance and the temple's portico bore a relief of three divine figures, usually identified as 'Aglibol, Iarhibol and Belti (the female consort of Bel), and the other figurative reliefs on the roof beams show an assortment of deities. Indeed, the epigraphic record implies that the Palmyrenes regarded this sanctuary as a temple of various Palmyrene gods rather than being restricted to the worship of Bel.

The thalamoi in the Temple of Bel are both flanked by towers in the angles of the cella, with staircases leading to a roof terrace. Possibly processions of priests and other celebrants made their way up and down while ceremonies were being performed in the court. Four corner towers are also to be observed in another eccentric temple, at Thelsea (Dmeir), on the road between Damascus and Palmyra (fig. 172). It was in use from the Severan period but not completed until AD 245, and consists of a rectangular cella with large arched portals at either end, allowing passage through the building. The design did not provide for a thalamos. One of the towers contains a staircase which presumably led to some sort of roof terrace. Whether it should be considered a temple at all is debatable; it may have been the monumental entrance to a sanctuary now buried or never built, or some variation on the tower altar, although the inscriptions on it, which outline details of legal cases, are all concerned with a temple of Zeus Hypsistos.

Baalbek and the Limits of Megalomania

During the first century BC and first century AD some truly enormous religious structures were built. The outer circuit of Herod's Temple at Jerusalem created a trapezoidal space whose maximum dimensions were about 310 by 510 metres (339 by 558 yards), making it the largest such structure in the region. The outer peribolos of the sanctuary of Zeus at Damascus, probably constructed under Augustus and his immediate successors, was about 305 by 385 metres (334 by 421 yards), and enclosed an inner circuit of about 100 by 150 metres (109 by 164 yards), the latter now forming the boundary wall of the great Umayyad Mosque. There may have been others, such as Elagabal at Emesa and Atargatis at Hierapolis, but we have little evidence for the dimensions of these sanctuaries. Slightly smaller in scale, but equally designed to impress, were the sanctuaries of Bel at Palmyra and Jupiter Heliopolitanus at Heliopolis. The builders of the Temple of Jupiter did not set out to compete with Jerusalem and Damascus, whose enormous enclosures resembled city walls. Instead they chose to increase the scale of the house of the god itself, to monstrous proportions. What they achieved still astonishes today, and is on a scale that has never since been surpassed; that they were unable to finish the building is perhaps not so surprising. Indeed, the most ambitious phase of the project was abandoned in its early stages, probably because the builders had reached the limits of what was physically and financially possible. In scaling up the size of the whole building, they had also intended to scale up the size of the building blocks used. The result is a monument so awe-inspiring that modern minds have difficulty conceiving how it was built, and as with the pyramids and other impressive feats of ancient engineering, the most speculative and least imaginative resort to the influences of visiting spacemen for an explanation.

Fig. 173. General view of the main religious complex at Heliopolis: the 'Temple of Bacchus' (in the foreground) and the Temple and courtyard of Jupiter Heliopolitanus, seen from the south. Beyond the temples, the plain of the Bekaa and the foothills of the Lebanon range.

Heliopolis may not have become an independent city until the end of the second century AD, but its role as a major religious centre was well established long before that time. The site is thought to have served as a religious centre for the Ituraeans, and may well have been part of the principality of Chalcis in the first century BC. Inscribed dedications mentioning the rulers of Emesa, and perhaps Arca, indicate that the sanctuary of Jupiter was attracting the attention of important regional figures in the first century AD, and the prodigious sums involved in constructing the temples and sanctuaries there must mean that the deities at Heliopolis could draw on much greater resources than those that could be provided by the hinterland and surrounding population. The elaborate ceiling of the portico around the 'Temple of Bacchus' (colour plate 10) is decorated with busts of deities, including a number of city-goddesses. One of these is labelled 'Antiochia', and it may honour one of a number of cities that provided funds for the building. That is speculation; but the scale of the structures at Heliopolis can only mean that the cults attracted substantial donations and a considerable following.

There were several monumental sanctuaries and temples at Heliopolis. Two massive temples were located on the western side of the city (fig. 173), the largest and tallest dedicated to 'Jupiter Optimus Maximus Heliopolitanus', and the other, generally called the 'Temple of Bacchus' and one of the best-preserved temples in the Roman world, to a deity or deities unknown (colour plates 8-10). Both appear to have been constructed before the end of the second century, and so both vast structures date mainly to the period when Heliopolis

Fig. 174. The Temple of Jupiter, seen from top of one of the tower altars of the great court.

did not have independent city status. Immediately to the south of these giant temples was a rectangular temenos containing temples of more modest size, including the unusual round temple known as the 'Temple of Venus'. Finally, on a hilltop to the east stood another large temple, located at the end of a long staircase. Only fragments remain, but the dimensions of one of its column bases suggest that it was not much smaller than the two great temples in the plain below.

There is no doubt that the principal cult at Heliopolis was that of Jupiter Optimus Maximus Heliopolitanus, because most of the surviving dedications are to this deity. There is also no doubt that the largest temple was dedicated to him. The courtyard of the temple is filled with dedications, and coins which depict the building (distinguishable from the others by the number of columns) are always accompanied by the initials of the deity, I.O.M.H. (fig. 175.1). The 'Temple of Bacchus' appears on some coins, alongside the Temple of Jupiter, but no identifying inscription accompanies the representation. The temple on the hill is also depicted on coins, identifiable by its staircase (which still survives) and the rocky landscape (fig. 175.2). The smaller temples do not appear at all. What is slightly unusual about these numismatic representations is that, unlike many other depictions of temples on civic coins, those of Heliopolis never show the deities within. Perhaps as suggested above the doors to the temples were not normally opened, and the deities were not meant to be viewed from the outside.

It seems absurd that the identity of the deities worshipped in such huge temples should be sought in little things like inscriptions and coins, but these provide some of our most important contemporary sources of evidence. Inscriptions attest a deity called Venus Heliopolitana, but the buildings and coins provide no clues as to which temple – if any – was hers. A colossal statue, thought to represent this deity, was found in the courtyard of the Temple of Jupiter (it is now in Istanbul), and perhaps part of the courtyard was given over to her. She may be the female Tyche figure which appears on coins, flanked by male figures and encircled by a veil held by two little figures on columns (fig. 175.3), but the identification is not explicit. Coins and inscriptions attest another deity, called Mercury, and representations of the temple on the hill are accompanied by a little symbol of Mercury: a herald's wand (caduceus: fig. 175.2). Consequently this has been dubbed the 'Temple of Mercury'. However, a caduceus is also found on the underside of the doorway of the 'Temple of Bacchus', where it is carried by an eagle. It is suggested that in this case the caduceus refers to the eagle as a messenger of the sun, which if correct highlights some of the difficulties encountered when trying to equate a divine symbol with a single meaning. The fact that the 'Temple of Bacchus' is well preserved only complicates matters, for it is decorated with a plethora of divine figures and symbols. Reliefs inside show what appear to be scenes from the myths of Dionysus, including the god's birth; hence the identification with Bacchus, the Roman equivalent of Dionysus. It is quite possible that these images refer to a young god of nature and regeneration, like Adonis at Byblus, and that 'Mercury', somehow assimilated to Dionysus, is the young god of a triad of deities which included Jupiter and Venus as father and mother. But other deities are also shown on coins: a city-goddess resembling the Tyche of Antioch; another Tyche between two military standards who may or may not be identical to the previous; and two naked male figures carrying uncertain objects, perhaps branches, who may be the same as those shown with the Tyche with the veil. Thus the coins confirm a cult of Jupiter Heliopolitanus (whose image is strangely absent), and of Mercury and a city Tyche, but the precise meaning of the remaining images is elusive, hinting at a cult of a female deity resembling a Tyche who may be Venus, and two unknown male figures who may be her acolytes. The conspicuousness of the monuments contrasts with our ignorance of the details.

175.1

175.2

175.3

Fig. 175. Civic bronze coins of Heliopolis.

Fig. 175.1. Coin of Septimius Severus (AD 193-211), showing the Temple of Jupiter, labelled I.O.M.H. BMC 3.

Fig. 175.2. Coin of Philip I (AD 244-9), showing the 'Temple of Mercury' on a hill covered in shrubs, approached by a long staircase. The temenos contains an altar and urn, with a caduceus outside, on the left. BMC 19.

Fig. 175.3. Coin of Philip I with a Tyche figure standing between two small naked male figures, an inflated veil held over her head by two small female figures on columns. BMC 21.

Fig. 176. Drawings of some of the votive lead figurines found at Ain al-Djouj near Heliopolis. From left to right: Jupiter Heliopolitanus (labelled 'Zeus') flanked by bulls, the façade of his temple at his feet; Mercurius Heliopolitanus, holding a caduceus (more classical-style versions are known); Tyche holding a cornucopia (Venus Heliopolitana?). Other figurines include Dionysus, animals and some curious ensigns resembling a caduceus topped by a disc and a bust of Helios. Their precise date is uncertain, but they are presumed to be Roman rather than Hellenistic.

The Jupiter sanctuary was the most excessive of the religious buildings at Heliopolis. A monumental temple, probably of the first century BC, was already standing when the first Roman phase of construction began. It is not known whether this earlier building had been completed, but its platform, measuring approximately 48 by 90 metres (52 by 98½ yards) and standing 12 metres (39½ feet) high, provided the core of the Roman temple's podium. A courtyard for worshippers lay to the east in front of this temple, constructed over a low hill which is presumed to have formed a place of worship in pre-Hellenistic times. It is possible that the builders of the Roman period intended to extend the

courtyard westwards to surround the new temple, but if so, this part of the project was abandoned.

The first and most outrageous phase of the Temple of Jupiter's construction was invisible to the worshippers in the great court. This, the so-called trilithon phase, expanded the width and length of the podium by about 10 metres (33 feet). But what was most remarkable about it was the preposterous size of the stones to be used. It seems like an undertaking to build the unbuildable; proof, perhaps, to contemporary observers of the power of the god. If completed, the outer facing of the podium, standing about 12 metres (39½ feet) high, would have been composed of a mere three courses of giant ashlars. Long after the temple fell into ruins these vast stones prompted wonder, particularly the three immense examples which form the second course of the western end (hence the name 'trilithon'). These are the largest stone blocks ever employed in a building, and two even larger ones lie in the quarry to the south (figs 68, 177).

Local geology enabled the builders to begin realizing their ambitious project. Good-quality building stone with few natural fissures, suitable for megalithic elements such as these, could be found next to the site where the temples were to be built. The quarries were also located at an elevation slightly above the temples, so that the journey between them could benefit from gravity at least part of the way. The two unused blocks were both quarried at an incline, which presumably made it easier to detach them from the bedrock. The first course of huge blocks was completed on all three sides of the podium, as was the second layer of the western end, but then, for reasons unknown, the construction technique was abandoned. Perhaps the higher courses were beyond the builders' capacity, or the project was too expensive. Further courses, assuming

Fig. 177. In 1994 workers digging for building aggregate in the ancient quarries at the base of the Sheikh Abdullah hill at Baalbek revealed an even larger stone than the famous 'Hajjar al-Hiblah' (fig. 68). This stone, dubbed 'Monolith II', is nearly 20 metres (65½ feet) long and about 4.5 metres (14¾ feet) in breadth and depth. It would have weighed about 1250 tonnes had it been released from the bedrock beneath it. The monolith itself was used as a quarry in later times; note that smaller blocks have been removed from its surface.

that the work was completed, were constructed with much smaller blocks. Some may have disappeared as a result of robbing when the temples were converted into a medieval citadel, but it is likely that the northern side of the podium was never built up. Coins giving an oblique view show the temple's 'better' southern side (fig. 175.1). The giant blocks of this trilithon phase are marked with guidelines for dressing, and some attempt was made to begin shaping the mouldings on the lowest course, but otherwise many of the blocks remained in their quarry state, which must have given the whole podium a rather crude appearance from ground level.

The temple itself was probably constructed over several decades, beginning in the mid-first century AD. As it was placed on the existing Hellenistic podium, it was not necessary to complete the trilithon before beginning on the temple, and the phases of their construction overlapped. In fact, the second course of the trilithon has etched on its upper surface a full-scale plan of the western pediment, on which the blocks were presumably laid out before being lifted into position some 28 metres (92 feet) above; and an unused column drum from the temple was incorporated into the trilithon foundations. The temple had a colonnaded portico around all four sides, ten columns along the front and rear, and nineteen along the sides (counting the corners twice), standing about 20 metres (65½ feet) high. From ground level to the top of the pediments the temple measured almost 48 metres (158 feet); and from the courtyard to the point of the roof about 40 metres (130 feet). Enormous blocks of stone continued to be employed. The four corner columns of the building, each 16.6 metres (54½ feet) high, are thought to have been monolithic shafts of limestone weighing about 130 tonnes. Although much of the sculptural detail on the outside of temple seems to have been finished, some features, such as a capital topping one of the *antae* (the projecting side walls of the cella, flanking the door), were not.

The courtyard itself was enlarged by throwing three large vaults around the original hill on all sides except the west, where the temple stood. Some of the keystones in the vaults have sculptures and inscriptions naming the teams that

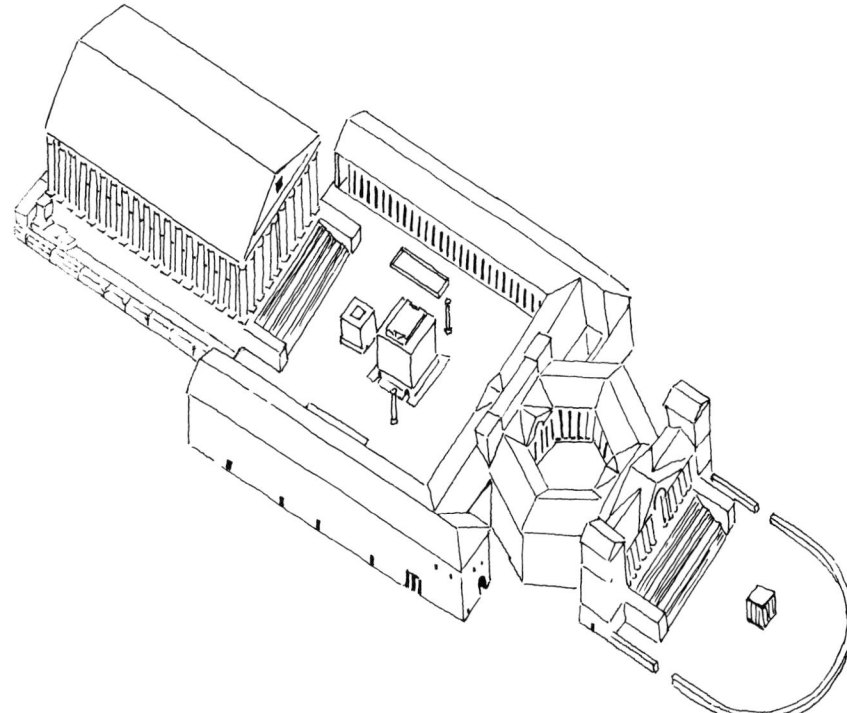

Fig. 178. Drawing of the Jupiter sanctuary at Heliopolis, showing it as it probably appeared in the middle of the third century AD, and assuming that the podium of the trilithon phase was never completed.

Fig. 179. Civic coin of Heliopolis, of the reign of Philip I (AD 244-9). Propylaeum to the Temple of Jupiter, identified by the letters I.O.M.H. The representation is fairly accurate, and the substantial remains of this entrance make the representation immediately recognizable. BMC 16.

constructed a section of vaulting: 'the Squad of Moschus'; 'the tenth squad of [the village of?] the Chonensii'.[60] As with the trilithon, the dressing of the vaults was begun but then abandoned. On three sides of the courtyard above, an immense wall, containing apsidal exhedras and colonnades of Aswan granite shafts, was fronted by a continuous portico of Aswan columns (fig. 162). The wall was decorated with niches for statues. Much of the construction here is later first or second century. The courtyard was embellished with two large water basins supplied by fountains (unfinished), a pair of honorific columns (or Hellenized versions of baetyls?) and the two impressive tower altars mentioned earlier in this chapter. This courtyard presumably had a monumental entrance; if so, it was dismantled in the third century to make way for an additional courtyard with an unusual hexagonal plan. This project too was never completed, with many of the blocks left undressed. Finally, a monumental colonnaded entrance with two corner towers was added to the hexagonal court, and before that, a semicircular courtyard containing a *monument à colonnettes* (figs 178, 179).

Like the sanctuaries at Damascus and Palmyra the Heliopolis ensemble provides us with an example of the strength of 'pagan' piety and the extraordinary vigour with which religions were pursued. Its builders appear to have experimented with the very limits of the possible, thanks to the presence of suitable stone near the site, but in doing so were unable to finish what they had started. There may have been no other motive than to demonstrate the immense potency and importance of the god, making his sanctuary as prominent and permanent as possible. Like the great civic monuments, gigantic religious sanctuaries perhaps tried to affirm the glory and perpetuity of a certain social organization through overweening architecture. The effort involved certainly betokens something more than mere caprice; but perhaps, like the builders of another giant sanctuary, the great fifteenth-century Gothic cathedral of Seville, the religious authorities at Heliopolis also could have claimed (with some justification) that they did it for no other reason than 'so that future generations will take us for madmen'.

THE IMPERIAL CULT

Worship of the emperor was an activity that Rome actively promoted and organized, which in the early empire provided some sort of unifying religious structure and identity in a fragmented polytheistic world of local or regional cults. The imperial cult was celebrated on various levels, chief among these being the city and the province. Individuals and other cults could demonstrate loyalty to the empire and ruling regime by dedications, prayers or setting up images of the rulers in houses, shrines or temples. Cities had honoured Hellenistic rulers or powerful Roman generals as divine or semi-divine beings right up to the inception of the principate, when this worship became focused on the figure of the emperor. Sanctuaries for municipal imperial cults are attested in various cities in the region, but these all functioned within the civic framework. The imperial cult was organized on a communal, provincial basis (called the *koinon* of Syria: fig. 180.1) from the reign of Augustus, when the tetrarch Dexandros, an ancestor of Lucius Julius Agrippa of Apamea (see p. 226), held its first high priesthood. Representatives of the Syrian cities would come together for provincial assemblies and celebrations, which consisted of festivities in honour of the emperor: official panegyrics, gladiatorial combats, or recitals of poems or prose works about him. The province showed its fidelity as a whole, setting aside civic rivalries and animosities. The imperial cult bound the individual and the city to the Roman hierarchy, defining the place of provincials within the power structure, but through its assemblies it also provided provincials with an additional channel of communication with the emperor. In this sense it acted as a mediating institution between the cities and the centre of power, and for this reason was likely to have been an important institution for provincials. It is worthy of note that on civic coins the *koinon* and sub-districts of the imperial cult are the only social and political entities commonly referred to other than the cities themselves. The institution provided provincials with an identity as members of a province of the Roman world, and rejection of the imperial cult was a very serious matter. Christianity's first serious problems were with this cult rather than others, and as a result Christians placed themselves in conflict with the hierarchical order of the empire.

The Syrian provincial cult was divided into smaller regional entities or sub-districts called – somewhat confusingly – provinces or eparchies. Before the reign of Vespasian there had been three, centred on Tarsus (eastern Cilicia being part of the province of Syria at this date), Antioch and Tyre. Under Vespasian the annexation of Commagene added a fourth eparchy, but this was quickly reduced to three again after eastern Cilicia was detached from Syria. By the reign of Hadrian the number had been raised once more to four, with the creation of an eparchy centred on Damascus. The names of the four were Commagene (presumably with its capital at Samosata, whose civic coins bear abbreviations which must be expanded to something like 'Metropolis, of Commagene'), Syria (Antioch), Phoenice (Tyre) and Coele-Syria (Damascus). Beyond these details the evidence is extremely fragmentary and incoherent. Delegates from each eparchy met at their respective capitals, and each eparchy had its sanctuary, president and high priest, although an inscription from Gerasa cites a high priest 'of the four eparchies', resident at Antioch. It seems therefore that Antioch had some sort of precedence over the other eparchies. It is also interesting to note that the four eparchies evolved independently of the Roman administrative provinces, as if they had gained some social or political identity of their own. The eparchy of Coele-Syria included a number of Decapolis cities which by the second century were in the administrative provinces of Arabia or Syria Palaestina, and as an entity this eparchy continued to exist after Septimius Severus created an administrative province with the same name in a different region (see chapter 3). Second- and third-century coins of various cities, Abila, Dium, Gadara, Scythopolis, Pella and Philadelphia advertise the fact that they are 'of Coele Syria', as if the eparchy provided them with a communal affiliation. There is also some evidence to suggest that after its punishment by Septimius Severus following the defeat of Pescennius Niger, Antioch lost its pre-eminent position to Laodicea (see p. 49). Some Severan coins of Laodicea call the city 'Metropolis of the Four Provinces', and some show four *Tychai*, perhaps representing the eparchies, standing before the city-goddess of Laodicea (fig. 180.2). However, it is difficult to imagine that Antioch failed to recover its original status during the Severan period, so perhaps Laodicea was granted honorary status, or shared its position with Antioch in some way.

There is no clear evidence for a provincial imperial cult in Judaea/Syria Palaestina, although cities of the province had their own municipal imperial cults. By analogy with the coins inscribed 'of Coele Syria', civic issues of Neapolis and Caesarea inscribed 'of Syria Palaestina' *might* support the existence of a provincial imperial cult there. Some slight evidence exists for Arabia in the third century, but this is not enough to give us an idea of its organization.

180.1

180.2

Fig. 180.1. Bronze coin of Trajan (AD 98-117), with a personification of the koinon *('the commune') of Syria.* BMC I.

Fig. 180.2. Civic coin of Laodicea of the reign of Philip I (AD 244-9). Four Tychai *standing before the city goddess of Laodicea.* BMC 110.

JEWS AND SAMARITANS

From Herod to Bar-Kokhba

If the evidence for pagan identities requires some considerable interpretation and speculation drawn from diverse and fragmentary sources, that is not so with the Jews. The enormous amount of literary evidence allows for more confident interpretations of the archaeological record, and shows how religion contributed to a sense of community and difference, and how knowledge of a pre-Hellenistic past could be used to justify activities in the present. Continuity was aided enormously by Jewish reverence for the written word, which imparted a degree of religious, moral and social authority and conformity in the form of the *Torah*. The Hasmonaean conquests in the late Hellenistic periods had expanded the Jewish presence, mainly, it seems, by forced conversion of locals such as the Galilaeans and Idumaeans. Although the greatest concentration of Jews was in Judaea and Galilee, there was no clear geographical boundary between gentile and Jewish settlement, and no zone that was entirely Jewish. Greek cities were established in predominantly Jewish Judaea and Galilee and pagans evidently lived in the countryside in these areas (although there is practically no archaeological evidence for them); conversely there were significant Jewish communities in cities and rural areas outside these regions. There were also plenty of Jews who had remained in Babylonia after the exile. In all these areas Jews and gentiles generally coexisted peacefully, but the political impositions of the gentiles could generate tensions and conflict (see chapter 8). Nevertheless the Romans took measures to accommodate Judaism, recognizing the rights of Jews within the empire, including exemption from military service, their payment of the Temple-tax, and the right not to appear in court on the Sabbath. They did not have to worship the emperor (although they might offer sacrifice to God in his name), or swear oaths on the emperor's name. The emperors themselves were not insensitive to the potency of the Jewish deity; Augustus provided for daily sacrifices in the Temple on his behalf. Boundaries between gentile and Jew were religious, social and cultural rather than political and geographical, but the coming of the Messiah promised political deliverance for the land as well.

Until the end of the first revolt, Judaism resembled some of the other cults of the region in that it was originally centred on a great sanctuary with its High Priests, and with festivals, sacrifices and pilgrimage as an important feature of religious observances. Where it differed crucially was in the Jewish rejection of all other deities. The High Priest presided over a supreme court, the Sanhedrin, which was responsible for making judgements on religious and civil matters and which provided a legal framework for the Jews of Judaea and a corporate body for regulating the faith. That Judaism was a unifying social force is evinced by the fact that during the first revolt the converts of Idumaea and Galilee, as well as the Judaeans, were prominent in fighting against Rome. However, there were also forces within Judaism tending towards disunity as well, some of which the Sanhedrin could not control. Even among the members of the Sanhedrin there were different opinions on a variety of practices and beliefs, and among all pious Jews there were disagreements and debates over interpretation of the *Torah* and over rituals and taboos, about whether there was an afterlife, and over when the Messiah would come and what would happen. The best-known groups are the Essenes, the Pharisees and the Sadducees, who held very different positions with regard to tradition, scriptural interpretation, and observance of the Law, but there were numerous other sects as well. Some saw resistance to Rome as a religious duty, while others accepted and co-operated with Roman hegemony. These vigorous debates and varying stances within Judaism were extremely difficult for the Sanhedrin to manage, let alone outside powers, but the Roman prefects and procurators do not appear to have handled the problems they faced with any great degree of competence. The popular belief that a Messiah would come to liberate the Jews from foreign domination naturally found little favour with the rulers, but gained popularity with the masses. Messianic claims abounded in the first half of the first century AD, leading to a chain of rebellions. During the first century those opposed to Roman dominion succeeded in swaying some of the religious leaders, and the emergence of extremists who specialized in assassinating moderate Jewish collaborators provided additional coercion. The first revolt witnessed a shortlived but remarkable experiment with an independent Jewish

181.1

181.2

Fig. 181.1. Silver shekel of the first Jewish revolt. The inscriptions are in archaic Palaeo-Hebrew script and the designs consciously avoid using Hellenizing symbols. The obverse reads 'shekel of Israel', with the date, year 5 (AD 70), above a chalice; the reverse has a stem with three flowers, around which is the inscription 'Jerusalem is holy'. BMC 20.

Fig. 181.2. Bronze coin of the emperor Vespasian (AD 69-79), from an uncertain mint (Caesarea?), showing a personification of Victory inscribing a shield set on a column. The Greek inscription is the equivalent of the Latin Judaea capta. BMC 1.

state, notable for its deliberate rejection of Hellenism. It also witnessed attacks on Jews by the Greek populations of the cities across the region, and, following the collapse of the revolt, the state's attitude towards Judaism was symbolized by the image found on millions of gold, silver and bronze coins across the Roman world: *Judaea capta*. Captured Judaea was an emblem fundamental in helping to legitimize the usurping Flavian dynasty.

The destruction of the Temple was a turning-point in the development of Judaism, bringing the sacrificial cult, the High Priesthood and the Sanhedrin to an end. Initially many Jews perhaps hoped it would be rebuilt, and rabbis continued to debate sacrificial ritual as if the Temple existed, but as time passed it must have become clear that restoration was not imminent. To some the restoration was perhaps not so important; the authority of the High Priest and Sanhedrin had been tarnished somewhat during the periods of Herodian and Roman rule, and various groups had contested their authority, including questioning the spiritual importance of sacrifice. Jews of the Diaspora generally lived too far away to participate in the sacrificial cult, although they might arrange for sacrifices to be performed on their behalf. The ground had already been prepared for a more decentred cult, for which a great sanctuary was no longer necessary. During the interval between the fall of Jerusalem in AD 70 and the outbreak of the Bar-Kokhba war, rabbinic academies were established in centres like Jamnia for the study and interpretation of the *Torah* and the preservation of commentaries on it, and it was these institutions that gradually came to take on the spiritual authority once enjoyed by the High Priests and the Sanhedrin. This process began at the same time as new Greek cities were being established in Jewish and Samaritan areas, continuing the Hellenizing project begun by the Herodian kings and Julio-Claudian emperors. We do not know what effect the Jewish rebellions of AD 115-17 in Cyprus, Cyrenaica, Egypt and Mesopotamia had in our region, although the Roman general responsible for putting down the Mesopotamian revolt was afterwards made governor of Judaea – a sign, perhaps, that trouble was expected. The Bar-Kokhba revolt saw another attempt to create a Jewish state, although this rebellion was more restricted and did not find such widespread support as the earlier one. With the defeat of Bar-Kokhba, the Jewish population of Jerusalem and its territory was expelled and a gentile population settled there, dashing any hopes that the Temple might be rebuilt. The installation of a legion at Caparcotna, in a position between Galilee to the north and Samaria and Judaea to the south, was probably intended to drive a wedge between the two regions and so check any potential uprising in one spreading to the other. Greek cities and Roman armies contributed to a redefinition of political geography in the region.

After Bar-Kokhba

Rabbinic Judaism was an adaptation to suit the changed circumstances after the fall of the Temple: there was no emphasis on the duty of sacrifice, and other rituals formerly exclusive to the Temple could now be performed elsewhere. The study of the *Torah* became central to religious devotion, and through it the rabbis set about defining Jewish religious identity and generating practical rules that allowed pious Jews to observe the Law and at the same time live in a world where coexistence with gentiles was a fact of life. After the Bar-Kokhba revolt most of the influential rabbinic academies were to be found in Galilee. A Hasmonaean conquest, the inhabitants of which had been forcibly converted,

Fig. 182. Silver shekel of the Bar-Kokhba revolt. The obverse type shows the Temple, with the Palaeo-Hebrew inscription 'Jerusalem'. The reverse reads 'year two of the freedom of Israel' – a clear reference to an independent Jewish state – and shows ritual symbols, a bundle of twigs (lulav) and a citron (ethrog). BMC 6.

Galilee had already become an important centre for interpretation of the Law by the first century AD (Jesus of Nazareth was one of the region's more famous radicals), and this position was maintained throughout the period of Roman rule. However, in spite of the copious literature discussing religious law generated by the rabbis, resulting in the authoritative *Mishnah* (*c.* AD 200), the third-century *Tosefta* (the 'Supplement' to the *Mishnah*) and the Palestinian or Jerusalem Talmud (interpretations of the *Mishnah*, completed *c.* 400), it is uncertain to what extent the writings and prescriptions of these sages influenced the daily behaviour and attitudes of other Jews. The rabbis do seem to have gained authority in religious matters, not least because they rendered a crucial service by determining the religious calendar, something that had formerly been determined by the High Priest and Sanhedrin. However, it is sometimes difficult to reconcile the image of Judaism in rabbinic sources with portrayals of Jews encountered in non-rabbinic sources. The ordinary people portrayed in the latter seem to belong to another world, often less concerned with the ritual purity and pious lifestyle advocated by the rabbis, and often less anxious to create strict cultural boundaries between themselves and the gentile population. The detailed prescriptions of the rabbis were in any case rather difficult to fulfil to the letter, especially as there was not always agreement. The rabbinic work was perhaps more important in helping to preserve and transmit traditions and in developing and shaping a coherent Jewish identity, particularly in late Roman times when the empire had adopted a religious offshoot of Judaism as its official religion. The centrality of religion to that Jewish identity is undeniable, and it is worthy of note that no significant body of *secular* Jewish writing survives in either Aramaic or Greek from late antiquity.

By the third century the restrictions imposed after the Bar-Kokhba war were relaxed, and a Jewish community was reinstalled in Jerusalem. The Jews were largely exempt from Roman persecutions of Christians in the third and early fourth centuries, which shows how far the two faiths had grown apart, and how successful both had been in separating themselves from each other in the eyes of the authorities. Unlike Christians, Jews did not have to sacrifice to the emperor to prove their loyalty to the state. By the fourth century the Roman state had come to recognize a leading rabbi as the patriarchal representative of all Jews, but it is far from clear what his powers and responsibilities were. However, the fourth century also witnessed the triumph of Christianity over the Roman world. While Jews were permitted as a sect, the Christian state nonetheless placed all sorts of restrictions on them, some of the more significant being aimed at preventing the spread of their religion. During the fifth and sixth centuries the Roman authorities became increasingly concerned with heresies (see below), and anyone who held religious views other than Chalcedonian Christianity was likely to fall under suspicion. From the time of Justinian onwards the government became progressively suspicious of, and more oppressive in its attitude towards, the Jews of the empire. They were accused of complicity in the Persian conquest in the early seventh century, and following the Roman reconquest Heraclius ordered the conversion of all Jews to Christianity (the rapid collapse of Roman authority in the region during the years that followed rendered the measure irrelevant).

In late antiquity Galilee retained its pre-eminence, but over the centuries emigration abroad saw the overall numbers of Jews in the region decline, so much so that rabbis began trying to encourage them to return to the Holy

Land. The Jewish population of the Palestinian provinces seems to have become increasingly urban too, abandoning the countryside in favour of the larger villages and cities. Jewish farmsteads (identified by their ritual baths) are common in the first century AD, but rare thereafter, suggesting that the suppression of the revolts could have triggered a major and permanent shift away from the land. It was in the Hellenized urban environments that later Judaism flourished, in places like Tiberias, which was a major centre of rabbinic Judaism in late antiquity, and where the Jewish patriarch was based until the early fifth century.

Samaritans

The evidence for the Samaritans is not so abundant. Since the return from exile Judaism and Samaritanism had developed separately. Samaritans had a distinct theology and in the late Hellenistic period there had been conflicts with the Jews, culminating in the Hasmonaean sack of their Temple on Mount Gerizim. This remained their sacred site, however. The Samaritans were not exempt from the impositions of Hellenism: Herod had founded the Greek city of Sebaste with foreign colonists, and under Vespasian another Greek city, Neapolis (Nablus), was founded near Mount Gerizim. By the second century a temple to Zeus Hypsistos stood on a peak of Mount Gerizim near the site of the Samaritan Temple. There are occasional references to Samaritan unrest in the early empire, but it is in the late fifth and sixth centuries that we encounter notable conflicts between them and the Roman authorities, of sufficient severity to induce the Romans to introduce anti-Samaritan measures and to convert their synagogue on Mount Gerizim into a church. Whereas the Christian state tolerated Jews, it seems to have had little fondness for Samaritans, although the authorities may sometimes have confused them with Jews. Major Samaritan revolts in 529 and 555 suggest a substantial population with a distinct sense of identity and a severe grudge.

A RELIGION OF STATE

Christianity: Early Division and Dissent

Christianity emerged from the radical ferment of Jewish apocalyptic and messianic traditions current during the first half of the first century AD. Jesus and his followers were all Jews, and in the early years after his crucifixion c. AD 30 his cult can scarcely be regarded as anything other than an offshoot of Judaism. Jewish followers were responsible for transmitting this cult of the 'Nazarenes' among the cities of the region, and at Antioch they seem to have first received the name 'Christians'. Wherever Jewish communities were to be found, soon there were also Christians, even among the diaspora communities of Babylonia. From Syria the cult spread to Asia Minor and the rest of the Mediterranean. However, during the first century the number of Christians in the Roman world must have been very small. Christianity was definitely a minority religion, yet it was strengthened early in its history when the church departed from mainstream Judaism by accepting gentiles into the Christian community. Not all Jewish Christians necessarily concurred with this policy, but within a few decades the number of gentile Christians came to outnumber Jewish ones, and following the disturbances of the first Jewish war (AD 66-70) identification with Judaism was not necessarily desirable. Further Jewish revolts in 115-17 and under Bar-Kokhba probably accelerated the process of separation. Communities of Jewish Christians continued to exist, steadfastly observing Jewish ritual, but they became isolated from the streams of universalizing Christianity.

Proselytism provided the cult with a new ambition. The move allowed Christianity to be viewed as a universal religion, open to all who embraced it. It proclaimed universal truths without employing obscure philosophical language (although, as Christian intellectuals discovered, obscure Greek philosophical concepts could be accommodated). Its texts were written in a language accessible to all. Cult practice did not require expensive public rituals or great temples (although the process of initiation might require lengthy tests of a neophyte's commitment). While no single explanation can adequately convey the reasons why Christianity became so successful in the Roman world in the second and third centuries, one must be that this univeralizing religion had no real challengers. Orthodox Jews do not appear to have been enthusiastic about proselytes. The religious philosophizing of the intellectual elites was open only to the highly literate. Many pagan religions were associated with a particular place or people and did not exclude other faiths, or, like Mithraism, were restricted to particular classes and gender.

Christianity soon came to straddle the Fertile Crescent and the boundaries of the Roman and Parthian empires. As noted above, Jewish Christians were established in Babylonia by at least the early second century AD and, on the opposite side of the Euphrates from the province of Syria, the kingdom of Osrhoene, which during the second century was brought under the control of Rome, hosted a variety of Christian sects. Its capital Edessa was a notable centre of pagan cult, but by the late second century various Christian groups were established there, including the ascetic Encratites, a sect established by the Syrian apologist Tatian. An Edessene aristocrat, Bardaisan, was a convert, and his king Abgar VIII (AD 179-214) reputedly took an interest in the religion. The third-century *Acts of Thomas* hint at Christian communities further east, in India and perhaps beyond.

If Christianity was a universal religion, its mission was to convert everyone. But what exactly was Christianity? Diversity was inherent in the faith from its early days, perhaps because its communities of worshippers were so dispersed, and because of a lack of any strong focal point from which orthodoxy could be disseminated. Christians identified with one another against non-Christians, but otherwise the different sects were concerned with differentiating themselves. The sects might agree that there were fixed, universal truths, but this did not naturally lead towards unity, because the body of truths themselves differed from one community to another. Christianity offered an eternal afterlife in a heavenly abode of perfection, but speculation about the exact relationship of the eternal realm to the everyday world led to a variety of interpretations. Some sects gravitated towards Platonic-style philosophies concerned with eternal truths far removed from the apparent material world. To grasp these truths required special knowledge (*gnosis*). A broad spectrum of beliefs is usually placed under the umbrella of the term 'Gnosticism', ranging from sects which drew heavily on orthodox Christianity to those whose monotheism was questionable, and whose teachings attracted the interests of pagan intellectuals. The principal elements of Gnosticism seem to be these: that a pre-cosmic catastrophe had resulted in a realm of purity, truth and light being mixed with corruption, falsehood and darkness, these latter qualities being equated with matter and the 'apparent' changing world around us. Sparks of the original pure light were trapped inside the material bodies of certain elect humans, and Gnostic teaching was supposed to awaken these trapped souls and prepare them for their journey to heaven. As a result, the body, being composed of matter, was generally regarded as irrelevant to salvation. Gnosticism usually required textual expurgation or elaborate theological acrobatics to reconcile Christian scriptures with its basic tenets; for a start, the very first chapter of the Old Testament claimed that God had created the material world. And was not the body of Christ Himself made of matter? The eponymous founder of a Gnostic sect called the Marcionites, which became well established in Syria and Mesopotamia in the second century, adopted a solution to such problems. Marcion taught that the God of the Old Testament had indeed created the world, but that this being was an inept demiurge, and not the true God (whose eternal realm was immaterial). Christ, as a pure being, could not have been made of matter or born of human flesh, and while the New Testament was witness to his coming, it had become corrupted through references to the wicked Jewish Old Testament and required judicious pruning. Marcion appears to have been the first Christian to form a canon of acceptable scriptures. He also insisted on celibacy to deny the inferior creator-being success through human procreation. Some have seen the Marcionite principle of celibacy as a precursor to later Christian ascetic traditions of self-mortification and denial of the body. From the fourth century asceticism became a major movement in Egypt, Syria and Mesopotamia (see below). Marcionite communities were certainly established in places like Edessa, which became an important centre for asceticism, and Epiphanius, the fourth-century bishop of Salamis in Cyprus, when listing the places where this heresy still existed, shows the Marcionites to have been concentrated in the Fertile Crescent. Tatian's Encratites, established at Edessa in the late second century, also practised self-denial and celibacy. The origins of asceticism, however, are much disputed, and some would see its development in Syria as being independent of the ascetic movement of Egypt. Furthermore, notions of purity through celibacy can also be found in pagan Syrian cult.

Dissent was to be found even among the more orthodox, and in particular the learned and influential. Bishops and church leaders held diverse opinions about the Trinity, and the precise relation between God the Father and God the Son. Origen (c. 185-253), bishop of Caesarea in Palestine, proposed that Christ was the Word, who had adopted human form to bring God to humanity. An opposite view, that Christ was a man in whom the Holy Spirit had taken up residence, was adopted by figures such as Paul of Samosata, bishop of Antioch (260-68). Paul's views were considered heretical, but in the decades that followed Antioch became the centre of a school of Biblical studies stressing the human aspect of Christ, in opposition to the belief that he was a purely metaphysical being.

Thus Christianity showed a tendency towards fragmentation rather than unity, long before Constantine adopted it as a religion of state. A historical Jesus was less important than a Christ who could be employed in the service of the various Christian communities. The influences of Judaism, Greek philosophies, and Hellenized Mazdaism, with its insistence on dualities of light and dark, good and bad, generated various interpretations of Christ and His message among the scattered communities of Christians. Bishops might gather to consult one another on matters of doctrine, but the scriptures available were wildly different and not all enjoyed common acceptance.

THE CONSEQUENCES OF EMPIRE

By the third century politics began to play a prominent role in the fortunes of the church. There is a tradition that the emperor Philip the Arab (AD 244-9) was Christian, and some have seen the actions of his successor and supplanter Trajan Decius (249-51) as a backlash against Philip's positive attitude towards Christianity, whether or not Philip was actually a believer. Rome had celebrated its thousandth anniversary in AD 247-8, but the empire was in crisis and now it was felt that subversive elements had to be purged. Trajan Decius decreed that all inhabitants of the empire were to sacrifice to the gods by a certain date, and to gain a receipt to show that they had done so. In this way they demonstrated loyalty to the state. Even if his edict was not intended as a direct attack on Christians, refusal to sacrifice was met with harsh punishment, and a number of Christians demonstrated their commitment by the supreme sacrifice of martyrdom. Persecution continued under Valerian (253-60), this time with edicts specifically against Christians, forbidding meetings and condemning senior clergy and influential members of the congregations. These persecutions ended with Valerian's capture by the Persians in 260, and shortly afterwards the emperor Gallienus issued an edict reversing his father's policies. In the latter part of the third century, the 'Little Peace of the Church' allowed Christian communities to assimilate themselves into the fabric of provincial society. The earlier persecutions had helped to define the orthodox Christian believer and the role of church leaders, and Christian apologists, anxious to demonstrate that they were not a threat to the traditional order, sought to harness Greek intellectual culture in the service of their faith. The church was now prominent enough to attract the criticisms of influential pagan intellectuals, and Christian apologists retaliated with Hellenized treatises of their own. By using Greek culture, Christian leaders forged an identity that could compete with Hellenism and win favours from the central powers. The most eloquent were eventually able to compete with traditional Greek rhetors for honours before emperors, and such defeats on their own territory forced pagans on to the defensive. Christians could also look to the emperor to arbitrate on their behalf. Aurelian (270-75) was the first emperor to whom the church appealed to solve an internal dispute, which was to rule in favour of the other bishops against Paul of Samosata, who had been accused of heresy for his beliefs but had refused to leave his church. Most important of all, the first three centuries witnessed the gradual development of a Hellenized Christian discourse that was relevant to the project of empire. The second-century Christian Tatian, himself from Syria or Mesopotamia, had written after his conversion that there should be one code of law and one political organization for all mankind, and these sorts of sentiments appealed when it was intimated that Rome was the political organization in question.

With the accession of Diocletian in AD 284 the late third-century atmosphere of tolerance began to dissolve. In AD 303, inspired by an oracle and coerced by his violently anti-Christian colleague Galerius, he issued a series of edicts which effectively outlawed Christianity. These commanded that 'churches be levelled to the ground and the Scriptures be destroyed by fire' and that 'those who held places of honour be degraded, and that imperial freedmen, if they persisted in the profession of Christianity, be deprived of freedom'.[61] The effectiveness of the edict seems to have depended on the inclinations of provincial governors, but the ensuing persecutions under Diocletian, Galerius and Maximinus were to claim numerous martyrs and may well have induced many Christians to move from the cities to the safer anonymity of the countryside, heralding a new era of monasticism and asceticism. Nevertheless this diffusion out from the urban centres was slow, and the persecutions cannot account for much of it. For example, epigraphic evidence from the north of Syria suggests the spread of Christianity into the countryside of Antioch in the first half of the fourth century, and in the territory of Apamea by the second half, reaching further south only in the fifth and sixth centuries – but this evidence relies on our being able to identify memorials and monuments as Christian.

The importance of Constantine's conversion and his triumph over his rivals cannot be overstated. The emperor's great achievement was to marry the religious force of Christianity with the secular powers of the Roman empire, giving the Roman world a new identity and a new mission. He also saw his role as that of a protector of Christians *outside* the empire, so that his rule transcended the boundaries of what was politically possible by invoking the spiritually possible. The Roman emperors had harboured the ideal of ruling the inhabited world; now Christianity aspired to make this reality. If the sources are to be believed, Christians in Iran identified with the emperor, so much so that following Constantine's death and his unrealized Persian campaign they were persecuted as subversives. The identification of a state with a religion was nothing new to the Jews, and during the third century an association between Zoroastrianism and the Sasanian royal house had gathered strength, though this relied very much on the personal whims of the kings. In the past Roman emperors (as the embodiment of state) had associated themselves with heavenly counterparts such as the sun or Jupiter. In some senses, then, Constantine was doing nothing original by conjoining emperor and empire with a particular religion. But this was a universal religion with a message for all of humanity, and the state was to define and embody the orthodoxy necessary for salvation. Emperors were not merely a figurehead for the church. From Constantine onwards the church sought their help in doctrinal disputes. Emperors took a keen interest in the councils, published letters setting out their opinions on matters of orthodoxy, and, if necessary, authorized persecutions of sects deemed heretical. There was no separation of church and state. An entirely new community – a politico-cultural commonwealth of Christians – had been created. It would be no exaggeration to say that this change in the nature of the empire had consequences for every one of its inhabitants.

Pagans and Christians

The fortunes of the Christian world depended on the will of God as much as on military power. A sinful empire would be punished, so it was important to eliminate sin wherever it lay. Pagans were obvious targets, although in the time of Constantine polytheists were still in the majority, making them difficult to attack. But paganism by its very nature consisted of a wide variety of unconnected cults; and while pagan intellectuals might seek some form of unity there was no universal pagan organization to oppose an assault by the highly organized and well-connected Christian church. The very concept of pagans and paganism was a Christian creation, an abstraction that the adherents of polytheistic cults would not have recognized. On the other hand the power of individual pagan 'demons' was felt to be very real, and it was sometimes necessary to demonstrate the power of the Christian God in metaphysical duels with these lesser spirits or by physically appropriating their sanctuaries. Some of the more famous centres of Syrian paganism were pointedly claimed for Christianity. At Heliopolis Constantine constructed a church and forbade ritual prostitution there. Constantius II interred the relics of the Christian martyr St Babylas at Daphne near Antioch, silencing the oracle of Apollo. Christianity began to encroach on the ritual landscape with more conspicuous churches and, in the countryside, monasteries. The plain of Dana, between Antioch and Beroea, was an important rural district into which Christianity intruded and established itself in the fourth century. This was a landscape dominated by a mountain (Jebel Sheikh Barakat) on which stood the pagan sanctuary of Zeus Madbachos and Selamanes. Some measures, even if not deliberately anti-pagan, were probably intended to demoralize pagan intellectuals whose writings and teachings could undermine Christian legitimacy. Apamea hosted a school of Neoplatonists; and in 331 Constantine executed the philosopher Sopatros, who came from that city. If the interpretation of the fourth-century mosaics under the cathedral at Apamea as Neoplatonic allegory is correct (see p. 321), it would seem that Christianity struck at their property as well.

Destroying temples had symbolic value, even if it did not always silence the demons. Urban and rural landscapes were converted into battlegrounds in which Jews and pagans often found themselves ranged against Christians. Much depended on the power structure – the religious interests of the emperor and, often more importantly, the governors. The activities of the emperor Julian (AD 360-63) briefly reversed the trend. He had been converted from Christianity to Greek intellectual paganism ('Hellenism') by Neoplatonists of the Apamene school in about 355, the year in which Constantius II made him deputy emperor, and on becoming sole emperor Julian worked actively to promote Hellenism. In order to prevent Christians appropriating Greek philosophy he forbade them to learn it. Temples were restored or reopened, as inscriptions attest: 'Under the rule of Flavius Claudius Julianus, Imperator, Augustus, the rites were restored, and the temple was rebuilt and consecrated in the year 256, the 5th of Dystros' [March AD 362].[62] Where Christians had formerly attacked pagans, now pagans attacked Christians. Constantine's church at Heliopolis was dismantled and Christian virgins killed; at Damascus Jews destroyed two churches; at Sebaste the tomb of St John the Baptist was profaned; and the pagan *comes Orientis* seized the sacred vases of the church at Antioch. At Arethusa on the Orontes the bishop Mark had tried to convert the pagan inhabitants by violence, and Julian commanded that an opulent temple which Mark had destroyed be rebuilt. The bishop and his followers were tortured and Mark was killed. Maiuma, the port of Gaza, had been rewarded with independent city status when its inhabitants converted to Christianity; Julian revoked this and rejoined it with pagan Gaza. But in spite of these measures, Julian seems to have misjudged the devotion of Christians and the apparent indifference of pagans to his universalist Hellenism. In any case the experiment faltered when

Fig. 183. Temple at Bziza in northern Lebanon, which was later converted into a church. Initially Christians destroyed temples and left them in ruins, preferring not to convert houses of 'demons' into churches, but in many cases the appropriation of the sacred space ultimately proved a more effective way of eradicating or assimilating the pagan spirits worshipped in such places.

he died in 363 and his successor Jovian returned fully to the Christian fold.

The anarchy of paganism made it fairly easy to contain, if not to eradicate. But in the fourth century Christianity also had to deal with a rival universal religion, a form of Gnosticism with Christian, Jewish and Persian elements called Manichaeism. Its originator, Mani, a third-century Syriac-speaking ascetic from the Sasanian province of Asorestan (Assyria-Babylonia), travelled with his disciples, winning converts wherever they could. The sect's organization appears to have been loosely structured, and the religion itself easily adapted to particular local conditions without compromising its integrity as a faith. It won many converts in Persia, but came into conflict with the ambitions of the Zoroastrian high priest Kartir. In AD 276 Mani was executed and the Sasanian state commenced its persecutions of the Manichaeans. But the failure of Manichaeism in the Sasanian empire led to the diffusion of its missionaries east to central Asia and China (where the sect continued into the fourteenth century) and west into Roman Mesopotamia and Syria, whence it spread to other parts of the Mediterranean, attracting sufficient attention for Diocletian in 297 to issue a rescript to the proconsul of Africa condemning the sect. Their proselytizing made them unpopular with Christians, and although Manichaeism was rife in the fourth century, the Christian empire managed to eliminate them by the fifth or sixth. Perhaps Manichaeism had never been a serious rival to Christianity. To become one of its Elect was a complex process, involving reincarnation; Christianity offered a simpler route to salvation.

In the later fourth century the increasing association of the Roman state with Christianity, particularly under Theodosius I (AD 379-95), intensified pressure on pagans. In 391 Theodosius prohibited them from visiting temples and sacrificing, effectively preventing them from practising the fundamental rituals of pagan cult, and in the following year pagan cults were officially banned. Like many imperial decrees, this one was probably difficult to enforce universally, and there is no evidence that it killed off paganism. But it did mean that paganism was officially unacceptable, and encouraged anti-pagans like Theodosius' prefect of Oriens, Cynegius, who saw to the closure or destruction of numerous pagan temples during the 380s. Bands of monks and ascetics were particularly effective at combating the 'demons' that haunted the pagan sanctuaries, and which were often defended by angry locals. Cynegius was prepared to provide Christians with military support to carry out their acts. Bishops were also key players in directing the vandalism. They were concerned among other things that they would have to atone in the next world not only for their own sins but also for those of the inhabitants of their sees, and did not want their reputation in heaven stained by the questionable activities of a heretical or pagan population.

Yet even in these circumstances polytheism retained its vitality. There were legal loopholes which allowed temples to remain open and cults to be observed. Local and even imperial officials could be bribed to ignore the emperor's orders. Famous pagan shrines were often protected by powerful interests, and sometimes exceptional zeal and daring was needed to overcome the powers of pagan elites and the 'demons' who lived in the sanctuaries. Gaza's best-known shrine, the Marneum, remained open for several years in spite of an appeal to the emperor Arcadius by its bishop and the presence of an imperial official charged with the closure of pagan shrines. Only by visiting Constantinople in person did the bishop obtain an imperial order to close the Marneum. He returned with a military escort, but the pagan priests put up a show of force and it took a miraculous sign from God to fire the Christians with sufficient courage to launch a successful assault and burn the house of the formidable demon (AD 402). Theodosius I had constructed a large basilica in the great court of the Temple of Jupiter at Heliopolis, and yet this flagrant appropriation of pagan space was unable to overcome the power of the deities worshipped there. Theodoret referred to Heliopolis as 'a city of demons', and the fifth-century bishop of Edessa, Rabbula, attempted to destroy its idols but was beaten up and thrown out of the sanctuary. In the later sixth century a pagan attack on local Christians in the city led to the discovery of a widely networked underground pagan organization covering a number of Syrian cities, with a 'high priest' based at Antioch. The investigations led to startling accusations and a witch hunt that implicated various elite figures, including the Antiochene patriarch.

Although late Syrian paganism lacks much in the way of material culture, it is quite clear from written sources that polytheism continued down to the Muslim conquest and beyond. In the early sixth century Jacob, bishop of Serug (Batnae) in Mesopotamia, could list an extensive catalogue of pagan deities and cult centres in the region. At Carrhae paganism included notable elements from Greek philosophy; the cult survived into the tenth century. The worshippers of 'demons' included intellectual Hellenes as well as uneducated rustics, and the fact that education in the Roman world continued to be entrusted to Hellenes was of sufficient concern for Justinian to forbid them to teach. Rustics could be overcome by force, but intellectual paganism was a more formidable source of corruption.

Jews and Samaritans were other natural targets. Jews could be seen as possible collaborators with enemies, be they pagans within the state or Persians without, and as such were vulnerable to attack. These Christian fears were not always groundless. Under Julian, and during the Persian invasion of Syria during the early seventh century, Jews were able to take advantage of anti-Christian movements. Consequently synagogues as well as temples were prey for marauding monks and ascetics.

Beyond the Frontiers

The adoption of Christianity as an imperial religion also affected the inhabitants of lands outside the empire. The emperors, through their support of missionaries, encouraged the Christianization of foreign communities and states. Religion, even if viewed as slightly heretical by the centre, was a useful tool with which to bind together peripheries and even states beyond the reach of Roman armies. The emperors could view themselves as the heads of a commonwealth of Christian states, exercising a new form of Roman hegemony. Relations were established with a wide spectrum of political, cultural and ethnic entities: with the Axumites of Ethiopia, whose rulers had converted to Christianity in the first half of the fourth century; with Christian communities in Mesopotamia and South Arabia; with Iberia (eastern Georgia) and Lazica (Colchis); and of course with Armenia, whose king Tiridates had been baptized in the early fourth century.

The danger that this new form of Roman hegemony posed to other states is evident in the reactions and counter-reactions it engendered. After Julian's defeat (AD 363) Shapur II officially banned Greek in Armenia, in an attempt to neutralize Armenian Christianity (the contemporary Armenian liturgical language being Greek). But under the religiously tolerant Yazdgard I (399-420), Persian Armenia adopted a written form of the Armenian language (previously it had used only Greek and Syriac), helping to spread Christianity there. The Sasanians subsequently abolished the Christian Arsacid dynasty in Persian Armenia, and tried to impose Zoroastrianism, without success. They then attempted to promote Nestorianism, which had been anathematized by the Romans (see p. 386) and could be regarded by the Sasanians as 'their' form of Christianity. This too failed, and the Armenians preferred to align themselves with the new Monophysite doctrine that had emerged in the Roman empire (see below). Sasanian attempts to impose Zoroastrianism in Christian Lazica achieved similar results: Lazica also adopted Monophysitism. The theatre of religious conflict extended even further afield: in the first half of the sixth century the emperor Justin encouraged an Axumite invasion of South Arabia to protect Christians there from their Jewish ruler, prompting a Sasanian invasion and ejection of the Axumites later in the century.

Christianization did not always work to Rome's advantage, particularly when it came to dealing with heresy. In the fifth century the Antiochene patriarchate had maintained links with Nestorian churches in the Persian empire, but the growth of Monophysitism (see p. 381) in northern Syria led to the Persian church formally breaking with the Roman empire in AD 484. Nestorianism had been condemned within the empire; in this way the Christians of the Sasanian empire, through commitment to Nestorianism, were able to demonstrate their separation from Roman political and spiritual hegemony. Their missionaries spread Nestorianism further east, as far as China, but in Mesopotamia and Babylonia they were soon in competition with the Monophysites. Yet by the sixth and seventh centuries Monophysites were also in conflict with the Chalcedonian Christian emperors and thus became acceptable to Sasanian rulers as a sect that was opposed to Roman hegemony. It is no doubt for this reason that during his invasion of Mesopotamia in the early seventh century, Khusrau II gave the Chalcedonian Christians of Edessa the choice of conversion to Nestorianism or Monophysitism.

THE SEARCH FOR UNITY

By the seventh century, during the struggle between the Persians and the Romans, the identification of the Roman state with Christianity had become firmly ingrained. Roman identity had become inseparable from the Christian faith. But behind the façade of unity the religion of the empire was in crisis, triggered by a doctrinal statement issued by a church council in the middle of the fifth century. There were basically two camps, one accepting the statement, and the other rejecting it. Although proponents of both positions existed all over the eastern empire, the split could be roughly characterized as geographical, dividing the northern areas of the empire from the Fertile Crescent. The emperors and court had become identified with the northern group, forcing the others to disassociate themselves from the centre of Roman power. A doctrinal problem had become a political, social and military hazard to the unity of the empire.

The alliance of empire and faith created its own special problems for the faithful. Religion was inseparable from politics, but the dynamics of politics were ill-suited to producing conformity in a universal religion of this sort. Christianity demanded certainty on important doctrinal matters, but politics often demanded compromise, being unable to impose absolute truths on a population with different notions of truth. When salvation was at stake, truth and compromise were incompatible bedfellows.

Christ himself proved to be the most intractable problem of all. Was he human? How exactly had he come to be filled with God's Spirit? When Christ had suffered on the cross, had God suffered as well? Consensus on these fundamental matters was virtually impossible to attain. The Christian scriptures were inadequate for the rigid demands made on them, because they left such important matters open to a variety of interpretations, giving potential heretics a leeway. Heresy was not only the enemy of truth; it was the enemy of the unity that was so deeply desired. The politics of absolute truth could not permit differential readings of the same texts, and contradictory opinions could not point the way to salvation. Hence the insistence on the true way, even though there was no ultimate authority recognized by the entire body of the church that was capable of defining the truth. Instead the search proceeded through a series of councils.

A desire for conformity had long been manifest, even before Constantine, through provincial councils of bishops who met to commune on matters of doctrine, but opinions on many fundamental articles of faith had always been too different for consensual certainty to emerge. Christian emperors themselves were not happy with uncertainties. They were keen to see Christianity consolidated and the collections of scriptures systematized and understood correctly. The truths of Christianity were the truths of the empire. Orthodoxy was not only God's intention; it was good for Rome. The great ecumenical councils, beginning with that of Nicaea (325), had tried to define Christianity, but the irony of these successive councils was that the doctrinal and organizational compromises to which the bishops communally agreed did not prevent dissent, and might even force church leaders into opposing camps. The search for doctrinal certainty became a search for compromise with those who would not compromise.

Thanks to the alliance of church and state, the personal convictions of emperors and their relatives contributed to the politico-religious tumult. In the fourth century the Arian heresy, which espoused the idea that the Son and the Father were metaphysically separate in substance, prospered for several decades under sympathetic emperors. Imperial religious inclinations had considerable influence on church affairs, and support for a particular doctrinal position in one reign might be reversed in a later reign. If the emperor had no strong convictions of his own, policies might be influenced by powerful figures at court, including those bishops who had the emperor's ear.

Aside from the profound doctrinal differences, regional factionalism also had a part to play in the disunity of the Christian domain. The primacy of the papacy in the church hierarchy was not disputed, but the later fourth and fifth centuries witnessed a struggle between the other patriarchates for primacy in the eastern empire. The great sees of Constantinople, Antioch and Alexandria jostled for supremacy, their bishops using doctrine as a weapon against one another. The success or failure of the parties often depended in part on the reigning emperor's views, but popular opinion could never be neglected. The details are far too complex to outline here, but the nature of Christ provided a decisive focus for allegiances. The council of Nicaea had ruled that Father and Son were the same, but the wording was such that this could be interpreted in different ways. Christ could be regarded as having two natures (human and divine) or a single nature (divine). The papacy tended to support the two nature, diphysite view, and was opposed to Christ having a single nature (*monophysis*). Its views were influential, but not incontrovertible. The pope, moreover, was far away from the centre of the dispute, and in the east popular support for Monophysitism reduced papal authority to a distant opinion.

During the fifth century Antioch lost ground in the power struggles between the patriarchates, partly on account of its association with diphysitism. The city had become a centre for adherents of the idea that Christ had two natures, and many bishops were followers of this school, such as the influential theologian Theodoret, bishop of Cyrrhus. But as patriarchs the bishops of Antioch, regardless of their personal inclinations, had to supervise bishops and Christian communities of both diphysite and Monophysite persuasions. Local Monophysites were frequently opposed to diphysite bishops, and, as the fifth century wore on, the opposition became increasingly violent. In addition many Syrians were still pagans. There were prosperous and important Jewish communities to contend with as well; and of those that considered themselves Christian many were regarded as heretics by both diphysites and Monophysites, being Gnostics, Marcionites or Manichees. A further problem for the Antiochene patriarchate was the ambition of the fifth-century bishop of Jerusalem, Juvenal (422-58). He wanted his own patriarchate, which could only be formed at the expense of Antiochene authority. In order to achieve his aim, he had to enlist the support of Antioch's opponents. His strongest allies were among the supporters of the Monophysite patriarch of Alexandria in Egypt, Cyril (412-44).

The patriarchate of Alexandria emerged in the fifth century as a powerful opponent of the Antiochene diphysite school, promoting the idea that Christ was the Word, and that God had suffered on the cross. Although the boundary between Monophysite and diphysite doctrines and identities grew ever more distinct over time, there were various different positions on points of doctrine between the two extremes. Many Syrian bishops supported Monophysitism in more or less extreme forms, aligning themselves with Alexandria rather than Antioch, and the influence of the Antiochene patriarchate was somewhat unfairly linked to the fortunes of the diphysite movement in the east. One of the more notable and bitter doctrinal battles was that between Cyril and Nestorius, patriarch of Constantinople, who was a pupil of the Antiochene school. Nestorius had influence at court, but his orthodoxy was questionable, and Cyril devoted his efforts to exposing Nestorius' heresy. Furthermore, Alexandria was not prepared to concede primacy in the east to Constantinople, a city which had not even existed at the time of the council of Nicaea. At the ecumenical council of Ephesus in 431 Nestorius was deposed and sent into exile by the emperor Theodosius II.

Although this was a defeat for Nestorian diphysitism, the council did not lead to a Monophysite triumph, as the Alexandrian patriarch was forced in the interests of unity to come to a compromise with the Antiochene diphysites. Proponents of both sides of the debate sought to gain control of the three great eastern sees, Rome being too distant to be seriously engaged in the struggle. Cyril's extremist successor Dioscorus (444-51) worked hard to cultivate the imperial court in Constantinople and undermine diphysite Christology, and in 449 the investment paid off. The emperor Theodosius II appointed Dioscorus president of the second council of Ephesus, and with military assistance Dioscorus was able to depose those bishops who opposed his Monophysite views. Juvenal was granted his patriarchate, consisting of jurisdiction in the two provinces of Phoenicia, the three provinces of Palestine, and Arabia. The patriarchs of Antioch and Constantinople were deposed, together with many of their supporters, including Theodoret of Cyrrhus. Dioscorus proved victorious, but his support diminished the following year when Theodosius II died. Pope Leo, who was opposed to Monophysite doctrine and had not been present at Ephesus, was furious, calling the council 'a band of robbers'. Dioscorus had gone too far. The new patriarch of Constantinople saw an opportunity to gain papal recognition as the chief patriarch in the east by summoning a new council, which would bring the heads of the church together to define its doctrine and organization once and for all.

In 451 the ecumenical council of Chalcedon was convened, at which Dioscorus was deposed. Juvenal switched sides and salvaged a patriarchate consisting of the three provinces of Palestine; Theodoret of Cyrrhus was restored to his see. Alexandria's power had been broken, Constantinople's had been reinforced and schism with Rome prevented. More importantly, a doctrinal statement emerged. It was probably not intended to be a creed like that of Nicaea, but Pope Leo was especially keen to see the problem of Christ resolved. The council ruled that Christ was 'truly God and truly Man', and that he was 'made known to us in two natures'. The reference to two natures had been insisted upon by papal legates and some of the bishops of the Antiochene school. This doctrinal statement proved to be the source of a protracted battle which eventually rent the eastern church in two. Had it been declared that Christ had been formed *out of* two natures rather than *in* two natures, all might have been well, since it could have been interpreted as one nature formed *out of* two by the supporters of *monophysis*. The distinction between the Greek words 'out of' (*ek*) and 'in' (*en*) appears trivial, but in a world where theological debate interested all Christians, and where only one version could be correct, such differences were crucial. Matters of personal salvation, orthodoxy and relations between the empire and churches beyond its borders were at stake. On this truth there could be no compromise.

It seems that all those who attended the council misjudged the difficulties involved in reconciling doctrinal differences. Chalcedon had defined orthodoxy, but the definition did not suit everyone. Monophysite rejection of 'Chalcedonian' doctrine led to riots in the cities and Monophysites taking matters into their own hands. Juvenal of Jerusalem, now seen as a supporter of Chalcedon, was driven from his patriarchate, and the Monophysites of Ascalon and Gaza appointed their own bishops in defiance. If schism had threatened before Chalcedon, the threat was now even greater. The church stood divided on the nature of Christ.

The later fifth and early sixth centuries saw a struggle to control the Antiochene patriarchate by proponents of both sides of the Christological debate. The authority of its Chalcedonian patriarchs declined, in contrast to the expanding influence of their colleagues in Constantinople and Alexandria. Some loss of influence was due to political changes: in the late fourth century the province of Syria Coele had been divided in two, Syria Prima and Syria Secunda. The creation of Syria Secunda, and the building of a major cathedral at Apamea, shifted some of the focus away from Antioch. Cyprus had been detached from the patriarchate at the council of Ephesus in 431, and Juvenal of Jerusalem's victory at the 'robber' council of 449 reduced Antioch's jurisdiction to Syria Prima and Secunda, although Chalcedon had returned the Phoenicias and Arabia to the Antiochene fold. But the doctrines of the Chalcedonian patriarchs of Antioch were also opposed locally, and sometimes savagely, by Monophysites. These people, who in their day were never known as Monophysites, but were instead politely called 'Hesitants', 'Those with Reservations', or less politely 'Dissidents' or 'Manichees', gained much ground in Syria during the fifth century. Imperial commitment to Chalcedon wavered, and this uncertainty led to open defiance on the streets. In 470/471 Bishop Martyrius resigned; in 479 Bishop Stephen was stabbed to death by fanatics wielding reed pens; and Stephen's successor Calendio was prevented from entering Antioch for a whole year. A Monophysite candidate, Peter the Fuller, was bishop three times between 470 and 489, the beneficiary and victim of changing imperial policies and doctrinal power struggles. The emperor Anastasius (491-518) appears to have had Monophysite sympathies, or at any rate it was he who appointed Severus to the Antiochene patriarchate in 512. Severus was the architect of an organized Monophysite sect, and although a highly educated man he was not above using violence and intimidation to compel others in his diocese to accept Monophysite beliefs. While Chalcedonians argued the essential unity of Chalcedonian and Monophysite views, Severus argued against any compromise. There were many who did not share this sentiment. Syria Secunda stayed faithful to Chalcedon, and in 516 several of its bishops declared Severus deposed and excommunicated, cutting all ties with him. The anti-Severan side, feeling isolated under an indifferent emperor, even looked to Rome for support. In 517 the monastery of Maro in Syria Secunda appealed to the authority of the pope rather than be forced to deal with Monophysite sympathizers in Constantinople, Alexandria or Antioch.

With the death of Anastasius in 518, and the accession of the Chalcedonian emperor Justin I, Severus' imperial support collapsed and he was deposed. He fled to Alexandria, where he continued to administer to the Monophysites as if he were still patriarch until his death in 538. Imperial sympathy for the doctrine was at a low ebb. Justin and his nephew Justinian were looking west, and their ambitions in this arena required the support of the pope, whose consent could be won only by a show of support for Chalcedon. In any case Justin was anxious to unify Christianity under Chalcedon as the expression of true faith. The imperial government was also especially keen to see that no Monophysite bishop should gain control of the Antiochene patriarchate, and Severus' post was filled by the Chalcedonian Paul, who initiated a persecution of Monophysites under his jurisdiction. Paul's excesses led to his removal from office, but Chalcedonian persecution of Monophysites was understood to be orthodox policy. Monks were forced to sign documents agreeing to comply with Chalcedon or be turned out of their monasteries. Some accepted imperial will, but others chose to leave and set up communities in remote places where they would be free to observe their beliefs. Intransigence reigned on both sides. The Monophysites had come to distinguish themselves by a special adaptation of a liturgical formula called the *Trisagion*, which originally stated: 'Holy God, Holy Mighty, Holy Immortal, have mercy upon us', but the Monophysites inserted the phrase 'who was crucified for us' after the invocation. This was an explicit reference to God crucified, and such a formula, which the Monophysites would not relinquish, was unacceptable to orthodox Chalcedonians. On the other hand Monophysitism in any form was unacceptable to the pope, whose opinion mattered greatly if the west was to be won. When Justinian became sole emperor he sought a reconciliation of the Chalcedonian and Monophysite camps (532), and even persuaded Severus to come to the capital. He seems to have been influenced by his wife Theodora, who was sympathetic to Monophysitism. But when Severus won over the patriarch of Constantinople, the pope intervened. However strong the emperor's personal desire for unity might have been, he bowed to pressure. The patriarch of Constantinople was deposed, Severus was anathematized, and his writings burned. In spite of this, the emperor still held out hope for compromise and was prepared to make conciliatory gestures. The Monophysites complained that Chalcedon had rehabilitated the writings of diphysites whom they considered heretical, among them Theodoret of Cyrrhus. Justinian hoped that an official condemnation of these writings might open up the door to reconciliation, but harmony remained beyond the emperor's grasp.

In spite of these problems, and the bouts of persecution during the sixth century, Monophysites remained loyal to the idea of a united Christian empire; as far as they were concerned, Constantinople was in error about Christianity's mission and needed correction. The two sides had had a common history before Chalcedon and this mutual heritage was not so easily cast aside. On the imperial side there can be little doubt that reconciliation was of the highest priority. However, some Syrian Monophysites fled to Persian territory to escape oppression, and in doing so placed themselves beyond the reach of Constantinople. Here they could operate independently and remain in communication with the faithful in Roman territory. Syrian Monophysites within the empire might identify with these other Monophysites outside it, but this did not, until the last decades of Roman rule in Syria, prevent them from identifying with the Roman empire as well.

The Monophysite Church

For Monophysite leaders a complete break with Chalcedonian Constantinople was a step too far. However, the Monophysite solution to the emergency under Justinian – the creation of a parallel church, with a Monophysite priesthood separate from the Chalcedonian – was a radical measure which sent clear signals to Constantinople: there would be no reconciliation without a refutation of Chalcedon. Initially they made no attempt to consecrate bishops, which could be seen as a direct challenge to imperial authority; the aim was simply to create a clergy who could minister to the faithful. However, the Monophysite bishop John of Tella was willing to travel beyond the empire to consecrate Monophysite bishops in Persian territory, with the result that the authority of this parallel Monophysite church transcended the limits of empire in a way that Chalcedonian Constantinople did not. The most significant departure was initiated by Jacob Baradaeus, bishop of Edessa, who from 542 until his death in 578 travelled widely throughout the eastern empire, dressed as a beggar to avoid detection by his Chalcedonian enemies, consecrating Monophysite bishops and organizing an underground Monophysite church. Although he did not intend to break with the church of the empire, the ordination of so many Monophysite clerics made it difficult, if not impossible, to reverse the process. A 'Jacobite' Monophysite patriarch of Antioch now held office concurrently with a Chalcedonian one, and because Monophysitism in northern Syria tended to be centred on monasteries and the countryside, these alternative patriarchs of Antioch resided in monasteries, often some distance from the city itself.

Until the end of the sixth century there had been notable communities of Monophysites at Constantinople and in Asia Minor, but these had presumably mostly converted to Chalcedon by *c.* 600, for after that we hear nothing more about them. However, by this time Monophysites outnumbered Chalcedonians along the eastern frontier and beyond, from Ethiopia to Armenia and Iberia. A coherent community had been forged through opposition to the centre of power. It may not have been planned as a separate political entity from the Roman empire, but in a state that identified with one particular doctrine any organized opposition took on political dimensions. Furthermore, the Arab tribes like the Ghassanids on whom the Romans relied for the defence of their desert frontier were predominantly Monophysite and the antagonism between the two sects thus gained a potential strategic dimension. Most importantly, the Monophysites came to discover that their religious identity did not have to be coterminous with the aspirations of Roman hegemony. The Monophysite movement created a cohesive Christian community at the periphery of the Roman and Sasanian empires, in which Syria and Mesopotamia played a central and unifying role. There were also linguistic differences with Chalcedon, however indistinct these might be. Many of the clergymen appointed by Jacob Baradaeus were Syriac-speakers, drawing a cultural line between Chalcedonian Greek-speakers and the Monophysites. It was not a strict boundary, because there were numerous Monophysites who were speakers of Greek and languages other than Syriac, not to mention Syriac-speaking Chalcedonians, but it drew another distinction between the Monophysites and the mission of imperial unity. A new Christian identity, transcendent of political boundaries, had been created in debate with the Greek, Chalcedonian Christianity of the empire.

Justinian's successor, Justin II, also tried to find common ground with the

Monophysites, but without a revocation of Chalcedon negotiations seemed doomed to failure. Thwarted, imperial policy reverted to persecution, particularly under the strongly Chalcedonian emperor Maurice. The Persian invasion and occupation of Syria in the early seventh century swept the pro-Roman Chalcedonians aside, their bishops often being replaced by Monophysites or Nestorians. The Monophysite church had become increasingly autonomous of the Roman state, which no longer formed an important part of its self-identity. When Heraclius recovered Syria and Mesopotamia he tried, like his predecessors, to find common ground without refuting Chalcedon. He met important Monophysite leaders, attempting to find a compromise, but Chalcedon remained an impossible obstacle, and before long the emperor's patience turned to persecution. The Roman state did not represent Monophysite interests, and there were many who welcomed the relief from persecution that the Muslim conquerors brought. When God 'saw that the measure of the Romans' sins was overflowing and that they were committing every sort of crime against our people and our churches,' wrote the ninth-century Monophysite patriarch Dionysus of Tel-Mahre, 'He stirred up the Sons of Ishmael and enticed them hither from their southern land ... it was by bargaining with them that we secured our deliverance. This was no small gain, to be rescued from the tyrannical kingdom of the Romans.'[63] In the long term however, relief from Chalcedonian persecution was all that Monophysites could expect from Muslim rule.

OUT OF CONTROL

Within the Roman world Christianity had developed alternative sources of power to those of the imperial government. This structure, however, was difficult to control, because whereas imperial officials were answerable to their seniors, church leaders and the pious were ultimately answerable only to God. The failure of the church to agree on a definitive power structure may be a consequence of its early history, when Christians were scattered in small autonomous communities across the Roman world and beyond, but this lack of a formal, well-defined hierarchy meant there was no ultimate authority capable of settling differences among the leaders, or of defining what was appropriate action and what was not. Nor was there any way for one leader to impose his will on the others. Appeals might be sent to emperors, but emperors could not always be relied on, and some tended towards what others viewed as heresy. At the same time the diffusion of Christianity out of the cities and into the countryside made it difficult for city-based church leaders to control.

This 'anarchy of the church'[64] might worry emperors, but it proved very useful to Christian leaders. Bishops were able to build up a power base in their see, because unlike imperial officials they often remained in their post for life. As experts in doctrine they could challenge emperors. Certain sees, such as those of Antioch or Alexandria, gained greater powers and influence and fought to promote their doctrinal views in the capital. Patriarchs could send missionaries outside the empire promoting doctrines that conflicted with current imperial ones. In turn episcopal authority could sometimes be challenged by   the bishops' own subordinates: the bishop tended to be based in, and thus represent, the authority of the city, but his power in the countryside was invested in assistants who might champion the independence of large villages in a bid to gain episcopal powers for themselves. At the same time the powers of appointed church leaders (and emperors) could be challenged by the spiritual authority of people and things that stood outside the existing structure of the church: by ascetics and monks, and by more abstract holy entities such as sacred images and relics.

Ascetics were Christian heroes, martyrs in times of peace. Focal points for ascetic expression were often in remote, out-of-the-way places: caves or abandoned tombs, or in some cases no shelter at all. The ascetic was superhuman and anti-city, enduring inhospitable environments where civilization did not exist. In fleeing the world the ascetic practised *anachoresis*, the withdrawal or removal of one's self from one's village (*chora*). He shared certain ideals with the Gnostics, by renouncing the world, which had fallen from God's grace, and with it bodily desires. Such Holy Men were inspirational to the masses. The ascetic did what they could not, even though he often came from a background as humble as theirs. Obeying the commandments of Christ literally, the ascetic life gave individuals from all sorts of backgrounds a direct link to God, and these Christian heroes were prepared to listen to and pray on behalf of all classes of people. The Holy Man could intercede on behalf of a local community, harnessing divine will for them. After eight years of fasting and solitude the aged Abraham the Recluse prevented a rainstorm from destroying village crops with a miraculous prayer. Prevention of a storm might seem a trivial reward for such

Fig. 184. A stump is all that remains of the column on which St Simeon Stylites stood in prayer. After his death the column became an object of veneration and a martyrium was built around it (see fig. 188).

prolonged asceticism, but to a local community an intercession like this could be a matter of survival or starvation. The Holy Man did not need any formal authority conferred upon him by the church; his power came directly from heaven.

Syrian asceticism took some extreme (and occasionally sensational) forms. Some ascetics became *boskoi*, 'grazers', living in the open without proper clothing, eating grass, nuts, berries and roots, like animals. Others loaded themselves with heavy iron chains. The Mesopotamian 'dendrite' David perched like a bird in a tree at Thessalonica in Greece. This unusual behaviour could lead to iconic, superstar status. Simeon the Stylite (*c*. 386-459), the pillar-dwelling saint, was Syria's most celebrated ascetic, whose renown spread from Gaul to Persia. A monk whose growing dissatisfaction with monastic life led him to increasingly strange acts of devotion, Simeon abandoned his monastery and became a hermit, living on a hill above the settlement of Telanissus (Deir Semaan), close to the plain of Dana, between Antioch and Beroea. He was unable to avoid the attentions of the crowds of devotees, and eventually, in order to divorce himself further from the world, he ascended a column (*c*. 412), on which he stood in almost continuous prayer. The first column was replaced by a second, higher one, and then a third, which reputedly raised him about 20 metres (65½ feet) off the ground (fig. 184). Here he lived an austere life of prayer and contemplation, but he also succeeded in attracting increasing numbers of pilgrims, who were eventually served by a monastery and hostel around the foot of the pillar. His assistants climbed a ladder to deliver messages and food. Twice daily Simeon would interrupt his prayer to listen to individuals or to address the crowds. He pronounced on problems of orthodoxy and heresy, and his opinions were sought at the ecumenical councils of Ephesus and Chalcedon. Emperors, elites and peasants alike wanted his advice, prophecies and judgements.

In spite of the extreme rigours of his lifestyle, Simeon lived on columns for nearly fifty years and was over seventy years old when he died. On his death the Antiochenes claimed his body, and it was borne in a slow procession to the city, with an escort of soldiers and bishops and the imperial *magister militum per orientem*. Simeon had become a relic, and his lifestyle an example to others. Imitators were to be found throughout Syria and Mesopotamia, among them a namesake, Simeon the Younger (AD 521-92), who began his vocation at the age of seven under the guidance of the stylite John. He established a column and a monastery on the Miraculous Mountain between Antioch and Seleucia Pieria, which even today bears his name (Samandag, 'Mount Simeon').

The fame and spectacle of stylitism was something that Simeon the Elder's hagiographers had difficulty explaining. It seemed to be deliberately seeking attention, rather than withdrawing from the world. Other ascetics achieved renown somewhat paradoxically by deliberately avoiding public notice and admiration, trying to live anonymously, such as the various 'holy fools' who set themselves up to be scorned or laughed at by day and, thus estranged from the world, spent the night in prayer. Their examples were less of a challenge to the authorities.

Monasticism was an institutionalized form of asceticism, but it too was difficult to regulate and absorb into the ecclesiastical framework. The monastic movement became an immensely powerful force in Syria in late antiquity, and it was crucial for the church to maintain communion with the monks, a communion which the patriarchs of Antioch more than any other had difficulty in maintaining because of differences of doctrine. Some Syrian abbots were powerful and independent voices, and influential figures at church councils, so their support was often vital to emperors and church leaders alike. Rural monasteries, where groups of holy men came together to observe communion with God through fasting, suffering, isolation and contemplation, were often a significant feature of village societies and their economies, and inevitably became social and political institutions serving a wider public than the monastery itself. Like the solitary ascetic, the holiness of the monk made him a suitable judge of morality in the local community, and by invoking God's authority monks could champion the rights of the poor. Monasteries were to be found in cities as well as in the countryside, but this did not make such institutions easier for the church authorities to control. Surrounded by the pleasures of urban life, the city monks were perhaps subjected to the rigours of self-denial even more than their country brethren were, and thus were equally holy and influential. There was nothing particularly meek about monks, especially when it came to matters of doctrine. Disagreements between the orders sometimes led to riots and street fights between them. Monks and abbots were all too obviously prepared to intervene in the affairs of cities, and bishops found it prudent to align themselves with the monasteries if they could. It was mostly monks, rather than ordinary Christians, who were instrumental in organizing the destruction of pagan temples and idols, for their holiness enabled them to combat demons effectively.

While the life of the ascetic or monk was impractical for the majority of the population, individuals could participate in holiness by observing some ascetic practices. Celibacy could be adopted by married folk after having a family. Laymen and women were encouraged to become consecrated 'covenanters' of the church, living strictly according to certain doctrines but otherwise participating in the life of the general community. As the bishops often discovered, personal religious experience was impossible to regulate and doctrinal concessions might have to be offered to religious communities in exchange for political support. Theodoret of Cyrrhus had to authorize the use of an expurgated version of the Gospels to satisfy the many Marcionites in his diocese. Miracles and religiously inspired individuals encouraged crowds to take the will of God into their own hands. Illegal actions of a religious nature such as the destruction of synagogues were difficult to punish when the faithful culprits claimed they were acting on God's orders.

The Christianization of the Landscape

Christian architecture rejected the temple as a model, and turned instead to assembly halls. This was appropriate, as the space was intended for an assembly (*ecclesia*) of the faithful, rather than for housing a cult image. While Christianity liberated architects from the conventions of classical temple design, it soon imposed new rules. Early Christian 'church houses' resemble domestic buildings, but by *c.* AD 350 distinct architectural forms had emerged. The commonest form of Christian religious building was the basilica, which derived its design from the earlier civic buildings of that name. Typically the basilica consisted of a rectangular nave, facing west, with aisles either side and an apse (either internal or projecting) at the eastern end (colour plate 24). The earliest known in the region was the cathedral at Tyre, built *c.* AD 314-17, and described by the church historian Eusebius, but the earliest surviving examples

Fig. 185. The basilica at Qalbloze, a village in the Jebel A'la of the limestone massif of northern Syria, close to the plain of Antioch.

belong to the second half of the fourth century, when the basilica became a formal design for places of Christian worship. While the basic concept eschewed the temple, there is some debate about whether certain features of the basilica owe anything to pagan shrines. The fine church at Qalbloze (fig. 185) provides us with an excellent example of a basilical form employing two towers flanking the main entrance, which recalls the façades of some Syrian temples (fig. 167). The tripartite thalamos of the temples appears to be repeated in the apses and side chapels of these churches (fig. 186). Some Syrian temples even end in an apse: Burkush and Rahle on Mount Hermon; or the temple at Slim in the Hauran, which also had towers flanking the entrance. While it is

Fig. 186.1. Plan of the first-century AD temple at Slim in the Hauran.
186.2. Plan of the fifth-century basilica at Dama in the Leja.
186.3. Plan of the basilica at Mshabbak in the Jebel Semaan, built c. 460 (see colour plate 24).

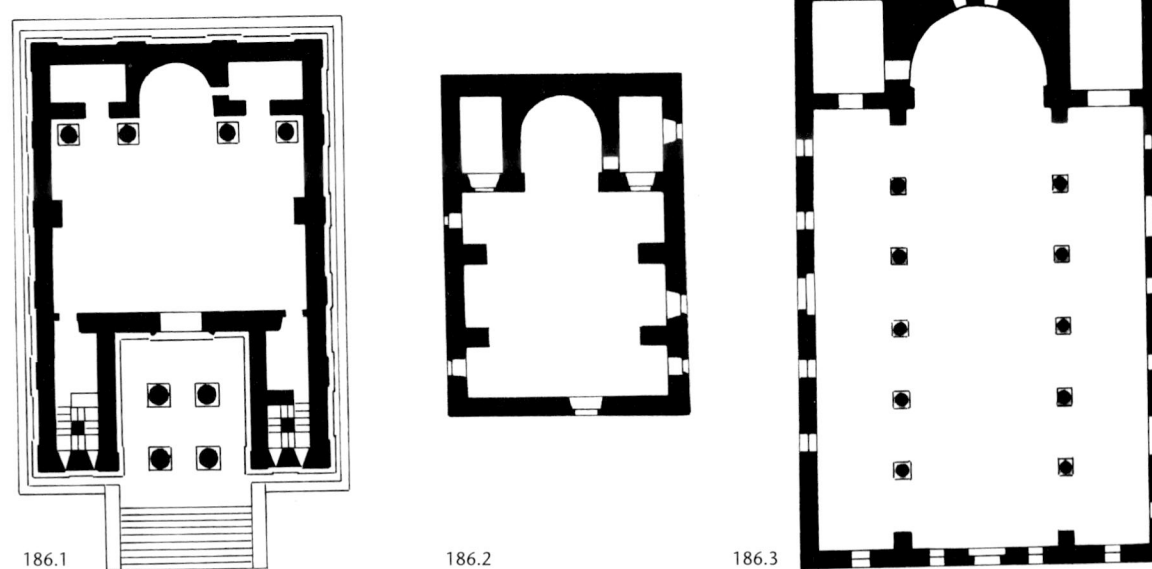

186.1   186.2   186.3

not unlikely that temples did inspire some of these elements, others were already present in civic basilicas, and the dates of many notable 'precursors' (such as those just cited) are all probably first century AD. No doubt some of these temples were still functioning, or their ruins were still visible in late antiquity, but there is no unequivocal evidence for transmission of a tradition, and it is not clear whether any physical affinities imply ritual similitude.

Other forms were completely new. The fourth-century Great Church of Constantine at Antioch was evidently built in the form of an octagon, for that was what it was commonly called. This may be an early example of the other

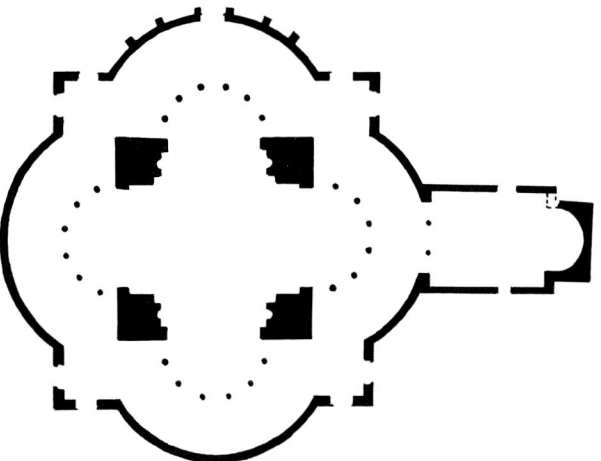

Fig. 187. Plan of the tetraconch church at Seleucia.

main tradition of churches, where a large central space is capped by a dome. There are a number of these buildings in the Hauran, of which the church at Zorava (modern Zoraa) is the best known and among the best preserved. Larger tetraconch churches were constructed in the cities: the cathedral at Apamea and a church at Seleucia (fig. 187) were both built to the same plan and virtually the same scale. Similar tetraconch plans are found at Bostra and Amida. The Syrian examples are poorly preserved, but a fourth-century church of comparable scale and plan that still stands is that of San Lorenzo in Milan, which gives one an impression of the original appearance of the Syrian ones.

Like temples the churches were often situated in an enclosure containing other buildings such as a baptistry. Some complexes were martyria, buildings constructed near or around holy places or relics, rather than simply churches for everyday worship. Like the great pagan sanctuaries before them, these special sites attracted pilgrims and wealthy donors. Among the most elaborate and famous is the cruciform complex built around the pillar of St Simeon Stylites at Qalaat Semaan. This martyrium resembled a set of four basilical halls meeting in a central octagon (colour plate 23; fig. 188). The main part of the shrine was probably constructed under the emperor Zeno (AD 474-91). The focal point was the octagon, perhaps roofed, perhaps open to the sky, which housed the saint's pillar (fig. 184). Three of the four arms of the martyrium were assembly halls for pilgrims; one arm on the east side formed a basilica church. The space between the eastern and southern arms was enclosed and contained a monastery and cloister for visiting priests. Pilgrims arrived at the hilltop

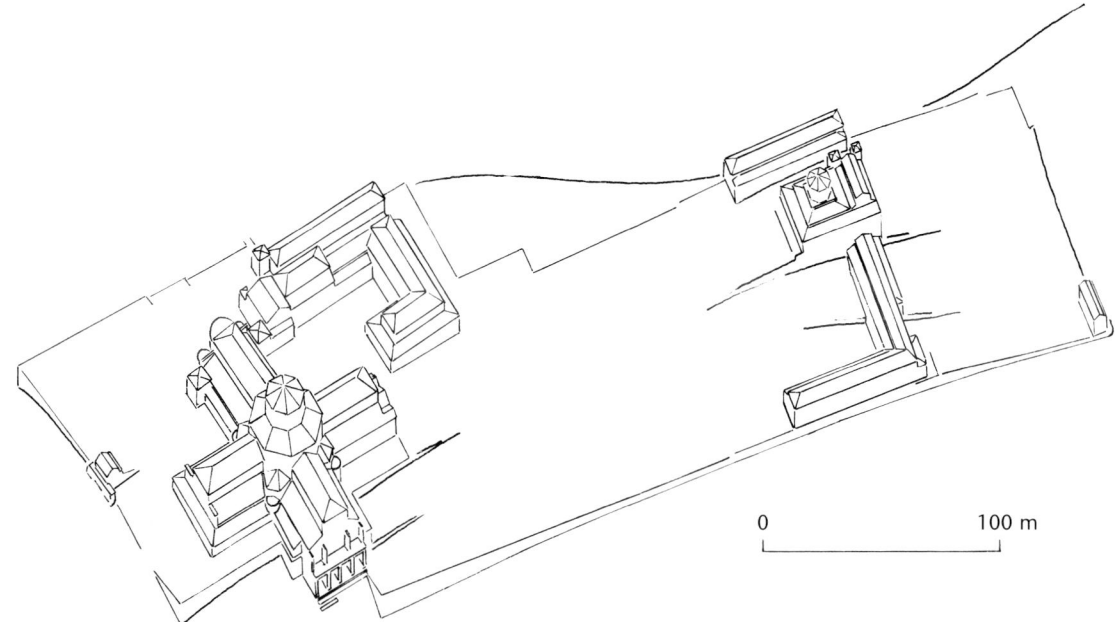

complex from the south via a series of monumental gateways, the third and innermost of which was surrounded by hostels, stables and a baptistry. These substantial arrangements, together with the hostels identified in the village of Deir Semaan at the foot of the hill, attest the enormous popularity of the saint's cult, which was a more than adequate Christian counterweight to the pagan Temple of Zeus Madbachos and Selamanes on the neighbouring hilltop.

No attempt will be made here to describe the immense variety of Christian buildings in Syria. Suffice to say that there were an enormous number of such structures, particularly churches. The latter are far commoner than pagan sanctuaries, or, at least, they are commoner than *identifiable* pagan sanctuaries, which does raise questions about the degree to which recognizable form inhibits our ability to discern the frequency of pagan shrines in the landscape. Some account must be taken of the growing population in late Roman times, of course. In addition it should be realized that the frequency with which one encounters churches (and, indeed, temples) across the region varies from place to place. Some villages have only one or two churches, others of comparable size (and presumably population) have many more. Their number and distribution in a settlement may reflect its social organization. Umm al-Jimal has fourteen, which may not be excessive for the estimated number of inhabitants (6000-8000), but most of these are contained within the irregular blocks of houses that constitute the late Roman village, and are thought to be the private places of worship for the inhabitants of those blocks. Thus most of the Umm al-Jimal churches were not strictly public places of worship, but more like the chapels for extended families or cells, and in this sense recalling the pagan *thiasoi*. These arrangements resemble the religious practice at Dura, where temples were located amid houses and were not major public buildings. The multiplicity of small Syrian churches may constitute the late antique successors to a large number of private or family pagan shrines which remain unidentified.

Church building was also important as a way of affirming the

Fig. 188. Drawing of the martyrium complex of St Simeon Stylites at Qalaat Semaan as it was in the early sixth century, restored here with a roof over the central octagon housing the saint's column. Further hostels and buildings were added to the complex during the course of the sixth century. After G. Tchalenko, Villages antiques de la Syrie du nord, *vol. II, plate lxxviii.*

Christianization of the landscape. The conversion of rural and urban temples into churches was one way of doing this (fig. 183), but during the early phases of this Christianizing process it was deemed more important to leave temples in ruins after assaulting them rather than rebuilding them as churches, to create powerful symbols of pagan decrepitude. There was also the matter of what to do about Old Testament sites venerated by both Jews and Christians. Generally these were treated with respect by the Christian authorities and existing arrangements were left intact. Within the cities Christians also adopted some of the paraphernalia of pagan ritual – such as public processions – to assert control of the *polis* and its civic spaces. That these processions could be the scene of zealous assaults on pagan shrines and statues by the crowd was further proof of their effectiveness in the competition with pagans for the mastery of urban space. The building of churches 'blocking' the main street, a sixth- or seventh-century characteristic observable in some cities, may be less a sign of urban degeneration than the deliberate appropriation of a key element of civic life. The street was a public area, and now Christians claimed it for their faith.

The Christianizing process of the fourth to sixth centuries need not be viewed as a total break with the classical tradition. People still inhabited a civic landscape filled with statues and images of 'pagan' myths. What is more, they continued to make things with 'pagan' images: for example, mosaic pavements. It was difficult to eliminate the pagan tradition entirely without ridding themselves of the classical city. Up to the end of Justinian's reign there were attempts to restore and even build new civic monuments in the classical tradition. The great transformation that began under Roman rule in the later sixth century, in which Christianity came to pervade almost all aspects of life within the empire, was cut short in our region by the Muslim conquest.

FROM POLYTHEISM TO MONOTHEISM

In the early empire no effort was made to regulate religious beliefs, except where they offered resistance or conflicted with imperial ideology. Many cults were considered ancestral to particular social groups or intimately bound up with particular social institutions such as villages or cities. The pagan religions of Syria appear timeless in contrast to the linear histories of Judaism and Christianity, but that is probably the consequence of our own ignorance. In general we know too little about them to be sure about the effects Roman rule and Hellenism had on iconography, liturgy and beliefs, or to what extent the communities of worshippers had a strong sense of identity (the example of Judaism may not be appropriate to other cases). But some form of identification with the cult and its observances will have been necessary for a display of piety. The essay of Lucian on the Syrian Goddess suggests pride in the distinction and antiquity of Syrian cults in contrast to those of the Greeks, and Hellenism's respect for indigenous cults may have been exploited by Syrian elites as an expression of their communal differences. The imperial cult acted as a loosely binding social force cutting across these differences: the emperors embodied the empire for their subjects.

Rome's adoption of Christianity was a radical departure. The empire had always been a pious institution, but piety had generally involved respect for the myriad religious traditions within its boundaries. Now the complex world of polytheism gave way to a more ordered identity of Roman Christianity. Rejecting all other cults, the empire attempted to make one religion synonymous with itself, but there were forces within Christianity over which the empire had little or no control. Christianity's own lack of unity on matters of doctrine led to the growth of separate and competing communities, not all of which were identical with the empire. In the Christian world ultimate authority lay with God, not the emperor, and direct communion with God was possible from all levels of society. Part of the transformation of the Roman world in late antiquity involved the state coming to terms with this new organization of authority.

The Christian tradition provided an alternative to the Greek, making it possible for relatively low-class, non-Hellenized individuals to win renown, something that had been difficult in the pre-Christian empire. The activities of monks and ascetics demonstrated that people did not require a sophisticated education to gain respect, and educated Greek-speaking Christians employed their literary talents to describe the lives of some of these ascetic heroes. At the same time Holy Men opened up a channel for the lower orders, who could not adopt the ascetic life, to express themselves. Christianity helped to provide a new identity for many Syrians, and gave authority to languages other than Greek or Latin. Greek domination of Christianity was to be resisted, even if Syriac Christianity was not independent of Greek and Hellenism.

The process of Christianization was far from complete when the region was lost to the Romans and its Christian inhabitants became subordinate to a new politico-religious empire. The long centuries of Islam succeeded in providing a sense of ethnic and spiritual community for the majority of inhabitants of the region where Christianity had been arrested.

10 THE MILITARY

THE COMPANY OF SOLDIERS

The Roman army was another major institution in Syria around which identities were organized. Soldiers tended to live together, and the culture of the army was relatively homogeneous across the empire. The state was responsible for arranging most of the supplies to the army. Such facts raise questions about the degree of integration or positive interaction between the military and the civilian population. Traditionally the Roman army has been seen as a force assisting the cultural and economic integration of civil societies in the provinces. It was responsible for developing provincial infrastructure (roads, canals, aqueducts), and in peripheral regions military bases or veteran colonies provided a framework for urbanization. Soldiers intermarried with the local population and their pay was spent in local markets. But much of Syria was urbanized and economically developed *before* it was incorporated into the Roman empire, and some recent studies have focused more on the *lack* of interaction between soldiers and civilians. For a start, the jobs which the soldiers had to do as official representatives of an often oppressive central power – such as policing, tax collection and surveillance – set them apart from the general population. In order to perform these tasks it was better for them not to be closely integrated into civilian society. Soldiers were identifiably different from civilians, even if they were often billeted in cities and in the countryside among the civilian population, and even if many would have been recruited from the region. The army, like other social institutions such as the *polis*, provided a communal identity, in this case for recruits from diverse backgrounds, who were given a common training, and schooled in common values, effectively creating a community of soldiers. Intermarriage with the locals did take place, but equally it was not uncommon – as many military tombstones attest – for soldiers to pass on their inheritances to comrades (implying that they had no other heirs), or for them to marry the daughters of other soldiers.

Like the local population most soldiers in Syria would probably have spoken Greek and/or Aramaic in everyday contexts, but they could also distinguish themselves through the use of Latin for official business (and commonly for military tombstones). At Bostra, where the *legio III Cyrenaica* had its headquarters, there is not much evidence for the mixing of military personnel and the locals. Even if the rank and file consisted of natives by the fourth century AD, it was considered unusual if a Roman officer spoke the local language (unless that language was Greek). As in the *polis*, festivals were used to help cement a sense of corporate identity among the soldiers. These had nothing to do with the cults of the region in which they were stationed. A papyrus calendar dated AD 225-35 found at Dura lists festivals observed by the *cohors XX Palmyrenorum*, an auxiliary unit which was stationed in the city. The celebrations are those of the imperial cult and traditional Roman feasts (fig. 189). Such observances may have been imposed on all army units from the time of Augustus. Even in private religious observances there were certain deities such as Mithras and Jupiter Dolichenus who were popular with the army but not so frequently encountered outside military contexts (see, however, the comments on p. 341).

Economic independence from civilians is rather harder to demonstrate, but equally the case for economic interaction with them is also difficult to prove. Locals may have produced goods to sell in bulk to the army, or items for individuals: for example, pottery or textiles. The state attempted to provide basic supplies through taxation in kind and control of production, and probably did so even in periods when soldiers were expected to buy equipment using their own salaries. Certainly by the late Roman period imperial factories at Antioch and Damascus supplied weapons and armour, and soldiers' clothing was provided by state workshops or through tax in kind (although commonly commuted to cash). So while the separation of soldiers from civilians was not complete, there were social, cultural, economic, religious and linguistic spheres of interaction among the military which were not characteristic of civilians.

The ethnic makeup of the army in Syria would have been diverse, and the various official practices mentioned above will have been necessary to provide coherence. The preference may have been for recruits from the Greek-speaking east rather than the Latin-speaking west, although Syria was a popular recruiting ground for auxiliary soldiers and their linguistic biases were no bar to their deployment, as they were posted all over the empire: Palmyrenes and Emesenes served in Numidia, Epiphaneians and Ituraeans in Mauretania Tingitana; there were archers from Epiphaneia on Hadrian's Wall; and Syrian soldiers were also posted to the Danube. Even highly Hellenized cities like Antioch and Caesarea furnished the army with auxiliaries.

Local or regional recruitment to the legionary and auxiliary forces stationed in Syria itself is noted from at least the early second century, breaking

Fig. 189. Drawing of a wall painting from the Temple of Bel at Dura Europus, showing Julius Terentius, tribune of the cohors XX Palmyrenorum, offering a sacrifice before three figures on pedestals. The latter have been identified as Palmyrene gods, but another suggestion is that they are images of Balbinus, Pupienus and Gordian III, emperors in AD 238, and that this scene shows military observance of the imperial cult. The seated figures below are the city-goddesses (Tychai) of Palmyra and Dura.

with an earlier tradition of ensuring that units did not serve in the province in which they were raised. Many of the late Roman units called *equites* were locally raised, as attested by their names: *indigenae*, *Saraceni*. On the other hand, some western barbarian auxiliary units are listed in the *Notitia Dignitatum* (on which, see below), though it is likely that after the division of the empire in AD 395 recruitment into these units was local, even if they retained their original ethnic names. The use of people from the region or the locality ought to have led to increased interaction between soldiers and civilians, and yet even on the matter of recruitment there is evidence for a certain degree of introversion. From as early as the second century the allocation of land to veterans might be conditional on their sons serving in the army. In late Roman times it was common for sons of veterans to be drafted into the military, meaning that the units were to some degree self-perpetuating. However, the absence of references to such practices in the sixth-century *Codex Justinianus* may mean that recruitment was largely voluntary by this period and that conscription or obligations had been abolished.

On joining the legions soldiers became Roman citizens, and auxiliaries acquired citizenship on retirement. In the first and second centuries this meant that ex-soldiers often had important social standing in local communities, but the importance of the army as a route to improving status through citizenship declined after Caracalla granted citizenship to all free inhabitants of the empire in AD 212. Although army veterans must commonly have received land in frontier areas, the notion that they had a great deal of cultural impact, or that their wealth helped stimulate agriculture in a given region, remains somewhat speculative. The presence of veterans, soldiers and administrators, particularly in the more remote or weakly Hellenized areas, probably had some effect on local communities, especially since these figures of authority were powerful in the locality and had influence outside it. This probably explains the occasional use of Latin for some civilian inscriptions in country areas: there it had a status value that Greek perhaps did not. However, the only real detectable *cultural* impact is in the colony and territory of Berytus. The main language of monumental inscriptions in Berytus following the foundation is Latin, there is evidence for obscure Italian cults, and Latin also spread to the countryside (fig. 90.2), yet by the fourth century Greek had taken over as the language of inscriptions, even if Latin remained a literary and legal language taught in the city (see chapter 7). Nevertheless the Roman nature of Berytus drew comment even in late antiquity. The city had a huge territory, and if the intent was to create some sort of dominant economic giant on the coast, there is not much evidence of export of surpluses, unless it was perishables that were not packaged in ceramic containers (see chapter 6). It was once thought that the early phase of development of the limestone massif in the north might be attributable to wealthy veterans moving into the area, but is far from clear whether the veterans recorded in inscriptions were living in the hills or whether they were absentee landlords. The evidence of veterans in the Hauran region suggests integration into the local communities, often as important figures, and here perhaps their investment did stimulate economic growth – but many may have been recruited from these communities in the first place, and thus their *cultural* impact may have been slight. Overall, when one takes into account the numbers of veterans, together with the fact that the state seems to have encouraged veterans to take up agriculture, especially in late Roman times, it is likely that these people assisted the economic growth of marginal zones in Syria, even if it did not foment cultural change.

The clearest evidence for interaction between the military and civilians comes from Dura Europus, but even here the indications are equivocal. Following the Roman conquest the north-western part of the city was taken over by the army and became a military base, which presumably involved ejecting any civilians from this quarter. There is evidence for a mud brick wall being constructed across part of the city to demarcate the military zone, although it is clear that certain personnel were also billeted, at least on an occasional basis, outside this zone. So while the soldiers did not occupy a purpose-built camp, there does seem to have been an attempt to create some form of physical separation from the rest of the city. However, the city walls were also manned by soldiers during conflicts, suggesting that in times of crisis the whole of Dura became a fortress. There is also a fair amount of evidence to suggest that soldiers were active in policing the city at all times. Within the confines of the camp were several purpose-built military structures, including a small amphitheatre. Former civilian houses were transformed into barracks. Other buildings housed officers, and a temple was used for keeping the archives of the *cohors XX Palmyrenorum*. Overlooking the Euphrates was a large complex with two courtyards which the excavators dubbed, on the basis of somewhat slender support, the 'Palace of the *dux ripae*'. The *dux ripae* was a military official recorded in texts from Dura (the Euphrates is known to have been divided for administrative purposes into a *ripa superior* and *ripa inferior*, and the *dux ripae* may have been a commander subordinate to the governor of Syria Coele, but nothing concrete is known of the duties of this official). Some temples seem to have been mainly or perhaps exclusively patronized by soldiers: a *mithraeum* in the military zone; and a *dolicheneum*. Other temples in the military zone appear to have been used by both military and civilians: the Temple of Azzanathkona (which housed the records of the *cohors XX Palmyrenorum*); and the Temple of Bel. Outside the military zone the evidence (dedications, graffiti) suggests that most temples were patronized by civilians, although the Temple of the Gaddé was frequented by some military personnel and the so-called 'Military Temple', which resembles a Roman temple more than the other religious structures at Dura, was built by auxiliary archers. Dura had several bath buildings, one in the military quarter, another next to the 'Palace of the *dux ripae*', and two others close to the main gates (which perhaps indicates that they were intended for use by soldiers coming off guard duty). It would seem that while soldiers and civilians lived side by side at Dura, the most 'Romanized' installations were built and used by soldiers.

Benefits and Burdens

There is no clear sign at Dura or other cities of military interference in civic government, but there is not much indication either way. The larger and more powerful cities may have been able to avoid military meddling in their affairs, and soldiers perhaps had more influence in more remote or smaller communities close to major bases. There is a number of dedications by local communities in the Hauran region to military personnel as benefactors or 'friends' of the community. Texts of the third and fourth century show comparatively low-ranking military personnel acting as judges in civilian legal disputes, but such cases may not have been accepted government procedure and it is difficult to say whether appeals to army officers represent choices exercised by civilians or constraints on civilians by the military. In remote areas soldiers may have been the only easily accessible official representatives of the state.

For the cities some military impositions were official burdens, others were not. In late Roman times the tax system required city councillors to undertake the transport of tax in kind to the army, which sometimes meant moving goods over long distances at considerable personal expense. Libanius refers to Antiochene councillors who took supplies to Barbalissus and Callinicum on the Euphrates, as if this were a regular obligation. It must have been an onerous and unrewarding task. Another way in which the military presence could have had an adverse affect on civic government is also encountered in the writings of Libanius. Presumably the state frowned upon the activity, but it was unable or unwilling to prevent soldiers from interfering with lives and profits of the Antiochene civic elites by defending smallholders and tenants against tax collectors and bailiffs. In exchange for this protection the villagers paid them cash or foodstuffs. Presumably the soldiers in question were billeted in the villages; and apparently such 'protected' communities also felt free to molest unprotected neighbours. Such developments were apparently accepted by the senior military officials at Antioch, who may even have sponsored these activities. Securing military patrons was one way for the weak to subvert the established structure of civic authority; whether this counts as positive soldier-civilian interaction or not depends on one's point of view.

However the military presence could have a negative impact on the fortunes of the masses as well as those of the elites. Soldiers were feared by the peasants. Military personnel had the right to requisition goods or means of transport, to commandeer guides from among the local people, to force them to act as porters or to supply beasts of burden or horses for the *cursus publicus*, or to demand food or billeting for soldiers. They were supposed to carry a diploma from the emperor which permitted them to make such demands, but people forged these, or used ones that had expired, and it was difficult for peasants to argue with armed soldiers. An inscription from Epiphanea (Hama) records the instructions of the emperor Domitian (AD 81-96) to an imperial procurator, that 'neither by the renting of beasts of burden nor by the distress of lodging should the provinces be burdened', and that 'nobody commandeers a beast of burden' or 'a guide unless he has a permit from me, for, when farmers are torn from their homes, the fields will remain without their attention'.[65] Some communities provided purpose-built accommodation for military and other persons on state business in the form of inns. An inscription of AD 185-6 from Phaena on the edge of Trachonitis preserves the letter from a governor telling the locals that they are not obliged to receive soldiers into their homes if their village has an inn. Public display of imperial orders in the form of inscriptions such as these may have helped settle some disputes, but the theme of unlawful military impositions keeps cropping up over the centuries. Soldiers are recorded as abusing their hosts, stealing from them and behaving in a drunken and threatening manner. They could extort extra taxes over and above the required amount or demand more rations from producers. In times of peace soldiers could draw foodstuffs from established state granaries (access and rations being strictly controlled), but when the number of soldiers swelled during a campaign, locals would find themselves competing with soldiers for food, and prices would rise. To alleviate the problem food and supplies might be brought in from outside the region by the state, but this in itself could also become a source of friction if imported foodstuffs undercut prices on the local markets. Sometimes local traders simply closed their shops if they deemed the prices too low. Even in peacetime soldiers might compete with locals for resources, particularly during shortages. Nevertheless the existence of soldier-farmers (if indeed such a category existed), particularly in late Roman times, will have seen some of the interests of soldiers and civilians converge.

The army's involvement in the construction of major works like roads and aqueducts was of benefit to communities, although it is not always easy to distinguish projects intended for civilians from those which incidentally benefited them. Sometimes military expertise and labour might be brought in for a civilian project, but it did not necessarily come free of charge. The state might require locals to finance necessary infrastructure works, even if they were built by the army; this certainly seems to have been the case in the late empire and

Fig. 190. The Hadrianic aqueduct at Caesarea, which brought water into the city from the north. Although intended for civilian use, inscriptions attest to its construction by soldiers of the legio VI Ferrata.

may well have been so in earlier times. A road from Damascus to the Bekaa valley which passes through the Wadi Barada (the ancient Chrysoroas river, flowing into Damascus) collapsed into the river during the second century and was repaired by soldiers of the *legio XVI Flavia*, but the community of Abila paid the bills.

The role of the military in the process of urbanization has been questioned above. In the early empire it seems that military bases were generally established in or added to existing urban communities, and the army appears to have had little effect on the urban framework of the provinces of the region (with the exception of Raphanea). However, in the late empire the military requirements of defence do seem to have had some influence on urbanization, with settlements being fortified as military strongholds and promoted to cities. Strategic requirements altered the urban framework in a way they had not in the early empire (although numerous new cities were not military bases and were promoted for various other reasons; see chapter 3).

The presence of soldiers with cash to spend will have offered opportunities to enterprising locals and local communities, but proving that any civilian material culture found at military bases was supplied by private entrepreneurs and not by requisition or tax in kind is often difficult. In Syria such research is also frustrated by the fact that the origins of many artefacts, particularly pots, are unknown. Even when origins are known, the objects do not necessarily provide us with the information we are seeking. The association of Late Roman C ware with military bases may point to an entrepreneurial enterprise taking advantage of an established trade route or its products riding 'piggy-back' on more important state supplies (see chapter 6), but as Late Roman C comes from western Asia Minor that is hardly evidence of *local* economic exchange. A relationship between issues of civic coins and military campaigns in the early empire might be adduced as evidence of the economic interests of civilians and soldiers converging, but this has also been seen as either testimony to the impositions forced on civilians by the army (civilian communities providing money for state employees) or, conversely, cities profiting by forcing soldiers to exchange silver and gold for local small change (which might have a lower value or no value at all outside the issuing community).

Clearly there are few certain answers to the question of whether the Roman army can be credited as a key factor in the assimilation and 'Romanization' of Syria. It depends on whether we view the acculturation and integration of locals as part of any greater Roman military mission or strategy. The most pessimistic stance sees the army as an institution largely separate from the civilian world and with its own systems of supply. Most interaction with locals was incidental to the role the army played in Syria, and it was the civilians themselves who played a major part in the development and integration of the region with the rest of the Roman world. The validity of this stance depends in part on the role of the army in the east. But as with the matter of interaction, the question of the army's role in the region has no easy answers.

STRATEGIES AND FRONTIERS

For many years the concept of a defensive imperial 'grand strategy' has dominated the study of Roman frontiers. Some scholars favour it, others are opposed to it, and yet others take the middle ground. In its best-known form the model advanced proposes that the Roman state had long-term policies for organizing and defending its borders, beginning with a system of client buffer states and highly mobile legions in the first century AD, shifting to a defensive cordon of more permanent, stationary forces on the frontiers in the second and early third centuries, and finally to a system of 'defence-in-depth', involving mobile cavalry units and permanent garrisons at points both on and behind the frontiers in the late empire. While the various phases of this model do seem to explain certain networks and dispositions of armies and fortresses in certain periods, there are enormous problems with the whole as an overall explanation of Roman strategies and objectives. In the first century it is clear that Rome relied quite heavily on the client kings for military support (their armies were later absorbed into the Roman army, although usually they were not posted in the places where they were recruited). But most client states in Syria were not positioned to be 'buffers' between Rome and her enemies, with the possible exception of Commagene, and some kingdoms, such as Osrhoene in

Mesopotamia, continued to exist long after the first model was supposed to have been abandoned. While some legionary bases of the second phase were located in places where they could intercept attacks by the Parthians and Sasanians, others were positioned far from any possible front line. At all times the location of fortresses and armies will have been dictated by three main factors: first, the need for adequate supplies without becoming too great a burden on local populations; second, the need to police those populations, particularly in the large cities, but also in the countryside; and third, the defence of the empire in the face of external attack. One could also add a fourth factor for the early empire: the concentration of too many armies under one governor was a potential danger to the ruling emperor, and thus it was prudent to distribute these armies among several provinces and governors, bringing them together only in an emergency. Some of these factors will have militated against a purely scientific defensive strategy with regard to the disposition of the imperial forces.

More importantly, one might question whether defence against external foes was always uppermost in the minds of those who managed the Roman army, and whether Rome ever viewed its frontier in Syria as a defensive cordon. The military presence was clearly for reasons of security, but the exact nature of the security threat is contended. Was it mainly external, or internal? To what extent did Rome perceive the Parthians and Sasanians as a serious threat to Syria? Was the Roman frontier in the east aimed at preventing powerful enemies penetrating the empire, or were the frontiers limited only by what peoples and kingdoms Rome could conquer and control? Was the army envisaged as a force aimed at supervising Rome's subjects more than defending them against outside enemies? Our understanding of the function and disposition of the Roman army in the east depends in large part on the answers to these questions, and views on these matters differ considerably. Some scholars prefer to see the empire as one geared towards *offence* rather than defence, and have pointed to imperial rhetoric and ideologies in support of this view. This rhetoric stresses eternal Roman victory and unlimited expansion, or the notion that the *oikoumene* or inhabited (and civilized) world, and the Roman empire or the realm ruled by its emperors, were the same. Perhaps the Roman government did not see the frontiers as defensive structures, but merely zones from which further conquests could be launched. Hence perhaps the apparently 'soft frontier' in Mesopotamia, lacking any fortified boundary but peppered with fortresses which both sides sought to control by means of garrisons and sieges, and from which Roman armies could advance into Armenia and to Ctesiphon. But the idea that the armies on the frontiers *did* protect the empire is also expressed in the sources. With the adoption of Christianity the empire gained a further mission: responsibility for protecting the interests of Christians, not only within the empire, but also beyond the physical and political frontiers.

However, there is a fundamental difference between the ideologies of empires and their realities. Reality, of course, forced the Romans to recognize practical limits to Roman power. There were zones that could be controlled directly, zones that could be controlled or influenced indirectly, and others that could not be controlled at all. Sometimes the uncontrollable areas lay outside the empire, and sometimes it would seem that areas well within the frontiers of empire (such as seems to have been the case with the Ituraeans of Mount Lebanon under Augustus) were also beyond the limits. The frontier provinces were made up of zones in which the degrees of control were potentially always shifting, and it is likely that the deployment of forces within the frontiers reflects this. Roman power, however, extended beyond the frontiers in the form of alliances with other states. The eastern frontier is easily cast as a nearly immobile structure constrained by hostile and invincible foes, the Parthians and Sasanians, but for the Romans it was also a place with opportunities for diplomatic influence and imperial expansion: into Mesopotamia and Armenia, and further north, into Colchis, Iberia and Albania. It was a place where the political and military boundaries of the empire might be transgressed by other sorts of social relations: religious and spiritual, cultural, and economic. The eastern frontier was contingent rather than planned, with the result that various allegiances and spheres of social interaction extended from the Roman world into what was enemy territory in political and military terms.

The term *limes* is commonly used to describe the defended frontier of the Roman empire, and especially any network of fortifications. But there is no evidence that the Romans themselves used this word to mean a linear defensive boundary. In the east it is not a term encountered before the fourth century, when it was used officially to mean an administrative frontier region under the command of a *dux* who commanded *limitanei* (troops of the *limes*), unconnected with any defensive or military installations that happened to be in it. In Syria it also came to have specific associations with the desert, regardless of whether this was occupied by any Roman forts or soldiers.

Traditionally the bulk of the army has been seen as a protective shield against barbarian aggression and infiltration. Forts and legionary bases were positioned so that their units would be able to react with maximum efficiency to an invasion. The alternative position argues that in our region there was no defensive barrier as such, that the presence of army units near the border of the Parthian and Sasanian empires was to facilitate Roman acts of aggression against these adversaries (both of which Rome did not consider a major threat), and that an important function of the army was to maintain security internally, policing the cities and the road network, putting down rebellions and suppressing banditry.

The Enemy Without

A simple review of the number of Parthian or Sasanian invasions of Syria compared to the number of Roman attacks on Ctesiphon lends support to the notion that external threats, while an ever-present danger, were less a part of the Roman military experience in Syria than Roman aggression (see chapter 2). Some of this may be due to poor historical records, especially in the late first and second centuries, but it would take a number of unrecorded Parthian and Sasanian attacks to match the known Roman invasions under Pompey, Crassus, Mark Antony, Trajan, Lucius Verus, Septimius Severus, Caracalla, Severus Alexander, Gordian III, Carus, Galerius and Julian (a number of which led to permanent conquests). The only securely recorded Parthian invasions of Syria are in 51 BC, in response the aggression of Crassus, 40 BC, in the company of the Roman renegade Labienus, and AD 161, and only one of these led to the annexation of territory (40 BC). There was certainly a threat in AD 62, and a possible attack *c.* AD 73-8, but these did not lead to Parthian conquests. The Sasanians are often painted as aggressors in their wars with Rome, but their rulers could maintain with justification that Rome was injuring their cause. Shapur I claimed that Gordian III attacked him, not vice-versa, and the pretext for his campaign that led to the fall of Antioch was Caesar's 'lie' concerning Armenia – presumably the violation of a treaty. Most Parthian and Sasanian attacks on the Roman empire seem more punitive than colonial in their intent, and like the Parthians, the Sasanians raided Roman Syria but attempted to conquer it only once.

One likely reason why there were few Sasanian attacks on Syria is that the Roman conquests in Mesopotamia shifted the main arena of conflict to the other side of the Euphrates. For the Romans, control of Mesopotamia presented a particular problem. There was no obvious natural or ethnic boundary between what was Roman and what was Sasanian. On the other hand the conquests made attacks on Sasanian territory easier – the army could march against Ctesiphon and be in Roman territory much of the way, as well as relying on supplies from the fertile lands on both sides of the Euphrates. From Ctesiphon it was a fairly short though arduous route up the Tigris back into Roman possessions. Mesopotamia also provided a base from which to threaten or influence whoever ruled in Armenia. Its strategic importance made the conflicts it created acceptable. Septimius Severus claimed that the conquest of Mesopotamia provided security for Syria. The historian Cassius Dio disagreed, insisting that it only brought more strife. Territorial disputes in Mesopotamia proved Dio right, but the fact that there were no Sasanian invasions of Syria between the third and sixth centuries also justified the claim of Severus.

The Parthians and Sasanians clearly constituted a threat to Roman ambitions in Mesopotamia, and to some extent they threatened northern Syria, particularly in the early empire when northern Syria *was* the frontier. The degree to which Roman emperors considered them a threat to the eastern provinces as a whole is debatable (see chapter 2), but any perception that the Parthians or Sasanians had a claim to Syria will have influenced Roman strategies there. More uncertain is the threat posed by nomads of the steppe and desert, especially in the early empire. Traditionally the network of roads and forts in the steppe between the Euphrates and the Red Sea has been seen as a defensive frontier aimed at controlling non-allied nomadic groups. But some scholars have questioned whether that was truly the purpose of these installations, which suggest considerable effort invested on the part of Rome. There must have been times when bands of nomads posed a threat to sedentary peoples, but this does not necessarily mean that the Romans considered the raids sufficiently threatening to warrant the construction of an elaborate defensive network against them. Forts could have housed soldiers whose job it was to police the roads, provide safety for travellers and protect strategic resources such as wells. At the same time the system would have permitted the soldiers to exercise some control over nomad activities, by placing forts at important water sources and regulating markets where the tribes came to buy or sell commodities. Nomad tribes and confederations are more prominent in the late empire, when they were used by Rome and the Persians (see chapter 2), but we often read more about disruption caused by those 'allied' groups in the pay of Rome than by independent non-aligned groups outside the empire. It is not certain how serious was the threat posed by nomads outside the sphere of the Roman-Sasanian conflict. As the Roman military advanced into the steppe in the late second and early third centuries it will have had more contact and potential conflicts with such groups, but were they the reason for the military presence in the first place? Or was the development of the Roman borderlands and

Roman alliances beyond the frontiers the reason why the tribes began gravi-
tating towards these regions?

Lack of references to conflicts with the nomads need not preclude them. The
corpus of Safaitic graffiti includes occasional mentions of the warrior life to
which nomads might aspire and suggests that the tribesmen sometimes came
into conflict with Roman soldiers. This evidence indicates that, as in times prior
to and after Rome, the nomads of the desert fringes saw raiding as part of their
way of life. A low-intensity threat of this sort could have devastating effects on
sedentary populations in the long term. Such raids would receive little or no
mention in literary sources, which were interested in major conflicts and
key events. The graffiti are occasionally accompanied by drawings showing
tribesmen fighting, on foot or on horse- or camel-back. Like bedouin of more
modern times, they probably fought each other and the settled communities,
perhaps also extorting protection-money from settled peoples.

Any temporary alliance by many tribes could pose a serious threat. Desert
tribes seem to have been involved in the rebellion of Palmyra, although the
details are very obscure. Two decades later Diocletian constructed a system of
roads and forts in this same area (see below), which may have been a response
to problems with nomadic tribes following Palmyra's fall. Some villages in the
eastern Hauran, closest to the nomadic regions, appear to have been fortified at
this time by the construction of walls around them; nomad raiding is a possible explanation. In the end it would seem that the nomads gained the upper
hand, or Rome found the use of regular troops to maintain security in such an
unproductive and arid environment too expensive, because the forts were
apparently abandoned by the end of the fourth century (see below).

The Enemy Within

The local population was a potential threat to Roman order. The poor or dispossessed had an interest in changing that order, or at the very least sought to
live outside its rules. Others saw resistance to Roman domination as a religious
or ideological duty. These enemies within the frontiers could be as disruptive as
barbarian invaders. Aside from the threat of internal rebellions and civil
unrest, such as the two Jewish conflicts in the early empire and the Samaritan
revolts under Zeno and Justinian, there was the perennial threat of banditry.
Travellers frequently ran the gauntlet of highwaymen; the story of the Good
Samaritan exemplifies the potential dangers of travel in the countryside.
Simple footpads operating in small groups were not necessarily of interest to
the authorities, and fortified inns and towers along roads could provide security
at night for people on the move. However, the evidence implies that bandits
could also operate in large units, putting cities and villages in jeopardy as well.

If left unchecked bandit groups could attract followings among the lower
classes and threaten the security of wide areas. It is difficult to assess the threat
posed by bandits in areas under direct Roman control from the scattered references, but in zones where direct control was difficult to achieve the impression
is that banditry was common. The lawlessness of these remote areas within the
empire could spill into the 'civilized' regions. For example, in about AD 400
bandits from Isauria, a part of the Cilician Taurus famous for brigandage,
plundered Cilicia and Syria and harried Antioch between about 404 and 405
(they were supposed to have penetrated Phoenicia and Galilee as well).

Some bandit leaders evidently enjoyed considerable successes and possibly achieved folk hero status. Outlaws rejected the established social order and as such had some romantic appeal; they were stock characters in Greek novels. Cassius Dio mentions one precocious commander named Claudius 'who was overrunning Judaea and Syria'[66] when Septimius Severus was campaigning in the east and who successfully evaded capture. The story of how he greeted and kissed the emperor while in disguise sounds like the impertinent exploit of some ancient Robin Hood; suffice to say that bandits were not necessarily regarded as the enemy by all sectors of the population, although their targets were more often likely to have been the weak and vulnerable rather than the rich and powerful.

Of course it is not always a simple matter to distinguish banditry from nomadic raiding by people from outside the empire, and within the frontiers remote areas of the sort haunted by large bandit groups were often almost as inaccessible to Roman forces as those outside. In the early empire the Ituraeans had a formidable reputation as robbers, and the bandits of Trachonitis, who as late as the reign of the Herodian Agrippa II (AD 48-c. 94) appear to be referred to in a fragmentary inscription from Canatha as living in a 'beast-like condition' and 'lurking in holes in many parts of the country',[67] were tamed only by a century of rule by client kings.

Policing the locals was therefore likely to have been a major preoccupation for the Roman authorities, although the provision of security in the provinces was not confined solely to the military. In the early empire much of the military policing seems to have been confined to the countryside; at any rate major cities appear to have had their own police forces. The civic authorities were expected to deal with their own unruly mobs while client kings and Roman army units attended to the hinterlands. But there are signs that security in the cities eventually became as important to the authorities as brigandage in rural areas, if not more so. By the third century there is some evidence to suggest that vexillations from the legions were being deployed in the larger cities and security seems a plausible reason for this. Soldiers become more prominent as civic police in the late empire, and in contrast the onus for policing the countryside increasingly seems to have shifted to civilians, who built fortified refuges and towers in rural areas. These civilian strongholds are difficult to distinguish from military installations, which further complicates the study of imperial strategies (see below).

Although it was the job of a governor and his forces to suppress organized bands of marauders, it is unclear whether the authorities commonly took any great interest in the activities of bandits unless they became a serious threat to people and regions that mattered, particularly in the late empire. Ammianus Marcellinus describes the ravages of the Maratocupreni, an entire village near Apamea whose inhabitants lived by plunder and who were 'exceedingly numerous, skilled in crafty wiles, and dreaded because they roamed about quietly under the guise of honourable traders and soldiers'.[68] That their activities continued unhindered for some considerable time is suggested by the fact that they built elaborate houses in their home village with their loot. When eventually the army intervened, harsh measures were exacted: the entire village was slaughtered, including the children, and their houses demolished. That banditry was such a severe problem in the territory of one of Syria's greatest cities is striking. It is all the more likely, then, that in more remote locations the local population may have had to make its own arrangements for security.

On balance it seems not unreasonable to propose that one of the most important functions of the Roman army in Syria and the Near East was to control the civilians. But the civilians themselves were also expected to make an effort, just as they were expected to contribute to the well being of the empire in other ways. The great military powers to the east, raiders in the frontier regions, unruly mobs in the cities and armed marauders in the countryside are all likely to have influenced the manner in which the Roman army was deployed in the region. The limits to imperial order lay both within and without.

THE ROMAN ARMY IN SYRIA, PALAESTINA AND ARABIA: UNITS AND DEPLOYMENTS

In the early empire the bulk of the Roman army consisted of legions (composed of heavy infantrymen who had Roman citizenship) and auxiliary troops (who gained citizenship after their term of service). Each legion contained about five thousand men, often divided up into detachments (vexillations) stationed throughout the province. Auxiliary infantrymen served in cohorts of either about a thousand or five hundred men, and the cavalry *alae* were organized into units of the same strengths (there were also mixed cavalry and infantry units). Army units would always have been dispersed in cities and in forts and camps along routes of communication, according to the factors outlined above (supply, coercion, defence and limiting the military power of governors). Legionary bases did not house armies up to full strength except when mustering troops for campaigns; in general they would have served as administrative centres, housing commanders and their staff and some units, while the rest of the legion served in detachments elsewhere. The forces of the republic and early empire were probably billeted in or near the major cities, moving from one location to another as circumstances dictated. There were perhaps two legions based in Syria initially, but the numbers fluctuated considerably in the civil wars at the end of the republic. There is somewhat scanty evidence for the number of legions under the Julio-Claudians – three, perhaps, under Augustus, and four under Tiberius, all stationed in the north: the *III Gallica, VI Ferrata, X Fretensis* and *XII Fulminata*. Another, the *IV Scythica*, seems to have come to Syria during Corbulo's Armenian campaigns. There were no legions in the south until the Jewish war, and the units stationed in places like Judaea prior to that conflict would have been composed of auxiliaries. The sources refer to armies being located at places like Cyrrhus, Laodicea and perhaps Beroea, but the legions of the period were highly mobile and these cities were probably not intended as permanent legionary bases, even if proper fortresses began to emerge at some locations in the later first century. From about the reign of Nero there was a legion, possibly two, at Raphanea (*XII Fulminata* and perhaps *VI Ferrata*), and this site remained a legionary base until the third century. Under Vespasian Zeugma became the headquarters of the *IV Scythica*; the city may have housed the *X Fretensis* before the latter was transferred to Judaea during the Jewish war. In other regions Rome relied on the armies of client kings, who were expected to maintain security within their kingdoms and provide assistance to Roman forces when necessary (see chapter 3). In addition there were some units working for the Roman army that did not properly belong to it, provided by indigenous groups such as the Palmyrenes.

As the kingdoms were annexed, the legionary presence moved into the south. By the reign of Hadrian the disposition of the legions was probably as follows: in the north, the *XVI Flavia* at Samosata, the former royal capital of Commagene, the *IV Scythica* at Zeugma, and the *III Gallica* at Raphanea; and in the south, the Judaean garrisons of the *X Fretensis* at Aelia Capitolina and the *VI Ferrata* at Caparcotna (Legio) in the Jezreel valley. For Trajan's new province of Arabia, the *III Cyrenaica* had been transferred from Egypt to Bostra. The legions were therefore distributed throughout the region, and only two were based on the Euphrates and so in a position to protect Syria from a Parthian invasion.

The practice of transferring entire legions from one province to another became rare after Hadrian, but details about their disposition in the region during the later second and third centuries is no less sketchy than before. A Severan legion, the *II Parthica*, seems to have wintered at Apamea during imperial campaigns of the third century, and was instrumental in leading Elagabalus' revolt against Macrinus in AD 218. In Syria Phoenice the *III Gallica* was suppressed for supporting a rebellion against the same emperor, but was later restored at Danaba near Damascus. The *IV Scythica* seems to have been transferred from Syria Palaestina to Alexandria by Severus Alexander, but is found at Oresa in the Syrian steppe in the fourth century.

Auxiliary units are attested mainly by inscriptions. Two military diplomas (documents given to veterans on their discharge) of AD 88 together record eight cavalry *alae* and nineteen infantry cohorts in Syria, an auxiliary force of about 14,500. Another diploma of AD 156-7 has three or four *alae* and sixteen cohorts, and it is likely that there were more in the province at the time. Many recruits in Syria seem to have come from the Balkans, particularly Thrace (renowned for its fierce warriors), although local recruitment into these auxiliary units is likely during the course of the second century. In the first century there was a marked preference for posting auxiliaries away from their province of recruitment, but this practice appears to have changed during the second. Soldiers of the *cohors III Thracum Syriaca* (Thracians based in Syria), attested in one of the diplomas of AD 88, might originally have been from Thrace, but over time new recruits could have come from diverse backgrounds, including Syria. Evidence for the location of units is largely based on finds of inscriptions, but these were often reused in later buildings, requiring the assumption that the stone had not travelled far from its original location. Wandering stones are a hazard of epigraphy in Syria; such stones could have been re-employed for their decorative appeal, even if they could not be read, and thus have a greater tendency to move long distances than unmarked stones. Does the presence of an inscription of the *cohors I Flavia Chalcidenorum equitata sagittariorum*,[69] reused in a large fortress near Thelsea (Dmeir) on the road between Damascus and Palmyra, provide evidence of the unit's presence there in *c.* AD 162 (the date of the inscription)? The surviving fortress may not even be Roman; recent research suggests it is an Umayyad desert palace. The inscription may have come from a nearby building in Thelsea, but that cannot yet be proved. These sorts of problems make the assessment of any strategy of auxiliary deployment very difficult. Overall the pattern suggests that the number of auxiliaries increased during the late first and second centuries, implying that Rome found these more lightly armed troops increasingly useful. The absorption of the armies of client kings into the *auxilia* is likely to have contributed to the increase in numbers. The auxiliaries were perhaps better suited to police work than heavy infantrymen of the legions. However in many of them were cavalry units and archers, and these forces may have been intended as a counterbalance to Parthian horse- and bowmen who had proved so successful against legionary armies in the past. Through auxiliary and non-legionary forces Rome sought to make up for any deficiencies in her traditional tactics, learning from mistakes and observing what was effective: hence units of *dromedarii* (camel corps) and *clibanarii* (heavily armoured cavalry) which could counter hostile nomads and Parthian or Sasanian forces.

Aside from the land-based forces, Syria also had a fleet, the *classis Syriaca*. It was perhaps established under Vespasian, although the earliest certain evidence is Hadrianic. It is thought that its main base was at Seleucia Pieria; however, its galleys were also stationed at other cities along the coast. Naval ships patrolled the Euphrates too. In addition detachments from the Italian fleets at Misenum and Ravenna were posted at Seleucia, their main purpose apparently to provide logistical support for eastern campaigns.

In the first century AD the royal armies of the client kings could be called upon to provide assistance to the Roman army, and these forces were also expected to defend Roman interests and maintain order in their respective kingdoms. The abundant literary evidence for the Herodian armies shows that like their imperial counterpart they too were stationed in both cities and remote places and were not necessarily intended for frontier defence. Like Roman troops they acted as a police force (the dynasty could not always rely on popular support, and Herod's fortress palaces like Masada could function as refuges if necessary), but they could also be used for aggression outside their kingdoms (provided the kings consulted the relevant Roman authorities and their aims did not conflict with Roman interests). On the annexation of the kingdoms many if not all of these royal armies were formed into auxiliary units. The *cohors I Ulpia Petraeorum*, listed in the diploma of AD 156-7, is likely to have been formed originally of Nabataean soldiers, who were then posted to Syria. Similarly a *cohors I Ituraeorum* found in one of the diplomas of AD 88 might have originated in the forces of a client ruler.

In the early empire Syria had the largest military presence of the eastern provinces, although the size of this army is difficult to calculate, given that in addition to the legionaries there was an unknown number of auxiliaries. One source (Tacitus) hints that under Tiberius the two types of soldier were present in equal numbers throughout the empire. There were four legions in the east at this time, a force of about 20,000 men, all based in the province of Syria; so together with the auxiliaries the army was perhaps about 40,000 strong. Using the same rule of thumb we can calculate that by the end of Hadrian's reign the number in the east had risen to 60,000 (three legions in Syria, one in Arabia and two in Syria Palaestina, plus an equal number of auxiliaries). The dissolution of the client kingdoms and the advance into more remote areas will have required additional forces, and the garrisoning of Mesopotamia will have raised the numbers to perhaps 80,000-90,000 by the early third century (there were also two legions stationed further north in Anatolia). With Severus' division of Syria in two, the concentration of forces in a single province of Syria ended (subsequently there were perhaps 20,000 in Syria Coele, and 10,000 in

Syria Phoenice). Attempts to calculate the ratio of soldiers to civilians involve calculations based on even vaguer rules of thumb, but it is unlikely that it ever rose above 1:100 and was probably considerably lower. The scope for interaction between the military and the local population was therefore in part limited by numbers, although the power soldiers could wield within a community will have helped compensate for any numerical deficiency.

In the late empire the legions declined in importance. Instead of legionaries and auxiliaries, the principal distinction in the Roman army was now between the units of the mobile field army (the *comitatus*), and the permanent garrisons under the command of provincial *duces*. The *comitatus* was commanded by the *magister militum per orientem*, based at Antioch, who was the chief military official for the eastern provinces. The *duces* were also answerable to him. Legions were now smaller units, sometimes perhaps no more than a thousand men, and while some served in the *comitatus*, others formed permanent garrisons and in general they were no longer the crack troops of the Roman army. Auxiliary cohorts and *alae* were also reduced in size. Fortunately we possess a list of civilian and military officials, the *Notitia Dignitatum*, which names the legions, auxiliary units and other forces of the provinces together with their locations. The sections in the *Notitia* for the east date to about AD 400, but it is thought that they largely reflect troop dispositions under Diocletian. It shows that in Syria most of the legions of the early empire were still in the same provinces or regions. Apart from the *III Cyrenaica* at Bostra in Arabia the other legions had by the fourth century moved to new bases, all of which were in more remote areas than the earlier ones. The Euphrates was covered by the *IV Scythica* at Oresa (at-Tayibeh) and the *XVI Flavia* at Sura; the steppe by the *III Gallica* at Danaba and the *I Illyricorum*, probably brought to Syria by Aurelian, at Palmyra. In Palestine the *X Fretensis* had moved to Aila on the Gulf of Aqaba, and Arabia was now listed with two legions, the *III Cyrenaica* and the *IV Martia* (at a place called Betthorus, perhaps modern Lejjun). Aside from units of auxiliary *alae* and cohorts, other forces of the permanent garrison of the provinces listed in the *Notitia* consisted of cavalry units referred to as *equites*. The units of the *comitatus* had no permanent bases (or at least, none is mentioned in the *Notitia*), and when not on campaign were billeted in cities. In contrast the permanent garrisons were settled in the regions which they defended and patrolled, and their interests tended to converge with those of the civilian population, regardless of state concerns: for example, when Jovian ceded Nisibis to the Sasanians the garrison of the city refused to comply and fought the enemy in a futile bid to save their home. It seems that like the civilian population the soldiers of the permanent garrison also farmed the land, for a law of AD 443 refers to an ancient right of the troops in the border regions, the *limitanei*, to cultivate land for their own profit free from the obligations of performing public services and paying land tax. In return for these concessions their sons were expected to provide the next generation of *limitanei*. Although they have sometimes been called a 'peasant militia' and were clearly secondary in status to the *comitatenses*, the *limitanei* were regular troops, and an effective fighting force. They could be called up to serve away from their homes, and were sometimes drafted into the field armies under the title of *pseudocomitatenses*.

Apart from commanding the provincial garrisons, the *duces* also seem to have been responsible for liaising with, and perhaps paying subsidies to, Arab allies and *foederati*. But the federates themselves were commanded by tribal leaders who had been either recognized or appointed by Rome. Paying tribal leaders had evidently become customary by the reign of Julian, when the emperor lost their support at the outset of his Persian campaign by withdrawing subsidies to some of them. Non-payment of subsidies might result not only in loss of support or revenge raids on friendly territory; it might also represent a very real loss of Roman influence over peripheral regions where the tribes operated. The activities of Justin II and Maurice in breaking the power of the Ghassanids led to the weakening of Roman control in the Syrian steppe and was likely to have been a factor assisting the Sasanian conquests of the early seventh century. Increasing reliance on Arab *foederati* from the fourth century is suggested archaeologically by the apparent abandonment of Roman forts and towers in some remote areas of the south like the Azraq oasis, about 80 kilometres (50 miles) south-east of Bostra and in the heart of what would later be Ghassanid territory.

By the sixth century references to legions, cohorts and *alae* had disappeared from the Roman military vocabulary, and Procopius, when writing the history of Justinian's wars, had to describe for his readers what an ancient Roman legion was. There is also evidence that numbers had seriously declined: at the beginning of the fifth century the strength of the *comitatus* in the east is estimated at about 104,000, but by the time of Justinian it may have been less than a quarter of that strength. There seems to be no way of estimating the size of the permanent garrison, although there is a tradition that Justinian also reduced their numbers. It is perhaps no surprise to find that after the troubles of the early seventh century the entire Roman army in the final battle against the Muslim forces at the Yarmuk in AD 636 numbered about 50,000.

FORTS AND GEOGRAPHIES

Physical remains attesting to the Roman army's presence in our region are confined mainly to the steppe and desert, and consequently they are mostly of the third century or later, when the Roman army advanced into these periph-eral zones. There are some earlier fortifications in these regions, but the overall purpose behind the Roman advance into such apparently unrewarding environments remains uncertain. If they were not aimed at controlling the activities of nomad raiders, they may have protected and policed trade routes and sedentary populations living in these marginal zones. The Severan period witnessed notable advances down the Euphrates (p. 55) and into the remote eastern regions of the province of Arabia. If there were motives for these advances other than imperial opportunism they are not clear to us, even though there are tantalizing indications of a rationale in some cases. The fortifications in and around the remote Azraq oasis in Arabia controlled valuable water resources in an otherwise arid basalt landscape, and the soldiers stationed there may have had an interest in traffic along the Wadi Sirhan, a depression which stretches into what is now the north of modern Saudi Arabia. Quite what form any Roman influence over the Wadi Sirhan took is difficult to say (manned posts and regular patrols?), although an inscription from Azraq gives distances from the fort to other locations and mentions Dumatha, modern Jauf, at the other end of the wadi about 400 kilometres (248 miles) to the south-east, and a Latin dedication by a centurion found at Jauf itself suggests a Roman military presence there, perhaps during the late second or early third century. Suffice to say that during the period from the late second to perhaps the early fourth century the Roman military had an interest in this area, whether for economic or security reasons, but they may have withdrawn during the course of the fourth century, perhaps in response to the growing power of nomad confederations and heavier dependence on 'Saracen' foederati.

The late third-century *Strata Diocletiana* and the legionary camp at Palmyra (fig. 191) may be related to whatever strategies were being pursued at Azraq. These look very much like a response on the part of the state to the collapse of Palmyrene control. Under Diocletian the Roman army stepped in to do the job that the Palmyrenes had formerly done, and of all the military systems in Syria, the *Strata Diocletiana* most resembles a scientific cordon, with roads linking a line of forts stretching from Sura on the Euphrates via Palmyra and south, passing east of Auranitis to reach the road linking Bostra and Azraq. Milestones along the route from Aracha southwards use the term '*Strata Diocletiana*' or '*Istrata Diocletiana*', implying that this was the official name of the road network. Yet even this is not certain, for there are also milestones in the name of Constantine and his co-rulers reading '*Istrata Constantini* [...?]', so the term may signify nothing more than the fact that there were various roads constructed under Diocletian and Constantine. But the evidence of so many roads and buildings under Diocletian, at least between Palmyra and Azraq, strongly suggests a programme and their conception as an integrated system. The best evidence comes from the section between Palmyra and Thelsea (Dmeir). At its northern end was the *legio I Illyricorum* at Palmyra; in the rear was the *legio III Gallica* at Danaba. The *Strata* itself was guarded by forts of auxiliaries and units of *equites*. Other units of *equites* were settled behind the *Strata*; their purpose may have been to provide strike forces to intercept raiders. Yet there is no certain indication of what threat such a network was intended to counter. Perhaps it was supposed to secure the settled areas against incursions by the Tanukh or other nomads, or simply to protect traffic and ensure a line of communication. Most of the forts cannot have been positioned so as to protect sedentary peasants in the vicinity, for there is little evidence of ancient farming in this arid landscape. Scattered though the evidence is, a case for the *Strata Diocletiana* between Palmyra and Thelsea being a reaction to problems with nomads is perceptible. The sixth-century chronicler Malalas says that Diocletian 'built arms factories at Damascus, bearing in mind the incursions of the Saracens',[70] and the emperor is known to have conducted a Saracen campaign in AD 290, though the precise location of the enemy in this case is unknown. It may well have been in this area; the Azraq inscription mentioning Dumatha also refers to the presence of soldiers from four Danubian legions, who are likely to have been there for some very special reason. When this network was abandoned is also unclear to us; it has been suggested that like the system at Azraq the forts fell out of use during the fourth century. Perhaps Diocletian's successors found the system of direct control ineffectual, and turned over responsibility for these regions to federate Arabs, so that henceforth the Roman military presence began only at Palmyra. The name, however, seems to have survived, for Procopius tells us that under Justinian there was a quarrel between the Ghassanids and Lakhmids over a district called Strata, which lay south of Palmyra and was named after a road.

Fig. 191. The Strata Diocletiana. *The network between Palmyra and the Euphrates is probably earlier than Diocletian; a milestone from Aracha (Arak) records road works in AD 75. This may have become a frontier zone after the fall of Palmyra to Aurelian. A milestone using the term* Strata Diocletiana *was found between Palmyra and Aracha, but otherwise all other certain Diocletianic installations associated with this system are found from Palmyra southwards. Recent work on the section between Palmyra and Sura on the Euphrates suggests that in late Roman times this section was probably intended to maintain security against Sasanian attacks; at any rate the main periods of occupation in the forts there coincide with known Sasanian invasions.*

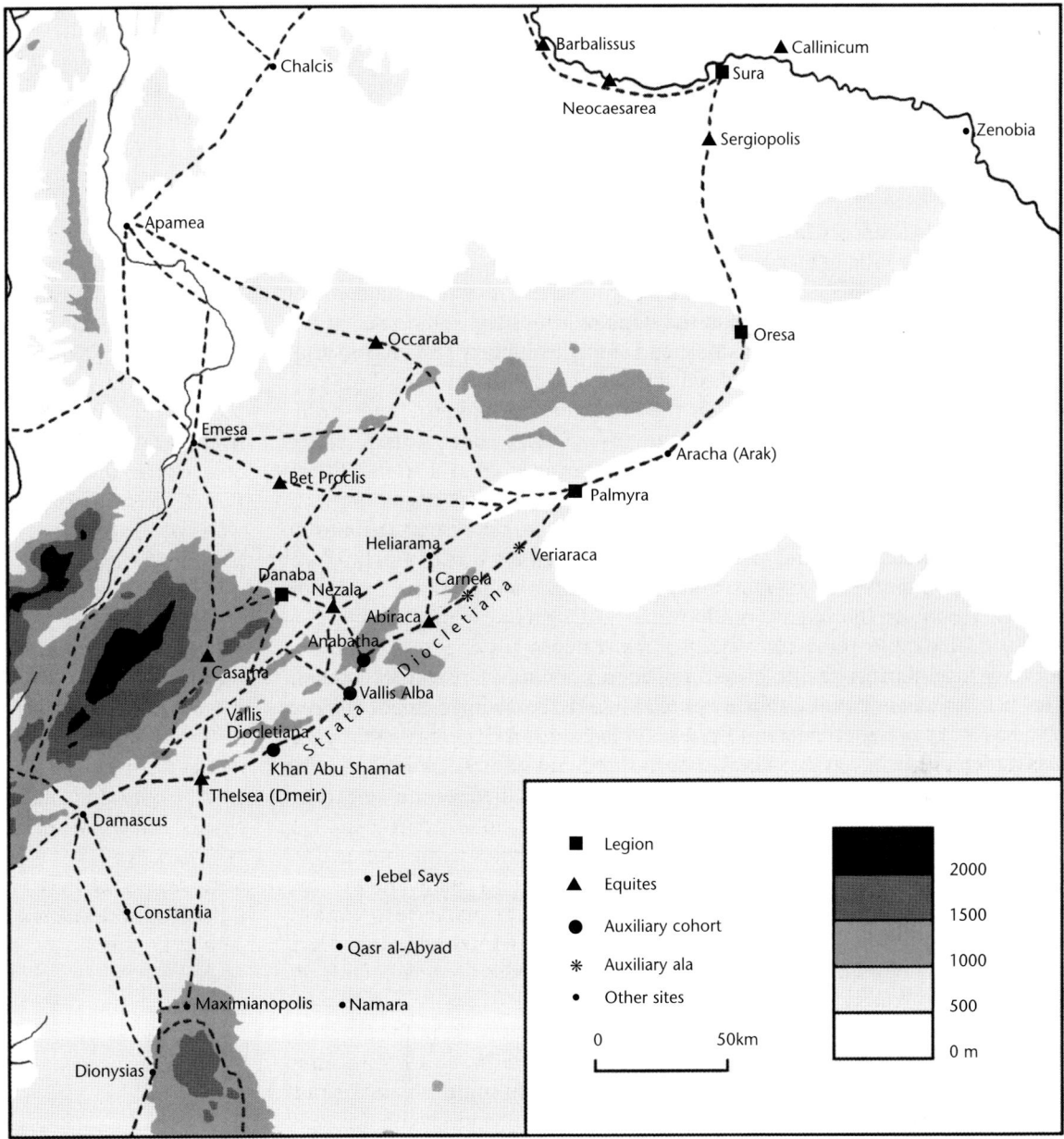

There are many differences between Roman military installations in the western empire and those found in the east. Comparisons between the two parts of the empire are often made on the assumption that those in the west represent the 'normal' types (for instance, fortresses of 'playing card' shape), and that eastern practices such as billeting armies in cities or building forts that do not conform to western designs is somewhat aberrant, or that the western-style forts have yet to be discovered. From an eastern perspective it may be the case that the western-style installations are the true aberrations, used mainly in provinces where urbanization had not yet taken root. However, the possibility of new discoveries in our region cannot be discounted, given the current state of knowledge. Legionary fortresses of the early empire are poorly known;

that at Samosata has disappeared under the floodwaters of a dam, as perhaps has that at Zeugma. Raphanea has barely been explored, and little is known about the fortresses at Caparcotna and Jerusalem. A large rectangular enclosure on the northern side of Bostra has been identified as the camp of the *legio III Cyrenaica* (fig. 36). The details of its interior have yet to be revealed, but this is the only fortress so far discovered in the region that is comparable in size and shape to the classic legionary bases of the western empire. Legionary fortresses of the late empire are slightly better known. Two substantial examples can still be seen at Lejjun and Udruh in Jordan, both of which lay east of the *via nova Traiana* in Arabia and Palaestina Tertia, away from major civilian settlements. Lejjun was probably constructed under Diocletian for the *IV Martia*, and is much smaller than the fortress at Bostra, being sufficient to accommodate between about 1000-1500 men. Nevertheless at 242 by 190 metres (265 by 208 yards) it is one of the largest military installations surviving in the east (fig. 192). Udruh, which is of comparable size though more irregular in shape, is something of a puzzle, because it seems to be superfluous (all of the legions in the *Notitia Dignitatum* are accounted for without it). One possibility is that this was the home of the *Legio VI Ferrata*, which is not mentioned at all in the *Notitia Dignitatum*. Perhaps it was transferred there in the third or early fourth century and then destroyed or suppressed. Other ruins associated with late Roman legions are the 'Camp of Diocletian' at Palmyra, probably the base of the *legio I Illyricorum*, and traces of a possible camp for the *IV Scythica* between Palmyra and Sura at a site called at-Tayibeh, identified as ancient Oresa. Internal buildings are not well preserved, although the *principia* (headquarters) can be distinguished at Palmyra, Lejjun and Udruh. The camp at Palmyra was monumentalized in keeping with the rest of the city, and was adapted from a pre-existing plan for that quarter. Its axial colonnades appear to be second

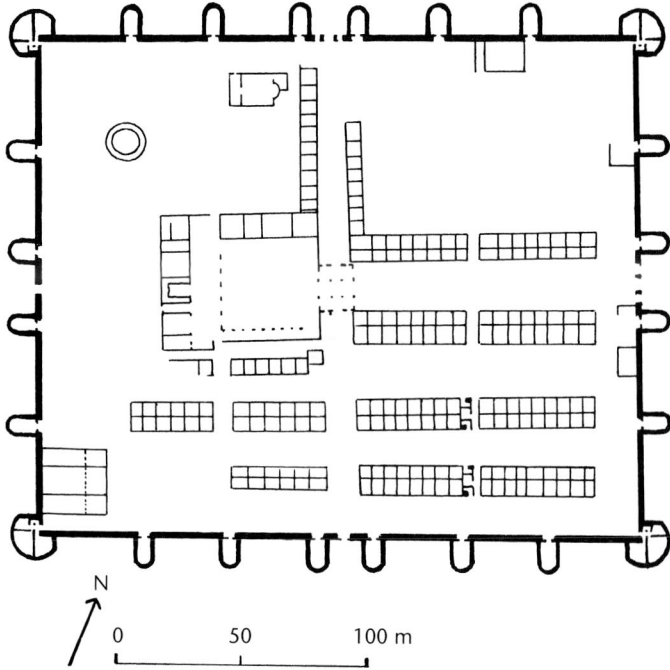

Fig. 192. Plan of the legionary fortress at Lejjun.

N

0   50   100 m

century; these met in a tetrapylon made of reused stones, probably a Diocletianic addition. On the north-western side at the end of an open square stood the *principia*, nestling against a hill on the very edge of the city; its impressive ruins still dominate that part of the site.

Most smaller forts are also of late Roman date, when they can be dated at all. An exception is the early auxiliary fort at Tell el-Hajj near the Euphrates between Zeugma and Sura. Some other forts which lack external towers (on these features, see below) are thought to belong to the early empire because in outline and size they resemble western imperial auxiliary forts, although few have been explored in order to confirm this. There are many forts and fort-like structures in the steppe and desert of Syria and Mesopotamia, most of which have not yet been investigated. The difficulties of establishing a chronology are exacerbated by the fact that many fortifications assumed to be Roman may instead be Parthian, Sasanian or Umayyad. Even when they can be assigned to the Roman empire it is not always clear whether the building in question was a military base, a fortified refuge built by locals, or a villa or monastery with a defensive circuit. Trying to delineate 'grand strategies' or speculating about relations between soldiers and civilians using such insecure evidence is particularly hazardous. The basic typologies remain very uncertain and rely on dated analogies from other regions of the Roman world. In the early empire towers tended to project inward, but the later forts (which basically means most of the examples in our region) have towers projecting outwards. However, the shape of the towers themselves (square in plan, pointed, rounded and so on) would seem to be no guide at all to the date of a fort. Small forts which are square or form a parallelogram and have four corner towers have traditionally been attributed to the Tetrarchy, but the design may have enjoyed long-standing popularity in the region. In some smaller forts the barracks are usually attached to the curtain wall (thought to be a late feature) rather than free-standing, others combine both forms; but larger bases like Lejjun retained the traditional pattern of free-standing barrack blocks and again such features are an unreliable indicator of date. In the countryside forts were often interspersed with towers positioned along roads frequented by travellers; apart from acting as guard posts they could also be used to send signals to each other and to the forts. Some towers were fairly substantial, with accommodation for soldiers, while others were more specifically designed for observation or signalling. In an experiment using towers in the vicinity of Lejjun archaeologists were able to discover that signals could be transmitted at night by burning torches to the fort of Khirbet el-Fityan, which in turn could relay messages to the legionary fortress at Lejjun to the south-east, from which the towers themselves could not be seen. Other signals were presumably used in daylight. Such installations helped to give the Roman army the edge over any hostile forces.

Apart from housing the units needed to counter any enemy forces, the smaller forts served as bases for patrols, local administrative centres, watering places, stopovers for travellers and couriers, and guard posts along the routes of communication. A combination of good communications and resources was no doubt important in the choice of sites for these smaller forts. In the drier regions control of water supplies was a significant factor: that at Azraq in Arabia was built on a lava ridge above a lake and natural springs, at the junction of roads from Damascus and Bostra, and a late third- or fourth-century inscription from Khan al-Abyad on the road from Damascus to

Fig. 193. The single entrance to Khan al-Manqoura (Vallis Alba), a fort of the Strata Diocletiana. *This large fort could have housed up to 500 auxiliaries of the* cohors I Julia Lectorum, *and guarded not only the* Strata *but also a pass in the Jebel Rawaq which dominates the western horizon. Although located in the dry steppe, it was at the centre of a complex system of water collection, and there is a large reservoir south of the gate.*

Palmyra praises a certain Silvinus for having constructed a *castrum* in the dry wasteland and ensuring 'that it abound with water celestial'[71] to provide for wayfarers and agriculture. While the forts on the *Strata Diocletiana* and around Azraq may have been deserted by the end of the fourth century, many others remained in use through the fifth century. But by the sixth a number of those in the south had been abandoned, particularly in Arabia and Palaestina Tertia. The latest certain involvement of the Roman army in Arabia is indicated by an inscription of AD 529 from Qasr el-Hallabat, about 60 kilometres (37 miles) south of Bostra (although this may be a 'wandering stone'). This suggests that the concerns of the empire were focused elsewhere, and the periphery was being increasingly left to the Arab allies and *foederati*, at least in the southern part of our region.

The army was one of the great rationalizing forces that Rome had at her disposal. If there were a series of strategies pursued by the Roman military during the centuries of Roman rule in Syria, they might have been as follows. During the first century there was a gradual buildup of legionary and auxiliary forces across the region. The initial focus was on the north because it was here that adequate supplies and infrastructure were to be found. At this point the army acted as the state's forces of coercion; the logistics required to support a Parthian war were as yet underdeveloped. The gradual expansion of the Roman military into the countryside was achieved only as the army gained mastery over and developed sufficient supply to rural areas. Increasing sedentarization of the indigenous population no doubt assisted these developments, even if the army did not encourage the process of settlement. By the early second century the infrastructure was sufficiently well developed to allow emperors to wage war on the Parthian kingdom, with the aim of conquering at least the land between the Euphrates and Tigris. This was partly achieved, and successive attacks weakened the Parthians, but their overthrow and replacement by the Sasanians checked the Roman advance. Consolidation recommenced in the later third century, and with the victory of Galerius over

Narseh Roman ambitions in Mesopotamia revived. However, with the partition of the empire and its resources under Constantine's sons the main concern was to defend this territory rather than attempt new conquests. After the treaty of Jovian and the partition of Armenia the boundaries between the Roman and Sasanian empires remained fairly static. Settlements in the border regions or potential enemy invasion routes such as the Euphrates valley were fortified and a number of these were promoted to city status. The smaller size of the forces, including legions, and their dispersal across the steppe, might be a consequence of problems of supply in the more remote areas where many were now stationed, so that the soldiers were encouraged to exploit local resources as much as possible. Crucial changes occurred in the sixth century, but their nature and extent are uncertain. They may well be connected with Justinian's costly wars of conquest in the western Mediterranean. The number of regular soldiers was probably reduced, and the *comitatus* was much smaller than before. The waning of Roman military presence in the south-east was probably connected with the growth of nomad federations, itself likely to have been a symptom of state reliance on these groups for security in remote areas. Periodic attempts to revise this strategy and revive direct Roman control further weakened the state's authority in these peripheral areas, because the nomads effectively held control whether the state paid them or not. There are also signs that the state was having financial difficulties by the beginning of the seventh century, if not before. The disruption of the Persian conquest in the early seventh century effectively put an end to any organized Roman strategy in the region, for Heraclius had barely succeeded in recovering the lost provinces before they were conquered by the armies of Islam. The successes of the Muslim armies altered the strategic makeup of the region completely. The project to unite the Fertile Crescent under a single power was finally achieved; not by Rome, nor by its Sasanian opponents, but by the peoples of the imperial peripheries.

EPILOGUE

THE END OF ROMAN SYRIA: AN HISTORICAL SKETCH

In AD 622, the year in which Heraclius launched his attack on the Sasanians, the Arab followers of a new monotheistic religion established themselves at Medina in the Arabian peninsula. Their leader was Muhammad, a citizen of Mecca who proclaimed submission to Allah, the one true god, and in doing so had angered the pagans of his native city. Inspired by this new faith, the Muslim followers of Muhammad recovered Mecca and began expanding their political and religious power over the whole peninsula. Soon they were looking northwards, to the Arab tribes inhabiting the fertile and populous lands of Syria, the *Bilad ash-Sham*.

The same period had witnessed the momentous struggle between the Romans and Sasanians. Against seemingly impossible odds Heraclius had prevailed (see chapter 2). In July 629 the Persian general Shahrbaraz and the Roman emperor met in Cappadocia to arrange a withdrawal of the Persian forces from Syria, Egypt and Asia. The terms of the peace treaty allowed the Romans to recover all the territory that had been lost to them in the previous two decades, at least as far as the Khabur river in Mesopotamia. A period of

instability ensued as the Persians withdrew and Roman forces moved southwards to re-establish garrisons in the Syrian cities. Most of these places had not
experienced Roman rule for many years.

On 21 March AD 630, Heraclius returned the remains of the True Cross to
Jerusalem, with great ceremony. Even so, Roman control of the south was not
yet fully consolidated. In September 629 the Romans had defeated a 'Saracen'
army of Muslims at Mu'ta near Charach Moba (Karak), east of the Dead Sea.
To the Romans, who were busy trying to consolidate their power in the region,
the precarious nature of their control and vulnerability of their situation were
probably not fully apparent, and the conflict at Mu'ta was in all likelihood
viewed as the latest in a long succession of skirmishes with Arab tribes and
federations. Islam, however, gave the tribes a new cohesion which the Romans
did not at first appreciate and probably did not understand. By the time the
threat became more evident, the southern periphery was already lost. In 630
Muhammad formed a peace with Christian and Jewish tribes in and around the
Gulf of Aqaba, and negotiated the surrender of Aila (Aqaba) and Udruh. There
is no sign of any Roman presence this far south, though it is likely that given
the chance a presence would have been re-established.

Muhammad died in 632, but political authority passed to his closest friend
and supporter Abu Bakr (632-4), the first caliph ('successor') of Islam. Late in
633 or early 634 the Muslim incursions into territory held by the Romans
began in earnest. A Roman army was defeated near Gaza, and at about the
same time Bostra submitted to another force which had crossed the Syrian
desert and next moved on to Damascus, where it crushed a Ghassanid army.
The Roman position in the south was suddenly in grave danger. A major defeat
of the Roman forces at Ajnadayn, near Eleutheropolis (Bet Guvrin) in
Palestine, followed in the summer of 634, and the fall of Damascus in 635. The
Muslims then moved north into the Orontes valley.

Heraclius, based at Antioch, mustered an army to repel the invaders. In the
face of a Roman advance the Muslim forces withdrew to the south, and after
numerous skirmishes in the summer of 636 the decisive battle took place north
of the Wadi Yarmuk on 20 August. The Roman army was led into a trap
between the deep gorges of the Yarmuk and its tributaries and destroyed. The
defeat was absolute: the Roman camp was overwhelmed, and those who managed to escape were quickly pursued. For the Romans the day, and the Syrian
provinces, were lost.

Heraclius did not attempt a counter attack. He decided instead that the best
course of action would be to evacuate and to consolidate his position in Asia
Minor. It might have been possible to defend the Syrian cities of the north, but
Heraclius abandoned them. It was probably a strategic trade-off: by leaving the
Muslims with plenty of territory to organize, he gave his own forces precious
time to regroup beyond the Taurus. With the departure of the emperor seven
centuries of Roman rule came to a close.

For most cities the transition from Roman to Muslim rule was relatively
peaceful, and there is no evidence of general resistance. Coastal ports, whose
garrisons could be supplied by sea, remained in Roman hands longest, but
within about five years most of these too had capitulated. Mesopotamia, the
keystone to the Fertile Crescent, fared little better. Its Roman *curator* had treated
with the Muslims, agreeing to pay them an annual bribe if they remained in
Syria. Heraclius, who had not been consulted, annulled the treaty. The Muslims

then crossed the Euphrates and between 638 and 640 took the whole of Mesopotamia, and from there began campaigning in Heraclius' homeland of Armenia. Heraclius died in early 641, a bitterly disillusioned man. The great military emperor, conqueror of the Persians, had been thoroughly worsted by this unexpected onslaught from Arabia.

The losses suffered by the Romans pale in comparison with the fate that befell their old adversary, the Sasanian kingdom. Defeat by Heraclius, and Khusrau's death, plunged the kingdom into a crisis. The threat from the Arabs on the south-western border, always prevalent since the suppression of the Lakhmids, now increased, and in 637 the Sasanians were defeated by the Muslim armies near al-Hira and lost Iraq. The king, Yazdgard III, fled to Iran. Defeated in further battles, Yazdgard was eventually assassinated, and so the Sasanian kingdom was effectively brought to an end.

WHY THE CONQUEST?

There are two main approaches to the problem. One emphasizes the specific political and historical circumstances. The sixth century was a difficult time for the eastern provinces, and the catalogues of earthquakes, famines, Persian invasions and plagues are seen as contributing to a general decline and increasing weakness in the social, economic and military structure of the empire. Antioch and Apamea were badly damaged by earthquakes in 526 and 528, and Berytus, Sidon and Tyre by an earthquake of 551. The cities continued to function, but in Berytus large areas of the city, including high-status residences, were only partly restored, with other parts being left in ruins or demolished. The pottery from Berytus shows that a narrower range of products was reaching the city after the earthquake than had done so before, suggesting a sudden decline in economic activity at the site. The Persians sacked Antioch in 540, and Apamea in 573. Apamea's great Cathedral of the East, probably containing a relic of the True Cross, was never restored. Whether this was through lack of will or resources is unclear. The Persians also deported large sections of the population of some of the cities to their own empire, leaving these centres with fewer inhabitants. The 'Justinianic Plague', which ravaged the empire beginning in 540, broke out repeatedly during the sixth and seventh centuries. Then, in the early seventh century, the empire suffered a major period of internal strife (rebellions against Maurice and Phocas) at a time when it was waging war on two fronts, against the Persians in the east and the Avars and Slavs in the north. The Persians were able to take advantage, and the major discontinuity of the Sasanian conquest weakened Roman authority over the eastern provinces, so that after Heraclius' victory the Muslim armies were able to exploit this weakness in order to assume control at the expense of Rome.

Formidable though the list of disasters is, the degree to which plagues, earthquakes and sackings were determining factors leading to the empire's decline is debatable; some studies of more recent catastrophes have indicated that they do not necessarily lead to the collapse of society, and can even stimulate growth. There are signs of urban continuity after some of these traumas, though as a rule building activity throughout the region appears to have been reduced in the second half of the sixth century. The porticos of Antioch's main street were rebuilt in the aftermath of the Persian sack of 540. The city's main baths may not have been rebuilt, but further south, in Berytus, the imperial baths remained in use when neighbouring residential neighbourhoods had been abandoned following the earthquake of 551. The baths of Gerasa were restored in 584.

So in some places essential 'Roman' elements of civic life persisted beyond horizons of destruction, natural or man-made. This is not to deny the significance of catastrophic events: disasters can, of course, deal serious blows to a way of life already in decline as a result of other factors.

Another approach stresses the empire's internal decline over 'assassination' by invaders and events beyond its control. Preceding chapters have looked at long-term changes to the cultural, political and military life and organization of the region in the late Roman period. Many changes were common to the empire as a whole, and some must have weakened the authority of the central government in the provinces, even though that was not what the state had intended. As we have seen, the erosion of traditional civic government and values, on which the Roman state had relied heavily during the early empire, was reflected in the transformation of the urban environment. But that was not all. Rigid rules governing expenditure of taxes made it difficult for the central government to divert resources in times of emergency, and the officials who oversaw expenditure did not always make their accounting procedures transparent. Army units, settled and dispersed throughout the region, were reluctant to serve elsewhere, and the state began to rely heavily on mobile forces of federate nomads for defence. The rule introduced by Marcus Aurelius that no one could be governor of their native province had been created to prevent governors from mobilizing regional loyalties against the central government. This rule was overturned in late Roman times, in response to pressures from the powerful grandees. This meant that the government in Constantinople increasingly devolved control to regional interests, which did not always concur with imperial concerns.

The rise of Christianity and sectarian conflicts led to changes in cultural allegiances and the organization of new identities. From Justinian onwards the drive to Christianize the empire strengthened, leading to fierce persecutions of pagans, Jews and heretics. The importance of the divide between Chalcedonians and Monophysites has often been downplayed, but it gave many Syrians reasons not to identify themselves with the emperors. Heraclius had tried to solve the rift by advancing a doctrine that Christ had one will (Monothelitism), a novelty which even many Chalcedonians resisted. The fact that the Muslim invaders encountered little resistance might suggest that the Romans had failed to provide Syrians of both persuasions with a good reason for identifying with Constantinople. If the empire was 'assassinated' by external foes in the seventh century, it had perhaps unwittingly developed a suicidal streak by the late sixth.

The weakness of the empire, brought about both by catastrophes and long term changes, was no doubt the reason why opportunistic invaders were able to succeed. The decline of one state inevitably gives others advantages. Another factor may be demographic: the late Roman period had witnessed the growth of powerful Arab groups on the desert fringes. Although Christian and in the pay of Rome, these groups had much in common with the conquerors, and could be easily assimilated with them. A recent thesis also stresses the proactive economic role of the invaders. The nomads of Arabia had depended on the economy of the settled areas, by participating in the long-distance trade in luxuries. The later sixth-century decline of the cities and their economic infrastructure affected the nomad economies, causing a 'crisis of mutuality' to develop between sedentary peoples and nomads. Islam gave the nomads the cohesion to take matters into their own hands, by conquering the economic centres on which they had previously depended. They aimed not to overthrow existing society, but to appropriate the economic system and revitalize it. Rather than being heavily regulated and state-controlled, the new system, led by 'entrepreneurs', became more competitive and dynamic than what had gone before. This is presented as an alternative to the idea that the Islamic state's finances initially comprised looting and acquisition of booty prior to the development of an organized system of taxation.

AFTERMATH

Within a century of the Roman defeat at the Yarmuk *Dar al-Islam*, the 'Abode of Islam', had become a vast domain, stretching from north Africa to Afghanistan. The Syrian navy that the Muslims employed gained mastery of much of the eastern Mediterranean, inflicting another major defeat on the Romans off the coast of Lycia in 655. The Muslim governor of Syria, Mu'awiya, was established as caliph in 661, marking the beginning of the Syrian-based Umayyad dynasty which was to control the Islamic world for almost a hundred years. He was a brilliant administrator who managed the diverse and potentially conflicting elements within his empire with considerable skill. His power base rested with the Arab armies in Syria, and it was to his former province that he transferred the seat of power, leaving Medina and Mecca as places of pilgrimage. Syria, formerly on the eastern periphery of the Roman empire, was now at the centre of a realm whose influence by the early eighth century extended from Spain to the Indus, with Damascus at its heart.

The idea that the Muslim conquest represents a dramatic break with the past, and that the region experienced a sharp cultural and demographic decline afterwards, no longer prevails. Cities in Umayyad Syria seem to have fared well (in contrast to those in Roman Anatolia), and archaeological excavations and surveys in the countryside convey a strong impression of continuity and dense occupation across the region. In the dry steppe and desert the Umayyads developed and improved late Roman water collection and irrigation techniques to create elaborate farmsteads and large residences (often rather misleadingly called 'desert castles'). These domains seem to have been part of a wider, integrated system including towns and villages of the steppe; but it is possible to see in the 'desert castles' a shift in the centres of power in these drier regions, from the emerging urban centres of late Roman times to the residences of aristocrats located in the countryside.

One striking element of continuity is afforded by the tradition of mosaics. Local authorities continued to decorate their churches with rich mosaic carpets, such as those at Deir el-Adas (fig. 146) or Kastron Mefaa (Umm ar-Rasas). The magnificent pavements in the nave and aisles of the church of St Stephen at Kastron Mefaa (fig. 145) are probably to be dated to AD 718 (the date of construction is given in an inscription, but the reading is unclear; a much later date of 785 has been proposed, though there are problems with this). Features such as the borders of Nilotic motifs are clearly derived from earlier classical versions, while others, such as the vine-scrolls, representations of cities (including Kastron Mefaa itself) and the elaborate geometric carpets are typical of the late Roman period. The Umayyad caliphs themselves also sponsored mosaics, among the most celebrated of which are those covering the upper walls of the porticos and façades of the great Umayyad mosque in Damascus (colour plate 29; only parts visible today are original). In accordance with Muslim rulings there are no people or animals in the scenes, but there are palatial pavilions, resembling the Hellenistic architecture of Alexandria, and towns set amid a lush landscape of trees and flowing water, all against a background of gilded glass tesserae. This was a version of paradise as promised to the righteous. The subject matter would not look out of place on a floor of the Roman period, but the sumptuous nature of the materials used, the skilful handling of colours and contrasts and the sheer extent of these mosaics must have outclassed all others in their magnificence.

Mosaics are merely one of many aspects of continuity that could be stressed here, but it should also be emphasized that the Umayyad world was a period of transition from a Hellenized culture to an Arabized one. Some features of that transition, such as the transformation of cities and urban lifestyles, had already commenced in the last century of Roman rule. Nor were the elements of continuity and change exclusively 'Graeco-Roman' or 'Arab'. The caliphs also borrowed extensively from the Sasanian world, whose values were in some respects closer to those of the Muslim warriors (admiration for the heroic deeds of great fighters, a strong tradition of court poetry). Though they might make use of its symbols, the Muslim rulers did not need Hellenism to bolster their legitimacy. A new and confident culture took shape within the bounds of the Umayyad empire, every bit as vigorous as that of the Romans. The Umayyads brought together the traditions from both sides of the Fertile Crescent and created something quite different, the final moment of late antiquity in Syria. The eternal domination of the Romans, celebrated by the provincials of Syria for 700 years, was at an end, but the Muslims did not break completely with that tradition. Instead it was a legacy they inherited and shaped as their own.

1. Contrasting landscapes: cedars of Lebanon on the Jebel Baruk, part of the Lebanon range . . .

2. . . . .and landscape west of Petra, looking towards the Wadi 'Araba.

3. The grand colonnade at Apamea, looking north. An honorific column stands in the middle of the street in the distance.

4. One of four entrances to the temenos of Zeus at Baetocaece in the Jebel Ansariyeh.
Note the monumental size of the ashlars used.

5. A small sanctuary at Sfire in northern Lebanon, which originally housed a *monument à colonnettes.*

6. *Monument à colonnettes* (heavily restored) at Fakra in Lebanon.

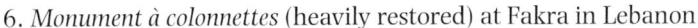

7. Late first-century BC funerary monument at Hermel, in the northern Bekaa Valley.

8. Southern side of the so-called 'Temple of Bacchus' at Heliopolis (Baalbek).

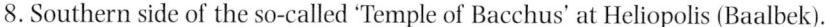

9. Interior of the 'Temple of Bacchus', showing the raised thalamos and the elaborate interior decoration.

10. Detail of the richly decorated ceiling between the peristyle and cella of the 'Temple of Bacchus'.

ABOVE
11. Temple at Ain Hersheh on the western slope of Mount Hermon. The rear of the cella is decorated with a bust of the moon-goddess Selene; the front bore a bust of the sun-god Helios. Note the burial in the foreground.

TOP RIGHT
12. General view of Palmyra and its oasis, showing the grand colonnade which stretches from the huge temenos of Bel (centre) to the so-called Funerary Temple (bottom right), changing direction twice along its course. The city wall can be discerned in the foreground.

BOTTOM RIGHT
13. The monumental arch of the grand colonnade at Palmyra.

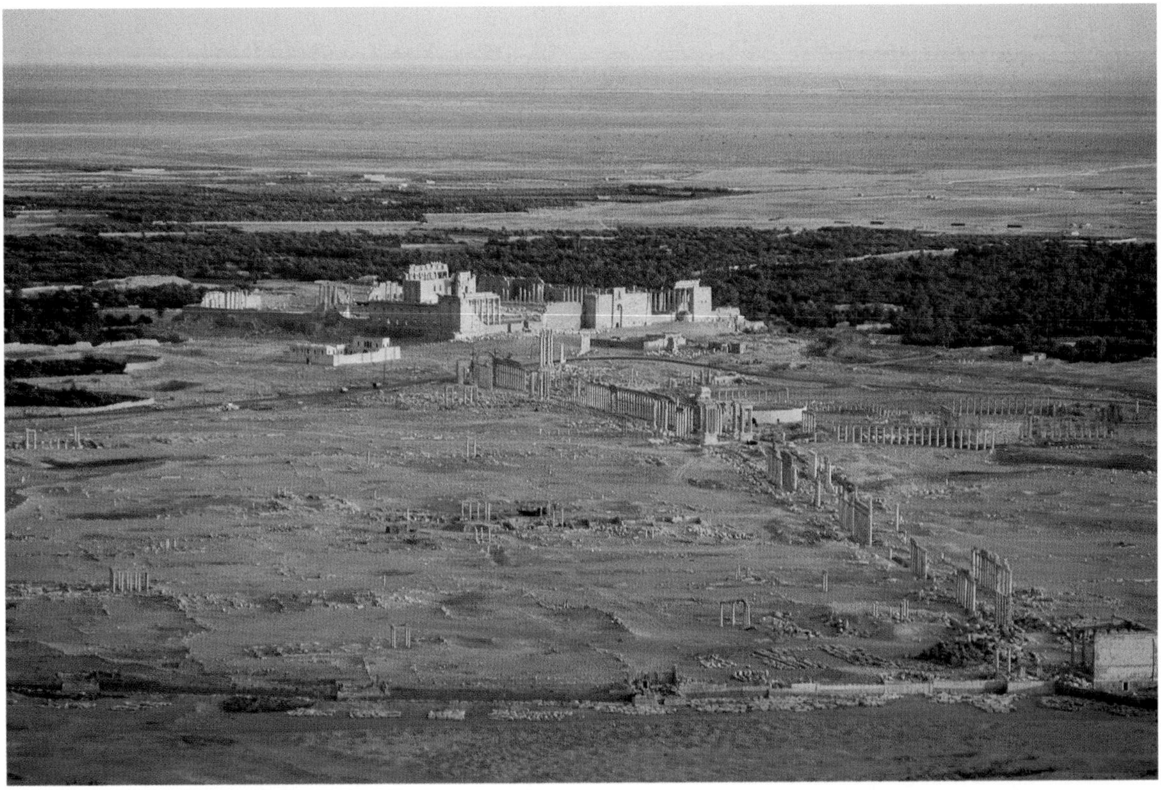

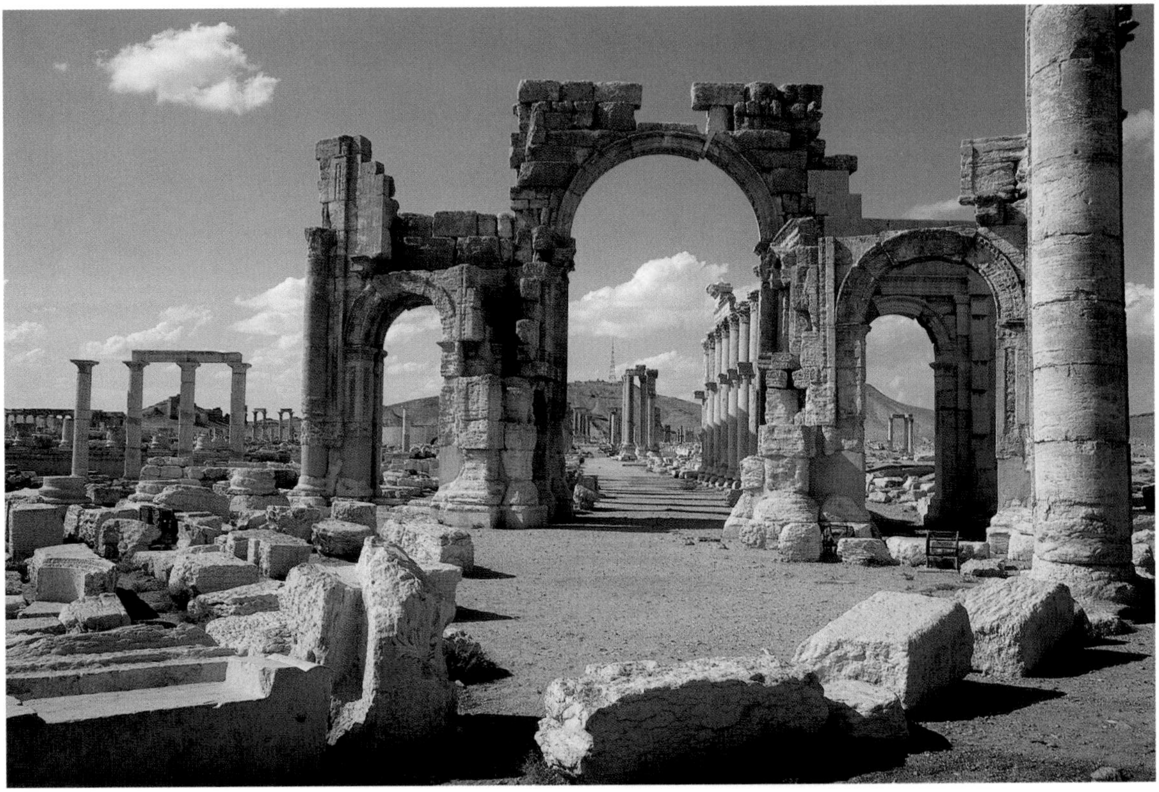

14. The so-called Funerary Temple at Palmyra. In the foreground, the collapsed remains of another monumental tomb.

15. Tower-tombs in the western necropolis at Palmyra. In the distance can be seen the well-preserved tower of Elahbel.

16. The interior of tower 19 in the city wall at Dura Europus. Persian sappers undermined the foundations of the south-western corner during the final siege of the city, but instead of collapsing the wall sank into the mine and remained standing. The finds from the tower were extraordinarily well-preserved, and included horse armour, a painted shield and weapons.

17. The well-preserved interior of the theatre at Bostra. Although built of black basalt, the façade of the *scenae frons* employed contrasting white limestone columns and entablatures.

18. Colonnaded street in Tyre, the chief city of Syria Phoenice. The columns and their capitals are all imported granites and marbles.

19. The north theatre at Jerash.

20. General view of the site of Pella. In the foreground, a late Roman church complex in the civic centre of the ancient city.

21. High Ptolemaic architectural style: the so-called Khazneh or 'Treasury' at Petra.

22. Tombs at Petra. Note the 'Assyrian' merlons on the tops of some of them.

23. General view of the martyrium complex at Qalaat Semaan. The focal point was the large octagon (on the right) which surrounded the pillar of the dead saint. Arranged around this, forming a cross, were four halls, of which two can be seen here. The eastern one (on the left) served as a church; the other three were used as assembly halls for pilgrims.

24. The well-preserved church at Mshabbak in the Jebel Semaan.

25. General view of Serjilla, a village in the Jebel Zawiye. The building to the left in the middle distance is a bath building; the one on the right is thought to be an *andron* (fig. 49) and the two buildings may have been conceived as a single complex. The other buildings are houses.

26. Ruined houses in the village of Jerade on the eastern edge of the Jebel Zawiye. On the left is a small tower.

27. Interior of the Church of the Holy Cross at Resafa.

28. House at Umm al-Jimal. Note the exterior staircase. The economy of this village in the dry steppe was based around raising livestock, and the settlement was under Ghassanid control in the sixth century.

29. Mosaics on the courtyard wall of the Great Mosque of the Umayyads in Damascus.

SELECT BIBLIOGRAPHY AND TEXT NOTES

The following is far from an exhaustive list of relevant publications. Many of the works cited have extensive bibliographies that can be consulted by those who wish to follow up specific topics in more detail.

General

One of the best introductions to the Roman world remains F. Millar's *The Roman Empire and its Neighbours* (London and New York, 2/1981), which approaches the subject from a provincial perspective. Also influential and important: P. Garnsey and R. Saller's *The Roman Empire: Economy, Society and Culture* (London, 1987). A scholarly, succinct and highly readable introduction to the early empire is M. Goodman's *The Roman World, 44 BC–AD 180* (London, 1997). An excellent and detailed introduction to the eastern empire is M. Sartre's *L'Orient romain: Provinces et sociétés provinciales en Méditerranée orientale d'Auguste aux Sévères* (Paris, 1991); and note also the collection of essays in S.E. Alcock (ed.), *The Early Roman Empire in the East* (Oxford, 1997). For the later empire see A.H.M. Jones, *The Later Roman Empire* (Oxford, 1964); P. Brown, *The World of Late Antiquity* (London, 1971); and especially the works by A. Cameron, *The Later Roman Empire (AD 284-430)* (London, 1993) and *The Mediterranean World in Late Antiquity, AD 395-600* (London, 1993). Recent general studies include two books by W. Treadgold, *A History of the Byzantine State and Society* (Stanford, CA, 1997) and *A Concise History of Byzantium* (New York, 2001). Expert essays are to be found in G.W. Bowersock, P. Brown, O. Grabar, *Late Antiquity: A Guide to the Postclassical World* (Cambridge, MA, 1999).

For Syria and the Near East, see in particular F. Millar, *The Roman Near East* (Cambridge, MA, 1993); M. Sartre, *D'Alexandre à Zénobie: Histoire du Levant antique, IVe siècle av. J.-C.- IIIe siècle ap. J.-C.* (Paris, 2001); G. Bowersock, *Roman Arabia* (Cambridge, MA, 1983). These detailed studies should be consulted at the outset by anyone interested in the region. For the south, there is the massive work by E. Schürer, *The History of the Jewish People in the Age of Jesus Christ*, rev. G. Vermes, F. Millar, M. Black, M. Goodman, 3 vols (Edinburgh, 1973-86). Other important studies include M. Sartre, *Trois études sur l'Arabie romaine et byzantine* (Brussels, 1982); D. Kennedy, 'Syria', in A.K. Bowman, E. Chaplin, A. Lintott (eds), *The Cambridge Ancient History*, x (Cambridge, 2/1996), pp. 703-36. An entire volume of the series *Aufstieg und Niedergang der römischen Welt*, ii/8 (Berlin and New York, 1977), is devoted to the region and contains important essays on a wide variety of topics. Likewise J.-M. Dentzer, W. Orthmann (eds.), *Archéologie et histoire de la Syrie, ii: La Syrie de l'époque achéménide à l'avènement de l'Islam* (Saarbrücken, 1989), provides an excellent and authoritative collection of essays on wide-ranging aspects of Hellenistic and Roman Syria, focused on the geographical territory of the modern Syrian Arab Republic. More wide-ranging, and illustrated with spectacular colour photographs, is O. Binst (ed.), *The Levant: History and Archaeology in the Eastern Mediterranean* (Cologne, 1999). A beautifully illustrated account of the Nabataean kingdom and Arabia is provided by J. Taylor, *Petra and the Lost Kingdom of the Nabataeans* (London and New York, 2001).

Older, but still important, works include H.C. Butler *et al., Publications of the American Archaeological Expedition to Syria in 1899-1900* (New York, 1903-14); and H.C. Butler *et al., Publications of the Princeton University Archaeological Expeditions to Syria in 1904-1905 and 1909* (Leiden, 1907-49); and R.E. Brünnow, A. von Domaszewski, *Die Provincia Arabia* (Strasbourg, 1904-9); see also the article by D. Kennedy, 'The Publications of the Princeton University Archaeological Expeditions to Syria in 1904-05 and 1909', *Palestine Exploration Quarterly* (1995), pp. 21-32. These early expeditions studied architecture and inscriptions. The most important source of epigraphic evidence is collected in the series *Inscriptions grecques et latines de la Syrie* (IGLS) of which various volumes have appeared since 1929 (a useful summary of the series is provided by H. MacAdam, 'The IGLS series then and now (1905-89)', *Journal of Roman Archaeology*, iii (1990), pp. 458-64). See also the summary by W. Van Rengen, 'L'épigraphie grecque et latine de la Syrie. Bilan d'un quart de siècle de recherches épigraphiques', *Aufstieg und Niedergang der römischen Welt*, II/8, pp. 31-53. Recently a subsidiary series of IGLS has also been initiated for Jordan, *Inscriptions grecques et latines de la Jordanie* (IGLJ). Other collections include the *Inventaire des inscriptions de Palmyre*, various authors (Beirut, Damascus and Paris, 1930–).

For the visitor to the region, a variety of guidebooks can be found. See, for example, R. Burns, *Monuments of Syria: An Historical Guide* (London and New York, 1992); W. Ball, *Syria: A Historical and Architectural Guide* (Buckhurst Hill, 1994); and S. Rollin, J. Streetly, *Blue Guide: Jordan* (London and New York, 1996). Old but still informative for the traveller are R. Boulanger's *The Middle East: Lebanon-Syria-Jordan-Iraq-Iran*, Hachette World Guides (Paris, 1966), and G. Lankester Harding, *The Antiquities of Jordan* (London, 1967). A highly detailed bibliography of sites is provided by G. Lehmann, *Bibliographie der archäologischen Fundstellen und Surveys in Syrien und Libanon*, Orient-Archäologie Band 9 (Rahden, 2002).

Foreword

p. 9 There are no generally agreed definitions of the chronological limits of terms like 'Roman' or 'Byzantine'. A justification, if one were needed, for extending use of the term 'Roman' down to the seventh century, is provided by D. Olster, 'From Periphery to Center: The Transformation of Late Roman Self-Definition in the Seventh Century', in R.W. Mathisen and H.S. Sivan (eds.), *Shifting Frontiers in Late Antiquity* (Aldershot, 1996), pp. 93-101. See also J. Haldon, *Byzantium in the Seventh Century: the Transformation of a Culture* (Cambridge, 1990). Likewise there is little agreement on how best to subdivide this period. 'Early', 'mid' and 'late' Roman are terms often encountered in archaeological studies, but definitions vary depending on the material and site being studied. I have chosen to circumvent these difficulties by dividing the chronology of the Roman empire into two main periods which seem to reflect two principal fields of scholarship, one focused on the early empire and another on 'late antiquity'.

pp. 9-10 A general concept of '**Syria**' was constructed by R. Dussaud (see, for example, *La Syrie antique et médiévale illustrée*, Paris, 1931), and 'Syria' or 'Roman Syria' is used extensively by modern scholars in a variety of ways, none of which suggests any rigid geographical or ethnic conception. See, for example, the comments by M. Sartre, *D'Alexandre à Zénobie*, pp. 11-12, 35. Modern boundaries do not help: Antioch, the foremost city of Roman Syria, is now in Turkey (but this identity is disputed by the Syrian Arab Republic); a large part of the Hauran is in the present-day state of Syria but for much of the period covered by this book most of it was in the province of Arabia (although the corpus of inscriptions for the city of Bostra is published as a volume in the series IGLS). Nor does the authority of the past provide a definition, because administrative names and boundaries changed. Judaea was part of the province of Syria during the first century but then became a separate province. It was renamed Syria Palaestina in the second century, but by the late Roman period the 'Syria' appellation had been dropped. By the sixth century the only provinces called Syria were two in the northwestern corner of what had been the first-century province of that name. Present-day political aspirations and antagonisms add to the confusion. In Lebanon there are many who want 'Phoenicia' to have a separate past and destiny from Syria, and others who deny the existence of Phoenicia. The region is a battleground for identities, ancient and modern; see, for example, G.W. Bowersock, 'Palestine: Ancient History and Modern Politics', in E.W. Said, C. Hitchens (eds), *Blaming the Victims. Spurious Scholarship and the Palestinian Question* (London, 1988), pp. 181-91.

p. 10 The term '**Fertile Crescent**' was coined by James Breasted (see, for example, his *The Oriental Institute*, Chicago, 1933).

pp. 11-15 For a general **geographical**

overview see the *Tübinger Atlas des Vorderen Orients* (TAVO) (Wiesbaden, 1988); and R.J.A. Talbert (ed.), *Barrington Atlas of the Greek and Roman World* (Princeton and Oxford, 2000). Other important surveys include E. Wirth, *Syrien* (Darmstadt, 1971); D. Kennedy, D. Riley, *Rome's Desert Frontier from the Air* (London, 1990); Y. Tsafrir, L. Di Segni, J. Green, *Tabula Imperii Romani: Iudaea-Palaestina* (Jerusalem, 1994). For **Mesopotamia:** L. Dilleman, *Haute-Mésopotamie orientale et pays adjacents* (Paris, 1962). On **water and human geography:** M. Moussly, *Le problème de l'eau en Syrie* (Lyon, 1951).

pp. 16-17 On the debate between **Hellenism and indigenous identity**, see in particular F. Millar, *The Roman Near East*; and W. Ball, *Rome in the East* (London, 2000). My approaches to the problem have been influenced by: I. Hodder, *Reading the Past. Current Approaches to Interpretation in Archaeology* (Cambridge, 1986); M. Mann, *The Sources of Social Power*, i: *A History of Power from the Beginning to AD 1760* (Cambridge, 1986); S. Swain, *Hellenism and Empire: Language, Classicism and Power in the Greek World, AD 50-250* (Oxford, 1996); I. Morris, *Archaeology as Cultural History* (Oxford, 2002).

Chapter 1: An Incidental Annexation

pp. 19-23 On **Pompey and the annexation:** A.R. Bellinger, 'The End of the Seleucids', *Transactions of the Connecticut Academy of Arts and Sciences*, xxxviii (1949), pp. 51-102; A.N. Sherwin-White, *Roman Foreign Policy in the East, 168 BC to AD 1* (Norman, OK, 1983); P.M.W. Freeman, 'Pompey's Eastern Settlement: A Matter of Presentation?', in C. Deroux (ed.), *Studies in Latin Literature and Roman History vii, Collection Latomus 227* (1994), pp. 143-79. The **political geography of Syria** in 64 BC is described in two works by J.D. Grainger: *The Cities of Seleukid Syria* (Oxford, 1990); and *Hellenistic Phoenicia* (Oxford, 1991). On **Parthian intentions and Roman interpretations**, see K. Butcher, 'A Vast Process: Rome, Parthia, and the Formation of the Eastern "Client" States', *Journal of Roman Archaeology*, vii (1994), pp. 447-53; see also notes to p. 51, below.

pp. 23-4 For the **Achaemenids** see R.N. Frye, *The History of Ancient Iran* (Munich, 1984); J. Wiesehöfer, *Ancient Persia from 550 BC to 650 AD* (London and New York, 1996); P. Briant, *From Cyrus to Alexander: a History of the Persian Empire* (Winona Lake, MN, 2002). For **Achaemenid Syria:** M. Sartre, 'La Syrie sous la domination achéménide', in J.-M. Dentzer, W. Orthmann (eds), *Archéologie et histoire de la Syrie*, ii (Saarbrücken, 1989), pp. 9-18; and his *D'Alexandre à Zénobie*, pp. 35-65; also J.D. Grainger, *The Cities of Seleukid Syria* (Oxford, 1990), pp. 15-30; and for the **Phoenician cities** S. Moscati, *The World of the Phoenicians* (London, 1973); G.E. Markoe, *Phoenicians* (London, 2000); and especially the works of J. Elayi, 'The Phoenician Cities in the Persian Period', *Journal of the Ancient Near Eastern Society of Columbia University*, xii (1980), pp. 13-28; *Recherches sur les cités phéniciennes à l'époque perse* (Naples, 1987); *L'économie des cités phéniciennes sous l'empire perse* (Naples, 1990).

pp. 25-31 **Seleucid and Ptolemaic Syria:** the best general introduction to the Hellenistic world in English is P. Green, *From Alexander to Actium: The Historical Evolution of the Hellenistic Age* (Berkeley and Los Angeles, 1990). For **political history**, see E. Will, *Histoire politique du monde hellénistique*, 2 vols (Nancy, 1972-89). An excellent and detailed **synthesis of Hellenistic Syria** is to be found in M. Sartre's *D'Alexandre à Zénobie*, pp. 67-433; note also an essay by the same author on the same subject, 'La Syrie à l'époque hellénistique', in J.-M. Dentzer, W. Orthmann (eds), *Archéologie et histoire de la Syrie*, ii (Saarbrücken, 1989), pp. 31-44. For the **Seleucids** in general, see A. Kuhrt, S. Sherwin-White (eds), *Hellenism in the East* (London, 1987) (in which note the chapter by F. Millar, 'The Problem of Hellenistic Syria'); and S. Sherwin-White, A. Kuhrt, *From Samarkhand to Sardis: A New Approach to the Seleucid Empire* (London, 1993). For **Ptolemaic Syria and Palestine:** R.S. Bagnall, *The Administration of Ptolemaic Possessions outside Egypt* (Leiden, 1979). For the lack of Ptolemaic development, see D. Graf, 'Hellenisation and the Decapolis', *Aram*, iv (1992), pp. 1-48.

p. 26 In using terms like '**the model of the Greek polis**' or 'Greek-style city state' I am not proposing that some sort of rigid blueprint was imposed on every city of the region, or that every city was a carbon-copy of democratic Athens in the fifth century BC. Nor does evidence for the adoption of Greek institutions necessarily mean that the population was essentially 'Hellenized'. It is clear that, as in so many other spheres of social life in the region, there were local variations on the general theme of the Greek *polis*. Note the comments by D. Graf, above, notes to pp. 25-31. See also P. Leriche, 'Urbanisme défensif et occupation du territoire en Syrie hellénistique', in E. Frézouls (ed.), *Sociétés urbaines, sociétés rurales dans l'Asie Mineure et la Syrie hellénistiques et romaines* (Strasbourg, 1987). For Seleucid urbanism, see the essays by H. Seyrig, 'Séleucos I et la fondation de la monarchie syrienne', *Syria*, xlvii (1970), pp. 290-311; 'Seleucus I and the Foundation of Hellenistic Syria', in H. Seyrig, *Scripta Varia: Mélanges d'archéologie et d'histoire* (Paris, 1985), pp. 335-46; the works by J.D. Grainger, *The Cities of Seleukid Syria* (Oxford, 1990) and *Hellenistic Phoenicia* (Oxford, 1991).

pp. 28-9 For the **final decline of the Seleucids** see in particular A.R. Bellinger, 'The End of the Seleucids' *Transactions of the Connecticut Academy of Arts and Sciences* 38 (1949), pp. 51-102, and R.D. Sullivan, *Near Eastern Royalty and Rome, 100-30 BC* (Toronto, 1990). **Concessions of independence to cities:** but note that this did not always mean total independence, as kings sometimes minted coins in these 'autonomous' cities.

p. 30 The evidence for the **growth of Seleucid cities** in the second century BC has not yet been synthesized, but can be detected at various sites such as Antioch, Berytus and Dura-Europus. See P. Leriche, 'Le Chréophylakeion de Doura-Europos et la mise en place du plan hippodamien de la ville', *Archives, Seals and Sealings in the Hellenistic World, Bulletin de correspondance Hellénique*, xxx

(1993), pp. 157-69. The **expansion of Berytus:** D. Perring, 'Excavations in the Souks of Beirut', *Berytus*, xliii (1997-8), pp. 9-34. **Demonetization of Ptolemaic coinage:** K. Butcher, 'Small Change in Ancient Beirut: The Coin Finds from BEY 006 and BEY 045', *Berytus*, xlv-xlvi (2001-2 (2003)), forthcoming.

p. 30-31 A general overview of **pottery in the Seleucid empire** is provided by L. Hannestad, *Ikaros: The Hellenistic Settlements*, ii/2: *The Hellenistic Pottery from Failaka. With a Survey of Hellenistic Pottery in the Near East* (Århus, 1983).

p. 31 The **Seleucids as an 'interlude':** J. Wiesehöfer, *Ancient Persia*, pp. 103-14.

Chapter 2: Rome, Syria, Parthia and Persia

For **Syria and the Near East in the early Roman period**, Fergus Millar's *The Roman Near East* is an indispensable source for the period from Augustus to Constantine. Likewise G. Bowersock, *Roman Arabia* (Cambridge, MA, 1983), and the monumental study by M. Sartre, *D'Alexandre à Zénobie* (Paris, 2001). The articles by J.-P. Rey-Coquais, 'Syrie romaine, de Pompée à Dioclétien', *Journal of Roman Studies*, lxviii (1978), pp. 44-73, and 'La Syrie, de Pompée à Dioclétien: histoire politique et administrative', in J.-M. Dentzer, W. Orthmann (eds), *Archéologie et histoire de la Syrie*, ii (Saarbrücken, 1989), pp. 45-61, are also essential for this period. A good overview in English is that provided by D. Kennedy, 'The East', in J. Wacher (ed.), *The Roman World* (London, 1990), i, pp. 266-308. Excellent discussions of **third-century history** are to be found in D.S. Potter, *Prophecy and History in the Crisis of the Roman Empire: A Historical Commentary on the Thirteenth Sibylline Oracle* (Oxford, 1990); and M. Christol, *L'empire romain du IIIe siècle: Histoire politique, 192-325 après J.-C.* (Paris, 1997). See also J. Eadie, 'One Hundred Years of Rebellion: the Eastern Army in Politics, AD 175-272', in D. Kennedy (ed.), *The Roman Army in the East* (Ann Arbor, 1996). For the **late Roman period** see M.H. Dodgeon, S.N.C. Lieu, *The Roman Eastern Frontier and the Persian Wars, AD 226-363: A Documentary History* (London, 1991) and its companion volume G. Greatrex, S.N.C. Lieu, *The Roman Eastern Frontiers and the Persian Wars*, ii: AD 363-630. A Narrative Sourcebook (London and New York, 2002); R.C. Blockley, *East Roman Foreign Policy, Formation and Conduct from Diocletian to Anastasius* (Leeds, 1992); G. Greatrex, *Rome and Persia at War, 502-532* (Leeds, 1998). See also the essay by G. Tate, 'La Syrie à l'époque byzantine: Essai de synthèse', in J.-M. Dentzer, W. Orthmann (eds), *Archéologie et histoire de la Syrie*, ii, pp. 97-116. For Rome's relations with the **Arabs**, see in particular the works of I. Shahid (below, notes to pp. 64-6 and 378). For **Armenia:** M.-L. Chaumont, 'L'Arménie entre Rome et Iran', *Aufstieg und Niedergang der römischen Welt*, xii/1 (1976), pp. 71-193. Sources for the **seventh century** are gathered together with a splendid commentary in A. Palmer, S. Brock, R. Hoyland, *The Seventh Century in the West-Syrian Chronicles* (Liverpool, 1993).

p. 32 For the debate about **Parthian and**

Sasanian ideology and empire, and the threat posed to Roman Syria: E. Dabrowa, *La politique de l'état parthe à l'égard de Rome* (Cracow, 1983); D.S. Potter, 'Alexander Severus and Ardashir', *Mesopotamia*, xxii (1987), pp. 147-57; B. Isaac, *The Limits of Empire* (Oxford, 1990, rev. 1992). For the **size of the Roman armies**, see Kennedy and Riley, *Rome's Desert Frontier* (London, 1990), pp. 43-4.

p. 33-5 For the **Parthians and Parthian history**, see N.C. Debevoise, *A Political History of Parthia* (Chicago, 1938); *The Cambridge History of Iran*, iii/1-2 (Cambridge, 1983); R.N. Frye, *The History of Ancient Iran* (Munich, 1984); M.A.R. Colledge, *The Parthians* (London, 1967); G. Hermann, *The Iranian Revival* (Oxford, 1977); J. Wolski, *L'empire des Arsacides*, Acta Iranica, 32 (1993); J. Wiesehöfer, *Ancient Persia from 550 BC to 650 AD* (London and New York, 1996). For **Roman relations with the Parthians** in the republican period: A. Keaveney, 'The King and the War Lords: Romano-Parthian Relations *c*. 64-53 BC', *American Journal of Philology*, ciii (1982), pp. 412-28.

p. 34 The **caution of Parthian kings**: D. Kennedy, 'Parthia and Rome: Eastern Perspectives', in D. Kennedy (ed.), *The Roman Army in the East* (Ann Arbor, 1996), pp. 67-90.

p. 35 **Culture change in the Parthian kingdom:** G. Hermann, *The Iranian Revival*, pp. 53-56.

p. 37 **Coins of Labienus and Pacorus:** K. Butcher, *Coinage in Roman Syria* (London, 2003), pp. 27, 49, 95.

pp. 40-41 For **Germanicus in Syria**, new epigraphic evidence has arisen in the form of the *senatus consultum de Cn. Pisone patre*, published by W. Eck, A. Caballos, F. Fernández, *Das Senatus Consultum de Cn Pisone Patre* (Munich, 1996); an English translation of this important document is provided by D.S. Potter, 'Senatus consultum de Cn. Pisone', *Journal of Roman Archaeology*, xi (1998), pp. 437-57. For **Corbulo**: M. Hammond, 'Corbulo and Nero's Eastern Policy', *Harvard Studies in Classical Philology*, xlv (1934), pp. 81-104.

pp. 41-2 For the **Jewish revolt** and the **Jewish elites**, see especially M. Goodman, *The Ruling Class of Judaea* (Cambridge, 1987).

p. 42 The **imperial portrait on coinage**: see A. Burnett, M. Amandry, P.P. Ripollès, *Roman Provincial Coinage*, i (London and Paris, 1992).

pp. 43-4 **Flavian consolidation**: G. Bowersock, 'Syria under Vespasian', *Journal of Roman Studies*, lxiii (1973), pp. 123-9; D. van Berchem, 'Le port de Séleucie de Piérie et l'infrastructure navale des guerres parthiques', *Bonner Jahrbücher*, clxxxv (1985), pp. 47-8.

p. 44 **Roman presence at Jauf**: M.P. Speidel, 'The Roman Road to Dumatha (Jawf in Saudi Arabia) and the Frontier Strategy of the *Praetensio Colligare*', *Historia*, xxxvi (1987), pp. 211-21; T. Bauzou, 'La praetensio de Bostra à Dumata (el-Jowf)', *Syria*, lxxiii (1996), pp. 23-35.

pp. 44-6 **Arabia**: G.W. Bowersock, 'A Report on Arabia Provincia', *Journal of Roman Studies*, lxi (1971), pp. 219-42. The reasons for the Roman annexation are unknown. Perhaps Trajan considered Rabbel II's successor unsatisfactory. See J.W. Eadie, 'Artifacts of Annexation: Trajan's Grand Strategy and Arabia', in *The Craft of the Ancient Historian: Essays in Honor of Chester G. Starr* (Washington, DC, 1985), pp. 407-23; M. Sartre, *Bostra: Des origines à l'Islam* (Paris, 1985), pp. 63-72; P. Freeman, 'The Annexation of Arabia and Imperial Grand Strategy', in D. Kennedy (ed.), *The Roman Army in the East* (Ann Arbor, 1996), pp. 91-118. **Trajan's Parthian war**: the standard reference is F.A. Lepper, *Trajan's Parthian War* (London, 1948). See also J. Guey, *Essai sur la guerre parthique (114-117)* (Bucharest, 1937); A. Maricq, 'La province d'Assyrie créée par Trajan', *Syria*, xxxvi (1959), pp. 254-63; C.S. Lightfoot, 'Trajan's Parthian War and the Fourth-Century Perspective', *Journal of Roman Studies*, lxxx (1990), pp. 115-26; J. Bennet, *Trajan. Optimus Princeps: A Life and Times* (London, 1997).

p. 46 **Characene** and its recapture by the Parthians: D. Schlumberger, 'Palmyre et la Mésène', *Syria*, xxxviii (1961), pp. 258-60; R. Black, 'The History of Parthia and Characene in the 2nd Century AD', *Sumer*, xliii (1984), pp. 230-34; G. Bowersock, 'La Mésène (Maisan) antonine', in T. Fahd (ed.), *L'Arabie préislamique et son environnement historique et culturel* (Leiden, 1989), pp. 159-68; D.S. Potter, 'The Inscription on the Bronze Herakles from Mesene: Vologeses IV's War with Rome and the Date of Tacitus' Annales', *Zeitschrift für Papyrologie und Epigraphik*, lxxxviii (1991), pp. 277-90. The **Bar-Kokhba** war: Y. Yadin, *Bar-Kokhba* (London, 1971); S. Applebaum, *Prolegomena to the Study of the Second Jewish Revolt* (Oxford, 1979); L. Mildenberg, *The Coinage of the Bar Kokhba War* (Aarau, 1984); W. Eck, 'The Bar Kokhba Revolt: the Roman Point of View', *Journal of Roman Studies*, lxxxix (1999), pp. 76-89, suggesting that the revolt was more widespread. For Hadrian commanding the war, see F. Millar, *The Roman Near East*, p. 107.

pp. 46-7 **Lucius Verus' Parthian war**: C.H. Dodd, 'Chronology of the Eastern Campaigns of the Emperor Lucius Verus', *Numismatic Chronicle* (1911), pp. 209-67; A. Birley, *Marcus Aurelius: A Biography* (London, 1987), pp. 184-9. **Avidius Cassius**: M.L. Astarita, *Avidio Cassio* (Rome, 1983).

p. 48 **Septimius Severus' Parthian wars**: Z. Rubin, 'Dio, Herodian, and Severus' Second Parthian War', *Chiron*, v (1975), pp. 419-41; A. Birley, *The African Emperor: Septimius Severus* (London, 1988). **Boundary stone of Osrhoene**: J. Wagner, 'Provincia Osrhoenae: New Archaeological Finds Illustrating the Military Organization under the Severan Dynasty', in S. Mitchell (ed.), *Armies and Frontiers in Roman and Byzantine Anatolia* (Oxford, 1983), pp. 103-30. **Siege of Hatra**: Z. Rubin (above); D.B. Campbell, 'What Happened at Hatra? The Problems of the Severan Siege Operations', in P. Freemen, D. Kennedy (eds), *The Defence of the Roman and Byzantine East* (Oxford, 1986), pp. 51-8. On **Severus and the east** see D. Kennedy, 'The Frontier Policy of Septimius Severus: New Evidence from Arabia', in S. Mitchell (ed.), *Armies and Frontiers in Roman and Byzantine Anatolia* (Oxford, 1983), pp. 879-88. **Cassius Dio on Mesopotamia**: 75.3.

p. 49 **Severus and Antioch**: R. Ziegler, 'Antiochia, Laodicea und Sidon in der Politik der Severer', *Chiron*, viii (1978), pp. 493-514.

p. 51 **Dura Europus receives a Parthian envoy**: M.-L. Chaumont, 'Un document méconnu concernant l'envoi d'un ambassadeur Parthe vers Septime Sévere (P. Dura 60 B)', *Historia*, xxxvi (1987), pp. 422-47. **Sasanian attitudes towards the Roman east**: E. Yarshater, 'Were the Sassanians Heirs to the Achaemenids?', in *La Persia nel Medioevo: Rome, 1970* (Rome, 1971), pp. 517-31; D.S. Potter, 'Alexander Severus and Ardashir', *Mesopotamia*, xxii (1987), pp. 147-57.

pp. 51-3 The **Sasanians**: G. Hermann, *The Iranian Revival* (Oxford, 1977); *The Cambridge History of Iran*, iii; R.N. Frye, *The History of Ancient Iran* (Munich, 1984); J. Wiesehöfer, *Ancient Persia from 550 BC to 650 AD* (London and New York, 1996).

p. 53 **Coins of Vologaeses VI**: D. Sellwood, *An Introduction to the Coinage of Parthia*, London, 1971, p. 290 and no. 88/16.

pp. 53-5 For the history of this period, see especially D.S. Potter, *Prophecy and History in the Crisis of the Roman Empire: A Historical Commentary on the Thirteenth Sibylline Oracle* (Oxford, 1990). For **Uranius Antoninus**: R. Delbrueck, 'Uranius of Emesa', *Numismatic Chronicle* (1948), pp. 11-29; H. Seyrig, 'Uranius Antonin: une question d'authenticité', *Revue numismatique* (1958), pp. 51-7; and H.R. Baldus, *Uranius Antoninus. Münzprägung und Geschichte* (Bonn, 1971). For the **Sasanian attack on Syria**: E. Honigmann, A. Maricq, *Recherches sur les Res Gestae Divi Saporis* (Brussels, 1953); E. Kettenhofen, *Die römischpersischen Kriege des 3. Jahrhunderts n. Chr.* (Wiesbaden, 1982); E. Winter, *Die sasanidischrömischen Friedensverträge des 3. Jahrhunderts n. Chr.* (Frankfurt am Main, 1988).

pp. 55-8 The **middle Euphrates:** see two works by M. Gawlikowski, 'Palmyre et l'Euphrate', *Syria*, xl (1983), pp. 53-68; and 'The Roman Frontier on the Euphrates', *Mesopotamia*, xxii (1987), pp. 77-80. For geography and place names, see A. Musil, *The Middle Euphrates* (New York, 1927); M.-L. Chaumont, 'Etudes d'histoire Parthe v. La route royale des Parthes de Zeugma à Séleucie du Tigre d'après l'itinéraire d'Isodore de Charax', *Syria*, lxi (1984), pp. 63-107. On **'Ana**, see: A. Northedge, A. Bamber, M. Roaf, *Excavations at 'Ana: Qal'a Island* (Warminster, 1988). For **Kifrin**, see: A. Invernizzi, 'Kifrin and the Euphrates *limes*', in P. Freeman and D. Kennedy (eds), *The Defence of the Roman and Byzantine East* (Oxford, 1986), pp. 357-81; E. Valtz, 'Kifrin, a fortress of the limes on the Euphrates', *Mesopotamia*, xxii (1987), pp. 81-90. For **Bijan**: M. Gawlikowski, 'L'île de Bidjan sur le moyen Euphrate: une forteresse assyrienne et romaine', *Archéologia*, 178 (May 1983), pp. 26-33; 'Began Island', *Archiv für Orientforschung*, xxix-xxx (1984), p. 207; 'Bijan in the Euphrates', *Sumer*, xlii (1985), pp. 15-21. **Brittle ware pottery**: S.L. Dyson, *Excavations at Dura-Europos, Final Report, iv/i.3: The Common Pottery. The Brittle Ware* (New Haven, 1968). On the **fall of Dura**: S. James, 'Dura-Europos and the Chronology of Syria in the 250s AD', *Chiron*, xv (1985), pp. 111-24; D. MacDonald, 'Dating the Fall of Dura-Europos', *Historia*, xxxv (1986), pp. 45-68; and, on the question of whether there was a Sasanian occupation of Dura, F. Grenet, 'Les Sassanides à Doura-Europos (253 ap. J.-C.)', in P.-L. Gatier, B. Helly, J.-P. Rey-Coquais (below, notes to pp. 108-21), pp. 133-58. For the **Roman alliance with Hatra**: D. Oates, 'A Note on Three Latin Inscriptions from Hatra', *Sumer*, xi (1955), pp. 39-43; A. Maricq, 'Classica et Orientalia, 2: Les dernières années de Hatra. L'alliance romaine', *Syria*, xxxiv (1957), pp. 288-96; M.-L. Chaumont, 'A propos de la chute de Hatra et du couronnement de Shapur Ier', *Acta Antiqua Academiae Scientiarum Hungaricae*, xxvii (1979), pp. 207-37.

pp. 58-60 **Palmyra**: E. Will, 'Le sac de Palmyre', in *Mélanges André Piganiol* (Paris, 1966), pp. 1409-16; L. de Blois, 'Odenathus and the Roman-Persian War of 252-64 AD', *Talanta*, vi (1975), pp. 7-23; R. Stoneman, *Palmyra and its Empire: Zenobia's Revolt against Rome* (Ann Arbor, 1994); E. Equini Schneider, *Septimia Zenobia Sebaste* (Rome, 1993); U. Hartmann, *Das palmyrenische Teilreich* (Stuttgart, 2001).

p. 58 The **career and family of Odaenathus**: M. Gawlikowski, 'Les princes de Palmyre', *Syria*, lxii (1985), pp. 251-61; D.S. Potter, 'Palmyra and Rome: Odaenathus' Titulature and the Use of *Imperium Maius*', *Zeitschrift für Papyrologie und Epigraphik*, cxiii (1996), pp. 271-85.

p. 59 **Roman and Sasanian goods in the Gulf**: D.T. Potts, 'The Roman Relations with the Persicus sinus from the Rise of Spasinou Charax (127 BC) to the Reign of Shapur II (AD 309-379)', in S.E. Alcock (ed.), *The Early Roman Empire in the East* (Oxford, 1997), pp. 89-107. The **Baths of Diocletian**: An inscription refers to such a building: see H. Seyrig, 'Antiquités syriennes, 2: Notes épigraphiques', *Syria*, xii (1931), p. 321, no. IV. For the suggestion that it was a palace, see R. Fellman, 'Der Palast der Königin Zenobia', in E.M. Ruprechtsberger (ed.), *Palmyra: Geschichte, Kunst und Kultur der syrischen Oasenstadt* (Linz, 1987), pp. 131-6.

pp. 61-4 The **Tetrarchy and Constantine**: T. Barnes, *The New Empire of Diocletian and Constantine* (Harvard, 1982); T. Barnes, 'Imperial Campaigns, AD 285-311', *Phoenix*, xxx (1976), pp. 174-93. For the **treaty between Narseh and the Romans**: E. Winter, 'On the Regulation of the Eastern Frontier of the Roman Empire in 298', in D.H. French, C.S. Lightfoot, *The Eastern Frontier of the Roman Empire* (Oxford, 1989). **Constantine's eastern plans**: T.D. Barnes, 'Constantine and the Christians of Persia', *Journal of Roman Studies*, lxxv (1985), pp. 126-36. **Constantius II**: B.H. Warmington, 'Objectives and Strategy in the Persian War of Constantius II', in J. Fitz (ed.), *Limes. Acts of the XI Limes Congress, 1976* (Budapest, 1977), pp. 509-20.

pp. 64-6 The **federate Arabs**: see three major works by I. Shahid, *Byzantium and the Arabs in the Fourth Century* (Washington, DC, 1984); *Byzantium and the Arabs in the Fifth Century* (Washington, DC, 1989); *Byzantium and the Arabs in the Sixth Century* (Washington, DC, 1995); also M. Sartre, *Trois études sur l'Arabie* (Brussels, 1982), pp. 121-203; and for differing views on the nomad menace, S.T. Parker, *Romans and Saracens: A History of the Arabian Frontier* (Winona Lake, MN, 1986); D.

Graf, 'Rome and the Saracens: Reassessing the Nomadic Menace', in T. Fahd (ed.), *L'Arabie préislamique et son environnement historique et culturel* (Leiden, 1989), pp. 341-400; B. Isaac, *The Limits of Empire: The Roman Army in the East* (Oxford, 1992). Note also D. Graf, M. O'Connor, 'The Origin of the Term Saracen and the Rawwafah Inscriptions', *Byzantine Studies*, iv (1977), pp. 52-66. Strictly speaking many of these 'Saracen' groups were 'allies' rather than federates, but I have not made that distinction here. On **Imru' al-Qays**, see H.I. MacAdam, 'The Nemara Inscription: Some Historical Considerations', *Al Abhath*, xxviii (1980), pp. 31-46; J.A. Bellamy, 'A New Reading of the Namarah Inscription', *Journal of the American Oriental Society*, cv (1985), pp. 31-48. On **Mavia**, see P. Mayerson, 'Mavia, Queen of the Saracens – A Cautionary Note', *Israel Exploration Journal*, xxx (1980), pp. 164-72; G.W. Bowersock, 'Mavia, Queen of the Saracens', *Studien zur antiken Sozialgeschichte: Festschrift F. Vittinghoff*, Kölner historische Abhandlungen 28 (1980), pp. 477-95. Her tribe may have been the Tanukh.

p. 66 **Division of Armenia**: R.C. Blockley, 'The Division of Armenia between the Romans and the Persians at the End of the Fourth Century AD', *Historia*, xxxvi (1987), pp. 222-34.

p. 67 **Protecting the Caspian Gates**: the evidence for Roman subsidies and a joint strategy is equivocal. For various views, see R.C. Blockley, 'Subsidies and Diplomacy: Rome and Persia in Late Antiquity', *Phoenix*, xxxix (1985), pp. 62-74; and Z. Rubin, 'Diplomacy and War in the Relations between Byzantium and the Sassanids in the Fifth Century AD', in P. Freeman, D. Kennedy (eds), *The Defence of the Roman and Byzantine East* (Oxford, 1986), pp. 677-95. **Huns**: see Greatrex and Lieu, *The Roman Eastern Frontier and the Persian Wars*, pp. 17-19.

p. 68 **Amorcesus**: Shahid, *Byzantium and the Arabs in the Fifth Century* (above, notes to pp. 64-6), pp. 59-81; P. Mayerson, 'The Island of Iotabe in the Byzantine Sources: A Reprise', *Bulletin of the American Schools of Oriental Research*, 287 (1992), pp. 1-4; D.G. Letsios, 'The Case of Amorkesos and the Question of Roman foederati in Arabia in the Vth century', in T. Fahd (ed.), *L'Arabie préislamique et son environnement historique et culturel* (Leiden, 1989), pp. 525-38.

pp. 68-71 For a history of this period, see M. Sartre, *Trois études sur l'Arabie*; G. Greatrex, *Rome and Persia at War, 502-532* (Leeds, 1998).

pp. 69-70 The **war under Anastasius**: Greatrex and Lieu, *The Roman Eastern Frontier*, pp. 62-77.

p. 70 The **Kindites**: M. Sartre, *Trois études*, pp. 155-62; C. Robin, 'Le royaume Hujride, dit "Royaume de Kinda" entre Himyar et Byzance', *Comptes rendus de l'Académie des inscriptions et belles-lettres* (1996), pp. 665-714.

pp. 70-71 The **Ghassanids**: Shahid, *Byzantium and the Arabs in the Sixth Century* (Washington, DC, 1995), pp. 95-124.

p. 71 **Sergiopolis**: see below, notes to pp. 266-9.

p. 73 **Roman weakness**: J.H.G.W. Liebeschuetz, 'The Defences of Syria in the Sixth Century', in C.B. Ruger (ed.), *Studien zu den Militärgrenzen Roms II* (Cologne, 1977), pp.

487-99. **Justinian's coinage in Palestine and Arabia**: P.J. Casey, 'Justinian, the *limitanei*, and Arab-Byzantine Relations in the 6th c.', *Journal of Roman Archaeology*, ix (1996), pp. 214-22.

pp. 75-6 **Maurice**: see in particular M. Whitby, *The Emperor Maurice and his Historian* (Oxford, 1988).

pp. 76-7 **Persian invasion**: M. Morony, 'Syria under the Persians, 610-29', in M.A. Bakhit (ed.), *Proceedings of the Second Symposium on the History of Bilad al-Sham during the Early Islamic Period up to 40 AH/ 640 AD* (Amman, 1987), i, pp. 87-95; J. Russell, 'The Persian Invasions of Syia/Palestine and Asia Minor in the Reign of Heraclius: Archaeological and Numismatic Evidence', in E. Kontoura-Galake (ed.), *The Dark Centuries of Byzantium (7th-9th c.)* (Athens, 2001), pp. 41-71; Greatrex and Lieu, *The Roman Eastern Frontier*, pp. 183-97.

Chapter 3: Political Entities

On Government in general: A.H.M. Jones, *The Later Roman Empire* (Oxford, 1964); F. Millar, *The Roman Empire and its Neighbours* (New York, 1981); P. Garnsey, R. Saller, *The Roman Empire: Economy, Society and Culture* (London, 1987); F. Millar, *The Emperor in the Roman World (31 BC–AD 337)* (London, 2/1992); A.W. Lintott, *Imperium Romanum: Politics and Administration* (London, 1993).

p. 79 Luke 2:2 ('And this taxing was first made when Cyrenius was governor of Syria'). 'Cyrenius' is presumably P. Suplicius *Quirinius*, who was governor in AD 6 and supervised the deposition of Herod's son Archelaus and the imposition of direct rule over Judaea; he also supervised a census in Syria (below, notes to p. 106). However in the Gospels the birth of Jesus is set in the kingdom of Herod, who died in 4 BC. It is unlikely that the Romans would have conducted a census in the kingdom of a 'client' ruler, which was politically separate from the province.

pp. 80-82 **Number of officials for the entire empire**: P. Garnsey, R. Saller, *The Roman Empire*, pp. 20-26. **Governors**: In general, see B.E. Thomasson, *Legatus: Beiträge zur römischen Verwaltungsgeschichte* (Stockholm, 1991). For the governors of Syria and other Near Eastern provinces, see J.-P. Rey-Coquais, 'Syrie romaine, de Pompée à Dioclétien', *Journal of Roman Studies*, lxviii (1978), pp. 44-73, at pp. 61-7; B.E. Thomasson, *Laterculi praesidum*, 3 vols (Göteborg, 1984-90); E. Dabrowa, *The Governors of Roman Syria from Augustus to Septimius Severus* (Bonn, 1998); M. Sartre, *Trois études sur l'Arabie* (Brussels, 1982), pp. 77-120; G. Bowersock, *Roman Arabia* (Cambridge, MA, 1983), pp. 161-3. See also J. Martindale et al., *The Prosopography of the Later Roman Empire*, 3 vols (Cambridge, 1971-3).

p. 81 **Tiberius' governor:** L. Aelius Lamia (Tacitus, *Annals*, 6.27.2). **Germanicus and Piso:** see notes to pp. 40-41.

pp. 82-7 the **division of the provinces** is discussed in many of the general works listed in chapter 2, to which add E. Kettenhofen, 'Zur Nordgrenze der Provincia Arabiae im 3. Jahrhundert n. Chr.', *Zeitschrift des Deutschen Palästina-Vereins*, xcvii (1981), pp. 62-73; T.

Barnes, *The New Empire of Diocletian and Constantine* (Harvard, 1982); E. Dabrowa, 'The Frontier in Syria in the First Century AD', in P. Freeman, D. Kennedy (eds), *The Defence of the Roman and Byzantine East* (Oxford, 1986), pp. 93-108; M. Sartre, *Trois études*, chapter 1; J. Balty, J.-Ch. Balty, 'L'Apamène antique et les limites de la Syria Secunda', in T. Fahd (ed.), *La géographie administrative et politique d'Alexandre à Mahomet: Colloque de Strasbourg 1979* (1983), pp. 41-75.

p. 83 **Village of the lord**: D. Feissel, J. Gascou, 'Documents d'archives romains inédits du Moyen Euphrate' (below, notes to pp. 142-5), at p. 541.

pp. 83-4 **Judaea**: F. Millar, *The Roman Near East*, pp. 44-8. **Arabia**: G. Bowersock, *Roman Arabia*, pp. 76-89; Millar, *The Roman Near East*, pp. 92-9. **Syria Palaestina**: Millar, *The Roman Near East*, pp. 108, 374. **Boundaries of Syria Coele and Phoenice**: J.-P. Rey-Coquais, *Arados et sa Pérée aux époques grecque, romaine et byzantine* (Paris, 1974), p. 120.

p. 85 **Diocletian**: T. Barnes (above, notes to pp. 82-7).

p. 86-7 **Late Roman civil administration**: A.H.M. Jones, *The Later Roman Empire*; J.H.W.G. Liebeschuetz, *Antioch: City and Imperial Administration in the Later Roman Empire* (Oxford, 1972).

pp. 87-98 **Client states**: The standard work in English is D. Braund, *Rome and the Friendly King* (London, 1983). I have chosen to maintain the terms 'client kings', 'client states', inadequate though these are. The essays by R.D. Sullivan in *Aufstieg und Niedergang der römischen Welt*, ii/8: 'The Dynasty of Commagene' (pp. 732-63), 'The Dynasty of Emesa' (pp. 198-219) and 'The Dynasty of Judaea in the First Century' (pp. 296-354), cover the relevant dynasties in detail. Sullivan's book *Near Eastern Royalty and Rome, 100-30 BC* (Toronto, 1990), deals with the Republican period. Other works on these states include, for **Commagene**: F. K. Dörner, *Kommagene: Ein wiederentdecktes Königreich* (Gundholzen, 1971); D.H. French, 'Commagene: Territorial Definitions', *Asia Minor Studien 3* (Bonn, 1991), pp. 11-19; **Emesa**: C. Chad, *Les dynastes d'Émèse* (Beirut, 1972); the **Ituraeans**: E. Schürer, *A History of the Jewish People*, i (Edinburgh, 1973), Appendix I, 'History of Chalcis, Ituraea and Abilene', pp. 561-73; J. Starcky, 'Arca du Liban', *Les Cahiers de l'Oronte* (1971/2), pp. 103-17; G. Schmitt, 'Zum Königreich Chalkis', *Zeitschrift des Deutschen Palästina-Vereins*, xcviii (1982), pp. 110-24; W. Schottroff, 'Die Ituräer', *ibid.*, pp. 125-52. Literature on the **Herodians** is extensive. See in particular Schürer, i; A.H.M. Jones, *The Herods of Judaea* (Oxford, 1938); and N. Kokkinos, *The Herodian Dynasty: Origins, Role in Society and Eclipse* (Sheffield, 1998). On the **Nabataeans**: P.C. Hammond, *The Nabataeans, their History, Culture and Archaeology* (Göteborg, 1973); A. Negev, 'The Nabataeans and the Provincia Arabia', *Aufstieg und Niedergang der römischen Welt*, ii/8 (1977), pp. 520-686; G.W. Bowersock, 'A Report on Arabia Provincia', *Journal of Roman Studies*, lxi (1971), pp. 219-42.

pp. 89-90 **Agrippa inscription**: J.-P. Rey-Coquais, 'Inscriptions grecques d'Apamée', *Les Annales archéologiques arabes syriennes*, xxiii (1973), pp. 39-84. For the **Rabbaeans** or **Rhambei**, see M.G. Astour, *The Rabbeans: A Tribal Society on the Euphrates from Yahdun-Lim to Julius Caesar*, Syro-Mesopotamian Studies 2/i (January 1978). For the **eras of Chalcis and Samosata**: K. Butcher, *Coinage in Roman Syria*, London, 2003, pp. 435, 467. For **Osrhoene and Edessa**, see F. Millar, *The Roman Near East*, pp. 472-81; S.K. Ross, *Roman Edessa: Politics and Culture on the Eastern Fringes of the Roman Empire, 114-242 CE* (London, 2001).

p. 91 **Antiochus IV's possessions**: R.D. Sullivan, 'The Dynasty of Commagene' (see notes to pp. 87-98 above). On the **acquisition of part of Armenia**: Tacitus, *Annals*, 14.26.1.

p. 92 **Arethusa inscription**: L. Jalabert, R. Mouterde, C. Mondésert, *IGLS*, v: *Émésène* (Paris, 1959), no. 2085. Recent excavation at **Homs**: P.-L. Gatier (below, notes to pp. 108-21, under Emesa). **Tomb inscription**: L. Jalabert, R. Mouterde, C. Mondésert (above), no. 2212. **Connections between the royal dynasty and later historical figures**: F. Millar, *The Roman Near East*, pp. 303.

p. 93 Location of **Chalcis**: E. Will, 'Un vieux problème de la topographie de la Beqâ' antique: Chalcis du Liban', *Zeitschrift des Deutschen Palästina-Vereins*, xcix (1982), pp. 141-6.

p. 94 **Military activity against the Ituraeans of Mount Lebanon**: An inscription outlining the career of Q. Aemilius Secundus refers to this: H. Dessau, *Inscriptiones Latinae Selectae* (Berlin, 1892), i, no. 2683.

pp. 98-108 **Cities**: In general see A.H.M. Jones, *The Cities of the Eastern Roman Provinces* (Oxford, 1971); J.D. Grainger, *The Cities of Seleukid Syria* (Oxford, 1990); M. Sartre, *L'Orient romain* (Paris, 1991), pp. 335-55; *D'Alexandre à Zénobie* (Paris, 2001), pp. 639-733; and the essays in E. Frézouls (ed.), *Sociétés urbaines, sociétés rurales dans l'Asie Mineure et la Syrie hellénistiques et romaines* (Strasbourg, 1987) (including the editor's own, 'Du village à la ville: Problèmes de l'urbanisation dans la Syrie hellénistique et romaine', pp. 81-93). **Regional studies**: A.H.M. Jones, 'The Urbanization of the Ituraean Principality', *Journal of Roman Studies*, xxi (1931), pp. 265-75; A. Segal, 'Roman Cities in the Province of Arabia', *Journal of the Society of Architectural Historians* (1981), pp. 108-21; M. Sartre, *Trois études sur l'Arabie* (Brussels, 1982); D. Urman, *The Golan: A Profile of a Region during the Roman and Byzantine Periods* (Oxford, 1985).

p. 99 **Village and city**: G. Dagron, 'Entre village et cité: La bourgade rurale des IVe-VIIe siècles en Orient', *Koinonia*, iii (1979), pp. 29-52. The character and status of **Androna**: M.M. Mango, 'Excavations and Survey at Androna, Syria: The Oxford Team 1999', *Dumbarton Oaks Papers*, lvi (2002), pp. 307-15.

pp. 99-100 The **Macedonian renaming** is considered in E. Frézouls, 'La toponymie de l'Orient syrien et l'apport des éléments macédoniens', in *La toponymie antique: Actes du Colloque de Strasbourg, 12-14 juin 1975* (Leiden, 1975), pp. 219-24. The **parallelism of the cities' situations** is examined by J.D. Grainger, *The Cities of Seleukid Syria* (Oxford, 1990).

p. 101 **Antioch as 'capital'**: against the notion of capitals: F. Millar, *The Roman Near East*, p. 123; but see comments of M. Sartre, *D'Alexandre à Zénobie*, p. 614, note 26. **Metropolis**: G. Bowersock, 'Hadrian and Metropolis', *Beiträge zur Historia-Augusta-Forschung*, xvii: Bonner Historia-Augusta-Colloquium 1982/1983 (1985), pp. 75-88; J.-P. Rey-Coquais, 'Syrie romaine', pp. 56-7; K. Butcher, *Coinage in Roman Syria* (London, 2003) pp. 220-1.

p. 102 **Disputing front-line positions**: R. Ziegler, 'Antiochia, Laodicea und Sidon in der Politik der Severer', *Chiron*, viii (1978), pp. 493-514. **Emesa and Seleucia as metropolis**: K. Butcher, *Coinage in Roman Syria* (London, 2003). **Rivalry of Berytus and Tyre**: L. Jones Hall, *Berytus, 'Mother of Laws': Studies in the Social History of Beirut from the Third to the Sixth Centuries AD*, unpubd PhD thesis, Ohio State University (1996), p. 77.

p. 106 **Estimates of population**: the census of AD 6 under the governor Quirinius recorded 117,000 in the territory of Apamea: H. Dessau, *Inscriptiones Latinae Selectae*, i (Berlin, 1892), no. 2683. **Umm al-Jimal**: B. de Vries, *Umm al-Jimal. 'Gem of the Black Desert': A Brief Guide to the Antiquities* (Amman, 1990), p. 11. **Lack of imperial involvement in urbanization**: B. Isaac, *The Limits of Empire* (Oxford, 1990), pp. 331-71. **Philippopolis**: see notes to pp. 233-4. **Colonies**: F. Millar, 'The Roman *Coloniae* of the Near East: a Study of Cultural Relations', in H. Solin, M. Kajava (eds), *Roman Eastern Policy and Other Studies in Roman History: Proceedings of a Colloquium at Tvärminne, 2-3 October 1987* (Helsinki, 1990), pp. 7-58.

p. 107 **Decline of Zeugma**: excavations have revealed much less evidence of occupation after the mid-third century. For an overview, see N. Basgelen, R. Ergeç, *Belkis/Zeugma. A Last Look at History* (Istanbul, 2000). **Emesa**: the only evidence for this city's decline would seem to be textual. Libanius claimed that Emesa was no longer an important city in his day, but see P.-L. Gatier, below, notes to pp. 108-21.

pp. 108-21 For **Syrian place names, cities, towns and villages** in general, see R. Dussaud, *Topographie historique de la Syrie antique et médiévale* (Paris, 1927); E. Will, 'Les villes de la Syrie à l'époque hellénistique et romaine', in J.-M. Dentzer, W. Orthmann (eds), *Archéologie et histoire de la Syrie*, ii (Saarbrücken, 1989), pp. 223-50; and the collection of essays in P.-L. Gatier, B. Helly, J.-P. Rey-Coquais (eds), *Géographie historique au Proche-Orient (Syrie, Phénicie, Arabie, grecques, romaines, byzantines)* (Paris, 1988). For a detailed study of the political entities in the south, see in particular E. Schürer, *The History of the Jewish People in the Age of Jesus Christ (175 BC–AD 135)*, English edn rev. and ed. G. Vermes and F. Millar, 3 vols (Edinburgh, 1973-87).

There are numerous books and articles dealing with individual cities. A selection are cited here, in alphabetical order of city: **Antioch**: G. Downey, *A History of Antioch in Syria: From Seleucus to the Arab Conquest* (Princeton, 1961); J.H.W.G. Liebeschuetz, *Antioch: City and Imperial Administration in the Later Roman Empire* (Oxford, 1972); J. Lassus, 'La ville d'Antioche à l'époque romaine d'après l'archéologie', *Aufstieg und Niedergang der römischen Welt*, ii/8, pp. 54-102; E. Will, 'Antioche sur l'Oronte, métropole d'Asie', *Syria*, lxxiv (1997), pp. 99-113; C. Kondoleon, *Antioch: The Lost City* (Princeton, 2000). **Apamea**: J. Balty, J.-Ch. Balty, 'Apamée de Syrie, archéologie et histoire, I: Des origines à la Tétrarchie', *Aufstieg und Niedergang der römischen Welt*, ii/8, pp. 103-34; J.-Ch. Balty, *Guide d'Apamée* (Brussels, 1981); and by the same author, 'Apamea in Syria in the Second and Third Centuries AD', *Journal of Roman Studies*, lxxviii (1988), pp. 91-104. **Aradus**: J.-P. Rey-Coquais, *Arados et sa pérée aux époques grecque, romaine et byzantine* (Paris, 1974). **Berytus**: J. Lauffray, *Beyrouth, ville romaine* (Beirut, 1953); N. Jidejian, *Beirut through the Ages* (Beirut, 1973); J. Lauffray, 'Beyrouth Archéologie et Histoire, époques gréco-romaines I', *Aufstieg und Niedergang der römischen Welt*, ii/8, pp. 135-63; K. Butcher, R. Thorpe, 'A Note on Excavations in Central Beirut, 1994-96', *Journal of Roman Archaeology*, x (1997), pp. 291-306; D. Perring, 'Excavations in the Souks of Beirut', *Berytus*, xliii (1997-8), pp. 9-34. **Bostra**: M. Sartre, *Bostra: Des origines à l'Islam* (Paris, 1985); H.I. MacAdam, 'Bostra Gloriosa', *Berytus*, xxiii (1985), pp. 169-85; K.S. Freyberger, 'Einige Beobachtungen zur städtebaulichen Entwicklung des römischen Bostra', *Damaszener Mitteilungen*, iv (1989), pp. 45-60. **Caesarea**: K.G. Holum *et al.*, *King Herod's Dream: Caesarea on the Sea* (New York and London, 1988); R.L. Vann (ed.), *Caesarea Papers I: Straton's Tower, Herod's Harbour, and Roman and Byzantine Caesarea* (Ann Arbor, 1992); K.G. Holum, A. Raban, J. Patrich (eds), *Caesarea Papers 2: Herod's Temple, the Provincial Governor's Praetorium and Granaries, the Later Harbor* (Portsmouth, RI, 1999). **Damascus**: D. Sack, 'Damaskus, die Stadt *intra muros*', *Damaszener Mitteilungen*, iv (1985), pp. 207-90; T. Weber, '"Damaskos Polis Episemos". Hellenistische, römische und byzantinische Bauwerke in Damaskos aus der Sicht griechischer und lateinischer Schriftquellen', *Damaszener Mitteilungen*, vii (1993), pp. 135-76; E. Will, 'Damas antique', *Syria*, lxxi (1994), pp. 1-43. **Dura Europus**: P.V.C. Baur, M. Rostovtzeff *et al.*, *The Excavations at Dura-Europos (1928-1933)* (New Haven, 1929-52); F. Cumont, *Fouilles de Doura-Europos* (Paris, 1926); C. Hopkins, *The Discovery of Dura-Europos* (New Haven, 1979); S. Matheson, *Dura-Europos* (New Haven, 1982); P. Leriche *et al.* (eds), *Doura-Europos: Etudes* (Paris, 1986-97) (some of which are published in *Syria*, lxiii-lxix). **Emesa**: H. Seyrig, 'Caractères de l'histoire d'Emèse', *Syria*, xxxvi (1959), pp. 184-92; P.-L. Gatier, 'Palmyre et Emèse ou Emèse sans Palmyre', *Annales archéologiques arabes syriennes*, xlii (1996), pp. 431-6. **Gadara**: T. Weber, R. Khouri, *Umm Qais: Gadara of the Decapolis* (Amman, 1989); T. Weber, *Gadara-Umm Qes, i: Gadara Decapolitana. Untersuchungen zur Topographie, Geschichte, Architektur und bildenden Kunst einer "Polis Hellenis" im Ostjordanland* (Wiesbaden, 2002). **Gerasa**: C.H. Kraeling (ed.), *Gerasa: City of the Decapolis* (New Haven, 1938); I. Browning, *Jerash and the Decapolis* (London, 1982); R. Khouri, *Jerash: A Frontier*

City of the Roman East (London, 1986); F. Zayadine, *Jerash Archaeological Project, 1981-1983* (Amman, 1986). **Heliopolis**: T. Wiegand (ed.), *Baalbek: Ergebnisse der Ausgrabungen und Untersuchungen in den Jahren 1898-1905*, 3 vols (Berlin and Leipzig, 1921-5); F. Ragette, *Baalbek* (London, 1980); M. von Ess, T. Weber, *Baalbek: Im Bann römischer Monumentalarchitektur* (Mainz, 1999). **Palmyra**: D. Krencker, O. Puchstein *et al.*, *Palmyra: Ergebnisse der Expeditionen von 1902 und 1907* (Berlin, 1932); I.A. Richmond, 'Palmyra under the Aegis of Rome', *Journal of Roman Studies*, liii (1963), pp. 43-54; I. Browning, *Palmyra* (London, 1979); J. Teixidor, *Un port romain du désert: Palmyre et son commerce d'Auguste à Caracalla* (Paris, 1984); J. Starcky, M. Gawlikowski, *Palmyre* (Paris, 1985); A. Schmidt-Colinet (ed.), *Palmyra: Geschichte, Kunst und Kultur der syrischen Oasenstadt* (Linz, 1987); A. Bounni, Kh. Al-As'ad, *Palmyra: History, Monuments and Museum* (Damascus, 1988); E. Will, *Les Palmyréniens: La Venise des sables* (Paris, 1992). A whole volume of *Aram* (vii/1, 1995) is dedicated to Palmyra. A recent and useful introduction to the site is Kh. al-As'ad, J.-B. Yon, *Inscriptions de Palmyre: Promenades épigraphiques dans la ville antique de Palmyre* (Beirut, Damascus and Amman, 2001). **Petra**: I. Browning, *Petra* (London, 1980); R.G. Khouri, *Petra: A Guide to the Capital of the Nabataeans* (London, 1986); T. Weber, R. Wenning (eds), *Petra: Antike Felsstadt zwischen arabischer Tradition und griechischer Norm* (Mainz, 1997); L. Nehmé, F. Villeneuve, *Petra* (Paris, 1999). **Scythopolis**: B. Lifshitz, 'Scythopolis: L'histoire, les institutions et les cultes de la ville à l'époque hellénistique et imperiale', *Aufstieg und Niedergang der römischen Welt*, ii/8, pp. 262-94; G. Foerster, Y. Tsafrir, 'Nysa-Scythorium in the Roman Period: "a Greek City of Coele Syria" – Evidence from the Excavations at Bet-Shean', *Aram*, iv (1992), pp. 117-39; Y. Tsafrir, G. Foerster, 'Urbanism at Scythopolis-Bet Shean in the Fourth to Seventh Centuries', *Dumbarton Oaks Papers*, li (1997), pp. 85-146. **Tripolis**: H.S. Sarkis, 'Histoire de Tripoli, i: Des origines à l'occupation franque', *Cahiers de l'Oronte*, x (1971-2), pp. 81-102. **Tyre**: A. Poidebard, *Un grand port disparu: Tyr* (Paris, 1939); M. Chehab, 'Tyr à l'époque romaine', *Mélanges de l'Université Saint-Joseph*, xxxviii (1962), pp. 13-40; N. Jidejian, *Tyre through the Ages* (Beirut, 1969). **Zeugma**: J. Wagner, *Seleukeia am Euphrat-Zeugma* (Wiesbaden, 1976); D.L. Kennedy, *The Twin Towns of Zeugma on the Euphrates* (Ann Arbor, 1998).

p. 110 **Laodicea Scabiosa**: Ptolemy, *Geography*, 5.16.

pp. 113-14 **The Decapolis**: An entire volume of *Aram* (iv, 1992) is dedicated to the Decapolis. See also S.T. Parker, 'The Decapolis Reviewed', *Journal of Biblical Literature*, xciv (1975), pp. 437-41; H. Bietenhard, 'Die syrische Dekapolis von Pompeius bis Trajan', *Aufstieg und Niedergang der römischen Welt*, ii/8, pp. 220-61.

p. 115 **Symeon the Fool**: see C. Mango, *Byzantium: The Empire of New Rome* (London, 1980), pp. 64-5.

p. 115-16 The **status of Heliopolis**: F. Millar, 'The Roman *coloniae* of the Near East' (above, notes to p. 106).

p. 117 **Hellenistic Palmyra**: the nature and extent of the settlement is at last beginning to emerge. See A. Schmidt-Colinet, Kh. al-As'ad, 'Zur Urbanistik des hellenistischen Palmyra: Ein Vorbericht', *Damaszener Mitteilungen*, xii (2000), pp. 61-93.

p. 117-18 **Raphanea**: N. Pollard, *Soldiers, Cities and Civilians in Roman Syria* (Ann Arbor, 2000), p. 268.

p. 120 **Random imperial responses to local petitions**: for various views, see notes to pp. 157-61 (cities in the Hauran).

Chapter 4: Time and Motion

pp. 122-7 On **eras and calendars**: V. Grumel, *Traité d'études byzantines* (Paris, 1958); E.J. Bickerman, *Chronology of the Ancient World* (London, 1968); A.E. Samuel, *Greek and Roman Chronology: Calendars and Years in Classical Antiquity* (Munich, 1972). Studies specific to the region include H. Seyrig, 'Sur les ères de quelques villes de Syrie', *Syria*, xxvii (1950), pp. 5-50; J.-P. Rey-Coquais, 'Calendriers de la Syrie gréco-romaine d'après des inscriptions inédites', *Akten des VI. Internationalen Kongresses für Griechische und Lateinische Epigraphik, Munich, 1972* (Munich, 1973), pp. 564-6; P.M.W. Freeman, 'The Era of the Province of Arabia: Problems and Solution?', in H.I. MacAdam, *Studies in the History of the Roman Province of Arabia* (Oxford, 1986), pp. 38-46; Y. Meimaris, *Chronological Systems in Roman-Byzantine Palestine and Arabia* (Athens, 1992). See also comments by A. Wallace-Hadrill, 'Mutatio morum: the Idea of a Cultural Revolution', in T. Habinek, A. Schlesaro (eds), *The Roman Cultural Revolution* (Cambridge, 1997), pp. 3-22.

p. 123 **Eras at Antioch**: K. Butcher, *Coinage in Roman Syria* (London, 2003) 302-6. **Mariamme**: see commentary to IGLS, v (above, notes to p. 92), no 2107. **'Ain as-Samake**: H. Seyrig, 'La date des mosaïques de 'Ain es-Samake', *Syria*, xxxix (1959), pp. 173-8.

pp. 127-34 On **travel**: L. Casson, *Travel in the Ancient World* (Baltimore, 2/1994); J.-M. André, M.-F. Baslez, *Voyager dans l'Antiquité* (Paris, 1993). On **roads and other works**: the seminal study is P. Thomsen, 'Die römischen Meilensteine der Provinzen Syria, Arabia und Palaestina', *Zeitschrift des Deutschen Palästinavereins*, xl (1917), pp. 1-106. A selection of other works on the road system includes, for **Syria**: A. Poidebard, *La trace de Rome dans le désert de Syrie: Le limes de Trajan à la conquête arabe* (Paris, 1934); R.G. Goodchild, 'The Coast Road of Phoenicia and its Milestones', *Berytus*, ix (1949), pp. 91-107; T. Bauzou, 'Les routes romaines de Syrie', in *Archéologie et histoire de la Syrie*, ii, pp. 205-11; D. Graf, 'The Persian Royal Road System', *Achaemenid History*, viii (1994), pp. 167-89; **Palestine/Judaea**: B. Isaac, I. Roll, *Roman Roads in Judaea*, i (Oxford, 1982); I. Roll, 'The Roman Road System in Judaea', *The Jerusalem Cathedra*, iii (1983), pp. 136-61; I. Roll, E. Ayalon, 'Roman Roads in Western Samaria', *Palestine Exploration Quarterly*, cxviii (1986), pp. 113-34; I. Roll, 'A Latin Imperial Inscription from the Time of Diocletian Found at Yotvata', *Israel Exploration Journal*, xxxix (1989), pp. 239-60; M. Fischer, B. Isaac, I Roll, *Roman Roads in*

Judaea, ii (Oxford, 1996); **Arabia**: D.L. Kennedy, *Archaeological Explorations of the Roman Frontier in North-Eastern Jordan* (Oxford, 1982); T. Bauzou, 'Les voies de communication dans le Hauran à l'époque romaine', in J.-M. Dentzer (ed.), *Hauran*, i (Paris, 1985), pp. 137-65; D.L. Kennedy, 'Roman Roads and Routes in North East Jordan', *Levant*, xxix (1997), pp. 71-93. For the *Via Nova Traiana*, see D. Graf, 'The Via Nova Traiana in Arabia Petraea', in J. Humphrey (ed.), *The Roman and Byzantine Near East: Some Recent Archaeological Research* (Ann Arbor, 1995), pp. 241-67. **On maps**: O.A.W. Dilke, *Greek and Roman Maps* (London, 1985).

p. 129 **Milestones**: B. Isaac, *The Limits of Empire* (Oxford, 1990), pp. 304-9.

p. 131-2 **Theophanes' accounts** are published in C.H. Roberts, E.G. Turner (eds), *Catalogue of the Greek and Latin Papyri in the John Rylands Library, Manchester*, iv: *Documents of the Ptolemaic, Roman, and Byzantine Periods (Nos. 552-717)* (Manchester, 1952), pp. 104-7, 117-49.

p. 132 **Travellers between Antaradus and Laodicea**: J.-P. Rey-Coquais, *Arados et sa Pérée* (Paris, 1974), pp. 28-9. The travellers in this case were St Peter and his disciples.

pp. 132-4 **Harbours and river traffic**: D. van Berchem, 'Le port de Séleucie de Piérie et l'infrastructure navale des guerres parthiques', *Bonner Jahrbücher*, clxxxv (1985), pp. 47-87; J. Rougé, 'La navigation intérieure dans le Proche Orient antique', in P. Louis (ed.), *L'homme et l'eau en Méditerranée et au Proche-Orient* (Lyon, 1986), pp. 39-49; A. Raban *et al.*, *The Harbours of Caesarea Maritima*, i: *The Site and Excavations* (Oxford, 1989).

p. 134 **Shipwright at Derkush**: L. Jalabert, R. Mouterde, *IGLS*, ii: *Chalcidique et Antiochène* (Paris, 1939), no. 665.

Chapter 5: Syrian Landscapes: Exploiting the Available

For some general views: J. Rich, A. Wallace-Hadrill (eds), *City and Country in the Ancient World* (London, 1991); Tamara Lewit, *Agricultural Production in the Roman Economy, AD 200-400* (Oxford, 1991); L. De Ligt, *Fairs and Markets in the Roman Empire: Economic and Social Aspects of Periodic Trade in a Pre-industrial Society* (Amsterdam, 1993). G.R.D. King, A. Cameron (eds), *The Byzantine and Early Islamic Near East*, ii: *Land Use and Settlement Patterns* (Princeton, 1994).

pp. 138-40 On **villages**: J.-M. Dentzer, F. Villeneuve, 'Les villages de la Syrie romaine dans une tradition d'urbanisme oriental', in J.-L. Huot, M. Yon, Y. Calvet (eds), *De l'Indus aux Balkans: Recueil à la mémoire de Jean Deshayes* (Paris, 1985), pp. 213-48; P.-L. Gatier, 'Villages du Proche-Orient protobyzantin (4ème–7ème s.): Etude régionale', in G.R.D. King, A. Cameron (eds), *The Byzantine and Early Islamic Near East*, ii: *Land Use and Settlement Patterns* (Princeton, 1994), pp. 17-48; G. Tate, 'The Syrian Countryside during the Roman Era', in S.E. Alcock (ed.), *The Early Roman Empire in the East* (Oxford, 1997), pp. 55-71. Other relevant studies include H.I. MacAdam, 'Some Aspects of Land Tenure and Social Development in the Roman Near East: Arabia, Phoenicia and Syria', in T. Khalidi (ed.), *Land Tenure and Social*

Transformation in the Middle East (Beirut, 1984), pp. 45-62; and G.W. Bowersock, 'Social and Economic History of Syria under the Roman Empire', in J.-M. Dentzer, W. Orthmann (eds), *Archéologie et histoire de la Syrie*, ii (Saarbrücken, 1989), pp. 63-80. For **regional studies**, see, for example, S. Applebaum, 'Judaea as a Roman Province: the Countryside as a Political and Economic Factor', *Aufstieg und Niedergang der römischen Welt*, ii/8, pp. 355-96; C.M. Dauphin, S. Gibson, 'Ancient Settlements and their Landscape: the Results of Ten Years of Survey on the Golan Heights (1978-1988)', *Bulletin of the Anglo-Israel Archaeological Society*, xii (1992-3), pp. 7-31; S. Dar, *Settlements and Cult Sites on Mount Hermon, Israel: Ituraean Culture in the Hellenistic and Roman Periods* (Oxford, 1993); Y. Hirschfeld, 'Farms and Villages in Byzantine Palestine', *Dumbarton Oaks Papers*, li (1997), pp. 33-71. See also the notes to pp. 145-53, 153-6, 157-61, below.

p. 137 The **Gerasa Macellum**: A. Uscatescu, M. Martín-Bueno, 'The Macellum of Gerasa (Jerash, Jordan): From a Market Place to an Industrial Area', *Bulletin of the American Schools of Oriental Research*, 307 (1997), pp. 67-88. **Cities setting prices**: D. Sperber, *Roman Palestine, 200-400: Money and Prices*, Bar Ilan University (1974).

pp. 137-8 **Julianus the Architect**: there are several versions of the text apart from Hermenopolus. See C. Saliou, *Le traité d'urbanisme de Julien d'Ascalon: Droit et architecture en Palestine au VIe siècle* (Paris, 1996). The English translation quoted here is the one provided by J.P. Brown, *The Lebanon and Phoenicia: Ancient Texts Illustrating their Physical Geography and Native Industries*, i: *The Physical Setting and the Forest* (Beirut, 1969), pp. 49-52 (see also his comments there on Rabbi Akiba). See also C. Saliou, *Les lois des bâtiments* (Beirut, 1994).

p. 138 A **land of villages**: emphasized by F. Millar, *The Roman Near East*; see also G. Bowersock, 'Social and Economic History of Syria' (above, notes to pp. 138-40). For **Syrians abroad identifying with their home village**, see D. Feissel, 'Remarques de toponymie syrienne d'après des inscriptions grecques chrétiennes trouvées hors de Syrie', *Syria*, lix (1982), pp. 319-43. On **villas**: J.J. Rossiter, 'Roman Villas of the Greek East and the Villa in Gregory of Nyssa *Ep.* 20', *Journal of Roman Archaeology*, ii (1989), pp. 101-10; J. Lassus, 'Une villa de plaisance à Daphné-Yakto', in R. Stillwell (ed.), *Antioch-on-the-Orontes*, ii (Princeton, 1938), pp. 95-147; R. Stillwell (ed.), *Antioch-on-the-Orontes*, iii (Princeton, 1941), pp. 1-34. For those south of Berytus, see M.H. Chéhab, *Mosaïques du Liban, Bulletin du Musée de Beyrouth*, xix, 2 vols (1957-9); Z. Safrai, *The Economy of Roman Palestine* (London, 1994); Y. Hirschfeld, 'Jewish Rural Settlement in Judaea in the Early Roman Period', in S.E. Alcock (ed.), *The Early Roman Empire in the East* (Oxford, 1995), pp. 72-88.

p. 139 The **elimination of peasant proprietors**: A.H.M. Jones, 'The Roman Colonate', *Past and Present*, xiii (1958), pp. 1-13 (reprinted in *The Roman Economy*, Oxford, 1974, pp. 293-307). **Growth in late Roman times**: C. Foss, 'The Near Eastern Countryside in Late Antiquity: A Review Article', in J.

Humphrey (ed.), *The Roman and Byzantine Near East: Some Recent Research* (Ann Arbor, 1995), pp. 213-34; see also notes to pp. 145-53, 153-6, 157-61, below. **Large hydraulic projects**: see comments by G. Tate, in S. Alcock (ed.) (above, notes to pp. 138-40), at pp. 62-4.

pp. 140-42 The **spread of sedentarization**: see G. Tate, in S. Alcock (ed.), pp. 57-8.

p. 141 *Limitanei* **cultivating their own fields**: some scholars debate this, but they certainly seem to have *owned* land: B. Isaac, *The Limits of Empire* (Oxford, 1990), pp. 208-9. See also N. Pollard, *Soldiers, Cities and Civilians in Roman Syria* (Ann Arbor, 2000), p. 222. **Rescript of Constantine**: Theodosian Code 7.20.3; see discussion in Pollard, *Soldiers, Cities and Civilians*, pp. 162, 248.

pp. 142-5 **Archives and documentary evidence**: A helpful list, with comments and bibliography, is provided by H.M. Cotton, W.E.H. Cockle and F.G.B. Millar, 'The Papyrology of the Roman Near East: a Survey', *Journal of Roman Studies*, lxxxv (1995), pp. 214-35. For documents from the **Babatha archive** see N. Lewis, *The Documents from the Bar Kochba Period in the Cave of Letters: Greek Papyri* (Jerusalem, 1989); G.W. Bowersock, 'The Babatha Papyri, Masada and Rome', *Journal of Roman Archaeology*, iv (1991), pp. 336-44; M. Goodman, 'Babatha's Story', *Journal of Roman Studies*, lxxxi (1991), pp. 169-75; M. Broshi, 'Agriculture and Economy in Roman Palestine: Seven Notes on the Babatha Archive', *Israel Exploration Journal*, xlii (1992), pp. 230-40. Another archive from the same find is published by H.M. Cotton, 'The Archive of Salome Komaise, Daughter of Levi: Another Archive from the "Cave of Letters"', *Zeitschrift für Papyrologie und Epigraphik*, cv (1991), pp. 171-208. For the **Euphrates archive**, see the articles by D. Feissel, J. Gascou, 'Documents d'archives romains inédits du Moyen Euphrate (IIIe siècle après J.-C.)', *Comptes rendus de l'Académie des inscriptions et belles-lettres* (1989), pp. 535-61; 'Documents d'archives romains inédits du Moyen Euphrate (IIIe siècle après J.-C.), i: Les pétitions (P. Euphr. 1 à 5)', *Journal des savants*, lxv (1995), pp. 61-119; 'II. Les actes de vente-achat (P. Euphr. 6 à 10)', *Journal des savants* 67 (1997), pp. 3-57; J. Teixidor, 'Deux documents syriaques du IIIe siècle après J.-C. provenant du moyen Euphrate', *Comptes rendus de l'Académie des inscriptions et belles-lettres* (1990), pp. 146-66; also S. Brock, 'Some New Syriac Documents from the Third Century AD', *Aram*, iii/1-2 (1991), pp. 259-67. **Dura documents**: C.B. Welles, R.O. Fink, J.F. Gilliam, *The Excavations at Dura-Europus. Final Report V.1: The Parchments and Papyri* (New Haven, 1958). For a summary of the **Petra archive**, see L. Koenen, 'The Carbonized Archive from Petra', *Journal of Roman Archaeology*, ix (1996), pp. 177-88. **Nessana**: C.J. Kraemer, *Excavations at Nessana*, iii: *Non-literary Papyri* (Princeton, 1958).

pp. 145-53 The **'Dead Cities' and the Antioch region**: for early approaches, see M. de Vogüé, *Syrie centrale, architecture civile et religieuse du Ier au VIIe siècle*, 2 vols (Paris, 1865-77); H.C. Butler, E. Litmann, D. Magie, D.R. Stuart (eds), *Publications of the Princeton University Archaeological Expeditions to Syria in 1904-1905 and 1909*, 4 vols (Leiden, 1907-49), and J. Mattern, *Villes mortes de Haute Syrie* (Beirut, 1944). The magisterial study of G. Tchalenko, *Villages antiques de la Syrie du nord: Le massif du Bélus à l'époque romaine*, 3 vols (Paris, 1953-8), deserves careful study. Important recent work includes: O. Callot, *Huileries antiques de Syrie du nord* (Paris, 1984); J.-P. Sodini *et al.*, 'Déhès (Syrie du nord) campagnes I-III (1976-1978): Recherches sur l'habitat rural', *Syria*, lvii (1980), pp. 1-304; J.H.G.W. Liebeschuetz, H. Kennedy, 'Antioch and the Villages of Northern Syria in the Fifth and Sixth Centuries AD: Trends and Problems', *Nottingham Medieval Studies*, xxxii (1988), pp. 65-90; G. Tate, *Les campagnes de la Syrie du nord, du IIe au VIIe siècle*, i (Paris, 1992); I. Peña, *The Christian Art of Byzantine Syria* (1996); C. Strube, *Die "Toten Städte": Stadt und Land in Nordsyrien während der Spätantike* (Mainz, 1996); M. Decker, 'Food for an Empire: Wine and Oil Production in North Syria', in S. Kingsley, M. Decker (eds), *Economic Exchange in the Eastern Mediterranean during Late Antiquity* (Oxford, 2001), pp. 69-86. For the sites, see also the studies by I. Peña, P. Castellana, R. Fernández, *Inventaire du Jébel Baricha* (Milan, 1987); *Inventaire du Jébel El-A'la* (Milan, 1990); and *Inventaire du Jébel Wastani* (Milan, 1999).

p. 146 **Broad trends**: see especially G. Tate (above, notes to pp. 145-53). **Estimates of population** are derived from Peña, (above, notes to pp. 145-53), p. 40.

p. 148 A summary of some of the changing views about the Dead Cities is provided by C. Foss (above, notes to p. 139). For another summary of Tchalenko, see K. Greene, *The Archaeology of the Roman Economy*, pp. 138-40.

pp. 148-9 **LRA 1 and the Dead Cities**: M. Decker, 'Food for an Empire: Wine and Oil Production in North Syria' (above, notes to pp. 145-53). **Presses and quality of oil**: O. Callot, *Huileries antiques de Syrie du nord* (Paris, 1984).

p. 151 **Zaero (Baziher)**: see H.C. Butler, *Publications of the Princeton University Archaeological Expedition to Syria in 1904-1905. Division II. Section B. Part 6* (Leiden, 1920), p. 330.

p. 153 On the **plain of Antioch**, see R.J. Braidwood, *Mounds in the Plain of Antioch* (Chicago, 1937), and in particular K. Aslihan Yener, C. Edens, T.P. Harrison, J. Verstraete, T.J. Wilkinson, 'The Amuq Valley Regional Project, 1995-1998', *American Journal of Archaeology*, civ (2000), pp. 163-220.

pp. 153-6 **Chalcidice and the steppe of north-eastern Syria**: H.C. Butler, *Publications of the Princeton University Archaeological Expedition to Syria, Division II. Section B. Parts 1-2* (Leiden, 1920 and 1908, respectively); R. Mouterde, A. Poidebard, *Le Limes de Chalcis: Organisation de la steppe en Haute Syrie romaine* (Paris, 1945); B. Geyer, 'Des fermes byzantines aux palais omayyades, ou l'ingénieuse mise en valeur des plaines steppiques de Chalcidique', in L. Nordiguian, J.-F. Salles (eds), *Aux origines de l'archéologie aérienne: A. Poidebard (1878-1955)* (Beirut, 2000), pp. 109-22; G.M. Schwartz, H.H. Curvers, F.A. Gerritsen, J.A. MacCormack, N.F. Miller, J.A. Weber, 'Excavation and Survey in the Jabbul Plain, Western Syria: The Umm el-Marra Project, 1996-1997', *American Journal of Archaeology*,

civ (2000), pp. 419-62. See also J. Lassus, *Inventaire archéologique de la région au nord-est de Hama*, 2 vols (Damascus, 1935).

pp. 155-6 **Qasr Ibn Wardan**: H.C. Butler *et al.*, *Publications of the Princeton University Expedition to Syria in 1904-5 and 1909 II.B* (Leiden, 1920), pp. 26-45; H.C. Butler, *Early Churches in Syria, 4th to 7th Centuries* (Amsterdam, 1969); C. Mango, *Byzantine Architecture* (London, 1986), pp. 80-82.

pp. 156-7 **Palmyrene**: A. Musil, *Palmyrena: A Topographical Itinerary* (New York, 1928); D. Schlumberger, *La Palmyrène du Nord-Ouest* (Paris, 1951).

pp. 157-61 The **Hauran**: J.-M. Dentzer, *Hauran*, i (Paris, 1988) (in which see in particular the essay by F. Villeneuve, 'L'économie rurale et la vie des campagnes dans le Hauran antique', pp. 63-136); F. Villeneuve, 'Économie et société des villages de la montagne hauranaise à l'époque romaine: l'apport des données archéologiques', *Annales archéologiques arabes syriennes*, xli (1997), pp. 31-7. A useful guide to the sites of the region is A. Abou Assaf, *The Archaeology of Jebel Hauran: The Mohafaza of Souweida* (Damascus, 1998). The main **arguments for and against a policy of urbanization** in the Hauran, and the meaning of various terms encountered in the inscriptions, are to be found in: G.M. Harper, 'Village Administration in the Roman Province of Syria', *Yale Classical Studies*, i (1928), pp. 105-68; H. MacAdam, 'Epigraphy and Village Life in Southern Syria during the Roman and Early Byzantine Periods', *Berytus*, xxxi (1983), pp. 103-15; H. MacAdam, 'Some Aspects of Land Tenure and Social Development in the Roman Near East: Arabia, Phoenicia and Syria', in T. Khalidi (ed.), *Land Tenure and Social Transformation in the Middle East* (Beirut, 1984), pp. 45-62; H. MacAdam, *Studies in the History of the Roman Province of Arabia* (Oxford, 1986); J. Grainger, '"Village Government" in Roman Syria and Arabia', *Levant*, xxvii (1995), pp. 179-95; M. Sartre, 'Les *metrokomiai* de Syrie du sud', *Syria*, lxxvi (1999), pp. 197-222. *Annales archéologiques arabes syriennes*, xli (1997) is devoted to the Hauran (Mohafazat as-Sweida).

p. 159 On **nomads in the Hauran**, see D. Graf, 'Romans and Saracens' (above, notes to pp. 64-6); M.C.A. MacDonald, 'Nomads and the Hawran in the Late Hellenistic and Roman Periods', *Syria*, lxx (1993), pp. 303-403; M. Sartre, 'Transhumance, économie et société de montagne en Syrie du sud', *Annales archéologiques arabes syriennes*, xli (1997), pp. 75-86; and H. Zeinaddin, 'Safaitische Inschriften aus dem Gabal al-'Arab', *Damaszener Mitteilungen*, xii (2000), pp. 265-89.

p. 161 **Sanamein inscription**: see M. Sartre, 'Les *metrokomiai*' (above, notes to pp. 157-61).

pp. 161-6 **Water**: in general: M. Moussly, *Le problème de l'eau en Syrie* (Lyon, 1951); Ö. Wikander (ed.), *Handbook of Ancient Water Technology* (Leiden, 2000). On **aqueducts**: A.T. Hodge, *Roman Aqueducts and Water Supply* (London, 1992); A. Wilson, 'Deliveries *extra urbem*: Aqueducts and the Countryside', *Journal of Roman Archaeology*, xii (1999), pp. 314-31.

p. 163-4 On **dams**: Y. Calvet and B. Geyer, *Barrages antiques de Syrie* (Lyon, 1992). For illustrations of the dam at Homs see M. Abdulkarim, 'Problems Relating to the Refoundation of the City of Emese (Homs) in the Hellenistic and Roman Periods' (in Arabic), *Annales archéologiennes arabes syriennes*, xliv (2001), pp. 45-53 (English summary on p. 193). **Antioch's canals**: D. van Berchem (above, notes to pp. 43-4); D. Feissel, 'Deux listes de quartiers d'Antioche astreints au creusement d'un canal (73-4 après J.-C.)', *Syria*, lxii (1985), pp. 77-103.

pp. 165-6 **Resafa's cisterns**: W. Brinker, 'Zur Wasserversorgung von Resafa-Sergiopolis', *Damaszener Mitteilungen*, v (1991), pp. 119-46. **Water management in the Negev**: P. Mayerson, *The Ancient Agricultural Regime of Nessana and the Central Negev* (London, 1960).

pp. 166-7 **Wheat from Syria regarded as superior**: implied by Heichelheim (below, notes to pp. 168-9), pp. 127-8. **Economic interdependence of cities**: M. Fulford, 'Economic interdependence among urban communities of the Roman Mediterranean', *World Archaeology*, xix (1987), pp. 58-75. **Gallus and the landowners**: Ammianus Marcellinus 14.7.2.

p. 167-8 **Grain shortages**: N. Pollard, *Soldiers, Cities and Civilians in Roman Syria* (Ann Arbor, 2000), pp. 222-5. **Julian and the landowners**: Ammianus Marcellinus 22.14.1; Libanius *Orations* 18.195; see comments by J.H.W.G. Liebeschuetz, *Antioch* (Oxford, 1972), pp. 127, 130, and N. Pollard, *Soldiers*, pp. 222-3.

pp. 168-9 On **field systems**: G. Tate, 'The Syrian Countryside', in S. Alcock (ed.) (above, notes to pp. 138-40), at pp. 60-62 (northern Syria); F. Villeneuve, 'L'économie rurale et la vie des campagnes dans le Hauran antique', in J.-M. Dentzer, *Hauran*, I (Paris, 1988), pp. 63-136 (Hauran); J. Leblanc, G. Poccardi, 'Étude de la permanence de tracés urbains et ruraux antiques à Antioche-sur-l'Oronte', *Syria*, lxxvi (1999), pp. 91-126 (Antioch). **Laws encouraging utilization of land**: G. Tate, in S. Alcock (ed.) (above). **Surveys of Diocletian**: F. Millar (below, notes to pp. 192-3). **Olive trees and vines valued at higher tax rate than grain**: see notes to pp. 192-3. A **detailed list of Syrian agricultural products** found in textual sources is to be found in F.M. Heichelheim, 'Roman Syria', in T. Frank (ed.), *An Economic Survey of Ancient Rome* (Baltimore, 1933-40), iv, pp. 121-257. **Carion**: J.-P. Rey-Coquais, *Arados et sa Pérée* (Paris, 1974), pp. 69, 86-8. **Herod importing apples**: H.M. Cotton, J. Geiger (eds), *Masada II. The Yigael Yadin Excavations 1963-1965: Final Reports: The Greek and Latin Documents* (Jerusalem, 1989), doc. no. 822.

p. 170-71 On **livestock**: A. King, 'Diet in the Roman World: a Regional Inter-site Comparison of the Mammal Bones', *Journal of Roman Archaeology*, xii (1999), pp. 168-202; T. Williams, M. Monk, M.A. Murray, J. Rackham, 'Preliminary Results of the Environmental Sampling Undertaken on the Souks Excavation (BEY 006), Beirut', *Berytus*, xliii (1997-8), pp. 211-20. On **nomads**: R. Cribb, *Nomads in Archaeology* (Cambridge, 1991).

pp. 171-3 For **olive presses** see especially: O. Callot, *Huileries antiques de Syrie du nord* (Paris, 1984). For **olive and wine presses** in the south, see R. Frankel, 'Presses for Oil and Wine in the Southern Levant in the Byzantine Period', *Dumbarton Oaks Papers*, li (1997), pp. 73-84.

pp. 173-4 **Chhim**: T. Waliszewski, 'Chhim: Explorations, 2000', *Polish Archaeology in the Mediterranean*, x (1999), pp. 297-306. The **process of wine making** is described by S. Kingsley, 'The Economic Impact of the Palestinian Wine Trade in Late Antiquity', in S. Kingsley, M. Decker (eds), *Economy and Exchange in the East Mediterranean during Late Antiquity* (Oxford, 2001), pp. 44-68. **Excellence of wines**: see F.M. Heichelheim, 'Roman Syria' (above, notes to pp. 168-9). For a possible contender for the **Laodicean wine amphora**, see R. Tomber, '"Laodicean" Wine Containers in Roman Egypt', in O.E. Kaper (ed.), *Life on the Fringe: Living in the Southern Egyptian Deserts during the Roman and Early Byzantine Periods* (Leiden, 1998), pp. 213-19. **Amphoras of Berytus**: P. Reynolds, 'The Beirut Amphora Type, 1st Century BC–7th Century AD: An Outline of its Development and some Preliminary Observations of Regional Economic Trends', *Rei Cretariae Romanae Fautorum Acta*, xxxvi (2000), pp. 387-95. On **Gaza**, see the article by Kingsley, above.

p. 174 **Specialized products**: See Heichelheim, above, notes to pp. 168-9. The process of **purple production** is described by Pliny the Elder, *Natural History* 9.62.133. The estimate of how many murex were needed for a garment is to be found in D.S. Reese, 'The Mediterranean Shell Purple-Dye Industry', *American Journal of Archaeology*, xc (1986), p. 183.

pp. 176-7 **Kaisariyeh at Shaqqa**: H.C. Butler, *Publications of an American Archaeological Expedition to Syria in 1899-1900* (New York, 1903), ii, pp. 370-75. **Regional trade in basalt mills**: O. Williams-Thorpe, R.S. Thorpe, 'Geochemistry and Trade of Eastern Mediterranean Millstones from the Neolithic to Roman Period', *Journal of Archaeological Science*, xx (1993), pp. 263-320. **Mud brick at Dura Europus**: A. Perkins, *The Art of Doura-Europos* (Oxford, 1973), pp. 10-32.

p. 178 **Lebanon inscriptions**: J.-F. Breton, *Les inscriptions forestières d'Hadrien dans le Mont Liban*, IGLS, viii/3 (1980).

pp. 178-9 **Mineral resources**: see Heichelheim, above, notes to pp. 168-9. The Romans certainly exploited **copper mines** in the Wadi 'Araba intensively: S.T. Parker, 'Preliminary Report on the 1994 Season of the Roman Aqaba Project', *Bulletin of the American Schools of Oriental Research*, 305 (1997), pp. 19-44, at p. 40. **Nabataean gold and silver**: Strabo, *Geography*, 16.4.26.

Chapter 6: Portable Antiquities

Writings on the Roman economy and tax system abound. For general views relevant here, see: M. Rostovtzeff, *The Social and Economic History of the Roman Empire*, rev. P. M. Fraser (Oxford, 2/1957); and M. I. Finley, *The Ancient Economy* (London, 1973). In spite of his 'primitivist' views of the Roman economy, the essays by A.H.M. Jones, *The Roman Economy: Studies in Ancient Economic and Administrative History*, ed. P.A. Brunt (Oxford, 1974), remain extremely valuable. More recent works include: P. Garnsey, K. Hopkins, C.R. Whittaker, *Trade in the Ancient Economy* (London, 1983); M. Fulford, 'Economic interdependence among Urban Communities of the Roman Mediterranean', *World Archaeology*, xix (1987), pp. 58-75; R. Duncan-Jones, *Structure and Scale in the Roman Economy* (Cambridge, 1990). A useful collection of recent views may be found in H. Parkins and C. Smith (eds), *Trade, Traders and the Ancient City* (London, 1998).

For Syria in general, a detailed survey of the evidence from texts is provided by F. Heichelheim, 'Roman Syria' (above, notes to pp. 168-9). See also L.C. West, 'Commercial Syria under the Roman Empire', *Transactions of the American Philosophical Association*, lv (1924), pp. 159-89. These essays were written before much of the evidence presented in this chapter had been assembled and assessed. A more recent synthesis is provided by G.W. Bowersock, 'Social and Economic History of Syria under the Roman Empire', in J.-M. Dentzer, W. Orthmann (eds), *Archéologie et histoire de la Syrie*, ii (Saarbrücken, 1989), pp. 63-80. See also N. Pollard, *Soldiers, Cities and Civilians in Roman Syria* (Ann Arbor, 2000), which contains excellent discussions of the Syrian economy; and Z. Safrai, *The Economy of Roman Palestine* (London, 1994).

pp. 181-2 The **'primitivist' and 'modernist' debate** is summarized by K. Greene (above, notes to p. 148), pp. 11-16. **Scale and complexity of trade**: J. Paterson, 'Trade and Traders in the Roman World', in Parkin and Smith (see above), pp. 149-67.

p. 183-4 **Transport**: R. Laurence, 'Land Transport in Roman Italy', in Parkin and Smith (see above), pp. 129-48. See also K. Greene (above, notes to p. 148), pp. 17-44.

pp. 184-6 For **Palmyra and the 'caravan trade'**: M. Rostovtzeff, *Caravan Cities* (Oxford, 1932); E. Will, 'Marchands et chefs de caravanes à Palmyre', *Syria* (1957), pp. 262-71; J. Teixidor, *Un port romain* (above, notes to pp. 108-21); J.F. Matthews, 'The Tax Law of Palmyra: Evidence for Economic History in a City of the Roman East', *Journal of Roman Studies*, lxxiv (1984), pp. 157-80; M.G. Raschke, 'New Studies in Roman Commerce with the East', *Aufstieg und Niedergang der römischen Welt*, ii/9 (1978), pp. 604-1361; and G.W. Bowersock, 'Social and Economic History of Syria', above, general notes for this chapter. Important recent work includes J.-M. Dentzer, 'Khans ou casernes à Palmyre', *Syria*, lxxi (1994), pp. 45-112; J. Bylinski, 'A IIIrd Century Open-Court Building in Palmyra: Excavation Report', *Damaszener Mitteilungen*, viii (1995), pp. 213-46; J.-B. Yon, 'Remarques sur une famille caravanière à Palmyre', *Syria*, lxxv (1998), pp. 153-60; F. Millar, 'Caravan Cities: the Roman Near East and Long Distance Trade by Land', in M. Austin *et al.*, *Modus Operandi: Essays in Honour of Geoffrey Rickman* (London, 1998), pp. 119-37; and G. Young, *Rome's Eastern Trade: International Commerce and Imperial Policy, 31 BC -AD 305* (London and New York, 2001). A volume of *Aram* (viii/1, 1996), is dedicated to trade routes in the region, as is a volume of *Annales archéologiques arabes syriennes* (xlii, 1996) entitled 'Palmyra and the Silk Road'. **Merchants and caravan chiefs**: see J.-B. Yon, *Les notables de Palmyre* (Beirut, 2002), pp. 100-18. For the Palmyrene-style tomb on **Kharg**: R. Ghirshman, 'L'île de Kharg (Ikaros) dans le golfe persique', *Revue Archéologique* (1959), pp. 70-77. **Roman imports to the Persian gulf**: D. Potts, above, notes to p. 59. **Palmyrenes at Berenice and other Red Sea ports**: G. Young (above), pp. 80-82. **Chinese silk from Palmyrene tombs**: A. Stauffer, 'Kleider, Kissen, bunte Tücher: Einheimische Textilproduktion und weltweiter Handel', in A. Schmidt-Colinet (ed.), *Palmyra: Kulturbegegnung im Grenzbereich* (Mainz, 1995), pp. 57-71; and, by the same author, 'Textiles from Palmyra: Local Production and the Import and Imitation of Chinese Silk Weavings', *Annales archéologiques arabes syriennes*, xlii (1996), pp. 425-30.

p. 186 **Berytus bankers in Italy**: see J. Lauffray (above, notes to pp. 108-21, under Berytus).

pp. 187-8 **Carrot amphora**: P. Vipard, 'Les amphores carottes (forme Schöne-Mau XV): Etat de la question', *Actes du Congrès du Rouen, 1995* (Marseilles, 1995), pp. 51-77. **Pompeii 5 amphora**: P. Reynolds, 'Levantine Amphorae from Cilicia to Gaza: A Typology and Analysis of Regional Production from the 2nd to 6th Centuries', *First International Conference on Late Roman Coarse Wares, Cooking Wares and Amphorae in the Mediterranean: Barcelona, 2002* (forthcoming). **Eastern exports to the west**: P. Reynolds, *Trade in the Western Mediterranean, AD 400-700* (Oxford, 1995).

pp. 189-93 On the **relationship of taxes to trade**, see the seminal article by K. Hopkins, 'Taxes and Trade in the Roman Empire (200 BC–AD 400)', *Journal of Roman Studies*, lxx (1980), pp. 101-25, and R. Duncan-Jones, *Structure and Scale in the Roman Economy* (Cambridge, 1990), esp. pp. 30-46 and pp. 187-210, where the evidence for taxation in kind is examined. For **Babatha and taxation in dates**, see notes to pp. 142-5; the archive of Salome Komaise also contains a reference to this form of taxation.

p. 190 **Gift of grain to Laodicea**: W. Wroth, *A Catalogue of Greek Coins in the British Museum. Catalogue of the Greek Coins of Galatia, Cappadocia, and Syria*, London, 1899, p. 260, no. 94. **Palmyra tariff**: see below, notes to pp. 193-4.

pp. 190-91 **Types of direct taxation**: Duncan-Jones, above, notes to pp. 183-93 (the problem of Appian's statement regarding Syria is considered by Duncan-Jones on p. 189); F. Millar, *The Roman Empire and its Neighbours* (London and New York, 2/1981), pp. 90-96. **Census of Quirinius**: above, notes to p. 106; see also notes to p. 79. Tacitus: *Annals*, 2.42.

p. 191 **Portorium and the 25% duty**: G. Young (above, notes to pp. 184-6).

pp. 192-3 On the **iugum** in the *Syro-Roman Lawbook*, see A. Vööbus, *The Syro-Roman Lawbook* (Stockholm, 1982); R. Duncan-Jones (above, notes to pp. 189-93), pp. 202-203; olives seem to have been assessed by the number of trees rather than by area of land that they occupied. The **cadastral stones of the**

Diocletianic surveyors are usefully gathered together by F. Millar, *Roman Near East*, Appendix I, pp. 535-44. **Reversion to cash in the sixth century**: S. Williams, G. Friell, *The Rome that did not Fall: The Survival of the East in the Sixth Century* (London, 1999), p. 204 (with references).

pp. 193-4 The **Palmyra tariff**: J.F. Matthews, 'The Tax Law of Palmyra: Evidence for Economic History in a City of the Roman East', *Journal of Roman Studies*, lxxiv (1984), pp. 157-80.

pp. 194-201 On **Roman pottery and exchange** in general: J. Hayes, *Late Roman Pottery* (London, 1972), and *Handbook of Mediterranean Roman Pottery* (London, 1997); D.P.S. Peacock, *Pottery in the Roman World: an Ethnoarchaeological Approach* (London, 1982); P. Reynolds, *Trade in the Western Mediterranean* (above, notes to pp 187-8).

p. 195 **Material from the Euphrates**: N. Pollard, *Soldiers, Cities and Civilians in Roman Syria* (Ann Arbor, 2000), pp. 190-91, 226-7. **Territorial distribution of amphoras**: A. Berlin, 'From Monarchy to Markets: The Phoenicians in Hellenistic Palestine', *Bulletin of the American Schools of Oriental Research*, 306 (1997), pp. 75-88. **Nabataean pottery**: P. Hammond, 'A Classification of Nabataean Fine Ware', *American Journal of Archaeology*, lxvi (1962), pp. 169-80; and, on the identification of a major kiln at Petra, K. 'Amr, *The Pottery from Petra: A Neutron Activation Analysis Study* (Oxford, 1987).

p. 196 **Beirut amphora**: P. Reynolds, 'The Beirut Amphora Type' (above, notes to pp. 173-4). For **Tyre**, see P. Reynolds, 'Pottery Production and Economic Exchange' (below, notes to pp. 196-9).

pp. 196-9 On **amphoras in general**, see D.P.S. Peacock and D.F. Williams, *Amphorae and the Roman Economy: An Introductory Guide* (London, 1986); and the publications by P. Reynolds, 'Pottery Production and Economic exchange in 2nd Century Berytus: some preliminary observations of ceramic trends from quantified ceramic deposits from the Anglo-Lebanese excavations in Beirut', *Berytus*, xliii (1997-8), pp. 35-110; 'Baetican, Lusitanian and Tarraconensian Imports from the Western Mediterranean in the Anglo-Lebanese Excavations in Beirut (BEY 006, 007 and 045)', *Congreso Internacional 'Ex Baetica Amphorae': Universidad de Sevilla, 17-20 December 1998* (Ecija, 2000) (see also notes to pp. 187-8 above); and S. Kingsley, 'The Economic Impact of the Palestinian Wine Trade in Late Antiquity', in S. Kingsley, M. Decker (eds), *Economy and Exchange in the East Mediterranean during Late Antiquity* (Oxford, 2001), pp. 44-58.

p. 197 On the **Beirut amphora** and the stamp COL BER, see notes to pp. 173-4. On the **wine of Berytus**, see Heichelheim (above, notes to pp. 168-9).

pp. 198-9 **Late Roman Amphora** 1: M. Decker, 'Food for an Empire: Wine and Oil Production in North Syria', in S. Kingsley, M. Decker (eds), *Economic Exchange in the Eastern Mediterranean during Late Antiquity* (Oxford, 2001), pp. 69-86. **Late Roman Amphora** 4 **and** 5: Kingsley (above, notes to pp. 196-9). **'Gazans'**: *Gazitoi* or *Gazitia*: see, for exam-

ple, the Nessana archive (see notes to pp. 142-5), and P. Mayerson, 'The Gaza "Wine" Jar (Gazition) and the "Lost" Ashkelon Jar (Askalonion)', *Israel Exploration Journal*, xlii (1992), pp. 76-80.

p. 199 **Caesarea levelling dump**: P. Reynolds, personal communication.

pp. 199-200 **Coarse wares**: for *mortaria* see J.W. Hayes, 'North Syrian Mortaria', *Hesperia*, xxxvi (1967), pp. 337-47; M. Vallerin, '*Pelves* estampillés de Bassit', *Syria*, lxxi (1994), pp. 141-204; for **brittle ware**, S.L. Dyson (above, notes to pp. 55-8).

pp. 200-1 **Eastern Sigillata A**: An excellent discussion may be found in K.W. Slane, 'The Fine Wares', in S.C. Herbert (ed.), *Tel Anafa*, ii/1: *The Hellenistic and Roman Pottery* (Ann Arbor, 1997), pp. 247-406. For the **classification and dating of late Roman fine wares**, see J. Hayes, *Late Roman Pottery* (London, 1972).

pp. 201-2 On **glass**: S. Abdul-Hak, 'Contribution d'une découverte archéologique récente à l'étude de la verrerie syrienne à l'époque romaine', *Journal of Glass Studies*, vii (1965), pp. 26-34; O. Dussart, *Le verre en Jordanie et en Syrie du Sud* (Beirut, 1998); M. O'Hea, 'The Glass Industry of the Decapolis', *Aram*, iv (1992), pp. 253-64. The **Beth Shearim slab** has recently been re-dated to the very end of the Roman or beginning of the early Islamic period: Y. Gorin-Rosen, 'The Ancient Glass Industry in Israel: Summary of the Finds and New Discoveries', in M.-D. Nenna (ed.), *La route de verre: Ateliers primaires et secondaires du second millénaire av. J-C. au Moyen Age* (Lyon, 2000), pp. 49-63. For the site of **Jalame**, see G.D. Weinberg (ed.), *Excavations at Jalame: Site of a Glass Factory in Late Roman Palestine* (Columbia, MO, 1988). Strictly speaking, 'cullet' is the term applied to recycled glass; 'raw' or 'chunk' glass is used by specialists to describe primary material. I have not made a distinction here. On **'Sidonian' glass**: S. Jennings, 'Late Hellenistic and Early Roman Glass from the Souks Excavations in Beirut, Lebanon', *Hyalos-Vitrumm-Glass* (Athens, 2002), pp. 127-32.

pp. 203-11 On **marble**: H. Dodge and B. Ward-Perkins (eds), *Marble in Antiquity: The Collected Papers of J.B. Ward-Perkins* (London [British School at Rome], 1992); H. Dodge, 'Palmyra and the Roman Marble Trade: Evidence from the Baths of Diocletian', *Levant*, xx (1988), pp. 215-30; J.C. Fant, 'The Roman Emperors in the Marble Business: Capitalists, Middle-Men or Philanthropists', in N. Herz, M. Waelkens (eds), *Classical Marble: Geochemistry, Technology, Trade* (Dordrecht, London and Boston, 1988), pp. 147-58; J.C. Fant (ed.), *Ancient Marble Quarrying and Trade* (Oxford, 1988); H. Dodge, 'Ancient Marble Studies: Recent Research', *Journal of Roman Archaeology*, iv (1991), pp. 28-50 (with extensive bibliography); L. Moshe Fischer, *Marble Studies: Roman Palestine and the Marble Trade* (Konstanz, 1998); O. Williams-Thorpe, M.M. Henty, 'The Sources of Roman Granite Columns in Israel', *Levant*, xxxii (2000), pp. 155-70.

pp. 204-5 On the **architecture of Masada**: Y. Yadin, *Masada: Herod's Fortress and the Zealots' Last Stand* (London, 1966); E. Netzer,

Masada III, the Yigael Yadin Excavations 1963-1965, Final Reports. The Buildings, Stratigraphy and Architecture (Jerusalem, 1991); and G. Foerster, *Masada V, Art and Architecture* (Jerusalem, 1995). On **Herodian palaces** and their *opus sectile* **floors**: E. Netzer, *Die Paläste der Hasmonaer und Herodes des Grossen* (Mainz, 1999).

pp. 208-11 **Sarcophagi**: in general, see the paper by J.B. Ward-Perkins, 'The Trade in Sarcophagi', in H. Dodge and B. Ward-Perkins (eds), *Marble in Antiquity: The Collected Papers of J.B. Ward-Perkins* (London, 1992), pp. 31-7; and for the **Near East**, G. Koch, 'Der Import kaiserzeitlicher Sarkophage in den römischen Provinzen Syria, Palästina und Arabia', *Bonner Jahrbücher*, clxxxix (1989), pp. 161-211. The **Tyre necropolis**: see the article by J.B. Ward-Perkins, 'The Imported Sarcophagi of Roman Tyre', in H. Dodge and B. Ward-Perkins (eds), *Marble in Antiquity*, pp. 129-51.

pp. 211-12 On **textiles**: A.H.M. Jones, 'The Cloth Industry under the Roman Empire', in his *The Roman Economy* (see introductory bibliography for this chapter, above), pp. 350-64. Two studies of Syrian textiles are by R. Pfister, *Textiles de Palmyre* (Paris, 1934-40) and *Textiles de Halabiyeh (Zenobia)* (Paris, 1951). See also A. Stauffer, 'Kleider, Kissen, bunte Tücher' (notes to pp. 184-6, above).

p. 212 **Diocletian's Price Edict**: the standard text with an English translation is E. Rose Graser, 'The Edict of Diocletian on Maximum Prices', in T. Frank, *An Economic Survey of Ancient Rome* v, (Baltimore, 1940), pp. 307-421. More fragments of the edict have come to light since, but these are not particularly relevant here. **House of Nebuchelus**: P. Baur, M. Rostovtzeff, A. Bellinger (eds), *The Excavations at Dura-Europos: Preliminary Report on the Fourth Season, 1930-31* (New Haven, 1933), pp. 79-145.

pp. 212-21 On **coins**: C. Augé, 'La monnaie en Syrie à l'époque hellénistique et romaine', in J.-M. Dentzer, W. Orthmann (eds), *Archéologie et histoire de la Syrie*, ii (Saarbrücken, 1989), pp. 149-90; C. Morrisson, 'La monnaie en Syrie byzantine', *ibid.*, pp. 191-204; K. Butcher, 'Coinage and Currency in Syria and Palestine to the Reign of Gallienus', in C.E. King, D.G. Wigg (eds), *Coin Finds and Coin Use in the Roman World* (Berlin, 1996), pp. 101-12; and *Coinage in Roman Syria* (London, 2003); K.W. Harl, *Civic Coins and Civic Politics in the Roman East* (Berkeley, 1987); C. Augé, F. Duyrat (eds), *Les monnayages syriens: Quel apport pour l'histoire du Proche-Orient hellénistique et romain? Actes de la table ronde de Damas, 10-12 novembre 1999* (Beirut, 2002). Standard catalogues include the Catalogues of Greek Coins in the British Museum (BMC: various authors, London, 1873-1927), of which four volumes (*Galatia, Cappadocia, and Syria*, 1899; *Phoenicia*, 1910; *Palestine*, 1914; and *Arabia, Mesopotamia, and Persia*, 1922) provide a general view of the provincial and civic coinages of the area; readers should be aware, however, that these do not constitute a complete listing of types and issues. Comprehensive lists are to be found in A.M. Burnett, M. Amandry *et al.*, *Roman Provincial Coinage* (RPC), of which two volumes (London and Paris, 1992, 1999) have appeared.

p. 213 **Dura Mithraeum**: on the interpretation of the value marks in this inscription, see K. Butcher, *Coinage in Roman Syria* (London, 2003), pp. 208-9

p. 215 **Coinages of Laodicea and Aradus**: F. de Callataÿ, *L'histoire des guerres mithridatiques vue par les monnaies* (Louvain-la-Neuve, 1997). **Tyrian tetradrachms**: D.R. Walker, *The Metrology of the Roman Silver Coinage*, i (Oxford, 1976), pp. 70-73; B. Levy, 'Tyrian Shekels: The Myth of the Jerusalem Mint', *SAN: Journal of the Society for Ancient Numismatics*, xix/2 (1995), pp. 33-5.

p. 216 **One mint striking silver for another**: K. Butcher, M. Ponting, 'Rome and the East: Production of Roman Provincial Silver Coinage for Caesarea in Cappadocia under Vespasian, AD 69-70', *Oxford Journal of Archaeology*, xiv (1995), pp. 63-77.

p. 218 **Greek value marks**: K. Butcher, *Coinage in Roman Syria* (London, 2003), pp. 207-9. For the notion of **coin types as monuments**, see A. Meadows, J. Williams, 'Moneta and Monuments: Coinage and Politics in Republican Rome', *Journal of Roman Studies*, xci (2001), pp. 27-49. On the question of **whom coin types were intended to address**, see K. Butcher, 'Information, Legitimation or Self-legitimation? Popular and Elite Designs on the Coin Types of Roman Syria', in A. Burnett, V. Heuchert, C. Howgego (eds), *Coinage and Identity in the Roman Provinces* (Oxford, forthcoming).

p. 219 **Trader moving between Berytus and Brundisium**: R. Duncan-Jones, *Structure and Scale in the Roman Economy* (Cambridge, 1990), p. 42.

pp. 220-21 Useful **summaries of late Roman and Byzantine coins in Syria** are provided by Augé and Morrisson, (above, notes to pp. 212-21). For the **coastal cities opting out of the post-512 system**, see K. Butcher, 'Coinage in Sixth Century Beirut', *Berytus*, xliii (1997-8), pp. 173-80; and *idem, Small Change in Ancient Beirut* (above, notes to p. 30). For coins of **Constans II and imitations**, good illustrations and a sound discussion may be found in T. Goodwin, M. Phillips, 'A Seventh-century Syrian Hoard of Byzantine and Imitative Copper Coins', *Numismatic Chronicle*, 157 (1997), pp. 61-87, and for **Arab-Byzantine coinage**, S. Qedar, 'Copper Coinage of Syria in the Seventh and Eighth Century AD', *Israel Numismatic Journal*, x (1988-9), pp. 27-39; and M. Bates, 'Byzantine Coinage and its Imitations, Arab Coinage and its Imitations: Arab-Byzantine Coinage', *Aram*, vi (1994), pp. 381-403.

p. 222 **Denarii of Vespasian**: see K. Butcher, M. Ponting (notes to p. 216, above).

Chapter 7: Public Values

On **ancient cities** in general: A.H.M. Jones, *The Greek City from Alexander to Justinian* (Oxford, 1940); J. Rykwert, *The Idea of a Town: The Anthropology of the Urban Form in Rome, Italy and the Ancient World* (London, 1976); R.T. Marchese (ed.), *Aspects of Greek and Roman Urbanism* (Oxford, 1983); E.J. Owens, *The City in the Greek and Roman World* (London, 1992); H. Parkins, *Roman Urbanism* (London, 1997). For an **outline of civic development** in the east-

ern empire: S. Mitchell, *Anatolia: Land, Men, and Gods in Asia Minor*, i: *The Celts and the Impact of Roman Rule* (Oxford, 1993), pp. 198-226.

On the **region**: H.C. Butler, *Architecture and other Arts: Part II of the Publications of an American Archaeological Expedition to Syria in 1899-1900* (New York, 1903); *Architecture and other Arts: Part II of the Publications of the Princeton University Archaeological Expeditions* (Leiden, 1907); J. Lauffray, 'L'urbanisme antique au Proche-Orient', *Proceedings of the Second International Congress of Classical Studies: Copenhagen, 1958*, iv, pp. 7-26; E. Will, 'Les villes de la Syrie à l'époque hellénistique et romaine', in J.-M. Dentzer, W. Orthmann (eds), *Archéologie et histoire de la Syrie*, ii, pp. 223-50; D. Sperber, *The City in Roman Palestine* (Oxford, 1998); M. Sartre, *D'Alexandre à Zénobie*, pp. 639-733.

For the **architecture at individual sites**, see bibliography for chapter 3 as well as those cited below, to which add the following works. **Apamea**: J.-Ch. Balty (ed.), *Apamée de Syrie: Bilan des recherches archéologiques 1965-1968* (Brussels, 1969); *1969-1971* (Brussels, 1972); *1973-1979* (Brussels, 1984). **Cyrrhus**: E. Frézouls, 'Cyrrhus et la Cyrrhestique jusqu'à la fin du Haut-Empire', *Aufstieg und Niedergang der römischen Welt*, ii/8, pp. 164-97.

p. 224 The **Greek *polis* as a model**: this should not be taken to mean that in social terms all Syrian cities were identical, or that there were no Semitic elements to the culture(s) of their populations. The evidence currently does not permit such assertions to be made. See notes to p. 26.

pp. 225-7 **Civic government**: F. Millar, *The Roman Empire and its Neighbours*, p. 87. For the region, see J.M.C. Bowsher, 'Civic Organization within the Decapolis', *Aram*, iv (1992), pp. 265-81; M. Sartre, 'Vie municipale et intégration des notables dans la Syrie et l'Arabie romaines', *Antiquitas*, xxii (1997), pp. 153-74, and, *idem, D'Alexandre à Zénobie*, pp. 649-54. It must be admitted that we have very little evidence for the workings of civic government in Syria and the Near East, and therefore it is assumed that the basic pattern follows civic government in other regions – that is, with a hereditary class of elite councillors dominating civic affairs. Excavations have revealed a *bouleterion* (council chamber) in several cities: for example Dura Europus, Dionysias, Gerasa and Petra. In the Hauran many councillors seem to have resided in their home villages rather than in the city itself. Some scholars would question whether all Syrian cities had the constitutional trappings of a Greek city: see D. Graf, 'Hellenisation and the Decapolis' (above, notes to pp. 25-31). Even where there is evidence, the nature of the officials and institutions continues to be contested: see, for example, the comments of M. Sartre, 'Palmyre, cité grecque', *Annales archéologiques arabes syriennes*, xlii (1996), pp. 385-405.

p. 226 The **search for benefactors**: Augustus served as a high priest at Antioch. See W. Wroth, BMC: *Galatia, Cappadocia, and Syria* (London, 1899), p. 167-8, where the coins record that: 'the Antiochenes bestowed the high priesthood on Caesar Augustus the high priest'. King Herod donated gifts to many cities

outside his kingdom. See, for example, Josephus, *Jewish War*, 1.422-5; D.W. Roller, *The Building Program of Herod the Great* (Berkeley, 1998). **Monumental writing as a monument**: G. Woolf, 'Monumental Writing and the Expansion of Roman Society in the Early Empire', *Journal of Roman Studies*, lxxxvi (1996), pp. 22-39. On **Lucius Julius Agrippa**: J.-P. Rey-Coquais, 'Inscriptions grecques d'Apamée', *Annales archéologiques arabes syriennes*, xxiii (1973), pp. 39-84.

p. 227 Work on the **canal at Antioch** is discussed by D. Feissel (above, notes to pp. 163-4).

p. 228 **Lack of public buildings in Hellenistic times**: G. Bowersock, 'Social and Economic History' (above, notes to pp. 138-40), at p. 65. The **early street at Apamea** is described by J.-Ch. Balty, 'Grande colonnade et quartiers nord d'Apamée à la fin de l'époque hellénistique', *Comptes rendus de l'Académie des inscriptions et belles-lettres* (1994), pp. 77-101.

pp. 228-9 **Civic festivals as an alternative**: S. Mitchell, *Anatolia* (Oxford, 1993), pp. 217-25. On the **evolution of festivals**: M. Sartre, *L'Orient Romain* (Paris, 1991), p. 343. **Palmyra and many Arabian cities not holding festivals**: F. Millar, *The Roman Near East*, p. 329, 425. As Millar points out, this may be a consequence of the poverty of our evidence.

pp. 229-34 On **Roman colonies**, the fundamental study is F. Millar, 'The Roman *Coloniae* of the Near East: a Study of Cultural Relations', in H. Solin, M. Kajava (eds), *Roman Eastern Policy and other Studies in Roman History: Proceedings of a Colloquium at Tvärminne, 2-3 October 1987* (Helsinki, 1990), pp. 7-58.

pp. 230-31 The **urban plan of Berytus**: K. Butcher, R. Thorpe, 'A Note on Excavations in Central Beirut 1994-96', *Journal of Roman Archaeology*, x (1997), pp. 291-306. For the ***pagus augustus***, see J.-P. Rey-Coquais, 'Des montagnes au désert: Baetocécé, la Pagus Augustus de Niha, la Ghouta à l'est de Damas', in E. Frézouls (ed.), *Sociétés urbaines, sociétés rurales dans l'Asie Mineure et la Syrie hellénistiques et romaines* (Strasbourg, 1987). **Exotic Roman cults at Berytus**: see comments by F. Millar, *The Roman Near East*, pp. 280-81. **Roman law at Berytus**: P. Collinet, *Histoire de l'École de droit de Beyrouth* (Paris, 1925); H. I. MacAdam, 'Studia et Circenses: Beirut's Roman Law School in its Colonial, Cultural Context', *Aram*, xiii-xiv (2001), pp. 193-226.

p. 232 **Inscription of Philippopolis**: R. Cagnat *et al.*, *Inscriptiones graecae ad res romanas pertinentes*, iii (Paris, 1906), no. 1196. Civic coins of Philippopolis were produced after Philip's son had been elevated to co-emperor in AD 246/7; they were probably made at Antioch, and share obverse dies with other cities: see K. Butcher, 'The Colonial Coinage of Antioch-on-the-Orontes, *c.* AD 218-53', *Numismatic Chronicle*, 148 (1988), pp. 63-75. **Laodicea using Latin letters to write Greek**: COL. LAOD. METROPOLEOS (W. Wroth, BMC: *Galatia, Cappadocia, and Syria* (London, 1899), pp. 261-3).

pp. 233-4 For **Philippopolis**, see H.C. Butler, *Architecture and Other Arts. Part II of the Publications of an American Archaeological Expedition to Syria in 1899-1900* (New York,

1903), pp. 376-96; and K.S. Freyberger, 'Die Bauten und Bildwerke von Philippopolis: Zeugnisse imperialer und orientalischer Selbstdarstellung der Familie des Kaisers Philippus Arabs', *Damaszener Mitteilungen*, vi (1992), pp. 293-311. Its sanctuary of the imperial cult is described by Gh. Amer, M. Gawlikowski, *Damaszener Mitteilungen*, ii (1985), pp. 1-15.

pp. 234-6 **City boundaries**: the boundary stone between Emesa and Palmyra is published by D. Schlumberger, 'Bornes frontières de la Palmyrène', *Syria*, xx (1939), pp. 43-73. The **boundary between Antioch and Apamea** is discussed by H. Seyrig, 'Inscriptions grecques', in G. Tchalenko (above, notes to pp. 145-53), iii (Paris, 1958), pp. 2-62, with map at p. 57. For **Latin inscriptions in the Bekaa**: J.-P. Rey-Coquais, *IGLS, Tome VI: Baalbek et Beqa* (Paris, 1967); C. Ghadban, 'Les frontières du territoire d'Héliopolis-Baalbek à la lumière de nouveaux documents', in T. Fahd (ed.), *La géographie administrative et politique d'Alexandre à Mahomet* (Leiden, 1982), pp. 143-68.

pp. 236-7 **Tyche**: T. Dohrn, *Die Tyche von Antiochia* (Berlin, 1960); R. Gersht, 'The Tyche of Caesarea Maritima', *Palestine Exploration Quarterly*, cxvi (1984), pp. 110-14; K. Parlasca, 'Die Stadtgöttin Palmyras', *Bonner Jahrbücher*, clxxxiv (1984), pp. 167-76. For the **Gad of Dura**, see M.I. Rostovtzeff, F.E. Brown, C.B. Welles, *The Excavations at Dura-Europos: Preliminary Report of the Seventh and Eighth Seasons* (New Haven, 1939), pp. 258-60, 277-8. Another scene which almost certainly shows Seleucus Nicator founding a city is discussed by H. Seyrig, 'Scène historique sur un chapiteau du Musée de Beyrouth', *Revue des Etudes Anciennes*, xlii (1940), pp. 340-44. The **Balanea inscription** is discussed by R. Fleischer, 'Die Tychegruppe von Balanea-Leukas in Syrien', *Archäologischer Anzeiger* (1986), pp. 707-9. **For the Aere Tychaion**: E. Littmann, D. Magie, D.R. Stuart, *Publications of the Princeton University Archaeological Expeditions, A.5: Greek and Latin Inscriptions in Syria* (Leiden, 1915), pp. 290-92, no. 652; K.S. Freyberger, 'Das Tychaïon von as-Sanamein', *Damaszener Mitteilungen*, iv (1989), pp. 87-108.

pp. 237-59 **Buildings**: A. Segal, *From Function to Monument: Urban Landscapes of Roman Palestine, Syria and Provincia Arabia* (Oxford, 1997); W. Ball, *Rome in the East* (London, 2000).

p. 239 **Pollution of death**: In some cities, such as Palmyra, the separation of the living from the dead was less rigorous than in the typical Greek-style city, hinting at different attitudes towards the defunct.

p. 240 **Hellenistic palaces**: I. Nielsen, *Hellenistic Palaces* (Århus, 1994). For Herodian palaces, see notes to pp. 204-5.

pp. 240-42 **Urban plans**: J. Sauvaget, 'Le plan de Laodicée-sur-Mer', *Bulletin d'études orientales de l'Institut français de Damas*, iv (1934), pp. 81-114; D. van Berchem, 'Le plan de Palmyre', in *Palmyre: Bilan et Perspectives, Travaux du Centre de recherche sur le Proche-Orient et la Grèce antiques*, iii (Strasbourg, 1976), pp. 165-73; A.S. Barghouti, 'Urbanization of Palestine and Jordan in Hellenistic and Roman Times', *Studies in the History and Archaeology of Jordan*, i (Amman,

1982), pp. 209-29; F.E. Peters, 'City Planning in Greco-Roman Syria: Some New Considerations', *Damaszener Mitteilungen*, i (1983), pp. 269-77; E. Will, 'Le développement urbain de Palmyre', *Syria*, lx (1983), pp. 69-81; A. Segal, *Town Planning and Architecture in Provincia Arabia* (Oxford, 1988).

p. 240 **Looking to non-Greek traditions**: see especially W. Ball, *Rome in the East* (London, 2000).

p. 241 **Sizes of city blocks**: Sauvaget, above, notes to pp. 240-42. **Antioch's city blocks**: Leblanc and Poccardi, above, notes to pp. 168-9. **Berytus**: K. Butcher, R. Thorpe (above, notes to pp. 230-31); D. Perring, 'Excavations in the Souks of Beirut', *Berytus*, xliii (1997-8), pp. 9-34. **Ptolemaic and Nabataean designs**: see F.E. Peters, notes to pp. 240-42, above; but note also J.-M. Dentzer, 'Les sondages de l'arc nabatéen et l'urbanisme de Bostra', *Comptes rendus de l'Académie des inscriptions et belles-lettres* (1986), pp. 62-87.

p. 242 **Irregularities of terrain a constraint on orthogonal layout**: see comments of Y. Tsafrir, G. Foerster, 'Urbanism at Scythopolis' (above, notes to pp. 108-21).

pp. 242-3 **Walls**: note the interesting inscriptions of the mid- to later third century from Adraa in Arabia, recording the building of fortifications through an imperial 'gift': H.-G. Pflaum, 'La fortification de la ville d'Adraha d'Arabie (259-260 à 274-275) d'après les inscriptions récemment découvertes', *Syria*, xxix (1959), pp. 307-30. **Apamea's walls**: J.D. Grainger, *The Cities of Seleukid Syria* (Oxford, 1990), pp. 82-3. **Palmyra's walls**: M. Gawlikowski, 'Les défenses de Palmyre', *Syria*, li (1974), pp. 231-42.

pp. 244-51 For **colonnaded streets** see the works of J. Lassus, *Les portiques d'Antioche: Antioch-on-the-Orontes Report V* (Princeton, 1972); 'Quelques remarques sur les rues à portiques', in *Palmyre: Bilan et perspectives* (Strasbourg, 1974), pp. 175-90; also Segal (above, notes to pp. 237-59), pp. 5-53. Other relevant studies: M. Broshi, 'Standards of street widths in the Roman-Byzantine period', *Israel Exploration Journal*, xxvii (1977), pp. 232-5.

pp. 244-5 **Apamea's cardo**: 'Apamea in Syria in the Second and Third Centuries AD', *Journal of Roman Studies*, lxxviii (1988), pp. 91-104. **Antioch's street**: J. Lassus, *Les portiques d'Antioche* (above, notes to pp. 244-51). **Gerasa**: R. Khouri, *Jerash: A Frontier City of the Roman East* (London and New York, 1986), pp. 67-9.

pp. 245-6 **Palmyra's colonnade**: van Berchem, above, notes to pp. 240-42; but see now M. Baranski, 'The Great Colonnade of Palmyra Reconsidered', *Aram*, vii (1995), pp. 37-46. It would now appear that the central part of the colonnade, around the area of the theatre, was the last part to be constructed. Work began at the western end of the colonnade in the mid-second century, and at the eastern end in the late second, but the central part was not completed until the mid-third or later.

p. 247 **Colonnades as an extension of the agora** (likened to a souk or bazaar): E. Will, 'Les villes de la Syrie à l'époque hellénistique et romaine', in J.-M. Dentzer, W.

Orthmann (eds), *Archéologie et histoire de la Syrie*, ii, pp. 223-50, at pp. 244-5. **Roofing over streets** suggested by W. Ball, *Rome in the East* (above, notes to p. 240), pp. 271, 274.

p. 248-9 **Arches**: A.L. Frothingham, 'The Roman Territorial Arch', *American Journal of Archaeology*, xix (1915), pp. 155-74; F.S. Kleiner, 'The Study of Roman Triumphal and Honorary Arches 50 Years after Kahler', *Journal of Roman Archaeology*, ii (1988), pp. 195-206. **Arch at Dura Europos**: M. Pillet, 'The Triumphal Arch', in P. Bauer, M. Rostovtzeff, A. Bellinger, *The Excavations at Dura-Europos: Preliminary Report of the Fourth Season, 1930-1931* (New Haven, 1933), pp. 3-4. **Church at Bab el-Hawa**: I am grateful to P.-L. Gatier (personal communication) for this information.

p. 249 For **nymphaea**, see A. Segal, *From Function to Monument*, pp. 151-68, and for the nyphaeum as an opportunity for self-advertisement, see S. Walker, 'Roman Nymphaea in the Greek World', in S. Macready, F.H. Thompson, *Roman Architecture in the Greek World* (London, 1987), pp. 60-71. **Apamea latrine**: J.-Ch. Balty, *Guide d'Apamée* (Brussels, 1981), pp. 77-8.

p. 250 **Gerasa street monuments**: R. Khouri (above, notes to pp. 244-5) provides a good general outline; R. Parapetti, 'Architectural and Urban Space in Roman Gerasa', *Mesopotamia*, xviii-xix (1983-4), pp. 37-84. The **cardo at Jerusalem**: A. Segal, *From Function to Monument* (Oxford, 1997), pp. 41-4. **Justinianic tetrakionion**: J.-Ch. Balty, 'Tetrakionia de l'époque de Justinien sur la grande colonnade d'Apamée', *Syria*, lxxvii (2000), pp. 227-37.

p. 252 The **agora at Palmyra**: H. Seyrig, 'Rapport sommaire sur les fouilles de l'agora de Palmyre', *Comptes rendus de l'Académie des inscriptions et des belles-lettres* (1940), pp. 237-49; Kh. As'ad, J.-B. Yon, *Inscriptions de Palmyre* (Beirut, Damascus and Amman, 2001), pp. 56-61.

p. 253 **Monumental setting for sculpture**: see Amer and Gawlikowski (above, notes to pp. 233-4). **Paradeisos**: A.-L. Bedal, 'A Paradeisos at Petra: New Light on the "Lower Market"', *Annual of the Department of Antiquities of Jordan*, xliii (1999), pp. 227-39. **Gardens in Hellenistic palaces**: see in general I. Nielsen, *Hellenistic Palaces* (Århus, 1994).

pp. 254-5 **Basilica at Sebaste**: J. W. Crowfoot, K. M. Kenyon, E. L. Sukenik, *The Buildings at Samaria*, London, 1942. **Basilicas at Canatha**: Gh. Amer, J.-L. Biscop, J. Dentzer-Feydy, J.-P. Sodini, 'L'ensemble basilical de Qanawat (Syrie du sud)', *Syria* 59 (1982), pp. 257-318.

pp. 255-9 **Entertainment and assemblies**: J.-Ch. Balty, *Curia Ordinis: Recherches d'architecture et d'urbanisme antique sur les curies provinciales du monde romain* (Brussels, 1991). For **Marathus**, see N. Salibi, 'Amrit', in J.-M. Dentzer, W. Orthmann (eds), *Archéologie et histoire de la Syrie*, ii (Saarbrücken, 1989), pp. 19-30. On **theatres**, see E. Frézouls, 'Recherches sur les théâtres de l'Orient syrien', *Syria*, xxxvi (1959), pp. 202-28, and xxxviii (1961), pp. 54-86; and, *idem*, 'Les édifices des spectacles en Syrie', in Dentzer and Orthmann, pp. 385-406. See also A. Segal, *Theatres in Roman Palestine and Provincia Arabia*, Leiden, 1995. The theatre at Philippopolis is the subject of a study by P. Coupel, E. Frézouls (ed.), *Le théâtre de Philippopolis en Arabie* (Paris, 1956). The **north theatre at Gerasa**: V. Clark *et al.*, 'The Jerash North Theatre: Architecture and Archaeology 1982-1983', in F. Zayadine (ed.), *Jerash Archaeological Project* (Amman, 1983). **Arena at Tyre**: M. Chehab, 'Tyr à l'époque romaine', *Mélanges de l'Université Saint Joseph*, xxxviii (1962), pp. 13-40. **Caesarea**: Y. Porath, 'Herod's "amphitheatre" at Caesarea: a multipurpose entertainment building', in J. Humphrey (ed.), *The Roman and Byzantine Near East: Some Recent Archaeological Research* (Ann Arbor, 1995), pp. 15-27. **On the Dura Europus 'odeum'**: P. Leriche, 'Salle à gradins du temple d'Artémis à Doura-Europos', *Topoi*, ix (1999), pp. 725-6; 'Doura-Europos: Bilan de la campagne 1998', *Annales archéologiques arabes syriennes*, xliv (2001), pp. 107-30, at pp. 113-15. **Baths**: F. Yegül, *Baths and Bathing in Classical Antiquity* (New York, Cambridge, MA, and London, 1992). **Kifrin's bath**: above, notes to pp. 55-8. **Bath at Serjilla**: G. Charpentier, 'Les bains de Serjilla', *Syria*, lxxi (1994), pp. 113-42.

pp. 259-61 **Dura-Europus**: See above, notes to pp. 108-21. P. Leriche (above, notes to p. 30) has proposed that the original foundation of Seleucus I was a small settlement around the fortified citadel, and that the formal plan and enlargement of the city occurred in the mid-second century BC. For social structure and lack of monumentality at Dura, see A.J. Wharton, *Refiguring the Post Classical City: Dura Europos, Jerash, Jerusalem and Ravenna* (Cambridge, 1995).

pp. 261-9 On the **late antique city**, see in particular J.H.W.G. Liebeschuetz, *The Decline and Fall of the Ancient City* (Oxford, 2001). Other important work includes S.J.B. Barnish, 'The Transformation of Classical Cities and the Pirenne Debate', *Journal of Roman Archaeology*, ii (1989), pp. 385-400; W. Liebeschuetz, 'The End of the Ancient City', in J. Rich (ed.), *The City in Late Antiquity* (London, 1992), pp. 1-49; L. Di Segni, 'The Involvement of Local, Municipal and Provincial Authorities in Urban Building in Late Antique Palestine and Arabia', in J.H. Humphrey (ed.), *The Roman and Byzantine Near East: Some Recent Archaeological Research* (Ann Arbor, 1995), pp. 312-32; C. Foss, 'Syria in Transition, AD 550-750: An Archaeological Approach', *Dumbarton Oaks Papers*, li (1997), pp. 190-269; L. Lavan, *Recent Research in Late Antique Urbanism* (Portsmouth, RI, 2001).

pp. 262 **Caracalla and the citizen of Byblus**: R. Duncan-Jones, *Structure and Scale in the Roman Economy* (Cambridge, 1990), p. 167. **Restrictions on the movement of councillors**: Theodosian Code 12.18.1-2. Until AD 386 councillors could freely sell their ancestral property, on which their membership of the council depended, and in this rather drastic way escape the burdens: Liebeschuetz, *Antioch* (Oxford, 1972), pp. 182-6. Councillors might even by whipped for failing in their duties: Liebeschuetz, *Antioch*, pp. 166 and 173.

pp. 262-3 I have used the term 'grandees' here rather than 'elites', to avoid confusion with the civic elites of the early Roman period. On the grandees' role in city government, I have followed Liebeschuetz, *The Decline and Fall of the Ancient City*, pp. 104-24.

p. 264 **The end of Greek festivals**: Liebeschuetz, *Antioch*, p. 140, noting that by the third quarter of the fourth century only Antioch and Apamea seem to have had sacred games. The Olympic Games of Antioch survived into the sixth century, long after the original Olympics of Greece had been suppressed. **Factions**: Liebeschuetz, *Decline and Fall*, pp. 203-20. **The Tyre hippodrome 'clubs'**: J.-P. Rey-Coquais, 'Inscriptions de l'hippodrome de Tyr', *Journal of Roman Archaeology*, xv (2002), pp. 325-35. **Public building**: see L. Di Segni (above, notes to pp. 261-9). **Elusa's theatre**: F. Millar, *The Roman Near East*, p. 425 note 47.

pp. 264-6 **Evidence for change**: see above, notes to pp. 261-9, and below, notes to pp. 424-5. **Re-employment of inscriptions to Agrippa**: J.-Ch. Balty, *Guide d'Apamée*, p. 205. **Berytus houses**: D. Perring (above, notes to p. 241), p. 30. **Gerasa**: the evidence is summarized in Liebeschuetz, *Decline and Fall*, pp. 61-2.

pp. 266-9 **Cities that developed in late Roman times**. Procopius: B. Croke, J. Crow, 'Procopius and Dara', *Journal of Roman Studies*, lxxiii (1983), pp. 143-59. **For Sergiopolis/Resafa**, see J. Sauvaget, 'Les Ghassanides et Sergiopolis', *Byzantion*, xiv (1939), pp. 115-30; W. Karnapp, *Die Stadtmauer von Resafa in Syrien* (Berlin, 1976); T. Ulbert, 'Rusafa-Sergiopolis: Pilgrimage Shrine and Capital', in H. Weiss (ed.), *Ebla to Damascus* (Washington, DC, 1985), pp. 452-6; and, *idem*, 'Villes et fortifications de l'Euphrate à l'époque paléo-chrétienne', in J.-M. Dentzer, W. Orthmann (eds.), *Archéologie et histoire de la Syrie*, ii (Saarbrücken, 1989), pp. 283-93. For **Zenobia**, see the splendid study by J. Lauffray, *Halabiyya-Zenobia, place forte du limes oriental et la Haute-Mésopotamie au VIe siècle*, 2 vols (Paris, 1983-91). The fortress is considered one of 'a number of sees which were not civil units' in A.H.M. Jones, *Cities of the Eastern Roman Provinces* (Oxford, 1971), p. 460; but Lauffray's work would seem to refute this.

Chapter 8: Impure Genres

The quest for identities and cultural traditions is a major theme in F. Millar, *The Roman Near East*, and several other important studies by the same author: 'The Phoenician Cities: a Case-study of Hellenisation', *Proceedings of the Cambridge Philological Society*, ccxix (1983), pp. 55-71; 'The Problem of Hellenistic Syria', in A. Kuhrt, S. Sherwin-White, *Hellenism in the East* (London, 1987), pp. 110-33; 'Empire, Community and Culture in the Roman Near East: Greeks, Syrian, Jews and Arabs', *Journal of Jewish Studies*, xxxviii (1987), pp. 143-64; 'Ethnic Identity in the Roman Near East, 325-450: Language, Religion, and Culture', *Mediterranean Archaeology*, xi (1999-2000), pp. 159-76. Other studies of the Near East include C. Dauphin, *La Palestine byzantine: Peuplement et populations* (Oxford, 1998).

For an overview of the region's contribution to classical culture, see E. Will, 'La Syrie à l'époque hellénistique et romaine: mille ans de vie intellectuelle et artistique', in J.-M. Dentzer,

W. Orthmann (eds), *Archéologie et histoire de la Syrie*, ii (Saarbrücken, 1989), pp. 567-79; and M. Sartre, *D'Alexandre à Zénobie*, pp. 867-77.

For some theoretical approaches to identity and culture: Frederik Barth (ed.), *Ethnic Groups and Boundaries: The Social Organisation of Culture Difference* (Oslo, 1969); A.P. Cohen, *The Symbolic Construction of Community* (London, 1985); T.H. Eriksen, *Ethnicity and Nationalism. Anthropological Perspectives* (London, 1993); R. Jenkins, *Social Identity* (London, 1996). For applications of anthropological and social theories to the Roman world, see J. Webster, N. Cooper, *Roman Imperialism: Post-Colonial Perspectives* (Leicester, 1996); R. Laurence, J. Berry (eds), *Cultural Identity in the Roman Empire* (London, 1998). See also the essays in S. Mitchell, G. Greatrex (eds), *Ethnicity and Culture in Late Antiquity* (London and Swansea, 2000).

pp. 270-72 **Syria, Syrians**: T. Noldeke, 'ΑΣΣΥΡΙΟΣ ΣΥΡΙΟΣ ΣΥΡΟΣ', *Hermes*, v (1871), pp. 443-68; F. Cumont, 'The Population of Syria', *Journal of Roman Studies*, xxiv (1934), pp. 187-90; R.N. Frye, 'Assyria and Syria: Synonyms', *Journal of Near Eastern Studies*, li (1992), pp. 281-5. **Antioch's corrupting influence**: see, for example, E.L. Wheeler, 'The Laxity of the Syrian Legions', in D. Kennedy (ed.), *The Roman Army in the East* (Ann Arbor, 1992), pp. 229-76; and, for some general remarks on ancient prejudices, B. Isaac, *The Limits of Empire* (Oxford, 1990), p. 21, note 8; and M. Sartre, *D'Alexandre à Zénobie*, pp. 850-51. **Strabo on Syrians and Assyrians**: 16.1.1-2. **Arabs**: D.S. Potter, *Prophecy and History*, pp. 216-18; F. Millar, *The Roman Near East*, pp. 512-14; J.F. Healey, 'Were the Nabataeans Arabs?', *Aram*, i (1989), pp. 38-44; D.F. Graf, 'The Origin of the Nabataeans', *Aram*, ii (1990), pp. 45-75. **Arab from Canatha**: L. Robert, 'L'épitaphe d'un Arabe à Thasos', *Hellenica*, ii (1946), p. 47; F. Millar, *Roman Near East*, pp. 419-20. The appellation may be because the city of Septimia Canatha was in the province of Arabia (I am grateful to Alexander Hourany for this suggestion). **Ethnic identity at Palmyra**: J.-B. Yon, *Les notables de Palmyre* (Beirut, 2002), pp. 57-97.

p. 272 **Three zones of material culture**: M. Gawlikowski, 'Some Directions and Perspectives of Research', *Mesopotamia*, xxii (1987), pp. 11-17.

pp. 273-7 On **Hellenism and the Second Sophistic**: G. Anderson, *The Second Sophistic: A Cultural Phenomenon in the Roman Empire* (London, 1993); S. Swain, *Hellenism and Empire: Language, Classicism and Power in the Greek World, AD 50-250* (Oxford, 1996). For the argument that Hellenism was a bonding cultural force, see the essays by G.W. Bowersock, *Hellenism in Late Antiquity* (Cambridge, 1990). See also G. Woolf, 'Becoming Roman, Staying Greek: Culture, Identity, and the Civilizing Process in the Roman East', *Proceedings of the Cambridge Philological Society*, xl (1994), pp. 116-43.

p. 274 For the **evidence from papyri**, see notes to pp. 142-5, above.

pp. 275-6 **Judaism and Hellenism**: see especially A. Momigliano, *Alien Wisdom: The Limits of Hellenization* (Cambridge, 1975); M. Hengel, *The 'Hellenization' of Judaea in the First*

Century after Christ (London and Philadelphia, 1989); and F. Millar, *The Roman Near East*, pp. 353-74.

p. 276 **Medaba mosaics**: M. Avi-Yonah, *The Madaba Mosaic Map* (Jerusalem, 1954). **Sarrïn**: J. Balty, below, notes to pp. 324-5. **Malalas**: E. Jeffreys, M. Jeffreys, R. Scott *et al.*, *The Chronicle of John Malalas: A Translation* (Melbourne, 1986).

p. 278 The **population of Dura Europus**: C.B. Welles, 'The Population of Roman Dura', in P.R. Coleman-Norton (ed.), *Studies in Roman Economic and Social History in Honor of A.C. Johnson* (Princeton, 1951), pp. 251-74; E. Will, 'La population de Doura-Europos: une évaluation', *Syria*, lxv (1988), pp. 315-21. **Hellenism and other identities in the Decapolis**: P.-L. Gatier, 'A propos de la culture grecque à Gérasa', in A. Invernizzi, J.-F. Salles (eds), *Arabia Antiqua: Hellenistic Centres around Arabia* (Rome, 1993), pp. 15-35; D. Kennedy, 'The Identity of Roman Gerasa: an Archaeological Approach', in G.W. Clarke, D. Harrison (eds) *Identities in the Eastern Mediterranean in Antiquity: Proceedings of a Conference held at the Humanities Research Centre in Canberra, 10-12 November, 1997, Mediterranean Archaeology*, xi (1998 [1999]), pp. 39-69. **Caesarea ad Libanum**: third-century coins read COL. CESARIA LIBANI ITVR.: G.F. Hill, *BMC: Phoenicia* (London, 1910), p. 110.

p. 279 **Abila coin** of Alexander and Seleucus: W. Leschhorn, 'Mythos und Stadtgründung im Nahen Osten', *Ο ΕΛΛΗ–ΝΙΣΜΟΣ ΣΤΗΝ ΑΝΑΤΟΛΗ: International Meeting of History and Archaeology, Delphi, 6-9 November 1986* (Athens, 1991), pp. 441-51, at p. 450, pl. 4, 3.

p. 280 **Coin types as monuments**: see above, notes to p. 218. For **Tyrian coin types** see G.F. Hill, above, notes to p. 278. The **Pygmalion type** on coins of Tyre is discussed by M. Robinson, 'Phoenician Inscriptions on the Late Roman Bronze Coinage of Tyre, Part I-A: Coin Depicting Pygmalion', *Spink's Numismatic Circular*, cv/7 (September 1997), pp. 234-6; and G. Bijovksi, 'More about Pygmalion from Tyre', *Quaderni Ticinesi*, xxix (2000), pp. 319-32. On **Philo of Byblos**: H.W. Attridge, R.A. Oden, *Philo of Byblos: The Phoenician History* (Washington, 1981).

pp. 281-3 **Signs of culture**: On semiotics in archaeology, see I. Hodder, *Symbols in Action* (Cambridge, 1992). For **semiotics and communication**: W. Leeds-Hurwitz, *Semiotics and Communication: Signs, Codes, Cultures* (Hillsdale, NJ, 1993. **Semiotics and communal identity**: A.P. Cohen, *The Symbolic Construction of Community* (London, 1985).

p. 281 For the **symbolism of Uranius Antoninus**, see D.S. Potter, *Prophecy and History in the Crisis of the Roman Empire: A Historical Commentary on the Thirteenth Sibylline Oracle* (Oxford, 1990), pp. 48-9, 325-6. For a more sceptical view: K. Butcher, 'Imagined Emperors: Personalities and Political Failure in the 3rd Century', *Journal of Roman Archaeology*, ix (1996), pp. 515-27.

p. 282 The **Temple of Bel**: H. Seyrig, R. Amy, E. Will, *Le temple de Bel à Palmyre*, 2 vols (Paris, 1968-75); for a summary of its construction see T. Kaizer, *The Religious Life of Palmyra* (Stuttgart, 2002), pp. 67-9. **Its**

Hellenized veneer: W. Ball, *Rome in the East*, pp. 336-7.

pp. 283-9 **Languages**: A.H.M. Jones, *The Later Roman Empire*, pp. 991-7; R. MacMullen, 'Provincial Languages in the Roman Empire', in R. MacMullen, *Changes in the Roman Empire* (Princeton, 1990), pp. 32-40; F.G.B. Millar, 'Il ruolo delle lingue semitiche nel vicino oriente tardo-romano (V-VI secolo)', *Mediterraneo Antico*, i (1998), pp. 71-94; M. Sartre, *D'Alexandre à Zénobie*, pp. 853-4. A colloquium entitled *Die Sprachen im römischen Reich der Kaiserzeit: Kolloquium vom 8. bis. 10. April 1974* (Cologne and Bonn, 1980) has some articles relevant to the region.

p. 284 **Bilingualism**: see J.-B. Yon, *Les notables de Palmyre* (Beirut, 2002), pp. 23-36. **Personal names**: J.-P. Rey-Coquais, 'Onomastique et histoire de la Syrie gréco-romaine', in D.M. Pippidi (ed.), *Actes du VIIe congrès international d'épigraphie grecque et latine* (Paris and Bucharest, 1979), pp. 171-83; A. Negev, *Personal Names in the Nabataean Realm. Qedem*, xxxii (1991). M. Sartre, 'Nom, langue et identité culturelle en Syrie aux époques hellénistique et romaine', in J.-B. Humbert, A. Desreumaux, *Khirbet es-Samra*, i (Turnhout, 1998), pp. 555-62. On the **use of Semitic and Greek names**, see D. Kennedy, 'Greek, Roman and Native Cultures in the Roman Near East', in J. Humphrey (ed.), *The Roman and Byzantine Near East*, ii (Portsmouth, RI, 1999), pp. 76-106. On **papyrus documents**, see notes to pp. 142-5, above.

p. 285 **Aramaic under the Achaemenids**: it is traditionally considered to have been the *lingua franca*, but see also D. Graf, 'Aramaic on the Periphery of the Achaemenid Realm', *Archäologische Mitteilungen aus Iran und Turan*, xxxii (2000), pp. 75-92. For a **survey of Aramaic**, see S. Brock, 'Three Thousand Years of Aramaic Literature', *Aram*, i (1989), pp. 11-23.

pp. 285-7 On **Syriac**, see especially the work of S. Brock, *Syriac Perspectives on Late Antiquity* (London, 1984); *From Ephrem to Romanos: Interactions between Syriac and Greek in Late Antiquity* (Aldershot, 1999); J.B. Segal, *Edessa: 'The Blessed City'* (Oxford, 1970); F. Millar, 'Ethnic Identity in the Roman Near East, 325-450: Language, Religion, and Culture', *Mediterranean Archaeology*, xi (1999-2000), pp. 159-76. The earliest known writer in Syriac to come from west of the Euphrates appears to be Balaeus, a fifth-century poet: see Millar, p. 163, n. 20. But Syriac inscriptions of the early imperial period are known from Birecik and Apamea (Zeugma) on the eastern bank of the Euphrates, and it would not be too astonishing if they should eventually turn up on the western bank as well. On **Bardaisan**: H.J.W. Drijvers, *Bardaisan of Edessa* (Assen, 1966); J. Teixidor, *Bardesane d'Edesse: La première philosophie syriaque* (Paris, 1992).

pp. 287-8 **Phoenician**: F. Millar, 'The Phoenician Cities: a Case-study of Hellenisation', *Proceedings of the Cambridge Philological Society*, ccxix (1983), pp. 55-71; F. Briquel-Chatonnet, 'Les derniers témoignages sur la langue phénicienne en Orient', *Rivista di Studi Fenici*, xix (1991), pp. 3-21. **Hebrew**: E. Schürer, *A History of the Jewish People*, ii (Edinburgh, 1979), pp. 19-23. **Arabic**: J.A.

Bellamy, 'A New Reading of the Namarah Inscription' (above, notes to pp. 64-6); and, *idem*, 'Arabic Verses from the First/Second Century: The Inscription of 'En 'Avdat', *Journal of Semitic Studies*, xxxv (1990), pp. 73-9; C. Robin, 'Les plus anciens monuments de la langue arabe', in C. Robin (ed.), *L'Arabie antique de Karaib'il à Mahomet, Revue du monde musulman et de la Méditerranée*, lxi (1991), pp. 113-16. Note a dated inscription (AD 267) from Hegra, south of our region: J.F. Healey, G. Rex Smith, 'Jaussen-Savignac 17: The Earliest Dated Arabic Document (AD 267)', *Al-Atlal*, xii (1989), pp. 77-84. It is likely that more evidence for Arabic in Syria and the Near East will emerge in future. **Safaitic**: There is a large literature. See especially M.C.A. Macdonald, 'Nomads and the Hawran in the Late Hellenistic and Roman Periods: a Reassessment of the Epigraphic Evidence', *Syria*, lxx (1993), pp. 303-403; also H. Zeinaddin, 'Safaitische Inschriften aus dem Gabal al-'Arab', *Damaszener Mitteilungen*, xii (2000), pp. 265-89.

pp. 289-307 **Architecture**: J. B. Ward-Perkins, *Roman Imperial Architecture* (London, 1981), has a chapter on the region; see also W. MacDonald, *The Architecture of the Roman Empire* (New York, 1986); and much of W. Ball, *Rome in the East*, is devoted to architecture. Other essays examining local traditions and outside influences: A. Schmidt-Colinet, 'Aspects of "Hellenism" in Nabatean and Palmyrene Funerary Architecture', in *Ο ΕΛΛ–ΗΝΙΣΜΟΣ ΣΤΗΝ ΑΝΑΤΟΛΗ: International Meeting of History and Archaeology, Delphi, 6-9 November 1986* (Athens, 1991), pp. 13-44; and, by the same author, 'East and West in Palmyrene Pattern Books', *Annales archéologiques arabes syriennes*, xlii (1996), pp. 417-23; K.S. Freyberger, 'Das kaiserzeitliche Damaskus: Schauplatz lokaler Tradition und auswärtiger Einflüsse', *Damaszener Mitteilungen*, xi (1999), pp. 123-38.

pp. 289-95 **Architectural style**: see the essays by J. Dentzer-Feydy, 'Le décor architectural en Syrie aux époques hellénistique et romaine', in J.-M. Dentzer, W. Orthmann (eds), *Archéologie et histoire de la Syrie*, ii (Saarbrücken, 1989), pp. 457-76; 'Le décor architectural en Transjordanie de la periode hellénistique à la création de la province d'Arabie en 106', *Studies in the History and Archaeology of Jordan*, iv (1992), pp. 227-32. For **Sia**, see H.C. Butler, *Publications of the Princeton University Archaeological Expeditions II.A.6*, pp. 365-402 (see also notes to pp. 359-60, below). **Fakra**: D. Krencker, W. Zschietzschmann, *Römische Tempel in Syrien* (Berlin and Leipzig, 1938), i, pp. 40-55; J.-P. Rey-Coquais, 'Qalaat Fakra: un monument du culte impérial dans la montagne libanaise', *Topoi*, ix (1999), pp. 632-8, arguing for a sanctuary of the imperial cult there. For the tower, see P. Collart, 'La tour de Qalaat Fakra', *Syria*, l (1973), pp. 137-61. **Yammoune**: the lintel was photographed by the author in 1995; I do not know if it is still visible. For the **Q. Longinus Nicon inscription**: C. Ghadban, 'Trois nouvelles inscriptions latines de Beyrouth', *Bulletin d'Archéologie et d'Architecture Libanaises*, ii (1997), pp. 206-35.

pp. 291 **Palmyrene architectural style**: A.

Schmidt-Colinet, *Palmyra: Kulturbegegnung im Grenzbereich* (Mainz, 1995); C. Saliou, 'Du portique à la rue à portiques. Les rues à colonnades de Palmyre dans le cadre de l'urbanisme romain imperial: originalité et conformisme', *Annales archéologiques arabes syriennes*, xlii (1996), pp. 319-27; and, in the same volume, A. Invernizzi, 'Les chapiteaux du temple de Bel de Palmyre dans le cadre des chapiteaux à éléments rapportés dans l'Asie hellénistique', pp. 355-61; M. Gawlikowski, 'Du hamana au naos: le temple palmyrénien hellénisé', *Topoi*, vii (1997), pp. 837-49; A. Schmidt-Colinet, 'Aspects of "Romanization": The Tomb Architecture at Palmyra and its Decoration', in S.E. Alcock (ed.), *The Early Roman Empire in the East* (Oxford, 1997), pp. 157-77.

pp. 291-2 **Architectural style in the Hauran**: J. Dentzer-Feydy, 'Décor architectural et développement du Hauran de Ier s. av. J.-C. au VIIe s. ap. J.-C.', in *Hauran*, i/2 (Paris, 1986), pp. 261-309; K.S. Freyberger, *Die frühkaiserzeitlichen Heiligtümer der Karawanenstationen im hellenisierten Osten* (Mainz, 1998).

pp. 292-3 For the **influence of Ptolemaic architecture and the architecture of Nabataea**, see J. McKenzie, *The Architecture of Petra* (Oxford, 1990).

p. 294 **Roman and other influences at Heliopolis**: H. Seyrig, 'Questions héliopolitaines', *Syria*, xxxi (1954), pp. 80-98; Y. Hajjar, *La triade d'Héliopolis-Baalbek*, 3 vols (Leiden, 1977-85); M. Wheeler, 'Size and Baalbek', in F. Ragette, *Baalbek* (London, 1980), pp. 7-11. **Influence of patterns in other media**: A. Schmidt-Colinet, 'East and West in Palmyrene Pattern Books' (above, notes to pp. 289-307). **Preference for ashlar masonry**: C. Mango, *Byzantine Architecture* (Milan, 1979), pp. 79-80.

pp. 294-5 **Architectural decoration in the late Roman period**: C. Strube, 'Die Formgebung der Apsisdekoration in Qalbloze und Qalat Siman', *Jahrbuch für Antike und Christentum*, xx (1977), pp. 181-91; and, by the same author, 'Baudekoration in den Kirchen des nordsyrischen Kalksteinmassivs', *Archäologischer Anzeiger* (1978), pp. 577-601; A. Naccache, J.-P. Sodini, 'Le décor architectural en Syrie byzantine', in J.-M. Dentzer, W. Orthmann (eds), *Archéologie et histoire de la Syrie*, ii (Saarbrücken, 1989), pp. 477-90; A. Naccache, *Le décor des églises de villages d'Antiochène du IVe au VIIe siècle*, 2 vols (Paris, 1992).

pp. 295-302 For **burials and tombs** in antiquity in general: J.M.C. Toynbee, *Death and Burial in the Roman World* (London, 1971); I. Morris, *Death-ritual and Social Structure in Classical Antiquity* (Cambridge, 1992). Excellent **overviews for the region** are provided by M. Gawlikowski, 'La notion de tombeau en Syrie romaine', *Berytus*, xxi (1972), pp. 5-15; and A. Sartre, 'Architecture funéraire de la Syrie', in J.-M. Dentzer, W. Orthmann (eds), *Archéologie et histoire de la Syrie*, ii (Saarbrücken, 1989), pp. 423-46. For a **detailed and systematic study of the Hauran**, which draws on comparisons with other parts of the Near East, see A. Sartre-Fauriat, *Des tombeaux et des morts: Monuments funéraires, société et culture en Syrie du sud du Ier s. av. J.-C. au VIIe s. apr. J.-C.* (Beirut, 2001). This

seems set to become a standard work on the subject of tombs and burials in Syria and the Near East.

p. 296 **Emesa necropolis**: H. Seyrig, 'Antiquités de la nécropole d'Emèse', *Syria*, xxix (1952), pp. 204-50 and xxx (1953), pp. 12-24. See also A. Sartre-Fauriat, *Des tombeaux et des morts*, i, p. 42. **Sarcophagi**: Sartre-Fauriat, i, pp. 217-40, and ii, p. 76 (on the rarity of single, freestanding sarcophagi in the Hauran).

p. 297 **Distribution of loculi and arcosilia**: but note that one form of burial did not exist to the exclusion of the other in different regions: Sartre-Fauriat, ii, pp. 91-2. **Ossuaries**: Sartre-Fauriat, ii, pp. 92-4; P. Figueras, *Decorated Jewish Ossuaries* (Leiden, 1983); L.Y. Rahmani, *A Catalogue of Jewish Ossuaries in the Collection of the State of Israel* (Jerusalem, 1994).

pp. 298-9 **Kidron valley**: N. Avigad, *Ancient Monuments in the Kidron Valley* (Jerusalem, 1954). **Seats at entrances to hypogea**: M. Griesheimer, 'Sociabilité et rites funéraires: Les porches à banquettes des maisons et des tombeaux du Massif Calcaire', in Castel *et al.* (below, notes to pp. 302-7), pp. 297-304. On **Rimet al-Lohf** see the works of A. Sartre-Fauriat, above, notes to pp. 295-302. Inscriptions attest to the existence of 'dovecots' or, more poetically, towers 'for swift-winged pigeons': Sartre-Fauriat, ii, p. 70.

pp. 299-301 **Funerary architecture of Palmyra**: see in particular the studies by M. Gawlikowski, 'Classement, chronologie et évolution de la tour funéraire à Palmyre', *Etudes et Travaux*, iii (1966), pp. 168-81; *Monuments funéraires de Palmyre* (Warsaw, 1970); and by A. Schmidt-Colinet, 'L'architecture funéraire de Palmyre', in J.-M. Dentzer, W. Orthmann (eds), *Archéologie et histoire de la Syrie*, ii (Saarbrücken, 1989), pp. 447-56; K. Parlasca, 'Beobachtungen zur palmyrenischer Grabarchitektur', *Damaszener Mitteilungen*, iv (1989), pp. 181-90; E. Will, 'La maison d'éternité et les conceptions funéraires des Palmyréniens', in *Mélanges Pierre Lévêque* (Besançon, 1990), pp. 433-40. **Tower-tombs**: E. Will, 'La tour funéraire de Palmyre', *Syria*, xxvi (1949), pp. 87-116. For tower-tombs elsewhere see E. Will, 'La tour funéraire de Syrie et les monuments apparentés', *Syria*, xxvi (1949), pp. 258-313; R. Gografe, 'Die Grabtürme von Sirrin (Osroëne)', *Damaszener Mitteilungen*, viii (1995), pp. 165-201. **Temple-tomb no. 36**: K. al-Asa'd, A. Schmidt-Colinet, 'Das Tempelgrab Nr. 36 in der Westnekropole von Palmyra: Ein Vorbericht', *Damaszener Mitteilungen*, ii (1985), pp. 17-35. The shift from tower-tombs to temple-tombs appears to have been driven by changing fashions among the elites: see J.-B. Yon, *Les notables de Palmyre* (Beirut, 2002), pp. 197-232.

pp. 301-2 The **textiles from Zenobia**: R. Fister, *Textiles de Halabiyeh (Zenobia)* (Paris, 1951). **Gold sheets at Heliopolis**: M. van Ess, *Heliopolis Baalbek, 1898-1998: Rediscovery and Ruins* (Berlin, 1998). For **gold face masks** as a 'Phoenician' feature: J. Curtis, 'Gold Face-Masks in the Ancient Near East', in S. Campbell, A. Green (eds), *The Archaeology of Death in the Ancient Near East* (Oxford, 1995), pp. 226-31. **Lead sarcophagi**: M. Avi-Yonah, 'Lead Coffins from Palestine', *Quarterly of the*

Department of Antiquities of Palestine, iv (1935), pp. 87-99; A.-M. Bertin, 'Les sarcophages en plomb syriens au Musée du Louvre', *Revue archéologique* (1974), pp. 43-82. For more recent studies which deal with questions of production and workshops, see L.Y. Rahmani, 'Roman Lead Coffins in the Israel Museum', *Israel Museum Journal*, vii (1988), pp. 47-55; D. White, 'The Eschatological Connection between Lead and Ropes as Reflected in a Roman Imperial Period Coffin in Philadelphia', *Israel Exploration Journal*, xlix (1999), pp. 66-91. For the **Tyre epitaphs**, see the works by J.-P. Rey-Coquais, *Inscriptions grecques et latines découvertes dans les fouilles de Tyr (1963-1974)*, i: *Inscriptions de la Nécropole*, *Bulletin du Musée de Beyrouth*, xxix (1977); 'Fouilles récentes, ville, hippodrome et nécropole: l'apport des inscriptions', *Revue archéologique* (1979), pp. 166-8. In general, however, occupations are rare in the corpus of funerary inscriptions from the region as a whole, except for soldiers. See comments by A. Sartre-Fauriat, *Des tombeaux et des morts*, ii, pp. 162-4.

pp. 302-7 **Domestic architecture**: see J.-Ch. Balty, 'La maison urbaine en Syrie', in J.-M. Dentzer, W. Orthmann (eds), *Archéologie et histoire de la Syrie*, ii (Saarbrücken, 1989), pp. 407-22; and the important collection of essays in C. Castel, M. al-Maqdissi, F. Villeneuve (eds), *Les maisons dans la Syrie antique du IIIe millénaire aux débuts de l'Islam. Pratiques et représentations de l'espace domestique: Actes du Colloque International, Damas 27-30 juin 1992* (Beirut, 1997). For the south, see especially Y. Hirschfeld, *The Palestinian Dwelling in the Roman-Byzantine Period* (Jerusalem, 1995).

p. 303 **Edifice au *triclinos***: J.-Ch. Balty, 'Palais et maisons d'Apamée', in Castel *et al.* (above, notes to pp. 302-7), pp. 283-95; see also C. Foss (above, notes to pp. 261-9), pp. 217-18. For **Julianus the Architect** of Ascalon, see notes to pp. 137-8, above.

pp. 303-4 **Dura Europus**: A. Perkins, *The Art of Dura-Europos* (Oxford, 1973), pp. 21-3; and the works of A. Allara, 'Les maisons de Doura-Europos: Questions de typologie', *Syria*, lxiii (1986), pp. 39-60; 'Domestic Architecture at Dura-Europus', *Mesopotamia*, xxii (1987), pp. 67-76. **Petra**: R. Stucky, 'The Nabataean House and the Urbanistic System of the Habitation Quarters in Petra', *Studies in the History and Archaeology of Jordan*, v (Amman, 1995), pp. 193-8.

pp. 304-5 **Palmyra**: E. Frézouls, 'A propos de l'architecture domestique à Palmyre', *Ktéma*, i (1976), pp. 29-52; M. Gawlikowski, 'L'habitat à Palmyre de l'antiquité au moyen-age', in Castel *et al.* (above, notes to pp. 302-7), pp. 161-6. **Apamea**: J. Balty (ed.), *Actes du IIIe Colloque Apamée de Syrie. Bilan des recherches archéologiques 1973-1979: Aspects de l'architecture domestique d'Apamée* (Brussels, 1984); and C. Foss, above, notes to pp. 261-9.

pp. 305-7 **Dead Cities**: see notes to pp. 145-53, especially the work of G. Tate, to which add J.-P. Sodini, G. Tate, 'Maisons d'époque romaine et byzantine (IIe-VIe siècle) du Massif Calcaire de Syrie du Nord: Etude typologique', in J. Balty (ed.), *Apamée de Syrie: Bilan des recherches archéologiques 1973-1979* (Brussels, 1984), pp. 377-429. **Hauran**: F. Villeneuve, 'L'économie rurale et la vie des campagnes dans le Hauran antique' (above, notes to pp. 157-61); and, by the same author, 'Les salles à alcôve dans les maisons d'époque romaine et byzantine en Syrie', in Castel *et al.* (above, notes to pp. 302-7), pp. 269-81.

pp. 307-27 **Art**: In general: J. Elsner, *Imperial Rome and Christian Triumph: The Art of the Roman Empire, AD 100-450* (Oxford, 1998). On the Near East: D. Schlumberger, 'Descendants non-méditerranéens de l'art grec', *Syria*, xxxvii (1960), pp. 131-66, 253-318; E. Will, 'La Syrie romaine entre l'Occident gréco-romain et l'Orient parthe', *Actes du VIIIe Congrès international d'archéologie classique* (Paris, 1965), pp. 511-25; H. Klengel, *The Art of Ancient Syria* (South Brunswick and New York, 1972); K. Parlasca, 'La sculpture grecque et la sculpture d'époque romaine impériale en Syrie' in J.-M. Dentzer, W. Orthmann (eds), *Archéologie et histoire de la Syrie*, ii (Saarbrücken, 1989), pp. 537-56; T. Weber, 'A Survey of Roman Sculpture in the Decapolis: Preliminary Report', *Annual of the Department of Antiquities of Jordan*, xxxiv (1990), pp. 351-5.

p. 308 **Kartaba sculpture**: C. Doumet-Serhal, A.-M. Maila-Afeiche, F. el-Dahdah, A. Rabate, *Stones and Creed: 100 Artefacts from Lebanon's Antiquity* (Beirut, 1998), p. 188. **Bronze feet** from the agora at Palmyra: M.A.R. Colledge, *The Art of Palmyra* (London, 1976), p. 90. **Agrippa's bronzes**: J.-P. Rey-Coquais, 'Inscriptions grecques' (above, notes to p. 226).

p. 309 **Imported marbles**: M. Fisher, 'Figured Capitals in Roman Palestine: Marble Imports and Local Stone. Some Aspects of "Imperial" and "Provincial" Art', *Palestine Exploration Quarterly*, cxxi (1989), pp. 112-32. **Byblus nymphaeum**: J. Lauffray, 'Une fouille au pied de l'acropole de Byblos', *Bulletin du Musée de Beyrouth*, iv (1940), pp. 7-36. **Imports to Caesarea Maritima and Scythopolis**: E.A. Friedland, 'Graeco-Roman Sculpture in the Levant: the Marbles from the Sanctuary of Pan at Caesarea Philippi (Banias)', in J. Humphrey (ed.), *The Roman and Byzantine Near East*, ii (Portsmouth, RI, 1999), pp. 7-22. **Allat temple at Palmyra**: see the discussions by M. Gawlikowski, 'Le Temple d'Allat à Palmyre', *Revue archéologique* (1977), pp. 253-74; 'Réflexions sur la chronologie du sanctuaire d'Allat à Palmyre', *Damaszener Mitteilungen*, i (1983), pp. 59-67; 'Le premier temple d'Allat', in *Resurrecting the Past: A Joint Tribute to Adnan Bounni* (Istanbul, 1990), pp. 101-9.

p. 310 **Zeugma sculptures**: K. Parlasca, *Syrische Grabreliefs hellenistischer und römischer Zeit: Fundgruppen und Probleme* (Mainz, 1982); various sculptures are illustrated in N. Basgelen, R. Ergeç, *Belkis/Zeugma: A Last Look at History* (Istanbul, 2000), pp. 16-17. For the basket and eagle, see E. Will, 'Les problèmes iconographiques de la Syrie romaine', in *EIΔ-ΩΛΟΠΟΙΙΑ: Actes du colloque sur les problèmes de l'image dans le monde méditerranéen classique, Lourmarin, 1982* (Rome, 1985), pp. 41-8, pl. 2, fig. 3. **Mount Nemrut**: D.H. Sanders, *Nemrut Dag: The Hierothesion of Antiochus I of Commagene*, 2 vols (Winona Lake, MN, 1996).

pp. 310-11 **Hauran sculptures**: A. Al Ush, A. Joundi, B. Zouhdi, *Catalogue du Musée National de Damas* (Damascus, 1969); M.

Dunand, *Le Musée de Soueïda* (Paris, 1934); G. Bolelli, 'La sculpture au musée de Suweida', in J.-M. Dentzer, J. Dentzer-Feydy, *Le djebel al-Arab: Histoire et patrimoine au Musée de Suweida* (Paris, 1991), pp. 63-80; K. Lembke, 'Römische Schreiberstatuen aus dem Hauran und ihr ägyptisierendes Umfeld', *Damaszener Mitteilungen*, xi (1999), pp. 255-64; A. Sartre-Fauriat, *Des tombeaux et des morts* (Beirut, 2001).

pp. 311-13 **Palmyrene sculpture**: H. Ingholt, *Studier over palmyrensk skulptur* (Copenhagen, 1928); E. Will, 'Le relief de la tour de Kithot et le banquet funéraire à Palmyre', *Syria*, xxviii (1951), pp. 70-100; M. Morehart, 'Early Sculpture at Palmyra', *Berytus*, xii (1956-8), pp. 53-83; M.A.R. Colledge, *The Art of Palmyra* (London, 1976); M. Pietrzykowski, 'The Origins of the Frontal Convention in the Arts of the Near East', *Berytus*, xxxiii (1985), pp. 55-9; K. Tanabe, *Sculptures of Palmyra*, i (Tokyo, 1987); A. Sadurska, A. Bounni, *Les sculptures funéraires de Palmyre* (Rome, 1994); K. Parlasca, 'Some Problems of Palmyrene Plastic Art', *Aram*, vii (1995), pp. 59-71. **Parthian sculpture**: M.A.R. Colledge, *Parthian Art* (London, 1977).

p. 313 **Dura Europus**: A. Perkins, *The Art of Dura-Europos* (Oxford, 1973); S.B. Downey, *The Herakles Sculptures: Excavations at Dura-Europos, Final Report III. I. I.* (New Haven, 1969); S.B. Downey, 'Cult Reliefs at Dura-Europos: Problems of Interpretation and Placement', *Damaszener Mitteilungen*, x (1998), pp. 201-10. **Antioch collection of sculpture**: D.M. Brinkerhoff, *A Collection of Sculpture in Classical and Early Christian Antioch* (New York, 1970).

pp. 313-25 **Mosaics**: two fundamental works are by J. Balty: *Mosaïques antiques de Syrie* (Brussels, 1977); and *Mosaïques antiques du Proche-Orient: Chronologie, iconographie, interprétation* (Besançon, 1995). An excellent general study is K.M.D. Dunbabin's *Mosaics of the Greek and Roman World* (Cambridge, 1999). For various regions and sites, see D. Levi, *Antioch Mosaic Pavements*, 2 vols (Princeton, 1947); S. Campbell, *The Mosaics of Antioch* (Toronto, 1988); N. Basgelen, R. Ergeç, *Belkis/Zeugma* (Istanbul, 2000); M. Chéhab, *Mosaïques du Liban*, 2 vols, *Bulletin du Musée de Beyrouth*, xiv-xv (1957-9); H. Stern, *Les mosaïques des maisons d'Achille et de Cassiopée à Palmyre* (Paris, 1977); J. Balty, *Mosaïques d'Apamée* (Brussels, 1985); M. Piccirillo, *The Mosaics of Jordan* (Amman, 1993); J. Balty, 'Les mosaïques de Shahba-Philippopolis: Chronologie, Ateliers, Commanditaires', *Annales archéologiques arabes syriennes*, xli (1997), pp. 49-61.

p. 316 **Cassiopeia in a Syrian context**: J. Balty, *Mosaïques antiques de Syrie* (Brussels, 1977); and, for eastern readings of Greek myths in mosaics, by the same author: 'Composantes classiques et orientales dans les mosaïques de Palmyre', *Annales archéologiques arabes syriennes*, xlii (1996), pp. 407-16.

p. 318 **Mosaic of the Evil Eye**: D. Levi, 'The Evil Eye and the Lucky Hunchback', in R. Stillwell (ed.), *Antioch-on-the-Orontes*, iii (Princeton, 1941), pp. 220-32. **House of the Buffet Supper**: D. Levi, *Antioch Mosaic Pavements*, pp. 127-36.

p. 319 **On *ekphrasis***: M. Krieger, *Ekphrasis: The Illusion of the Natural Sign* (Baltimore,

1992); J. Hefferman, *Museum of Words* (Chicago, 1992). **Mariamme mosaic**: A.R. Zaqzuq, M. Duchesne-Guillemin, 'La mosaïque de Miriamin', *Annales archéologiques arabes syriennes*, xx (1970), pp. 93-125. **Metiochos and Parthenope**: S. Campbell, R. Ergeç, E. Csapo, 'New Mosaics', in D. Kennedy (ed.), *The Twin Towns of Zeugma on the Euphrates: Rescue Work and Historical Studies* (Portsmouth, RI, 1998), pp. 109-28.

pp. 319-21 **Philippopolis mosaic**: E. Will, 'Une nouvelle mosaïque de Chahba-Philippopolis', *Annales archéologiques arabes syriennes*, iii (1953), pp. 27-48; for a recent interpretation of this pavement, see M.-H. Quet, 'La mosaïque dite d'Aion de Shahba-Philippopolis, Philippe l'Arabe et la conception hellène de l'ordre du monde, en Arabie, à l'aube du christianisme', *Cahiers Glotz*, x (1999), pp. 269-30; and, by the same author, 'Le Triptolème de la mosaïque dite d'Aion et l'affirmation identitaire hellène à Shahba-Philippopolis', *Syria*, lxxvii (2000), pp. 181-200.

p. 322 **Past, present and future mosaic**: D. Levi, 'Aion', *Hesperia*, xiii (1944), pp. 269-314. **Neoplatonist mosaics**: J. Balty, J.-Ch. Balty, 'Un programme philosophique sous la cathédrale d'Apamée: l'ensemble néo-platonicien de l'empereur Julien', in *Texte et image: Actes de colloque* (Paris, 1984), pp. 167-76. **Heliopolis mosaics**: M. Chéhab (above, notes to pp. 313-25), pp. 29-50.

pp. 323-4 **Sasanian motifs**: K.M.D. Dunbabin (above, notes to pp. 313-25), p. 178. **Influences in other media**: J. Balty, 'Mosaïque et textiles en Syrie du nord', *Annales archéologiques arabes syriennes*, xliii (1999), pp. 185-92; **Medaba mosaic**: see above, notes to p. 276. Eusebius' *Onomasticon* is another unlikely influence. **Huarte mosaic**: M.T. and P. Canivet, 'La mosaïque d'Adam dans l'église syrienne de Huarte (ve s.)', *Cahiers Archéologiques*, xxiv (1975), pp. 49-69. For churches in general: P. Donceel-Voûte, *Les pavements des églises byzantines de Syrie et du Liban: Décor, archéologie et liturgie* (Louvain-la-Neuve, 1988). **Synagogues**: Dunbabin (above, notes to pp. 313-25). **Hammath Tiberias mosaics**: M. Dothan, *Hammath Tiberias: Early Synagogues and the Hellenistic and Roman Remains* (Jerusalem, 1983).

pp. 324-5 **Edessa mosaics**: see the articles by J. Leroy, 'Mosaïques funéraires d'Edesse', *Syria*, xxxiv (1957), pp. 306-42; 'Nouvelle découvertes archéologiques relatives à Edesse', *Syria*, xxxviii (1961), pp. 159-69; see also S.K. Ross, *Roman Edessa: Politics and Culture on the Eastern Fringes of the Roman Empire, 114-242 CE* (London, 2001). **Sarrîn mosaics**: J. Balty, *La mosaïque de Sarrîn (Osrhoène): Inventaire des mosaïques de Syrie*, i (Paris, 1990).

pp. 325-7 **Painting**: An essay by J. Balty, 'La peinture en Syrie', in J.-M. Dentzer, W. Orthmann (eds), *Archéologie et histoire de la Syrie*, ii (Saarbrücken, 1989), pp. 525-36 provides an overview. For sites, particularly **Dura**, see C.H. Kraeling, *The Excavations at Dura-Europos*, viii/1: *The Synagogue* (New Haven, 1956), and viii/2: *The Christian Building at Dura-Europos* (New Haven, 1967); M.I. Rostovtzeff, *Dura and its Art* (Oxford, 1938); A. Perkins, *The Art of Dura-Europos* (Oxford,

1973); A.J. Wharton, *Refiguring the Post Classical City: Dura Europos, Jerash, Jerusalem and Ravenna* (Cambridge, 1995). For **Zeugma**, see N. Basgelen, R. Ergeç, *Belkis/Zeugma: A Last Look at History* (Istanbul, 2000); and for **Petra**, M. Lindner, *Petra: Neue Ausgrabungen und Entdeckungen* (Munich-Bad Windsheim, 1986). For **Huarte**: M. Gawlikowski, 'Un nouveau Mithraeum récemment découvert à Huarte près d'Apamée', *Comptes rendus de l'Académie des inscriptions et des belles-lettres* (2000), pp. 161-71; 'Hawarti: Preliminary Report', *Polish Archaeology in the Mediterranean*, x (1999), pp. 197-204; 'Hawarte: Third Interim Report on the Work Done in the Mithraeum', *Polish Archaeology in the Mediterranean*, xii (2001), pp. 309-14. **Palmyra**: C.H. Kraeling, 'Color Photographs of the Paintings in the Tomb of the Three Brothers at Palmyra', *Annales archéologiques arabes syriennes*, xi-xii (1961-2), pp. 13-18. **Masyaf**: F. Chapouthier, 'Les peintures murales d'un hypogée funéraire près de Massyaf', *Syria*, xxxi (1954), pp. 172-211. For other paintings from the region, not discussed here, see J.P. Peters, H. Thiersch, *Painted Tombs in the Necropolis of Marissa* (London, 1905); A. Barbet, C. Vibert-Guigue, *Les peintures des nécropoles romaines d'Abila et du nord de la Jordanie*, 2 vols (Beirut, 1988-94).

p. 327 **Shai al-Kaum**: E.A. Knauf, 'Dushara and Shai' al-Qaum', *Aram*, ii (1990), pp. 175-83; J.F. Healey, *The Religion of the Nabataeans: A Conspectus* (Leiden, 2001), pp. 143-7. Perhaps relevant in this context is the remark put into the mouth of Pescennius Niger by the writer of the *Historia Augusta* about 'Saracens' drinking water rather than wine: 7.8. **Epispasm**: E. Schürer, *A History of the Jewish People*, I (Edinburgh, 1973), pp. 148-9, note 28.

p. 328 **Loincloths in Hauran sculpture**: G. Bolelli (above, notes to pp. 330-11), p. 65.

p. 329 **Cultural links between Palmyra and Mesopotamia**: H.J.W. Drijvers, 'Hatra, Palmyra und Edessa', *Aufstieg und Niedergang der römischen Welt*, ii/8 (1977), pp. 799-906; J.-B. Yon, below, notes to p. 331, pp. 134-5.

pp. 331 **Priestly dress**: R.A. Stucky, 'Prêtres syriens I: Palmyre', *Syria*, l (1973), pp. 163-80; 'II: Hiérapolis', *Syria*, liii (1976), pp. 127-40. R. Krumeich, 'Darstellung syrischer Priester an den kaiserzeitlichen Tempeln von Niha et Chehim im Libanon', *Damaszener Mitteilungen*, x (1998), pp. 171-200; K. Chéhadeh, M. Griesheimer, 'Les reliefs funéraires du tombeau du prêtre Rapsônès', *Syria*, lxxv (1999), pp. 171-92; J.-B. Yon, *Les notables de Palmyre* (Beirut, 2002), pp. 132-4. For **costume as a form of resistance**, see J.-Ch. Balty, 'Palmyre entre orient et occident: Acculturation et résistances', *Annales archéologiques arabes syriennes*, xlii (1996), pp. 437-41.

p. 333 **Senators and equestrians**: G. Bowersock, 'Roman Senators from the Near East: Syria, Judaea, Arabia, Mesopotamia', in S. Panciera (ed.), *Epigrafia e ordine senatorio* II, *Tituli* 5 (1982), pp. 651-68; H. Devijer, 'Equestrian Officers from the East', in P. Freeman, D. Kennedy, *The Defence of the Roman and Byzantine East* (Oxford, 1986), i, p. 109-225. **South Shields**: M.A.R. Colledge, *The Art of Palmyra* (London, 1976), pp. 231-3.

Chapter 9: The Pious World

For general works on pagan religion: R. MacMullen, *Paganism in the Roman Empire* (New Haven, 1981); M. Beard, J. North (eds), *Pagan Priests: Religion and Power in the Ancient World* (London, 1990); M. Beard, J.A. North, S. Price, *Religions of Rome* (Cambridge, 1998).

For Syrian deities and religion, see in particular the works of H. Seyrig, for example, 'Hiérarchie des divinités de Palmyre', *Syria*, xiii (1932), pp. 190-95; 'Le culte de Bêl et de Baalshamin', *Syria*, xiv (1933), pp. 238-52; 'Divinités de Sidon', *Syria*, xxxvi (1959) pp. 48-56; 'Les grands dieux de Tyr à l'époque grecque et romaine', *Syria*, xl (1963), pp. 19-28. Other important works include D. Sourdel, *Les cultes du Hauran à l'époque romaine* (Paris, 1952); H.J.W. Drijvers, *Cults and Beliefs at Edessa* (Leiden, 1970); J.T. Milik, *Dedicaces faites par des dieux (Palmyre, Hatra, Tyr) et des thiases sémitiques à l'époque romaine* (Paris, 1972); J. Teixidor, *The Pagan God: Popular Religion in the Ancient Near East* (Princeton, 1977); and, by the same author, J. Teixidor, 'Sur quelques aspects de la vie religieuse dans la Syrie à l'époque hellénistique et romaine', in Dentzer and Orthmann (eds), *Archéologie et histoire de la Syrie*, ii, pp. 81-95; L. Dirven, *The Palmyrenes of Dura-Europos: A Study of Religious Interaction in Roman Syria* (Leiden, 1999). Important works on cults and the design of temples by Ernest Will are gathered together in his *De l'Euphrate au Rhin: Aspects de l'hellénisation et de la romanisation du Proche-Orient* (Beirut, 1995). *Aufstieg und Niedergang der römischen Welt*, xviii/4, has various essays about religions in the Near East.

pp. 335-6 **Lucian's reverence for Atargatis**: J. Elsner, 'The Origins of the Icon: Pilgrimage, Religion and Visual Culture in the Roman East as "Resistance" to the Centre', in S.E. Alcock (ed.), *The Early Roman Empire in the East* (Oxford, 1997), pp. 178-99. **'Superstar'** cults and others abroad: R. Turcan, *Les cultes orientaux dans le monde romain* (Paris, 1989); J.R. Hinnells, *Mithraic Studies* (Manchester, 1975).

p. 337 **Glycon**: Lucian, *Alexander*. **Lucian on Syrian and Phoenician cults**: Elsner, above, notes to pp. 335-6. **Jupiter Dolichenus**: M.P. Speidel, *The Religion of Iuppiter Dolichenus in the Roman Army* (Leiden, 1978); F. Millar, *The Roman Near East*, pp. 248-9; P.-L. Gatier, 'Monuments du culte "dolichénien" en Cyrrhestique', *Syria*, lxxv (1998), pp. 161-9.

pp. 337-8 On **Jupiter Heliopolitanus**, see notes to p. 366 below.

p. 339 The **Malakbel altar**: M.A.R. Colledge, *The Art of Palmyra* (London, 1976), pp. 231-2.

p. 340 For **Nabataean deities**, see in particular: G.W. Bowersock, 'The Cult and Representation of Dusares in Roman Arabia', in F. Zayadine (ed.), *Petra and the Caravan Cities* (Amman, 1990), pp. 31-3; E.A. Knauf, 'Dushara and Shai' al-Qaum', *Aram*, ii (1990), pp. 175-83; J.F. Healy, *The Religion of the Nabataeans: A Conspectus* (Leiden, 2001).

pp. 340-41 **Solar cults**: H. Seyrig, 'Le culte du Soleil en Syrie à l'époque romaine', *Syria*, xlviii (1971), pp. 337-73; E. Will, 'Une figure du culte solaire d'Aurélien: *Jupiter consul vel con-*

sulens', *Syria*, xxxvi (1959), pp. 193-201. **Mithras and Mithraic temples**: there are numerous essays on the subject by E. Will, gathered together in his *De l'Euphrate au Rhin* (Beirut, 1995). See also L.M. Hopfe, 'Mithraism in Syria', *Aufstieg und Niedergang der römischen Welt*, xviii/4; I. Roll, 'The Mysteries of Mithras in the Roman Orient: The Problem of Origin', *Journal of Mithraic Studies*, ii (1977-8), pp. 53-68; M. Sartre, *D'Alexandre à Zénobie*, pp. 897-9. For recent finds at Doliche: E. Winter, 'Mithraism and Christianity in Late Antiquity', in S. Mitchell, G. Greatrex (eds), *Ethnicity and Culture in Late Antiquity* (London and Swansea, 2000), pp. 173-82. For the Huarte *mithraeum*, see M. Gawlikowski (above, notes to pp. 325-7).

p. 342 **Triads**: scepticism expressed by F. Millar, *The Roman Near East*, pp. 281-2.

p. 343 **Zeus Carmelus Heliopolitanus**: F. Millar, *The Roman Near East*, p. 270.

pp. 343-4 **Elagabal**: M. Frey, *Untersuchungen zur Religion und zur Religionspolitik des Kaisers Elagabal* (Stuttgart, 1989); see also F. Millar, *The Roman Near East*, pp. 300-9. **'God-Mountain'**: J. Starcky, 'Stèle d'Elahagabal', *Mélanges de l'Université Saint Joseph*, xlix (1975/6), pp. 501-20. W. Ball, *Rome in the East* (London, 2000), pp. 37-47, suggests that the temple of Elagabal is in fact the temple of Jupiter Heliopolitanus at Heliopolis, but on civic coins of Emesa the temple is consistently depicted with a façade of six columns, whereas on civic coins of Heliopolis the temple specifically labelled as that of Jupiter Optimus Maximus Heliopolitanus has a façade of ten (which corresponds to the number at the site).

pp. 344-5 On the **process of syncretism**: for the view followed here, see J. Webster, 'A Negotiated Syncretism: Readings on the Development of Romano-Celtic Religion', in D.J. Mattingly (ed.), *Dialogues in Roman Imperialism* (Portsmouth, RI, 1997), pp. 165-84. The **Syrian Goddess**: M. Avi-Yonah, 'Syrian Gods at Ptolemais-Accho', *Israel Exploration Journal*, ix (1959), pp. 1-12; H. Seyrig, 'Les dieux de Hiérapolis', *Syria*, xxxvii (1961), pp. 233-52; H. Seyrig, 'Bas-relief des dieux d'Hiérapolis', *Syria*, xlix (1972), pp. 105-8; R.A. Oden, *Studies in Lucian's De Syria Dea*, Harvard Semitic Monographs 15 (Cambridge, MA, 1977); P. Bilde, 'Atargatis/Dea Syria: Hellenization of her Cult in the Hellenistic-Roman Period?', in P. Bilde, T. Engberg, L. Hannestad, J. Zahle (eds), *Religion and Religious Practice in the Seleucid Kingdom* (Århus, 1990), pp. 151-87; F. Millar, *The Roman Near East*, pp. 242-7. For depictions of the deities on coins of the late Persian-early Hellenistic periods, see L. Mildenberg, 'A Note on the Coinage of Hierapolis-Bambyce', in M. Amandry, S. Hurter, D. Bérend (eds), *Travaux de numismatique grecque offerts à Georges Le Rider* (London, 1999), pp. 277-84. On the **bearded Apollo**: H. Seyrig, 'Sur une idole hiérapolitaine', *Syria*, xxvi (1949), pp. 17-28; also Elsner, above, notes to p. 335-6.

pp. 345-6 **Cults at Palmyra**: there are numerous works by H. Seyrig, for example, 'Hiérarchie des divinités de Palmyre', *Syria*, xiii (1932), pp. 190-95; 'Le culte de Bêl et de Baalshamin', *Syria*, xiv (1933), pp. 238-52; 'Bêl de Palmyre', *Syria*, xlviii (1971), pp. 85-114. Other important works: H.J.W. Drijvers, *The Religion of Palmyra* (Leiden, 1976); J. Teixidor,

The Pantheon of Palmyra (Leiden, 1979); M. Gawlikowski, 'Les dieux de Palmyre', *Aufstieg und Niedergang der römischen Welt*, II.xviii/4 (1990), pp. 2605-58; and the recent excellent discussion by T. Kaizer, *The Religious Life of Palmyra* (Stuttgart, 2002).

pp. 348-9 **Keraunophors**: L. Jalabert, R. Mouterde, IGLS, ii/2: *Antioch, Antiochène* (Paris, 1953), no. 1184B. **Festival of Adonis at Byblus**: E. Will, 'Le rituel des Adonies', *Syria*, lii (1975), pp. 93-105; B. Soyez, *Byblos et la fête des Adonies* (Leiden, 1977). **Hocmaea**: J.-P. Rey-Coquais, 'Des montagnes au désert' (below, notes to pp. 351-2). **Zosimus**: 1.58; some have suggested that the location for this event is at Yammoune, on the opposite side of the Lebanon range from Aphaca, where there is also a temple, a spring and pools.

pp. 349-50 **Banquets**: H. Seyrig, 'Les tessères palmyréniennes et le banquet rituel', *Mémorial Lagrange* (1940), pp. 51-8; J.T. Milik, *Dedicaces faites par des dieux* (Paris, 1972) (but note also the comments of T. Kaizer, *The Religious Life of Palmyra*, Stuttgart, 2002, p. 258); E. Will, 'Les salles de banquet de Palmyre et d'autres lieux', *Topoi*, vii (1997), pp. 873-87; and D. Tarrier, 'Banquets rituels en Palmyrène et en Nabatène', *Aram*, vii (1995), pp. 165-82. **Disputes at Dmeir**: P. Roussel, F. De Visscher, 'Les inscriptions du temple de Dmeir', *Syria*, xxiii (1942-3), pp. 173-200. **Iabruda**: Jalabert *et al.* (above, notes to p. 92), no. 2707.

pp. 351-2 **Origins of temple designs**: W. Ball, *Rome in the East*, pp. 317-56. **High Places**: O. Callot, J. Marcillet-Jaubert, 'Hauts-lieux de Syrie du nord', in G. Roux (ed.), *Temples et sanctuaires* (Paris, 1984), pp. 185-202. **Hierapolis and temple estates**: M. Sartre, *D'Alexandre à Zénobie*, pp. 744-5. **Baetocaece**: H. Seyrig, 'Arados et Baetocaece', *Syria*, xxviii (1951), pp. 191-206; J.-P. Rey-Coquais, 'Des montagnes au désert: Baetocécé, la Pagus Augustus de Niha, la Ghouta à l'est de Damas', in E. Frézouls (ed.), *Sociétés urbaines, sociétés rurales dans l'Asie Mineure et la Syrie hellénistiques et romaines* (Strasbourg, 1987), pp. 191-216; F. Millar, *The Roman Near East*, pp. 271-3; D. Feissel, 'Les privilèges de Baitokaike', *Syria*, lxx (1993), pp. 13-26.

pp. 352-63 On **Syrian and Near Eastern temples** in general: D. Krencker, W. Zschietzschmann, *Römische Tempel in Syrien* (Berlin, 1938). G. Taylor, *The Roman Temples of Lebanon* (Beirut, 1971); M. Le Glay, *Villes, temples et sanctuaires de l'Orient romain*, Paris, 1986; J.-M. Dentzer, 'Le sanctuaire syrien', J.-M. Dentzer, W. Orthmann (eds), *Archéologie et histoire de la Syrie*, ii (Saarbrücken, 1989), pp. 297-322; M. Gawlikowski, 'Les temples dans la Syrie à l'époque hellénistique et romaine', in Dentzer and Orthmann, pp. 323-46; E. Will, 'L'espace sacrificiel dans les provinces romaines de Syrie et d'Arabie', in *L'espace sacrificiel dans les civilisations méditerranéennes de l'Antiquité*, Publications de la Bibliothèque Salomon Reinach (Lyon, 1991), pp. 259-63; K.S. Freyberger (above, notes to pp. 291-2).

pp. 353-4 **Temples at Dura Europus**: P. Leriche, 'Matériaux pour une réflexion renouvelée sur les sanctuaires de Doura-Europos', *Topoi*, vii (1997), pp. 889-913. **Private nature of worship**: see Wharton, above, notes to pp. 259-61. See also L. Dirven, *The Palmyrenes of*

Dura-Europos: A Study of Religious Interaction in Roman Syria (Leiden, 1999).

p. 354 **Sanctuary of Baalshamin at Palmyra**: P. Collart, J. Vicari, *Le sanctuaire de Baalshamin à Palmyra*, i-ii: *Topographie et architecture* (Rome, 1969). **Inscriptions on the Jebel Sheikh Barakat**: W.K. Prentice, *Part III of the Publications of an American Archaeological Expedition to Syria in 1899-1900* (New York, 1906), nos 100-104.

pp. 355-6 **Tower altars**: see two works by P. Collart, P. Coupel, *L'autel monumental de Baalbek* (Paris, 1951); *Le petit autel de Baalbek* (Paris, 1977). For **monuments à colonnettes**: E. Will, 'A propos de quelques monuments sacrés de la Syrie et de l'Arabie romaines', in F. Zayadine (ed.), *Petra and the Caravan Cities* (Amman, 1990), pp. 197-205; K.S. Freyberger, 'Zur Funktion der Hamana im Kontext lokaler Heiligtümer in Syrien und Palästina', *Damaszener Mitteilungen*, ix (1996), pp. 143-61. See also the comments of J.-M. Dentzer, 'Edicules d'époque hellénistico-romaine et tradition des pierres cultuelles en Syrie et en Arabie', in P. Matthiae, M. van Loon, H. Weiss, *Resurrecting the Past: A Joint Tribute to Adnan Bounni* (Istanbul, 1990), pp. 65-83.

p. 356 **Theatron**: E. Will, 'Théâtres sacrés de la Syrie et de l'Empire', *Mélanges de l'Université Saint Joseph*, xxxvii (1961), pp. 209-19. For **Sia**: above, notes to pp. 289-95; for **Sahr**: Butler (above, notes to pp. 289-95), II.A.7 (Leiden 1919), pp. 441-6; for **Dura**: M.I. Rostovtzeff (ed.), *The Excavations at Dura-Europos: Preliminary Report of Fifth Season of Work, 1931-1932* (New Haven, 1934), pp. 131-200; P. Arnaud, 'Les salles W9 et W10 du temple d'Azzanathkona à Doura-Europos', in P. Leriche, M. Gelin (eds), *Doura-Europos Études*, iv (Beirut, 1997), pp. 117-44.

pp. 357-8 For the **Petra Great Temple**, M.S. Joukowski, *Petra Great Temple*, i: *Brown University Excavations, 1993-1997* (Providence, RI, 1998). **Temple of Bel at Palmyra**: see notes to pp. 361-3 below. **Temple of Nebo at Palmyra**: A. Bounni, *Le sanctuaire de Nabu* (Damascus, 1982). **Thalamos**: E. Will, 'L'adyton dans le temple syrien de l'époque impériale', *Études d'archéologie classique*, ii, *Annales de l'Est*, University of Nancy, mémoire 22 (1959), pp. 136-45.

pp. 359-60 **Niha model**: E. Will, 'La maquette de l'adyton du temple A de Niha (Beqa)', in *Le dessin d'architecture dans les sociétés antiques: Actes du colloque de Strasbourg, 1984* (Strasbourg, 1985), pp. 277-81. **Nabataean temples**: N. Glueck, *Deities and Dolphins* (London, 1966); P.C. Hammond, *The Temple of the Winged Lions, Petra, Jordan, 1973-1990* (Fountain Hills, 1996). The Baalshamin temple at Sia has now been almost completely obliterated by a modern house: J.-M. Dentzer, F. Braemer, J. Dentzer-Feydy, F. Villeneuve, 'Six campagnes de fouilles à Si': Développement et culture indigène en Syrie méridionale', *Damaszener Mitteilungen*, ii (1985), pp. 65-83.

pp. 360-61 **Kalybé**: M. Gawlikowski, 'Les temples dans la Syrie' (above, notes to pp. 352-63), pp. 333-4. Various monuments in the Hauran have been dubbed a *kalybé*, but the only certain examples are at Umm ez-Zeitun, Hayyat and Maximinopolis-Shaqqa. On the possible origin of this form, see J.-M. Dentzer,

'Naiskoi du Hauran et qubbah arabe', in F. Zayadine (ed.), *Petra and the Caravan Cities* (Amman, 1990), pp. 207-19.

pp. 361-3 **Bel Temple at Palmyra**: above, notes to p. 282; to which add E. Will, 'Le temple de Bel de Palmyre et sa place dans l'histoire de l'art de la Syrie romaine', *Annales archéologiques arabes syriennes*, xxi (1971), pp. 261-8; M.A.R. Colledge, 'Le temple de Bel à Palmyre: qui l'a fait, et pourquoi?', in *Palmyre: Bilan et perspectives* (above, notes to pp. 240-42), pp. 45-52. As a **temple to the Palmyrene gods**: T. Kaizer (above, notes to pp. 345-6), pp. 69-79.

p. 363 **Dmeir**: E. Brümmer, 'Der römische Tempel von Dmeir: Vorbericht', *Damaszener Mitteilungen*, ii (1985), pp. 17-35; M. Klinkott, 'Ergebnisse der Bauaufnahme am "Tempel" von Dmeir', *Damaszener Mitteilungen*, iv (1989), pp. 109-61. The inscriptions are published by P. Roussel, F. De Visscher (above, notes to pp. 349-50).

pp. 363-4 **Jerusalem Temple**: T. Busink, *Der Tempel von Jerusalem von Salomo bis Herodes* (Leiden, 1980). **Damascus temple**: K.S. Freyberger, 'Untersuchungen zur Baugeschichte des Jupiter-Heiligtums in Damaskus', *Damaszener Mitteilungen*, iv (1989), pp. 61-86.

pp. 363-70 There are many works on **Heliopolis**. See above, notes to pp. 108-21; to which add N. Jidejian, *Baalbek: Heliopolis, 'City of the Sun'* (Beirut, 1975); K.S. Freyberger, 'Im Licht des Sonnengottes: Deutung und Funktion des sogenannten "Bacchus-Tempels" im Heiligtum des Jupiter Heliopolitanus in Baalbek', *Damaszener Mitteilungen*, xii (2000), pp. 95-133. For inscriptions from the site, see J.-P. Rey-Coquais, IGLS, vi: *Baalbek et Beqa'* (Paris, 1967).

p. 366 For the **cults at Heliopolis**, see the articles by H. Seyrig, 'La triade héliopolitaine et les temples de Baalbek', *Syria*, x (1929), pp. 314-56; 'Bas-relief de la triade de Baalbek trouvé à Fneidiq', *Bulletin du Musée de Beyrouth*, xii (1955), pp. 25-8; and Y. Hajjar, *La Triade d'Héliopolis-Baalbek*, 3 vols (Leiden, 1977-85). The two naked male figures on coins have been identified as Hermes and Dionysus: see E.M. Ruprechtsberger, below, notes to pp. 367-9.

p. 367 For the **lead figurines**: H. Seyrig, 'La triade héliopolitaine' (above, notes to p. 366); L. Badré, 'Les figurines de plomb de 'Ain-al-Djouj', *Syria*, lxxvi (1999), pp. 181-96.

pp. 367-9 For details about the **Temple of Jupiter**, see (in addition to the sources cited above, notes to pp. 363-70) A. Hoffman, 'Terrace and Temple: Remarks on the Architectural History of the Temple of Jupiter in Baalbek', in H. Sader, T. Scheffer, A. Neuwirth (eds), *Baalbek: Image and Monument, 1898-1998* (Beirut, 1998), pp. 279-304; and E.M. Ruprechtsberger, *Vom Steinbruch zum Jupitertempel von Heliopolis/Baalbek (Libanon)* (Linz, 1999).

pp. 370-71 **The imperial cult**: S.R.F. Price, *Rituals and Power: The Roman Imperial Cult in Asia Minor* (Cambridge, 1984); F. Millar, 'State and Subject: the Impact of the Monarchy', in F. Millar, A. Segal (eds), *Caesar Augustus: Seven Aspects* (Oxford, 1984), pp. 37-60. On the evolution of the eparchies, see J.-P. Rey-Coquais,

'Syrie romaine' (above, notes to pp. 80-82), pp. 53-4; M. Sartre, *L'Orient romain* (Paris, 1991), pp. 339-40. On the coins of cities of Coele-Syria, see A. Spijkerman, *The Coins of the Decapolis and Provincia Arabia* (Jerusalem, 1978). On Laodicea as 'Metropolis of the Four Provinces', see K. Butcher, *Coinage in Roman Syria* (London, 2003), p. 234. For the continuation of the imperial cult after Constantine, see J.H.W.G. Liebeschuetz, 'The Syriarch in the Fourth Century AD', *Historia*, viii (1959), pp. 113-26; and, by the same author, *Antioch* (Oxford, 1972), pp. 141-3. G.W. Bowersock, 'Polytheism and Monotheism in Arabia and the Three Palestines', *Dumbarton Oaks Papers*, li (1997), pp. 1-10. It was gradually shorn of its pagan aspects in order to suit Christian sensibilities, but the games of the provincial assembly at Antioch continued to be financed by a civic magistrate until AD 465, when responsibility was assigned to an imperial official.

pp. 371-5 **Jews and Samaritans**: The literature on Judaism is considerable, and cannot be dealt with in detail here. See especially E. Schürer, *The History of the Jewish People in the Age of Jesus Christ*, rev. G. Vermes, F. Millar, M. Black, M. Goodman, 3 vols (Edinburgh, 1973-87); E.M. Smallwood, *The Jews under Roman Rule* (Leiden, 1976); M. Avi-Yonah, *The Jews under Roman and Byzantine Rule* (New York, 1976, R/1984); G. Alon, *The Jews in their Land in the Talmudic Age (70-640 CE)*, 2 vols (Jerusalem, 1980-84); M. Goodman, *The Ruling Class of Judaea* (Cambridge, 1987); L.I. Levine, *The Rabbinic Class of Roman Palestine in Late Antiquity* (Jerusalem and New York, 1989); F. Millar, *The Roman Near East*, pp. 337-86; M. Sartre, *L'Orient romain*, pp. 357-407; *D'Alexandre à Zénobie*, pp. 530-607, 927-48. Other recent studies: L.H. Feldman, *Jew and Gentile in the Ancient World* (Princeton, 1997); S. Schwartz, *Imperialism and Jewish Society, 200 BCE to 640 CE* (Princeton, 2000). For some points discussed here see Y. Hirschfeld, 'Jewish Rural Settlement in Judaea in the Early Roman Period', in S.E. Alcock, *The Early Roman Empire in the East*, pp. 72-88 (which in fact discusses early and late Roman settlement); and, by the same author, 'Early Roman Manor Houses in Judaea and the Site of Khirbet Qumran', *Journal of Near Eastern Studies*, lvii (1998), pp. 161-89. On the Samaritans, see A.D. Crown (ed.), *The Samaritans* (Tübingen, 1989); Y. Magen, 'Mount Garizim and the Samaritans', in F. Manns, E. Alliata (eds), *Early Christianity in Context: Monuments and Documents* (Jerusalem, 1993), pp. 91-147. **For Samaritan strife in late antiquity**: B. Isaac, *The Limits of Empire* (Oxford, 1990), pp. 89-90; G.W. Bowersock, above, notes to pp. 370-71.

pp. 375-98 The literature on **Christianity** is immense. For the narrative presented here, see in particular: H. Chadwick, *The Early Church* (London, 1967); P. Brown, *The World of Late Antiquity, AD 150-750* (London, 1971); R. Lane Fox, *Pagans and Christians* (London, 1986); R. MacMullen, *Christianity in the Roman Empire* (New Haven, 1984); and G. Fowden, *Empire to Commonwealth. Consequences of Monotheism in Late Antiquity* (Princeton, 1993). On **Syria and the Near East** specifically: P. Canivet, 'Le christianisme en Syrie des origines à l'avènement de l'islam', in J.-M. Dentzer, W.

Orthmann (eds), *Archéologie et histoire de la Syrie*, ii (Saarbrücken, 1989), pp. 117-48; M. Sartre, *D'Alexandre à Zénobie*, pp. 948-58. For various regional studies: D.S. Wallace-Hadrill, *Christian Antioch: A Study of Early Christian Thought in the East* (Cambridge, 1982); R. Schick, *The Christian Communities of Palestine from Byzantine to Islamic Rule* (Princeton, 1995); and the works of A.J. Festugière: *Antioche païenne et chrétienne: Libanios, Chrysostome et les moines de Syrie* (Paris, 1959); *Les moines d'Orient* (Paris, 1960-65).

p. 375 On the **small number of Christians in the first century**: K. Hopkins, *A World Full of Gods* (London, 1999), p. 84.

pp. 376-7 **Gnosticism**: H. Jonas, *The Gnostic Religion* (Boston, 1958); M.A. Williams, *Rethinking Gnosticism* (Princeton, 1996). **Marcion**: H.J.W. Drijvers, 'Marcionism in Syria', *The Second Century*, vi (1987-8), pp. 153-72. **Tatian**: M. Whittaker, *Tatian: 'Oratio ad Graecos' and Fragments* (Oxford, 1982).

p. 377 **Origen**: Chadwick (above, notes to pp. 375-98) provides a summary of Origen's position. **Paul of Samosata**: F. Millar, 'Paul of Samosata, Zenobia and Aurelian: the Church, Local Culture and Political Allegiance in Third-Century Syria', *Journal of Roman Studies*, lxi (1971), pp. 1-17.

p. 378 The **Christianity of Philip the Arab**: H.A. Pohlsander, 'Philip the Arab and Christianity', *Historia*, xxix (1980), pp. 463-73; I. Shahid, *Rome and the Arabs* (Washington, DC, 1984). The **Decian persecution**: D.S. Potter, *Prophecy and History in the Crisis of the Roman Empire* (Oxford, 1990), pp. 42-3, 261-7; J.B. Rives, 'The Decree of Decius and the Religion of Empire', *Journal of Roman Studies*, lxxxix (1999), pp. 135-54. **Christian discourse**: A. Cameron, *Christianity and the Rhetoric of Empire: The Development of Christian Discourse* (Berkeley, 1991).

p. 379 **Spread of Christianity into the countryside**: J.H.G.W. Liebeschuetz, 'Epigraphic Evidence on the Christianisation of Syria', *Akten des XI. Internationalen Limeskongresses* (Budapest, 1981), pp. 458-508.

p. 380 **Julian**: G. Bowersock, *Julian the Apostate* (London, 1978).

p. 381 **Manichaeism**: P. Brown, 'The Diffusion of Manichaeism in the Roman Empire', *Journal of Roman Studies*, lix (1969), pp. 92-103; S.N.C. Lieu, *Manichaeism in the Later Roman Empire and Medieval China* (Tübingen, 1992).

pp. 381-3 **Christian assaults on paganism**: G. Fowden, 'Bishops and Temples in the Eastern Roman Empire, AD 320-435', *Journal of Theological Studies*, xxix (1978), pp. 53-78; H.J.W. Drijvers, *Cults and Beliefs at Edessa* (Leiden, 1980); F.R. Trombley, *Hellenic Religion and Christianization AD 320-529*, i (Leiden, 1993), pp. 246-82. **Carrhae's cult**: G. Fowden, *From Empire to Commonwealth*, pp. 62-5.

pp. 383-4 For **Rome's relations with Christians beyond the frontiers**, see Fowden, *From Empire to Commonwealth*.

pp. 384-90 **Monophysitism**: see in particular W.H.C. Frend, *The Rise of the Monophysite Movement* (Cambridge, 1979).

p. 387 **'Ek' and 'en'**: the critical wording in the council's doctrinal statement was *ek duo physeon* ('out of two natures') in the first draft,

emended to *en duo physesin* ('in two natures') in the second.

pp. 390-93 **Asceticism**: H. Delehaye, *Les saints stylites* (Brussels, 1923); A. Vööbus, *A History of Asceticism in the Syrian Orient* (Leuven, 1958-60); P. Brown, 'The Rise and Function of the Holy Man in Late Antiquity', *Journal of Roman Studies*, lxi (1971), pp. 80-101. For architecture associated with ascetics, see the works of I. Peña, P. Castellana, R. Fernández, *Les stylites syriens* (Milan, 1975); *Les reclus syriens* (Milan, 1980); *Les cénobites syriens* (Milan, 1983).

pp. 393-7 **Christian architecture**: H.C. Butler, *Early Churches in Syria: Fourth to Seventh Centuries* (Leiden, 1929); J. Lassus, *Sanctuaires chrétiens de Syrie* (Paris, 1947); R.P.C. Hanson, 'The Transformation of Pagan Temples into Churches in the Early Christian Centuries', *Journal of Semitic Studies*, xxiii (1978), pp. 257-67; J. Wilkinson, 'What Butler Saw', *Levant*, xvi (1984), pp. 113-27; J.-P. Sodini, 'Les églises de Syrie du nord', in J.-M. Dentzer, W. Orthmann (eds), *Archéologie et histoire de la Syrie*, ii (Saarbrücken, 1989), pp. 347-72; and, in the same volume, M. Restle, 'Les monuments chrétiens de la Syrie du Sud', pp. 373-84; J.-L. Biscop, *Deir Déhès, monastère d'Antiochène* (Beirut, 1997). **Temple at Slim**: K.S. Freyberger, 'Der Tempel in Slim: Ein Bericht', *Damaszener Mitteilungen*, v (1991), pp. 9-38. **Qalaat Semaan**: J.-P. Sodini, 'Travaux récents au sanctuaire syrien de St. Syméon le Stylite', *Comptes rendus de l'Académie des inscriptions et belles-lettres* (1983), pp. 335-72.

p. 396 **Umm al-Jimal churches**: B. de Vries (above, notes to p. 106), p. 11.

Chapter 10: The Military

The literature on this subject is large. In general: E.N. Luttwak, *The Grand Strategy of the Roman Empire* (Baltimore, 1976); J.C. Mann, 'Power, Force and the Frontiers of the Empire' (review of Luttwak), *Journal of Roman Studies*, lxix (1979), pp. 175-83; C.R. Whittaker, *Frontiers of the Roman Empire: A Social and Economic Study* (London, 1994); H. Elton, *Frontiers of the Roman Empire* (London, 1996).

For the **eastern provinces**: P. Freeman, D. Kennedy (eds), *The Defence of the Roman and Byzantine East* (Oxford, 1986); D.H. French, C.S. Lightfoot (eds), *The Eastern Frontier of the Roman Empire*, 3 vols (Oxford, 1989); B. Isaac, *The Limits of Empire: The Roman Army in the East* (Oxford, 1990, rev. 1992); D. Kennedy, 'The East', in J. Wacher (ed.), *The Roman World*, i (London, 1987), pp. 266-308; E. Dabrowa (ed.), *The Roman and Byzantine Army in the East* (Cracow, 1994); P. Southern, K.R. Dixon, *The Late Roman Army* (London, 1996); D.L. Kennedy (ed.), *The Roman Army in the East* (Ann Arbor, 1996). **Syria**: E. Dabrowa, 'The Frontier in Syria in the First Century AD', in P. Freeman, D. Kennedy (eds), *The Defence of the Roman and Byzantine East*, pp. 93-108; M. Gawlikowski, 'The Roman Frontier on the Euphrates', *Mesopotamia*, xxii (1987), pp. 77-80; N. Pollard, *Soldiers, Cities, and Civilians in Roman Syria* (Ann Arbor, 2000). **Palestine and Arabia**: M.P. Speidel, 'The Roman Army in Arabia', *Aufstieg und Niedergang der römischen Welt*, ii/8 (1978), pp. 687-730; D. Kennedy,

Archaeological Explorations on the Roman Frontier in North East Jordan (Oxford, 1982); M.P. Spiedel, 'The Roman Army in Judaea under the Procurators: The Italian and the Augustan Cohort in the Acts of the Apostles', *Ancient Society*, xiii-xiv (1982-3), pp. 233-40; D. Graf, *Rome and the Arabian Frontier: From the Nabataeans to the Saracens* (Ashgate, 1997). **Mesopotamia**: J. Wagner, 'Provincia Osrhoenae: New Archaeological Finds Illustrating the Military Organisation under the Severan Dynasty', in S. Mitchell (ed.), *Armies and Frontiers in Roman and Byzantine Anatolia* (Oxford, 1983), pp. 103-30; D. Kennedy, 'The Garrisoning of Mesopotamia in the Late Antonine and Early Severan Periods', *Antichthon*, xxi (1987), pp. 57-66.

For early ideas (and spectacular **aerial photographs**) about defences in the region see A. Poidebard, *La trace de Rome dans le désert de Syrie. Le limes de Trajan à la conquête Arabe: Recherches aériennes (1925-1932)*, 2 vols (Paris, 1934); and R. Mouterde, A. Poidebard, *Le limes de Chalcis: Organisation de la steppe en Haute Syrie romaine* (Paris, 1945). A number of these early photographs have been collected and published with expert commentaries and plans by D. Kennedy, D. Riley, *Rome's Desert Frontier from the Air* (London, 1990).

pp. 399-400 **Lack of integration of soldiers and civilians**: this is a theme explored by N. Pollard, 'The Roman Army as a "Total Institution" in the Near East? Dura-Europos as a Case Study', in D. Kennedy, *The Roman Army in the East*, pp. 211-27; and his book *Soldiers, Cities and Civilians in Roman Syria*. See also S. James, 'The Community of Soldiers: a Major Identity and Centre of Power in the Roman Empire', in P. Baker, S. Jundi, R. Witcher, *TRAC 98: Proceedings of the Eighth Annual Theoretical Roman Archaeology Conference, Leicester 1998* (Oxford, 1998), pp. 14-25. **Soldiers billeted in cities among civilians**: some scholars question whether this was commonplace, and indeed there is not much evidence. **Mixing of military and locals at Bostra**: at least, not in the realms of religion or marriage: M. Sartre, IGLS, xiii: *Bostra* (Paris, 1982); and, by the same author, *Bostra* (Paris, 1985), p. 156. **Papyrus of the cohors XX Palmyrenorum**: R.O. Fink, A.S. Hoey, W.S. Snyder, 'The Feriale Duranum', *Yale Classical Studies*, vii (1940), pp. 1-222; and C.B. Welles, R.O. Fink, J.F. Gilliam (above, notes to pp. 142-5), pp. 191-212.

p. 400-2 **Ethnic makeup**: Pollard, *Soldiers, Cities and Civilians*, pp. 110-34, 138-42. **Recruitment of Syrians**: D. Kennedy, 'The Military Contribution of Syria to the Roman Army', in D.H. French, C.S. Lightfoot (eds), *The Eastern Frontier of the Roman Empire* (Oxford, 1989), pp. 235-46. **Sons of veterans serving**: N. Pollard, *Soldiers, Cities and Civilians*, p. 249. **Standing of soldiers in local communities**: a theme explored by H.I. MacAdam, *Studies in the History of the Roman Province of Arabia: The Northern Sector* (Oxford, 1986). **Veterans in the limestone massif**: evidence summarized in Pollard, pp. 247-8. **In the Hauran**: H.I. MacAdam, *Studies*. **Dura Europus**: Pollard, *Soldiers, Cities and Civilians*.

p. 402-3 **Military interference**: Pollard, *Soldiers, Cities and Civilians*, pp. 85-96. **Barbalissus and Callinicum**: Pollard, p. 222;

Liebeschuetz, *Antioch*, p. 163.

pp. 404-5 **Abila**: W.H. Waddington, *Inscriptions grecques et latines de la Syrie, recueillies et expliquées* (Paris, 1870), no. 1874. **Civic coins and soldiers**: R. Ziegler, 'Civic Coins and Imperial Campaigns', in D. Kennedy, *The Roman Army in the East*, pp. 119-34.

pp. 405-11 **Strategies**: see in particular the works of E.N. Luttwak, *The Grand Strategy of the Roman Empire* (Baltimore, 1976); and B. Isaac, *The Limits of Empire: The Roman Army in the East* (Oxford, 1990, rev. 1992). The case for defence against **external foes**, particularly nomads, is presented in the works of S.T. Parker: *Romans and Saracens: A History of the Arabian Frontier* (Winona Lake, MN, 1986); *The Roman Frontier in Central Jordan: Interim Report on the Limes Arabicus Project 1980-1985* (Oxford, 1987). The case for **internal policing**: B. Isaac, *The Limits of Empire*; D. Graf, 'Rome and the Saracens: Reassessing the Nomad Menace', in T. Fahd (ed.), *L'Arabie préislamique et son environnement historique et culturel* (Leiden, 1989), pp. 344-400. **Summary** of the debates: P.-L. Gatier, 'Une frontière sans *limes*?', in L. Nordiguian, J.-F. Salles (eds), *Aux origines de l'archéologie aérienne: A. Poidebard (1878-1955)* (Beirut, 2000), pp. 139-49. See also P. Mayerson, 'Saracens and Romans: Micro-Macro Relationships', *Bulletin of the American Schools of Oriental Research*, 274 (1989), pp. 71-9.

p. 407 **Limes**: B. Isaac, 'The Meaning of the terms Limes and Limitanei', *Journal of Roman Studies*, lxxviii (1988), pp. 125-47.

p. 408 **Cassius Dio on Mesopotamia**: 75.3. See also comments on pp. 48-9.

p. 409 **Safaitic graffiti**: M.C.A. MacDonald (above, notes to pp. 287-8).

pp. 409-10 On **bandits** in general: B.D. Shaw, 'Bandits in the Roman Empire', *Past and Present*, 105 (1984), pp. 3-52; and, by the same author, 'The Bandit', in A. Giardina (ed.), *The Romans* (Chicago and London, 1993), pp. 300-41. For regional studies, see the works of B. Isaac, 'Bandits in Judaea and Arabia', *Harvard Studies in Classical Philology*, lxxxviii (1984), pp. 171-203; *The Limits of Empire*, pp. 77-99. **Isaurian bandits**: B. Isaac, *The Limits of Empire*, pp. 75-6.

pp. 411-15 **Units and deployments**: J.-P. Rey-Coquais, 'Syrie romaine' (above, notes to pp. 80-82), pp. 67-71; L.J.F. Keppie, 'Legions in the East from Augustus to Trajan', in P. Freeman, D. Kennedy, *The Defence of the Roman and Byzantine East*, pp. 411-29; J.-Ch. Balty, 'Apamée (1986): Nouvelles données sur l'armée romaine d'Orient et les raids Sassanides du milieu du IIIe siècle', *Comptes rendus de l'Académie des inscriptions et belles-lettres* (1978), pp. 213-42.

pp. 412-13 I have not attempted to give a list of **auxiliary units** and their locations. A summary is provided by J.-P. Rey-Coquais, 'Syrie romaine' (above, notes to pp. 80-82), pp. 68-9; see also E. Dabrowa, 'Les troupes auxiliaires de l'armée romaine en Syrie au Ier s. de notre ère', *Dialogue d'Histoire Ancienne*, v (1979), pp. 233-54. **Diplomas**: N. Pollard, *Soldiers, Cities and Civilians*, pp. 120-25. The **camp at Dmeir** is reassessed by M. Lenoir, 'Dumayr, faux camp romain, vraie résidence palatiale', *Syria*, lxxvi (1999), pp. 227-36. **Fleet**: H. Seyrig, 'Le cimi-

tière des marins à Séleucie de Piérie', in *Mélanges syriens offerts à René Dussaud* (Paris, 1939), pp. 451-9; C.G. Starr, *The Roman Imperial Navy* (New York, 1941); N. Pollard, *Soldiers, Cities and Civilians in Roman Syria*, pp. 279-283. Vespasian may have been the creator of the classis Syriaca: see F. Millar, *The Roman Near East*, pp. 89-90. **Royal armies**: M.H. Gracey, 'The Armies of the Judaean Client Kings', in P. Freeman, D. Kennedy, *The Defence of the Roman and Byzantine East*, pp. 311-23; J. Bowsher, 'The Nabataean Army', in D.H. French, C.S. Lightfoot (eds), *The Eastern Frontier of the Roman Empire*, pp. 19-30.

pp. 413-15 **Estimates of overall strength of armies**: D. Kennedy, D. Riley, *Rome's Desert Frontier*, pp. 43-6. **Notitia Dignitatum**: O. Seeck, *Notitia Dignitatum* (Frankfurt, 1962) [repr. of the 1876 edition].

pp. 414-15 **Law of AD 443**: Novels of Theodosius 24.1.4. **Limitanei**: see Isaac (above, notes to p. 407). **Reduction in troop numbers**, and 50,000 at the Battle of the Yarmuk: D. Kennedy, D. Riley, *Rome's Desert Frontier*, p. 45. But see also B. Isaac, 'The Army in the Late Roman East', in A. Cameron (ed.), *The Byzantine and Early Islamic Near East*, iii: *States, Resources and Armies* (Princeton, 1995), pp. 125-55.

pp. 415-20 **For fortifications and other installations**, see especially S. Gregory, *Roman Military Architecture on the Eastern Frontier*, 3 vols (Amsterdam, 1995-7), and D. Kennedy, D. Riley, *Rome's Desert Frontier*.

pp. 415-16 For **Azraq and Jauf**, see D.L. Kennedy, H.I. MacAdam, 'Some Latin Inscriptions from the Azraq Oasis, Jordan', *Zeitschrift für Papyrologie und Epigraphik*, lx (1983), pp. 253-63; M.P. Speidel, 'The Roman Road to Dumatha (Jawf in Saudi Arabia) and the Frontier Strategy of the *Praetensione Colligare*', *Historia*, xxxvi (1987), pp. 211-21, and T. Bauzou, 'La praetensio de Bostra à Dumata (el-Jowf)', *Syria*, lxxiii (1996), pp. 23-35. An important essay on the **Strata Diocletiana** is by T. Bauzou, 'La "Strata Diocletiana"', in L. Nordiguian, J.-F. Salles (eds), *Aux origines de l'archéologie aérienne* (Beirut, 2000), pp. 79-91. See also R. Mouterde, 'La Strata Diocletiana et ses bornes milliaires', *Mélanges de l'Université Saint-Joseph*, xv (1930), pp. 221-33, 339-40; D. van Berchem, *L'armée de Dioclétien et la réforme constantinienne* (Paris, 1952); J. Eadie, 'The Transformation of the Eastern Frontier, 260-305', in R.W. Mathisen, H.S. Sivan (ed.), *Shifting Frontiers in Late Antiquity* (Aldershot, 1996), pp. 72-82. On the northern section from Palmyra to Sura, see M. Konrad, 'Research on the Roman and Early Byzantine Frontier in North Syria', *Journal of Roman Archaeology*, xii (1999), pp. 392-410; and, for evidence of pre-tetrarchic occupation in the area of the 'strata', M. Konrad, 'Frühkaizerzeitliche Befestigungen an der Strata Diocletiana? Neue Kleinfunde des 1. Jahrhunderts n. Chr. aus Nordsyrien', *Damaszener Mitteilungen*, ix (1996), pp. 163-80. See also the comments of G. Tate, 'Le problème de la défense et du peuplement de la steppe et du désert, dans le nord de la Syrie, entre la chute de Palmyre et le règne de Justinien', *Annales archéologiques arabes syriennes*, xlii (1996), pp. 331-7. On the southern section of the 'Strata', see T. Bauzou, 'Les voies de communication dans le Hauran à l'époque romaine', in J.-M. Dentzer (ed.), *Hauran*, i (Paris, 1985), pp. 137-65, especially at p. 153. **Procopius and the Strata**: *History of the Wars*, 2.1.6.

p. 417 On assumptions about **forts**: S. Gregory, 'Was there an Eastern Origin for the Design of Late Roman Fortifications? Some Problems for Research on Forts of Rome's Eastern Frontier', in D. Kennedy, *The Roman Army in the East*, pp. 169-209, and, by the same author, *Roman Military Architecture* (above, notes to pp. 415-20).

pp. 418-19 **Lejjun**: S.T. Parker, 'Legio IV Martia and the Legionary Camp at el-Lejjun', *Byzantinsche Forschungen*, viii (1982), pp. 185-210. **Udruh**: A. Killick, *Udruh: Caravan City and Desert Oasis* (Romsey, 1987). **Palmyra**: M. Gawlikowski, *Palmyre*, viii: *Les Principia de Dioclétien ('Camp des Enseignes')* (Warsaw, 1984). **Tell el-Hajj**: R. Stucky, 'Erster vorlaüfiger Bericht über die auf Tell el-Hajj durchgeführten Schweizerischen Archäologischen Ausgrabungen', *Annales archéologiques arabes syriennes*, xxiii (1973), pp. 161-200; R. Stucky, 'Tell el-Hajj 1972', *Annales archéologiques arabes syriennes*, xxv (1975), pp. 165-81. **On the typology and dating of forts**: Gregory (above, notes to p. 417); J. Lander, *Roman Stone Fortifications: Variation and Change from the First Century AD to the Fourth* (Oxford, 1984); P. Leriche, 'Les fortifications grecques et romaines en Syrie', J.-M. Dentzer, W. Orthmann (eds), *Archéologie et histoire de la Syrie*, ii, pp. 267-82. **Experiments in signalling**: S.T. Parker, *Limes Arabicus Project 1980-85* (Oxford, 1987).

Epilogue

For the early Islamic period in general, see H. Kennedy, *The Prophet and the Age of the Caliphates* (London and New York, 1986), and P.K. Hitti, *History of the Arabs* (London, 1970). A useful collection of primary sources for the period is provided by A. Palmer, S. Brock, R. Hoyland, *The Seventh Century in the West-Syrian Chronicles* (Liverpool, 1993).

pp. 422-3 On the **Muslim conquest**, see F.M. Donner, *The Early Islamic Conquests* (Princeton, 1981); W. Kaegi, *Byzantium and the Early Islamic Conquests* (Cambridge, 1992); and, by the same author, *Heraclius, Emperor of Byzantium* (Cambridge, 2002). There is some uncertainty about where the boundary between Rome and the Sasanian realm lay after the treaty of 629. In spite of the treaty Shahrbaraz seems to have resisted its implementation, briefly usurping the kingdom in 630: see G. Greatrex and S.N.C. Lieu, *The Roman Eastern Frontier and the Persian Wars* (London, 2002), pp. 226-8.

p. 424 For the **Berytus evidence**: K. Butcher, R. Thorpe, 'A Note on Excavations in Central Beirut, 1994-96', *Journal of Roman Archaeology*, x (1997), pp. 291-306; D. Perring, 'Excavations in the Souks of Beirut', *Berytus*, xliii (1997-8), pp. 9-34. The **'death' and 'assassination'** contrast was drawn by A. Piganiol, *L'empire chrétien (325-395)* (Paris, 1947), p. 422. See also M. Whittow, *The Making of Orthodox Byzantium, 606-1025* (London, 1996).

pp. 424-5 For the **transition from Roman to Islamic cities**, see especially H. Kennedy, 'From "Polis" to "Madina": Urban Change in Late Antique and Early Islamic Syria', *Past and Present*, 106 (Feb 1985), pp. 3-27, and, by the same author: 'The Last Century of Byzantine Syria: A Reinterpretation', *Byzantinische Forschungen*, x (1985), pp. 141-83; H.I. MacAdam, 'Settlements and Settlement Patterns in Northern and Central Transjordania, ca. 550-ca. 750', in G.R.D. King, A. Cameron (eds), *The Byzantine and Early Islamic Near East*, ii: *Land Use and Settlement Patterns* (Princeton, 1994), pp. 49-94; and C. Foss (above, notes to pp. 261-9), especially his conclusions, pp. 258-69. Other works: P. Canivet, J.-P. Rey-Coquais, *La Syrie de Byzance à l'Islam, VIIe – VIIIe siècles* (Damascus, 1992); G.P. Brogiolo, B. Ward-Perkins (eds), *The Idea and Ideal of the Town between Late Antiquity and the Early Middle Ages* (Leiden, 1999). For the **Berytus baths**, see K. Butcher, R. Thorpe, (above, notes to p. 424). The **role of the nomad economy** in the conquest is advanced by P. Pentz, *The Invisible Conquest: The Ontogenesis of Sixth and Seventh Century Syria* (Copenhagen, 1992).

pp. 425-6 **The Umayyads** An entire volume of *Aram* (6.1 1994) is dedicated to the Umayyads in Bilad al-Sham. **The Survival of Hellenism**: G.W. Bowersock, *Hellenism in Late Antiquity*, Ann Arbor, 1990. **Kastron Mefaa mosaics, date of**: J. Balty, 'Les mosaïques d'Umm al-Rasas et la date de 718', *Journal of Roman Archaeology* II (1998), pp. 700-2. **Damascus mosque and its mosaics**: R Förtsch, Die Architekturdarstellungen der Umaiyadenmoschee von Damaskos und die Rolle ihrer antiken Vorbilder,' *Damaszener Mitteilungen* 7 (1993), pp. 177-212.

ENDNOTES

1 F. Braudel, *La Méditerranée*, Paris, 1985, vol. II, p. 131.
2 W. Ball, *Rome in the East*, London, 2000, p. 448.
3 Justin 40.2.2-5.
4 *Annals* 6.31.
5 Cassius Dio, 54.7.6. The details are not known.
6 D. Sellwood, *An Introduction to the Coinage of Parthia*, London, 1971, p. 168, no. 55.
7 *A Catalogue of the Greek Coins in the British Museum*, 28. *Arabia, Mesopotamia, Persia*, London, 1922, pp. 92-93 and 137-139.
8 Cassius Dio, 72.31.1.
9 M. H. Dodgeon, S. N. C. Lieu (eds.), *The Roman Eastern Frontier and the Persian Wars (AD 226-363). A Documentary History*, London, 1991, pp. 84-85.
10 M. Gawlikowski, 'Inscriptions de Palmyre', *Syria* 48 (1971), pp. 407-26, at p. 420. English translation in Dodgeon and Lieu, above, note 9.
11 'Government without bureaucracy' is the title of chapter 2 of Garnsey and Saller, *The Roman Empire*. It would be exaggerating, however, to claim that there was no bureaucracy; in the provinces the army had an effective administrative structure that could be applied to civilian administration if necessary.
12 *Natural History* 5, 81-82.
13 *A Catalogue of the Greek Coins in the British Museum*, 26. *Phoenicia*, London, 1910, p. lxxiii.
14 J. Derrida, *Of Grammatology*, Baltimore, 1997, p. 113.
15 *Codex Justinianus*, 11. 22. 1.
16 *Oration* xxvii.42 (no longer a city); *Epistles*, 846.1 (sending crowns).
17 A.H.M. Jones, *Cities of the Eastern Roman Provinces*, Oxford, 1971, p. 286.
18 Strabo, 16. 2. 16.
19 F. Braudel, *Civilization and Capitalism, 15th-18th Century. Vol. I. The Structures of Everyday Life. The Limits of the Possible*, New York, 1981, pp. 482.
20 Strabo, 16.2.23.
21 For Julianus the Architect, see bibliography to this chapter.
22 A. H. M. Jones, *The Cities of the Eastern Roman Provinces*, Second Edition, Oxford, 1971, pp. 293-4.
23 Libanius, *Orations* 11.230.
24 G. W. Bowersock, 'Social and economic history of Syria under the Roman empire', in J.-M. Dentzer, W. Orthmann (eds), *Archéologie et histoire de la Syrie* II, Saarbrücken, 1989, pp. 63-80, at p. 67.
25 V.6.9.
26 H. Dessau (ed.), *Inscriptiones Latinae Selectae*, 3 vols., Berlin, 1892-1916, nos. 4301-3, 9284 (dedications to the god Jupiter Dolichenus).
27 A. H. M. Jones, *The Roman Economy*, Oxford, 1974, pp. 38-9.
28 Luke 2. 1-2.
29 Philostratus, *Life of Apollonius*, 1.20. The

English translation quoted is that of C. P. Jones, *Philostratus. Life of Apollonius*, London, 1970, p. 46.
30 *Descriptio Totius Orbis*, quoted in A. H. M. Jones, The Roman Economy (above, note 27), p. 147.
31 Pliny, *Natural History*, 36.27.
32 *The Roman Economy*, p. 39.
33 K. Butcher, *Coinage in Roman Syria*, London, 2003, p. 208.
34 Avienus, *Descriptio Orbis Terrae*, 1083.
35 I. Nielsen, *Hellenistic Palaces*, Aarhus, 1994, p. 213.
36 Spiro Kostof, *The City Shaped. Urban Patterns and Meanings Through History*, London, 1991, p. 95.
37 16.1.1.
38 *Antiquities of the Jews*, 1.121.
39 *Lives of the Sophists*, 625-6.
40 S. Swain, 'Hellenism in the East', *Journal of Roman Archaeology* 6 (1993), pp. 461-6, at p. 463.
41 16. 3. 1.
42 The phrase is from G. Bowersock, *Hellenism in Late Antiquity*, p. 82.
43 E. Littmann, *Publications of the Princeton University Archaeological Expeditions to Syria in 1904-5 and 1909, Division III. Greek and Latin Inscriptions, Section A. 2 Southern Hauran*, Leiden, 1907, p. 59, no. 56 (inscription from Burd, near Bostra).
44 *Questiones in Librum Judicum*, 19.
45 English translation in W. Cureton, *Spicilegium Syriacum*, London, 1855, p. 74.
46 J. Baudrillard, *America*, London, 1988, p. 21.
47 C. Kramsch, *Language and Culture*, Oxford, 1998, p. 62.
48 J.-P. Rey-Coquais, *Inscriptions grecques et latines découvertes dans les fouilles de Tyr (1963-1974). I. Inscriptions du nécropole* (Bulletin du Musée de Beyrouth 29 (1977)), p. 12, no. 17A.
49 R. Stucky, 'The Nabataean house and the urbanistic system of the habitation quarters in Petra', *Studies in the History and Archaeology of Jordan* 5, Amman, 1995, pp. 193-8, at p. 197.
50 F. Alpi, 'Bey 006. La mosaïque inscrite', *Bulletin d'archéologie et d'architecture libanaises* 1 (1996), pp. 215-217.
51 E. Littmann, *Publications of the American Archaeological Expedition to Syria in 1899-1900. Semitic Inscriptions*, New York, 1903, p. 70, Palmyrene inscription no. 6 (an altar of AD 132). See also D. R. Hillers, E. Cussini, *Palmyrene Aramaic Texts*, Baltimore and London, 1996, no. 0319.
52 *Natural History*, 11.50.136.
53 5.3.5 (Loeb version).
54 5.3.5 (Loeb version).
55 *De Dea Syria* 33.
56 English translation in W. Cureton, *Spicilegium Syriacum*, London, 1855, p. 45.
57 *De Dea Syria* 35.
58 J.-P. Rey-Coquais, *Inscriptions grecques et latines de la Syrie VII. Arados et régions*

voisines, Paris, 1970, no 4002.
59 J.-P. Rey-Coquais, *Inscriptions grecques et latines de la Syrie VI. Baalbek et Beqa'*, Paris, 1967, nos. 2804 and 2801.
60 *Inscriptions grecques et latines de la Syrie* VI, nos. 2805 and 2807. The reading of the latter is not certain.
61 Eusebius, *Martyrs of Palestine*, 1.3.
62 E. Littmann, *Publications of the Princeton University Archaeological Expeditions to Syria in 1904-5 and 1909, Division III. Greek and Latin Inscriptions, Section A. 2 Southern Hauran*, Leiden, 1907, p. 108, no. 186 (Greek inscription reused as a door lintel in a modern house at 'Anz in the southern Hauran, about 8 kilometres south of Salkhad).
63 English translation in R. Palmer, S. Brock, R. Hoyland, *The Seventh Century in the West Syrian Chronicles*, Liverpool 1993, p. 141.
64 A. H. M. Jones, *The Later Roman Empire*, Oxford, 1964, p. 888.
65 L. Jalabert, R. Mouterde, C. Mondésert, *Inscriptions grecques et latines de la Syrie V. Émésène*, Paris, 1959, no. 1998. English translation by R. K. Sherk, *The Roman Empire: Augustus to Constantine*, Cambridge, 1988, no. 95.
66 75.2.4.
67 R. Cagnat, *Inscriptiones Graecae ad Res Romanas Pertinentes* III, Paris, 1906, no. 1223. Alternatively the inscription may be referring to local nomads.
68 28.2.11 (Loeb translation).
69 W. H. Waddington, *Inscriptions grecques et latines de la Syrie*, Paris, 1870, p. 585, no. 2562d.
70 Malalas 12.38 (307-8 Bonn Edition).
71 L. Jalabert, R. Mouterde, C. Mondésert, *Inscriptions grecques et latines de la Syrie V. Émésène*, Paris, 1959, no. 2704.

INDEX